W9-BCY-008

murach's

Dreamweaver
CC 2014

TRAINING & REFERENCE

murach's
Dreamweaver
CC 2014

Zak Ruvalcaba

MIKE MURACH & ASSOCIATES, INC.

4340 N. Knoll Ave. • Fresno, CA 93722
www.murach.com • murachbooks@murach.com

Author: Zak Ruvalcaba

Writer/Editor: Anne Boehm

Production: Maria Spera

Books for web developers

Murach's Dreamweaver CC 2014
Murach's HTML5 and CSS3
Murach's JavaScript and jQuery
Murach's JavaScript and DOM Scripting
Murach's PHP and MySQL (2nd Edition)

Books for Java programmers

Murach's Java Programming
Murach's Android Programming
Murach's Java Servlets and JSP (3rd Edition)

Books for .NET programmers

Murach's C# 2012
Murach's ASP.NET 4.5 Web Programming with C# 2012

Murach's Visual Basic 2012
Murach's ASP.NET 4.5 Web Programming with VB 2012

Books for database developers

Murach's MySQL
Murach's Oracle SQL and PL/SQL (2nd Edition)
Murach's SQL Server 2012 for Developers

Books for IBM mainframe programmers

Murach's OS/390 and z/OS JCL
Murach's Mainframe COBOL
Murach's CICS for the COBOL Programmer

Please check www.murach.com for the most up-to-date Murach books

© 2014, Mike Murach & Associates, Inc.
All rights reserved.
Printed in the United States of America

10 9 8 7 6 5 4 3 2 1
ISBN-13: 978-1-890774-77-6

Content

Expanded contents

Section 3 How to create interactive and mobile web pages

Introduction

Since 1996, Dreamweaver has been the leading product for web developers who want to build web pages by using a visual interface instead of writing the HTML code themselves.

Now, Dreamweaver CC takes that to a new level, with tools that are designed to support today's best web design practices. For instance, the new CSS Designer provides an intuitive interface for adding CSS and CSS3 to embedded and external style sheets. Responsive Web Design is supported with media queries as well as Fluid Grid Layouts. jQuery and jQuery UI have replaced Adobe's proprietary Spry. And that's just the start.

Because Dreamweaver's visual interface lets the user get by with a minimal knowledge of HTML and CSS, it's a great product for beginning web developers. But that interface is also popular with experienced developers who like to use it whenever that's faster than writing the HTML and CSS code themselves. And when it isn't, they use the HTML and CSS editors that come with Dreamweaver to write their own code more efficiently.

The trick, of course, is in learning how to use all of the windows, panels, and toolbars that Dreamweaver provides and in integrating those navigational skills with all the design skills that you need to build modern, standards-compliant websites. That's where this book comes in. Unlike other Dreamweaver books, this one blends *all* of the skills that you need with the proven instructional approach that makes Murach books so effective.

That's why this book is the right book for beginning web developers who want to learn how to use Dreamweaver. It's also the right book for HTML and CSS developers who want to work more efficiently by using the Dreamweaver interface. It's even the right book for JavaScript and jQuery programmers who are looking for a better way to build and enhance web pages.

What this book does

- To get you started right, section 1 presents a crash course in Dreamweaver that has you developing web pages at a professional level after just six chapters. These chapters don't just show you how to use Dreamweaver to build web pages. They also show you how to use Dreamweaver so it generates the HTML and CSS for a page in a way that is consistent with the best practices of modern website development. That includes the use of HTML5 semantics, external style sheets, and CSS3.

- When you finish the first 6 chapters, you will have the perspective and skills you need for developing professional web pages in Dreamweaver. Then, you can add to those skills by reading any of the chapters in the next two sections...and you don't have to read those sections or chapters in sequence. In other words, you can skip to any of the chapters in the last two sections after you finish section 1. The one exception is that you should read chapter 7 before chapter 8 since they are closely related.

- The seven chapters in section 2 let you learn new Dreamweaver skills whenever you need them. If, for example, you want to learn how to use Responsive Web Design so your web pages work right in desktop browsers as well as in mobile devices, you can start by reading chapters 7 and 8. If you want to learn how to deploy an application to a web server, you can skip to chapter 13. If you want to learn how to add audio or video to a page by using HTML5 elements instead of plugins, you can skip to chapter 10. And if you want to learn how to use templates and library items to save time and build consistent web pages, you can skip to chapter 9.

- The four chapters in section 3 show you how to use Dreamweaver to create interactive and mobile web pages. Chapter 14, for example, shows how to add forms to your pages that send data to your web server for processing. Chapter 15 shows how to use Dreamweaver to add JavaScript features like image galleries to a web page...without knowing how to code JavaScript. Chapter 16 shows how to use Dreamweaver to add jQuery and jQuery UI features like accordions and tabs to your pages...without knowing how to use jQuery or jQuery UI. And chapter 17 shows how to use jQuery Mobile to build mobile websites, which in some cases is a practical alternative to Responsive Web Design.

Why you'll learn faster and better with this book

Like all our books, this one has features that you won't find in competing books. That's why we believe you'll learn faster and better with our book than with any other. Here are just a few of those features.

- From the first page to the last, this book shows you how to use the best HTML and CSS practices, even though you're using Dreamweaver to generate the HTML and CSS. That way, you'll be developing web pages at a professional level from the start. In contrast, most competing books focus on the Dreamweaver visual interface without worrying about the code that it generates.

- Chapter 2 presents the least any Dreamweaver user should know about HTML and CSS. That's because you can't be an effective Dreamweaver user without understanding the HTML and CSS that Dreamweaver generates. In fact, you will often want to review the generated code to make sure everything works correctly. In particular, this chapter presents the proper use of HTML5 semantics and external style sheets...essential web development skills that are treated too late or too lightly in most Dreamweaver books.

- If you page through this book, you'll see that all of the information is presented in "paired pages," with the essential syntax, guidelines, and examples on the right page and the perspective and extra explanation on the left page. This helps you learn faster by reading less...and this is the ideal reference format when you need to refresh your memory about how to do something.

- The exercises at the end of each chapter guide you through the development of web pages using the skills that have been presented in the chapter. Because Dreamweaver has a complicated visual interface that can be hard to master, these exercises are an essential part of the learning process. Unlike the exercises in other books, most of our exercises start from partial pages so you can get more practice in less time. They never introduce new skills because that's what the text and figures are for. And they never just tell you to "click here, click there" because that's not the kind of practice you need to get ready for your own projects. Instead, they build both your skills and your confidence.

What software you need

To develop web pages with Dreamweaver CC, you first need to subscribe to the Adobe Creative Cloud (CC). Then, you can pick a Dreamweaver CC payment plan that fits your budget. These plans start at $19.99 per month if you're willing to commit to a full-year plan. Or, if you aren't ready to commit, you can sign up for 30-day free trial. For more information on installing Dreamweaver, you can go to appendix A.

Then, to test a web page, you need multiple web browsers. Because Internet Explorer is the browser that is the least standard, you should test all of your web pages in that browser. You should also test your web pages in one or more of the standard browsers, including Chrome, Firefox, Opera, and Safari. All of these browsers are free, and appendix A shows how to install them.

How our downloadable files can help you learn

If you go to our website at www.murach.com, you can download all the files that you need for getting the most from this book. These files include:

- the files for all of the examples in this book

- the files that you will use as the starting points for the chapter exercises

- the files that provide the solutions to the exercises

These files let you test, review, and copy the code. In addition, if you have any problems with the exercises, the solutions are there to help you over the learning blocks. Here again, appendix A shows you how to download and install these files.

Support materials for trainers and instructors

If you're a corporate trainer or a college instructor who would like to use this book for a course, we offer an Instructor's CD that includes: (1) a complete set of PowerPoint slides that you can use to review and reinforce the content of the book; (2) instructional objectives that describe the skills a student should have upon completion of each chapter; (3) test banks that test how well your students have mastered those skills; (4) extra exercises that prove whether your students have mastered those skills; and (5) solutions to the extra exercises.

To learn more about this Instructor's CD and to find out how to get it, please go to our website at www.murach.com. Or, if you prefer, you can call Kelly at 1-800-221-5528 or send an email to kelly@murach.com.

Two companion books

Frankly, you can't be a good Dreamweaver developer without understanding the HTML and CSS that it generates. In fact, the more you know about HTML and CSS, including HTML5 and CSS3, the more productive you'll be with Dreamweaver. That's why *Murach's HTML5 and CSS3* is the perfect companion to our Dreamweaver book.

Similarly, you will be able to get more from the Dreamweaver behaviors and jQuery features if you understand the JavaScript and jQuery that they generate. That's why we recommend *Murach's JavaScript and jQuery* as the third book in the set. With all three books on your desk, you'll have the answers to all of your client-side questions and you'll be able to take Dreamweaver to the next level.

Please let us know how this book works for you

In 1996, I developed my first web pages with Dreamweaver. In 2002, I wrote my first Dreamweaver book, called *The Ten Minute Guide to Dreamweaver 4*. And now, eight Dreamweaver versions later, I still have the same passion for Dreamweaver that I had when I first started using it.

So, when I started this project, my first goal was to share my passion for Dreamweaver and its support of the modern web technologies. To that end, I've done my best to get the most from the Murach "paired-pages" format. Now, I'm hoping that this, my seventh Dreamweaver book, is everything you expected... and more.

I thank you for buying this book. I wish you all the best with your web development. And if you have any comments, I would appreciate hearing from you.

Zak Ruvalcaba
zak@modulemedia.com

Section 1

A crash course in Dreamweaver

The six chapters in this section are designed to get you off to a fast start. First, chapter 1 presents the concepts and terms that you need for developing web applications. In addition, it introduces you to the Dreamweaver interface, and it shows you several ways that you can customize the Dreamweaver workspace so you can use it efficiently.

Next, chapter 2 presents an introduction to HTML and CSS. Although Dreamweaver generates the HTML and CSS you need as you use its interface, it's important that you have a solid understanding of this code. That way, as you gain more experience building websites with Dreamweaver, you can view the HTML and CSS to pinpoint problems, and you can change this code directly.

With this as background, chapter 3 presents the basic skills for using Dreamweaver to build a website. Then, chapter 4 shows you how to use Dreamweaver to work with text, images, and links. Next, chapter 5 shows you how to use CSS to format text. Finally, chapter 6 shows you how to use CSS to control the layout of a web page and to add borders and backgrounds.

When you complete these chapters, you'll be able to develop web pages that use a variety of layouts and formatting. Then, you can expand your skills by reading the other chapters in this book.

Please note, however, that you don't have to read the chapters in the other sections in sequence. Instead, you can skip to the chapter that presents the skills that you want to learn next. In other words, the six chapters in this section present the prerequisites for all of the other chapters, and all of the other chapters are written as independent learning modules. As a result, you can read any of those chapters whenever you need its skills.

1

An introduction to web development with Dreamweaver

This chapter introduces you to the concepts and terms you need to understand how web applications work. In addition, it introduces you to the Dreamweaver interface and shows you some ways that you can customize it so it's easy for you to use.

How web applications work

The *World Wide Web*, or web, consists of many components that work together to bring a web page to your desktop over the *Internet*. Before you start building web pages of your own, you should have a basic understanding of how these components work together.

The components of a web application

The first diagram in figure 1-1 shows that web applications consist of *clients* and a *web server*. The clients are the desktop computers, tablets, and mobile devices that use the web applications. They access the web pages through programs known as *web browsers*. The web server holds the files that make up a web application.

A *network* is a system that allows clients and servers to communicate. The Internet in turn is a large network that consists of many smaller networks. In a diagram like this, the "cloud" represents the network or Internet that connects the clients and servers.

In general, you don't need to know how the cloud works. But you should have a general idea of what's going on. That's why the second diagram in this figure gives you a conceptual view of the architecture of the Internet.

To start, networks can be categorized by size. A *local area network* (*LAN*) is a small network of computers that are near each other and can communicate with each other over short distances. Computers on a LAN are typically in the same building or in adjacent buildings. This type of network is often called an *intranet*, and it can be used to run web applications for use by employees only.

In contrast, a *wide area network* (*WAN*) consists of multiple LANs that have been connected together over long distances using *routers*. To pass information from one client to another, a router determines which network is closest to the destination and sends the information over that network. A WAN can be owned privately by one company or it can be shared by multiple companies.

An *Internet service provider* (*ISP*) is a company that owns a WAN that is connected to the Internet. An ISP leases access to its network to other companies that need to be connected to the Internet.

The Internet is a global network consisting of multiple WANs that have been connected together. ISPs connect their WANs at large routers called *Internet exchange points* (*IXP*). This allows anyone connected to the Internet to exchange information with anyone else.

This diagram shows an example of data crossing the Internet. Here, data is being sent from the client in the top left to the server in the bottom right. First, the data leaves the client's LAN and enters the WAN owned by the client's ISP. Next, the data is routed through IXPs to the WAN owned by the server's ISP. Then, it enters the server's LAN and finally reaches the server. All of this can happen in less than 1/10th of a second.

The components of a web application

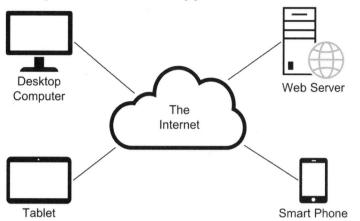

The architecture of the Internet

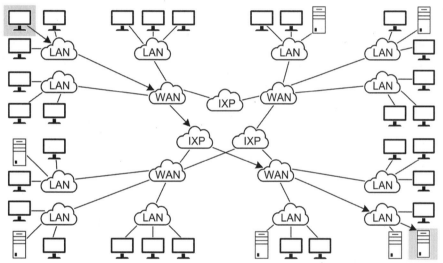

Description

- A web application consists of clients, a web server, and a network. The *clients* use programs known as *web browsers* to request web pages from the web server. The *web server* returns the pages that are requested to the browser.

- A *local area network* (LAN) directly connects computers that are near each other. This kind of network is often called an *intranet*.

- A *wide area network* (WAN) consists of two or more LANs that are connected by *routers*. The routers route information from one network to another.

- The *Internet* consists of many WANs that have been connected at *Internet exchange points* (IXP). There are several dozen IXPs located throughout the world.

- An *Internet service provider* (ISP) owns a WAN and leases access to its network. It connects its WAN to the rest of the Internet at one or more IXPs.

Figure 1-1   The components of a web application

How static web pages are processed

A *static web page* like the one at the top of figure 1-2 is a web page that only changes when the web developer changes it. This web page is sent directly from the web server to the web browser when the browser requests it.

The diagram in this figure shows how a web server processes a request for a static web page. This process begins when a client requests a web page in a web browser. To do that, the user can either type the address of the page into the browser's address bar or click a link in the current page that specifies the next page to load.

In either case, the web browser builds a request for the web page and sends it to the web server. This request, known as an *HTTP request*, is formatted using the *HyperText Transport Protocol* (HTTP), which lets the web server know which file is being requested.

When the web server receives the HTTP request, it retrieves the requested file from the disk drive. This file contains the *HTML (HyperText Markup Language)* for the requested page. Then, the web server sends the file back to the browser as part of an *HTTP response*.

When the browser receives the HTTP response, it *renders* (translates) the HTML into a web page that is displayed in the browser. Then, the user can view the content. If the user requests another page, either by clicking a link or typing another web address into the browser's address bar, the process begins again.

In this book, you'll learn how to use Dreamweaver to create static web pages. You can spot these pages in a web browser by looking at the extension in the address bar. If the extension is .htm or .html, the page is a static web page.

A static web page at http://www.modulemedia.com/ourwork/

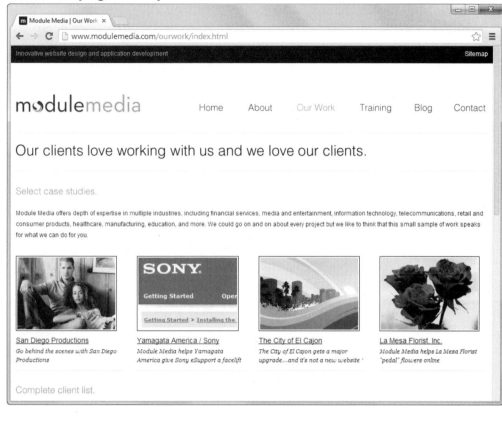

How a web server processes a static web page

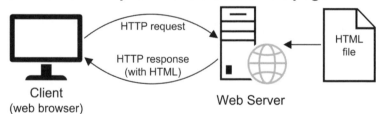

Client
(web browser)

Web Server

Description

- *Hypertext Markup Language* (*HTML*) is used to semantically mark up web pages.
- A *static web page* is an HTML document that's stored on the web server and doesn't change. The filenames for static web pages have .htm or .html extensions.
- When the user requests a static web page, the browser sends an *HTTP request* to the web server that includes the name of the file that's being requested.
- When the web server receives the request, it retrieves the HTML for the web page and sends it back to the browser as part of an *HTTP response*.
- When the browser receives the HTTP response, it *renders* the HTML into a web page that is displayed in the browser.

Figure 1-2   How static web pages are processed

How dynamic web pages are processed

A *dynamic web page* like the one in figure 1-3 is a page that's created by a program or script on the web server each time it is requested. This program or script is executed by an *application server* based on the data that's sent along with the HTTP request. In this example, the HTTP request identified the book that's shown. Then, the program or script retrieved the image and data for that book from a *database server*.

The diagram in this figure shows how a web server processes a dynamic web page. The process begins when the user requests a page in a web browser. To do that, the user can either type the URL of the page in the browser's address bar, click a link that specifies the dynamic page to load, or click a button that submits a form that contains the data that the dynamic page should process.

In each case, the web browser builds an HTTP request and sends it to the web server. This request includes whatever data the application needs for processing the request. If, for example, the user has entered data into a form, that data will be included in the HTTP request.

When the web server receives the HTTP request, the server examines the file extension of the requested web page to identify the application server that should process the request. The web server then forwards the request to the application server that processes that type of web page.

Next, the application server retrieves the appropriate program or script from the hard drive. It also loads any form data that the user submitted. Then, it executes the script. As the script executes, it generates the HTML for the web page. If necessary, the script will request data from a database server and use that data as part of the web page it is generating.

When the script is finished, the application server sends the dynamically generated HTML back to the web server. Then, the web server sends the HTML back to the browser in an HTTP response.

When the web browser receives the HTTP response, it renders the HTML and displays the web page. Note, however, that the web browser has no way to tell whether the HTML in the HTTP response was for a static page or a dynamic page. It just renders the HTML.

When the page is displayed, the user can view the content. Then, when the user requests another page, the process begins again. The process that begins with the user requesting a web page and ends with the server sending a response back to the client is called a *round trip*.

Dynamic web pages let you create interactive *web applications* that do all of the types of processing that you find on the Internet including eCommerce applications. Although you won't learn how to develop dynamic web pages in this book, you will learn how to create the forms that send user data to the web server. Once you master static web page development, you can learn how to use server-side languages like JSP, ASP.NET, or PHP to create the dynamic pages that a website needs.

A dynamic web page at amazon.com

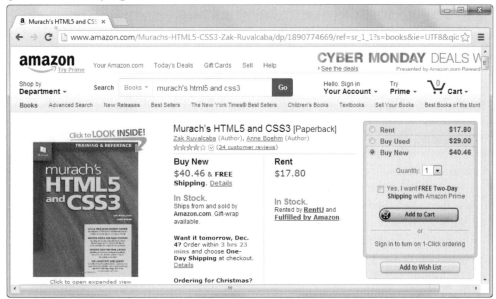

How a web server processes a dynamic web page

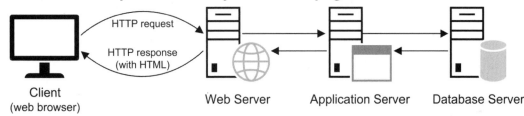

Client (web browser)   Web Server   Application Server   Database Server

Description

- A *dynamic web page* is a page that's generated by a server-side program or script.

- When a web server receives a request for a dynamic web page, it looks up the extension of the requested file to find out which *application server* should process the request.

- When the application server receives a request, it runs the specified script. Often, this script uses the data that it gets from the web browser to get data from a *database server*. This script can also store the data that it receives in the database.

- When the application server finishes processing the data, it generates the HTML for a web page and returns it to the web server. Then, the web server returns the HTML to the web browser as part of an HTTP response.

Figure 1-3   How dynamic web pages are processed

A survey of web browsers
and server-side scripting languages

Figure 1-4 summarizes the five web browsers that are used the most today. Google's Chrome is the most popular, even though it's a relatively recent addition to the choice of browsers. It has a clean, simple interface, it provides for searching directly from the address bar, and it has a large library of extensions and add-ons for developers. Plus, it's lightweight so it starts quickly and has a fast response time. Chrome is based on the WebKit rendering engine, and it's available for all major operating systems including Windows, Mac OS, and Linux.

Microsoft's Internet Explorer (IE) is the browser that comes with Windows. It was the most widely-used browser for many years, but Firefox has been catching up in recent years and Chrome has now surpassed it.

Like Chrome, Firefox is available for all major operating systems. Firefox was built using source code from the original Netscape Navigator web browser, and many web developers use it as their primary browser because they like its many features including its debugging features.

Safari and Opera are used by a smaller percentage of users. Safari is the default web browser on Mac OS, but it is also available for Windows. Opera is available for Windows, Mac OS, Linux, and other operating systems.

Next, this figure summarizes the most common *scripting languages* for web servers. These are the languages that let you develop dynamic web pages. For instance, ASP.NET is a Microsoft product. JSP is a free, open-source language that is commonly used with Java servlets. And PHP is another free, open-source language. To develop dynamic web pages, you need to choose the scripting language that you will use for *server-side processing*.

When you choose the scripting language, you also determine what web server you're going to need. For instance, JSP and PHP run on an *Apache web server*, which was developed by the Apache Software Foundation. It is an open-source software project that's available for free, and it runs on most operating systems, especially Linux systems. In contrast, ASP.NET runs on Microsoft's *Internet Information Services* (*IIS*), which isn't open source and runs on a Windows system.

Web browsers

Browser	Published by	Available on
Chrome	Google	All major operating systems
Internet Explorer	Microsoft	Windows
Firefox	Mozilla Corporation	All major operating systems
Safari	Apple	Macintosh and Windows
Opera	Opera Software	All major operating systems

Server-side scripting languages

Language	Description
ASP.NET	Runs on a Microsoft IIS web server. Its pages have the .aspx extension.
JSP	A free, open-source language that is commonly used with Java servlets. It runs on an Apache web server, and its pages have the .jsp extension.
PHP	A free, open-source language that is typically used with an Apache web server. Its pages have the .php extension.
ColdFusion	A commercial scripting language from Adobe that integrates well with Adobe Flash and Flex. Its pages have the .cfm or .cfml file extension.
Ruby	A free, open-source language that is typically combined with the Rails framework to simplify development. Its pages have the .rb extension.
Perl	A free, open-source language that was originally designed for use at the UNIX command line to manipulate text. Its pages have the .pl extension.
Python	A free, open-source language that can be used to develop many types of applications besides web applications. Its pages have the .py extension.

Description

- When you develop a website for general use, you need to test it on all five of the web browsers listed above including all versions that are still in common use.

- To develop dynamic web pages, you use a *server-side scripting language* like ASP.NET, JSP, or PHP. You can use Dreamweaver's text editor to work with all of these languages.

- The scripting languages are designed to run on specific web servers. The two most popular web servers are Microsoft *IIS* (*Internet Information Services*) and *Apache*.

Figure 1-4   A survey of web browsers and server-side scripting languages

How JavaScript and jQuery fit into web development

In contrast to the server-side processing that's done for dynamic web pages, *JavaScript* is a scripting language that provides for *client-side processing*. In the website in figure 1-5, for example, JavaScript is used to change the panel that's displayed when a tab is clicked within the *tabbed panel* in the web page.

To make this work, all three panels are loaded into the browser, and code is used to hide all but one of the panels when the page is first displayed. Then, when a user clicks the tab for a panel that isn't displayed, the panel that's currently displayed is hidden and the panel for the tab that was clicked is displayed.

The diagram in this figure shows how JavaScript processing works. When a browser requests a web page, both the HTML and the related JavaScript are returned to the browser by the web server. Then, the JavaScript code is executed in the web browser by the browser's *JavaScript engine*. This takes some of the processing burden off the server and makes the application run faster. Often, JavaScript is used in conjunction with dynamic web pages, but it can also be used with static web pages.

Besides tabbed panels, there are many other uses for JavaScript. For instance, another common use is to validate the data that the user enters into an HTML form before it is sent to the server for processing. This saves unnecessary round trips to the server. Other common uses of JavaScript are to run slide shows, rotate headlines or products in one area of a web page, and provide animation. In fact, whenever you see a portion of a web page cycle through a series of text blocks or images, that's probably being done by JavaScript.

jQuery is a free, open-source JavaScript library that provides dozens of methods for common web features that make JavaScript programming easier. Beyond that, the jQuery functions are coded and tested for cross-browser compatibility, so they will work in all browsers. These are two of the reasons why jQuery is used by most websites today. And that's why jQuery is commonly used by professional web developers. In fact, you can think of jQuery as one of the four technologies that every web developer should know how to use: HTML, CSS, JavaScript, and jQuery. But don't forget that jQuery is actually JavaScript.

In this book, you won't learn how to program with JavaScript and jQuery. In section 3, though, you'll learn how to use Dreamweaver to add JavaScript and jQuery features to your pages, even though you won't know how the code works. Then, if you want to learn how to program in JavaScript and jQuery so you can develop your own features, you can read *Murach's JavaScript and jQuery*.

A web page with a jQuery UI tabbed panel

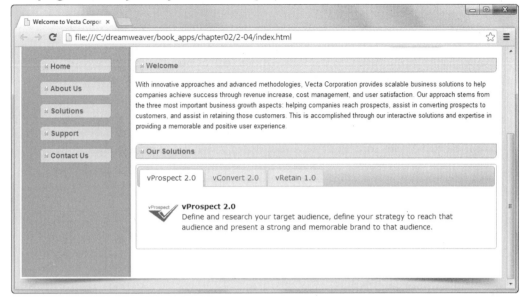

How JavaScript and jQuery fit into this architecture

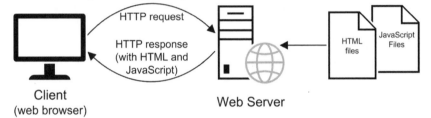

Some of the common uses of JavaScript and jQuery

- Data validation, date pickers, auto completion, and dialogs
- Image swaps, image rollovers, and slide shows
- Drop-down menus, tabbed panels, and accordions

Description

- *JavaScript* is a *client-side scripting language* that is run by the *JavaScript engine* of a web browser and controls the operation of the browser.
- *jQuery* is a popular JavaScript-based library that helps streamline web development.
- When the browser requests an HTML page that contains JavaScript or a link to a JavaScript file, both the HTML and the JavaScript are loaded into the browser.
- Because JavaScript runs on the client, not the server, it provides functions that don't require a trip back to the server. This can help an application run more efficiently.

Figure 1-5   How JavaScript and jQuery fit into web development

Web development and Dreamweaver CC

One way to develop a website is to use a text editor like Aptana Studio 3, Notepad++, or TextWrangler. If you do that, you have to code all of the HTML and CSS yourself. In contrast, Dreamweaver provides an *Integrated Development Environment (IDE)* that generates code for you as you work with its visual interface. This IDE is shown in figure 1-6.

Dreamweaver also provides the starting code for an HTML document whenever you start a new file. It helps you manage the folders and files for the website. It provides for transferring files between local and remote sites. And it has many other features. Because of that, Dreamweaver can help you make dramatic improvements in your productivity. That's why professional web developers often use Dreamweaver for web development.

Although you can use Dreamweaver independently of other web development products, it's often used with other products in the *Adobe Creative Cloud (CC)* suite of software. The Creative Cloud provides a new way of using Adobe's software. Instead of purchasing software as you did previously, Creative Cloud is a subscription-based service that lets you "rent" software and other services directly from Adobe.

In addition to Dreamweaver, web developers may be interested in using Photoshop or Fireworks for editing photos and images, Illustrator for creating and editing illustrations, Flash and Animate for adding animation and interactivity to web pages, and Edge Inspect for remote testing. All of these programs are installed and uninstalled from the Creative Cloud application that runs silently in the background of your computer.

The Dreamweaver IDE

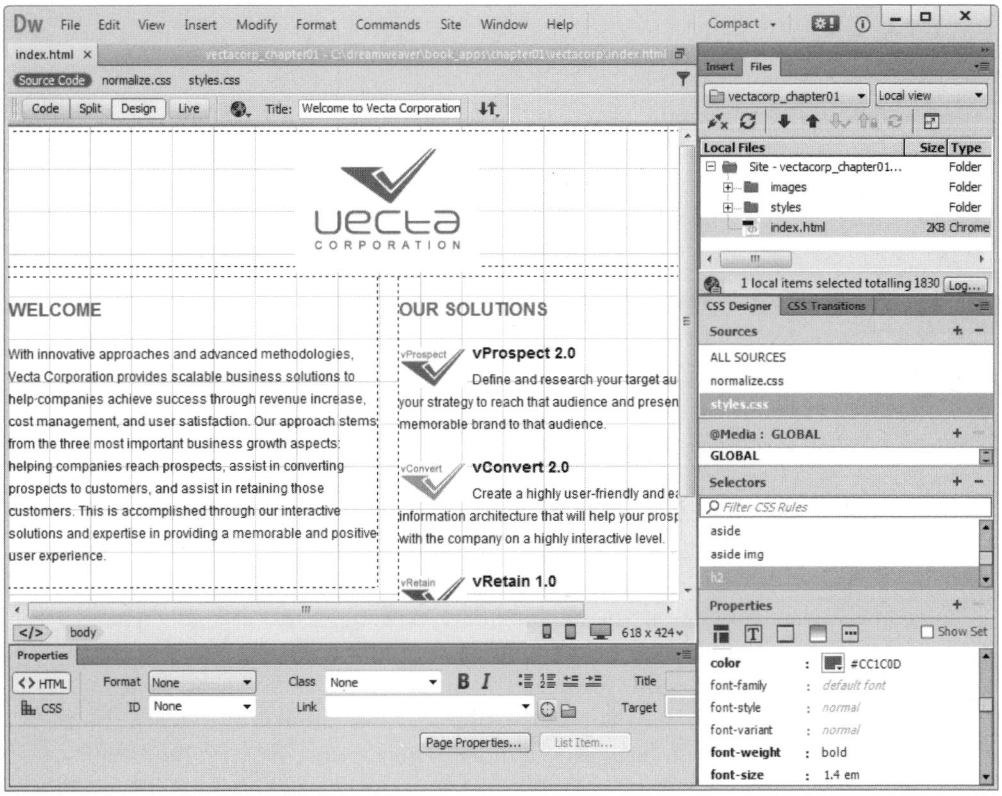

Description

- Dreamweaver is one of the few remaining *Integrated Development Environments (IDEs)* for web development. It provides a visual interface that helps you design pages more quickly by generating the required code. It also includes a text editor that you can use to work with the generated code directly.

- Dreamweaver also includes features for managing files, previewing pages, automating tasks, transferring and synchronizing files between local and remote websites, and more.

- *Dreamweaver CC (Creative Cloud)* is one of the products in the *Adobe Creative Cloud* suite of software. Adobe Creative Cloud is a subscription-based service that lets you rent graphic design, web development, and video editing software as well as cloud services directly from Adobe.

Variations between the Windows and Mac editions of Dreamweaver

- In this book, all of the screen illustrations are from the Windows version of Dreamweaver. However, there are some minor differences between this version and the Mac version. We'll point out these differences as they come up in each chapter.

Figure 1-6   Web development and Dreamweaver CC

A tour of the Dreamweaver interface

With that as background, you're ready to take a tour of the Dreamweaver IDE. Along the way, you'll learn some of the basic techniques for working in this environment. Then, as you progress through this book, you'll learn more about using the Dreamweaver IDE.

How to use the Welcome screen

Each time you start Dreamweaver, the *Welcome screen* shown in figure 1-7 is displayed in the center of the IDE. This screen provides access to a number of operations and resources. To start, you can click a file name in the Recent Files list to open that file. Or, you can click the Open button at the bottom of this list to display the Open dialog box so you can open a file that isn't in the list.

You can also create new files from the Welcome screen. To do that, you can click the appropriate icon in one of the first two rows of the Create New list. You can also create a new site by clicking the Site Setup icon, you can create a page with a fluid grid layout by clicking the Fluid Grid icon, and you can create a template by clicking the Site Templates icon. In each of these cases, a dialog box is displayed and you must enter the required information. You'll learn about creating a site in the next topic, and you'll learn about working with fluid grid layouts and templates later in this book.

If you want to learn more about Dreamweaver, you can use the links in the Learn list. The first link displays a quick tour of the new features of Dreamweaver CC 2014. You're also asked if you want to display this tour the first time you start Dreamweaver. The second link provides access to several videos that show you how to use some of the new features. The third link displays a page on the Adobe website that provides access to a variety of articles, tutorials, and projects. And the fourth link takes you to a page on the Adobe website that provides access to documentation and Adobe community forums.

The Welcome screen that's displayed when you start Dreamweaver

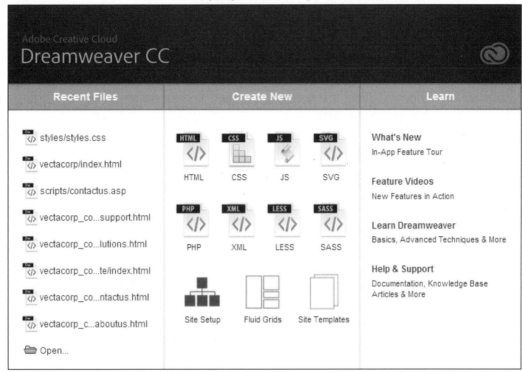

Description

- When Dreamweaver starts, the *Welcome screen* in displayed. You can use this screen to quickly open a recent file, create a new file, or learn more about Dreamweaver.

- If you don't want the Welcome screen displayed each time you start Dreamweaver, you can use the Preferences dialog box to turn this option off as shown in figure 1-17.

Figure 1-7   How to use the Welcome screen

How to create a Dreamweaver site

Before you begin building web pages in Dreamweaver, you'll want to create a Dreamweaver *site*. To do that, you choose Site→New Site to display the Site Setup dialog box shown in figure 1-8. (Incidentally, this notation means to drop down the Site menu and select the New Site item, and this notation will be used throughout this book.) At the least, you need to use the Site category of this dialog box to enter a name for the site and identify the folder on your local computer that will contain the files for the site. Later, you can use the Servers category to define a remote server where your site will be hosted.

When you define a site, Dreamweaver creates a *cache* where it stores information about the files and assets used by the site. (In Dreamweaver, an *asset* refers to any object that you use on a web page, such as an image, link, or JavaScript file.) The cache makes it possible for Dreamweaver to detect changes that you make to a site and automatically update references to assets whenever that's necessary.

Although you can work with individual files from Dreamweaver, you have access to several additional features when you create a site. Those features include templates, library items, global find and replace, the Assets panel, a built-in FTP program for uploading files to a remote server, site synchronization, and team collaboration. You'll learn about all of these features later in this book.

The Site Setup dialog box

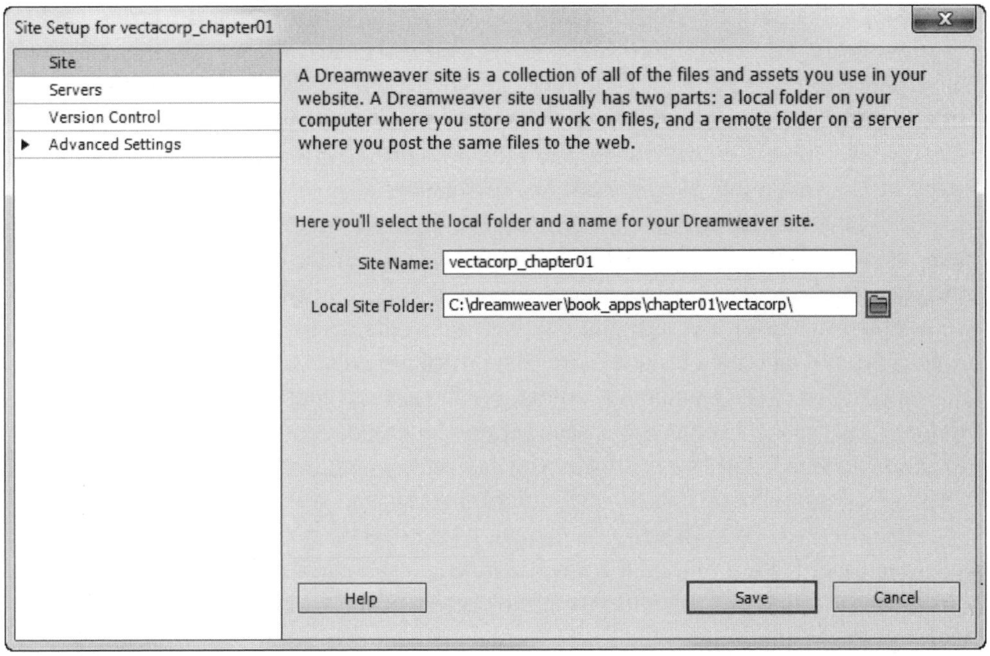

How to create a new site

1. Choose Site→New Site to display the Site Setup dialog box.
2. Enter a name for the site in the Site Name text box.
3. Click the Browse for Folder icon (▦) to the right of the Local Site Folder text box, and then browse to and select the top-level folder for the site. Or, enter the path for this folder into the text box.
4. Click the Save button to create the new site.

Description

- In general, each Dreamweaver *site* contains the folders, files, and *assets* for one website. Information about the site is stored in the site's *cache*.
- You can create a Dreamweaver site from a folder with existing files. You can also create an empty site from a folder with no files or from a new folder that you specify.

Figure 1-8   How to create a Dreamweaver site

How to work with the Document window in Design view

To develop web pages in Dreamweaver, you'll use the *Document window* shown in figure 1-9. Here, the Document window shows the index.html file in *Design view*. In this view, you can see a visual representation of the page. You'll work in this view often as you learn Dreamweaver.

You can also display a page in Code view, Split view, and Live view using the buttons in the Document toolbar. In *Code view*, you can see the HTML that defines the page. In *Split view*, the Document window is split into two panes: one that shows the HTML for the page and one that shows the design for the page. And in *Live view*, you can see a browser-like preview of the page.

In addition to the Document toolbar, the Document window can also contain a *Related Files bar*. This bar is displayed if the document contains one or more links to assets. In this figure, for example, you can see that the document contains links to two *Cascading Style Sheets* (*CSS*): normalize.css and styles.css. To see the code for either of these style sheets, you can click on its name in the Related Files bar.

One other feature of the Document window you should be familiar with is the *Tag selector* found in the *status bar* at the bottom of the window. The Tag selector displays the hierarchy of *HTML tags* for the element that's currently selected in the Document window. In this figure, for example, an h2 element is selected. This element is nested within a section element, which is nested within the body element.

You'll learn more about HTML tags and elements in the next chapter. For now, just realize that you can click on any tag in the Tag selector to select that element in the document. You can also click the Element Quick View icon at the left side of the Tag selector to display a hierarchical view of the HTML for the page. You'll learn more about working with Element Quick View in chapter 12.

This figure also shows some of the panels you can use as you develop a web page in the Document window. To start, you can use the *Insert panel* to add objects to a web page. In this figure, for example, you can see some of the structural objects you can add to a page. You'll learn more about using the Insert panel in chapter 3.

Below the Insert panel is the *CSS Designer panel*, or just *CSS Designer*. You can use this panel to create Cascading Style Sheets (CSS) and to apply *styles* to the web page. You'll learn more about styles and Cascading Style Sheets in the next chapter.

Below the Document window is the *Property Inspector panel*, or just *Property Inspector*. You can use the Property Inspector to format portions of a web page using either HTML or CSS. In chapter 4, you'll learn how to use the Property Inspector to work with text, links, and images. Then, in later chapters, you can learn how to use it to work with other types of objects.

Although only one document is open in the Document window in this figure, you should know that you can open multiple documents at the same time. Then, each document is displayed in its own tab, and you can click the tab for a document to display it. To close a tab, just click the Close button in its upper right corner.

Dreamweaver with a document displayed in Design view

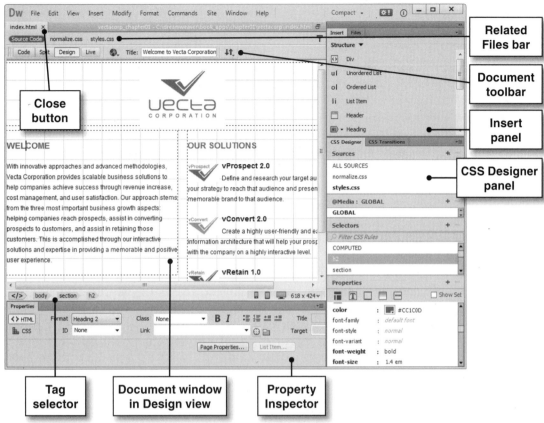

Description

- The *Document window* is the main Dreamweaver workspace and can contain one or more tabbed windows.

- To display a document in the Document window, you double-click on it in the *Files panel*. You'll learn more about the Files panel in figure 1-12.

- To display a different tab, just click on it. To close a tab, click its Close button.

- You can display the Document window in *Design view*, *Code view*, *Split view*, or *Live View*. To switch from one view to another, you use the four buttons in the Document toolbar.

- Design view provides a WYSIWYG interface that you can use to design your pages. From this view, you can use the *Insert panel* to insert objects into a document, you can use the *Property Inspector* to format the object that's selected in the Document window, and you can use the *CSS Designer panel* to create *Cascading Style Sheets* (*CSS*) and change style properties for one or more objects.

- If a document has related files such as Cascading Style Sheets, those files are displayed in the *Related Files bar*. Then, you can click on the name of a file to display it in Split view along with the document, and you can click on "Source Code" to close the related file.

Figure 1-9   How to work with the Document window in Design view

How to work with the Document window in Code view

Figure 1-10 shows the Document window you saw in figure 1-9 in *Code view*. Dreamweaver's Code view is a full-featured text editor that lets you work with the HTML that defines a page. You can also use it to work with other client-side languages including CSS, JavaScript, and jQuery. And you can use it to work with several server-side scripting languages such as PHP, ASP.NET, and ColdFusion. Although you probably won't use this view when you first start learning Dreamweaver, it can be an invaluable tool as you progress in your web development skills.

Dreamweaver provides a number of features that make it easy to work in Code view. If you click in an HTML tag, for example, Dreamweaver automatically highlights the opening and closing tags. In this figure, you can see that the cursor is in the <h2> tag, and both that tag and the closing </h2> tag are highlighted.

For most languages, Dreamweaver also provides *code hints*. For example, if you type "<" into an HTML document, Dreamweaver assumes you want to enter a tag and it displays a list of the tags that are available. Then, you can scroll through the list, highlight the tag you want to insert, and press the Enter key to insert it. You can also enter one or more characters of the tag you want to insert when the list of tags is displayed to scroll to the first tag in the list with those characters.

Dreamweaver also makes it easy to enter the closing tag for an element. To do that, just type the characters "</" and press the Enter key. Then, Dreamweaver adds the name of the previous unclosed tag, along with the ">" character.

The Coding toolbar at the left side of the Document window also contains some useful features for working with code. For example, you can use this toolbar to collapse and expand portions of code, locate the parent tag of the current tag, hide and display the line numbers, wrap a long line of code, add and remove comments, and automatically format the code. You'll want to experiment with these features after you gain more experience using Dreamweaver.

Dreamweaver with a document displayed in Code view

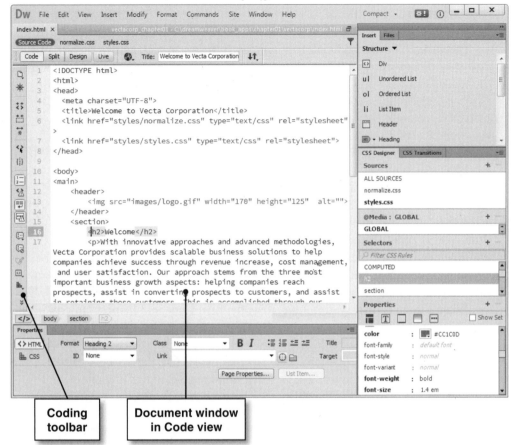

Coding toolbar

Document window in Code view

Description

- *Code view* provides a full-featured text editor that you can use to work with the HTML that Dreamweaver generates as you work in Design view.

- The text editor provides a variety of code editing features, including color coding, indentation, and *code hints*. You can access many of these features from the Coding toolbar.

- Although you can use the Insert panel, Property Inspector, and CSS Designer in Code view, you're more likely to use them in Design view.

- You can also use Code view to edit other types of files, including Cascading Style Sheets, JavaScript, and many of the server-side scripting languages.

Figure 1-10   How to work with the Document window in Code view

How to work with the Document window in Live view

Figure 1-11 shows the Document window you saw in the last two figures in *Live view*. This view provides a built-in browser that's based on the Chromium Embedded Framework (CEF). With this framework, the page will look the same as when displayed in the Chrome browser. That includes interactive elements such as video and Flash animation, which you can't see in Design view. This view can be useful for quickly previewing a page.

In addition to previewing a page in Live view, Dreamweaver CC 2014 lets you edit a page in Live view. That includes inserting new elements using the Insert panel, formatting a page using the Property Inspector, and working with styles using the CSS Designer. It includes editing text elements. And it includes using Element Live Display to work with the ID and classes for an element. (You'll learn about IDs and classes in the next chapter.) In this figure, for example, you can see the Element Live Display that appears when you select the "Welcome" heading. You'll learn more about how you use all of these features of Live view in chapters 3 and 4.

When a page is displayed in Live view, the Live Code and Inspect buttons become available in the Document toolbar. If you click the Live Code button, the Document window is displayed in Split view so you can see the HTML for the page. At first, this HTML may look just like the HTML that's displayed when you display the code for Design view. If the page contains any interactive elements, though, you'll be able to see how the HTML changes as you interact with the page. This can be useful for understanding how interactive elements work as well as for troubleshooting those elements. In section 3 of this book, you'll learn how to work with many of the interactive elements that Dreamweaver provides.

If you click the Inspect button, you can quickly review the HTML and CSS that's applied to an element. To do that, you simply point to the element in the Document window. Then, the HTML for that element is highlighted if you have the window displayed in Split view, and the styles that have been applied to the element are displayed in the CSS Designer.

Dreamweaver with a document displayed in Live view

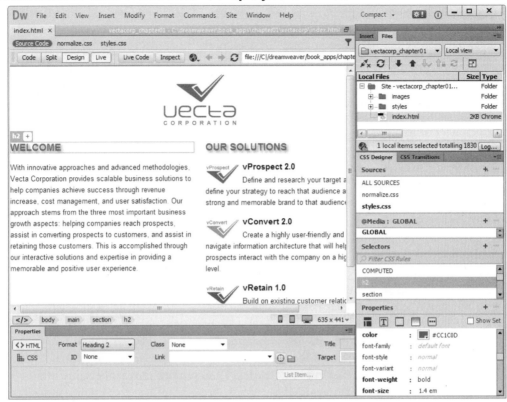

Description

- *Live view* provides a preview of a page as it would appear in the Chrome browser. You turn Live view on and off by clicking the Live button in the Document toolbar.

- You can use the Insert panel, Property Inspector, and CSS Designer in Live view just as you can in Design view. You can also display a related file in Split view by clicking on it in the Document toolbar.

- If you select an element in Live view, an Element Live Display appears above the element as shown above. This display includes the element name along with any ID or classes that have been assigned to the element. You can use this display to add or remove a class or ID.

- You can edit a text element in Live view by double-clicking on it and then entering the changes.

- You can click the Live Code button that becomes available in Live view to display the HTML that would be displayed for a page in a live browser. It's useful for reviewing the changes that occur when the user interacts with a dynamic web page.

- You can click the Inspect button that becomes available in Live view to quickly review the HTML for an element and the styles that are applied to it by simply pointing to that element in the Document window.

Figure 1-11   How to work with the Document window in Live view

How to use the Files panel

Figure 1-12 shows the *Files panel*, which you can use to manage your sites and the folders and files they contain. To display the folders and files for a site, you select it from the first menu at the top of the panel. Here, I selected the site named vectacorp_chapter01. This site includes two folders named images and styles that contain the images and style sheets used by the site, and a file named index.html that is the only HTML document for the site. To open the HTML document or a style sheet in the Document window, you just double-click on it in the Files panel.

Once you create a site in Dreamweaver, you'll want to be sure to use the Files panel for all file management tasks. If you need to move a file, for example, you'll want to do that from the Files panel rather than from outside of Dreamweaver. That's because Dreamweaver checks the cache for the site when you make this type of change to determine if any references to the file need to be updated as a result of the change. If so, it asks if you want it to update these references. In contrast, if you make a change from outside of Dreamweaver, the cache isn't checked and you may end up with incorrect references.

By default, the Files panel displays the local files for a website as indicated by the second menu at the top of this panel. However, you can also use it to display the files on other servers that are defined for the site. In particular, you can use it to display the files on the remote server where the website is hosted. You can also display the files for both the local and remote sites at the same time and then upload files to or download files from the remote site. You'll learn more about this in chapter 13.

The Files panel

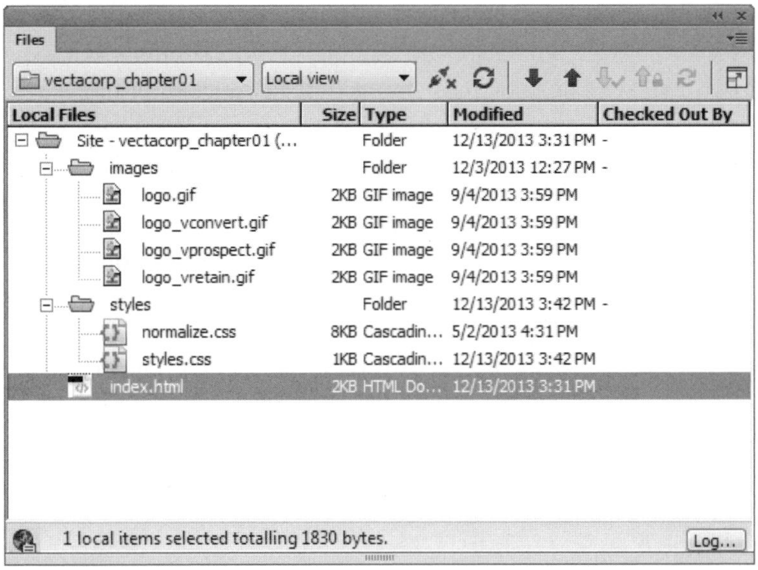

Description

- The *Files panel* lists all of the files and folders that make up a site. You can use it to manage and display those files and folders.
- The first menu at the top of the Files panel lets you choose from the sites that you've defined in Dreamweaver.
- Many of the other controls at the top of the Files panel let you work with a website on a remote server. For example, you can copy selected files to or from the remote server, or you can synchronize the local files with the files on the remote server. See chapter 13 for more information.
- To display a file in the Document window, just double-click on it in the Files panel.

Figure 1-12   How to use the Files panel

How to preview a web page

When you preview a web page, you display it in a browser to be sure it looks the way you want. You should also test the page by making sure that all of the links work.

To preview a page in a browser, you just display the Preview in Browser menu shown in figure 1-13 and then select the browser you want to use. By default, this list includes all of the browsers that were installed on your system when you installed Dreamweaver. If you install other browsers after installing Dreamweaver, you can add them to this list. For more information, please see chapter 3.

As you develop a web page, you should preview it in each browser that's likely to be used to access the page. When you do that, you will often find that the page is formatted differently in some browsers than in others. You can usually fix this type of problem by making some minor adjustments or improvements to the CSS for the page. Note, however, that learning how to adjust the CSS so a page looks the same in every browser isn't always an easy task. But it will become easier with experience.

Even if a web page looks the same in each browser, it may work in some browsers but not others. That's usually because some of the browsers make some assumptions that other browsers don't. If, for example, you have a slight coding error in an HTML file, one browser might make an assumption that fixes the problem, while the other doesn't. To fix problems like these, it often helps to validate the web page. You'll learn how to do that in chapter 3.

After you make changes to a page, you'll need to preview it again. The easiest way to do that is to click the Reload or Refresh button in each browser. Before you do that, though, you should be sure to save any changes you made to the page.

Remember that you can also preview a web page in the Document window by displaying it in Live view. Live view provides a way to quickly preview a page and test advanced features as you develop a page. Before you deploy a web page, though, you'll want to test it in all of the browsers that are in common use.

The Preview in Browser menu

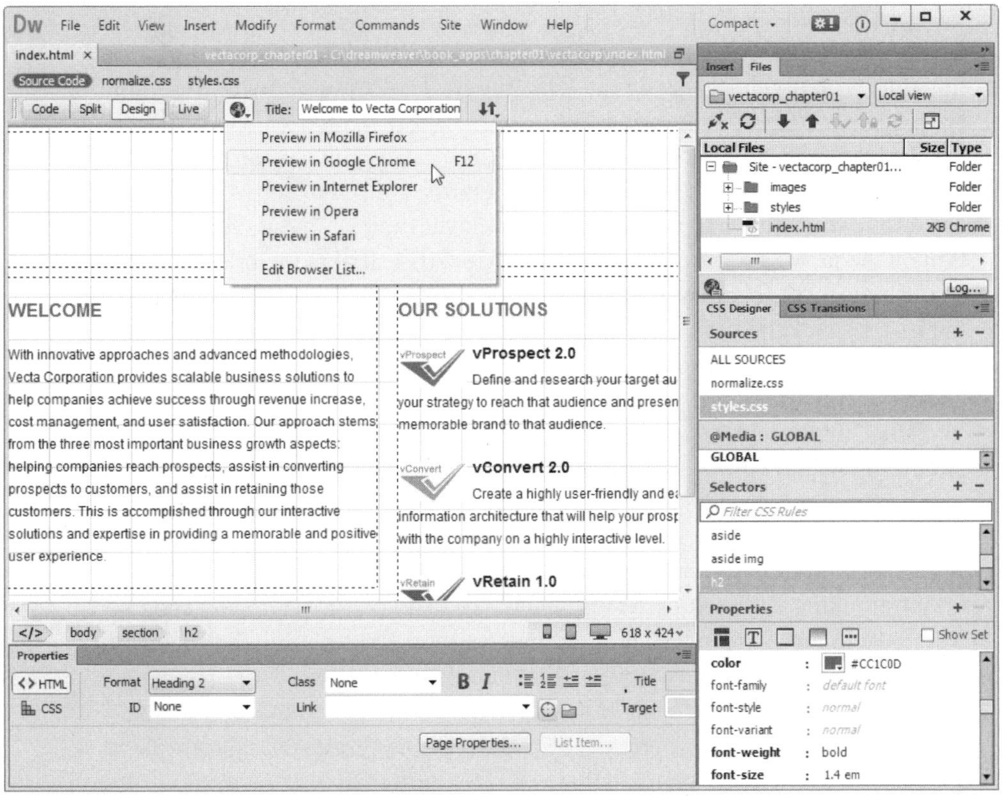

How to preview a web page in a browser

- To preview a web page in a browser, click the icon for the Preview in Browser menu (🌏.) in the Document toolbar, and then choose the browser that you want to use. Or, select a browser from the File→Preview in Browser menu.

- Before you preview a web page in a browser, you should save your work. To do that, you can choose File→Save or File→Save All. If you forget to save a file, Dreamweaver will warn you.

- You can customize the Preview in Browser menu so it includes the browsers you want to use and so it includes keyboard shortcuts for the primary and secondary browsers. For more information, see chapter 3.

How to preview a web page in the Document window

- To preview a web page in the Document window, click the Live button in the Document toolbar to display the page in Live view. To exit from Live view, click the Live button again.

- Because Live view uses the Chromium Embedded Framework, it will display the page exactly as it will appear in the Chrome browser.

Figure 1-13   How to preview a web page

How to get help

As you develop websites in Dreamweaver, you're likely to need some additional information about using the IDE. Figure 1-14 shows how to use Adobe's Help website to get this information.

To display the main help page for Dreamweaver, you can choose Help→Help and Support→Dreamweaver Online Help. From this page, you can get information about a variety of Dreamweaver topics. That includes information on the new features of Dreamweaver CC 2014. It also includes an overview of Dreamweaver CC as well as information on specific topics like how to use the Insert panel and the CSS Designer. You can also display the Dreamweaver CC 2014 manual in PDF format and access the community forums and Dreamweaver tutorials.

The Dreamweaver support page provides access to a variety of online articles, tutorials, and projects from contributors in the Dreamweaver community. You can also get answers to common questions asked by other Dreamweaver users, get solutions to top issues with the current release of Dreamweaver, access the community forums, and even contact Adobe if you have a problem or question that isn't addressed elsewhere. To display this page, you can choose Help→Help and Support→Dreamweaver Support Center or click the "Learn Dreamweaver CC tutorials" link on the main help page.

You can also display context-sensitive help from the panels and dialog boxes that are part of the Dreamweaver IDE. For example, the options menu in the upper right of every panel includes a Help item that you can use to display information about that panel. Similarly, each dialog box includes a Help button that displays information about using that dialog box. You'll find yourself using this context-sensitive help frequently as you learn Dreamweaver.

Adobe also provides an online forum for Dreamweaver that you can use to get answers that you can't find anywhere else. You can access this forum by choosing Help→Help and Support→Adobe Online Forums, by clicking the "Community Forums" link on the main help page, or by clicking the "Ask the Community" icon on the support page. Then, you can search the forum to find the answer you need. If you need additional help, you can ask your own question. Because this forum is moderated by thousands of web development professionals who use Dreamweaver, one of them is likely to have an answer to your question.

The main help page for Dreamweaver CC 2014

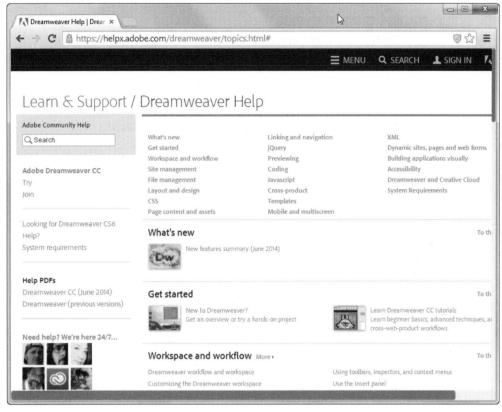

Description

- Adobe's Help website provides a variety of resources for learning about Dreamweaver. You can access these resources from Dreamweaver's Help menu.

- To display Dreamweaver's main help page, choose Help→Help and Support→Dreamweaver Online Help. From this page, you can get information about a variety of topics, including the new features of Dreamweaver CC 2014.

- To display the support page for Dreamweaver help, choose Help→Help and Support→Dreamweaver Support Center. From this page, you can access a variety of tutorials, projects, and articles, get answers to common questions, get solutions to top issues, access the community forums, and contact Adobe support personnel.

- You can use the Dreamweaver support forum to get answers to frequently asked questions, to search for previously asked questions and answers, and to ask your own questions. To display the Dreamweaver support forum, you can choose Help→Help and Support→Adobe Online Forums.

- You can also access help on specific topics from many of Dreamweaver's panels and dialog boxes.

Figure 1-14   How to get help

How to change the workspace and set preferences

In the remaining topics of this chapter, you'll learn three ways that you can customize the Dreamweaver workspace so you can work with it efficiently. To start, you'll learn about the two workspace layouts that Dreamweaver provides by default. Next, you'll learn how to rearrange Dreamweaver's panels so they're easy for you to work with. Finally, you'll learn how to set Dreamweaver's preferences so Dreamweaver works just the way you want it to.

How to use a predefined workspace layout

A *workspace layout* determines how the various panels of the Dreamweaver IDE are displayed and organized. As you saw in figure 1-9, for example, the Insert and Files panels are grouped together by default and are displayed at the right side of the IDE. Similarly, the CSS Designer and CSS Transitions panels are grouped together and displayed below the Insert and Files panels. Finally, the Property Inspector is displayed below the Document window. This is Dreamweaver's *compact layout*.

In contrast to compact layout, figure 1-15 presents the Dreamweaver IDE in *expanded layout*. With this layout, the CSS Designer panel is displayed in two columns, and all four panels at the right side of the IDE are wider to accommodate these two columns. Here, you can see that these panels take up about half the width of the screen, which makes the Document window hard to use. Because of that, you'll probably use expanded view only if you have a wide screen monitor.

To change from one layout to another, you can use the Workspace Layout menu shown in this figure to select a layout. You can also use this menu to reset the current layout to its default if you've made changes to it that you don't want to save.

The Dreamweaver workspace in expanded layout

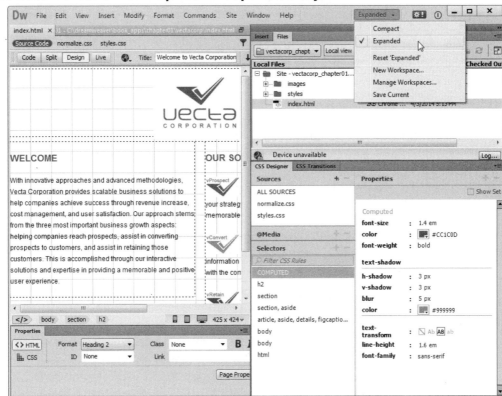

Description

- By default, the Dreamweaver *workspace* is displayed in *compact layout*. With this layout, all four panes of the CSS Designer panel are displayed in a single column so they take up a minimum amount of space on the screen.

- If you're using a widescreen monitor, you may want to use *expanded layout*. With this layout, the panes of the CSS Designer panel are displayed in two columns so they're easier to work with, but the panel takes up more space on the screen.

- To change to a different layout, you can use the Workspace Layout menu near the right side of Dreamweaver's menu bar, or you can use the Window→Workspace Layout submenu. You can also use these menus to reset the current layout if you made changes to it.

Figure 1-15   How to use a predefined workspace layout

How to work with panels

As a seasoned Dreamweaver developer, I prefer to have my workspace organized a certain way. Specifically, I like to have the Files panel open and displayed below the CSS Designer on smaller monitors. In contrast, I like to have the CSS Designer docked at the left side of the Dreamweaver interface on larger monitors. In either case, I close the CSS Transitions panel because I don't use it often, and I close the Insert panel because I don't use it at all. (As you'll learn later, Dreamweaver provides ways to insert objects other than using the Insert panel.) To create this type of layout, you use the skills presented in figure 1-16.

To start, you can undock a panel or a group of panels that's docked at an edge of the application window. To *undock a panel*, you drag it by its tab. To undock a group of panels, you drag it by the group's title bar to the right of the tabs for the panels. In this figure, for example, the group that includes the Insert and Files panels has been undocked from the right edge of the window so it's floating on the screen. You can also undock a panel or group of panels from one edge of the window and then dock it at another edge. You'll know when the panel or group is ready to be docked when it becomes semitransparent.

In addition to undocking and docking a panel or group of panels, you can undock and dock a *stack of panels*. In Dreamweaver, a stack of panels consists of panels that are stacked on top of each other. For example, the Insert and Files group of panels and the CSS Designer and CSS Transitions group of panels form a stack by default. To undock or dock a stack of panels, you drag it by the title bar above the panels in the top group of panels.

You can also collapse panels and stacks of panels. To collapse a panel, you double-click its tab. Then, only the tab for that panel and any other panels in the same group are displayed. To expand a panel, you simply click its tab.

To collapse a stack of panels, you click the Collapse to Icons button in its upper right corner. Then, an icon is displayed for each panel. In this figure, the stack that includes the CSS Designer and CSS Transitions panels is collapsed. Note that because the group that contains the Insert and Files panels has been undocked from the right edge of the window, the CSS Designer and CSS Transitions panels are the only two panels left in this stack. To expand the icons to panels again, you click the Collapse to Icons button again, which changes to Expand Panels when the stack is collapsed.

You can also reposition a panel within a group or move it to another group by dragging the panel's tab, and you can reposition a panel within a stack or move a panel to another stack by dragging it by its title bar. Finally, you can close a panel by choosing Close from its options menu, and you can close a group of panels by choosing Close Tab Group from its options menu. If a panel or group of panels is floating on the screen, you can also close it by clicking its Close button. To redisplay a closed panel, you select it from the Window menu.

If you experiment with these techniques for a few minutes, you'll see that they're easy to master. Then, as you get more comfortable with Dreamweaver, you can adjust the panels so they work best for you.

Floating panels, a docked panel, and two panels collapsed to icons

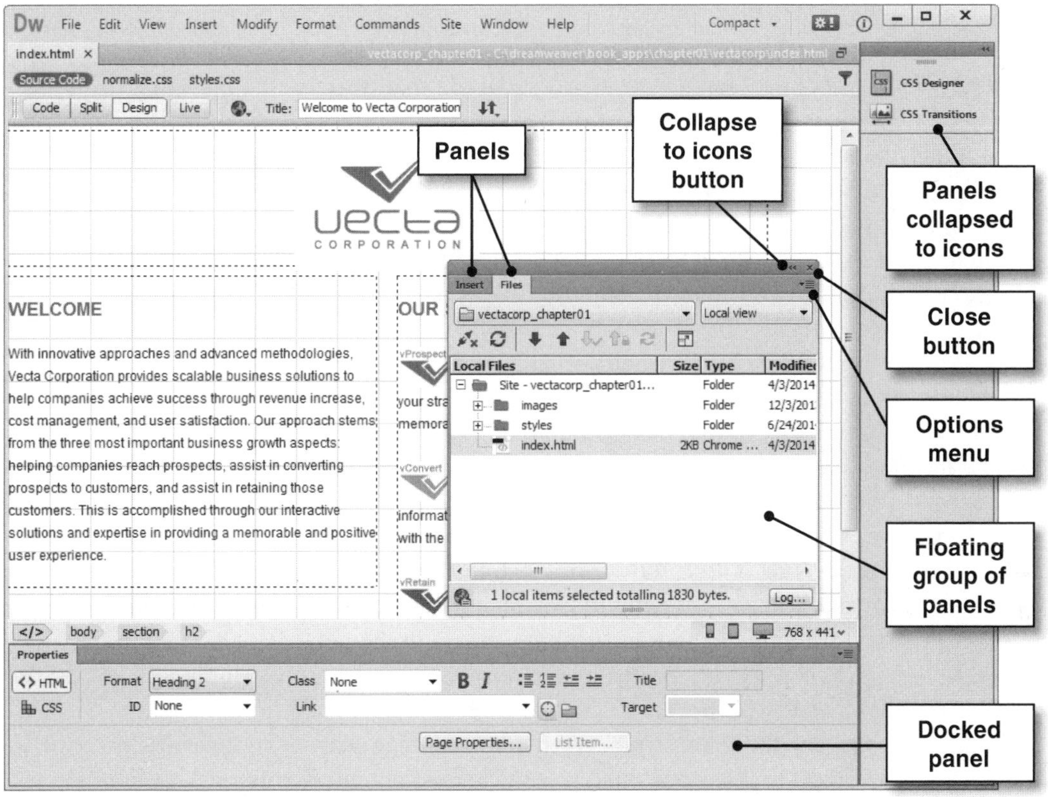

Description

- To undock a *docked panel* so it floats on the screen, drag it by its tab away from the edge of the application window. To undock a group of panels or a *stack of panels*, drag it by its title bar.

- To dock a *floating panel* or a floating group or stack of panels, drag it by its title bar to the edge of the application window until it becomes semitransparent.

- To reposition a panel within a group or move it to another group, drag its tab. To reposition a group within a stack or move it to another stack, drag it by its title bar.

- To collapse a stack so its panels are displayed as icons, click its Collapse to Icons button. To expand the stack, click this button again.

- To collapse a panel so that only its tab is displayed, double-click its tab. To expand the panel, click its tab.

- To close a panel or group of panels, use its options menu. You can also close a floating panel or group of panels by clicking its Close button.

- To display a panel in a group, click its tab. To redisplay a closed panel, select its name from the Window menu.

Figure 1-16   How to work with panels

How to set preferences

In addition to rearranging panels, you may want to change some of the preferences that affect how Dreamweaver works. To do that, you use the Preferences dialog box shown in figure 1-17. As you can see, the options that are available from this dialog box are organized into categories. To display the options for a category, you just click on it.

In this figure, you can see the options in the General category. One option you might want to change in this category is the Show Welcome Screen option. This option determines whether the Welcome screen is displayed when Dreamweaver starts.

Another option you might want to change is the Reopen Documents on Startup option. This option determines if the documents you have open when you close Dreamweaver are opened again the next time you start Dreamweaver.

One more option you may want to change is the Allow Multiple Consecutive Spaces option. To understand how this option works, you need to realize that when you enter one or more spaces into Design view, Dreamweaver treats them as a single space by default. If that's not what you want, you can select this option. Then, every space you enter in Design view is treated as a *non-breaking space*. You'll learn more about non-breaking spaces in the next chapter.

As you gain more experience using Dreamweaver and start developing more complex pages, you'll want to change other options in addition to those mentioned here. By doing that, you can customize Dreamweaver so it works the way you want it to. For now, though, you can just review the options in each category to see what's available.

The General category of the Preferences dialog box

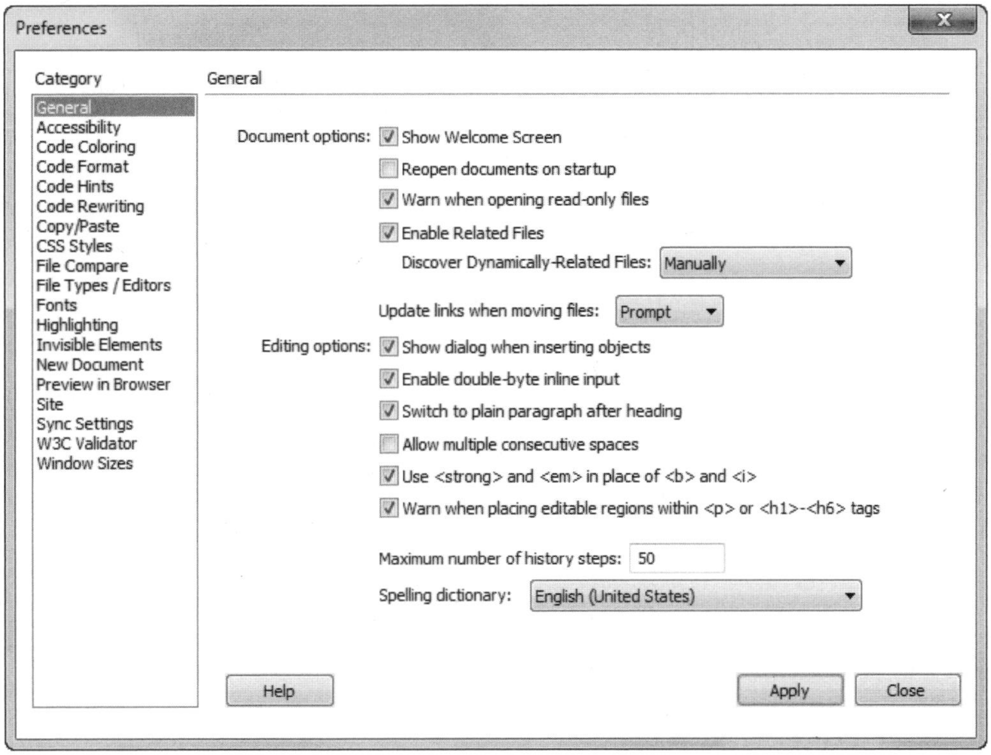

Description

- Dreamweaver provides a number of options you can use to control how it works. You can set these options from the Preferences dialog box.

- To display the Preferences dialog box, select Edit→Preferences (Windows) or Dreamweaver→Preferences (Mac).

- To display the options for a particular category, select the category from the Category pane.

- To prevent the Welcome screen from being displayed when Dreamweaver starts, uncheck the Show Welcome Screen option.

- To open any documents that were displayed when you closed Dreamweaver the next time Dreamweaver starts, check the Reopen Documents on Startup option.

- To provide for inserting multiple consecutive spaces from Design view, check the Allow Multiple Consecutive Spaces option.

- After you change one or more options, you can click the Apply button to apply them. Then, you can click the Close button to close the dialog box.

- Although many of Dreamweaver's options are set the way most beginning developers want them, you may want to review the options in each category so you know what's available.

Figure 1-17   How to set preferences

Perspective

In this chapter, you learned the concepts and terms that you need for developing websites with Dreamweaver. In addition, you learned about the Dreamweaver IDE and some of its basic windows and panels. And you learned how to customize the Dreamweaver workspace so it works the way you want it to.

With that as background, the next chapter presents the HTML and CSS concepts and skills you need to know before you begin developing your own web pages. Then, chapter 3 presents the basic skills for using Dreamweaver to create web pages that use HTML and CSS. After that, you'll be ready to learn how to use Dreamweaver for specific tasks.

Terms

World Wide Web
Internet
client
web server
web browser
network
local area network (LAN)
intranet
wide area network (WAN)
router
Internet service provider (ISP)
Internet exchange point (IXP)
static web page
HTTP request
HTTP (HyperText Transport Protocol)
HTML (HyperText Markup Language)
HTTP response
render a web page
dynamic web page
application server
database server
round trip
web application
server-side scripting language
server-side processing
Apache web server
IIS (Internet Information Services)
JavaScript
client-side processing
client-side scripting language
tabbed panel
JavaScript engine

jQuery
Integrated Development Environment (IDE)
Adobe Creative Cloud (CC)
Dreamweaver CC
Welcome screen
site
cache
asset
Document window
Design view
Code view
Split view
Live view
Related Files bar
Cascading Style Sheets (CSS)
Tag selector
status bar
HTML tag
Insert panel
CSS Designer
style
Property Inspector
code hints
Files panel
preview a web page
workspace layout
compact layout
expanded layout
undock a panel
floating panel
stack of panels
docked panel
non-breaking space

Summary

- A web application consists of clients, a web server, and a network. *Clients* use *web browsers* to request web pages from the web server. The *web server* returns the requested pages.

- A *local area network* (*LAN*) connects computers that are near to each other. This is often called an *intranet*. In contrast, a *wide area network* (*WAN*) uses *routers* to connect two or more LANs. The *Internet* consists of many WANs.

- To request a web page, the web browser sends an *HTTP request* to the web server. Then, the web server retrieves the HTML for the requested page and sends it back to the browser in an *HTTP response*. Last, the browser *renders* the HTML into a web page.

- A *static web page* is a page that is the same each time it's retrieved. The file for this type of page has html or htm as its extension, and its HTML doesn't change.

- The HTML for a *dynamic web page* is generated by a server-side program or script, so its HTML can change from one request to another.

- *JavaScript* is a *scripting language* that is run by the *JavaScript engine* of a web browser. It provides for *client-side processing*.

- *jQuery* is a JavaScript-based library that makes writing JavaScript easier.

- Dreamweaver's *Integrated Development Environment* (*IDE*) helps you design pages quickly using its visual interface.

- *Adobe Creative Cloud* is a subscription-based suite of tools managed by Adobe that allows users to "rent" software including *Dreamweaver CC*.

- Dreamweaver's *Welcome screen* lets you open documents, create new documents, and access a variety of resources.

- When you work in Dreamweaver, you typically create a *site* that consists of the folders and files for a single website. You can manage these folders and files from the *Files panel*.

- You work with the files of a website in the *Document window*. To work with a file using a visual interface, you display this window in *Design view*.

- You can also display the Document window in *Code view*. This view provides a full-featured text editor that you can use to work with several file types, including HTML and CSS.

- You can also display the Document window in *Live view*. In this view, the page is displayed as it would be in the Chrome browser. You can also edit a web page from Live view so you can preview the changes immediately.

- You can customize Dreamweaver's *workspace* so it's organized the way you like it. You can also change Dreamweaver's preferences so Dreamweaver works the way you want it to.

Before you do the exercises for this book...

Before you do the exercises for this book, you should download and install Dreamweaver CC 2014. You will also need to download and install the applications for this book. The procedures for installing the software and applications for this book are described in appendix A.

Exercise 1-1   Tour Dreamweaver

In this exercise, you'll create a Dreamweaver site and work with the panels of the Dreamweaver interface to get a feel for how they work. You'll also get a chance to experiment with the Dreamweaver workspace and review the preferences.

Start Dreamweaver and create a site

1. Start Dreamweaver. When the quick tour starts, click the "Skip the tour" link to close it.

2. When the Welcome screen is displayed, notice that the Recent Files list is empty except for the Open button since you haven't opened any files. Then, review the icons in the Create New list to see the types of files you can create.

3. Choose Site→New Site to display the Site Setup dialog box. Next, enter Exercise 1-1 in the Site Name text box, and click the Browse for Folder icon to locate and select this folder:

    `C:\dreamweaver\exercises\ex01-01\`

    Then, click the Save button.

Review the files for the site

4. Display the Files panel and then double-click the index.html file to display it in the Document window. If necessary, switch to Design view by clicking on the Design button in the Document toolbar.

5. Click the Code button in the Document toolbar to display the HTML for the page. Review this code to see that it provides the content for the page. Then, click the Design button to return to Design view.

6. Click the styles.css file in the Related Files bar to see that the code in this style sheet is displayed in Split view along with the design for the page. Then, click the Code button to show the styles in Code view. If you know some CSS, you might want to review this code to see that it provides the formatting for the content.

7. Click Source Code in the Related Files bar to show the HTML code in Code view.

8. Click the Live button to preview the page in Live view. Then, click in the Welcome heading to display the Element Live Display for that heading. This display indicates that the heading is an h2 element.

9. Double-click in the paragraph below the Welcome heading and make a change to this text to see that you can do that. Then, press the Esc key to cancel the change. When you're done, return to Design view.

Test the web page

10. Press F12 to display the page in your default browser. In this case, the page looks the same in the browser as it does in Live view, but that isn't always true. Now, leave the browser open, but return to Dreamweaver.

11. Click on the Preview in Browser icon and choose a different browser to display the page in that browser. Switch between the browsers to make sure the page looks the same in both browsers. In this case, it should look the same, but that may not always be true.

Experiment with the Property Inspector and Tag selector

12. Click in the Welcome heading, and review the properties for this heading in the Property Inspector when the HTML button on the left side of the Inspector is on. For instance, you can tell that this item has Heading 2 formatting. Also, notice that the Tag selector indicates that an h2 element is selected.

13. Click on other headings and text to see how the Property Inspector and Tag selector change for each item.

14. Click on the CSS button on the left side of the Inspector to see how the display for the selected item changes. Then, click on other headings and text to see how the Property Inspector changes.

Experiment with the workspace and its preferences

15. Change the Workspace Layout menu to display the workspace in expanded layout to see how this looks. Now, double-click the tab for the Files panel to collapse that panel and the Insert panel it's grouped with.

16. Use the Workspace Layout menu to reset the expanded layout to its default. Then, return to the compact layout. As you use Dreamweaver, you will probably use both of these layouts, depending on which layout works better for what you're trying to do.

17. Display the Preferences dialog box, review the options that are available, and make any changes. If you don't want the Welcome screen to be displayed the next time you start Dreamweaver, be sure to uncheck the Show Welcome Screen option. Then, close this dialog box.

18. Continue to experiment on your own. When you're finished, use the File→Close All command to close all files that are open. Then, close Dreamweaver.

Exercise 1-2   Run the book applications

In this exercise, you'll set up a site for the book applications and run some of them. That's something you may want to do as you do the exercises for this book.

1. Choose Site→New Site to display the Site Setup dialog box. Next, enter Book applications in the Site Name text box, and click the Browse for Folder icon to locate and select this folder:

    `C:\murach\dreamweaver\book_apps\`

    Then, click the Save button.

2. This sets up a site that gives you access to all of the applications presented in the book. That way, you can review and run any of them without creating a site for each one. Although you wouldn't do this for production sites, this makes it easy to review the book applications when you're learning.

3. In the Files panel, open the chapter06 folder by clicking on the plus sign in front of it. Notice that this folder contains other folders that contain the applications for the figures in the chapter. For instance, the 6-14 folder contains the application for figure 6-14.

4. Open the folder for figure 6-14, and double-click on the index file that it contains to open that file. Note that the navigation bar near the top of the page is scrambled in Design view, but looks okay in Live view. Then, move the mouse pointer over "Solutions" in the navigation bar, and notice the drop-down menu. That's what figure 6-14 shows you how to develop. When you're learning, running the application for a figure helps you see exactly how it works.

5. Try one more. Open the chapter08 folder, the 8-09 folder, and the index file that it contains. Then, run the application in a browser. If you vary the size of the browser window, you'll see that this application uses responsive web design to automatically adjust the content to the size of the window.

6. If you want to review other applications, you can do that now. But the applications will make more sense after you read about them. When you're through experimenting, close all open files and close Dreamweaver.

2

An introduction to HTML5 and CSS3

All web pages consist of HTML and CSS that can be displayed by a browser. When you use Dreamweaver, though, you can create web pages without writing the HTML and CSS code. Instead, you use the Dreamweaver interface to enter and format the content for a page, and Dreamweaver generates the HTML and CSS that gets the results that you want.

To use Dreamweaver effectively, though, you need to know the basics of HTML and CSS. That way, you can fix problems when something goes wrong. You can also do some Dreamweaver operations more precisely if you know how to work with the HTML and CSS code. For those reasons, this chapter presents the basics of HTML and CSS that every Dreamweaver designer should know.

If you already know HTML and CSS, most of the information in this chapter should be familiar to you. In that case, you may just want to skim the topics in this chapter to pick up any skills you don't already have. In particular, if you haven't been using HTML5, you should read the topics on the HTML5 semantic elements and how to make HTML5 work with older browsers. And if you haven't been using the normalization.css style sheet, you should read that topic too.

How web pages developed with Dreamweaver work

When you use Dreamweaver, you can build a web page without entering any HTML and CSS. Nevertheless, you'll work more efficiently and be able to fix more problems if you know how the generated HTML and CSS works. To get you started with that, this chapter starts by presenting a web page, its HTML, and its CSS.

A web page developed with Dreamweaver

Figure 2-1 presents a web page that was built by using Dreamweaver. This is a home page for a fictitious company called Vecta Corporation. Although this web page is simpler than most of the ones that you'll see on the Internet, it illustrates many of the basic features of a web page.

Here, you can see that the content below the heading for the page is displayed in two columns. The left column contains a welcome message, and the right column presents information about the three solutions offered by the company.

This page uses four images: one at the top of the page and one for each of the three solutions. Beyond that, though, this page consists entirely of HTML and CSS.

A web page developed with Dreamweaver

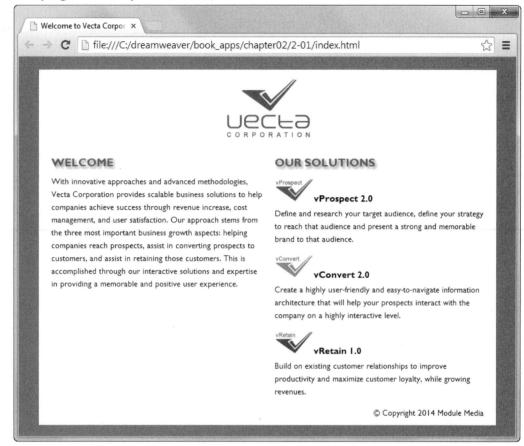

Description

- This is a simple home page for a fictitious company named Vecta Corporation.
- This page uses HTML5 for the content and CSS3 for the page layout and formatting.
- When you use Dreamweaver, you can build this page without coding any HTML or CSS. Instead, Dreamweaver will generate it for you.
- Nevertheless, you should have a basic understanding of how the generated HTML and CSS works. Often, that will help you work more efficiently and fix some problems when the generated code doesn't work the way you expected.

Figure 2-1   A web page developed with Dreamweaver

The HTML for the web page

Figure 2-2 presents the HTML for the web page, which defines the content and structure of the page. As you progress through this chapter, you'll learn many of the details of how this code works. For now, here's a brief introduction to what's going on.

To start, the code for the entire page is called an *HTML document*. This document starts with a *DOCTYPE declaration* that is followed by *tags* that identify the *HTML elements* within the document.

The basic structure of an HTML document consists of head and body elements that are coded within the html element. The head element contains other elements that provide information about the document. In this case, the head element contains a meta element that's generated by Dreamweaver, a title element that contains the title for the page, and two link elements that refer to the two style sheets used by the page.

The body element contains the elements that will be displayed in the web browser. Here, the body element starts with a main element that contains all the code for the page. Within that element are header, section, aside, and footer elements. These are all HTML5 *semantic elements* that provide the structure for the contents of a page.

Within these semantic elements are other elements that provide the content for the page. For example, the img element in the header identifies the image that's displayed at the top of the page. The first h2 element provides the text for the Welcome heading, and the <p> element provides the text that follows this heading.

Note that some of these elements are coded with *attributes* that define the way the content in the element is displayed. These attributes are coded within the opening tag for an element. For example, the four img elements contain src attributes that identify the image that's displayed.

If you review this HTML in the context of the web page displayed in the previous figure, you should be able to see how this HTML code relates to the page. Except for the four images, all of the text is supplied right in the HTML.

The HTML in the index.html file

```
<!DOCTYPE html>
<html>
<head>
    <meta charset="UTF-8">
    <title>Welcome to Vecta Corporation</title>
    <link href="styles/normalize.css" type="text/css" rel="stylesheet">
    <link href="styles/styles.css" type="text/css" rel="stylesheet">
</head>

<body>
<main>
    <header>
        <img src="images/logo.gif" width="170" height="125"
            alt="Vecta Logo">
    </header>
    <section>
        <h2>Welcome</h2>
        <p>With innovative approaches and advanced methodologies, Vecta
            Corporation provides scalable business solutions to help
            companies achieve success through revenue increase, cost
            management, and user satisfaction. Our approach stems from
            the three most important business growth aspects: helping
            companies reach prospects, assist in converting prospects to
            customers, and assist in retaining those customers. This is
            accomplished through our interactive solutions and expertise
            in providing a memorable and positive user experience.
        </p>
    </section>
    <aside>
        <h2>Our Solutions</h2>
        <h3><img src="images/logo_vprospect.gif" width="63" height="36"
            alt="">vProspect 2.0</h3>
        <p>Define and research your target audience, define your
            strategy to reach that audience and present a strong and
            memorable brand to that audience.</p>
        <h3><img src="images/logo_vconvert.gif" width="63" height="36"
            alt="">vConvert 2.0</h3>
        <p>Create a highly user-friendly and easy-to-navigate
            information architecture that will help your prospects
            interact with the company on a highly interactive level.</p>
        <h3><img src="images/logo_vretain.gif" width="63" height="36"
            alt="">vRetain 1.0</h3>
        <p>Build on existing customer relationships to improve
            productivity and maximize customer loyalty, while growing
            revenues.</p>
    </aside>
    <footer>&copy; Copyright 2014 Module Media</footer>
</main>
</body>
</html>
```

Description

- This page uses the HTML5 *semantic elements* to a define the main area of the page, as well as a header, section, aside, and footer.

Figure 2-2   The HTML for the web page

The CSS for the web page

Figure 2-3 presents the CSS that's in the styles.css file that the HTML for the page refers to. (You'll learn more about the normalize.css file later in this chapter.) This CSS file determines how the content for the web page is formatted. You'll learn the details of how this code works later in this chapter. But here's a brief description of it.

To start, you should know that CSS consists of one or more *rule sets*. Each rule set includes a *selector* that identifies the element or elements it applies to. In addition, it includes one or more *rules* that specify the formatting to be applied to those elements.

To illustrate, take a look at the first rule set, which is for the body element. The four rules in this rule set specify the font family, font size, line height, and background color. Here, the font and line height rules apply to the text for the entire web page, and the background color specifies the blue background that shows behind the web page. Note, however, that the font rules can be overridden by rules that appear later in the style sheet. For example, a larger font size is specified for the h2 element.

The next rule set is for the main element. Its first rule specifies a white background, which you can see over the blue background of the body element. Then, the next rule specifies the width for the main element (700 pixels), and the rest of the rules set the margins and padding for the main element. Here, the margin-left and margin-right rules are set to "auto", and that's what centers the main element in the browser window.

The third rule set is for the header. It sets the height of the header to 120 pixels and aligns the text in the center. That's why the image is centered when the page is displayed in a browser.

The fourth and fifth rule sets are for the section and aside elements. The widths of both are set to 340 pixels, and the float for both is set to left. That's why these elements are side by side when the web page is displayed in a browser. Then, the rule set for the footer element clears this float so the footer is always displayed at the bottom of the page.

If you're familiar with CSS, you'll realize that some of the rules shown here could be combined. For example, the margin rules for the main rule set could be combined into just one rule, and the same is true for the padding rules. When you use Dreamweaver, though, it doesn't combine rules like this. Instead, if you want to combine rules like this, you have to enter them explicitly

The CSS in the styles.css file

```css
body {
    font-family: "Gill Sans", "Gill Sans MT", "Myriad Pro",
                 "DejaVu Sans Condensed", Helvetica, Arial, sans-serif;
    font-size: 0.8em;
    line-height: 1.6em;
    background-color: #1C8CDC;
}
main {
    background-color: #FFFFFF;
    width: 700px;
    margin-top: 20px;
    margin-right: auto;
    margin-bottom: 0px;
    margin-left: auto;
    padding-left: 20px;
    padding-right: 20px;
    padding-top: 0px;
    padding-bottom: 10px;
}
header {
    height: 120px;
    text-align: center;
}
section {
    float: left;
    width: 340px;
    margin-right: 20px;
}
aside {
    float: left;
    width: 340px;
}
h2 {
    font-size: 1.4em;
    color: #CC1C0D;
    text-shadow: 3px 3px 5px #999999;
    text-transform: uppercase;
    margin-bottom: 0.5em;
}
h3 {
    margin-bottom: 0.2em;
}
p {
    margin-top: 0px;
}
footer {
    clear: left;
    text-align: right;
}
```

Figure 2-3   The CSS for the web page

The HTML skills that you need

With that as background, you're ready to learn how to code HTML. Although Dreamweaver can generate the HTML for you, you'll use Dreamweaver more effectively if you understand the code that's generated. You'll also be able to work with the code in Code view whenever you need to do that.

The basic structure of an HTML document

Figure 2-4 presents the basic structure of an *HTML document*. As you can see, every HTML document consists of two parts: the DOCTYPE declaration and the document tree.

When you use HTML5, the *DOCTYPE declaration* will appear exactly as it's shown in this figure. It will be the first line of code in every HTML document Dreamweaver creates, and it tells the browser that the document is using HTML5. If you've developed web pages with earlier versions of HTML, XHTML, or Dreamweaver, you will be pleased to see how much this declaration has been simplified.

The *document tree* starts right after the DOCTYPE declaration. This tree consists of the HTML elements that define the content and structure of the web page. The first of these elements is the html element itself, which contains all of the other elements. This element can be referred to as the *root element* of the tree.

The html element should always contain a head element and a body element. The head element contains elements that provide information about the page itself, while the body element contains the elements that provide the structure and content for the page. You saw examples of that in figure 2-2, and you can see additional examples in the document in this figure.

Every web page that you create will contain at least the elements shown at the top of this figure. In addition, it will contain meta and title elements like the ones shown in the HTML code. These are required elements for every web page, and Dreamweaver generates them for you when you create a new document.

The basic structure of an HTML5 document

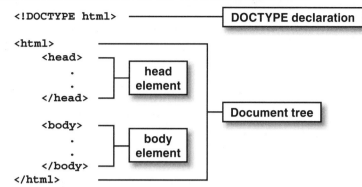

A simple HTML5 document

```
<!DOCTYPE html>
<html>
    <head>
        <meta charset="utf-8">
        <title>Welcome to Vecta Corporation</title>
    </head>
    <body>
        <h1>Vecta Corporation</h1>
        <p>Vecta Corporation provides scalable business
        solutions to help companies achieve success through
        revenue increase, cost management, and user satisfaction</p>
        <p><a href="solutions.html">Our Solutions</a></p>
    </body>
</html>
```

Description

- An *HTML document* contains HTML elements that define the content and structure of a web page.

- Each HTML5 document consists of two parts: the DOCTYPE declaration and the document tree.

- The *DOCTYPE declaration* shown above indicates that the document is going to use HTML5. Dreamweaver includes this declaration at the start of every HTML document.

- The *document tree* starts with the html element, which marks the beginning and end of the HTML code. This element can be referred to as the *root element* of the document.

- The html element always contains one head element that provides information about the document and one body element that provides the structure and content of the document.

Figure 2-4   The basic structure of an HTML document

How to code HTML elements

Figure 2-5 shows you how to code elements like those shown in the table. As you have already seen, most HTML elements start with an *opening tag* that consists of an opening bracket (<), the element name, one or more optional *attributes* that provide additional information for the tag, and a closing bracket (>). After the opening tag is the *content*, which is usually displayed when the page is rendered. After the content is the *closing tag* that marks the end of the element. The closing tag is like the opening tag but has a slash within it. Thus, <h1> is the opening tag for a level-1 heading, and </h1> is the closing tag.

Some elements, however, have no content or closing tag. These tags are referred to as *empty tags*. For instance, the <br> tag is an empty tag that starts a new line, and the <img> tag is an empty tag that identifies an image that should be displayed.

Most attributes are coded with an attribute name, an equals sign, and a value in quotation marks, as shown in the second group of examples in this figure. Here, for example, the <a> element has an href attribute that provides the URL that the link should go to when it is clicked, as well as a title attribute that provides the content for the link.

Boolean attributes, however, can be coded with just the name of the attribute. For instance, the checked attribute for the input element in the second group indicates that the checked attribute is "on", so the check box that this element represents will be checked. If a Boolean attribute isn't coded, the attribute is considered to be "off".

You can also code *comments* within an HTML document as shown in the last example in this figure. That way, you can describe sections of code that might be confusing. You can also use comments to *comment out* a portion of HTML code. That way, the code is ignored when the web page is displayed in a browser. That can be useful when testing a web page. Remember too that when you're using Dreamweaver, you can add comments using the Coding toolbar that's displayed at the left side of the Document window in Code view.

In the table at the top of this figure, you can see that some of the elements are *block elements* and some are *inline elements*. The difference is that by default, block elements are displayed on their own lines. In contrast, inline elements flow to the right of preceding elements and don't start new lines. As a result, you need to use a br element after an inline element if you want to start a new line after it.

Incidentally, you may have noticed that we refer to HTML elements by the name used in the opening tag. For instance, we refer to h1 and img elements. To prevent misreading, though, we enclose one-letter element names in brackets. As a result, we refer to <a> elements and <p> elements. That will continue throughout this book.

Common HTML elements

Element	Type	Defines
h1	Block	A level-1 heading with content in bold at 200% of the base font size.
h2	Block	A level-2 heading with content in bold at 150% of the base font size.
p	Block	A paragraph at 100% of the base font size.
img	Inline	An image that will be displayed on the page.
a	Inline	A link that goes to another page or a location on the current page when clicked.
em	Inline	Emphasizes the content by displaying it in italics.
strong	Inline	Strongly emphasizes the content by displaying it in bold.
br		A line break that starts a new line.

How to code HTML elements

Two block elements with opening and closing tags

```
<h1>Vecta Corporation</h1>
<p>Here is a list of links:</p>
```

Two self-closing tags

```
<br>
<img src="logo.gif" alt="Vecta Corp Logo">
```

How to code the attributes for HTML elements

How to code an opening tag with attributes

```
<a href="contact.html" title="Click to Contact Us">
```

How to code a Boolean attribute

```
<input type="checkbox" name="mailList" checked>
```

How to code an HTML comment

```
<!-- The text in a comment is ignored -->
```

Description

- An HTML element is coded within a *tag* that starts with an opening bracket (<) and ends with a closing bracket (>).
- Most HTML elements consist of an *opening tag*, the *content*, and a *closing tag*. The opening tag consists of the element name plus one or more optional *attributes*. The closing tag consists of a slash followed by the element's name.
- Some elements can be coded without content or a closing tag. These can be referred to as *empty tags*.
- By default, *block elements* are displayed on new lines, but *inline elements* flow to the right of the elements that precede them.
- *Comments* can be used to describe or *comment out* portions of HTML code.

Figure 2-5   How to code HTML elements

How to use the div and span elements

Figure 2-6 shows how to code the div and span elements that have traditionally been used to structure a page and to format portions of inline content. You need to know how these elements are used because you're sure to see them in the HTML for pages that haven't yet been converted to HTML5. In addition, Dreamweaver uses the div element when it implements features like fluid grid layouts that you'll learn about in chapter 8. In most cases, though, you should use the HTML5 elements that are presented in the next figure.

The div element is a block element that you can use to divide an HTML document into logical divisions. In the example in this figure, you can see that the content of the document is divided into three divisions. The first division contains the header for the page, the second division contains the main contents of the page, and the third division is for the footer. If you look at this web page as it's displayed in the browser, you can see that these div elements don't affect the appearance of the page.

For each div element, the id attribute is used to indicate the contents of the division. As you'll see later in the chapter, this id can be used as the selector for applying CSS formatting to each division. In the next figure, though, you'll see how the new HTML5 structural elements can simplify this. As a result, the use of div elements like those shown here should be avoided.

The other element that's presented in this figure is the span element. This inline element has traditionally been used to identify content so CSS can be used to format it. For instance, the <p> element in the main division in this figure contains an inline span element. Here again, the span element doesn't affect the appearance of the page, but its class attribute can be used as the selector for CSS formatting.

Like the div element, though, the use of the span element should be avoided. Instead, you should use the block and inline elements of figure 2-5 to identify the content types. Then, you can use CSS to give these elements the proper formatting.

The div and span elements

Element	Description
div	A block element that lets you divide a page into divisions that can be formatted and positioned with CSS.
span	An inline element that lets you identify text that can be formatted with CSS.

A page that's structured with div and span elements

```
<body>
    <div id="header">
        <h1>Welcome to Vecta Corporation</h1>
    </div>
    <div id="content">
        <p><span class="bold_title">Vecta Corporation</span> provides
        scalable business solutions to help companies achieve success
        through revenue increase, cost management, and user
        satisfaction</p>
    </div>
    <div id="footer">
        <p>&copy; Vecta Corp. - All Rights Reserved.</p>
    </div>
</body>
```

The page displayed in a web browser

Welcome to Vecta Corporation

Vecta Corporation provides scalable business solutions to help companies achieve
success through revenue increase, cost management, and user satisfaction

© Vecta Corp. – All Rights Reserved.

Description

- Before HTML5, div elements were used to define divisions within the body of a document. Now, the HTML5 semantic elements will be replacing div elements.

- Before HTML5, span elements were used to identify portions of text that you could apply formatting to. Today, a better practice is to use elements that identify the contents, like the cite, code, and <q> elements. Then, you can use CSS to format that content.

- You can add the div element in Dreamweaver using the Insert panel or the Insert→Div command. You have to add span elements manually using Code view.

Figure 2-6   How to use the div and span elements

How to use the HTML5 semantic elements

By default, Dreamweaver CC uses HTML5 when you create a new web page, and figure 2-7 presents the new HTML5 *semantic elements* that improve the way you can structure a page. For instance, the example in this figure shows how the header, main, and footer elements can be used to replace the three div elements of the previous figure. This makes it easier to see the structure of the page by looking at the HTML tags. This also makes it easier to code the selectors that you need for formatting these elements.

The use of the new structural elements is often referred to as *HTML5 semantics*. The implication here is that you do a better job of creating meaning when you use the new elements. In contrast, the div elements were generic elements with no meaning implied. In the long run, using HTML5 semantics may mean that search engines will be able to do a better job of coming up with relevant pages. For that reason, you should start using the semantic elements right away. You'll learn how to do that in the next chapter.

Does this mean that you shouldn't ever use div elements? There's debate about that. Some developers say that you should use the div element when you need to group generic content that doesn't fit the meaning of one of the HTML5 structural elements. Others say that you should use section elements for those groupings.

In this book, we use the div element when required by Dreamweaver, such as when working with fluid grid layouts. In all other cases, though, we encourage you to use HTML5 semantics.

The primary HTML5 semantic elements

Element	Contents
header	The header for a page.
main	The main section for a page. This element is new with HTML5.1.
section	A generic section of a document that doesn't indicate the type of content.
article	A composition like an article in the paper.
nav	A section of a page that contains links to other pages or placeholders.
aside	A section of a page like a sidebar that is related to the content that's near it.
figure	An image, table, or other component that's treated as a figure.
footer	The footer for a page.

A page that's structured with header, main, and footer elements

```
<body>
    <header>
        <h1>Welcome to Vecta Corporation</h1>
    </header>
    <main>
        <p>Vecta Corporation provides scalable business
        solutions to help companies achieve success through
        revenue increase, cost management, and user satisfaction</p>
    </main>
    <footer>
        <p>&copy; Vecta Corp. - All Rights Reserved.</p>
    </footer>
</body>
```

The page displayed in a web browser

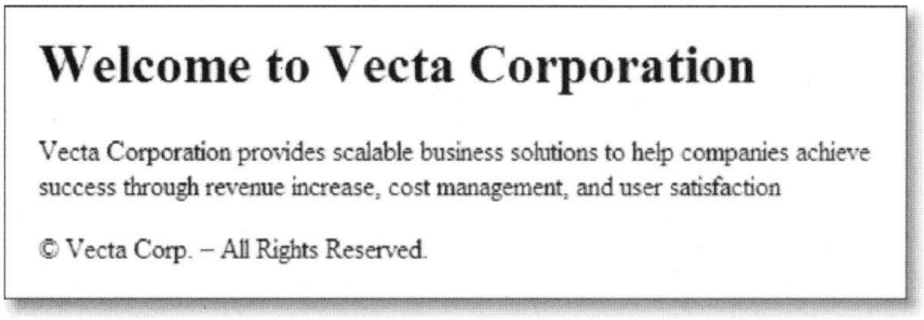

Welcome to Vecta Corporation

Vecta Corporation provides scalable business solutions to help companies achieve success through revenue increase, cost management, and user satisfaction

© Vecta Corp. – All Rights Reserved.

Description

- HTML5 provides new *semantic elements* that you should use to structure the contents of a web page.
- All of the HTML5 elements in this figure are supported by the modern browsers. They will also work on older browsers if you use the workarounds in figure 2-12.
- Two benefits that you get from using the semantic elements are (1) simplified HTML and CSS, and (2) improved *search engine optimization* (*SEO*).
- You can use Dreamweaver to add all of the semantic elements to a page.

Figure 2-7   How to use the HTML5 semantic elements

The CSS skills that you need

When you develop a website using Dreamweaver, you can use the CSS Designer to generate the CSS that's used to format the pages of the site. Before you can use the CSS Designer, though, you need to understand the three different ways that styles can be provided for a web page. In addition, you need to understand how to code CSS rule sets and selectors.

Three ways to provide CSS styles for a web page

Figure 2-8 shows three ways to provide CSS styles for a web page. First, you can code a link element that refers to an *external style sheet*. That's a separate file that contains the CSS for the page. This separates the content from the formatting and makes it easy to use the same styles for more than one page.

The attributes for a link element that links to an external file are the rel attribute with a value of "stylesheet" and the href attribute that locates the file. The href attribute is usually coded with a URL that is relative to the current file. As a result, the relative URL in the first example goes down one folder to the styles folder and locates a file named styles.css.

Second, you can embed a CSS style sheet in the HTML for a page. This is referred to as an *embedded style sheet*. When you embed a style sheet, the CSS rule sets are coded in a style element in the head section of the HTML. For instance, the embedded style sheet in the second example in this group contains one rule set for the body element and another for the h1 element. This works okay if the styles are only going to be used for that one document, but otherwise it's better to use an external style sheet.

Third, you can use *inline styles* within an HTML document as shown by the third example. When you use an inline style, you code a style attribute for the HTML element with a value that contains all the CSS properties that apply to the element. For instance, the inline style in this example applies two properties to the h1 element. Unfortunately, this type of formatting means that the content and formatting are tightly linked, so this can quickly get out of control.

If you use more than one way to provide styles for a page, the styles that are applied last override the styles that are applied earlier. If, for example, an inline style sets the font size for h1 elements, that will override an embedded style that sets the font size for h1 elements.

The next example in this figure shows that you can include more than one style sheet in a single document. Then, the styles are applied from the first external style sheet to the last. This means that a style in a later sheet will override the same style in an earlier style sheet.

Three ways to provide styles

Use an external style sheet by coding a link element in the head section

```
<link rel="stylesheet" type="text/css" href="styles/styles.css">
```

Embed the styles in the head section

```
<style type="text/css">
    body {
        font-family: Arial, sans-serif;
        font-size: 87.5%;
    }
    h1 {
        font-size: 250%;
    }
</style>
```

Use the style attribute to apply styles to a single element

```
<h1 style="font-size: 500%; color: red;">Our Solutions</h1>
```

The sequence in which styles are applied

Styles from an external style sheet

Embedded styles

Inline styles

A head element that includes two style sheets

```
<head>
    <title>Welcome to Vecta Corp.</title>
    <link rel="stylesheet" type="text/css" href="normalize.css">
    <link rel="stylesheet" type="text/css" href="styles.css">
</head>
```

The sequence in which styles are applied

From the first external style sheet to the last

Description

- When you use *external style sheets*, you separate content (HTML) from formatting (CSS). That makes it easy to use the same styles for two or more documents.

- If you use *embedded styles*, you have to copy the styles to other documents before you can use them a second time.

- If you use *inline styles*, the formatting is likely to get out of control.

- If more than one rule for the same property is applied to the same element, the last rule overrides the earlier rules.

- When you specify a relative URL for an external CSS file, the URL is relative to the current file.

- The type attribute for link and style elements isn't required by HTML5, but Dreamweaver uses it anyway.

Figure 2-8   Three ways to provide CSS styles for a web page

How to code CSS rule sets and comments

A CSS file consists of *rule sets*. As the diagram in figure 2-9 shows, a rule set consists of a *selector* followed by a set of braces. Within the braces are one or more *declarations*, and each declaration consists of a *property* and a *value*. Note that the property is followed by a colon and the value is followed by a semicolon.

In this diagram, the selector is h1 so it applies to all h1 elements. Then, the rule set consists of a single property named color that is set to the color navy. The result is that the content of all h1 elements will be displayed in navy blue.

In the CSS code that follows, you can see six other rule sets. Four of these contain only one declaration (or *rule*), but the first and fourth rule sets each include two rules. The first one includes rules for the width and margin properties, and the fourth one includes rules for the float and margin properties. You'll learn how these properties work in chapter 6.

Within a CSS file, you can also code *comments* that describe or explain what the CSS code is doing. For each comment, you start with /* and end with */, and anything between those characters is ignored. In the example in this figure, you can see how CSS comments can be coded on separate lines or after the lines that make up a rule set.

You can also use comments to comment out portions of code that you want disabled. This can be useful when you're testing your CSS code just as it is when you're testing your HTML code. In addition, just as when you're working with HTML code, you can add comments to CSS code using the Coding toolbar that's displayed in Code view.

The parts of a CSS rule set

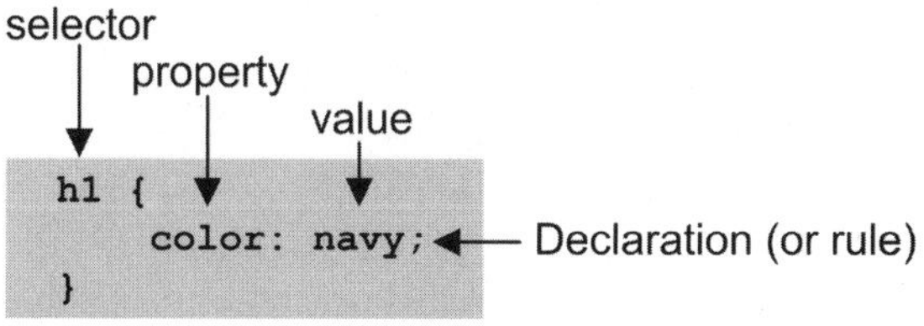

```
selector
    property
        value

h1 {
    color: navy;    ← Declaration (or rule)
}
```

A simple CSS document with comments

```css
/*****************************************************
* Description: Simple style sheet for vectacorp.com
* Author:        Anne Boehm
*****************************************************/
/* Adjust the styles for the body */
body {
    width: 700px;
    margin: 0 auto;                    /* Center the page horizontally */
}
/* Adjust the styles for the sections */
#welcome {
    width: 500px;
}
#solutions {
    width: 340px;
}
aside img {
    float: left;
    margin: 5px 5px 0 0;
}
/* Adjust the styles for the headings */
h1 {
    color: #CC1C0D;
}
h2 {
    border-bottom: 3px solid #CC1C0D;  /* Add a line below h2 headings */
}
```

Description

- A CSS *rule set* consists of a selector and a declaration block.
- A CSS *selector* consists of the identifiers that are coded at the beginning of the rule set.
- A CSS *declaration block* consists of an opening brace, zero or more declarations, and a closing brace.
- A CSS *declaration* (or *rule*) consists of a *property*, a colon, a *value*, and a semicolon.
- To make your code easier to read, you can use spaces, indentation, and blank lines within a rule set.
- CSS *comments* begin with the characters /* and end with the characters */. A CSS comment can be coded on a single line, or it can span multiple lines.

Figure 2-9   How to code CSS rule sets and comments

How to code selectors for elements, ids, and classes

The selector of a rule set identifies the HTML element or elements that the rules should be applied to. To give you a better idea of how this works, figure 2-10 presents the four types of selectors you'll use the most. All of these selectors can be applied to the HTML document shown at the top of this figure. This also shows how the use of CSS separates the formatting from the content and structure that is defined by the HTML.

The rule set in the first example uses the *universal selector*. This type of selector is identified by an asterisk. It instructs the browser to apply the properties to all elements on the web page.

The two rule sets in the second set of examples select elements by type. To code a *type selector*, you just code the name of the element. As a result, the first rule set in this group selects all h1 elements, and the second rule set selects all <p> elements.

The rule set in the third group selects an element by its id. An *id selector* consists of a pound sign (#) followed by an id value that uniquely identifies an element. As a result, this rule set selects the section element that has an id of "solutions".

The two rule sets in the last group of examples select HTML elements by class. A *class selector* consists of a period (.) followed by the class name. As a result, the first rule set selects all elements that have been assigned to the "black" class, which are all three <a> elements. The second rule set selects any elements that have been assigned to the "right" class, which is the paragraph in the footer.

One of the key points here is that a class attribute can have the same value for more than one element on a page. Then, if you code a selector for that class, it will be used to format all the elements in that class. In contrast, since the id for an element must be unique, an id selector can only be used to format a single element.

As you progress through this book, you'll learn all of the details for working with rule sets using the CSS Designer. But to give you an idea of what's going on in this example, here's a quick review of the code.

Here, the rule set for the universal selector sets the top and bottom margins of all elements on the page to .5em and the left and right margins to 1em. The rule set for the h1 element sets the font-family to either Arial (if the browser has access to that font) or the sans-serif font that is the default for the browser. So in this example, the font for "Our Solutions" will be Arial or sans-serif, and you can see that font in the browser display. Similarly, the p elements will have an additional left margin of 3em.

The rule set for the section element (#solutions) specifies a 2-pixel wide solid black border. Additionally, the padding between the contents and the border is set to 1em, which is the height of the default font. Here again, you can see how these rule sets are applied in the browser display.

Last, the rule set for the class named black sets the color to black. This means that the three <a> elements that have this class name are displayed in black. Similarly, the right class is applied to the <p> element in the footer. This class aligns the content within the element to the right side of the screen.

HTML that can be selected by element, id, or class

```
<section id="solutions">
    <h1>Our Solutions</h1>
    <p><a href="solutions.html" class="black">vProspect 2.0</a></p>
    <p><a href="solutions.html" class="black">vConvert 2.0</a></p>
    <p><a href="solutions.html" class="black">vRetain 1.0</a></p>
</section>
<footer>
    <p class="right">Copyright &copy; 2013</p>
</footer>
```

CSS rule sets that select by element type, id, and class

All elements
```
* { margin: .5em 1em; }
```

Type selectors
```
h1 { font-family: Arial, sans-serif; }
p { margin-left: 3em; }
```

ID selectors
```
#solutions { border: 2px solid black; padding: 1em; }
```

Class selectors
```
.black { color: black; }
.right { text-align: right; }
```

The elements displayed in a browser

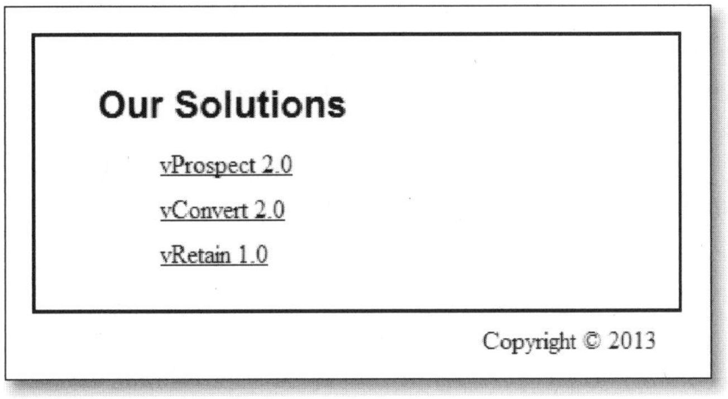

Our Solutions

vProspect 2.0

vConvert 2.0

vRetain 1.0

Copyright © 2013

Description

- You code a selector for all elements by coding the *universal selector* (*).
- You code a selector for all elements of a specific type by naming the element. This is referred to as a *type selector*.
- You code a selector for an element with an id attribute by coding a pound sign (#) followed by the id value.
- You code a selector for an element with a class attribute by coding a period followed by the class name. Then, the rule set applies to all elements with that class name.

Figure 2-10   How to code selectors for elements, id, and classes

How to code descendant, pseudo-class, and combination selectors

Figure 2-11 shows how to code some of the other types of selectors you'll use as you work with Dreamweaver. To start, you can use a *descendant selector* to select elements that are contained within another element. For instance, the h1 element and the first three <p> elements in the HTML in this figure are descendents of the section element, and the fourth <p> element is a descendent of the footer element.

To code a descendant selector, you code a selector for the parent element, followed by a space and a selector for the descendent element. This is illustrated by the first group of examples. Here, the first selector selects all <p> elements in the section with the id "solutions". Then, the second descendant selector selects the <p> element that is a descendant of the footer element.

Another type of selector you'll need to use is a *pseudo-class selector*. To code pseudo-class selectors, you use the *pseudo-classes* in the table at the top of this figure. These classes represent conditions that apply to the elements on a page. For example, you can use the :link pseudo-class to refer to a link that hasn't been visited, the :hover pseudo-class to refer to the element that has the mouse hovering over it, and the :focus pseudo-class to refer to the element that has the focus.

In the second group of examples, the rule set for the :link pseudo-class selector causes all links that haven't been visited to be displayed in blue. Then, the rule set for the :hover pseudo-class selector causes any link with the mouse hovering over it to be displayed in red. And the rule set for the :visited pseudo-class selector causes all visited links to be displayed in green.

The third type of selector you'll need to use is a *combination selector*. This type of selector lets you code multiple selectors for the same rule set. To do that, you separate the selectors with commas as shown in the third group of examples. The rule set in this example uses multiple selectors to apply its rules to all h1 and h2 elements.

Common CSS pseudo-classes

Class	Description
`:link`	A link that hasn't been visited. By default, blue, underlined text.
`:visited`	A link that has been visited. By default, purple, underlined text.
`:active`	The active link (mouse button down but not released). By default, red, underlined text.
`:hover`	An element with the mouse hovering over it. Code this after :link and :visited.
`:focus`	An element like a link that has the focus.

HTML that can be selected by context or by using pseudo-classes

```
<section id="solutions">
    <h1>Our Solutions</h1>
    <p class="blue"><a href="solutions.html">vProspect 2.0</a></p>
    <p class="blue"><a href="solutions.html">vConvert 2.0</a></p>
    <p class="blue"><a href="solutions.html">vRetain 1.0</a></p>
</section>
<footer>
    <p class="blue right">Copyright &copy; 2013</p>
</footer>
```

Descendant selectors

```
#solutions p { font-size: 110%; }
footer p {
    margin: 0;
    padding: .5em;
    background-color: silver;
    font-size: 90%; }
```

Pseudo-class selectors

```
a:link { color: blue; }
a:hover { color: red; }
a:visited { color: green; }
```

A combination selector

```
h1, h2 { color: navy; }
```

Description

- To select elements only when they are descendants of a higher-level element, use a *descendant selector* that consists of the higher element, a space, and the descendent element.

- *Pseudo-classes* are predefined classes that apply to specific conditions. You code a *pseudo-class selector* for an element by coding the element name followed by one of the pseudo-classes shown above.

- A *combination selector* consists of two or more selectors separated by commas.

Figure 2-11   How to code descendant, pseudo-class, and combination selectors

How to provide for cross-browser compatibility

The last two topics in this chapter present two skills that help you provide for *cross-browser compatibility*. This means that your web pages will look and work the same in all browsers. Although you won't need to use these skills while you're learning how to use Dreamweaver, they are useful when you're developing professional websites. That's why you should be aware of them.

How to make HTML5 pages work with older browsers

To provide for cross-browser compatibility, you need to make sure that the HTML5 semantic elements will work in older browsers. Since these elements are ignored by older browsers, the semantic tags won't work correctly in them. However, figure 2-12 provides an easy way to fix this problem.

All you have to do is add the script element shown at the top of this figure to the head element of each HTML document that uses HTML5 elements. This script element points to a JavaScript file known as a *shiv* (or *shim*). Then, when the web page is loaded, the JavaScript file is loaded and executed.

When the shiv is executed, it forces the browser to recognize the HTML5 semantic elements. It does that by issuing a series of createElement methods that add the HTML5 elements to the *Document Object Model* (*DOM*) that the browser builds from the HTML elements for each page.

This shiv also adds the CSS rule set shown in this figure to a style element for the page. This tells older browsers that these elements are block elements, not inline elements. Otherwise, since the older browsers don't recognize the HTML5 elements, they may assume that they're inline elements.

Eventually, all browsers will support the HTML5 elements so you won't need to use a JavaScript shiv for compatibility with older browsers. But until then, adding one script element to each HTML document is an easy way to fix this problem.

The JavaScript shiv for using HTML5 semantics with older browsers

```
<head>
    ...
    <script src="http://html5shiv.googlecode.com/svn/trunk/html5.js">
    </script>
</head>
```

The effect of the shiv

```
<head>
    <script>
        document.createElement(article);
        document.createElement(aside);
        document.createElement(figure);
        document.createElement(figcaption
        document.createElement(footer);
        document.createElement(header);
        document.createElement(main);
        document.createElement(nav);
        document.createElement(section);
    </script>
    <style>
        article, aside, figure, figcaption, footer, header, main, nav,
        section {
            display: block;
        }
    </style>
</head>
```

How to add the shiv to a web page in Dreamweaver

1. In Code view, place your cursor before the closing </head> tag and choose Insert→Script to display the Select File dialog box.

2. Paste this URL into the File Name text box and then click OK:

    `http://html5shiv.googlecode.com/svn/trunk/html5.js`

3. When Dreamweaver displays a dialog box asking if you would like to copy the script to your website's root folder, click No.

Description

*   To make older browsers recognize the HTML5 semantic elements, you can use the JavaScript *shiv* (also known as a *shim*) shown above.

*   The script element above gets the shiv from another site so you don't have to include its JavaScript file in your website. However, you can copy this file to your website and access it from that location.

*   The effect of the shiv is to issue createElement methods that add the HTML5 semantic elements to the *DOM* (*Document Object Module*) in the browser and also to add a CSS rule set for the page that tells the browser to treat the HTML5 elements as block elements.

Figure 2-12   How to make HTML5 pages work with older browsers

How to use the normalize.css style sheet

A problem that faces web developers today is that the five modern browsers render some elements of a web page differently. One example is the inline abbr element that's used to define abbreviations.

In Firefox, the textual content for this element is displayed with a dotted line below it. Then, when the user points to the element with the mouse, a tooltip that defines the abbreviation is displayed. In contrast, a dotted line isn't displayed under the abbreviation in Internet Explorer. Because of that, the user won't know that there is an abbreviation on the page unless he happens to point to it. Then, a tooltip appears just as it does in Firefox.

To standardize how elements like this are displayed, you can use the normalize.css style sheet that's described in figure 2-13. This style sheet applies styles to elements like the abbr element so they appear exactly the same in all browsers. This can save you a lot of time dealing with small rendering issues near the end of a web development project.

In this figure, you can see the start of the normalize style sheet. This shows that its rule sets are identified by comments. As you can see, the first rule set is the same as the rule set in the previous figure. It sets the HTML5 elements to block elements. So, if you combine the JavaScript shiv with the normalize style sheet, you go a long ways toward providing cross-browser compatibility.

In fact, the normalize style sheet fixes many of the problems with older versions of Internet Explorer, like IE 9 and IE 10, without the need for the JavaScript shiv. That's why the normalize style sheet is used in most of the exercise solutions for this book, but the JavaScript shiv isn't.

The start of the normalize.css style sheet

```
/*! normalize.css v2.1.1 | MIT License | git.io/normalize */
/* ===================================================================
   HTML5 display definitions
   =============================================================== */
/**
 * Correct `block` display not defined in IE 8/9.
 */
article,
aside,
details,
figcaption,
figure,
footer,
header,
hgroup,
main,
nav,
section,
summary {
    display: block;
}
```

The URL for downloading normalize.css

http://necolas.github.io/normalize.css/

How to download normalize.css and save it to your website

- Open a browser, browse to the URL shown above, and click the Download button.
- If CSS files are associated with a program that's installed on your computer, the normalize.css file will be opened in that program. Then, you can use that program to save the file to your website.
- If CSS files aren't associated with a program on your computer, the normalize.css file will be displayed on a page within the browser. Then, you can right-click the page, choose Save As, and use the dialog box that's displayed to save the normalize.css file to your website.
- Once you save the normalize.css file to your website, you can attach it to each web page.

Description

- Normalize.css is a CSS file that forces all browsers to render HTML elements the same way.
- The normalize style sheet also fixes many of the problems with older browsers, like Internet Explorer 9 and 10, without the need for the JavaScript shiv.
- Normalize.css is used by some of the most popular CSS frameworks, including Twitter Bootstrap, HTML5 Boilerplate, and YUI. It's also used by NASA, The United Kingdom's government site, and others.

Figure 2-13   How to use the normalize.css style sheet

Perspective

This chapter has presented the HTML and CSS concepts and skills that you need for working effectively with Dreamweaver and for understanding the HTML and CSS code that it generates. In the chapters that follow, you'll learn how to use Dreamweaver to provide the HTML and CSS for a page...without having to code the HTML and CSS yourself. Later, when you want to learn more about HTML and CSS, you can read *Murach's HTML5 and CSS3*.

Terms

HTML (HyperText Markup
   Language)
HTML document
tag
HTML element
Cascading Style Sheets (CSS)
DOCTYPE declaration
document tree
root element
opening tag
attribute
content
closing tag
empty tag
HTML comment
comment out
block element
inline element
HTML5 semantics
search engine optimization (SEO)
external style sheet
embedded style sheet

inline style
rule set
selector
declaration block
declaration
property
value
rule
CSS comment
universal selector
type selector
id selector
class selector
descendant selector
pseudo-class
pseudo-class selector
combination selector
cross-browser compatibility
Document Object Model (DOM)
HTML5 shiv
HTML5 shim

Summary

- An *HTML document* consists of a *DOCTYPE declaration* that indicates what version of HTML is being used and a *document tree* that contains the *HTML elements* that define the content and structure of a web page.

- The *root element* in a document tree is the html element, which always contains a head element and a body element. The head element provides information about the page, and the body element provides the structure and content for the page.

- Most HTML elements consist of an *opening tag* and a *closing tag* with *content* between these tags. An opening tag can also include one or more *attributes* that provide optional values.

- *Block elements* are the primary content elements of a website, and each block element starts on a new line when it is rendered by a browser. Headings and paragraphs are common block elements.

- *Inline elements* are coded within block elements, and they don't start on new lines when they are rendered. A common inline element is <a>, which creates a link.

- Historically, the div element has been used to divide the code for an HTML document into divisions, and the span element has been used to identify portions of text so formatting can be applied to them.

- The HTML5 *semantic elements* provide a new way to structure the content within an HTML document. This makes it easier to code and format elements. In the long run, it may also improve the way search engines rank your pages.

- If you're going to use a style sheet for more than one HTML document, it's usually best to store the styles in an *external style sheet*. However, you can also *embed a style sheet* in the HTML for a page, and you can apply styles to individual elements by using *inline styles*.

- A *CSS rule set* consists of a selector and a declaration block. The *selector* identifies the HTML elements that are going to be formatted.

- The *declaration block* in a CSS rule set contains one or more *declarations* that do the formatting. Each declaration (or *rule*) consists of a *property*, a colon, a *value*, and a semicolon.

- To select all elements, you code the *universal selector*, which consists of an asterisk (*).

- To select all elements of a specific type, you code a *type selector*, which consists of the element name.

- To select an element whose id attribute has a specific value, you code an *id selector*, which consists of a pound sign (#) followed by the id value.

- To select all elements that are assigned to a class, you code a *class selector*, which consists of a period followed by the class name.

- You can use a *pseudo-class selector* to apply CSS formatting when certain conditions occur or have occurred, like when the mouse hovers over an element or the focus is on an element.

- To provide *cross-browser compatibility* with older browsers when you use the HTML5 semantic elements, you can add a script element that accesses a JavaScript *shiv* to the head element of each HTML document.

- You can attach the normalize.css style sheet to your web pages to make sure that all elements will be rendered the same in every browser.

Before you do the exercises for this book...

If haven't already installed the software and applications for this book, you need to do that now. The procedures for doing that are in appendix A.

Exercise 2-1   Use Dreamweaver to work with HTML and CSS

In this exercise, you'll review the application that's presented in figures 2-1 through 2-3. You'll also use Code view to make some modifications to the HTML and CSS code for this application.

Review the application

1. Start Dreamweaver, and choose Site→New Site to display the Site Setup dialog box. Next, enter Exercise 2-1 in the Site Name text box, and click the Browse for Folder icon to locate and select this folder:

   `C:\dreamweaver\exercises\ex02-01\`

   Then, click the Save button.

2. Display the Files panel and then double-click the index.html file to display it in the Document window. If necessary, switch to Design view by clicking on the Design button in the Document toolbar.

3. Click the Code button in the Document toolbar to display the HTML for the page. Note that the head element includes two link elements that attach the normalize.css and styles.css files to the document. Then, review the rest of the HTML code to see that it provides the content for the page.

4. Click the styles.css file in the Related Files bar to see the code in this style sheet. Then, click the normalize.css file in the Related Files bar to see the code for this style sheet.

5. Return to Design view, note the Welcome heading, and switch to Live view to see that shadows are added to this heading in Live view. Then, turn off Live view by clicking on the Live button again, and run the application in your default browser by pressing F12. Note that the shadows are displayed. Now, return to Dreamweaver.

Modify and comment out some of the HTML code

6. Switch to Code view, and click Source Code in the Related Files bar to display the HTML for the page. Then, change the content for the first h2 element from "Welcome" to "Welcome to Vecta Corp", and switch to Design view to make sure this worked. (But note that this heading is displayed with all capital letters in Design view although it isn't coded that way in Code view. It's the CSS that makes that happen.)

7. Switch to Code view, select the entire h2 element that you just changed, find the Apply Comment button in the vertical toolbar to the left of the HTML, click on it, and select Apply HTML Comment. Then, switch to Design view to see that the heading is no longer displayed.

8.   Switch back to Code view, select the entire commented-out h2 element, and click on the Remove Comment button in the vertical toolbar. Then, check this change in Design view.

Modify and comment out some of the CSS code

9.   Switch to Code view, and click on styles.css in the Related Files bar to display the CSS for that style sheet. Then, in the rule set for the body element, change the background-color rule to #DFE3E6, and check this change in Design view.

10. In Code view, scroll down to the h2 rule set, and note the text-transform rule. That's the one that converts the text in the HTML to all caps. Select this entire rule, click on the Apply Comment button in the toolbar, and click on Apply /* */ Comment to comment out this rule. Then, switch to Design view and note the change in the way the heading is displayed.

11. In Code view, comment out the float rules in the rule sets for the section and aside elements, and review this change in Live view. Note that it is the float rules that implement the two-column formatting for the page.

12. Go back to Code view and undo this change by issuing the Undo command twice. To do that, you can either select the Edit→Undo command or press the shortcut key for the Undo command (Ctrl+Z for Windows, Cmd+Z for Macs). Then, check the change in Design view.

13. Comment out the background-color rule in the main rule set, and note the change in Design view. This shows that the background color for the body shows through the main element unless a background color for the main element is set too. In this case, that background color was white (#FFFFFF). Now, undo this change to restore the white background.

14. In Code view, comment out the margin-right and margin-left rules for the main rule set. Then, switch to Design view, run the application in your default browser, and note that the application is no longer centered in the browser window.

15. Return to Dreamweaver, and undo the changes to the margin-right and margin-left rules so they're reset to "auto". That's the value that centers the application between the left and right sides of the window.

Experiment on your own

16. If you want to experiment with some of the HTML and CSS code, you can do that now. This is fail-safe because you can always undo the changes that you've made.

17. When you're through experimenting, close all of the files.

How to build a website with Dreamweaver

In chapter 2, you learned how HTML and CSS are used to build web pages. Now, you'll learn how to build web pages with Dreamweaver and have it generate the HTML and CSS code for you.

How to create a site and add a web page

When you use Dreamweaver to develop a website, you typically start by creating a Dreamweaver *site* that will contain all the files for the website. Then, you can add pages to the site, define the basic appearance of each page, and add content to each page.

How to create a Dreamweaver site

In chapter 1, you learned how to create a Dreamweaver site. Figure 3-1 presents this information again so you can see how it's used to create the site for this chapter.

First, because each site must have a unique name, I included the chapter number in the site name. Then, I stored the websites for each chapter in a folder with a name that identifies the chapter number. Finally, although you can't see it here, I stored each website for a chapter in a separate folder within the chapter folder. For example, the application that you'll see in figure 3-4 is stored in a folder named 3-04 in the chapter03 folder.

When you create a site, Dreamweaver establishes a reference between that site and the folder you specify. If that folder contains other folders and files, they're automatically included in the site. However, you can also create a site from scratch. To do that, just specify a folder that doesn't already exist. Then, Dreamweaver creates that folder, and you can add any folders and files you want to that site. In the next figure, for example, you'll learn how to add a file that defines a web page to a site.

The Site Setup dialog box

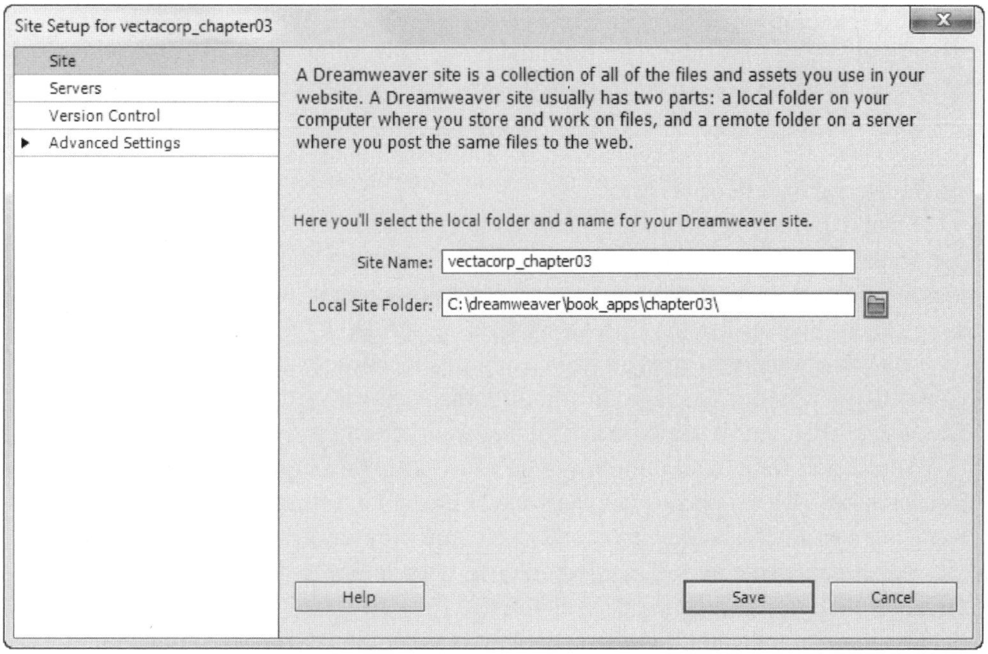

How to create a new Dreamweaver site

1. Choose Site→New Site to display the Site Setup dialog box.
2. Enter a name for the site into the Site Name text box.
3. Click the folder icon to the right of the Local Site Folder text box, and then browse to and select the top-level folder for the site. Or, enter the path for this folder into the text box.
4. Click the Save button to create the new site.

Description

- Although you can use Dreamweaver to work with individual files, you typically define a site for each website that contains the folders and files for that website. Then, you can use Dreamweaver's features for working with sites as you develop and maintain the website.

- If you create a site for a folder that already contains folders and files, those folders and files are included in the site.

- If you create a site for a folder that doesn't exist, that folder is created. Then, you can add any folders and files you need.

- After you create a Dreamweaver site, you can use the first menu at the top of the Files panel to display it if another site is currently displayed.

Figure 3-1   How to create a Dreamweaver site

How to create a new web page

Figure 3-2 presents the New Document dialog box that you can use to add a variety of page types. To add a basic HTML page, you choose the Blank Page category and then select HTML for the page type and <none> for the layout. You can also select a document type using the DocType menu. In most cases, though, you'll use the default of HTML5.

Finally, if your site already contains one or more external style sheets, you can attach those style sheets by clicking the Attach Style Sheet icon and then identifying each style sheet you want to attach. If you don't do that, you can attach style sheets using the CSS Designer as described later in this chapter.

Note that when you create a page using this technique, a default name like Untitled-1 is used for the page. In addition, the page isn't saved in the site. Because of that, you'll want to save the file right after you create it.

You'll also want to save the files you're working on frequently as you use Dreamweaver. That's because Dreamweaver doesn't automatically save your work at given intervals like many other software programs do.

When you create an HTML document as shown here, it includes the basic elements that you learned about in chapter 2. To start, it includes a DOCTYPE declaration that indicates that the document is going to use HTML5. In addition, it includes an html element for the document tree. Within this element is a head element and a body element. And within the head element is a meta element and a title element with a default title. If you attach a CSS file when you create the page, a link element that identifies that file is also included in the head element.

If you just want to create a basic page with the settings shown here, you can do that without displaying the New Document dialog box. To do that, just right-click on the folder in the Files panel where you want to add the page and select New File from the shortcut menu that's displayed. Then, enter a name for the page in the Files panel. Note that when you use this technique, the page is automatically saved in the site.

Instead of creating a web page from scratch, you should know that you can also create a page from another page. To do that, just select the existing page in the Files panel and then choose File→Save As to save the page with a different name. This can be helpful if you want to create a new page that's similar to an existing page.

The New Document dialog box

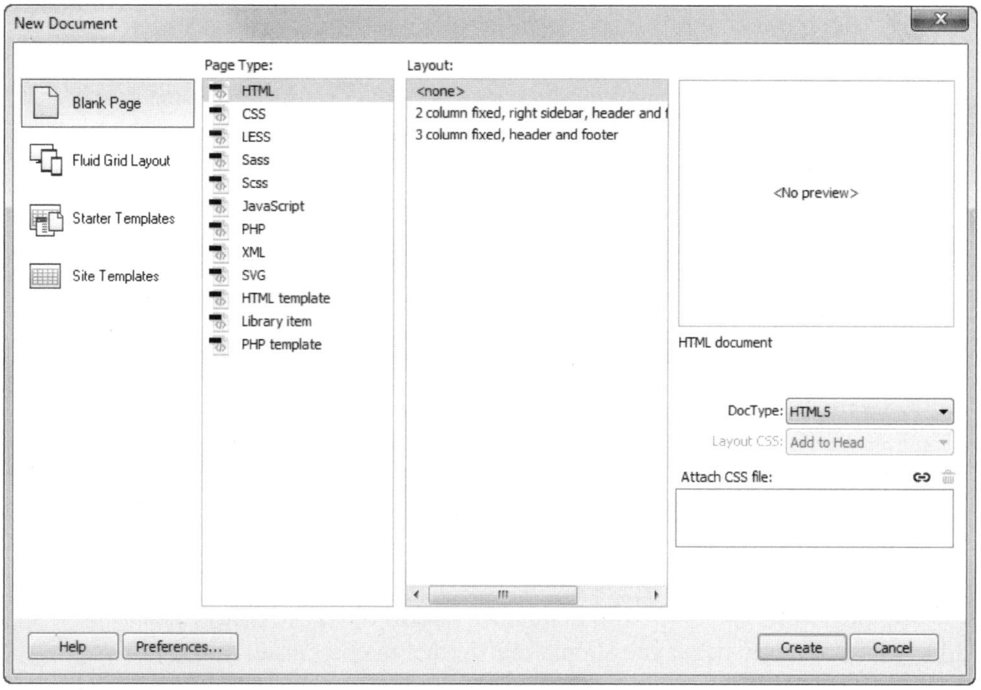

How to create a new HTML5 document

- Choose File→New to display the New Document dialog box.
- To create a document with basic starting code, choose the Blank Page category, make sure the HTML page type is selected, and choose <none> for the layout.
- Click the Create button to create the new document.
- Save your page by choosing File→Save As or by clicking the Save button in the Standard toolbar to display the Save As dialog box. Then, select the location where you want to save the file, enter a name for the file, and click the Save button.
- You can also choose File→Save As to create a new page from the page you select in the Files panel.
- To quickly create a new, blank page, right-click on the folder where you want to add the page in the Files panel, select New File, and enter a name for the file.

Description

- When you create a web page with Dreamweaver, the page uses HTML5 by default.
- If the site that will contain the new page includes external style sheets, you can attach them by clicking on the Attach Style Sheet icon (⊖).
- In addition to creating a web page with basic starting code, you can create pages with 2- and 3-column layouts. Because the code that's generated for these layouts is cumbersome, though, we recommend that you don't use them.
- If the Standard toolbar isn't displayed, you can display it by right-clicking the Document toolbar and choosing Standard or by choosing View→Toolbars→Standard.

Figure 3-2   How to create a new web page

How to define the basic appearance of a web page

Before you start adding content to a page, you may want to set some properties that define the basic appearance of the page. To do that, you can use the Page Properties dialog box shown in figure 3-3. As you can see, the page properties are divided into several categories. The three categories you're most likely to use are Appearance (CSS), Links (CSS), and Headings (CSS).

In this figure, you can see the properties that are available from the Appearance (CSS) category. Here, the font, font size, background color, and margins for the page have been set. In addition to these properties, you can set other font properties, the text color, and properties for background images.

From the Links (CSS) category, you can set properties that define the appearance of the links on the page. That includes the font and font size and the colors of the links in various states. It also includes when links are underlined.

From the Headings (CSS) category, you can define the appearance of the six levels of headings. That includes the font that's used for all headings, as well as the font size and color for each heading.

Although the Page Properties dialog box makes it easy to define the basic appearance of a web page, you should realize that the properties you specify here are included in an embedded style sheet. Because of that, you'll typically want to move the CSS rule sets that contain these properties to an external style sheet as described later in this chapter. Or, you can use the CSS Designer to create the rule sets you need in an external style sheet. You'll learn how to do that later in this chapter too, and you'll learn more about the properties that you can use with text and links in chapter 5.

The Appearance (CSS) category of the Page Properties dialog box

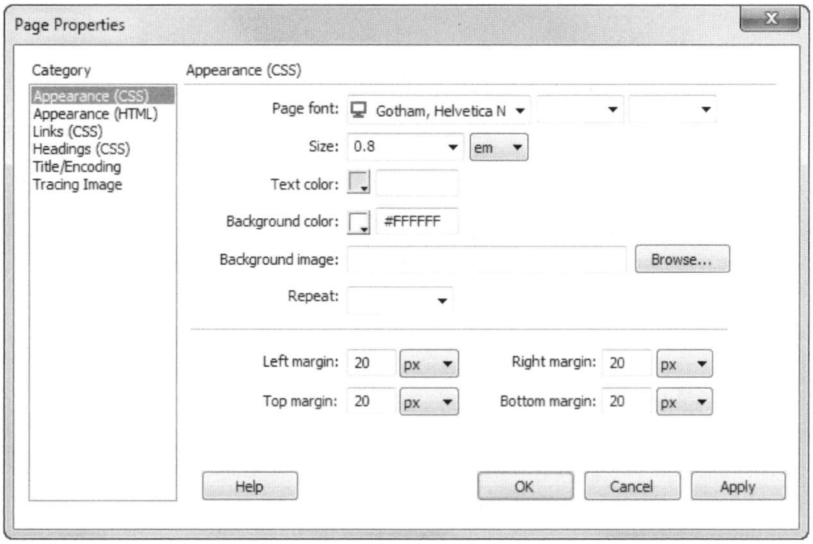

Categories of the Page Properties dialog box

Category	Description
Appearance (CSS)	CSS styles for fonts, backgrounds, and margins.
Appearance (HTML)	HTML attributes for backgrounds, text, links, and margins. You should avoid using this category because it results in invalid HTML5 code.
Links (CSS)	CSS styles for links, including those for fonts, link states, and underline style.
Headings (CSS)	CSS styles for headings, including fonts, sizes, and colors for heading levels 1 through 6.
Title/Encoding	The title for the document, as well as the document type (usually HTML5) and encoding (usually UTF-8).
Tracing Image	An image that you can use as a guide for designing a page.

Description

- You can use the Page Properties dialog box to set the basic properties for a page. Then, you can use CSS to apply formatting to individual elements.

- To display the Page Properties dialog box, choose Modify→Page Properties or click the Page Properties button in the Property Inspector.

- The CSS properties you specify from the Page Properties dialog box are included in an embedded style sheet. Then, you can move the CSS rule sets that contain these properties to an external style sheet as described later in this chapter.

- If you prefer, you can use the CSS Designer as shown later in this chapter to create the CSS rule sets for a page in an external style sheet.

- Instead of entering the title for a page from the Title/Encoding category, you can enter it in the Title text box in the Document toolbar.

Figure 3-3   How to define the basic appearance of a web page

How to add content to a web page

The easiest way to add content to a web page is to place your cursor within the page and begin typing. If you do that, you should know that you can press the Enter or Return key to create a paragraph for the text you're currently typing and to start a new paragraph. In other words, the text is structured with <p> elements. You can also enter a line break (a br element) by holding down the Shift key and pressing the Enter or Return key.

Often, though, the content is provided to you in the form of one or more files. If the content is plain text, you can add it to a web page by copying it from the original file and pasting it into the page. Note that if you use this technique, any text that's separated by two line breaks is formatted as paragraphs. Also note that you can copy content from the original file by opening it outside of Dreamweaver, or you can add the file to the site and then open it in Dreamweaver. In figure 3-4, for example, a text file named welcome.txt has been added to the site, and the content of this file has been added to the page.

Three images have also been added to the page in this figure. (You can only see the first two here.) These images have been added to the images folder of the website. Then, you can add an image to the page by dragging it from the Files panel and dropping it on the page where you want it to appear.

Of course, there are other ways that you can add text and images to a page. You'll learn more about that in the next chapter. For now, though, you can use the techniques shown here to quickly add the text and images you need.

A page after text and three images have been added to it

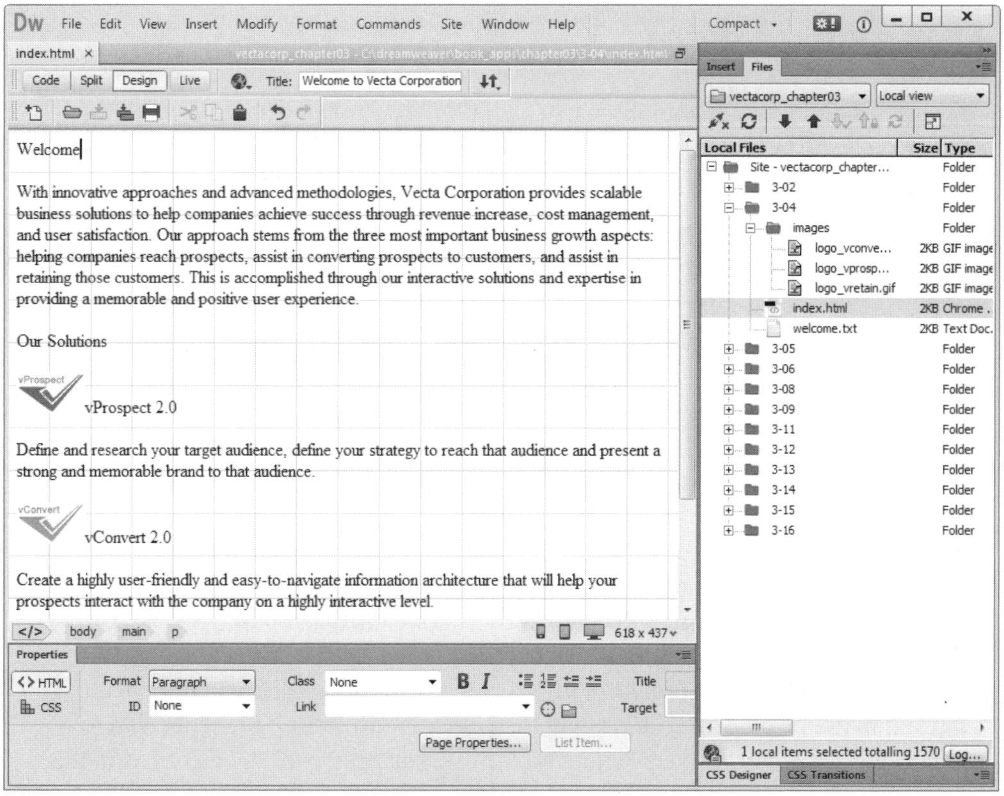

How to add plain text to a web page

- Open the file that contains the text, select the text you want to copy, and click the Copy button in the Standard toolbar or press Ctrl+C (Windows) or Cmd+C (Mac).

- Position the cursor where you want to add the text in Dreamweaver, and click the Paste button in the Standard toolbar or press Ctrl+V (Windows) or Cmd+V (Mac). Portions of text that are separated by two line breaks are formatted as paragraphs.

- You can also enter text directly into the Document window. When you do that, you can press the Enter key (Windows) or Return key (Mac) to start a new paragraph and Shift+Enter (Windows) or Shift+Return (Mac) to start a new line.

How to add an image to a web page

- Drag the image from the Files panel to the location in the page where you want the image to appear and then drop it.

Description

- The text for the web pages you develop will often be written for you by someone else. Then, you can copy the text from a file inside or outside of Dreamweaver, and paste it into a page within Dreamweaver.

Figure 3-4   How to add content to a web page

How to work with HTML in Dreamweaver

In this topic, you'll learn how to use the *HTML Property Inspector* and the *Insert panel* to work with the HTML in a web page.

How to use the Property Inspector to work with HTML

Figure 3-5 shows a web page after two paragraphs have been formatted as headings. To create these headings, I started by clicking in the paragraph to place the cursor in that paragraph. Then, I selected the Heading 2 option from the Format menu in the Property Inspector. When I did that, the <p> element was changed to an h2 element.

The other controls in the Property Inspector also generate HTML code for you. For example, you can add an id or class attribute to the element that contains the cursor by entering it in the ID or Class combo box.

In addition to formatting the element that contains the cursor, you can use the Property Inspector to format selected text or one or more selected elements. To enclose text with a <strong> or <em> element, for example, you drag over the text in the Document window and then click the Bold or Italic icon. And to generate HTML that formats elements as a list, you drag over the elements in the Document window and then click the Unordered List or Ordered List icon. To format a single element, you can drag over it or you can click in it and then click on its tag in the Tag selector at the bottom of the Document window.

The properties that are available in the Property Inspector change depending on what's selected in the Document window, and you'll learn more about these properties as you progress through this book. For now, you just need to understand the basic skills for using the HTML Property Inspector.

By the way, you should notice that the HTML category of the Property Inspector is displayed in this figure, as indicated by the HTML button on the left of the Inspector. That's why we refer to this view of the Inspector as the *HTML Property Inspector*. In contrast, the CSS category provides for formatting a page using CSS, and you'll see how that works later in this chapter.

The Property Inspector when the HTML option is selected

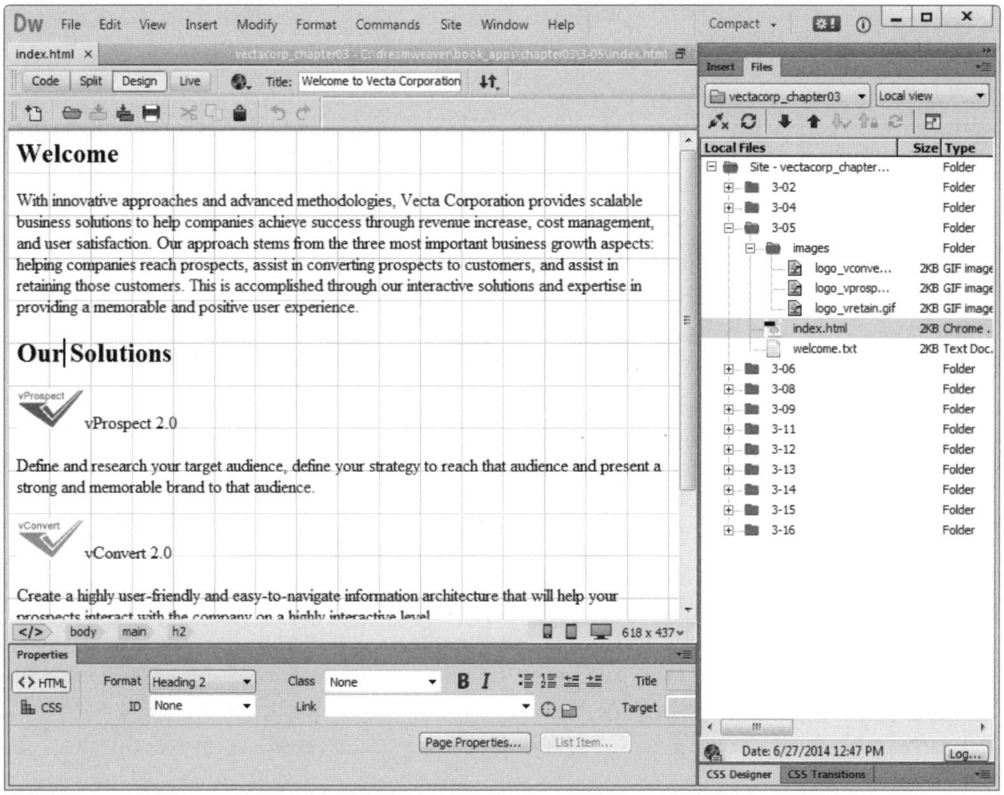

Description

- The *HTML Property Inspector* applies basic formatting to a page by generating HTML code based on the selections you make. To turn the HTML version of the Inspector on, click the HTML button on the left of the Inspector.

- To use the HTML Property Inspector to format an element, place the cursor in the element in the Document window and then use the controls that are displayed. For example, to change a <p> element to a heading element, you place the cursor in the element and then select a heading level from the Format menu.

- You can also use the HTML Property Inspector to format the text for all or part of an element or for two or more elements. To do that, you must select the text in the Document window.

- The formatting that's available from the Property Inspector depends on the element that's selected.

Figure 3-5   How to use the Property Inspector to work with HTML

How to use the Insert panel to work with HTML

As you develop a web page, you'll need to work with many different types of objects. One way to do that is to use the Insert panel shown in figure 3-6. This panel groups the available objects into several categories. You can see the objects in the Structure category here, but you'll want to review the objects in the other categories so you know what's available.

You can use the *Insert panel* to format existing content or insert new objects. To format existing content, you select the content in the Document window and then select an object from the Insert panel. For example, instead of using the Property Inspector to change a paragraph to a heading, you can click in the paragraph and then select a heading from the Heading menu in the Insert panel.

As another example, suppose you want to format two or more paragraphs as a bulleted list. To do that, you can just select those paragraphs in the Document window and then click the Unordered List object in the Insert panel. You'll learn more about lists and how to format them in chapter 6.

You can also use the Insert panel to add new objects. To do that, you position the cursor in the Document window where you want the element added and select the object from the Insert panel. Then, if no additional information is needed to insert the object, the HTML for the object is added to the document along with a placeholder that indicates where the object was inserted. If you insert a heading, for example, the placeholder consists of text that indicates where to place the content for the heading. Then, you can replace this text with the text for the heading.

In some cases, a dialog box will be displayed when you insert an object so you can enter information about the object. If you insert an image, for example, a dialog box is displayed that lets you select the image you want to insert. In most cases, that's what you want. If not, you can turn off the Dreamweaver preference that controls the display of these dialog boxes as described in this figure. Then, you can use the Property Inspector to specify the required information.

A dialog box is also displayed if you insert a div element or one of the HTML5 semantic elements. You'll learn more about how that works next.

The page as a new section is being inserted

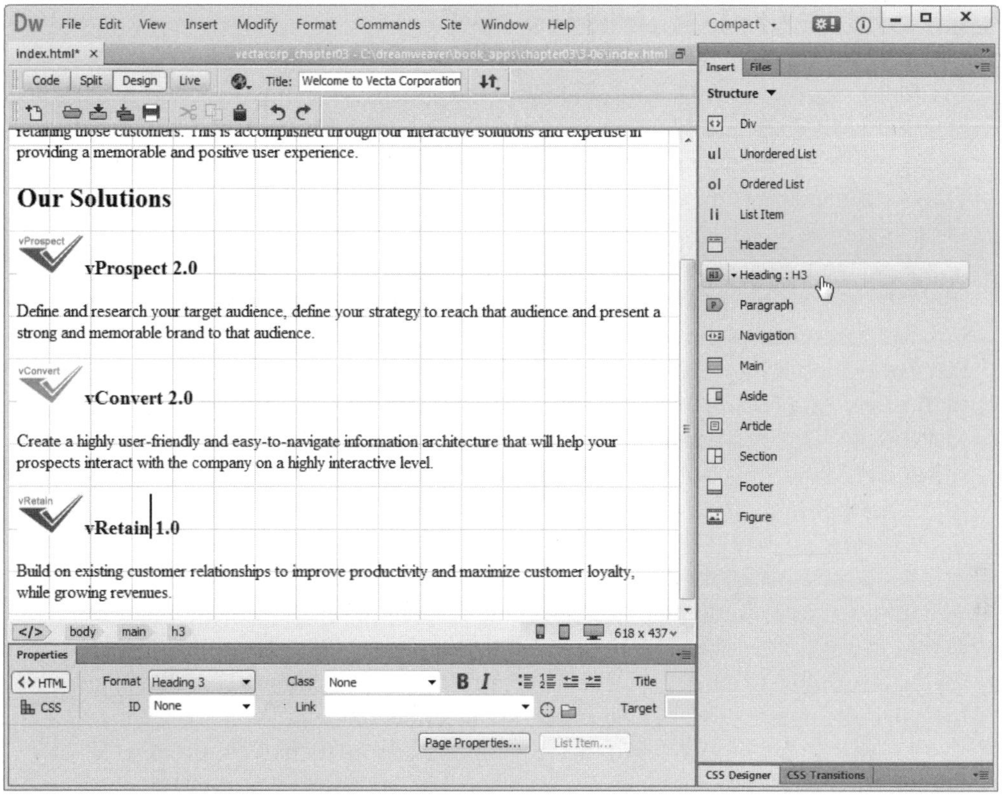

Description

- You can use the *Insert panel* to insert and apply HTML elements.

- To display the objects for a category of HTML elements, select the category from the menu at the top of the Insert panel.

- To insert the HTML for most objects, you can click in the Document window where you want to insert an object and then click the object in the Insert panel. Or, you can drag the object from the Insert panel and drop it in the Document window.

- To change the HTML element for existing content, select the item and then click an object in the Insert panel.

- To insert some objects, you select an item from a menu within a category. To insert an h3 element, for example, you use the Heading menu in the Structure category.

- By default, Dreamweaver displays a dialog box when you insert some objects so you can provide information about that object. If that's not what you want, you can remove the check mark from the Show Dialog When Inserting Objects option in the General category of the Preferences dialog box (Edit→Preferences). Then, you can use the Property Inspector to specify the required properties.

- In figure 3-7, you can learn about the special techniques that are required when you insert structural elements like the HTML5 semantic elements.

Figure 3-6   How to use the Insert panel to work with HTML

How to use the Insert panel to add structural elements

In the last topic, you learned the basic techniques for using the Insert panel to add HTML elements. Now, you'll learn about some special techniques for adding structural elements like the HTML5 semantic elements. The techniques you use depend on whether you're working in Design view, Live view, or Code view. Figure 3-7 presents the techniques for each of these views.

When you insert a structural element in Design view, a dialog box like the one shown at the top of this figure is displayed. The Insert menu in this dialog box lets you select where you want the element inserted. Although the options that are available vary, the standard options are At Insertion Point, After Start of Tag, and Before End of Tag. If the document contains one or more tags with id attributes, Before Tag and After Tag options are also available. Then, if you select one of the Tag options, a second menu becomes available that lets you select the tag. In this figure, a section will be inserted after the section with an id of "welcome".

You can also enclose existing content in a div element or an HTML5 semantic element. To do that, just select the content in the Document window before you select an object from the Insert panel. Then, the Insert menu in the dialog box that's displayed includes a Wrap Around Selection option that causes the selected content to be placed inside the inserted element.

Because it can be difficult to insert structural elements in the correct location when you use Design view, you may want to use Live view or Code view instead. To insert an element in Live view, you start by selecting the element relative to which the new element will be inserted. Then, when you insert the new element, the four icons shown in the second example in this figure are displayed. The first two icons let you insert the new element before or after the selected element. The third icon lets you wrap the new element around the selected element. And the fourth icon lets you nest the new element within the selected element.

Note that you don't have to identify elements by ID when you work in Live view like you do sometimes in Design view. However, you can't assign an ID or class to a structural element when you create it in Live view like you can in Design view. Instead, you have to use the Property Inspector or Element Live Display to assign an ID or class to an element after you create it.

If you want to have complete control over where an element is added, you can insert it in Code view. To do that, you simply position the cursor where you want to insert the element and then click on the element in the Insert panel. When you do, the Insert dialog box is displayed just like it is when you work in Design view. In this case, though, you can just select the default option to insert the element at the insertion point.

You can also wrap a new element around existing content in Code view. To do that, just select the content before you insert the element. Then, the default option in the dialog box that's displayed will be to wrap the element around the selected content.

The Insert dialog box that's displayed in Design view and Code view

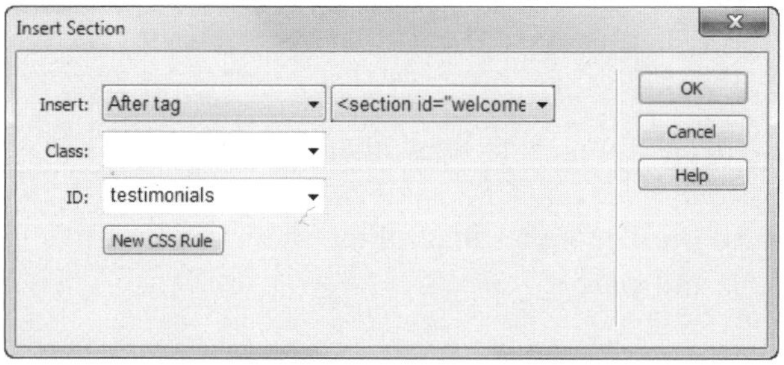

The icons that are displayed in Live view

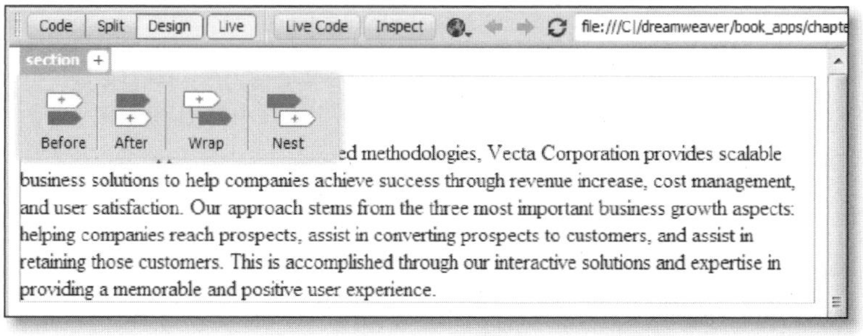

How to insert elements in Design view

- When you insert a div or an HTML5 structural element in Design view, Dreamweaver displays a dialog box that lets you choose where to place the element.

- By default, the options in the Insert menu let you insert an element at the insertion point, after the start of a tag, or before the end of a tag. You can use the after and before options with the body element or any element that has an ID.

- If any elements in the document have IDs, options that let you insert an element before or after those elements are also available.

- If content is selected in the Document window when you insert one of these elements, an option is available that lets you wrap the element around the selection.

How to insert elements in Live view

- When you insert a div or an HTML5 structural element in Live view, Dreamweaver displays icons that let you insert the element before the selected element, insert the element after the selected element, wrap the element around the selected element, or nest the element within the selected element.

How to insert elements in Code view

- Position the cursor where you want to insert the element and click on the element in the Insert panel. When the Insert dialog box is displayed, accept the default "At insertion point" option.

- You can also select content before you insert an element and then accept the default "Wrap around selection" option to wrap the new element around the selection.

Figure 3-7   How to use the Insert panel to add structural elements

How to work with CSS in Dreamweaver

When you work with Dreamweaver, you need to know that Dreamweaver typically refers to CSS rule sets as *style rules* and CSS rules as *styles*. Because of that, I'll use those terms from now on. The topics that follow show you how to create, modify, and delete style rules and styles.

How to use the CSS Designer to create style rules and styles

Figure 3-8 shows how to create a style rule with the *CSS Designer*. To start, if you need to create an external or embedded style sheet, you can use the first procedure in this figure.

Then, to add a style rule to an external style sheet, you select the style sheet from the Sources pane. Or, if you're using an embedded style sheet, you select <style> from this pane. This is a critical step when you create a style rule because you can accidentally add a style rule to the wrong style sheet if you forget to select the one you want.

To add a style rule to the selected style sheet, you click the Add Selector icon at the top of the Selectors pane. Then, a selector is displayed for the element that's selected in the Document window. If that's the selector you want to add, just press the Enter or Return key. Otherwise, enter the selector you want and press Enter or Return.

When you click the Add Selector icon, the selector for the current element often includes one or more parent elements. For example, if you selected the first heading element in the document in this figure, the selector would look like this:

`body section h2`

If you don't want to include the parent elements, you can omit them one at a time by pressing the Up Arrow key. In this example, the first time you pressed the Up Arrow key, the body element would be omitted from the selector. The second time you pressed this key, the section element would be omitted. This can make it easier to work with complex selectors.

If necessary, you can also add parent elements that you've omitted back to a selector. To do that, you press the Down Arrow key. Then, the parent elements are added back in the reverse order that they were omitted.

After you add the selector, you can add styles to the style rule by using the Properties pane of the CSS Designer. In this figure, for example, you can see that I've set the font-family, font-size, and line-height properties for the body element. (These properties are displayed in bold.) In the next figure, you'll learn how to work with the Properties pane.

A page after styles have been added for the body element

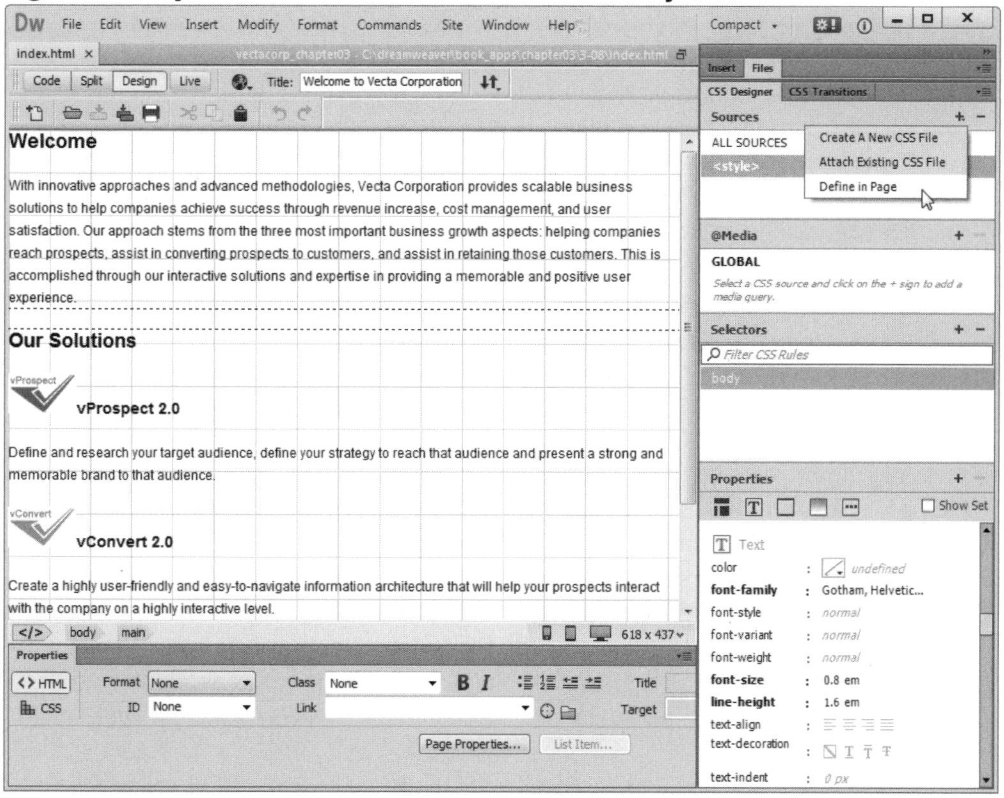

How to create a style sheet

- Click the Add CSS Source (+) icon in the Sources pane and select Create a New CSS File to create an external style sheet or select Define in Page to embed the styles in the page.

How to create a style rule and add styles

1. Select the name of the style sheet you want to add the style to from the Sources pane of the CSS Designer. To add the style to an embedded style sheet, select <style>. This is a critical step because it determines where the style rule is added.

2. Click the Add Selector (+) icon in the Selectors pane and enter a selector in the box that's displayed. By default, the box will contain a selector for the element that's selected in the Document window, but you can modify that.

3. Use the Properties pane to set the styles for the selector. This pane lets you set all of the properties that apply to the element or elements that are selected.

Notes

- In Dreamweaver, a CSS rule set is often referred to as a *style rule*, and a rule is referred to as a *style*.

- You can use the Up Arrow key to omit parent elements from a selector when you create it, and you can use the Down Arrow key to add omitted elements back.

Figure 3-8   How to use the CSS Designer to create style rules and styles

How to use the CSS Designer to modify, add, and delete styles

Figure 3-9 shows how you can use the CSS Designer to modify, add, and delete styles. This assumes that the style rule has already been created. Then, you start by selecting the style rule.

To display the styles for a style rule, you select its style sheet from the Sources pane and its selector from the Selectors pane. In figure 3-9, for example, you can see the properties for the body element in the external style sheet named styles.css. Notice here that the Show Set option at the top of the Properties pane is checked. That way, only the properties that have been set are displayed.

To modify a property, you change its value in the Properties pane. To do that, you can use the icons at the top of this pane to scroll to the properties in five different categories: Layout, Text, Border, Background, and Custom. Note that only the Layout and Background icons are shown here because these are the only categories that contain properties that have been set. If you look back to figure 3-8, though, you can see the icons for all five categories.

Later, if you want to disable or delete a style, you use the icons that appear when you point to the property. In this example, you can see these icons to the right of the padding property. If you click the Remove icon, the style is deleted from the style rule. If you click the Disable icon, the property is commented out in the style sheet. Then, if you ever want to enable the property, you just click this icon again.

If you decide that you don't want to keep the changes that you've made to one or more properties, you can choose Edit→Undo or use the shortcut key for your system to reverse the changes. With previous releases of Dreamweaver CC, you couldn't do that. Instead, you had to display the code for the style sheet, move the focus to that code, and then undo the change.

In chapter 2, you learned that the formatting that's applied to an element can be overridden by other elements that it contains. To explain how this works, consider the font-family property that's shown in this figure for the body element. Unless this property is overridden, it will be inherited by all text elements in the body of the document. If that's not what you want, you can change this property for specific elements.

When you display the properties for a specific selector in the Properties pane, only the properties that are applied directly by that selector are listed. But you can also display the properties that an element inherits from any containing elements. To do that, just select the element in the Document window and then select the COMPUTED option in the Selectors pane. Then, all the properties that apply to that element are displayed.

As you work with the CSS Designer, you should know that you can collapse individual panes by clicking on the header for the pane. Then, the item that's currently selected in that pane will be displayed in the header along with the name of the pane. This is particularly useful with the Sources pane. If I collapsed the Sources pane shown in this figure, for example, the header would look like this:

`Sources: styles.css`

The CSS Designer with just the set properties in the Properties pane

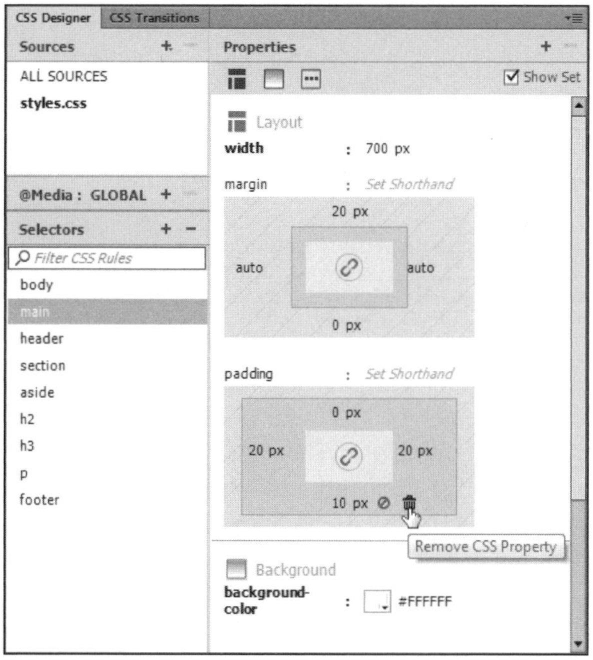

How to display the styles for a style rule

- Select the style sheet in the Sources pane, and select the selector in the Selectors pane. Then, the styles are displayed in the Properties pane.
- To display the properties in a specific category, click on the appropriate icon at the top of the Properties pane.
- To display just the properties that have been set, check the Show Set box.

How to modify, add, comment out, or delete a style in a style rule

- To modify a style, select it in the Properties pane and change its value.
- To add a new style, find the property in the Properties pane and set its value.
- To comment out or remove a property from a style sheet, point to the property in the Properties pane and click on the Disable or Remove icon that appears.
- To reverse a change, choose Edit→Undo or use the keyboard shortcut.

How to display all of the styles for a selected element

- Select the element in the Document window, and select the COMPUTED option in the Selectors pane. Then, the Properties window includes the properties that have been inherited from containing elements.

Description

- The Properties pane lets you set all of the properties that apply to the selected element or elements without writing any CSS code.

Figure 3-9   How to use the CSS Designer to modify, add, and delete styles

This can keep you from inadvertently selecting the wrong style sheet as you apply styles. Then, when you need to select a different style sheet, you can click the header again to expand the pane.

How to use the Property Inspector to display and modify styles

Although you're most likely to use the CSS Designer to work with styles as described in the previous figure, you can also use the *CSS Property Inspector* to work with some of the most common styles for an element. Figure 3-10 shows you how.

To start, you click the CSS icon at the left side of this panel to display the controls for working with CSS. Then, you select the style rule whose properties you want to display from the Targeted Rule combo box. Then, the properties for that style rule are displayed and you can modify them any way you like.

It's important to note that the properties that are available in the Property Inspector vary depending on the style rule that you select. In this example, the text-based properties are available because the style rule for the body element is selected. You'll learn more about the properties that are available for different types of objects as you proceed through this book.

In addition to modifying styles, you can use the Property Inspector to add a class attribute to an element. You can also remove a class from an element, and you can add multiple classes.

Finally, you can use the Property Inspector to add inline styles to an element. Since inline styles aren't a practical way to format elements, though, you probably won't use them.

The Property Inspector when the CSS option is selected

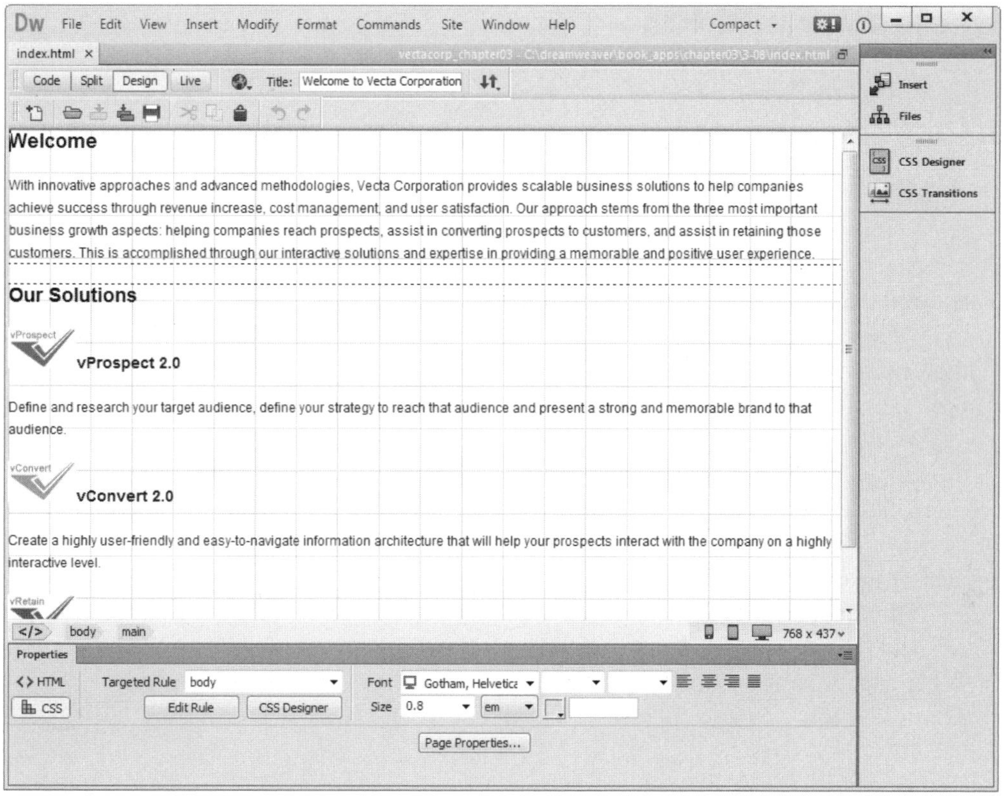

Procedures

- To display the CSS Property Inspector, click the CSS icon in the Properties pane.
- To display the styles for a style rule, select the rule from the Cascade category of the Targeted Rule combo box.
- To set or modify the styles for a selected style rule, use the controls in the Property Inspector.
- To apply a class to a selected element, select that class from the Apply Class category of the Targeted Rule combo box. To remove a class from a selected element, select the <Remove Class> option. And to apply multiple classes to a selected element, select the Apply Multiple Classes option and then select the classes from the dialog box that's displayed.
- To display the CSS Designer for a style rule, click the CSS Designer button. To display the Page Properties dialog box, click the Page Properties button. And to display the classic CSS Rule editor, click the Edit Rule button.

Description

- The *CSS Property Inspector* lets you apply basic formatting to a page by generating CSS based on the selections you make.

Figure 3-10   How to use the Property Inspector to display and modify styles

How to use Element Live Display to work with classes and IDs

One of the new features of Live view in Dreamweaver CC 2014 is *Element Live Display*. This display lets you work with the classes and ID of the selected element using a simple interface. Figure 3-11 shows how Element Live Display works.

In the example in this figure, a section element with an ID of "solutions" was selected by clicking on it in the Tag selector. Then, the Element Live Display showed the name of the element along with its ID. If an ID hasn't been assigned to an element, though, you can assign one by clicking the Add Class/ID icon and then entering the ID in the space that's provided. When you do that, be sure to prefix the ID with a pound sign (#) just like you do in the selector for an ID.

You can use the same technique to assign a class to an element. In this case, though, you must precede the class name with a period. In addition, if one or more classes already exist when you enter the period, a class list is displayed as shown in the first example in this figure. Then, you can select one of these classes to assign it to the element.

You can also use Element Live Display to remove an ID or class from an element. To do that, just point to the right side of the box for the ID or class. When you do, a Remove Class/ID icon will appear as shown in the second example. Then, you can click this icon to remove the class or ID.

An Element Live Display with a class list displayed

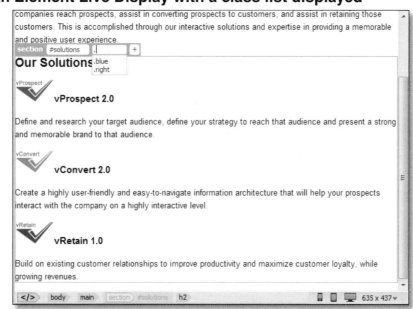

An Element Live Display with the Remove Class/ID icon

How to add a class or ID

- Click the Add Class/ID icon (+) at the right side of the Element Live Display. Then, enter the class or ID in the space that's provided. A class name must be preceded by a period, and an ID must be preceded by a pound sign (#).

- If one or more classes already exist, a class list is displayed when you enter a period. Then, you can select a class to assign it to the element.

How to remove a class or ID

- To remove a class or ID, point to the right side of the box that contains the class or ID and click the Remove Class/ID icon (x) that's displayed.

Description

- When you select an element in Live view, an *Element Live Display* is displayed above that element. This display includes the element name, along with the ID and classes assigned to the element, if any.

- You can use Element Live Display to add and remove classes and IDs.

Figure 3-11   How to use Element Live Display to work with classes and IDs

How to work with external style sheets

In figure 3-7, you learned the basics of how to create a style sheet. Now, you'll learn more about creating and working with external style sheets.

How to create an external style sheet

Figure 3-12 shows how to create an external style sheet. After you click on the plus icon in the Sources pane of the CSS Designer, you select Create a New CSS File. That will display the dialog box shown at the top of this figure.

In this dialog box, you can enter a name for the CSS file. In addition, you can identify a folder within the website where you want to store the file. In this example, I didn't specify a location, so the file will be stored in the root folder for the site. However, CSS files are typically stored in a folder named styles within the root folder.

By default, a link element is added to the head element of a document when you create a new CSS file. It will attach the file to the document. For example, the link element that's generated for the file in this figure will look like this:

```
<link href="styles.css" rel="stylesheet" type="text/css">
```

Remember, though, that the type attribute isn't required for HTML5.

You can also use the Create a New CSS File dialog box to specify a condition under which a style sheet is used. For example, you may want the style sheet to be applied only when a page is being printed. You'll learn more about that later in this chapter.

After you create a style sheet, it will appear in the Sources pane of the CSS Designer. Then, you can select it to add style rules to it. If more than one style sheet is associated with a document, you can also click the ALL SOURCES option in the Sources pane to display all the selectors in all the style sheets.

The Create a New CSS File dialog box

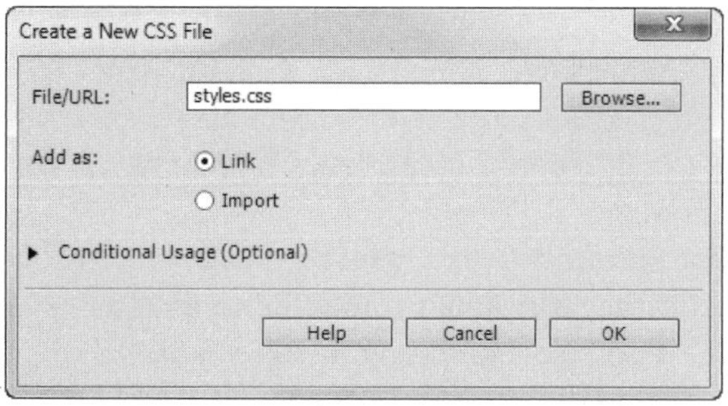

An external style sheet in the CSS Designer

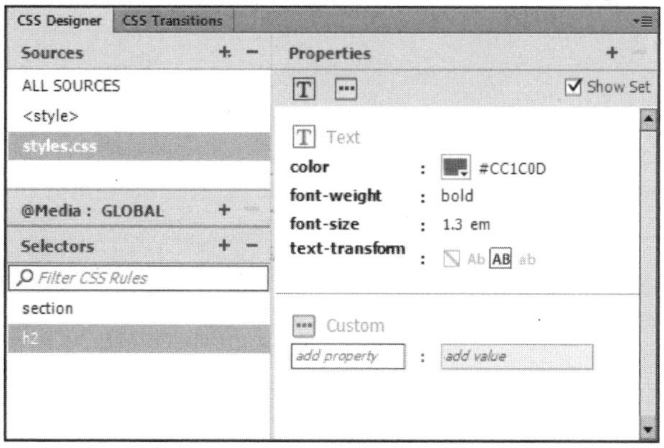

How to create an external style sheet using the CSS Designer

1. Click the Add CSS Source (+) icon in the Sources pane and select Create a New CSS File to display the dialog box shown above.

2. Enter the name of the file in the File/URL text box to add it to the root folder of the website, and click OK. Or, click the Browse button, select a location from the Save Style Sheet As dialog box that's displayed, enter the name of the file in the File Name text box, and click Save.

Description

- When you create an external style sheet with the Link option selected, a link element that identifies the style sheet is added to the head element of the document.

- If a document is associated with more than one style sheet, you can click the ALL SOURCES option in the Sources pane to display the selectors in all the style sheets.

- External style sheets are often stored in a separate folder of a website. To add a folder, right-click on the folder that will contain it, select New Folder from the menu that's displayed, and then enter a name for the folder.

- Because an external style sheet separates the formatting (CSS) from the content (HTML), we recommend that you use them for all production applications. External style sheets can also be attached to more than one web page.

Figure 3-12   How to create an external style sheet

How to move style rules and copy styles

As you create the style rules for a document, you may decide that you want to store one or more of them in a style sheet other than the one where they were originally created. In that case, you can use the procedure in figure 3-13 to move the style rules from one style sheet to another.

This is particularly useful if you start to format a document by using an embedded style sheet and then later decide that you want to store the style rules in an external style sheet. It's also useful if you have two or more external style sheets attached to a document and you want to move styles between those style sheets.

After you move style rules from one style sheet to another, you may want to remove a style sheet from the Sources pane as described in this figure. Note, however, that this doesn't delete the CSS file for the style sheet. As a result, you can still attach it to your web pages.

In addition to moving style rules from one style sheet to another, you can copy styles from one style rule to another. To do that, you use the shortcut menu that's displayed when you right-click a selector in the Selectors pane. You can use this menu to copy all the styles in a style rule or just the styles in a specific category, such as layout styles or text styles. Then, you can right-click on another selector and choose Paste Styles to paste the copied styles to the style rule for that selector. This is useful if you need to include similar styles in two or more style rules. After you copy the styles, of course, you can change them any way you want.

An embedded style rule as it's being moved to an external style sheet

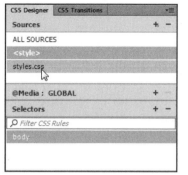

The shortcut menu for copying styles

How to move style rules

1. Select the style sheet that contains the style rules you want to move in the Sources pane of the CSS Designer to display the selectors it contains in the Selectors pane. ·

2. Select the selectors you want to move to another style sheet and then drag and drop them onto that style sheet in the Sources pane.

How to copy styles

1. Right-click the selector whose style rules you want to copy in the Selectors pane, and choose Copy All Styles to copy all the styles, or choose an item from the Copy Styles submenu to copy a specific type of style.

2. Right-click the selector where you want to copy the styles and choose Paste Styles.

Description

- You can use the first procedure shown above to move style rules from any style sheet to any other style sheet.

- If you move all of the style rules in a style sheet to another style sheet, you can remove the style sheet from the Sources pane by selecting it and then clicking the Remove CSS Source icon (−). Note that this doesn't delete the style sheet.

- You can use the second procedure shown above to copy styles from one style rule to another.

Figure 3-13   How to move style rules and copy styles

How to attach an external style sheet to a web page

Figure 3-14 shows two ways to attach an external style sheet to a web page. If you use the CSS Designer, you can use the dialog box to identify the style sheet that you want to attach and set conditions for using the style sheet. If you use the drag-and-drop method, you can't specify any options. Either way a link element is added to the head section of the HTML document.

When you use the CSS Designer to attach an external style sheet, though, the link element is added after any other link elements. Because of that, you may need to change the order of the link elements. If, for example, you attach the normalize.css style sheet to a web page that you've built, its link element will come last, even though it is supposed to come first. Unfortunately, the only way to change the order of link elements is to work in Code view.

Before you attach a style sheet like the normalize.css style sheet, you may want to add it to the website. However, that isn't a requirement. Instead, if you've already downloaded it to another location, you can use the dialog box to locate it. Then, when you click OK, Dreamweaver will display a message that asks if you want to copy the file to your site. In almost all cases, that's what you'll want to do.

The Attach Existing CSS File dialog box

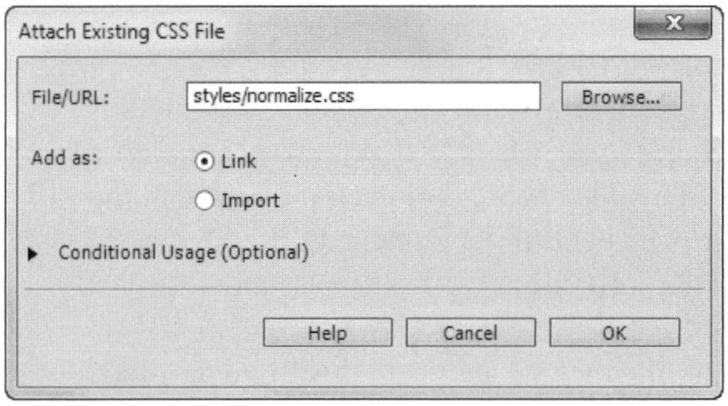

```
Attach Existing CSS File                                    [ X ]

File/URL:      styles/normalize.css                    [ Browse... ]

Add as:        ⊙ Link
               ○ Import

▶ Conditional Usage (Optional)
─────────────────────────────────────────────────────────

                          [ Help ]  [ Cancel ]  [  OK  ]
```

How to attach an external style sheet to a web page

1. Choose Attach Existing CSS File from the Add CSS Source menu (**+**) in the Sources pane to display the Attach Existing CSS File dialog box.

2. Click the Browse button and then locate and select the CSS file you want to attach. The file you select will be displayed in the File/URL text box.

3. Make sure the Link option is selected, and then click OK to attach the style sheet. This adds a link element for the style sheet to the head element of the HTML after any other link elements for the page.

How to use drag-and-drop to attach an external style sheet

- Switch to Code view for the HTML document. Then, drag the external file sheet from the Files panel and drop it in its proper place in the head element of the HTML. This adds a link element for the style sheet in that location.

Description

- If you want to use an existing style sheet for a website, you can add the style sheet to the website and attach it to each page that uses it.

- When you use the CSS Designer to attach a style sheet, its link element is added after any other link elements. Then, if you want to change the sequence of the link elements, you can use Code view.

- If you use the normalize.css style sheet for a page, the link element for this style sheet should be placed before any other link elements.

───

Figure 3-14   How to attach an external style sheet to a web page

How to create a style sheet for printing

If you develop a web page that users are likely to print, you may want to create a separate style sheet that will be applied to the page when it's printed. To do that, you can use the procedure in figure 3-15. Here, you start by creating a style sheet just as you would any other style sheet. Then, you indicate that the style sheet should be used only if the page is printed by selecting the Media and Print options from the two menus in the Conditional Usage (Optional) section of the Create a New CSS File dialog box.

When you're done, a link element like the one shown in this figure is added to the document. Here, the media attribute tells the browser that the style sheet should only be used if the page is printed.

This figure also presents some basic recommendations for formatting printed pages. As you can see, the first three recommendations have to do with changing the fonts so they're more readable. In particular, a serif font should be used for text because that makes the printed text easier to read (although sans-serif text is more readable on the screen).

The fourth recommendation is to remove site navigation. That makes sense because navigation can't be used when the page is printed. You may, however, want to print links that link to other topics to show the reader what is available.

The last recommendation is to remove any images that aren't needed for the printed version of the page. To remove an element, you can set its display property to "none".

The Vecta Corp web page of figure 2-1 after it's formatted for printing

WELCOME

With innovative approaches and advanced methodologies, Vecta Corporation provides scalable business solutions to help companies achieve success through revenue increase, cost management, and user satisfaction. Our approach stems from the three most important business growth aspects: helping companies reach prospects, assist in converting prospects to customers, and assist in retaining those customers. This is accomplished through our interactive solutions and expertise in providing a memorable and positive user experience.

OUR SOLUTIONS

vProspect 2.0

Define and research your target audience, define your strategy to reach that audience and present a strong and memorable brand to that audience.

vConvert 2.0

Create a highly user-friendly and easy-to-navigate information architecture that will help your prospects interact with the company on a highly interactive level.

vRetain 1.0

Build on existing customer relationships to improve productivity and maximize customer loyalty, while growing revenues.

The link element for the printing style sheet

```
<link href="styles/print.css" rel="stylesheet" type="text/css"
      media="print">
```

How to create a style sheet for printing

1. Create a new style sheet, but in the Create a New CSS File dialog box, expand the Conditional Usage (Optional) section. Then, select Media from the first menu, select Print from the second menu, and click OK.

2. Set the styles for printing by selecting the print style sheet in the Sources pane and adding the required styles.

Recommendations for formatting printed pages

- Change the text color to black and the background color to white.
- Change text other than headings to a serif font to make the text easier to read when printed.
- Use a base font size that's easy to read when printed.
- Remove site navigation since it can't be used from a printed page.
- Remove any unnecessary images, particularly Flash and animated images.

Description

- When you create a style sheet for printing, a link element is added to the head element for the page and its media attribute is set to "print".
- If you don't want an element to be included when a page is printed, you can set its display property to "none". Then, no space is allocated for the element.
- To see what a page will look like when it's printed, display the page in a browser and select the File→Print Preview command. (In Chrome, click the Customize button and then select Print.)

Figure 3-15   How to create a style sheet for printing

Other skills for working with Dreamweaver sites

In the last three topics of this chapter, you'll learn some other skills for working with Dreamweaver sites. Specifically, you'll learn how to validate a web page, how to set browser preferences, and how to delete, edit, and duplicate sites.

How to validate a web page

To *validate* a web page, you use a program or website for that purpose. When you use Dreamweaver, for example, the page is validated using the W3C Markup Validation Service. Figure 3-16 describes how this works.

When you run a validation scan for a page from Dreamweaver, Dreamweaver sends the page to the W3C Markup Validation Service. Then, if any errors are detected, they're returned to Dreamweaver and displayed in the *Validation panel*. In this figure, for example, you can see that the validation service detected three errors. In contrast, if no errors are detected, a single line is displayed in the Validation panel to indicate that.

In this example, I forced the three errors to occur by omitting the closing tag for the header element. The first error indicates that the footer element is contained within the header element. The second error indicates that the closing tag for an element contained within the main element (in this case, the header element) wasn't found before the closing tag for the main element. And the third error indicates that the header element isn't closed.

Notice that the line number where each error occurs is included in the Validation panel. That makes it easier to locate the errors. In addition, if you double-click on an error in the Validation panel, Dreamweaver will display the page in Split view and place the cursor in the line that contains the error. Then, after you fix all the errors, you can save your work and run the validation scan again.

Although it's estimated that 99% of all pages on the Web today haven't been validated, we think it's worth validating every page you develop. That's because validating your pages can avoid testing problems later on. And, because Dreamweaver makes validating pages so easy, there's no reason not to do it.

The Validation panel with three errors

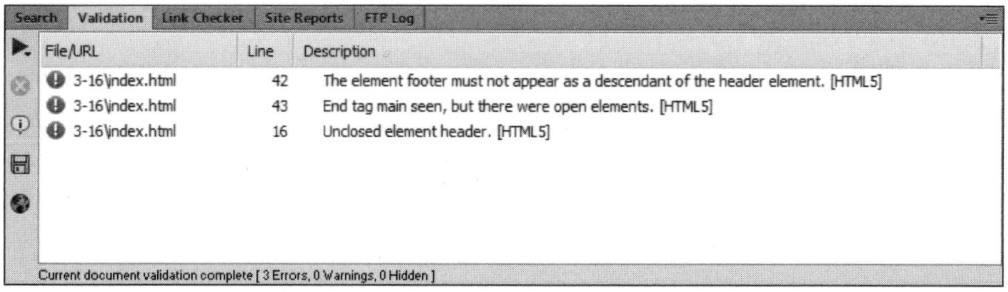

Search	Validation	Link Checker	Site Reports	FTP Log		

▶	File/URL	Line	Description
	❶ 3-16\index.html	42	The element footer must not appear as a descendant of the header element. [HTML5]
	❶ 3-16\index.html	43	End tag main seen, but there were open elements. [HTML5]
	❶ 3-16\index.html	16	Unclosed element header. [HTML5]

Current document validation complete [3 Errors, 0 Warnings, 0 Hidden]

How to run a validation scan for a web page

- Choose File→Validate→Validate Current Document (W3C). When a message is displayed alerting you that the web page will be sent to the W3C Markup Validation Service for validation, click OK.

- After the page is validated, a new group of panels will be displayed at the bottom of the Dreamweaver IDE and the *Validation panel* will be displayed. This panel lists any errors that were found.

- To move to the line of code that contains an error in the Document window, double-click on the error in the Validation panel.

Description

- You should *validate* your web page to be sure that the code it contains is compliant with the current HTML standards. Before you validate a web page, you should save it.

- After you fix the errors, you can rerun the validation directly from the Validation panel by selecting the Validate Current Document (W3C) command from the W3C Validation menu (▶) at the left side of the panel.

- The *W3C (World Wide Web Consortium)* is an international community in which member organizations, a full-time staff, and the public work together to develop Web standards.

Figure 3-16   How to validate a web page

How to set browser preferences

When you install Dreamweaver, it scans your system to determine what browsers you have installed, and it includes those browsers in the Preview in Browser menu. If you install a browser after you install Dreamweaver, though, you can add that browser to this menu using the Preview in Browser category of the Preferences dialog box.

Figure 3-17 describes how you do that. It also describes how you can remove a browser from the list of browsers. You'll want to do that if you remove the browser from your system. You can also change the name of a browser or the location of its executable file, but you're not likely to do that.

The Preferences dialog box also lets you specify the browsers you want to use as your primary and secondary browsers. Then, you can display a page in these browsers using a keyboard shortcut. When you set a primary browser, for example, you can preview a page by pressing the F12 key (Windows) or Option+F12 (Mac). And when you set a secondary browser, you can preview a page by pressing Ctrl+F12 (Windows) or Cmd+F12 (Mac). In this figure, you can see that Google Chrome is set as the primary browser.

The Preview in Browser category of the Preferences dialog box

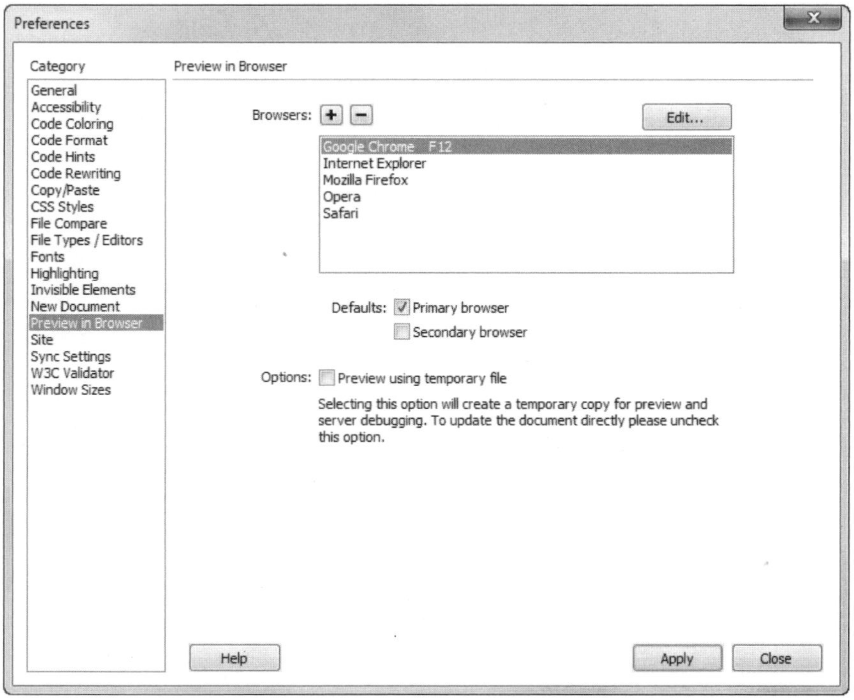

Description

- To display the Preview in Browser category of the Preferences dialog box, choose Edit Browser List from the Preview in Browser menu in the Document toolbar.

- To add a browser to the list, click the Add Browser button (+) to display the Add Browser dialog box. Then, enter a name for the browser and click the Browse button to browse for and select the executable file for the browser.

- To remove a browser from the list, select the browser and then click the Remove button (−).

- To change the name of the browser or the location of its executable file, select the browser and then click the Edit button to display the Edit Browser dialog box.

- By default, the primary browser is set to your system's default browser. To change that, select another browser and then select the Primary Browser option. To preview a page in that browser, press F12 (Windows) or Option+F12 (Mac).

- To set a browser as the secondary browser, select the browser and then select the Secondary Browser option. To preview a page in that browser, press Ctrl+F12 (Windows) or Command+F12 (Mac).

- You can also use the Add Browser and Edit Browser dialog boxes to set a browser as the primary or secondary browser.

Figure 3-17   How to set browser preferences

How to delete, edit, and duplicate sites

As you learn Dreamweaver, you'll probably create a variety of sites. Then, you'll want to know how to manage the sites you create. Figure 3-18 presents the basic skills for doing that. Specifically, it describes how to use the Manage Sites dialog box to delete, edit, and duplicate sites.

In addition to these functions, you can use the Manage Sites dialog box to import and export Dreamweaver sites. You'll learn how to do that in chapter 13. You can also add a new Dreamweaver site or import or add a Business Catalyst site. Business Catalyst is Adobe's cloud-based hosting service that features content management-type functionality for your sites. For more information, see the Adobe website.

The Manage Sites dialog box

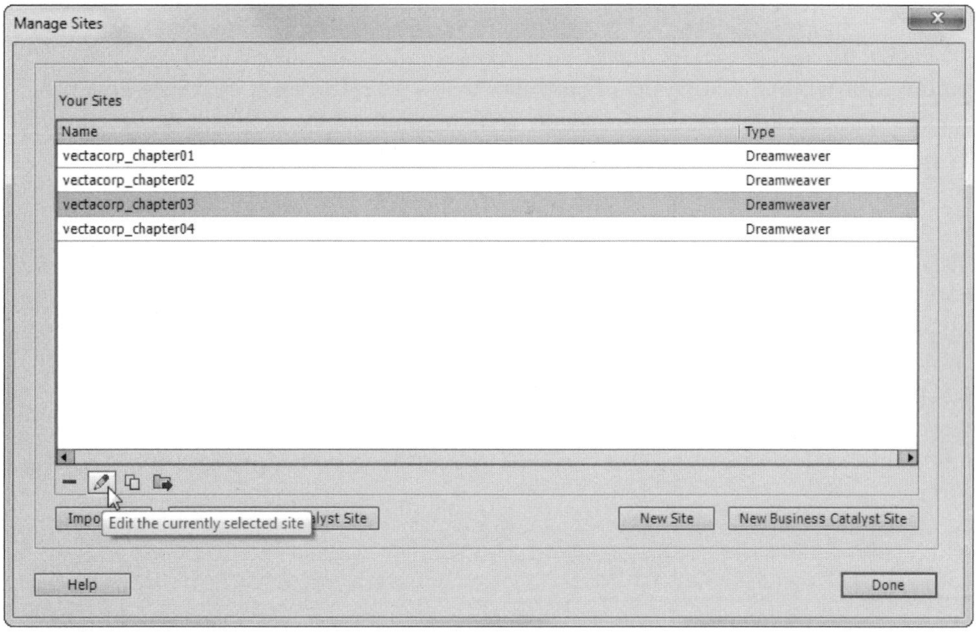

Description

- The Manage Sites dialog box lists all of your current Dreamweaver sites. To display this dialog box, choose Site→Manage Sites.

- To delete a site, select the site from the Your Sites list and then click the Delete icon (–). That deletes the Dreamweaver site, but not the files it contains.

- To edit a site, select the site from the Your Sites list and then click the Edit icon (🖉). This displays the Site Setup dialog box you saw in figure 3-1. You can edit any of the site settings from this dialog box.

- To create a copy of a site, select the site from the Your Sites list and then click the Duplicate icon (🗐). Another site with "copy" appended to the name will be added to the list. Then, you can select this site and click the Edit icon to change its settings.

- You can also use the Manage Sites dialog box to import and export sites. See chapter 13 for more information.

Figure 3-18   How to delete, edit, and duplicate sites

Perspective

This chapter has presented the critical skills for building websites in Dreamweaver without coding the HTML and CSS yourself. If you already know HTML and CSS, you can use these skills to build substantial web pages right now. In the next three chapters, though, you'll learn the other skills that you'll use for most of the websites that you build.

Terms

Dreamweaver site	Element Live Display
HTML Property Inspector	Code Navigator
Insert panel	validate a web page
style rule	Validation panel
style	World Wide Web Consortium (W3C)
CSS Designer	preview a web page
CSS Property Inspector	Live view

Summary

- When you create a Dreamweaver *site*, Dreamweaver establishes a reference between that site and the files for the website on your computer.
- After you create a site, you can add web pages to it, define the basic appearance of the pages using the Page Properties dialog box, and add content like text and images to the pages.
- The *HTML Property Inspector* generates HTML code based on the selections you make. You can also use the *Insert panel* to add HTML to a page.
- You can use the *CSS Designer* to create and modify *style rules* and *styles*. You can also modify some of the styles for a style rule by using the *CSS Property Inspector*.
- You can use *Element Live Display* to add an ID or class to an element or to remove an ID or class.
- You can use the CSS Designer to create external style sheets, move style rules from one style sheet to another, copy styles from one style rule to another, and attach an external style sheet to a web page.
- If you create an external style sheet for printing, you should change the text so it's easy to read and remove unnecessary elements like images.
- When you *validate a web page*, Dreamweaver sends your web page to the W3C Markup Validation Service and then displays any errors in the *Validation panel*.
- You can use the Manage Sites dialog box to delete, edit, and duplicate any sites you've created.

Exercise 3-1   Build a web page

In this exercise, you'll use the Dreamweaver skills that you learned in this chapter to build a web page that looks like the one below. This is an important exercise because it starts the process of mastering the Dreamweaver IDE. As you do the steps in this exercise, remember that you can undo any HTML or CSS change that doesn't work right by using the Edit→Undo command or its shortcut keys.

Create a site and start a new page

1. Start Dreamweaver, and choose Site→New Site to create a new site named Exercise 3-1 for this folder:

    ```
    C:\dreamweaver\exercises\ex03-01\
    ```

2. In the Files panel, review the folders and files for this site. Note the normalize.css file in the styles folder and the four images in the images folder.

3. With figure 3-2 as a guide, use File→New to create a new html file, and use File→Save As to save the file as index.html in the ex03-01 folder.

Add the HTML5 structure for the page

4. In Design view, put the insertion point in the upper left corner, and use the Insert panel to insert a main element.

5. Delete the text that Dreamweaver put into the main element, leave the insertion point in the main element, and use the Insert panel to insert a header element.

6. Switch to Code or Split view to make sure that a header element is within the main element. Then, start a new line after the header element, leave the insertion point at the start of this line, and use the Insert panel to insert a section element.

7. Switch to Live view, click anywhere in the section, and use the Tag selector to select the section element. Then, use the Insert panel to insert a footer element, and click the After icon to insert it after the section element. Now, check the code to make sure this worked right.

At this point, the HTML code should have header, section, and footer elements within the main element, and the main element should be within the body element. This is a typical structure for an HTML5 document.

Add the HTML content

8. Switch to Design view, delete the Dreamweaver text in the section element, open the welcome.txt file in the ex03-01 folder, and copy and paste the text into the section element of the index.html file. Then, switch to Code view to see that the text paragraphs are within HTML <p> elements. Check also to make sure that the paragraphs are within the section element.

9. In Design view, use the HTML Property Inspector to change the "Welcome" paragraph to a Heading 1 paragraph, the "Our Solutions" paragraph to a Heading 2 paragraph, and the three product name paragraphs to Heading 3 paragraphs. Live view now shows the default formatting for these headings.

10. In Design view, delete the Dreamweaver text in the header, drag the logo.gif file from the images folder, and drop it into the header.

11. In Design view, drag and drop the product gif files in the images folder to the left of the related product names in the Heading 3 elements. If the elements are dropped within the Heading 3 elements, the images and headings will stay on the same line.

12. In Live view, double-click on the footer element. Then, replace the Dreamweaver text in the footer with this text:

    Copyright 2014 Module Media

13. In the Document toolbar in Design view, enter this title in the Title text box:

    Vecta Corp Home Page

14. Display the Standard toolbar by right-clicking on the right side of the Document toolbar and selecting Standard. Then, click the Save button to save the changes that you've made, and preview the page in your default browser. Note the title in the title bar or tab for the page, and note that the page has all of the required content. That content just needs to be formatted.

Add the CSS that formats the text

15. With figure 3-8 as a guide, use the CSS designer to create an external style sheet named styles.css in the styles folder. This automatically adds a link element to the HTML that attaches the style sheet to the page.

16. In Live view so you can see the changes, create a style rule and style for the body tag, as shown in figure 3-8. To do that, select the styles.css style sheet in the Sources pane, click the + icon in the Selectors pane, and enter "body". Then, in the Properties pane, select the Text icon, set the font-family property to the option that starts with Gill Sans, and note the changes in Live view.

17. Use the CSS Designer to create a style rule for the h1 element that sets its color to red. To start, select the styles.css file in the Sources pane, and click on the Sources header so all of the styling that follows will apply to the styles.css style sheet. Then, click on the h1 element in Live view, click the + icon in the Selectors pane, and note that "main section h1" is the default selector. To change that to just "h1", press the up-arrow key on the keyboard twice, and then press the Enter key. Last, select the Text category in the Properties pane, and set the color property to #CC1C0D.

18. Create a style rule for the h2 element that sets its color to the same red as the h1 element, and note the change in Live view.

19. Create a style rule for the footer that sets the text-align property to "right". This should align the footer text on the right of the page. Then, check the Show Set box to display just the properties that have been set for the footer.

20. Create a style rule for the header that sets its text-align property to "center". This should center the image in the header.

21. Test the page in your default browser so see how it's coming along.

Add the CSS that provides background colors and centers the page

22. Create a style rule for the main element. Then, set its width property to 700 pixels, and test that change in your default browser. That property and the ones that follow are in the Layout category.

23. Set the left and right margins for the main selector to "auto" and test that change in your default browser. The page should now be centered in the window.

24. Set the padding for all four sides of the main selector to 25 pixels. One way to do that is to click "Set Shorthand" for the padding property, and then enter 25px to set the padding for all four sides. The other way to do that is to click in the center of the padding box, and then set the padding for one of the sides. That should set the padding for all of the sides.

25. Set the background-color property of the main selector to white (#FFFFFF). This property is the first one in the Background category. Then, set the background color of the body selector to #DFE3E6, and test these changes in your default browser. The page should now be centered with a white background that's surrounded by a darker background, but that may not be true for all browsers or for Live view.

Finish the page

26. Attach the normalize.css style sheet that's in the styles folder, but make sure it's before the styles.css style sheet. An easy way to do that is to switch to Code view, start a new line before the link element for the styles.css sheet, and drag the normalize.css file from the Files panel to the start of the new line. Now, test the page again to see that this fixed any browser differences.

27. With figure 3-16 as a guide, validate the web page to see if it has any errors. If it does, be sure to fix them.

28. Test the page one last time to make sure everything looks the same as the page shown at the start of this exercise. Then, review the HTML and CSS code that you've created.

29. If you want to make other modifications to the page, by all means experiment. When you're through, close all of the files.

Exercise 3-2   Create an Exercises site and delete the old sites

In this exercise, you'll create one site that you can use for all of the exercises so you won't have to create a separate site for each one. You'll also delete the sites that you've already created because you won't need them anymore.

Create a site for all of the exercises

1. Choose Site→New Site to create a new site named Exercises that starts with this folder:

    `C:\dreamweaver\exercises\`

2. Open the ex03-01 folder to see that it contains the folders and files for the exercise that you just finished.

Delete the sites you no longer need

3. With figure 3-18 as a guide, delete the sites that you created for specific exercises, like the Exercise 1-1, Exercise 2-1, and Exercise 3-1 sites.

Create a site for all of the solutions

4. At this point, you should have a Book applications site for accessing all the book applications and an Exercises site for accessing all of the exercises. Now, if you want to create a third site named Solutions for accessing all of the exercise solutions, they should be in this folder:

    `C:\murach\dreamweaver\solutions\`

4

How to work with text, images, and links

In chapter 3, you learned the basic features for using Dreamweaver to build a website. Now, this chapter expands on those skills by presenting the details for working with text, images, and links. These are the three objects you'll work with most often as you develop web pages.

How to work with text

In chapter 3, you learned a simple technique for adding text to a web page. Now, you'll learn some additional techniques for adding text. In addition, you'll learn how to edit text, insert special characters, use the Property Inspector to work with text, and check the spelling in a web page.

How to add text to a web page

Figure 4-1 presents three techniques for adding text to a web page. To start, you can add plain text by copying it from a text file and then pasting it into the web page. If you do that, Dreamweaver typically maintains the basic structure of the text. For example, if two returns appear after a block of text, Dreamweaver will format the text as a paragraph.

You can also insert *rich text* into a web page. This is the type of text that's created by word processors such as Microsoft Word and Apple's TextEdit. To work with this type of text, you can use the Paste Special dialog box shown in this figure. You can use this dialog box to remove any structure and formatting that has been applied to the text. You can also include just the structure, the structure plus basic formatting, or the structure plus all formatting.

Note that if you paste text that was copied from a Word document with structure or structure plus basic formatting, Dreamweaver will add space between paragraphs. If that's not what you want, you can select the Clean Up Word Paragraph Spacing option. In addition, if you want Dreamweaver to maintain line breaks in pasted text, you can select the Retain Line Breaks option. This option isn't available if you paste the text only. Finally, if you want Dreamweaver to replace smart, or "curly", quotes with straight quotes, you can select the Convert Smart Quotes to Straight Quotes option. In most cases, though, you'll want to keep the curly quotes.

If you're a Windows user and you want to insert the entire contents of a file that you've included in the site, you can do that by dragging the file from the Files panel onto a web page. When you do, the Insert Document dialog box is displayed. This dialog box provides many of the same options as the Paste Special dialog box. However, it also includes an option that lets you create a link to the document rather than inserting it into the page. You'll learn more about working with links later in this chapter.

Of course, you can also add text to a web page by typing it directly into the Document window. In most cases, though, you'll add text that someone else has written for you.

The Paste Special and Insert Document dialog boxes

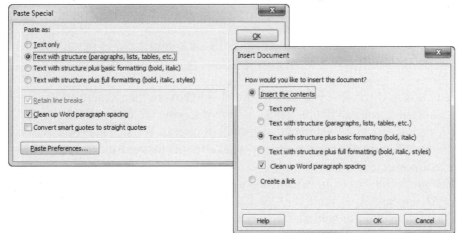

How to add plain text to a web page

- Copy the text from a text file and paste it into the web page as described in figure 3-4 of chapter 3. Dreamweaver will maintain the basic structure of the text.

How to add rich text to a web page

1. Open the file that contains the text, select the content you want to copy, and press Ctrl+C (Windows) or Cmd+C (Mac).

2. Open the document you want to add the text to, position the cursor where you want to add it, and choose Edit→Paste Special or press Ctrl+Shift+V (Windows) or Cmd+Shift+V (Mac) to display the Paste Special dialog box.

3. Choose how you want the text to be pasted and then click OK.

How to add text by dragging the file that contains it onto a web page

1. Drag the file from the Files panel onto the Document window in Design view to display the Insert Document dialog box.

2. Choose how you want the text in the file to be added to the document and then click OK. You can also create a link to the file instead of adding its text by selecting the Create a Link option. Then, the file will be displayed when you click the link.

Description

- If some or all of the text you need for a web page is already written for you, you can insert that text using one of the techniques above. The technique you use and the options you choose depend on the type of text you're adding and whether you want to include formatting.

- You can also enter text directly into the Document window. Then, you can press the Enter (Windows) or Return (Mac) key to start a new paragraph or the Shift+Enter (Windows) or Shift+Return (Mac) keys to add a line break.

Figure 4-1   How to add text to a web page

How to edit the text in a web page

When you work in Dreamweaver, you can use the same skills to edit text as you would from any basic text editor. These skills are summarized in figure 4-2. In addition to these skills, Live view provides some features that make it easy to work with text.

To edit text in Live view, you start by double-clicking in the element you want to edit. Then, you can double-click on a word to select it, and you can triple-click anywhere in the element to select all of its text. You can also drag across text to select it just as you normally would. In this figure, for example, two words are selected.

When you select text in an editable element, the *Quick Property Inspector*, or *Quick PI*, appears. By default, the Quick PI includes three buttons. You can use the first two buttons to boldface or italicize the selected text, and you can use the third button to make the selected text a hyperlink. When you click the third button, Dreamweaver provides controls that you can use to specify the page that will be displayed when the link is clicked as shown here.

The Document window in Live view with the Quick PI displayed

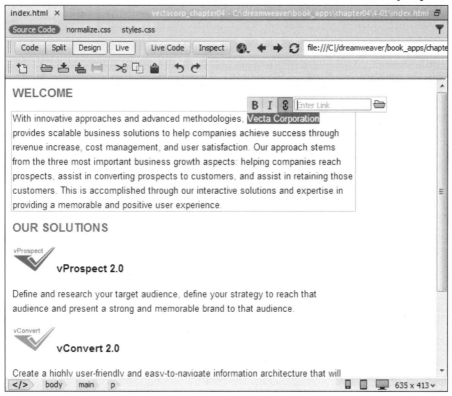

How to edit text in Design view or Code view

- To add text, just enter it as you normally would.
- To replace text, select it and then enter the new text.
- To delete text, select it and then press the Delete key.
- You can also use standard cut, copy, and paste techniques.

How to edit text in Live view

- To make a text element editable, double-click on it. When you do, an orange outline appears around it and you can edit the text just as you would in Design view or Code view.
- If you select text in an editable element, the *Quick Property Inspector* is displayed. This inspector lets you boldface or italicize the selected text or make it a link. If you click the Hyperlink button, you can specify the page you want to display when the link is clicked as shown above.
- To select a word in an editable element, you can double-click on it. To select all of the text in an editable element, you can triple-click anywhere in the element.

Figure 4-2   How to edit the text in a web page

How to insert special characters

Many of the web pages you develop will require *special characters*. These are characters that you can't insert using the keyboard, such as a copyright symbol, opening and closing "curly" quotes, and even non-breaking spaces. Instead, you can use the techniques described in figure 4-3.

At the top of this figure, you can see the list of special characters that Dreamweaver can insert. In addition to these characters, you can insert other, seldom-used characters by selecting the Other option. This displays a dialog box that includes all the special characters that Dreamweaver can insert.

Special characters are added to a web page as HTML *character entities*. This figure also lists the character entities for the most common special characters and shows how they're rendered in a web page. As you can see, all character entities start with an ampersand (&) and end with a semicolon (;). Then, the rest of the entity identifies the character it represents. To insert the copyright symbol (©), for example, Dreamweaver uses the © character entity.

Remember from chapter 2 that a line break (<br>) isn't implemented as a character entity. Even so, it's included in the list of special characters that you can insert from Dreamweaver.

One thing you should realize is that some character entities are inserted automatically when you add text in Design view. If the text contains an ampersand, for example, the ampersand is converted to its character entity. That makes sense because the ampersand identifies the start of a character entity, so you don't want to use it to represent an ampersand. Similarly, a character entity is inserted if you add text that contains a less-than sign (<) or a greater-than sign (>). That's because these characters are used to identify HTML tags.

The menu that lists special characters

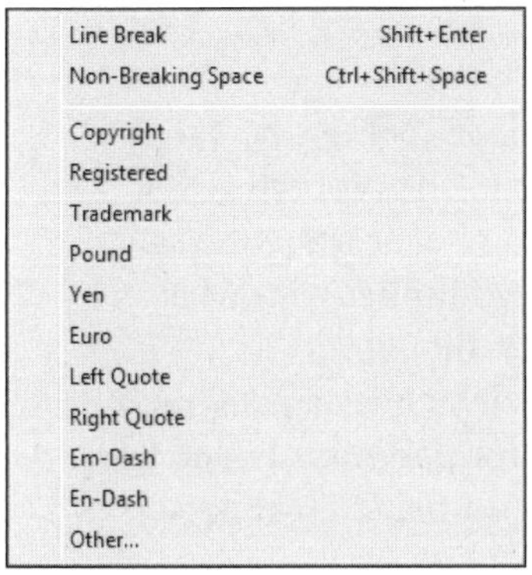

Line Break	Shift+Enter
Non-Breaking Space	Ctrl+Shift+Space
Copyright	
Registered	
Trademark	
Pound	
Yen	
Euro	
Left Quote	
Right Quote	
Em-Dash	
En-Dash	
Other...	

The character entities for some common special characters

Character	Renders as...	HTML character entity
Non-Breaking Space		` `
Copyright	©	`&copy;`
Registered	®	`&reg;`
Trademark	™	`&#8482;`
Pound	£	`&pound;`
Yen	¥	`&yen;`
Euro	€	`&#8364;`
Left Quote	"	`&#8220;`
Right Quote	"	`&#8221;`
Em-Dash	—	`&#8212;`
En-Dash	–	`&#8211;`

Description

- *Special characters* are characters for which a keyboard key does not exist. To insert a special character, you can use the Insert→Character menu or the Character menu in the Common category of the Insert panel.

- To insert a special character other than the ones that are available from the Character menu, you can choose Other and then select the character you want to insert from the dialog box that's displayed.

- When you insert a special character, a *character entity* like the ones shown above is added to the HTML document.

- You can use a non-breaking space to force the browser to display a space when it wouldn't normally be displayed.

- Although the line break isn't a character entity, it can be inserted from the Character menu.

- When you enter or paste text that contains an ampersand (&), less-than sign (<), or greater-than sign (>), the character is converted to a character entity.

Figure 4-3   How to insert special characters

How to use the Property Inspector to work with text

In chapter 3, you learned the basic skills for using the HTML Property Inspector to add HTML to a page. Now, figure 4-4 presents the properties that are available when text is selected in the Document window. These are the same properties you saw in chapter 3, so you should already be familiar with what most of them do. I'll present some additional details here, though.

To start, you can use the Format menu to format an element as a paragraph, heading, or preformatted text. Preformatted text is used for portions of code that are formatted with line breaks and spaces. A block of preformatted text preserves whitespace and is displayed in a monospaced font.

Next, you can use the ID combo box to enter an ID for an element or assign an id selector that already exists in an embedded or external style sheet for the page. Similarly, you can use the Class combo box to enter or assign a class. You can also use it to assign multiple classes, rename a class, remove a class, or attach an external style sheet.

The HTML Property Inspector also lets you apply boldface and italics to selected text. Remember, though, that you should use this technique to format text only when no special meaning is implied. Otherwise, you should use the CSS font-weight and font-style properties that you'll learn about in the next chapter.

Although they're not available from the HTML Property Inspector, you should know about some other formatting elements that you can apply to text. These elements are available from the Format→HTML Style menu. For example, this menu includes options for underlining and striking through text. These aren't options that you'll need to use often, though.

You can also use the HTML Property Inspector to create lists. To do that, just select the content you want to include in the list and then click the Unordered List or Ordered List icon. By default, an unordered list is formatted with bullets and an ordered list is formatted with decimals. You'll learn how to change this formatting in chapter 6.

This figure also shows you the CSS Property Inspector that's displayed when text is selected. You can use the controls it provides to generate styles for the style rule you select from the Targeted Rule combo box. For example, you can use it to set the font-family, font-style, and font-weight properties. You can also use it to set the font-size and color properties. And you can use it to set the text-align property. You'll learn about all of these properties in the next chapter.

Before I go on, you should notice the two icons that are always available in the upper right corner of the Property Inspector. You can use the Help icon to display help information about the type of content that's currently selected. If text is selected, for example, clicking this icon displays information about working with text.

The Quick Tag Editor icon lets you quickly add the tags for an element to a web page. If you click this icon, a list is displayed with the available elements. Then, you can select an element and press the Enter or Return key to insert the element into the page at the current location.

The HTML Property Inspector when text is selected

Common controls in the HTML Property Inspector for working with text

Control	Description
Format menu	Formats the selected text as a paragraph (<p>), a heading (<h1> through <h6>), or preformatted text (<pre>).
ID combo box	Adds an id attribute to the selected element with the value you specify.
Class combo box	Adds a class attribute to the selected element with the value you select. Can also be used to apply multiple classes, remove the current class, rename a class, or attach an external style sheet.
Boldface icon (**B**)	Boldfaces the selected text (<strong>).
Italic icon (*I*)	Italicizes the selected text (<em>).
Unordered List icon (▤)	Creates a bulleted list (<ul>), where each selected paragraph is a separate bulleted item (<li>).
Ordered List icon (▤)	Creates a numbered list (<ol>), where each selected paragraph is a separate numbered item (<li>).

The CSS Property Inspector when text is selected

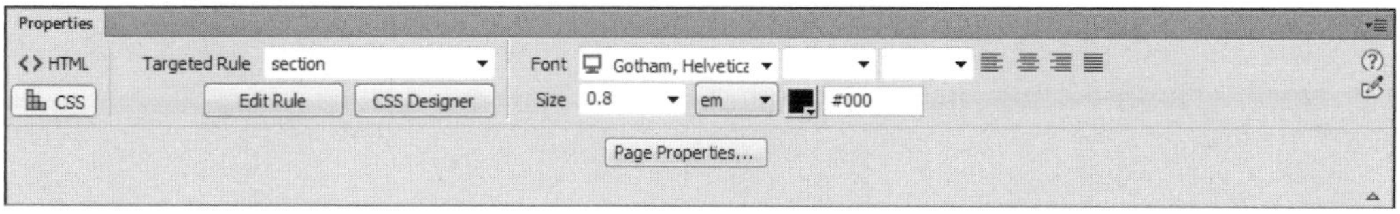

Common controls in the CSS Property Inspector for working with text

Control	Description
Targeted Rule combo box	Lets you select the style rule you want to modify.
Font combo boxes	Set the font-family, font-style, and font-weight properties.
Alignment icons (▤, ▤, ▤, and ▤)	Set the text-align property.
Size combo box and menu	Set the font-size property.
Text color menu and text box	Set the color property.

Description

- You can use the Link, Target, and Title controls in the HTML Property Inspector to work with text links as described later in this chapter.
- You can use the Help icon (⊘) in the upper right corner of the Property Inspector to display help information on text formatting.
- You can use the Quick Tag Editor icon (⊿) below the Help icon to quickly add the tags for the element you choose.

Figure 4-4 How to use the Property Inspector to work with text

How to check the spelling in a web page

In the last chapter, you learned that you should validate a web page to be sure that the code it contains is compliant with the current HTML standards. You should also preview a page in all current browsers to be sure that it looks the way you want it to and that it works correctly. In addition, you should check the spelling of the text in the page to be sure there aren't any errors. This can help make your page look more professional and improve your search engine rankings.

Figure 4-5 shows you how to use Dreamweaver's *spell checker* to check the spelling in a page. Because this spell checker works like the ones that come with most word processing applications, you shouldn't have any trouble using it. So I'll just summarize the basic skills here.

When you launch the spell checker, Dreamweaver starts to scan the text in your web page. If it detects a misspelled word, it stops and displays the Check Spelling dialog box shown here. Then, to change the word to one of the replacement words Dreamweaver suggests, you can select the replacement word and click the Change button to change just the current occurrence of the word or the Change All button to change all occurrences. You can also change the word to one other than those that Dreamweaver suggests by entering the word in the Change To text box.

If you don't want to change a word, you can click the Ignore button to skip the current occurrence of the word or the Ignore All button to skip all occurrences of the word. You can also click the Add to Personal button to add the word to your personal dictionary. Then, Dreamweaver will no longer detect a spelling error when it finds this word.

The Check Spelling dialog box

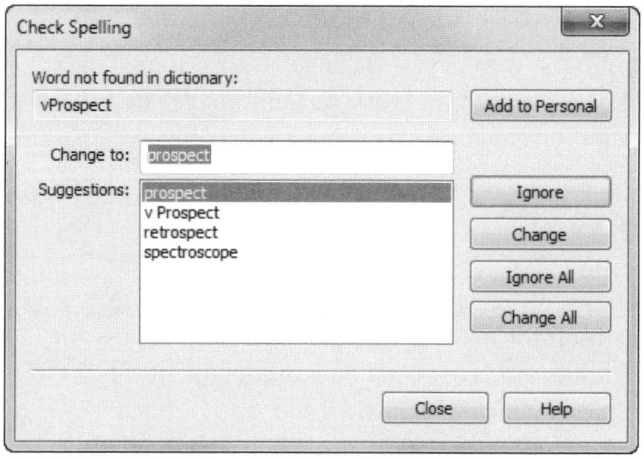

How to check the spelling in a web page

- Choose Commands→Check Spelling to begin the spelling check.
- If a word is found that isn't in Dreamweaver's dictionary, the Check Spelling dialog box is displayed.
- To change a word to one of the suggested replacement words, select the replacement word in the Suggestions list. Then, click the Change button to change just that occurrence of the word or the Change All button to change all occurrences of the word.
- If Dreamweaver doesn't suggest any replacement words or you want to use a word that isn't suggested, you can enter a replacement word directly into the Change To text box.
- If you don't want to change a word, you can click the Ignore button to skip just that occurrence of the word or the Ignore All button to skip all occurrences of the word. You can also click the Add to Personal button to add the word to your personal dictionary so Dreamweaver will no longer recognize it as a spelling error.

Description

- Like most word processing applications, Dreamweaver includes a *spell checker* that you can use to be sure that all the words in a document are spelled correctly.
- Before you check the spelling in a document, you should save it.

Figure 4-5   How to check the spelling in a web page

How to work with images

Images are an important part of most web pages. Because of that, the topics that follow teach you the skills you need for working with images in Dreamweaver.

Types of images for the Web

Figure 4-6 presents the three types of images you can use on a web page. To start, *JPEG files* are commonly used for photographs and scanned images, because these files can represent millions of colors and they use a type of compression that can display complex images with a small file size.

Although JPEG files lose information when they're compressed, they typically contain high quality images to begin with so this loss of information isn't noticeable on a web page. Similarly, although JPEG files don't support transparency, you usually don't need it for any of the colors in a photograph.

In contrast, *GIF files* are typically used for simple illustrations or logos that require a limited number of colors. Two advantages of storing images in this format are (1) they can be compressed without losing any information, and (2) one of the colors in the image can be transparent.

A GIF file can also contain an *animated image*. An animated image consists of a series of images called *frames*. When you display an animated image, each frame is displayed for a preset amount of time, usually fractions of a second. Because of that, the image appears to be moving. For example, the two globes in this figure are actually two of 30 frames that are stored in the same GIF file. When this file is displayed, the globe appears to be rotating.

Unlike the GIF and JPEG formats, which have been used for years in print materials, *PNG files* were developed specifically for the Web. In particular, this format was developed as a replacement for the GIF format. The advantages of the PNG format over the GIF format include better compression, support for millions of colors, and support for variable transparency.

Keep in mind as you develop the images for a website that you can use more than one format in the same site. As a rule of thumb, you should use the GIF format for images that contain a small number of colors such as line art or background images. You should use the JPEG format for photographs. And you should use the PNG format for images that require advanced features such as transparency.

You may also use different formats for the same image when displayed in a different size. For example, suppose you have a small thumbnail image that displays a larger version of the image when clicked. Then, you might want to save the thumbnail image as a GIF file and the larger image as a JPEG file. As you gain more experience working with images, you can decide which format works best for you.

Image types

Type	Description
JPEG	Typically used for photographs and scanned images because it uses a type of compression that can display complex images with a small file size. A JPEG file can represent millions of colors, loses information when compressed, and doesn't support transparency.
GIF	Typically used for logos, small illustrations such as clip art, and animated images. A GIF file can represent up to 256 colors, doesn't lose information when compressed, and supports transparency on a single color.
PNG	Typically used as a replacement for still GIF images. Compressed PNG files are typically smaller than GIF compressed files, although no information is lost. This format can represent millions of colors and supports transparency on multiple colors. PNG files are supported by all modern browsers, as well as mobile devices.

Typical JPEG and PNG images

Typical GIF images

Description

- *JPEG* (Joint Photographic Experts Group) images are commonly used for the photographs and images of a web page. Although information is lost when you compress a JPEG file, the reduced quality of the image usually isn't noticeable.

- *GIF* (Graphic Interchange Format) images are commonly used for logos and small illustrations. They can also be used for *animated images* that contain *frames*.

- The *PNG* (Portable Network Graphics) format was developed specifically for the web as a replacement for GIF files.

Figure 4-6   Types of images for the Web

How to insert images

Figure 4-7 describes three ways that you can insert an image into a web page. The easiest way is to drag the image file from the Files panel and then drop it on the web page. Then, the path that's generated for the image's src attribute is relative to the current document. If that's not what you want, you can use the Property Inspector to change this attribute as shown in the next figure.

If you use the Insert menu or Insert panel to insert an image as described in this figure, Dreamweaver displays the Select Image Source dialog box. From this dialog box, you can select the image you want to insert. You can also display the available images in different views to be sure you select the right one. And you can use the Relative To menu to determine if the path that's generated for the image is relative to the document or the site's root directory.

In addition to the src attribute that's generated for an image when it's inserted, Dreamweaver generates width and height attributes. These attributes are set to the actual width and height of the image, which helps the browser lay out the page as the image is loaded. In the next figure, you'll learn more about when and how you should resize an image.

The Select Image Source dialog box for inserting an image

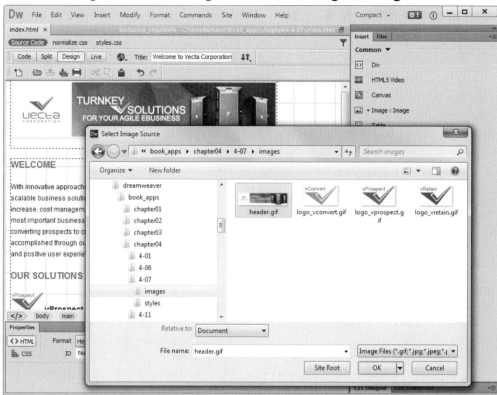

Three ways to insert an image into a web page

- Drag the image from the Files panel and drop it onto the web page.
- Position the cursor where you want to insert the image, and choose Insert→Image→Image to display the Select Image Source dialog box. Then, locate and select the image you want to insert and click OK to add it to the page.
- Position the cursor where you want to insert the image, and select the Image option from the Image menu in the Common category of the Insert panel to display the Select Image Source dialog box. If the Image option is already selected, you can just click the Image menu. Then, locate and select the image and click OK.

Description

- If you drag an image from the Files panel, the path that's generated for the image is relative to the current document. If you want to use a path that's relative to the root folder for the site, you can use one of the other techniques and then select the Site Root option from the Relative To menu.
- When you insert an image, it's displayed at its original size by default.
- If you select an image that's outside the website, Dreamweaver will give you the opportunity to copy that image into the site.

Figure 4-7   How to insert images

How to use the Property Inspector to work with images

Figure 4-8 shows the Property Inspector when an image is selected. Here, the Src text box specifies the path to the image. As you just learned, this value is set for you when you insert an image. If you need to change it, though, you can do that by entering the new value directly into the Src text box. Alternatively, you can drag the Point to File icon to the right of this text box to the Files panel and then drop it on the image you want to use. Or, you can click the Browse for File icon to display the Select Image Source dialog box you saw in figure 4-7.

Just as when you work with text, you can use the ID text box for an image to specify a unique ID for it. However, a list isn't provided to let you assign an existing ID. You can also use the Class combo box to assign one or more classes to the image, rename a class, remove a class, or attach a style sheet.

As you learned in the last topic, the width and height attributes of an image are set to the actual width and height of the image by default. If you want to change the size of an image, you can do that using the W and H controls. To start, if a closed lock icon is displayed to the right of the unit menus for the width and height as shown here, it means that the width and height are constrained so the aspect ratio of the image remains the same. So, if you change the width, the height changes accordingly. If that's not what you want, you can click the lock icon to unlock this constraint. Then, you can change the width and height any way you want. Since this distorts the image, though, you're not likely to do that.

When you enter a different value for the width or height and then press Enter or Return, the image is displayed at its new size in Design view. If it looks the way you want, you can click the Commit Image Size icon that appears to the right of the lock icon to commit the change. Otherwise, you can click the Reset to Original Size icon to cancel the change.

Note that if you change the size of an image in a web page, the actual image file is updated to reflect that change. So, if you insert the image again, it will be inserted at the new size. In addition, if the original image file is specified in the Original text box, the size of that image will we updated as well. You'll learn more about using this text box in just a minute.

The alt attribute is also included by default when you insert an image, but its value is set to an empty string. Then, you can use the Alt text box to provide information about the image in case it can't be displayed or the page is being accessed using a screen reader. This is essential for visually-impaired users. If an image is just for decoration, however, you can leave this attribute as an empty string.

Like the alt attribute, the title attribute is used to provide additional information about an image. If you specify a value in the Title text box, though, it's displayed in a tooltip when the cursor hovers over the image.

The Property Inspector also features some editing tools that you can use to modify an image directly within Dreamweaver. These tools include the ability to sharpen an image, change an image's brightness and contrast, crop an image, and resample an image, which improves the quality of a picture after you resize it. You can also optimize an image as shown in the next figure, and you can launch

The Property Inspector when an image is selected

Common controls for formatting images

Control	Description
ID text box	Adds an id attribute to the image with the value you specify.
Src text box	Sets the path to the image. You can change the file or path by typing it in, by dragging the Point to File icon (⊕) to the image in the Files panel and then dropping it on an image, or by clicking the Browse for File icon (📁) to display the Select Image Source dialog box.
Class combo box	Adds a class attribute to the image with the value you specify.
Edit tools	Provide access to advanced editing features. Options include launching the image within a previously defined image editor (Ps), optimizing the image (✿), cropping the image (✄), adjusting the image's brightness and contrast (◑), and adjusting the image's sharpness (△).
W and H controls	Lets you adjust the image's width and height.
Alt text box	Adds the text you specify to the alt attribute for the image. This text is displayed if the image can't be displayed for any reason.
Title text box	Adds a title attribute to the image with the text you specify. This text is displayed if you place the mouse pointer over the image in a browser.
Original text box	Sets the path to the original image that the image in the Src text box was created from. If you enter a value here and then click the Edit button, the original image is opened in your image editor so you can edit it. When you're done, the image in your web page is updated based on the changes you made.

Description

- If you change the width or height of an image from the Property Inspector, the aspect ratio of the image is maintained by default. If that's not what you want, you can click the Toggle Size Constrain icon (🔒) to unlock this constraint.
- When you change the height or width, the Reset to Original Size icon (◌) and Commit Image Size icon (✔) are displayed so you can cancel or commit the change after you preview it in Design view.
- If you change the size of an image in a web page, the size of the image in the source file is changed as well. In addition, if a path to the original image is specified, the size of that image is changed.
- You can use the Link, Target, and Map controls to work with image links as described later in this chapter.

Figure 4-8   How to use the Property Inspector to work with images

an image editor that you have installed on your computer to edit the original image. The first Edit icon indicates what editor is available. In figure 4-8, that editor is Photoshop. If a non-Adobe image editor is installed, a generic pencil icon is shown instead.

Before you can launch an external image editor from Dreamweaver, you must specify the location of the original image file in the Original text box. This value is also used to resize the original image if the image that's used in the web site is resized in Dreamweaver. Finally, if you edit the image specified here in an editor that's launched from outside of Dreamweaver, Dreamweaver detects that the images are out of sync and displays an Update From Original icon that you can use to update the image in the web page.

How to use the Quick Property Inspector to work with images

Earlier in this chapter, you learned how to use the Quick Property Inspector to work with text in Live view. Now, figure 4-9 shows how to use the Quick PI to work with images.

When you select an image in Live view, an Element Live Display appears. In addition to working with classes and IDs, you can use the Element Live Display for an image to work with other common attributes. To do that, you click the Edit HTML Attributes icon to display the Quick PI shown here. Then, you can set the value of any of the available attributes.

The Document window in Live view with the Quick PI for an image

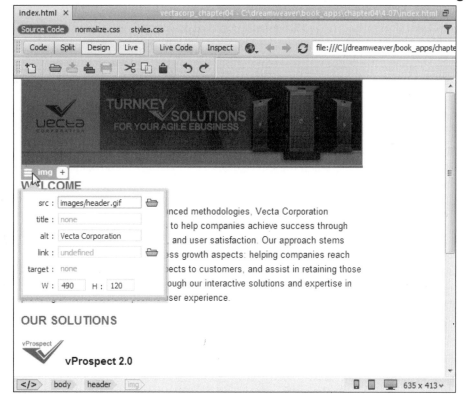

Description

- If you select an image in Live view, the Element Live Display includes an Edit HTML Attributes icon (▤) that lets you display the Quick Property Inspector for the image.

- The Quick Property Inspector for an image provides quick access to many of the properties that are available from the Property Inspector.

Figure 4-9   How to use the Quick Property Inspector to work with images

How to optimize images

Figure 4-10 shows the Image Optimization dialog box that you can use to optimize images within Dreamweaver. *Image optimization* involves removing features of an image file to reduce its size without sacrificing too much quality. This Dreamweaver CC feature makes it easy to adjust an image without having to use an image editor.

The table in this figure describes the options you can set to optimize an image. Note that the options that are available depend on the option you choose from the Preset or Format combo box. In this figure, for example, you can see the options that are available when the GIF format is selected, which includes most of the available options. Also notice that the current file size is shown at the bottom of the dialog box. That way, you can tell how a change affects the size of the file.

The preset configurations let you optimize an image quickly without having to think too much about the various settings. These configurations include 32-bit, 24-bit, and 8-bit PNG files that support various options; two types of JPEG configurations that vary only in their quality settings; and a GIF configuration. Most of the time, you'll want to use preset configurations that match the original image type. For instance, if you're optimizing a GIF image, you'll want to select the GIF option from the Preset combo box and then adjust the Palette, Color, Loss, Transparency, and Matte options to reduce the image size.

After you optimize an image, you'll want to check it to see how it looks in the web page. Then, if the quality is too degraded, you can undo the changes (Edit→Undo), or you can display the Image Optimization dialog box again and make some additional adjustments. You can continue this process until the quality of the image is acceptable.

The Image Optimization dialog box

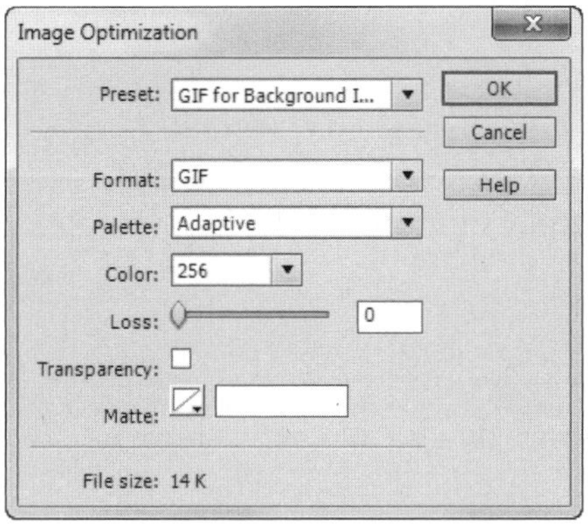

Options for image optimization

Option	Description
Format	The format for the image. Options are PNG 32, PNG 24, PNG 8, JPEG, and GIF.
Palette	Determines whether the image is displayed in color (Adaptive) or shades of gray (GrayScale). Available for GIF and PNG 8 files only.
Color	The number of colors used to display the image. Options range from 2 to 256. You can choose a number that's less than the original number of colors in the image to reduce the size of the image. Available for GIF and PNG 8 files only.
Loss	The percent of loss in image quality. The higher the value, the smaller the file. Available for GIF files only.
Transparency	If selected, indicates that the image contains a transparent color. Available for GIF and PNG 32 files only.
Matte	The color for the matte that's displayed behind an image. Typically used for an image with a transparent color that's displayed over a colored background to help the image blend into the background. Available for GIF and PNG 32 files only.
Quality	A value from 1 to 100 that determines the quality of the image. The higher the quality, the larger the file. Available for JPEG files only.

Description

- *Image optimization* is the process of reducing the size of an image file while maintaining acceptable quality.
- To display the Image Optimization dialog box, select the image you want to optimize and then click the Edit Image Settings icon (✿) in the Property Inspector or choose Modify→Image→Optimize.
- To optimize an image, you can choose a preset configuration or create a custom configuration using the options shown above.
- The options that are available from the Image Optimization dialog box depend on the Preset or Format option you choose.

Figure 4-10   How to optimize images

How to work with hyperlinks

One of the most critical skills that you will learn as a web developer is how to create and work with hyperlinks. The ability to link pages and resources together is what powers and connects the billions of pages on the Web. In the topics that follow, you'll learn how to create a variety of links.

How to create text links

Most web pages contain *hyperlinks*, or just *links*, that go to other web pages or resources. Figure 4-11 describes the process of creating text-based links. As you can see, you can create a link for existing text or for new text.

You can create a link for existing text in one of three ways. In all three cases, you start by selecting the text you want to create the link for. Then, you can enter the path to the file you want to link to in the Link combo box of the HTML Property Inspector, you can use the Browse for File icon to the right of the Link combo box to display a dialog box that lets you locate and select the file, or you can drag the Point to File icon to the right of the Link combo box to the file you want to link to in the Files panel.

After you create a link, you can use the Property Inspector to change some of its properties. To start, you can use the Target combo box to set the *target window* where the file will be loaded. The default is _self, which loads the file in the window that contains the link. The _blank option causes the file to be loaded in a new browser window or tab. The other options are related to a structuring method known as frames. Because frames are rarely used anymore, you probably won't need to use these options.

You can also enter a description of the link in the Title text box. Then, this description is displayed in a tooltip when the user hovers the mouse over the link. That can help clarify where the link is going. In addition, including a title will help users who use assistive technologies such as text-to-speech readers. It will also help improve search engine rankings.

To create a link for new text, you use the Hyperlink dialog box shown here. This dialog box lets you enter the text for the link and specify the path to the linked file. It also lets you specify a target and title as described above. And it lets you specify an access key and tab index, which aren't available from the Property Inspector.

An *access key* lets the user activate a link using the keyboard. The key you specify in the Access Key text box must be used in combination with other keys that depend on the operating system and browser. If the access key is set to the letter "C", for example, the link can be activated by pressing Ctrl+Option+C in Chrome under Mac, Alt+C in IE or Chrome under Windows, and Alt+Shift+C in Firefox.

The *tab index* sets the sequence in which the links and form controls on a page receive the focus when the user presses the Tab key. By default, this *tab order* is the sequence in which the links and controls appear in the HTML. To

Linked text within a web page

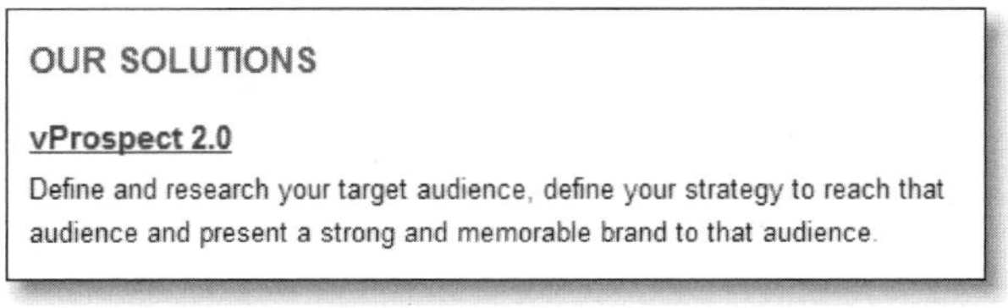

OUR SOLUTIONS

<u>vProspect 2.0</u>
Define and research your target audience, define your strategy to reach that
audience and present a strong and memorable brand to that audience.

The Hyperlink dialog box

Hyperlink

Text: more...

Link: aboutus.html

Target:

Title: Corp. including company history

Access key:

Tab index:

OK

Cancel

Help

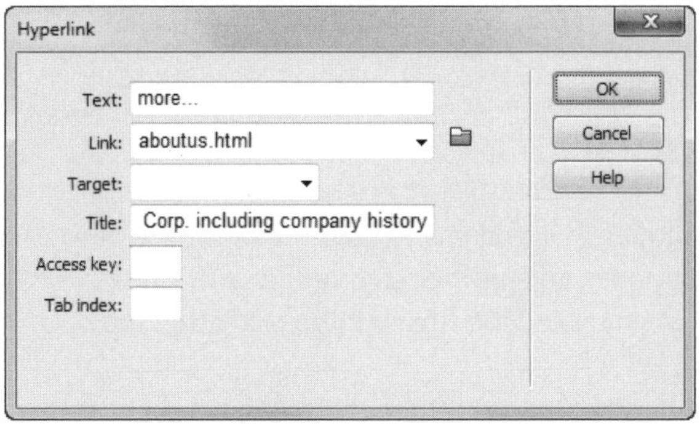

Three ways to create a link for existing text

- Select the text that you want to create a link for, and then enter the path to the file you want to link to in the Link combo box of the HTML Property Inspector.
- Select the text that you want to create a link for, and click the Browse for File icon (⌷) to the right of the Link combo box to display the Select File dialog box. Then, locate and select the file you want to link to.
- Select the text that you want to create a link for. Then, drag the Point to File icon (⊕) to the right of the Link combo box to the Files panel and drop it on the file you want to link to.

How to create a link for new text

1. Place the cursor within the document where you want to create the link, and choose Insert→Hyperlink or select Hyperlink from the Common category of the Insert panel to display the Hyperlink dialog box.
2. Enter the text for the link in the Text text box, and enter the name of the file it will link to in the Link text box or click the Browse icon to locate and select the file.

Description

- When the user clicks in a text *link*, the document or web page associated with that link is displayed.
- When you use the Hyperlink dialog box, you can also specify the *target window* where the file will be loaded, a title that's displayed when the user points to the link, an *access key* that can be used to select the link in a browser, and the *tab index* for the link.

Figure 4-11   How to create text links

change that order, though, you can set the tab index to a whole number starting from 0. If you want to exclude a link from the tab order, enter a negative number instead.

By default, links are underlined when they're displayed in a browser to indicate that they're clickable. As a result, most users have been conditioned to associate underlined text with links. Because of that, you should avoid underlining any other text. In addition, a link has a default color depending on its state. For instance, a link that hasn't been visited is displayed in blue, and a link that has been visited is displayed in purple. However, you can use CSS as described in the next chapter to change these settings.

How to create image links

You can use the same three techniques that you use to create a link for text to create a link for an image. These techniques are summarized in figure 4-12. As you can see, the only difference is that you select an image before creating the link instead of selecting text.

Traditionally, browsers rendered linked images with a blue border if the link was unvisited and a purple border if the link was visited. This is consistent with the appearance of text-based links. However, most web developers removed these borders so they didn't detract from the image. Because of that, most modern browsers have updated their built-in styles so borders aren't displayed. You may want to continue to remove these borders so they're not displayed in older browsers, though. You'll learn how to work with borders in chapter 6.

In addition to creating a link for an entire image, you can create a link for a portion of an image called a *hotspot*. To do that, you use the procedure in this figure. Here, I created a hotspot for the company logo within the header.

To create a hotspot, you use one of the hotspot tools in the Property Inspector. These tools let you create a hotspot that's a rectangle, a circle, or a polygon. When you do that, Dreamweaver places a pound sign (#) in the Link combo box. As you'll learn later in this chapter, you use the pound sign to indicate that the link will jump to a placeholder on the same page. For now, you can just create a link for a hotspot using the same techniques you use to create a link for an image. When you're done creating hotspots, be sure that the pointer hotspot tool is selected.

When you create a hotspot, you should realize that Dreamweaver creates an *image map* for the entire image using a map element. Then, it creates the hotspot within the map element using an area element that includes the coordinates of the hotspot. You can see these elements in the Tag selector shown here. You should also realize that you can add more than one hotspot to the same image. Then, each hotspot is coded within the image map for that image.

An image map with a hotspot

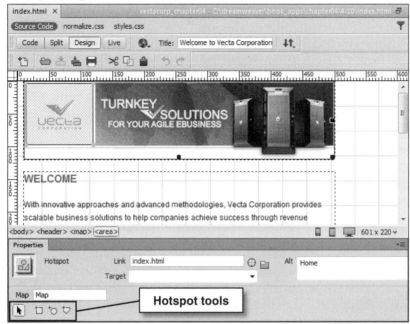

How to create a link for an image

- Select the image. Then, enter the path to the file you want to link to in the Link combo box of the Property Inspector. Or, use the Point to File icon (⊕) or the Browse for File icon (📁) to the right of the Link combo box to identify the file you want to link to.

How to create a link for a hotspot in an image map

1. Select the image that will contain the image map and hotspot. Then, select the rectangle, circle, or polygon hotspot tool from the Property Inspector, and draw a shape for the hotspot within the image.

2. With the hotspot selected, enter the path to the file you want to link to in the Link combo box of the Property Inspector. Or, use the Point to File icon or the Browse for File icon to the right of the Link combo box to identify the file you want to link to.

Description

- Dreamweaver lets you create a link for an image or an area within an image.

- To create a link for an area within an image, you create an *image map* for the image. An image map contains one or more *hotspots* that link to other files.

- When you create a hotspot, Dreamweaver reminds you to set its alt attribute to aid visually impaired users. You can do that using the Property Inspector. You can also use the Property Inspector to change the target window and the id attribute for the hotspot. To select a hotspot, be sure the pointer hotspot tool is selected.

Figure 4-12   How to create image links

How to create email, phone, and Skype links

Figure 4-13 shows how to create three additional types of links. To start, you can create a link that opens the user's default email client and sets the To address to the address you specify. To create this type of link, you can use the Email Link dialog box shown in this figure. Then, code like that shown in the first example in this figure is added to the Link combo box in the HTML Property Inspector. Of course, you can also enter code like this directly into this combo box.

You can also add one or more parameters to an email address to include additional information in the email. In the second code example in this figure, for instance, you can see that a CC address and a subject are included after the To address. Note that to include parameters, you must code a question mark following the To address. In addition, if you code two or more parameters, they must be separated by an ampersand (&).

As you can see, an email link always begins with the mailto: prefix. But you can also create other types of links using other prefixes. To create a phone link, for example, you code the tel: prefix followed by the phone number. This type of link is most useful for users who are viewing the website from a mobile device. Then, the device will automatically open its call functionality and attempt to dial the phone number.

To create a Skype link, you code the skype: prefix followed by the name of a registered Skype user. Then, if Skype is installed on the user's computer and that user is registered with Skype, the two users can communicate using Skype.

A web page with links for email, phone, and Skype

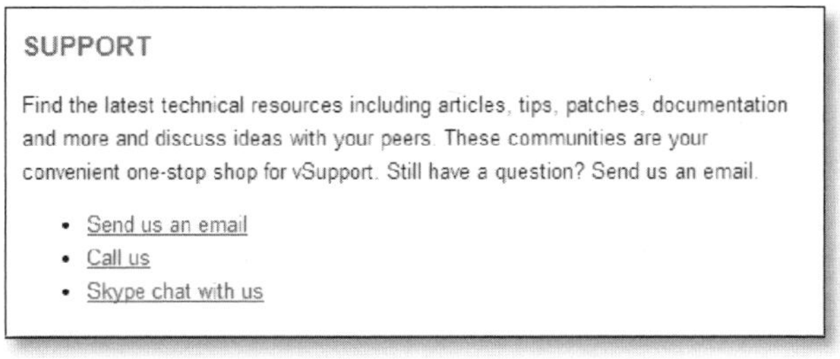

SUPPORT

Find the latest technical resources including articles, tips, patches, documentation and more and discuss ideas with your peers. These communities are your convenient one-stop shop for vSupport. Still have a question? Send us an email.

- Send us an email
- Call us
- Skype chat with us

The Email Link dialog box

Email Link

Text: Send us an email

Email: support@vectacorp.com

OK
Cancel
Help

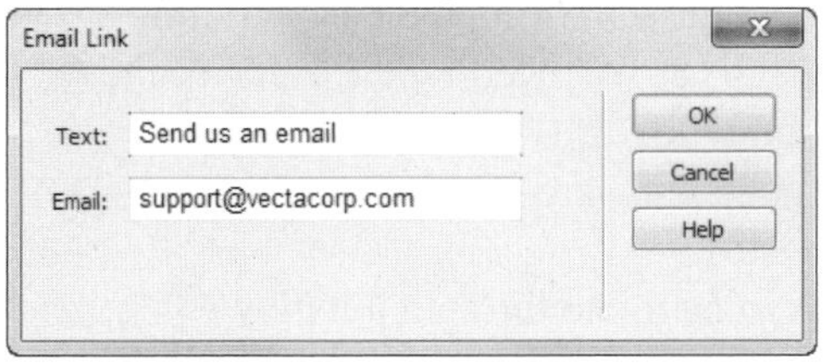

How to create an email link

1. Place the cursor within the document where you want to insert the link, and choose Insert→Email Link to display the Email Link dialog box.
2. Enter the text for the link in the Text text box, enter the email address in the Email text box, and click OK.

How to create phone and Skype links

- Create a link like you would for text, but enter code like that shown below into the Link combo box of the HTML Property Inspector.

Codes for inserting email, phone, and Skype links

Link type	Code
Email	`mailto:support@vectacorp.com`
Email with Parameters	`mailto:support@vectacorp.com?cc=herb@vectacorp.com&subject=I need help`
Phone	`tel:555-555-5555`
Skype	`skype:vectacorpsupport`

Description

- You can use the Email Link dialog box to create a link that opens the user's default email client. To create other types of links, you have to use the Link combo box in the HTML Property Inspector.
- You can include parameters on an email link to populate the subject, body, CC, and BCC for the email. To do that, you add a question mark after the email address, followed by the parameter name, an equal sign, and the parameter value. To include additional parameters, precede each one with an ampersand (&).

Figure 4-13   How to create email, phone, and Skype links

How to create and link to placeholders

Besides displaying another page or document, you can create links that jump to a location on the same page. To do that, you first create a *placeholder* that identifies the location you want the link to jump to. Then, you create a link that points to that placeholder. This is illustrated in figure 4-14.

To create a placeholder, you set the id attribute for the element that will act as the placeholder. In this figure, the headings vProspect 2.0, vConvert 2.0, and vRetain 1.0 (not shown) were selected and the id attributes were set to "vprospect", "vconvert", and "vretain".

To create a link to a placeholder, you select the text or image that will link to the placeholder. Then, you enter a pound sign (#) followed by the value of the id attribute of the placeholder in the Link combo box. If, for example, the user clicks on the vRetain link in this figure, the page will scroll to the heading with "vRetain" as its id.

Placeholders can make it easier for users to navigate through a long web page. For pages like these, it's common to include a placeholder at the top of the page along with navigation links for each section of the page. Then, at the end of each section, it's common to include a link to return to the top of the page.

Although placeholders are typically used for navigating within a single page, they can also be used to go to a location on another page. For instance, suppose you had a link for each solution on the main page of the Vecta Corporation website that displayed the solutions.html page shown here. Then, when you clicked one of these links, you could display the solutions.html page and jump to the placeholder for the solution that was clicked. To do that, you just code the value of the placeholder's id attribute at the end of the path for the link. To jump to the placeholder with an id attribute of "vretain" on the solutions.html page, for example, you would code this link: solutions.html#vretain.

Incidentally, placeholders were called *named anchors* in previous versions of Dreamweaver just as they were in HTML4. But since <a> tags are also known as anchor tags, this could be confusing. In HTML5 and Dreamweaver CC, the term *placeholder* makes this clearer.

A web page with a navigation menu that links to placeholders

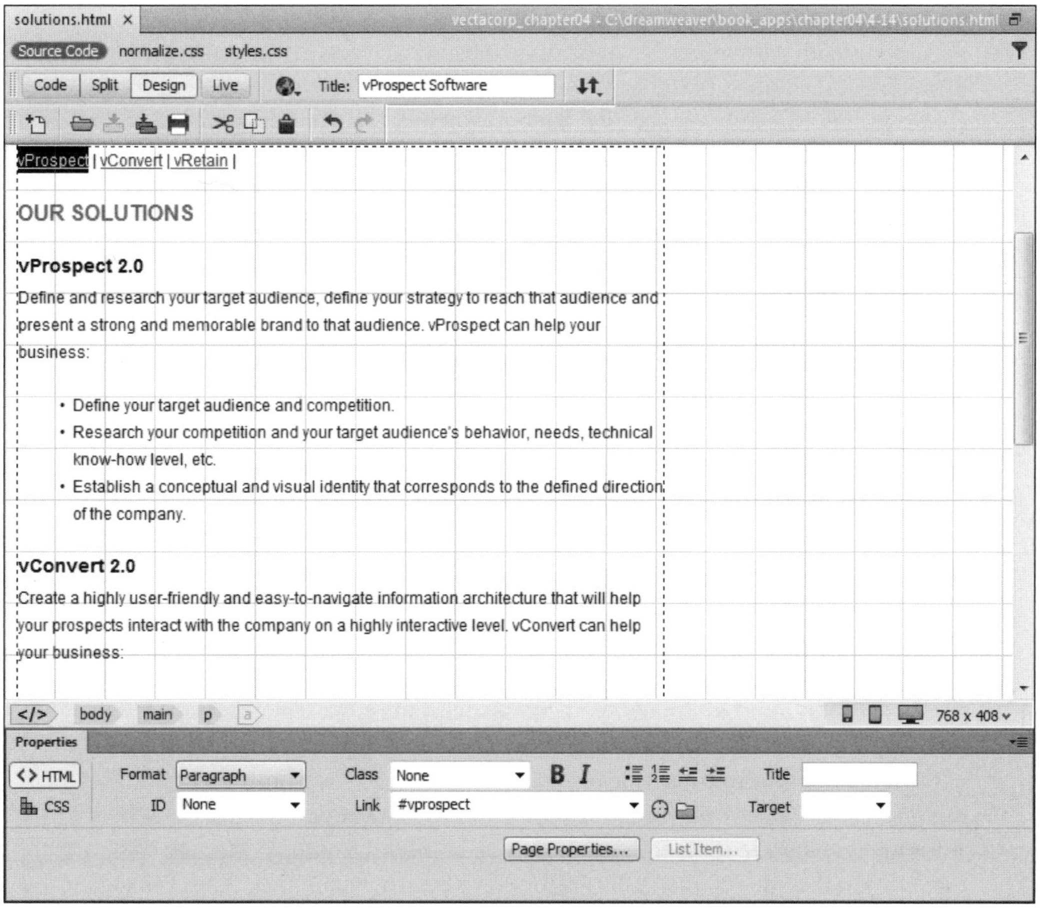

Description

- A *placeholder* identifies a location on a page that can be linked to. To create a placeholder, highlight a portion of text or select an image within the page and then set its id attribute to a unique value.

- To create a link that will jump to the placeholder, highlight the portion of text or select an image for the link. Then, enter the id of the placeholder, preceded by the pound sign, in the Link text box in the Property Inspector.

- You can also use the Point to File icon (⊕) to the right of the Link combo box to create a link to a placeholder. To do that, highlight the portion of text or select an image for the link, and then drag the Point to File icon to the element that contains the placeholder.

- You can also link to a placeholder on another page. To do that, enter the page name followed by the pound sign and the id of the placeholder.

Figure 4-14   How to create and link to placeholders

How to check and change links site wide

Along with validating the web pages in a site and testing them on multiple browsers as described in the last chapter and checking the spelling as described earlier in this chapter, you should check for *broken links* before a site goes live. When you check for broken links, Dreamweaver scans the cache and checks the paths to files for items like images and web pages. If a file isn't found at the specified path, it's listed as a broken link in the *Link Checker panel* shown in figure 4-15.

Here, one broken link to the solutions.html file was found in the index.html file. To fix this link, you can click on it in the Link Checker panel and then enter the correct path. Or, you can click the Browse for File icon to display a dialog box that lets you locate and select the file. When a link it corrected, it is removed from the Link Checker panel.

If you want to run another scan, you can do that by selecting an option from the Check Links menu at the left side of the Link Checker panel. These options let you check the links in the current page, check the links in the entire site, and check the links for the documents you select in the Files panel. You can also stop a scan by clicking the Stop icon below the Check Links menu. You may want to do that if a scan is taking too long to run. Then, you might want to rerun the scan on selected documents.

In addition to broken links, you can also use the Link Checker panel to display external links and orphaned files. To do that, you just select the appropriate option from the Show menu. *External links* are links that Dreamweaver can't verify because they point to an outside resource. You may want to review these links to be sure they're correct. *Orphaned files* are files that exist in the site but that aren't referred to by any web pages. These files can typically be deleted.

In addition to checking for broken links, you can change a link wherever it occurs in a site. To do that, you use the Change Link Sitewide dialog box, also shown in this figure. From this dialog box, you simply enter the old and new link. Or, you can use the Browse to File icons to locate and select the files. Here, all links that are currently pointing to the file named aboutus.html will be changed so they point to a file named about.html. Note that after you change a link site wide, you may want to check for broken links to be sure that all links were changed successfully.

The Link Checker panel with a broken link

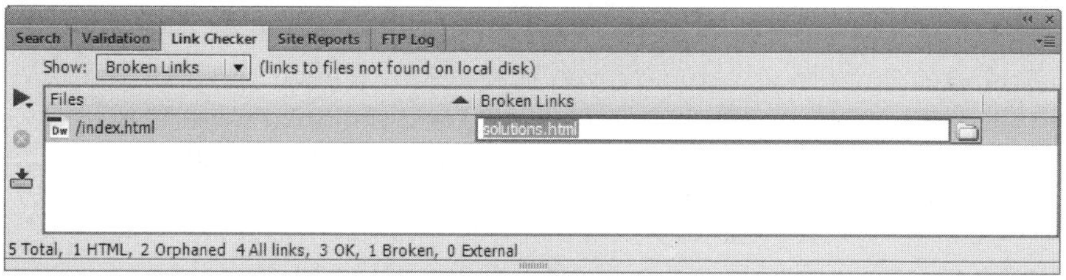

The Change Link Sitewide dialog box

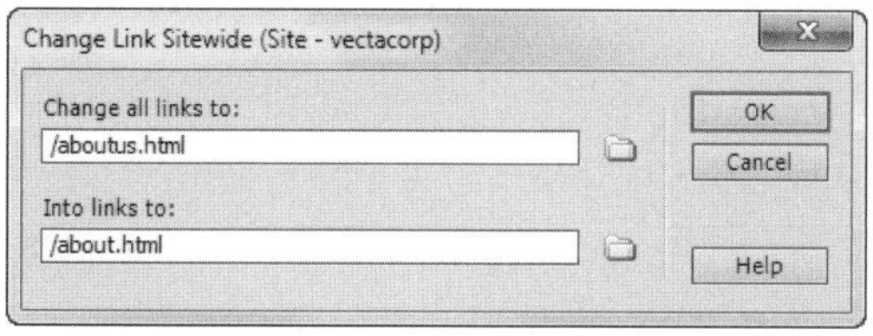

How to check for broken links within a website

- Choose Site→Check Links Sitewide to start the link check. If any broken links are found, they're displayed in the Link Checker panel at the bottom of the Dreamweaver window.

- To correct a broken link, click on it and enter a new path, or use the Browse for File icon (📁) to locate and select the file.

How to change a link site wide

1. Choose Site→Change Link Sitewide to display the Change Link Sitewide dialog box.

2. Use the Change All Links To text box or Browse to File icon to identify the file whose links you want to change.

3. Use the Into Links To text box or Browse to File icon to identify the file you want to change the links to.

4. When you click OK, the Update Files dialog box will be displayed with a list of all the links within your site that will be affected by the change. To change the links, click the Update button.

Description

- You should check for *broken links* within your website periodically to maintain its integrity.

- After you fix any broken links, you can recheck the links directly from the *Link Checker panel* by selecting Check Links For Entire Current Local Site from the Check Links menu (▶) at the left side of the panel. You can also check the links for just the current document or for selected documents from this menu.

- If you change the name of a page within a website, you can change any links to that page using the Change Link Sitewide dialog box.

Figure 4-15   How to check and change links site wide

Perspective

Now that you've completed this chapter, you should have a good perspective on how to use Dreamweaver to work with text, images, and links. With that as background, the next two chapters present the skills you need for formatting text and laying out pages.

Terms

rich text	target window
Quick Property Inspector (PI)	access key
special character	tab index
character entity	tab order
spell checker	hotspot
JPEG file	image map
GIF file	placeholder
animated image	named anchor
frame	broken link
PNG file	Link Checker panel
image optimization	external link
hyperlink	orphaned file
link	

Summary

- You can add plain text or *rich text* to a web page in Dreamweaver. You can also enter text directly into the Document window.

- You can now edit text in Live view as well as in Design view. When you do, you can use the *Quick Property Inspector* to quickly boldface or italicize selected text or create a link for the text.

- Dreamweaver provides for inserting *special characters* that can't be entered from the keyboard. Special characters are represented by *character entities* in HTML.

- To be sure that all the words in a document are spelled correctly, you should use Dreamweaver's *spell checker*.

- The three common formats for images are *JPEG* (for photographs and scanned images), *GIF* (for small illustrations, logos, and *animated images*), and *PNG* (typically used as a replacement for still GIF images).

- You can use the Element Live Display for an image to display the Quick Property Inspector for the image. The Quick PI for an image lets you set the most common properties for the image.

- To reduce the file size and loading time for an image, you can *optimize the image*. The options for optimizing an image in Dreamweaver depend on the image format.

- A *hyperlink*, or just *link*, typically loads another web page or resource when clicked. You can create links for text and images. You can also create links that start email messages, dial telephone numbers, and start Skype communications.

- The *target window* for a link determines where the file will be loaded. An *access key* provides access to a link using the keyboard. And the *tab index* for a link determines the order in which it receives focus when the Tab key is pressed.

- You can create a link for an area within an image by creating an *image map* that defines the clickable *hotspots*.

- A *placeholder* is a location on a page that can be linked to. A placeholder is identified by the value of its id attribute. To create a link that will jump to the placeholder, you specify the id of the placeholder as the path for the link.

- Before a website goes live, you should check for *broken links* to be sure that all the paths to files are correct. Then, if broken links are found, you can use the *Link Checker panel* to correct them.

- To change all occurrences of a link within a site, you use the Change Link Sitewide dialog box.

Exercise 4-1   Work with text, images, and links

In this exercise, you'll use the skills that you learned in this chapter to build
a web page like the one below and link it to two other pages. Along the way,
you'll use both placeholder and hotspot links.

Open the folder for this exercise and review its files

1. Open the Exercises site, and open the folder for this exercise.

2. Review the folders and files for this exercise. Note the two files in the styles
    folder, the five images in the images folder, the three html pages, and the one
    RTF file.

3. Open the index.html file in Design view, and note that it is a partial web page.
    Then, look at the HTML for the page in Code view, and note that it has a main
    element that contains header, section, and footer elements, but the section
    element is empty.

Add the content to the section element

4. Double-click on the welcome.rtf file to open it in your word processing program, and copy all of its contents. Then, go back to Dreamweaver, right-click in the section element in Code view, select the Paste Special command, and click on OK to paste the text into the HTML document.

5. Still in Code view, note that the formatting for the RTF file has been converted to the right HTML elements...just the way you would want them. Then, switch to Design view, and note that the styles that were set for those HTML elements work just as they did for exercise 3-1.

6. In Design view, move the insertion point to the start of the text in the footer. Then, use the Insert→Character→Copyright command to insert the copyright symbol, and enter one space after the symbol.

7. In Design view, put the insertion point anywhere in the footer, and use the CSS Property Inspector to center the text as shown in figure 4-4.

8. Use Commands→Check Spelling to check the spelling for the page. Then, fix the errors that are found, but ignore the suggestions for the company and product names.

Work with the images for the page

9. In Design view, delete the image in the header of the page. Then, use Insert→Image→Image to insert the header.gif file into the header.

10. With figure 4-8 as a guide, use the Property Inspector to set the Alt attribute to Vecta Logo. Then, with figure 4-9 as a guide, use the Quick PI to change the Alt attribute to Vecta Corp Logo. That's just two ways of doing the same thing.

11. With figure 4-10 as a guide, optimize the header.gif image. In the Image Optimization dialog box, use the Preset for GIF Background images and set the Loss to 20. In the Image Optimization dialog box, note that the file size goes down as the Loss value goes up.

12. Add the three product images in front of the headings for the products so they look the way they do in the page at the start of this exercise.

Add a navigation bar

13. In Live view, click in the header, use the Tag selector to select the header element, and use the Insert panel to add a nav element after that element.

14. In Design view, replace the text that Dreamweaver generated for the nav element with "Solutions". Then, select that text, and use the HTML Property Inspector to create a link that links to the solutions.html file.

15. Put the insertion point to the right of the Solutions link, and use the Insert panel to add an About Us hyperlink that goes to the aboutus.html file.

16. Use the CSS Designer to create a style for the hyperlinks in the nav element that sets the right margins to 20 pixels. (The selector should be: nav a).

17. With figure 4-13 as a guide, add an Email Us link to the right of the About Us link. This email should go to support@vectacorp.com.

18. Test these links in your default browser. To return to the index page, use the browser's Back button.

Add placeholder and hotspot links to the About Us page

19. In Design view for the About Us page, add a hotspot link to the image in the header, as shown in figure 4-12. The hotspot should be just for the logo portion of the image, and it should link to the index.html page.

20. To prepare for placeholder links, use the HTML Property Inspector in Design view or the Quick PI in Live view to add id attributes to the three h2 headings. In sequence, the ids should be "overview", "management", and "careers".

21. With figure 4-14 as a guide, use the HTML Property Inspector to set the navigation links at the top of the page to the three h2 headings. For instance, the Company Overview link should go to #overview, which is the selector that refers to the element with "overview" as its id.

22. Add a "Back to Top" link at the bottom of the page, right before the footer. This link should be within a paragraph, and it should link to the aboutus.html page.

23. If you haven't tested these enhancements after each step, test them all now.

Do some final checking

24. Do a final test of the About Us page in both Internet Explorer and another browser. Depending on your version of IE, you may see some problems or variations.

25. To resolve those differences, attach the normalize style sheet to the page. Then, test again. Now, attach the normalize style sheet to the index and solutions pages too.

26. Use the Site→Check Links Sitewide command to check the links for the site, although you shouldn't find any broken links. If you want to see how this works when you do have a broken link, change one of the links so it points to a file that doesn't exist, and check the links again. Then, fix the broken link as shown in figure 4-15.

27. When you're through experimenting, close all of the files.

5

How to use CSS to format text

In chapter 3, you learned how to use the CSS Designer to create style sheets and add selectors and styles to those style sheets. Now, you'll learn the details for working with the styles for formatting text as well as how to manage the fonts that you use.

How to specify measurements and colors

For many of the properties of a style rule, you will need to know how to specify measurements and colors. So, this chapter starts by presenting the most common units of measure and showing you how to specify them in Dreamweaver. Then, it shows you how to use Dreamweaver to specify colors.

How to specify measurements

Figure 5-1 shows the four units of measure that are commonly used with CSS: pixels, points, ems, and percent. Here, the first two are *absolute units of measure*, and the second two are *relative units of measure*. Dreamweaver provides for other absolute units, such as picas, but they aren't used as often in web development.

When you use relative units of measure like ems or a percent, the measurement will change if the user changes the browser's font size. If, for example, you set the size of an element's font to 80 percent of the browser's default font size, the size of that element will change if the user changes the font size in the browser. Because this lets the users adjust sizes to their own preferences, we recommend that you use relative measurements for most sizes.

In contrast, when you use an absolute unit of measure like pixels or points, the measurement won't change even if the user changes the font size in the browser. If, for example, you set the width of an element in pixels and the font size in points, the width and font size won't change.

When you use pixels, though, the size will change if the screen resolution changes. That's because the screen resolution determines the number of pixels that are displayed on the monitor. For instance, the pixels on a monitor with a screen resolution of 1280 x 1024 are closer together than the pixels on the same monitor with a screen resolution of 1152 x 864. That means that a measurement of 10 pixels will be smaller on the screen with the higher resolution. In contrast, a point is $1/72^{nd}$ of an inch no matter what the screen resolution is.

The example in this figure shows how to set units of measure with the CSS Designer. Here, the font size for the body element is being set to .8 ems. To do that, em is selected from the list that's displayed when the unit column is clicked. Then, the value column is highlighted so you can enter a value.

Common units of measure

Symbol	Name	Type	Description
px	pixels	absolute	A pixel represents a single dot on a monitor. The number of dots per inch depends on the resolution of the monitor.
pt	points	absolute	A point is 1/72 of an inch.
em	ems	relative	One em is equal to the font size for the current font.
%	percent	relative	A percent specifies a value relative to the current value.

How to specify a size with the CSS Designer

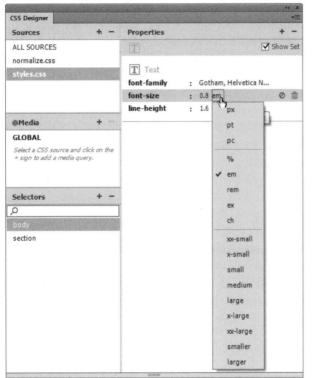

Description

- You use the units of measure to specify a variety of CSS properties, including font-size, line-height, width, height, margin, and padding.
- To specify an *absolute measurement*, you can use pixels or points.
- To specify a *relative measurement*, you can use ems or percent. This type of measurement is relative to the size of another element.
- To set a size in the CSS Designer, click the unit to the right of the property you want to set and select a unit from the list that's displayed. Then, enter a value for the size.

Figure 5-1   How to specify measurements

How to specify colors

When you work in Dreamweaver, you typically specify a color using the color picker. You can display the color picker for a property by clicking its color box. In figure 5-2, for example, the color picker is displayed for the color property of the h2 element.

When you use the color picker, you can specify a color using one of three color models. The default is to use the traditional *hexadecimal*, or *hex*, *values* to specify colors using the *RGB* (red, green, blue) *color model*, and this is the method that's preferred by most web designers. Then, each two-digit hex value is equivalent to a decimal value from 0 through 255. When you use this technique, the entire value must be preceded by the pound sign (#) as shown in this figure.

The second color model that you can use to specify a color in Dreamweaver is *RGBA* (red, green, blue, alpha), which became available with CSS3. With this model, the red, green, and blue values are specified as percents. Then, the alpha value indicates the opacity of the color. If, for example, you set this value to 0, the color is fully transparent so anything behind it will show through. Or, if you set this value to 1, nothing will show through.

Finally, you can use another color model that became available with CSS3, called the *HSLA* (Hue, Saturation, Lightness, and Alpha) color model. With this model, the hue, which is the main property of a color, is represented by a number from 1 to 359. Then, the saturation is a value from 0 through 100 that represents a percent. The lightness is a value from 0 through 100 that represents a percent with 50 being normal, 100 being white, and 0 being black. Finally, like an RGBA value, the alpha value indicates the opacity and can range from 0 to 1.

Now that you understand these three color models, you should realize that you don't have to specify their values directly when you use the color picker. Instead, you can use the Saturation and Brightness box and the three sliders to generate these values. You should realize, though, that if you choose the Hex option, you won't be able to set the opacity since it isn't supported by the RGB color model.

Another option for setting the color is to use the Sample tool. This tool lets you select a color from anywhere on your desktop. Once you do that, you can adjust the color using any of the other controls that are available from the color picker.

Once you get a color the way you want it, you may want to save it so you can use it again. To do that, you create a swatch as described in this figure. Here, you can see that I've created swatches for three colors. Then, to use a color again, I can simply click on its swatch.

The color picker in the CSS Designer

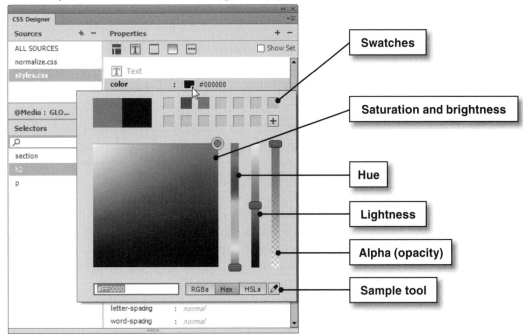

Accessibility guideline

- Remember the visually-impaired. Dark text on a light background is easier to read, and black type on a white background is easiest to read.

Description

- By default, Dreamweaver uses *hexadecimal*, or *hex*, values to specify colors using the *RGB* (red, green, blue) *color model*. Dreamweaver also lets you use the *RGBA* (red, green, blue, alpha) and *HSLA* (Hue, Saturation, Lightness, and Alpha) color models to provide for opacity.

- To display the color picker in the CSS Designer, click a color box. Then, select a color model and use the large box and the three slider controls in the color picker to specify the color you want to use. You can also use the Sample tool to select a color from anywhere on your desktop. To apply the color, press Enter or Return.

- If you know that you will want to reuse the same color again, you can save it as a swatch by clicking the Add Color as a Swatch button (+) near the upper right corner of the color picker. Then, you can apply the color again by clicking its swatch.

- As you use the color picker, Dreamweaver displays the new and current colors in the upper left corner.

- If you know the hex value for the color you want to use, you can enter it directly into the CSS Designer.

Figure 5-2   How to specify colors

How to work with text

Now that you know how to specify measurements and colors, you're ready to learn how to use CSS to style fonts and format text.

How to set the font family

Figure 5-3 shows how to use the CSS Designer to set the *font family* for text elements. In addition, the table in this figure lists the five generic font families, and the example below the table shows what typical fonts in three of these families look like when displayed in a browser.

When you develop a web page, your primary font family should be a sans-serif font family. That's because sans-serif fonts are easier to read in a browser than the other types of fonts, including serif fonts, even though serif fonts have long been considered the best for printed text. You can also use serif and monospace fonts for special purposes, but you should avoid the use of cursive and fantasy fonts.

The value for the font-family property consists of a list of the fonts that you want to use. In this figure, for example, you can see the list of font families that Dreamweaver provides by default. To set the font family, you simply select it from this list.

Notice that each font family in this list ends with a generic font name such as serif or sans-serif. Then, the browser will use the first font in the list that's available to it. But if none of the fonts are available on the user's computer, the browser will substitute its default font for the generic font that's coded last in the list.

The default font for most browsers is a serif font. Because of that, you'll typically want to set the font-family property for the body element of a web page to a sans-serif font. Then, because this property is inherited by all descendant elements, it will be used by all the elements on the page. If that's not what you want, you can change the font-family property for specific elements.

How to choose a font family in the CSS Designer

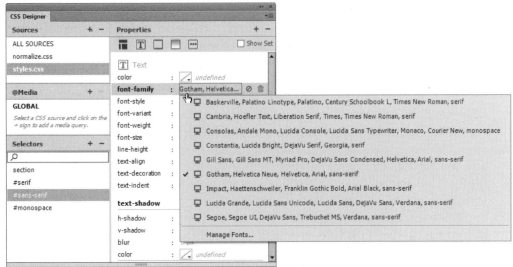

The five generic font families

Name	Description
`serif`	Fonts with tapered, flared, or slab stroke ends.
`sans-serif`	Fonts with plain stroke ends.
`monospace`	Fonts that use the same width for each character.
`cursive`	Fonts with connected, flowing letters that look like handwriting.
`fantasy`	Fonts with decorative styling.

Examples of serif, sans-serif, and monospace fonts

The default font for most web browsers is a serif font.

Sans-serif fonts are best for web pages.

Monospace fonts are used for code examples.

Description

- The font-family property specifies a list of the fonts you want to use. The browser will use the first font in the list that's available to it. If none of the fonts are available, the browser will substitute its default font for the generic font that's coded last in the list.

- To select a font family, click to the right of the font-family property in the Properties pane and then select a family from the list that's displayed.

- Because the font-family property is inherited by all of its descendants, it's typically a good idea to set this property for the body element.

- To display the font-family and other text properties in the CSS Designer, click the Text icon at the top of the Properties pane.

Figure 5-3   How to set the font family

How to set other properties for styling fonts

The table in figure 5-4 summarizes the other properties that you can use for styling a font. Like the font-family property, these properties are inherited by their descendants. The CSS Designer in this figure shows four of these properties after they're set for an h2 element. Notice that the COMPUTED selector has been selected here so any properties that are inherited by the h2 element are included. Then, the example in this figure illustrates how this heading differs from a standard paragraph of text when displayed in a browser.

To set the font size for a font, you use the font-size property. For this property, we recommend relative measurements so the users will be able to change the font sizes in their browser. The font-size property for the h2 element shown here, for example, is set to 1.2 ems.

When you use a relative measurement for the font size, it's relative to the parent element. So, if the parent element for the h2 element is .8 ems, the actual font size is 1.2 x .8, or .96 ems. Note that this is the same as coding the font size as 120%.

In addition to specifying a measurement for the font size, you should know that you can also specify one of several keywords. For example, you can use the x-small keyword to use an extra small font size, and you can use the x-large keyword to use an extra large font size. You can also use the smaller keyword to use a font size that's smaller than the size used by the parent element, and you can use the larger keyword to use a font size that's larger than the size used by the parent element. Because the size that's actually used can vary from one browser to another, though, you're not likely to use these keywords.

The font-weight property determines the boldness of a font. In most cases, you'll use the bold keyword as shown here. But if you want to use varying degrees of boldness, you can select a multiple of 100. You can also specify the boldness of a font relative to the boldness of the parent font by using the lighter or bolder keyword. All of the keywords and numbers you can use are available from the list in the CSS Designer for this property.

You can also set the font-style and font-variant properties by selecting a keyword from the list for that property. The font-style property lets you apply a slant to the font. If you want to italicize a font, for example, you can set this property to italic. The font-variant property lets you apply small caps to a font.

You can use the last property shown here, line-height, to increase or decrease the amount of vertical space that's used for a font. If, for example, you set the line height to 24 pixels for a font that is set to 12 pixels, there will be 12 extra pixels of space for the font. This space will be divided equally above and below the text within any block elements that are displayed on more than one line.

Like the font-size property, it's usually better to set the line-height property with a relative measurement like a percent or ems. That way, all modern browsers will be able to adjust the line height relative to the font size. In this figure, for example, the line height is set to 1.6 ems.

Common properties for styling fonts

Property	Description
`font-size`	A relative or absolute value or a keyword that specifies the size of the font.
`font-weight`	A keyword or number that determines the boldness of the font: normal, bold, bolder, lighter, or multiples of 100 from 100 through 900, with 400 equivalent to normal. Bolder and lighter are relative to the parent element.
`font-style`	A keyword that determines how the font is slanted: normal, italic, and oblique.
`font-variant`	A keyword that specifies whether small caps will be used: normal and small-caps.
`line-height`	A relative or absolute value that specifies the amount of vertical space for each line, or the normal keyword. The excess space is divided equally above and below the font.

A heading with properties for styling fonts

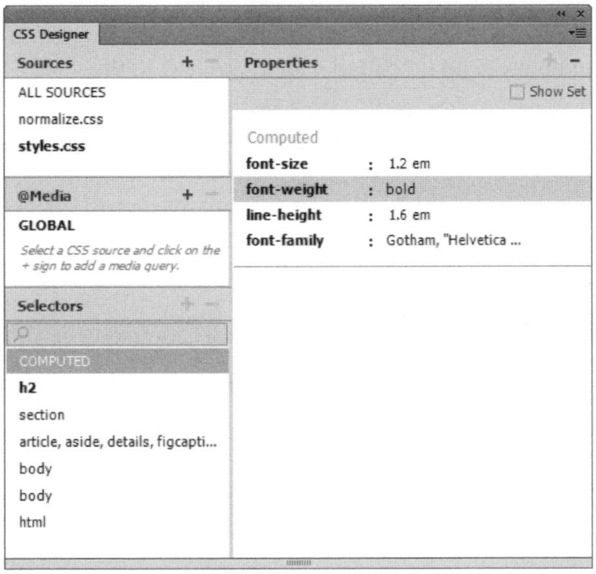

The heading and a paragraph in a web browser

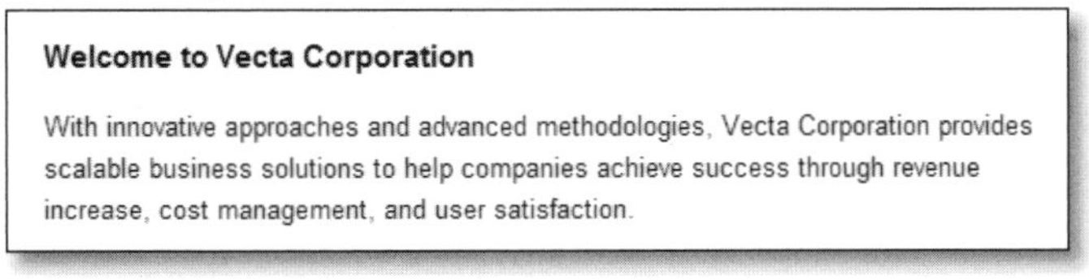

Welcome to Vecta Corporation

With innovative approaches and advanced methodologies, Vecta Corporation provides
scalable business solutions to help companies achieve success through revenue
increase, cost management, and user satisfaction.

Description

- If you select the normal keyword for the font-style, font-weight, font-variant, or line-height property, any formatting that has been applied is removed.
- Because the font-size property is inherited by all of its descendants, it's typically a good idea to set this property for the body element.

Figure 5-4   How to set other properties for styling fonts

How to indent and align text

Figure 5-5 presents the properties for indenting and aligning text. You can use the text-indent property to indent the first line of text in a paragraph. When you set this property, it usually makes sense to use a relative unit of measure. That way, if the size of the current font changes, the indentation will also change. In the example in this figure, the text-indent property has been set to 8%. Note that Dreamweaver doesn't provide for the use of ems with this property.

To align text horizontally, you can use the text-align property. By default, most elements are left-aligned, but you can click on one of the icons in the CSS Designer to center an element, right-align it, or justify it. Note, however, that when you justify text, the spacing between words is adjusted so the text is aligned on both the left and right sides as shown here. Since this makes the text more difficult to read, justified text should be avoided.

You can also align inline elements vertically. To illustrate, suppose that you had a span element within a paragraph, and you created a style rule that sets the font size for the text in the span element so it's smaller than the text in the paragraph. Then, the vertical-align property determines how the span element is aligned relative to its parent element. If, for example, you set the vertical-align property to "text-bottom", the bottom of the text in the span element will be aligned with the bottom of the text in the paragraph. Another alternative is to specify a relative or absolute value for this property to determine how far above or below its normal position the element should be displayed.

Properties for indenting and aligning text

Property	Description
text-indent	A relative or absolute value that determines the indentation for the first line of text.
text-align	A keyword that determines the horizontal alignment of text. Possible values are left, center, right, and justify.
vertical-align	A relative or absolute value or a keyword that determines the vertical alignment of text. Possible keywords are baseline, bottom, middle, top, text-bottom, text-top, sub, and super. If you use pixels, points, or ems to specify the value for the vertical-align property, the text is raised if the value is positive and lowered if it's negative. If you specify a percent, the text is raised or lowered based on the percentage of the line height.

A paragraph with text-align and text-indent properties set

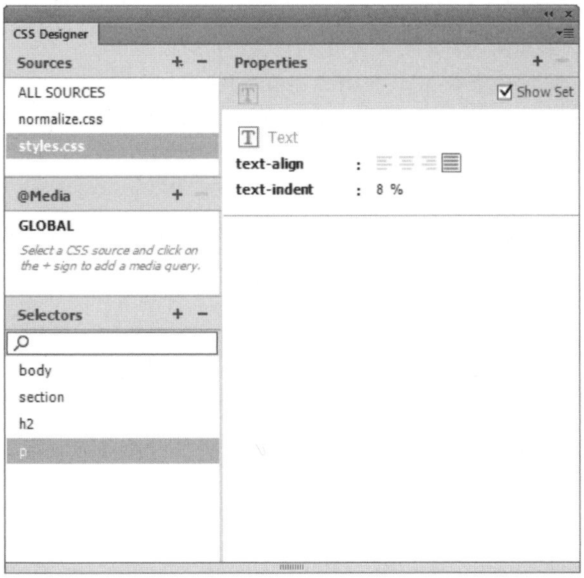

The paragraph in a web browser

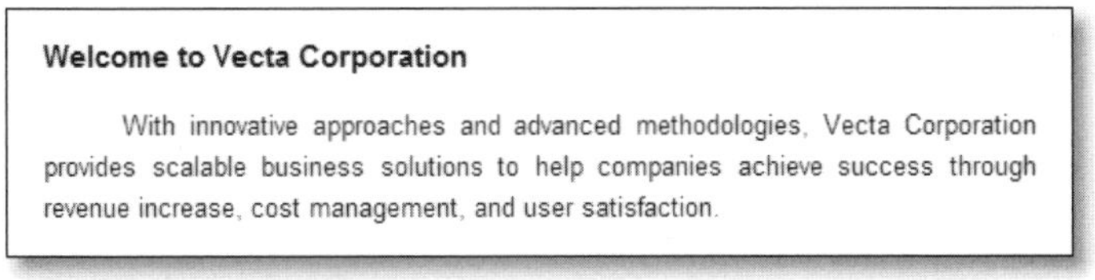

Welcome to Vecta Corporation

With innovative approaches and advanced methodologies, Vecta Corporation provides scalable business solutions to help companies achieve success through revenue increase, cost management, and user satisfaction.

Usability guidelines

- In general, you should avoid justified text because it isn't as easy to read as left-aligned text, which is ragged on the right.
- Web designers generally don't indent the first paragraph after a heading, but indenting the paragraphs that follow can improve readability.

Figure 5-5   How to indent and align text

How to transform and decorate text

Figure 5-6 shows two more properties for formatting text. To start, you can use the text-transform property to display text in all uppercase letters, all lowercase letters, or with the first letter of each word capitalized. To do that, you simply click the icon for the capitalization you want to use.

You can use the text-decoration property to display a line under, over, or through text. You can set this property by clicking an icon as well. However, this property has limited value for two reasons. First, you usually shouldn't underline words that aren't links. Second, you can use borders as shown in the next chapter to put lines over and under a block element, and that gives you more control over the lines.

The example in this figure illustrates how the text-transform and text-decoration properties work. Here, the text-transform property for the h2 element is set so the text is displayed in all uppercase letters. In addition, the text-decoration property is set so a line is drawn below the heading.

If you want to remove any text decorations and transformations that have been applied to an element, you can just click the None icons for these properties. For example, the text-decoration property of an <a> element is set to "underline" by default. If that's not what you want, you can click the None icon to set this property to "none".

Properties for transforming and decorating text

Property	Description
`text-transform`	A keyword that determines how text is capitalized. Possible values are uppercase, lowercase, capitalize, and none. This property is inherited.
`text-decoration`	A keyword that determines special decorations that are applied to text. Possible values are underline, overline, line-through, and none.

A heading with text-decoration and text-transform properties set

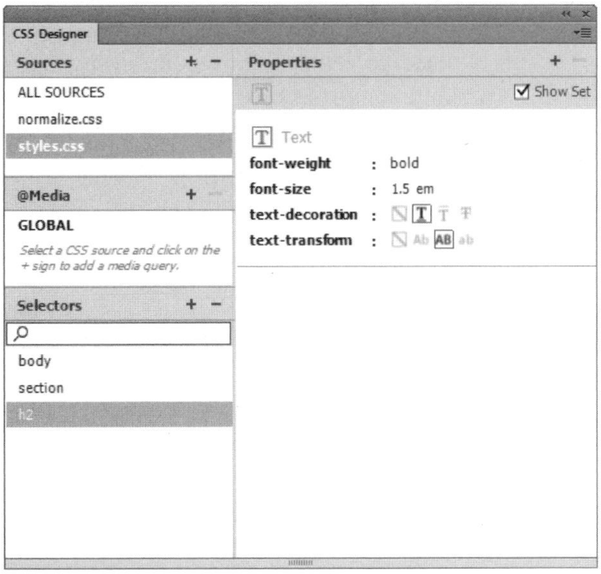

The heading in a web browser

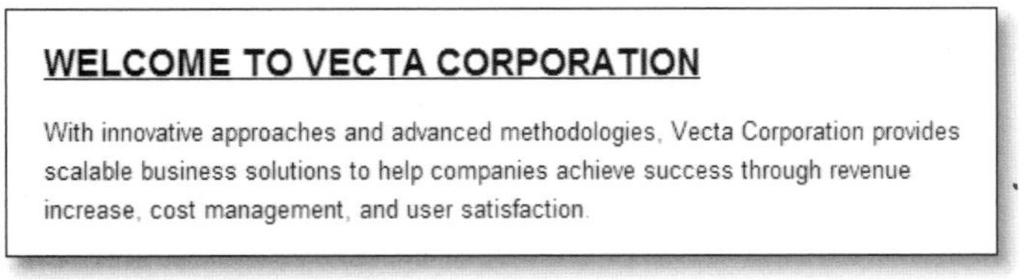

Usability guideline

- Avoid using the text-decoration property to underline elements. Users might think that the text is supposed to be a link and may become frustrated when they click it and aren't redirected to another page.

Figure 5-6   How to transform and decorate text

How to add shadows to text

Before CSS3, you had to use an image to display text with shadows. But now, CSS3 offers the text-shadow property for this purpose. That makes it much easier to provide shadows without the need for images that just increase the file size of the web page.

Figure 5-7 shows how to use this property in Dreamweaver. To start, it shows you the four values that are supported by the text-shadow property. These values are available from the text-shadow group in the CSS Designer.

The first value (h-shadow) specifies how much the shadow should be offset to the right (a positive value) or left (a negative value). The second value (v-shadow) specifies how much the shadow should be offset down (a positive value) or up (a negative value). The third value (blur) specifies how big the blur radius for the shadow should be. And the last value (color) specifies the color for the shadow.

The example in this figure shows a heading with a shadow applied. Here, the shadow is offset 3 pixels to the right and down, it has 5 pixels of blur, and it is light gray in color.

This property is supported by all modern browsers except Internet Explorer 9. But if a browser doesn't support this property, it is simply ignored so no harm is done: the heading is just displayed without the shadow. That's why you can start using this property right away.

When you use this property, though, remember the visually-impaired. If the offsets or blur are too large, the shadow can make the text more difficult to read.

Values specified on the text-shadow property

Value	Description
h-shadow	The position of the horizontal shadow. Positive values offset the shadow to the right. Negative values offset the shadow to the left.
v-shadow	The position of the vertical shadow. Positive values offset the shadow down. Negative values offset the shadow up.
blur	Determines how much the shadow is blurred (optional).
color	The color of the shadow (optional).

A heading with text-shadow values set

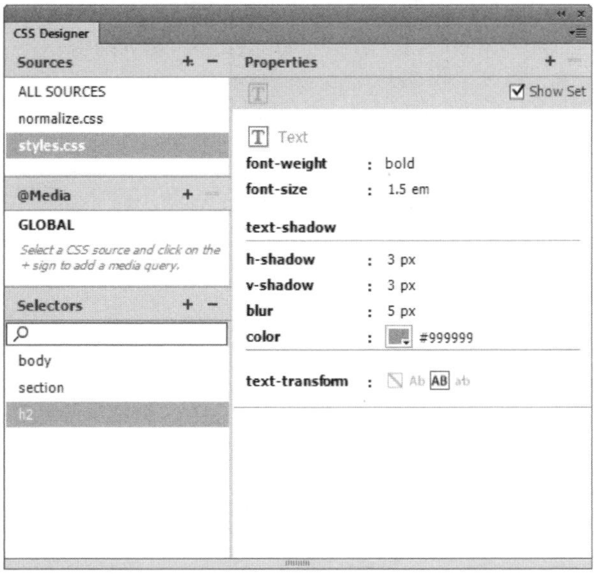

The heading in a web browser

Accessibility guideline

- Remember the visually-impaired. Too much shadow or blur makes text harder to read.

Description

- To set the text-shadow property in the CSS Designer, you set the four values in the text-shadow group.
- The text-shadow property is supported by all modern browsers. If it isn't supported by a browser, it is ignored so there's no shadow, which is usually okay.

Figure 5-7   How to add shadows to text

A web page with formatted text

Now that you've learned how to use Dreamweaver to format the text on a web page, you're ready to see a web page that uses formatted text.

The page layout for the web page

Figure 5-8 presents a web page that uses several of the properties you've just learned about. If you study this web page, you'll see that the default font has been set to a sans-serif font and the line height for the text has been increased. In addition, a larger font size, a color, and a text shadow have been applied to the first two headings, and the headings have been converted to uppercase. Overall, the page is simple but the formatting makes the web page look pretty good.

A web page with formatted text

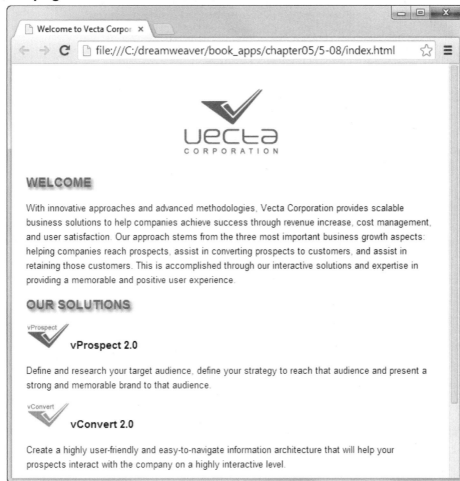

Description

- A sans-serif font has been applied to all of the text on this page because that's the most readable type of font for web pages. Also, relative font sizes have been applied to the elements on the page.
- The image in the header has been centered.
- A color has been applied to the first two headings, the headings have been transformed to all caps, and a shadow has been applied.

Figure 5-8   The page layout for the web page

The HTML for the web page

Figure 5-9 presents the HTML for the body of the web page shown in figure 5-8. The body consists of two elements: header and main. The header element contains the image that's displayed at the top of the web page. Then, the main element contains the remaining content for the page.

The main element starts with an h2 element for the "Welcome" heading, followed by a <p> element with the welcome text. Then, another h2 element is used for the "Our Solutions" heading. Each of the three solutions that follow consists of an h3 element with an img element for the solution's image and the solution's name, and a <p> element with the solution's description.

The CSS for the web page

Figure 5-9 also presents the CSS for the web page. Here, you can see that the style rule for the body selector sets three font styles: font-size, line-height, and font-family. All three of these properties are inherited by all the text elements on the page, since all the elements are descendants of the body element. In addition to these three properties, the margin property is used to set the margins for the body. You'll learn more about how this works in the next chapter.

In this example, the font-family property for the body is set to one of the lists of sans-serif fonts that's available from the CSS Designer. Then, the font-size property is set to .8 ems. This reduces the size of the text to eight tenths of the browser's default size. Finally, the line-height property is set to 1.6 ems. This results in a line with .4em of space above the text and .4em below.

The style rule for the h2 selector overrides the font-size property set in the style rule for the body selector. Here, the font size is set to 1.5 ems, or 1.5 times the size of the body font. In addition, the color property is set to #CC1C0D so the headings are displayed in a shade of red. Then, the font-weight property is set to "bold" so the headings are displayed in boldface. Note that this isn't really necessary because headings are automatically displayed in boldface. Finally, the text-shadow property is used to apply a shadow to the headings, and the text-transform property is used to convert the text for the headings to all upper-case. If you compare the text for the headings in the HTML to the headings that are displayed in the web page, you'll see how this works.

The last style rule shown here is for the header element. The height property sets the height for the element, and you'll learn more about this property in the next chapter. Then, the text-align property centers the contents of the header element. Note that this works even though the header element contains an image rather text.

The HTML for the body of the web page

```html
<body>
    <header><img src="images/logo.gif" width="170" height="125" alt=""/>
    </header>
    <main>
        <h2>Welcome</h2>
        <p>With innovative approaches and advanced methodologies,...</p>
        <h2>Our Solutions</h2>
        <h3><img src="images/logo_vprospect.gif" width="63" height="36"
                alt=""/>vProspect 2.0</h3>
        <p>Define and research your target audience, define ...</p>
        <h3><img src="images/logo_vconvert.gif" width="63" height="36"
                alt=""/>vConvert 2.0</h3>
        <p>Create a highly user-friendly and easy-to-navigate ...</p>
        <h3><img src="images/logo_vretain.gif" width="63" height="36"
                alt=""/>vRetain 1.0</h3>
        <p>Build on existing customer relationships to improve ...</p>
    </main>
</body>
```

The CSS for the web page

```css
body {
    font-family: Gotham, "Helvetica Neue", Helvetica, Arial, sans-serif;
    font-size: 0.8em;
    line-height: 1.6em;
    margin: 20px;
h2 {
    font-size: 1.5em;
    color: #CC1C0D;
    font-weight: bold;
    text-shadow: 3px 3px 5px #7D7D7D;
    text-transform: uppercase;
}
header {
    height: 120px;
    text-align: center;
}
```

Description

- The font family for the body element has been set to a list of sans-serif fonts. If none of the first four fonts in the list are supported by the browser, the browser's default sans-serif font is used.

- The font size for the body element has been reduced to eight tenths of the default size for the browser.

- The line-height for the body element has been increased to 1.6 ems.

- Because the font-size, line-height, and font-family properties are specified for the body element, they're inherited by all the other text on the page. However, the font-size property for the h2 element overrides the font size for the body element.

Figure 5-9   The HTML and CSS for the web page

How to manage web fonts

As you saw in figure 5-3, the choice of fonts that Dreamweaver provides by default is limited. In addition to these fonts, though, you can use Adobe Edge Web Fonts and local web fonts. You can also add your own custom font families to the list that Dreamweaver provides.

How to work with Adobe Edge Web Fonts

Adobe Edge Web Fonts are collections of fonts that are available through a commercial web font service called *Adobe Typekit*. These fonts are available free of charge to anyone who wants to use them in their websites. As figure 5-10 shows, Dreamweaver makes it easy to work with these fonts.

Before you can use an Adobe Edge Web Font in your website, you have to add it to your site. To do that, you use the Adobe Edge Web Fonts tab of the Manage Fonts dialog box. You can use several techniques to find the fonts you need from this dialog box. To start, if you know one or more characters of the font name, you can use the search bar to filter the list of fonts to those that contain those characters.

You can also display just the fonts that are recommended for headings or paragraphs using the first two buttons at the left side of the tab. And you can use the buttons in the next group of buttons to filter the fonts by style. If you click the first button in this group, for example, just the sans-serif fonts are displayed. And if you click the second button, just the serif fonts are displayed. Finally, you can click the last button at the left side of this tab to display just the fonts that you've already added.

Note that you can also use the search bar and the buttons in combination. If you enter the letter "n" in the search bar, for example, all the fonts that contain that letter will be displayed. Then, you could click the first button to display the fonts whose names contain the letter "n" that are recommended for headings. And so on.

Once you locate the font you want to use, you click on it to select it. When you do, a check mark is displayed in its upper right corner. In this figure, for example, the Actor font has been selected.

When you're done, you click the Done button to close the Manage Fonts dialog box. Then, the fonts will appear at the bottom of the list that's displayed for the font-family property in the CSS Designer, and you can use them just like any other font. Note that when you use an Adobe Edge Web Font on a page, a script is added to that page. This script will cause the font to be downloaded from the Adobe Edge Web Fonts server so it can be displayed in the user's browser.

The Adobe Edge Web Fonts tab of the Manage Fonts dialog box

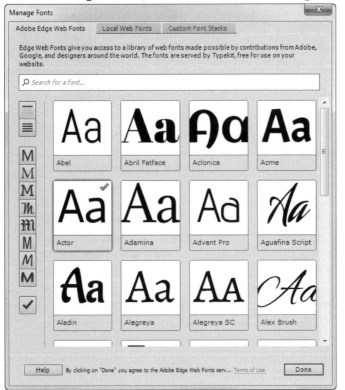

How to work with Adobe Edge Web Fonts

- To display the Manage Fonts dialog box, choose Modify→Manage Fonts.
- To add a font, click on it. A check mark will appear in the upper right corner. To remove a font, click it to remove the check mark.
- To filter the fonts by one or more characters in the font name, use the search bar.
- To filter the fonts so only those recommended for headings are displayed, click the first button along the left side of the tab. To filter the fonts so only those recommended for paragraphs are displayed, click the second button.
- To filter the fonts by style, click one of the buttons with an "M" on it.
- To filter the fonts so only those that have already been added are displayed, click the button with the check mark on it.

Description

- *Adobe Edge Web Fonts* are a collection of fonts provided by Adobe and the global design community.
- After you add an Adobe Edge Web Font, it will appear in the list of fonts for the font-family property so you can use it in your websites.
- When you use an Adobe Edge Web Font on a page, a script is added to the page that downloads the font from the Adobe Edge Web Fonts server.

Figure 5-10   How to work with Adobe Edge Web Fonts

How to work with local web fonts

Unlike Adobe Edge Web Fonts, which are downloaded from the Adobe Edge Web Fonts server each time a page that uses them is displayed, *local web fonts* are fonts that you have downloaded to your computer and that you can add directly to a website. Figure 5-11 shows how to work with local web fonts.

To start, you should know that you can download many different web fonts from the Internet. Some of these fonts are available free of charge and can be used on any website. Others require that you pay a license fee, though, so you'll want to be sure you have an appropriate license before you use them.

You should also know that when you download a font, you typically get several files. Most of the files are for different versions of the font, such as regular, bold, and italics. You also get an executable file that you can use to install the font on your system if you want to use it outside of Dreamweaver. In addition, you may get a text file that describes the license agreement.

After you download a font, you use the Local Web Fonts tab of the Manage Fonts dialog box to add it to a website. From this tab, you can use the Browse buttons to locate and select the font file in one of four formats: EOT (Embedded Open Type), WOFF (Web Open Font Format), TTF (TrueType Font), and SVG (Scalable Vector Graphics). In this figure, for example, I selected a font file named Aller_Rg.ttf. When I did that, the default name for this font was displayed in the Font Name text box. If you want to use a different name, of course, you can change this default.

Before I go on, you should realize that because of license restrictions, Dreamweaver won't let you browse directly to your system fonts. Because of that, you can't include these fonts in your websites. In addition, you'll want to store the font files you download in a directory other than the directory that contains the system fonts, since this directory contains installed fonts and not font files. In this figure, for example, you can see that my font files are stored in a Fonts directory that I created on my C drive.

After you select a font, you need to select the check box to indicate that you are licensed to use the font in your website. Finally, you click the Add button to add the font. Then, it will appear in the list of local web fonts at the bottom of this tab. In addition, when you click the Done button, the font will be available from the list for the font-family property in the CSS Designer.

When you add a local web font to a website, the font file is stored in a subfolder of a folder named webfonts that has the same name as the font. This subfolder also contains a style sheet named stylesheet.css that includes a CSS3 @font-face selector for the font. Then, when you use the font in a web page, this style sheet is imported into the last style sheet for the page. This causes the font to be embedded into the web page.

The Local Web Fonts tab of the Manage Fonts dialog box

```
Manage Fonts                                              [ x ]

 Adobe Edge Web Fonts    Local Web Fonts    Custom Font Stacks

   Add fonts from your computer. The added fonts will be available in all Font lists in Dreamweaver.

        Font Name:   [ Aller Rg                    ]

         EOT Font:   [                              ]   [ Browse... ]

        WOFF Font:   [                              ]   [ Browse... ]

         TTF Font:   [ C:\Fonts\Aller\Aller_Rg.ttf  ]   [ Browse... ]

         SVG Font:   [                              ]   [ Browse... ]

                     [✓] I have properly licensed the above font(s)
                         for website use.
                         What's this?
                                              [ Add ]

   ─────────────────────────────────────────────────────────

   Current list of    ┌──────────────────────────┐
   Local Web Fonts:   │                          │
                      │                          │
                      │                          │
                      │                          │
                      └──────────────────────────┘

                              [ Remove ]



   [ Help ]                                    [ Done ]
```

How to work with local web fonts

- To display the Manage Fonts dialog box, choose Modify→Manage Fonts.
- To add a font, use one of the Browse buttons to locate it on your computer by type and then be sure the font name is what you want. Click the check box to indicate that you are licensed to use the font, and then click the Add button to add the font.
- To remove a local web font, select it from the list in the bottom half of the tab and then click the Remove button.

Description

- A *local web font* is one that's available from your computer. You can download a variety of web fonts from the Internet.
- After you add a local font, it will appear in the list of fonts for the font-family property so you can use it in your websites.
- When you add a local font to a website, a webfonts folder is added to the site. This folder contains a subfolder that has the same name as the font, and that folder contains the font file and a file named stylesheet.css that contains a CSS3 @font-face selector for the font. This style sheet is imported into the last style sheet for the page where the font is used.
- The most common type of font is a True Type Font (TTF).

Figure 5-11   How to work with local web fonts

How to work with custom font stacks

In addition to adding fonts to a website, Dreamweaver lets you create custom font stacks. A *font stack* is simply a list of fonts like the ones that are available for the font-family property. The fonts used in the default font stacks are the ones that are considered web safe, because 90 percent or more of all computers have these fonts installed.

That's not the case with custom font stacks that include other fonts, though. Because of that, custom font stacks are typically used for websites that will be deployed to an intranet rather than the Internet. Then, the people who manage the computers that will have access to the site can be sure that the necessary fonts are installed.

To create and work with font stacks, you use the Custom Font Stacks tab of the Manage Fonts dialog box shown in figure 5-12. The list at the top of this tab includes all of the current font stacks. Then, to create a new font stack, you select each font you want to include from the Available Fonts list and add it to the Chosen Fonts. When you do that, be sure to add the fonts in the sequence you want them to appear in the stack. Otherwise, you may have to remove one or more fonts from the Chosen Fonts list and then add them back in sequence. Also, be sure to end the list with a generic font. In this figure, for example, I'm getting ready to add the serif font to the font stack.

Once your font list is complete, you can click the plus icon near the upper left of the tab to add it to the list of font stacks. You can also click the up and down icons near the upper right of the tab to move the stack up and down in the list of font stacks. You can modify a font stack by selecting it in the list so it's displayed in the Chosen From list. And you can delete a font stack by selecting it and then clicking the minus icon. Note that you can change the sequence of the font stacks that come with Dreamweaver too. You can also modify and delete these font stacks, although you're not likely to do that.

The Custom Font Stacks tab of the Manage Fonts dialog box

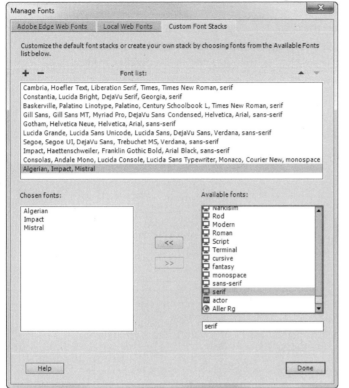

How to work with custom font stacks

- To display the Manage Fonts dialog box, choose Modify→Manage Fonts.
- To create a custom font stack, select each font from the Available Fonts list in the order you want them to appear in the stack, and then click the **<<** button to add the font to the Chosen Fonts list. Then, click the **+** icon to add the stack to the font list.
- To modify a custom font stack, select it in the Font List list to display its fonts in the Chosen Fonts list. Then, use the **<<** and **>>** buttons to add and remove fonts. You can also use the ▲ and ▼ icons to move the font stack up and down in the list.
- To remove a custom font stack, select it in the Font List list and then click the **–** icon.

Description

- A *font stack* is a customizable font family that you can create from fonts that are available on your computer.
- After you add a custom font stack, it will appear in the list of fonts for the font-family property so you can use it in your websites.
- Custom font stacks are typically used for sites that will be deployed to an intranet so the fonts can be made available on each computer that needs them.

Figure 5-12   How to work with custom font stacks

Perspective

Now that you've completed this chapter, you should know how to use the CSS properties for formatting text. Although that gets you off to a good start with CSS, there's still more to learn. So, in the next chapter, you'll learn how to use CSS to lay out pages and add borders and backgrounds.

Terms

absolute unit of measure	font family
relative unit of measure	Adobe Edge Web Fonts
hexadecimal (hex) value	Adobe Typekit
RGB color model	local web font
RGBA color model	font stack
HSLA color model	

Summary

- You can use *absolute measurements* like pixels or *relative measurements* like ems or percents to specify the CSS properties for sizes. For fonts, it's better to use relative measurements so the user can change the font sizes by changing the browser's default font size.

- Most graphic designers use *hex values* for the *RGB color model* that represent the colors that they want because that gives them the most control.

- Dreamweaver also lets you use the *RGBA* and *HLSA color models* that became available with CSS3 to specify colors. This gives the web designer more control over colors and transparency.

- The default font for most browsers is a serif font. However, because sans-serif fonts are easier to read in a browser, you normally change the *font family*.

- The colors and font properties of a parent element are inherited by all descendant elements. But those properties can be overridden by the style rules for the descendant elements.

- Text properties can be used to indent, align, transform, and decorate the text in a block element like a heading or paragraph. Dreamweaver also lets you use the CSS3 property for adding shadows to text.

- *Adobe Edge Web Fonts* are a collection of royalty-free fonts provided by the *Adobe Typekit* service. When you add an Adobe Edge Web Font to a web page, a script is added to the page that downloads the font onto each user's computer.

- *Local web fonts* are fonts that exist on your computer that can be embedded in a web page using the CSS3 @font-face selector.

- You can create custom lists of fonts, called *font stacks*, that consist of fonts that are available from your computer. Custom font stacks are typically used for websites that will be deployed to an intranet.

Exercise 5-1   Work with text

In this exercise, you'll use the skills that you learned in this chapter to style the text for an About Us web page so it looks something like the page below. This will show you how you can work with text until you're satisfied that it's easy to read.

Open the folder for this exercise and change its body font

1. Open the Exercises site, and open the folder for this exercise. Then, review its folders and files.

2. Open the aboutus.html file in Design view. Then, use the CSS Property Inspector to change the body font to the font family that starts with Gotham.

Style the text in the paragraphs

3. Use the CSS Designer to add a style for <p> elements that sets the line-height property to 1.2 ems.

4. Use the CSS Designer to create a new selector for a class named "indent" (the selector will be .indent). Then, set its text-indent property to 5%.

5. Select all of the paragraphs for the Company Overview, and use the HTML Property Inspector to add a class attribute for the "indent" class to all of them. This should indent all of the paragraphs.

6. Use the HTML Property Inspector to remove the class attribute from the first paragraph. That should remove the indentation from the first paragraph, which is the way the first paragraphs after headings are usually treated. At this point, the paragraphs in the web page should look like the ones at the start of this exercise.

Style the text in the navigation bar

7. Use the CSS Designer to display the styles that have been set for the nav a selector in the styles.css style sheet. Then, set the text-decoration property to none to remove the underlines from the links, set the font size to 120%, and set the font weight to bold.

8. Staying with the CSS Designer and the nav a selector, change the color of the links to the red that's in the Vecta logo. To do that, you can use the Sample tool as explained in figure 5-2. And while you're at it, add the color to the swatches so it's easy to use again.

9. To center the navigation bar on the page, create a style rule for just the nav element, and set its text-align property to center.

Style the h2 headings with shadows

10. Use the CSS Designer to display the styles that have been set for the h2 headings. Then, set the color of these headings to one of the blues in the image that's in the header, set the font size to 160%, and set the font family to the one that starts with Gill Sans.

11. With figure 5-7 as a guide, add shadows to the h2 headings. To start, add a shadow of .1 em to the right and below the headings, don't use any blur, and use the red of the navigation bar links as the shadow color. Those are the settings for the links in the web page at the start of this exercise. But experiment with them to see if you can do better in terms of readability. (Message: Use shadows with caution and remember the visually-impaired.)

Create and apply a custom stack

12. With figure 5-12 as a guide, create a custom stack that consists of the Verdana, Arial, and sans-serif font families. To find a font family in the Available Fonts list, you can type its name in the text box below the list.

13. Apply the custom stack you just created to the links in the navigation bar.

Do a final test of all three pages

14. Open the index.html page and run it in your browser. Then, click its links to go to the Solutions and About Us pages. Note that the changes that you made to the About Us page have been applied to all three pages because the same style sheet is used for all three. Then, return to Dreamweaver and close all files.

6

How to use CSS
for page layout, borders,
and backgrounds

In this chapter, you'll learn how to use the properties for controlling page layout. That includes controlling the space between elements, floating and positioning elements, and displaying borders and backgrounds. When you finish this chapter, you should be able to implement sophisticated page layouts.

How to size and space elements

When a browser displays a web page, it places each HTML block element in a box. That makes it easy to control the size, spacing, borders, and other formatting for elements like headers, sections, footers, headings, and paragraphs. Some inline elements like images are placed in a box as well. Other inline elements like hyperlinks can be made to be treated like a box in the browser using CSS. To work with these boxes, you use the CSS *box model*.

An introduction to the box model

Figure 6-1 presents a diagram that shows how the box model works. By default, the box for a block element is as wide as the block that contains it and as tall as it needs to be based on its content. However, you can explicitly specify the size of the content area for a block element by using the height and width properties. You can also use other properties to set the borders, margins, and padding for a block element.

If you look at the diagram in this figure, you can see that *padding* is the space between the content area and a border. Similarly, a *margin* is the space between the border and the outside of the box.

If you need to calculate the overall height of a box, you can use the formula in this figure. Here, you start by adding the values for the margin, border width, and padding for the top of the box. Then, you add the height of the content area. Last, you add the values for the padding, border width, and margin for the bottom of the box. The formula for calculating the overall width of a box is similar.

When you set the height and width properties for a block element, you can use any of the units that you learned about in the last chapter. Often, though, pixels are used so the sizes are fixed. That way, the size of the page won't change if the user changes the size of the browser window. This is referred to as a *fixed layout*.

When you use a fixed layout, you can use either absolute or relative units of measure for margins and padding. If you use a relative unit such as ems, the margins and padding will be adjusted if the font size changes. If you use an absolute unit, the margins and padding will stay the same.

The CSS box model

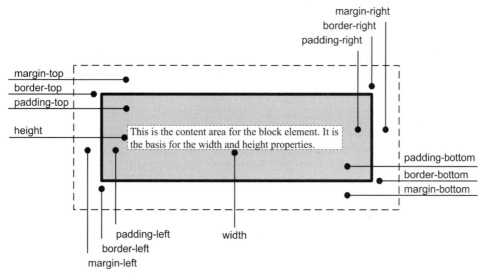

The formula for calculating the height of a box

```
top margin + top border + top padding +
height +
bottom padding + bottom border + bottom margin
```

The formula for calculating the width of a box

```
left margin + left border + left padding +
width +
right padding + right border + right margin
```

Description

- The CSS *box model* lets you work with the boxes that a browser places around each block element as well as some inline elements. This lets you add formatting such as widths, heights, margins, padding, and borders.

- By default, the box for a block element is as wide as the block that contains it and as tall as it needs to be based on its content.

- You can use the height and width properties to specify the size of the content area for a block element explicitly.

- You can use other properties to control the margins, padding, and borders for a block element. Then, these properties are added to the height and width of the content area to determine the height and width of the box.

Figure 6-1   How the box model works

How to set heights and widths

Figure 6-2 presents the properties for setting heights and widths. The two properties you'll use most often are width and height. By default, these properties are set to a value of "auto". As a result, the size of the content area for the element is automatically adjusted so it's as wide as the element that contains it and as tall as the content it contains. To change that, you can use the width and height properties to specify either an absolute or relative value. If you specify a relative value for these properties, the height and width are based on the height and width of the *containing block*.

In addition to the width and height properties, you can use the min-width, max-width, min-height, and max-height properties to specify the minimum and maximum width and height of the content area. Like the width and height properties, you can specify either a relative or an absolute value for these properties.

The example in this figure shows how some of these properties can be applied to two boxes in Dreamweaver. Here, both the width and the minimum height of the left box are set to 200 pixels. As you can see, when the first line of text within the box fills the width of the box, the text is continued onto the next line since the width is set to an absolute value. Note, however, that the box is taller than what's needed for the text. That's because this box is always at least 200 pixels tall. If the content expanded so it would no longer fit in the box, though, the height would be increased to accommodate the content.

Like the left box, the width of the right box in this figure has been set to an absolute value, so that width will never change. Unlike the left box, though, no minimum height has been set for this box. That means that the height of the box is never more than what's required to accommodate its contents.

Properties for setting heights and widths

Property	Description
width	A relative or absolute value that specifies the width of the content area. You can also specify auto if you want the width of the area calculated for you based on the width of its containing block. This is the default.
height	A relative or absolute value that specifies the height of the content area. You can also specify auto if you want the height of the area calculated for you based on its content. This is the default.
min-width	A relative or absolute value that specifies the minimum width of the content area. The area will always be at least this wide regardless of its content.
max-width	A relative or absolute value that specifies the maximum width of the content area. You can also specify none to indicate that there is no maximum width.
min-height	A relative or absolute value that specifies the minimum height of the content area. The area will always be at least this tall regardless of its content.
max-height	A relative or absolute value that specifies the maximum height of the content area. You can also specify none to indicate that there is no maximum height.

A web page in Dreamweaver that uses heights and widths

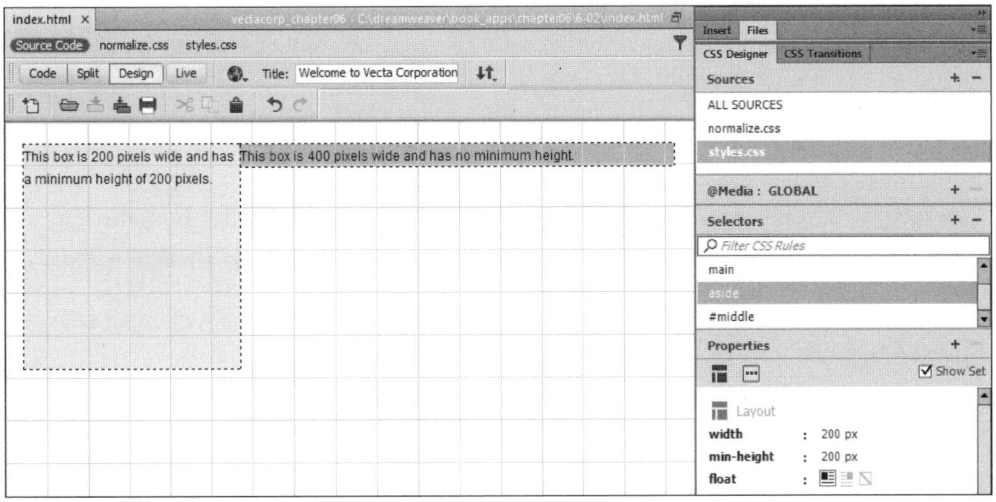

Description

- If you specify a percent for the width property, the width of the content area for the block element is based on the width of the block that contains it, called the *containing block*. In that case, the width of the containing block must be specified explicitly.

- If you specify a percent for the height property, the height of the content area for the block element is based on the height of the containing block. Then, if the height of the containing block isn't specified explicitly, "auto" is substituted for the percent.

- You can temporarily view your boxes in color by choosing View→Visual Aids→CSS Layout Backgrounds.

Figure 6-2   How to set heights and widths

How to set margins

Figure 6-3 presents the properties for setting margins. As you can see, you can use individual properties like margin-top or margin-left to set the margin for each side of an element. You can also set all four margins by using the margin property.

The easiest way to set margins with the CSS Designer is to use the margin tool shown in this figure. To set the margin for one side of an element, you select an absolute or relative unit of measure and then enter a value. In this figure, for example, I set the top margin for the main element to 2 ems. That's why this element doesn't start at the top of the page, even though it's the only element in the body of the page.

In addition to setting individual margins, you can set all of the margins for an element to the same value at once. To do that, you click the chain icon in the middle of the margin tool so it changes to a closed chain. Then, if you enter a value for any one margin, it will be applied to all the margins. If you want to switch back to entering a margin for a single side of the element, just click the chain icon again.

One situation where you'll want to set all the margins at once is if you need to set the top or bottom margin to 0. That's because the margin tool makes it difficult to set an individual margin to 0. In that case, you can set all the margins to 0 and then change any individual margins so they're the way you want them.

You can also specify the keyword "auto" for any margin. In most cases, you'll use this keyword to center a page in the browser window or a block element within its containing block. To do that, you specify auto for both the left and right margins. For this to work, you must also set the width of the element. In this figure, for example, the width of the main element is set to 500 pixels and the left and right margins are set to "auto". Because of that, this element is centered in the body of the page.

If you're familiar with CSS, you can also enter the margins directly into the CSS Designer instead of using the margin tool. To do that, you click to the right of the margin property where it says "Set Shorthand" and then specify the margins. When you do, a margin property that sets the margins for all four sides of the element is generated.

You can enter from one to four values when you use this technique. If you enter one value for the margin property, all four margins are set to that value. If you enter two values, the top and bottom margins are set to the first value and the left and right margins are set to the second value. If you enter three values, the top margin is set to the first value, the left and right margins are set to the second value, and the bottom margin is set to the third value. To set the margins shown in this figure, for example, I could have entered these three values since the left and right margins are the same:

```
2em auto 0
```

Finally, if you enter all four values, the margins are applied in a clockwise order: top, right, bottom, and left. To remember this order, you can think of the word *trou*b*le.

Properties for setting margins

Property	Description
margin-top	A relative or absolute value that defines the space between the top border of an element and the top of the containing block or the bottom of the element above it.
margin-right	A relative or absolute value that defines the space between the right border of an element and the right side of the containing block or the left side of the element to its right.
margin-bottom	A relative or absolute value that defines the space between the bottom border of an element and the bottom of the containing block or the top of the element below it.
margin-left	A relative or absolute value that defines the space between the left border of an element and the left side of the containing block or the right side of the element to its left.
margin	A shorthand property for setting all four margins.

A web page in Dreamweaver that uses margins

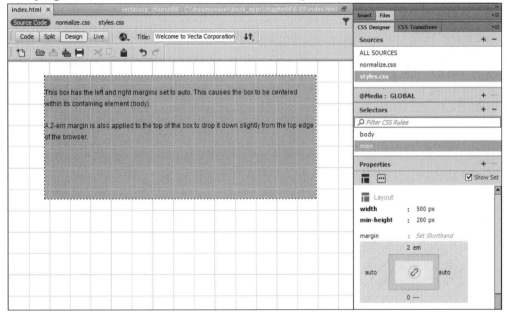

Description

- Margins should be taken into consideration when setting the width and height of a block element because they add to the overall width and height of the box.

- You can use the "auto" keyword on the margin-left and margin-right properties to center an element in its containing block. To do that, you must also specify the width of the element.

- To set an individual margin in the CSS Designer, select a unit and then enter a value. To set all margins to the same value, click the chain icon (🔗) in the middle of the margin tool and then set one margin. Click the icon again to switch back to setting one margin.

Figure 6-3   How to set margins

If you want to have Dreamweaver generate a shorthand property for margins, you can do that too. Just display the CSS Styles category of the Preferences dialog box (Edit→Preferences) and then select the Margin and Padding option in the Use Shorthand For group of options.

One more thing you should know about margins is that different browsers have different default margins for the block elements. Because of that, it's a good practice to explicitly set the top and bottom margins of the elements that you're using. That way, you can control the space between elements like headings and paragraphs.

Finally, if you specify a bottom margin for one element and a top margin for the element that follows it, the margins are *collapsed*. That means the smaller margin is ignored, and only the larger margin is applied. In that case, there may not be as much space between the two elements as you expected. One solution to this problem is to set the margins to zero and use padding for the spacing.

How to set padding

The properties for setting padding are similar to the properties for setting margins. These properties are presented in figure 6-4. As you can see, you can use individual properties to set the padding for each side of an element. Or, you can use a single property to set the padding for all four sides.

Dreamweaver provides a padding tool for setting the padding that works just like the margin tool. In this figure, for example, you can see the padding tool for the left box on the web page. Here, the padding for all four sides of the element have been set to 1 em. Because of that, there's space between the content area for the element and its side. In contrast, only the padding for the top of the right box has been set, so there's no space between the content area for the element and its other sides. However, a 1em margin has been added to the left side of the element. That creates space between the left box and the right box.

Notice in this figure that the float property of the left box has also been set. Although you can't see it here, the float property of the right box has been set as well. That's what caused the two boxes to be displayed next to each other, and you'll learn more about that later in this chapter.

Just as you can when you set margins, you can set padding by entering one to four values for the padding property. Since all four sides of the left box shown in this figure have the same padding, for example, I could have just entered that value for the padding property. In contrast, only the padding for the top of the right box is set. Because of that, I would have had to enter all four values to set the padding property:

```
1em 0 0 0
```

You can also have Dreamweaver generate a shorthand property for padding by selecting the Margin and Padding option in the Preferences dialog box as described above.

Properties for setting padding

Property	Description
padding-top	A relative or absolute value that defines the space between the top of an element and its top border.
padding-right	A relative or absolute value that defines the space between the right side of an element and its right border.
padding-bottom	A relative or absolute value that defines the space between the bottom of an element and its bottom border.
padding-left	A relative or absolute value that defines the space between the left side of an element and its left border.
padding	A shorthand property for setting the padding on all four sides of an element.

A web page in Dreamweaver that uses padding

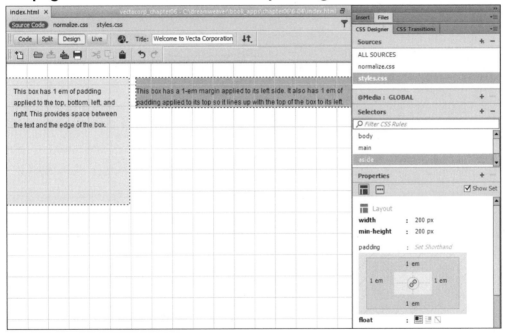

Description

- Padding can be applied to block elements to create space between the edge of the element and the content within the element.

- Like margins, padding should be taken into consideration when setting the width and height of a block element because it adds to the overall width and height of the box.

- You use the same techniques to set padding in the CSS Designer as you use to set margins.

Figure 6-4   How to set padding

A web page that illustrates sizing and spacing

To illustrate the use of the properties for sizing and spacing, figure 6-5 presents a web page that uses many of these properties. This web page is similar to the one shown in the last chapter. In fact, the HTML for the two pages is identical. However, the CSS has been modified so the page has been centered in the browser window and the spacing between the elements has been improved.

To center the page in the browser window, the width of the body element was set to 500 pixels and the left and right margins were set to "auto". To improve the spacing above and below the h2 headings, the margin top was set to 0 ems and the margin bottom was set to .5 ems. Similarly, to improve the spacing above and below the h3 headings, the margin top was set to 0 ems and the margin bottom was set to .5 ems. Finally, to improve the spacing above and below the paragraphs, the margin top was set to 0 ems and the margin bottom was set to 1 em.

To set the margin properties for each element, I started by clicking the chain icon in the middle of the margin tool and setting all the margins to 0 ems. Then, I set the margin-bottom property as appropriate. That way, the top and bottom margins will be the same in any browser. Although this also sets the left and right margins to 0 ems, these margins are zero by default so this doesn't affect the layout of the page. If you don't want to include these properties in your style sheet, though, you can click the Remove CSS Property icon for a property in the CSS Designer to delete it.

A web page that uses widths, heights, margins, and padding

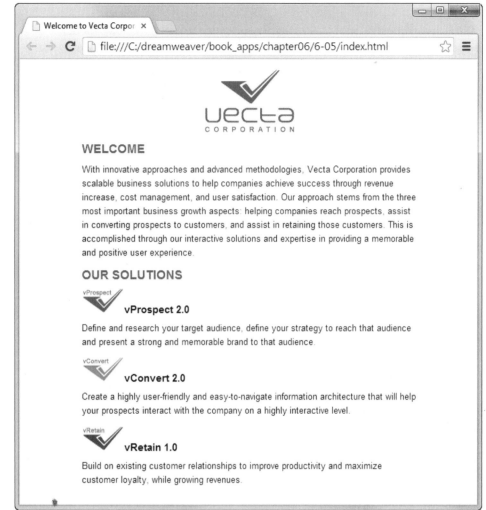

Description

- This page is centered in the browser window and uses margins and padding to improve the spacing before and after headings and paragraphs.

Figure 6-5   A web page that illustrates sizing and spacing

How to set borders and backgrounds

Now that you know how to size and space elements using the box model, you're ready to learn how to apply other formatting to boxes. That includes adding borders and setting background colors and images.

How to set borders

Figure 6-6 presents the properties for setting *borders* and illustrates how they work within the CSS Designer. To start, you can click the Border icon at the top of the Properties pane to display the border properties. Then, you can use the properties in the first tab to apply the same width, style, and color to each side of the box.

In this example, I applied a 1-pixel wide, solid gray border to h2 elements. When I did that, Dreamweaver generated a shorthand border property. You can also enter this property directly by clicking to the right of the border property and then entering the appropriate values.

In addition to specifying a relative or absolute value for the width of a border, you can specify the width using a keyword. Note that different browsers interpret these keywords differently, though. Because of that, you'll typically set the width of a border to a specific value as shown in this example.

Instead of setting the width, style, and color for all sides of a box at once, you can set each side independently. To do that, you use the other tabs for setting the border in the CSS Designer. If, for example, you want to set just the bottom border for an element, you can use the tab with the bottom border on it to set the width, style, and color for that border. Then, Dreamweaver generates a border-bottom property for you with all three values.

Properties for setting borders

Property	Description
border-width	One to four relative or absolute values (excluding a percent) or keywords that specify the widths of each side of a border. Possible keywords are thin, medium, and thick.
border-style	One to four keywords that specify the styles for each side of a border. Possible keywords are dotted, dashed, solid, double, groove, ridge, inset, outset, and none. The default is none.
border-color	One to four color values that specify the colors for each side of a border. The default is the color of the element.
border	A shorthand property for setting the border width, border style, and border color for all four sides of a border.
border-*side*-width	A relative or absolute value (excluding a percent) or a keyword that specifies the width of the indicated side of a border.
border-*side*-style	A keyword that specifies the style for the indicated side of a border.
border-*side*-color	A color value or keyword that specifies the color of the indicated side of a border.
border-*side*	Border width, style, and color values for the specified side of a border.

The Border properties in the CSS Designer

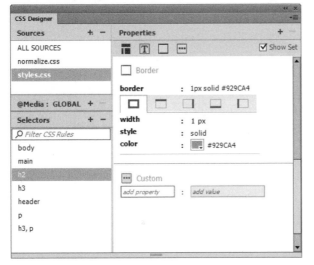

A heading with borders in a web browser

Welcome

Description

- The CSS Designer lets you set borders using a tabbed interface. To set all four borders at once, you use the properties in the first tab. To set the properties for an individual side, you use the tab for that side.

Figure 6-6   How to set borders

How to add rounded corners and shadows

Figure 6-7 shows how to use the properties for adding rounded corners and shadows to a box. These properties were added with CSS3, and they let you supply these graphic effects without using images. These properties are currently supported by all modern browsers. But if an older browser doesn't support them, it just ignores them, which is usually okay. That's why you can start using these properties right away. Note, however, that you can only see the effect of these properties in Live view.

To round the corners of a box, you can use the border-radius tool in the CSS Designer. To apply the same radius to all four corners of the border as shown here, you click the chain icon in the middle of the control and then enter a value for one corner that indicates the curvature you want to use. The heading shown in this figure illustrates the result of applying a 5-pixel radius to each corner. You can also set the curvature for each corner separately if you don't want them all to be the same.

You should also notice the two values at the top of the border-radius tool. By default, 4r is selected, which means that the same curvature will be applied to both sides of each corner. If you want to apply different curvatures to each side, you can click on 8r. Then, you can set a total of 8 radiuses: one on each side of each corner.

If you're familiar with the syntax of the border-radius property, you can also enter this property directly into the CSS Designer. To do that, you just click to the right of this property and then enter one or more values. If you enter a single value, it will be assigned to all four corners as shown here. You can also enter a separate value for each corner. Then, the values are applied to the corners in this order: top left, top right, bottom right, and bottom left.

To add shadows to a box, you use the box-shadow property. This works much like the text-shadow property that you learned about in the last chapter. You use the h-shadow and v-shadow values to specify the horizontal and vertical offsets for the shadow. You use the blur value to set the blur radius. And you use the color value to set the color of the shadow. In this figure, the box for the heading has a gray shadow with 3-pixel horizontal and vertical offsets and a 5-pixel blur.

You can also specify two additional values for a box shadow. The spread value specifies how far the blur is spread. And the inset keyword indicates that the shadow should be added inside the box so the box appears inset.

When you add a box shadow to an element, you should realize that Dreamweaver generates a -webkit-box-shadow property in addition to the box-shadow property. This property provides for box shadows in older versions of Chrome and Safari. If you want to provide for box shadows in older versions of Firefox, you can also add a -moz-box-shadow property directly to your style sheet. And you can add a -moz-border-radius property to provide for rounded corners in older versions of Firefox. A property isn't available to provide for rounded corners in older versions of Chrome and Safari, though.

CSS3 properties for adding round corners and shadows

Property	Description
`border-radius`	Specifies the curvature of the corners of a box.
`box-shadow`	Adds a drop shadow to a box. Works like the text-shadow property, but includes a spread value, which determines how far the blur is spread, and the inset keyword, which places the shadow inside the box so the box appears inset.

The border-radius and box-shadow properties in the CSS Designer

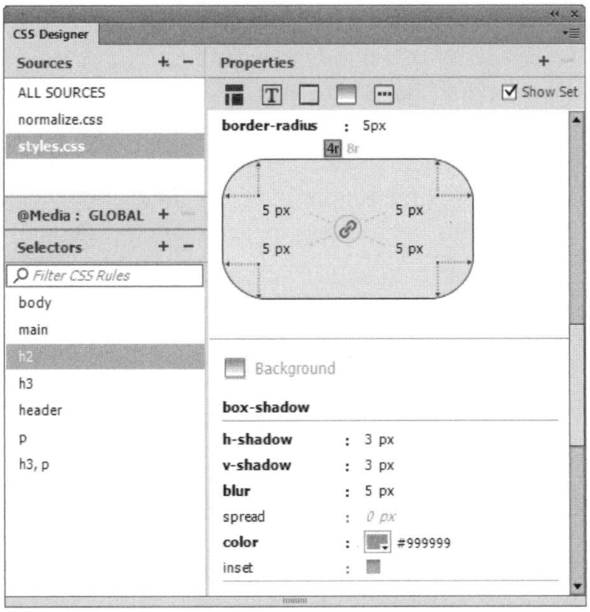

A heading with a border radius and a drop shadow in a web browser

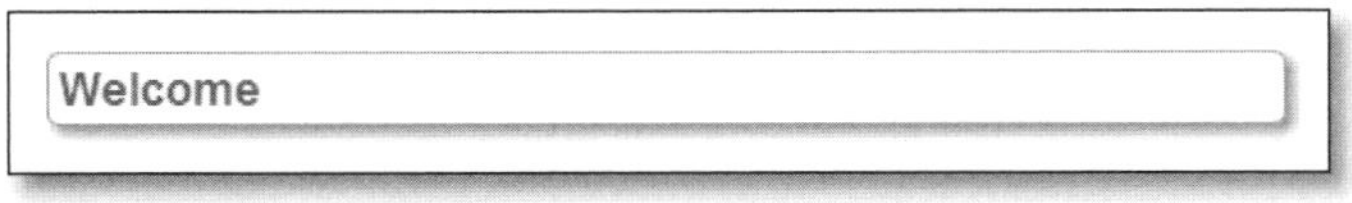

Description

- When you set the border-radius property, you can assign the same rounding radius to all four corners or a different radius to each corner.
- When you set the box-shadow property, positive values offset the shadow to the right or down, and negative values offset the shadow to the left or up.
- These properties are supported by all modern browsers. If they aren't supported by a browser, they are ignored, which is usually okay.

Figure 6-7   How to add rounded corners and shadows

How to set background colors and images

Figure 6-8 presents the properties you can use to set the *background* for a box. You can display these properties in the CSS Designer by clicking the Background icon at the top of the Properties pane.

When you set a background, it's displayed behind the content, padding, and borders for the box, but it isn't displayed behind the margins. You can set a background color, a background image, or both, but if you set both, the browser displays the background color behind the image. As a result, you can only see the background color if the image has areas that are transparent or the image doesn't occupy the entire element.

. By default, the background-color property for a box is transparent. As a result, you can see through the box to the color that's behind it, which is usually what you want. If you look back to figure 6-7, for instance, you'll see that the white color of the page shows through the transparent background of the box that contains the heading. In the example in this figure, however, a light background color is applied to the box that contains the heading, so the white behind the heading doesn't show through.

If you want to display a background image, you need to specify a path to the file for the image. To do that, you specify a url value for the background-image property as shown in this figure. Here, the icon_checker.gif file is used to display a small decorative icon near the left side of the box.

If you add a background image to a box, it will repeat horizontally and vertically to fill the box by default. This works well for small images that are intended to be tiled across or down a box. If you want to change this behavior, you can set the background-repeat property so the image is only repeated horizontally, so it's only repeated vertically, or so it isn't repeated at all. In the CSS Designer, you change the value of this property by clicking on one of the available icons. In this figure, for example, the no-repeat icon has been selected so the image appears just once.

If an image doesn't repeat horizontally and vertically, you may need to set additional properties to determine where the image is positioned and whether it scrolls with the page. By default, an image is positioned in the top left corner of the box. To change that, you use the background-position property. This property lets you specify both a horizontal and a vertical position. In the example in this figure, the background-position property is set so the image is positioned 7 pixels from both the left and top of the box.

The background-size property was added with CSS3. You can use this property to change the size of the background image that's displayed on the web page without changing the actual size of the image. That way, you can display the image in different sizes on different pages. This is similar to using the CSS height and width properties for sizing images that aren't displayed in the background.

In most cases, you'll want a background image to scroll as you scroll the box that contains it. For example, if you use a background image for an entire page and the page is larger than the browser window, you'll usually want the image to scroll as you scroll through the page. If not, you can set the background-attachment property to "fixed". Then, the image won't scroll with the page.

Common properties for setting the background color and image

Property	Description
background-color	A color value that specifies the color of an element's background.
background-image	A path to the image to use as a background for an element or a linear gradient to use for the background. See figure 6-9 for information on using linear gradients.
background-repeat	A keyword that specifies if and how an image is repeated. Possible values are repeat, repeat-x, repeat-y, and no-repeat. The default is repeat, which causes the image to be repeated both horizontally and vertically to fill the background.
background-position	One or two relative or absolute values or keywords that specify the initial horizontal and vertical positions of an image. Keywords are left, center, and right; top, center, and bottom.
background-size	One or two relative or absolute values that specify the width and height of a background image. The defaults are auto.
background-attachment	A keyword that specifies whether an image scrolls with the document or remains in a fixed position. Possible values are scroll and fixed. The default is scroll.

The Background properties in the CSS Designer

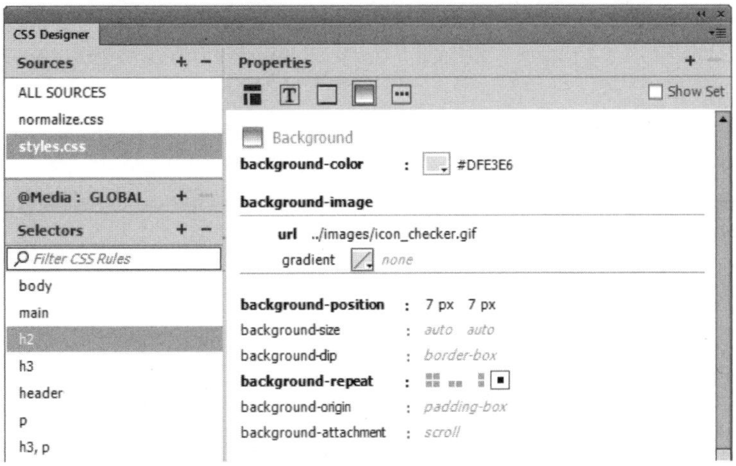

A heading with a background color and image in a web browser

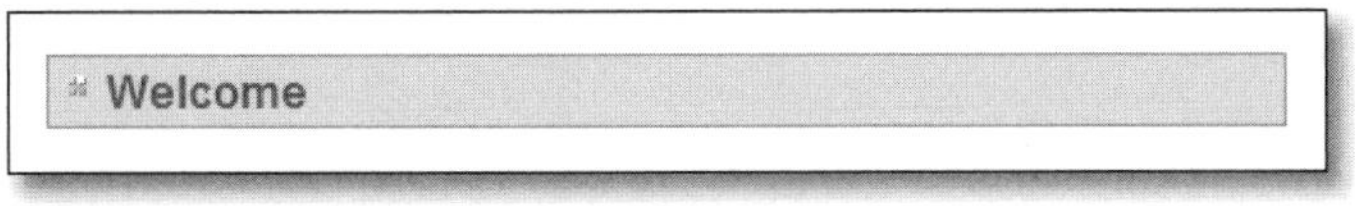

Accessibility guideline

- Don't use a background color or image that makes the text that's over it difficult to read.

Figure 6-8   How to set background colors and images

How to set background gradients

Figure 6-9 shows the basics of how to use the new CSS3 feature for *linear gradients*. Here again, this feature lets you provide interesting backgrounds without using images. At present, all modern browsers support this feature except Internet Explorer 9. And if a browser doesn't support this feature, it just ignores it, which is usually okay.

To create a linear gradient in Dreamweaver, you use the gradient editor shown in this figure. From this editor, you can choose the angle of the gradient by setting the degree value. You can choose the starting and ending colors for the gradient by clicking a color stop and then using the color controls at the right side of the editor. And you can choose the portion of the box the gradient occupies by dragging the color stops. If the gradient occupies less than the entire box, you can cause it to repeat by selecting the Repeating option.

The example in this figure illustrates how this works. Here, the gradient is set to an angle of 270 degrees so it will be applied from the right side of the box to the left side of the box. If I had set the angle to 90 degrees instead of 270 degrees, the gradient would have been applied from left to right instead. Next, the color stops are set so the color starts as a dark gray and ends as a light gray. The result is shown in the heading in this figure. Note that, like the CSS3 properties that let you round the corners of a border and apply a shadow to a box, you can't see the result of a gradient in the Document window unless you display it in Live view.

To create more complex gradients, you can add additional color stops by clicking between two other color stops. For example, you could use this technique to create a gradient that changes from red to white and then from white to blue. If you experiment with this feature, you'll see the interesting effects that you can get with it.

The gradient editor dialog box within the CSS Designer

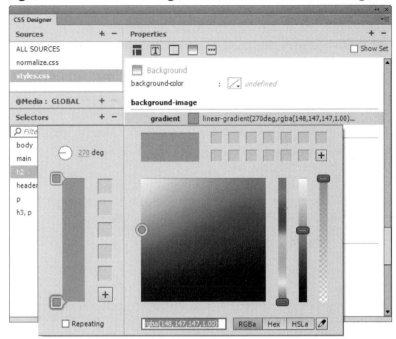

A header with a gradient background in a web browser

> Welcome

Description

- CSS3 lets you create *linear gradients* for backgrounds without using images. To do that, you specify a gradient for the background-image property.

- To create a linear gradient, you use the gradient editor. To display this editor, click the gradient box in the CSS Designer.

- To change the angle for the gradient, click the degree value and then enter a new value, or drag the degree line within the circle.

- To set the starting value for the gradient, click the top color stop at the left side of the editor and then set the color using the controls at the right. To set the ending value, click the bottom color stop and then set the color.

- You can also control the percent of the box each color occupies by dragging the color stops, and you can check the Repeating option to have the gradient repeat within the box.

- To create additional color stops, just click between two other color stops. To delete a color stop, drag it outside the editor.

- To save a gradient as a swatch, click the Add button (**+**).

Figure 6-9   How to set background gradients

A web page that uses borders and backgrounds

Figure 6-10 presents a web page that's similar to the one in figure 6-5. In fact, the HTML for these two pages is identical. However, the page in this figure has some additional formatting.

First, this page uses a linear gradient for the background behind the body. This gradient is applied to the html element at an angle of 180 degrees so it changes from a light grey at the top of the page to a darker gray at the bottom of the page. It also uses white as the background color for the body element. That way, the gradient doesn't show behind the body content. In addition, the body element has a black, 1-pixel, solid border.

Second, a background color, a border with rounded corners, and a drop shadow are added to the h2 elements within the page. The result is a web page that provides more visual interest than the pages you've seen previously.

A web page that uses borders, background colors and gradients, and drop shadows

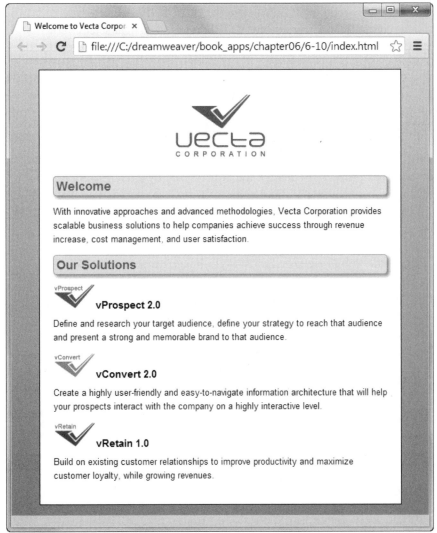

Description

- The body for this web page has a border around it, and the background behind the body is a linear gradient. For this to work, the linear gradient must be applied to the html element for the page.

- The main headings also have a border around them, and the box for these headings has a background color, rounded corners, and a drop shadow.

Figure 6-10   A web page that uses borders and backgrounds

How to format lists

In chapter 3, you learned that you can use the Property Inspector to create ordered (numbered) and unordered (bulleted) lists for the text you select. Now, you'll learn how to use CSS to format lists, and you'll see some examples of formatted lists. In addition, you'll learn how to use lists to create navigation menus.

The properties for formatting lists

Figure 6-11 presents the CSS properties for formatting lists. To start, you can use the list-style-type property to change the bullets used by a list. By default, an unordered list uses a solid circle (·), and an ordered list uses decimal numbers (1, 2, 3.). You'll learn about other types of bullets you can use in the next figure.

If you're working with an unordered list and the predefined bullet types aren't adequate, you can use a custom image for the bullet instead. To do that, you specify the path to the image on the list-style-image property.

The last property, list-style-position, lets you set the position of the bullets or numbers relative to the flow of the content for each list item. The default value for this property is "outside", which means that the bullets or numbers are placed outside the content flow. In contrast, if you select "inside" for the value of this property, the bullets or numbers are placed inside the content flow. You'll understand better how this works when you see the examples in the next figure.

To work with the list properties in the CSS Designer, you can click the Text button at the top of the Properties pane. Then, these properties are displayed after the other text properties. Here, you can see the properties for an unordered list (a ul element) that uses default values. To change the list-style-position property, you can click one of the two icons. To change the list-style-image property, you can select the url keyword from the list for this property. Then, you can enter the url in the text box that's provided or click the Browse icon that appears to locate and select the image. To change the list-style-type property, you can select a keyword from the list.

Properties for formatting lists

Property	Description
list-style-type	Determines the type of bullet that's used for the items in the list. See figure 6-12 for common values.
list-style-image	The path to the image that's used as the bullet in an unordered list.
list-style-position	Determines if the list item bullets should appear inside or outside the content flow. The default is outside.

The list properties in the CSS Designer

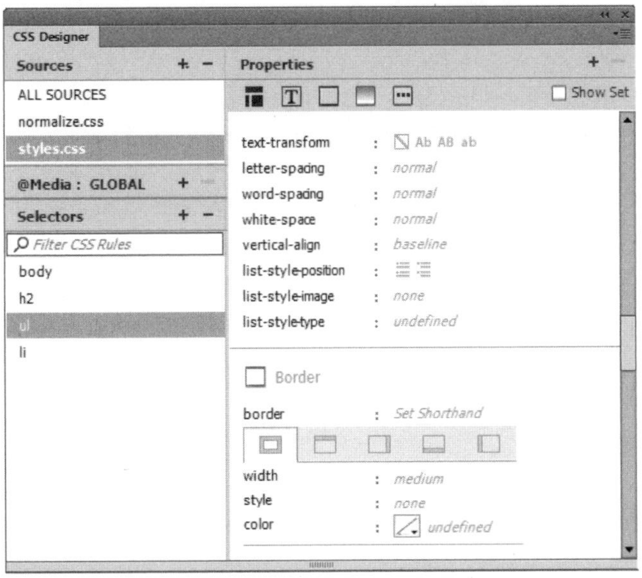

Description

- You can change the bullet that's displayed for an unordered list or the numbering system that's used for an ordered list by using the list-style-type property.
- To display an image for the bullet in an unordered list, use the list-style-image property.
- You can set the list-style-position property of a list to indent the first line of each list item so the bullet is aligned with the content of the lines that follow.
- To display the properties for formatting lists in the CSS Designer, click the Text icon at the top of the Properties pane.

Figure 6-11   The properties for formatting lists

Examples of unordered and ordered lists

The two tables in figure 6-12 present the values you can specify for the list-style-type property of an unordered list and some of the most common values you can specify for this property of an ordered list. Then, it presents an example of each of these types of lists.

The first example uses an unordered list with standard bullets. However, the list-style-position property for this list has been set to "inside". Because of that, the bullets appear inside the flow of the content for each list item. If you compare this list with the ordered list in the second example, you'll see how they differ.

The list-style-type property for the ordered list shown in this figure has been changed to "lower-alpha" so the list uses lowercase alphabetic characters. In addition, the padding-left property of the items in this list (the li elements) has been changed so the space between the alphabetic character and the content of the list item is increased slightly. Although it's not shown here, you can also use the padding-left property of a list (a ul or ol element) to change how far the list is indented.

Values for the list-style-type property of an unordered list

Value	Description
disc	solid circle
circle	hollow circle
square	solid square
none	no bullet

Common values for the list-style-type property of an ordered list

Value	Example
decimal	1, 2, 3, 4, 5 ...
decimal-leading-zero	01, 02, 03, 04, 05 ...
lower-alpha	a, b, c, d, e, ...
upper-alpha	A, B, C, D, E ...
lower-roman	i, ii, iii, iv, v ...
upper-roman	I, II, III, IV, V ...

An unordered list with the bullets inside the content flow

Our Solutions

• **vProspect 2.0:** Define and research your target audience, define your strategy to reach that audience and present a strong and memorable brand to that audience.

• **vConvert 2.0:** Create a highly user-friendly and easy-to-navigate information architecture that will help your prospects interact with the company on a highly interactive level.

• **vRetain 1.0:** Build on existing customer relationships to improve productivity and maximize customer loyalty, while growing revenues.

An ordered list with spacing added between the bullets and text

How to create an executable file

a. Run the WinZip Self Extractor program and click through the first three dialog boxes.

b. Enter the name of the zip file in the fourth dialog box.

c. Click the Next button to test the executable.

Description

- The default bullet type for an unordered list is disc, and the default numbering system for an ordered list is decimal.
- You can use the padding-left property of a list to change the left alignment of the list, and you can use the padding-left property of a list item to change the space between the bullet and the text.

Figure 6-12   Examples of unordered and ordered lists

How to use an unordered list to create a navigation menu

Unordered lists are commonly used to create navigation menus like the ones shown in figure 6-13. A *navigation menu* is just a vertical or horizontal list of links that often provides the primary navigation for a website. This is the preferred way to create a navigation menu, because a list is a logical container for the links.

This figure describes how you create a navigation menu from an unordered list. To start, you create a link for the text for each item in the list. Then, you remove the bullets from the list items. To do that, you set the list-style-type property for the list to "none". This creates a vertical menu like the first one shown in this figure.

You use a similar technique to create a horizontal menu. To get the list items to display horizontally, though, you have to change them from block elements to inline elements. To do that, you change the display property for the list items (the li elements) to "inline". You'll typically want to add padding to the right or left of each list item too to add space between them.

The horizontal menu in this figure illustrates how this works. Here, I added 1.4 ems of space to the right side of each list item. In addition, I added .5 ems of space above and below the list, along with 2-pixel solid black borders. Finally, I centered the list within its containing element (in this case, a nav element).

A web page with a vertical menu

A web page with a horizontal menu

Description

- To create a navigation menu from an unordered list, you highlight the text for each list item and then use the HTML Property Inspector to create a link for the item. If you're working in Live view, you can also use the Quick PI to create the link.

- To remove the bullets from the list items, set the list-style-type property to "none".

- To create a horizontal navigation menu, set the display property of the list items to "inline" so they are treated as inline elements instead of block elements. You can also set the padding for the line items to add space between them.

Figure 6-13   How to use an unordered list to create a navigation menu

How to create a multi-tier navigation menu

In addition to navigation menus like those shown in the previous figure, you can create multi-tier navigation menus like the one shown in figure 6-14. In a *multi-tier navigation menu*, each list item in the main menu can contain a submenu. For example, the Solutions item in the menu in this figure contains a submenu that displays a list of the solutions. This menu is displayed when the mouse hovers over the Solutions item.

To create a multi-tier navigation menu, you *nest* an unordered list within a list item of another unordered list. In this figure, for example, you can see the HTML for the nested list shown in this figure. Unfortunately, you can't add a nested list in Design view. Instead, you have to work in Code view. Remember, though, that you can insert the elements you need in Code view using the same techniques you use in Design view. In addition, you can use the Property Inspector to work with the generated elements.

The most difficult part of creating a multi-tier navigation menu is understanding the required selectors and CSS properties. The table in this figure lists these selectors and properties. Note that you can set properties in addition to the ones shown here so the submenu is formatted the way you want. For example, the background-color property for the submenu shown here is set so its background is the same color as the background of the main menu. In addition, the underlines have been removed from all the links in the menu and submenu. Although it's a good practice to keep the underlines for links because that makes it clear that they're links, it's okay to remove the underlines if the formatting makes that clear.

Because you don't want a submenu to be displayed until the mouse hovers over the item in the main menu that contains the submenu, you need to set the display property of the unordered list for the submenu (ul li ul) to "none". Then, when the mouse hovers over the item in the main menu, you need to set the display property of the submenu (ul li:hover ul) to "block" so the submenu is displayed vertically. In addition, you need to set the display property of the links within the submenu (ul li:hover ul li a) to "block" since links are inline elements by default.

In addition to the display property, you need to set the position property of the list item that contains the submenu (ul li) to "relative". This is done so you can position the submenu within this list item. Here, you can see that when the mouse hovers over the unordered list for the submenu (ul li:hover ul), the position property of this list is set to absolute. In addition, the left property is set to 0 ems and the top property is set to 1 em. This causes the submenu to be positioned absolutely within the closest containing block that is also positioned. In this case, that's the list item that contains the submenu. You'll learn more about how positioning works later in this chapter, but for now, this should be enough for you to understand how this menu works.

A web page with a multi-tier navigation menu

HTML for the nested list

```
<li><a href="solutions.html">Solutions</a>
    <ul>
        <li><a href="solutions.html#vprospect">vProspect 2.0</a></li>
        <li><a href="solutions.html#vconvert">vConvert 2.0</a></li>
        <li><a href="solutions.html#vretain">vRetain 1.0</a></li>
    </ul>
</li>
```

Selectors and CSS properties for creating a multi-tier menu

Descendant selector	CSS properties
ul li	position: relative
ul li ul	display: none
ul li:hover ul	display: block position: absolute left: 0em top: 1em
ul li:hover ul li a	display: block

Description

- To create a multi-tier navigation menu, you add an unordered list within the list item for another unordered list. This can be referred to as a *nested list*.
- To hide the nested list when the page is first displayed, you set its display property to "none".
- To display the nested list when the mouse hovers over the list item in the main list, you change the display property of the nested list to "block".
- To display the nested list directly below the main list, you set the position property of the main list to "relative". Then, you set the position property of the nested list to "absolute", the left property to 0, and the top property as appropriate.
- To format the links in the nested list so they appear as shown above, you set the display property of the links to "block"
- See figure 6-18 for more information on positioning elements.

Figure 6-14   How to create a multi-tier navigation menu

How to float elements

To create a page layout with two or more columns, you usually float the block elements that make up the columns of the page. You'll learn how to do that in the topics that follow.

The properties for floating and clearing elements

By default, the block elements defined in an HTML document flow from the top of the page to the bottom of the page, and inline elements flow from the left side of the block elements that contain them to the right side. When you *float* a block element, though, it's taken out of the flow of the document. Because of that, any elements that follow the floated element flow into the space that's left by the floated element.

Figure 6-15 presents the basic skills for floating an element on a web page. To do that, you use the float property to specify whether you want the element floated to the left or to the right. You also have to set the width of the floated element. For example, the first web page in this figure includes a sidebar with a width of 150 pixels that's floated to the right. As a result, the content that follows flows into the space to the left of the sidebar.

Note, however, that the footer at the bottom of the page doesn't flow to the left of the sidebar. That's because the clear property for the footer has been set to "right", which keeps the element from flowing into the space left by an element that's floated to the right. I could also have set this property to "both" to keep it from flowing into the space left by an element that's floated to either the left or the right. Similarly, if an element is floated to the left, you can set the clear property of an element that follows to either "left" or "both".

Although you can use the float property with any block element, you can also use it with some inline elements. For example, the second web page in this figure includes three images that are floated to the left. This causes the text that follows the images to flow into the space to the right of the images. Note that when you float an image, you don't have to set the width property because an image always has a default size.

The properties for floating and clearing elements

Property	Description
float	A keyword that determines how an element is floated. Possible values are left, right, and none. None is the default.
clear	A keyword that determines whether an element is cleared from flowing into the space left by a floated element. Possible values are left, right, both, and none. None is the default.

A web page with a sidebar floated to the right

Welcome

With innovative approaches and advanced methodologies, Vecta Corporation provides scalable business solutions to help companies achieve success through revenue increase, cost management, and user satisfaction.

For information about obtaining 30-day trials of our products, please see the Contact Us page.

© Copyright 2013 Module Media

A web page with images floated to the left

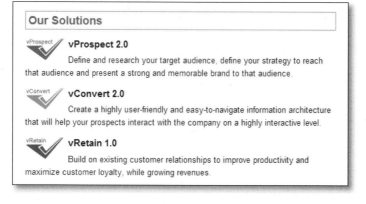

Our Solutions

vProspect 2.0
Define and research your target audience, define your strategy to reach that audience and present a strong and memorable brand to that audience.

vConvert 2.0
Create a highly user-friendly and easy-to-navigate information architecture that will help your prospects interact with the company on a highly interactive level.

vRetain 1.0
Build on existing customer relationships to improve productivity and maximize customer loyalty, while growing revenues.

Description

- When you *float* a block element to the right or left, the content that follows flows around it.

- When you use the float property for an element, you also need to set its width. The exception is an image element, since the width can be implied from the width of the image.

- To stop the floating before an element, use the clear property.

- In the first example above, if the clear property for the footer isn't set, its content will flow into the space beside the floated element.

- Even if an element that follows a floated element doesn't flow into the space beside the floated element, it's a best practice to clear the element in case the content of the page changes.

Figure 6-15   The properties for floating and clearing elements

How to use floating in a 2-column layout

Figure 6-16 shows how floating elements can be used to create a 2-column page layout. Here, the HTML in the body of the page consists of four elements: header, nav, main, and footer.

For this to work, the widths are set for the body, nav, and main elements. Here, the width of the body must be at least as wide as the sum of the widths of the nav and main elements, plus the widths of any margins, padding, and borders for these elements. In this case, the width of the nav element is set to 140 pixels, and it doesn't contain margins, padding, or borders. The width of the main element is set to 350 pixels, and it has a left padding of 10 pixels but no other padding and no borders. So the width of the body is set to 500 pixels (140 + 350 + 10).

After you set up the widths for the body and the two columns, you can create the columns by floating the nav element to the left and the main element to the right. This will work whether the nav or main element is coded first in the HTML. In that case, you must set the clear property of the footer element to "both" so it's displayed below both floated elements.

Another alternative is to float both the nav and the main elements to the left. In that case, though, the nav element must come first in the HTML. Note that if you float both elements to the left, the clear property for the footer element could be set to "left" instead of "both".

A web page with two columns

Description

- The navigation menu on this page is floated to the left and the main section is floated to the right. Then, it doesn't matter whether the navigation menu comes before or after the main section in the HTML.

- An alternative is to float both the navigation menu and the main section to the left, but then the navigation menu has to be coded before the main section in the HTML.

- To ensure that the footer is always displayed below the floated elements, its clear property is set to both. If the main section was floated to the left, the footer's clear property could be set to left.

Figure 6-16   How to use floating in a 2-column layout

How to use floating in a 3-column layout

Figure 6-17 shows how to take floating one more level to create a 3-column page layout. The web page shown here is like the one in the previous figure, but an aside element has been added after the main element.

In this example, the width of the body is 740 pixels, which is the sum of the nav element in the first column (140 pixels), the main element in the second column (390 pixels + 10 pixels of left padding), and the aside element in the third column (180 pixels + 20 pixels of left padding). Once those widths are set, the nav and main elements are floated to the left and the aside element is floated to the right. Note that the aside element could also have been floated to the left, though.

One of the keys here is getting the widths right. If, for example, you set the body width to 730 pixels instead of 740 pixels, the nav, main, and aside elements won't fit into the width of the body. In that case, the aside element will flow beneath the main element.

A web page with three columns

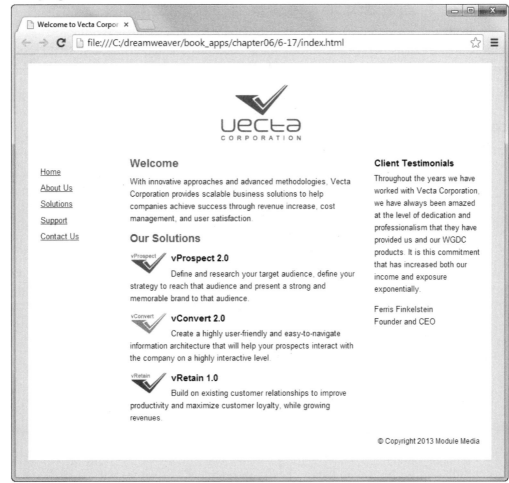

Description

- The navigation menu and the main section on this web page are floated to the left and the sidebar is floated to the right.

- You could get the same result by floating all three elements to the left.

- To ensure that the footer is always displayed below the floated elements, its clear property is set to both. If all three elements were floated to the left, the footer's clear property could be set to left instead.

Figure 6-17   How to use floating in a 3-column layout

How to position elements

Although floating provides an easy way to create pages with two or more columns, you may occasionally need to use other positioning techniques. That was the case with the multi-tier navigation menu you saw earlier in this chapter. You'll learn more about using techniques like this in the topics that follow.

Four ways to position an element

To position the elements on a page, you use the properties shown in the first table in figure 6-18. The position property determines the type of positioning that will be used. This property can have four different values as shown in the second table.

The first value, static, is the default. This causes elements to be placed in the normal flow.

The second value, absolute, removes the element from the normal flow and positions it based on the top, bottom, right, and left properties you specify. When you use *absolute positioning*, the element is positioned relative to the closest containing block that is also positioned. If no containing block is positioned, the element is positioned relative to the browser window.

The third value, fixed, works like absolute in that the position of the element is specified using the top, bottom, left, and right properties. Instead of being positioned relative to a containing block, however, an element that uses *fixed positioning* is positioned relative to the browser window. That means that the element doesn't move when you scroll through the window.

The fourth value, relative, causes an element to be positioned relative to its normal position in the flow. When you use the top, bottom, left, and right properties with *relative positioning*, they specify the element's offset from its normal position.

One more property you can use to position elements is z-index. This property is useful if an element that you position overlaps another element. In that case, you can use the z-index property to determine which element is on top.

Properties for positioning elements

Property	Description
`position`	A keyword that determines how an element is positioned. See the table below for possible values.
`top`, `bottom`, `left`, `right`	For absolute or fixed positioning, a relative or absolute value that specifies the top, bottom, left, or right position of an element's box. For relative positioning, the top, bottom, left, or right offset of an element's box.
`z-index`	An integer that determines the stack level of an element whose position property is set to absolute, relative, or fixed.

Possible values for the position property

Value	Description
`static`	The element is placed in the normal flow. This is the default.
`absolute`	The element is removed from the flow and is positioned relative to the closest containing block that is also positioned. The position is determined by the top, bottom, left, and right properties.
`fixed`	The element is positioned absolutely relative to the browser window. The position is determined by the top, bottom, left, and right properties.
`relative`	The element is positioned relative to its position in the normal flow. The position is determined by the top, bottom, left, and right properties.

Description

- By default, static positioning is used to position block elements from top to bottom and inline elements from left to right.

- To change the positioning of an element, you can code the position property. In most cases, you also code one or more of the top, bottom, left, and right properties.

- In the CSS Designer, you'll find the positioning properties right below the margin and padding properties.

- When you use absolute, relative, or fixed positioning for an element, the element can overlap other elements. Then, you can use the z-index property to specify a value that determines the level at which the element is displayed. An element with a higher z-index value is displayed on top of an element with a lower z-index value.

- Fixed positioning isn't supported by versions of Internet Explorer before version 7.

Figure 6-18   Four ways to position an element

How to use absolute positioning

To give you a better idea of how positioning works, the first example in figure 6-19 presents a page that uses absolute positioning. Here, a div element with a graphic for a Live Chat service is added to the body of the web page before the header element. This element is positioned absolutely within its containing element, which is the body element.

For this to work, the containing element must also be positioned. However, the positioning can be either relative or absolute, and the top, bottom, left, and right properties don't have to be set. Since they aren't set in this example, the body is positioned where it is in the natural flow. In other words, nothing changes. However, because the body is positioned, the elements that it contains can be absolutely positioned within it.

In the example in this figure, the div element that contains the graphic is positioned 35 pixels from the top of the body and 0 pixels from its left side. Then, when the user scrolls down the page as shown in the second browser window, the graphic doesn't scroll with the content. Because of that, the graphic may not always be visible, which probably isn't what you want in this case.

You're more likely to use absolute positioning when the element is related to another element on the page. Then, you can position the element absolutely based on the position of the other element or its containing element. In the multi-tier navigation menu you saw in figure 6-14, for example, the unordered list for the submenu was positioned absolutely within the list item for the main menu. This is something that you can't do with fixed positioning.

Although the position property of the body element in this example has been set to relative, you should realize that this is the one case in which you don't need to position the containing element. That's because the body element is positioned relative to the browser window by default. However, if you position an element within the body element, we recommend that you set the position property of the body element to make it clear that it is positioned.

How to use fixed positioning

If you want an element to always be visible on a web page regardless of what portion of the page is displayed, you can use fixed positioning instead of absolute positioning. With fixed positioning, an element is positioned relative to the browser window, not the containing element. So, you can change the first example in figure 6-19 from absolute to fixed positioning by making just two modifications. First, you delete the position property for the body element since fixed positioning is relative to the browser window. Second, you change the position property for the div element that contains the graphic to "fixed".

The second example in this figure illustrates how fixed positioning works. Here, even though the page has been scrolled down, the graphic is still displayed in its original position relative to the top and left sides of the browser window. Note that if you use fixed positioning, you can code the fixed element anywhere within the body of the document since it isn't positioned relative to the other elements.

A web page with an image that uses absolute positioning

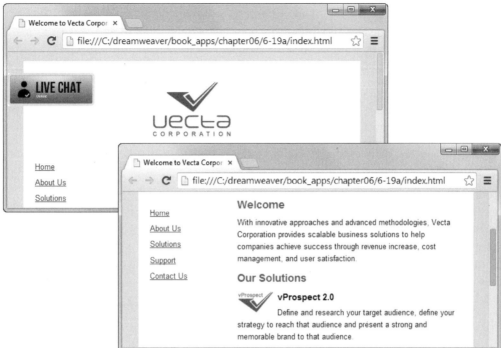

The same page using fixed positioning

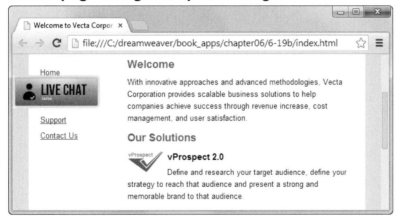

Description

- When you use *absolute positioning*, the remaining elements on the page are positioned as if the element wasn't there. As a result, you may need to make room for the positioned element by setting the margins or padding for other elements.

- Because an absolutely positioned element is positioned relative to its containing element, it will move in the browser window when you scroll through the page.

- When you use *fixed positioning*, the element is positioned relative to the browser window so it doesn't move even when you scroll.

Figure 6-19   How to use absolute and fixed positioning

Perspective

This completes the first section of this book, which we think of as a crash course in Dreamweaver. With these skills, you should be able to develop web pages at a professional level. Then, to add to these skills, you can read any of the chapters in the rest of this book in whatever sequence you prefer. In other words, you can learn those skills whenever you need them.

Terms

box model	linear gradient
padding	navigation menu
margin	multi-tier navigation menu
fixed layout	nested list
containing block	float
collapsed margins	absolute positioning
border	fixed positioning
background	relative positioning

Summary

- The CSS *box model* refers to the box that a browser places around each block element as well as some inline elements. Each box includes the content of the element, plus optional padding, borders, and margins.

- To set the height and width of a content area, you can use absolute measurements like pixels or relative measurements like percents. If you use a percent, the percent applies to the block that contains the box you're formatting.

- You can set the *margins* for all four sides of a box. Because different browsers have different default values for margins, it's good to set the margins explicitly.

- If you specify a bottom margin for one element and a top margin for the element that follows, the margins are *collapsed* to the size of the largest margin.

- You can also set the *padding* for all four sides of a box. One way to avoid margin collapse is to set the margins to zero and use padding for the spacing.

- A *border* can be placed on any of the sides of a box. That border goes on the outside of the padding for the box and inside any margins, and you can set the width, style, and color for a border.

- When you set the *background* for a box, it is displayed behind the content, padding, and border for the box, but not behind the margins. The background can consist of a color, an image, or both.

- With CSS3, you can round corners and add shadows to borders. You can also provide *linear gradients* as backgrounds.

- To create a *navigation menu*, you create a series of links within an unordered list. Then, you can use CSS to remove the bullets from the list items and to change the list items to inline elements so they're displayed horizontally.

- To create a *multi-tier navigation* menu, you *nest* an unordered list within a list item for another unordered list.

- When you use the float property to *float* an element, any elements after the floated element will flow into the space left vacant. To make this work, the floated element has to have a width that's either specified or implied.

- To stop an element from flowing into the space left vacant by a floated element, you can use the clear property.

- When you use *absolute positioning* for an element, the remaining elements on the page are positioned as if the element weren't there. When you use *relative positioning* for an element, the remaining elements leave space for the moved element as if it were still there.

- When you use *fixed positioning* for an element, the element doesn't move in the browser window, even when you scroll.

Exercise 6-1   Build pages with navigation bars and two-column layouts

In this exercise, you'll build pages that have navigation bars and two-column layouts like the one that follows. This will give you a chance to practice some of the skills that you learned in this chapter.

Open the folder for this exercise and review its pages

1. Open the Exercises site, and open the folder for this exercise.

2. Open the three HTML files for this site, review the HTML and CSS code, and run the pages in your browser. At this point, the pages aren't linked, and they don't have two columns.

Convert the index.html page to two columns

3. In Design view for the index.html page, select the Welcome heading and the paragraph that follows it including the final </p> tag. Then, use the Insert panel to enclose this selection in an aside element. When the dialog box shows Wrap around Selection, click OK, and check the HTML code to make sure that this worked correctly.

4. In Design view, select the Our Solutions heading and all of the elements that follow it up to the footer element. Then, use the Insert panel to enclose this selection in a section element, and check the HTML to make sure this worked.

5. Use the CSS Designer to increase the width of the style rule for the main selector in the styles.css file to 960 pixels. Then, in Design view, click on the image in the header, and use the Property Inspector to increase the width of the image to 960 pixels while maintaining the aspect ratio.

6. Use the CSS Designer to create a style rule in the styles.css style sheet for the aside selector. Then, set its width to 400 pixels, its float property to left, and its bottom margin to 1em. Now, create a style rule in that style sheet for the section selector, and set its width to 500 pixels, its float property to right, and its bottom margin to 1em.

7. Use the CSS Designer to set the clear property for the footer in the styles.css style sheet so it clears the float to the left and the right. At this point, the page should have two-column formatting.

8. Use the CSS Designer to add a top border to the footer with a 3 pixel width, the solid style, and the same color as the gray line in the image in the header. Then, set the top padding to 1em to provide space between the border and the text.

Add the navigation bar

9. In Live view, use the Insert panel to add a nav element after the header element and before the aside element. Next, add an unordered list inside the nav element, which will also add the first list item. Then, replace the text in the list item with "Home", and note the changes in the HTML code.

10. In Design view, move the insertion point to the end of the bulleted item for Home, press the Enter key, and type Solutions. Then, repeat for About Us and Support, and note that three more list items have been added.

11. In Design view, select the text for the first list item ("Home"), and use the Property Inspector to link it to the index.html page. Do the same for the next three items, and link them to these pages: solutions.html, aboutus.html, and support.html (even though that page hasn't been developed yet).

12. To remove the bullets from the list items, create a style rule in the styles.css file for the unordered list in the nav element (nav ul). Then, set its list-style-type property to none.

13. To convert the list from vertical to horizontal, create a style rule for the list items (nav ul li) that sets the display property to inline. Then, set the right margin for these items to 3em to provide spacing between them.

14. To improve the formatting for the links, create a style rule for them (nav ul li a). Then, to remove the underlines, set the text-decoration property to none. And to improve the appearance, set the font size to 120%, the font weight to bold, and the font color to the red color in the Vecta Logo in the header.

15. Add a border and background color to the nav element so it looks like the one at the start of this exercise. The background color should be the same as the one for the footer border, and the border color should be the same as the one for the h2 elements. The border should be solid, 3 pixels wide, with a border radius of 10 pixels for rounding the corners.

Convert the Solutions and About Us pages to two columns

16. Using whichever view you prefer for the Solutions page, enclose the Testimonial heading and the paragraphs that follow it in an aside element, and enclose the Our Solutions heading and everything that follows it up to the footer in a section element. Then, use the Property Inspector to set the width for the image in the heading to 960 pixels. Last, copy the nav element from the index.html page into the Solutions page between the header and aside elements. The page should now be formatted in two columns with a navigation bar, but check the HTML to make sure this worked right.

17. Repeat the last step for the About Us page. This time, enclose the Company Overview heading and the paragraphs that follow in the aside; the Management Team heading and the paragraphs that follow in a section; and the Careers heading and the paragraph that follows in another aside.

18. Run these pages in your browser to make sure the first three links in the navigation bar work okay. Note that the Careers aside for the About Us page is below the Company Overview in the first column of that page.

Improve the formatting for the headings, text, and lists

If you study the pages now, you should see some ways in which you can improve the formatting, like reducing the amount of space after h2 and h3 headings.

19. To reduce the amount of space after the h2 and h3 headings, set their bottom margins to .25em. Then, check this change on all three pages.

20. To improve the formatting for the bulleted list on the Solution page, create a style rule for the list (section ul). Then, to reduce the space before the list, set the top margin to .5em. And to move the bulleted list to the left, set the left padding to 1em.

21. To improve the formatting of the list items in the bulleted list on the Solutions page, create a style rule for those items (section ul li). Then, to add vertical space between the items, set the bottom padding to .5em. To adjust the space between the bullet and the text, set the left padding to .25em. And just for fun, change the list style type to "circle".

22. In Design view for the About Us page, if you look at the text under Company Overview, you can see that it's difficult to read. To fix that, use the CSS Designer to create a new style sheet named aboutus.css. That will also link the style sheet to the About Us page so the styles won't affect the other pages. Then, add a style rule for the paragraphs (p), and set the margin bottom property to .5em. That's a quick way to make the paragraphs easier to read, but you could also indent the paragraphs.

23. Test the pages in your browser to be sure that they look and work the way you want them to. If you want to make other improvements, do that now. Then, close all files.

Section 2

More Dreamweaver skills as you need them

In section 1, you learned the core Dreamweaver skills that you'll need for developing most web pages. Now, this section presents some additional skills that you can learn as you need them. Except for chapters 7 and 8, each chapter in this section is independent of the other chapters. As a result, you can read these chapters in whatever sequence you prefer.

In chapter 7, you'll learn how to use media queries to create web pages that adapt to the size of a screen. This is referred to as Responsive Web Design, and it's critical if you're developing a website that will be displayed on mobile devices such as smart phones and tablets as well as on PCs and Macs. Then, in chapter 8, you'll learn how to use a feature of Dreamweaver that implements a responsive design using fluid layouts. Because this feature works partly by using media queries, it's important that you read chapter 7 before reading this chapter.

In chapter 9, you'll learn how to design templates that you can use as the basis for two or more pages in a website. You'll also learn how to use library items, which contain HTML code that can be used in two or more pages of a website.

Next, chapter 10 shows how to add audio, video, and animations to a website. Chapter 11 shows how to work with tables. And chapter 12 shows how to use some of the features of Dreamweaver that can help improve your productivity. Finally, chapter 13 shows how to deploy a website to a web host as well as how to collaborate with the members of a team.

7

How to use media queries to create a responsive design

In section 1, you learned how to create and format web pages that will be displayed on desktop computers. Now, you'll learn how to create web pages whose layouts adapt to the screen sizes on smaller devices such as tablets and smart phones. To create these types of pages, you can use media queries.

An introduction to Responsive Web Design

Many different types of mobile devices are in use today, and these devices are frequently used to access websites. Because the screens on these devices can be much smaller than standard desktop screens, a website that's designed to be used on the desktop can be difficult to work with on a mobile device. To accommodate mobile users, then, web developers should design their web pages to adapt to different screen sizes.

How to provide pages for mobile devices

Figure 7-1 presents six ways to provide web pages for mobile devices. To start, you can use a style sheet for the handheld media type. But the problem here is that the handheld media type is considered antiquated and not all mobile browsers recognize it. That includes the Safari browser used by Apple's iPhone, the Opera Mobile and Opera Mini browsers, as well as others.

The second technique in this figure requires that you develop a separate website for mobile devices. When you use this technique, you include a link on the home page that lets the user switch to the mobile version of the site. The trouble with this is that users don't always enter a site at the home page, so you may need to provide links to the mobile site on other pages as well.

When you use the third, fourth, and fifth techniques in this figure, the website detects when a mobile device is being used and then redirects the user to the mobile version of the site automatically. This is the way detection has been performed on most commercial websites that service many mobile device users for years. The downside to these techniques is twofold. First, as more and more devices become available, it becomes increasingly difficult to detect them all. Second, the mobile version of a website is typically designed for a fixed-size screen. Because of that, it isn't appropriate for all devices.

The last technique is to use CSS3 *media queries*. Media queries are blocks of code within a style sheet that use conditional statements to "query" the device size and apply CSS based on the detected size. This lets you design a website using traditional methods for the desktop, and then adjust that design for a range of other screen sizes. The use of media queries is an important part of Responsive Web Design.

Define a style sheet for the handheld media type

- When you use this technique, you don't have to maintain a separate version of the website for mobile devices. However, many mobile browsers don't recognize the handheld media type.

Include a link to a mobile version of the website

- When you use this technique, you display the desktop version of the website no matter what device accesses it. Then, you include a link to a mobile version of the site near the top of the home page.

Use JavaScript to detect mobile devices and redirect

- When you use this technique, you use JavaScript to detect mobile devices. Then, if a mobile device is detected, the user is redirected to the mobile version of the website.
- The problem with this is that there are so many different mobile devices that it's difficult to detect them all. Also, some mobile devices don't support JavaScript.

Use a server-side scripting language to detect and redirect

- With this technique, you use a server-side scripting language such as PHP or ColdFusion to detect mobile devices. Then, if a mobile device is detected, the user is redirected to the mobile version of the website.
- The problem with this is that there are so many different mobile browsers that it's difficult to detect them all.

Use the WURFL to detect mobile devices

- The *WURFL* (*Wireless Universal Resource File*) is an XML configuration file that contains information about a variety of mobile devices, including the features and capabilities they support. This file is updated frequently with new devices.
- To use the WURFL, you implement the API (Application Programming Interface) using languages such as Java, PHP, C++, or .NET. Among other things, the API lets you determine the browser that's being used and then retrieve information about that browser from the XML file. When you use this technique, you have to download the XML configuration file periodically so it's up-to-date.

Use CSS3 media queries

- CSS3 provides a new feature called *media queries* that gives you the ability to adapt a page to a device's screen size.
- Although older browsers don't support CSS3, you can use third-party JavaScript libraries to force older browsers to recognize the queries.

Description

- Until recently, the best way to provide for mobile devices was to redirect users to a mobile version of the main website using a variety of less-than-elegant techniques. Now, you can use CSS3 media queries instead.

Figure 7-1   How to provide pages for mobile devices

The need for Responsive Web Design

The term *Responsive Web Design*, or *RWD*, was first coined by Ethan Marcotte in an article in the May 2010 issue of *A List Apart Magazine*. It refers to the theory and practice of creating websites that adapt gracefully to all viewing mediums, from desktop computers to mobile phones. The idea is to provide a website that is easy to read and navigate and that requires a minimum amount of resizing and scrolling.

According to Marcotte, the layout of a website that's designed with RWD in mind should adapt to the viewing environment by using fluid, proportion-based grids, flexible images, and CSS3 media queries. His idea for RWD has now become one of the hottest trends in web development. In fact, it has been touted as a cost-effective alternative to the development of mobile applications for specific platforms like iOS and Android, called *native mobile applications*. In addition, several popular open-source web design frameworks such as Skeleton, Foundation, Gumby, and Twitter Bootstrap incorporate RWD principles as a base for developing responsive websites.

So why should you consider using Responsive Web Design as you develop your websites? First, as you'll see in this chapter, Dreamweaver makes working with RWD easy. More importantly, though, statistics prove that mobile devices are being used more every day to access the Web. Some of these statistics are listed in figure 7-2. Consider, for example, that within the next four years, mobile devices will be used to access the Internet 26 times more than they are today. Also consider that 2.2 billion smart phones are expected to be sold in 2014 alone.

This figure also illustrates how a site that uses RWD adapts to the size and orientation of the screen. Here, you can see the home page of the Vecta Corp. website in a desktop browser. This page is similar to some of the other pages you've already seen in this book. Because it uses RWD, though, the layout of the page changes when it's displayed on a device with a smaller screen size. In this figure, for example, you can see how the page appears in an iPhone 5 in both portrait and landscape orientation. Note that the basic look and feel of the page remains the same across the different screen sizes. That way, users won't feel that they're visiting completely different sites from different devices. That's the beauty of Responsive Web Design!

The Vecta Corp website displayed on a desktop and a mobile phone

Statistics that prove the need for Responsive Web Design

- Web access from a mobile device outpaced the growth of web access from a desktop by 8 to 1 in 2013.
- 1 in 5 people worldwide access the Internet from a mobile device every day.
- In the next 4 years, mobile Internet usage will increase by a factor of 26.
- In 2013, desktop sales worldwide totaled 303 million, an 11 percent drop from 2012. 2014 desktop sales are expected to drop even lower to 281 million.
- In 2013, 2 billion tablets and smart phones were sold, a 20 percent increase from 2011. In 2014, tablet and smart phone sales are expected to rise to 2.2 billion.
- By 2015, more users will browse the web from a mobile device than from a desktop.

Description

- *Responsive Web Design* refers to websites that are designed to adapt gracefully to the screen size.
- Typically, the overall look-and-feel of a website will remain consistent from one screen size to the next.
- Flexible layouts, visual media that adapts to the layout, and media queries are the backbone of Responsive Web Design.

Figure 7-2   The need for Responsive Web Design

How to plan a responsive design

In contrast to websites that are designed to be displayed on desktop browsers alone, websites that use a responsive design require more thought and planning. That makes sense, because the pages of the site will need to work well regardless of the size of the screen they're displayed on. As figure 7-3 indicates, you need to focus on four areas as you plan a responsive design: content, navigation, functionality, and layout.

The traditional thought behind adding content to a website was to simply "throw it all up there" and let the user sort through it. Fortunately, as the use of the Web has grown, design guidelines have been developed that make web pages more usable. For example, one basic guideline is that the user should be able to access all critical information quickly, with a minimum of scrolling. Because guidelines like this can be difficult to attain when designing for mobile devices, careful planning is required.

As you plan the content for each web page, keep in mind too that not all mobile users have unlimited data plans. So the less content you have on a web page, the less data a mobile user will have to use to display it. On the other hand, you don't want too little content on a page either because then it won't work well on larger screens.

Navigation also plays a critical role in planning for a responsive design. As you plan the navigation for a site, then, you need to keep in mind that the more complex the navigation is for the desktop, the more difficult it will be to implement on smaller devices. In fact, third-party tools are often required to convert traditional navigation menus to drop-down menus to make them more usable. You'll learn more about that later in this chapter.

When you develop for mobile devices, you also need to keep in mind the additional functionality they provide. For example, most modern mobile devices include phone support, text messaging, GPS, Geolocation, and more. You can use these features to enhance the usability of a website for mobile users. In chapter 4, for example, you learned how to create a link to a phone number. Then, a smart phone user can click on this link to call the number. As you plan a website, you should decide which of these features it makes sense to use.

One of the most critical phases of planning is developing a wireframe for each range of resolutions that the website will provide for. A *wireframe* shows the basic layout of the information on each page and is typically developed using image editing software. In this figure, you can see basic wireframes for a page at four different sizes. Keep in mind, though, that wireframes are often more detailed than what's shown here.

Although you can design for any screen size when you use media queries, the four ranges of screen widths shown here are the ones that are used most often. They provide for desktops and for tablets in landscape orientation (960 pixels or more), tablets in portrait orientation (768 to 959 pixels), smart phones in landscape orientation (480 to 767 pixels), and smart phones in portrait orientation (up to 479 pixels). Although figuring out where to place content, imagery, and navigation for each of these sizes can be challenging, it's worth the effort to make your sites more accessible to mobile users.

A Vecta Corp wireframe shown at different screen resolution ranges

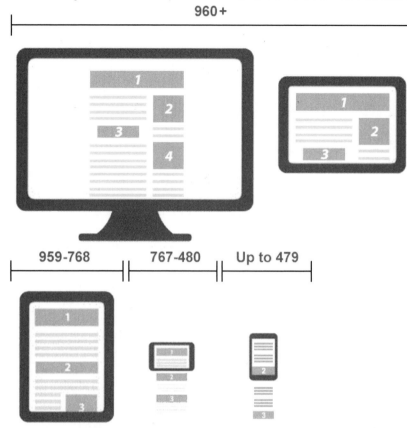

Description

- When planning a responsive design, you should focus on four distinct areas: content, navigation, functionality, and layout.

- Content should be written so users can access information quickly. That means presenting the most important information first, using headings and subheadings to identify portions of text, and using lists to make information more accessible.

- Navigation menus can be a challenge at smaller screen resolutions, and special options such as the use of drop-down menus may be required.

- Because mobile devices provide functionality like GPS and phone support, you'll want to decide early on what functionality to include.

- Before you begin developing a website that will use responsive design, you should create a *wireframe* for each range of screen resolutions that shows how the information will be laid out on each page.

- When creating the wireframes for a site, you should pay special attention to the placement of content areas, headings, logos, rotating banner ads, and navigation.

Figure 7-3   How to plan a responsive design

How to use CSS3 media queries

In the topics that follow, you'll learn how to use media queries to control the appearance of a page in various screen sizes. But first, you'll learn how to control the mobile viewport so it works in conjunction with media queries.

How to control the mobile viewport

When you develop a website that uses Responsive Web Design to provide for various screen sizes, you'll want to be sure it configures the *viewport* appropriately for mobile devices. To do that, you can use the meta element that's presented in figure 7-4.

To start, you should know that the viewport on a mobile browser works differently from the viewport on a desktop browser. On a desktop browser, the viewport is the visible area of the web page. The user can change the size of the viewport by changing the size of the browser window.

In contrast, the viewport on a mobile device can be larger or smaller than the visible area. In this figure, for example, you can see that the first web page is displayed so the entire width of the page is visible. Some mobile browsers such as Safari reduce a page like this automatically if no meta element is included. In contrast, other mobile browsers don't reduce the page at all, so it extends beyond the visible area of the screen as shown in the second web page in this figure.

When you use media queries, you want to be sure that the entire web page is displayed on the screen, since the media queries will adjust the appearance of the page based on the screen size. In other words, you want the page to look like the first one in this figure. To do that, you add a meta element like the one shown in this figure.

In this example, the name attribute is set to "viewport" to indicate that the element applies to the viewport. Then, the content attribute specifies the properties for the viewport. The first property, width, indicates that the width of the viewport should be set to the width of the device. That way, if the web page is wider than the browser, it will be reduced to fit within the screen.

The second property, initial-scale, determines the initial zoom factor, or *scale*, for the viewport. In this case, this scale is set to 1, which represents the default width for the viewport. This is what keeps the browser from scaling the page automatically.

When you add a meta element for the viewport from Dreamweaver, it automatically adds the width and initial-scale properties with the values shown here. In addition to these properties, you may want to set some of the other properties that are presented in this figure. Specifically, when you use RWD, the user-scalable property is often set to "no" so the user can't zoom in or out of the display. Or, if you want to let the user zoom in or out, you can set the minimum-scale and maximum-scale properties to limit how much the user can zoom. To set these properties, you have to enter them in Code view.

A web page on a mobile device without and with scaling

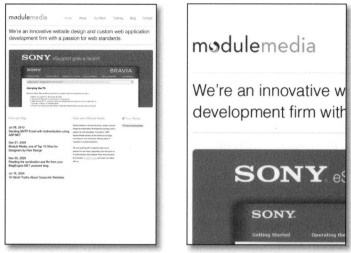

Content properties for viewport metadata

Property	Description
width	The logical width of the viewport specified in pixels. You can also use the device-width keyword to indicate that the viewport should be as wide as the screen.
height	The logical height of the viewport specified in pixels. You can also use the device-height keyword to indicate that the viewport should be as tall as the screen.
initial-scale	A number that indicates the initial zoom factor that's used to display the page.
minimum-scale	A number that indicates the minimum zoom factor for the page.
maximum-scale	A number that indicates the maximum zoom factor for the page.
user-scalable	Indicates whether the user can zoom in and out of the viewport. Possible values are yes and no.

A meta element that sets viewport properties

```
<meta name="viewport" content="width=device-width, initial-scale=1">
```

Description

- The *viewport* on a mobile device determines the content that's displayed on the screen. It can be larger or smaller than the actual visible area of the screen.
- You use a meta element to control the viewport settings for a device. To add a meta element for controlling the viewport from Dreamweaver, choose Insert→Head→Viewport or use the Common category of the Insert panel.
- When you use media queries, you should set the width property of the content attribute to "device-width", and you should set the initial-scale property to 1. You can also prevent or limit scaling with the user-scalable, minimum-scale, and maximum-scale properties.

Figure 7-4   How to control the mobile viewport

An introduction to media queries

Media queries are a new CSS3 feature that allows you to write conditional expressions directly within your CSS code. These conditional expressions can be used to query the device's screen size. Then, if the size falls within a range specified by a media query, the CSS for that media query can be used to adjust the appearance of the web page so it's appropriate for that screen size.

For example, a media query for a tablet in portrait orientation would look like this:

```
@media screen and (min-width: 768px) and (max-width: 959px)
{
    ...styles go here
}
```

This media query starts with an @media selector, followed by a media type. In this case, the media type is set to "screen", so the media query will only be used if the page is displayed on a screen.

In addition to a media type, a media query can include one or more conditional expressions, where each expression specifies the value of a property. In this example, the two expressions use the min-width and max-width properties to indicate that the media query will be used if the width of the device isn't less than 768 pixels or greater than 959 pixels. Note that additional properties are available for use with media queries, but these are the two you'll use most often with Responsive Web Design.

Figure 7-5 shows the media queries that are used most often with RWD. That includes one media query for full-size tablets in portrait orientation (768 to 959 pixels), one for mobile phones in landscape orientation (480 to 767 pixels), and one for mobile phones in portrait orientation (479 pixels or less). In addition, you could include a media query for the desktop (960 pixels or larger), but the styles for the desktop are typically coded outside the media queries as you've seen throughout this book. Finally, you could include a media query for all mobile phones. Then, that query would contain styles that apply to any mobile phone, and the other two queries would contain styles specific to phones in landscape or portrait orientation.

This figure also lists all the desktop browsers that support media queries. This includes all the current versions of all the major browsers. Because of that, you can use any of these browsers to test that the media queries used by a web page work correctly. To do that, you just change the width of the browser window to the width specified by a media query. Then, the styles defined by that media query will be applied. Of course, Dreamweaver also provides support for displaying a page at different screen sizes so the different media queries are applied. You'll learn about that later in this chapter.

Before I go on, you should realize that all the desktop browsers except for Internet Explorer are updated automatically when a new version becomes available. Because of that, you don't need to check what version you have before testing media queries. If you want to use Internet Explorer for testing, though, you need to be sure that you have at least version 9.

The most commonly used media queries

```
/* GLOBAL STYLES FOR ANYTHING 960 PIXELS OR LARGER (OPTIONAL) */
@media screen and (min-width: 960px) {
    ...global styles go here
}


/* TABLET PORTRAIT */
@media screen and (min-width: 768px) and (max-width: 959px) {
    ...styles go here
}


/* ALL MOBILE PHONE SIZES (OPTIONAL) */
@media screen and (max-width: 767px) {
    ...global styles go here
}


/* MOBILE PHONE LANDSCAPE */
@media screen and (min-width: 480px) and (max-width: 767px) {
    ...styles go here
}


/* MOBILE PHONE PORTRAIT */
@media screen and (max-width: 479px) {
    ...styles go here
}
```

Desktop browsers that support media queries

- Internet Explorer 9 and later
- Firefox 3.6 and later
- Safari 4 and later
- Opera 10 and later
- Chrome 5 and later

Description

- A media query is defined by a CSS3 @media selector. This selector specifies the media type for the query and, for the screen media type, the minimum, maximum, or both minimum and maximum widths that the query applies to.

- Media queries let you control the styles that are applied to a page based on conditional expressions such as the size of the screen.

- The screen size at which a media query is used to change the appearance of a page can be referred to as a *breakpoint*.

- Media queries are supported by all the current versions of all the major desktop browsers. That makes media queries easy to test in those browsers.

- Media queries are also supported by all the current versions of all mobile browsers.

- For a historical list of the browsers that support media queries, see http://caniuse.com/css-mediaqueries.

Figure 7-5   An introduction to media queries

How to create media queries in the CSS Designer

Figure 7-6 presents the procedure for creating a media query in Dreamweaver. To do that, you use the Define Media Query dialog box. As you can see, this dialog box lets you specify the conditions for the media query.

To create a media query that detects a specific screen size, you select "media" from the first menu and "screen" from the second menu. Then, you can add conditions for the minimum width, the maximum width, or both the minimum and maximum widths. As you do, the @media selector that will be generated is displayed at the bottom of the dialog box. Then, when you click OK, the media query will be listed in the @Media pane of the CSS Designer and the @media selector will be added to the selected style sheet.

After you add one or more media queries, you can use the CSS Designer to add style rules and styles to the queries. To do that, you select the style sheet that contains the media query from the Sources pane, and then select the media query from the @Media pane. Then, you can use the Selectors and Properties panes just as you normally would to add style rules and styles to the media query. As you do that, you can display the page at the appropriate size as described in the next topic to be sure it looks the way you want it to.

Once you add media queries to a style sheet, you may need to use the GLOBAL option that's available from the @Media pane. When you select this option, all of the selectors that are coded outside of the media queries are listed in the Selectors pane. Then, you can add and modify style rules without affecting the media queries. For example, if you implement the design of a web page for the desktop and then add media queries for the other screen sizes, you can modify the styles for the desktop design by selecting the GLOBAL option.

The Define Media Query dialog box and the media query it defines

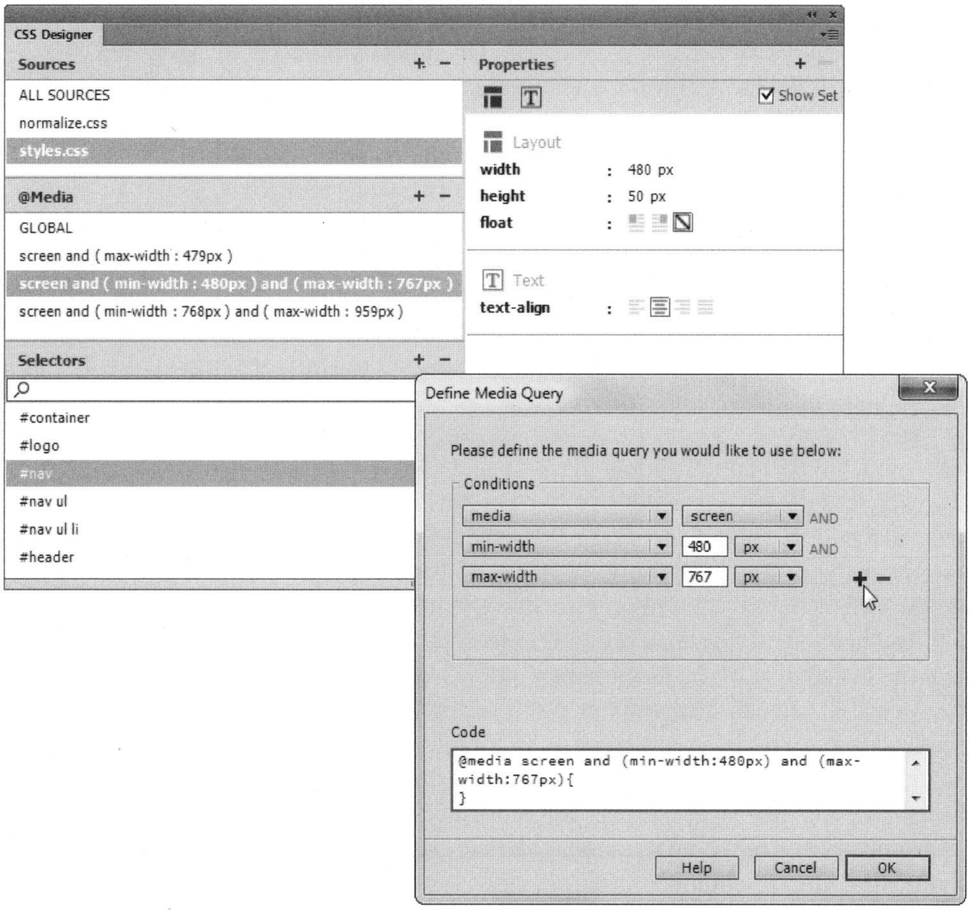

How to create a media query that detects screen size

1. Select the style sheet you want to add the media query to. Then, click the Add Media Query (+) icon at the top of the @Media pane of the CSS Designer to display the Define Media Query dialog box.

2. Select the Media option from the first menu, and select the Screen option from the second menu.

3. Click the Add Condition (+) icon that appears when you point to the right of the menus with the mouse. Then, use the additional controls that appear to specify conditions such as minimum and maximum width.

4. Repeat step 3 as necessary, then click OK. The query will appear in the @Media pane of the CSS Designer, and the @media selector for the query will be added at the end of the style sheet.

5. Select the style sheet that contains the media query in the Sources pane, select the media query in the @Media pane, and then use the Selectors and Properties panes to add style rules and styles to the query.

Figure 7-6   How to create media queries in the CSS Designer

How to display a page at different screen sizes

By default, Dreamweaver displays the Document window at desktop size, which is usually what you want when you're first designing a page. When you develop the media queries for a web page, though, you'll want to display this window at different screen sizes so you can see how the media queries affect the appearance of the page. Figure 7-7 describes three ways to do that.

The best way to display the Document window at a different size is to click on a media query in the @Media pane. Then, the page is displayed in a window whose size is determined by the conditions specified in the query. If a range of screen sizes is specified, for example, the width of the window is set to the average of those sizes. If just a minimum or maximum size is specified though, the width of the window is set to that size.

In this figure, the media query for a screen with a maximum width of 479 pixels is selected, so the window that's displayed is 479 pixels wide. Note, however, that the page is wider than the window. That's because no styles have been added to the media query to modify the page from desktop size. At this point, then, you would start applying styles to the media query to change the appearance of the page based on your design plan.

Another way to display a different screen size is to click one of the icons near the lower right of the Document window's status bar. These icons display the page at the standard smart phone size in portrait orientation (480 x 800 pixels), standard tablet size in portrait orientation (768 x 1024 pixels), and at standard desktop size (1000 x 835 pixels). If a media query exists for the size you choose, the page is displayed using that media query.

Notice here that the maximum width that Dreamweaver uses for a smart phone in portrait orientation is 480 pixels. In contrast, the standard maximum width for a smart phone when using Responsive Web Design is 479 pixels. Because of that, if you click the Mobile Size icon, the styles associated with the media query for a smart phone in portrait orientation won't be applied. That's one reason to use the @Media pane to test your media queries.

The third way to display a different screen size is to use the Window Size menu. This menu is available from Dreamweaver's View menu and from the status bar in the Document window as shown in this figure. This menu lets you select the specific screen size you want to display. It also lets you switch between portrait and landscape orientation. And it lets you create your own custom list of sizes using the Edit Sizes option. You might want to do that, for example, to change the standard screen size for a smart phone from 480 x 800 pixels to 479 x 800 pixels. Note, however, that this doesn't affect the size that's used by the Mobile Size icon.

A web page that's displayed in the Document window at mobile size

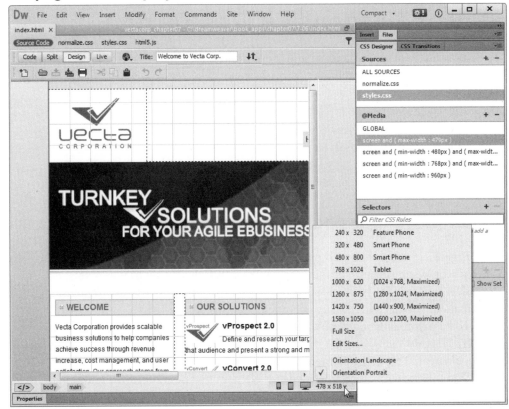

Three ways to display a page in different screen sizes

- Select a media query in the @Media pane to display the screen at the size specified by that query.

- Click one of the icons near the right side of the Document window's status bar to display the screen in mobile (smart phone) size (🗎), tablet size (▯), or desktop size (🖵).

- Use the Window Size menu to choose a size, to create your own custom size, or to switch between portrait and landscape orientation. To display this menu, click the size specification in the lower right corner of the Document window's status bar, or choose View→Window Size.

Description

- You can change the size of the Document window to see how a page looks in different screen sizes.

- If styles have been assigned to the media query for the selected screen size, they're applied to the page in the Document window.

Figure 7-7   How to display a page at different screen sizes

A web page that uses Responsive Web Design

Now that you understand what Responsive Web Design is and you know how to create the media queries for a responsive design in Dreamweaver, you're ready to see a web page that uses RWD. Here, I'll start by showing you the desktop design for the page. Then, I'll show you how the page design changes for a tablet in portrait orientation, for a smart phone in landscape orientation, and for a smart phone in portrait orientation. After you review these designs, you'll have a better idea of the types of changes you need to make when developing a responsive design.

The web page in a desktop browser

Figure 7-8 presents a web page that was designed to be displayed in a desktop browser. Because of that, the width of this page is set to 960 pixels, which is too wide for most mobile devices. The exception is a tablet in landscape orientation, which can typically accommodate this width.

To help you understand how this page is structured, this figure also presents the HTML for the body of the page. To start, the entire content is coded within a main element. This is the element that determines the width of the page.

Within this main element is a header element that contains three additional elements. The first div element contains an image of the company's logo. This image is floated to the left of a nav element that contains a horizontal navigation menu. Then, another div element that occupies the entire width of the page is used to display another image.

Notice here that the img element for the second image doesn't include width and height attributes. That's because this is a *scalable image* whose size will change based on the width of the page. To create a scalable image, you set its max-width property to 100% so the image will expand to fill the width of the page. Then, you set its height property to "auto" so the aspect ratio of the image is maintained.

The header element is followed by two section elements and an aside element. These elements are all floated to the left, and their widths, padding, and margins are set so they fit within the width of the page.

The last element, footer, doesn't include any content. Instead, it's implemented in CSS using the background-image property. Although I could have used a scalable image here as well, the effect of the raised corners wouldn't have been maintained. Because of that, I wasn't able to use the same background image for the different page widths.

A web page in a desktop browser

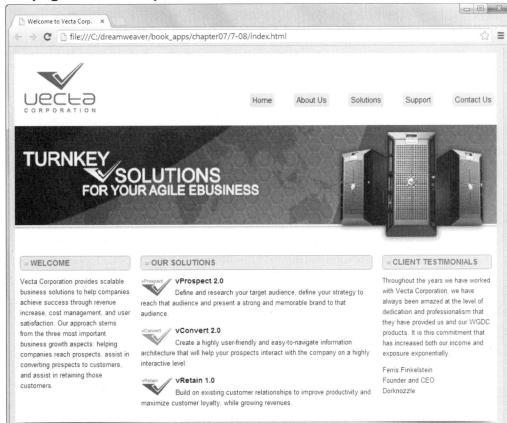

The basic structure of the HTML for the body of the page

```
<main>
  <header id="header">
    <div id="logo"><img src="images/logo.gif" width="180" height="133"
        alt="Vecta Corporation"/></div>
    <nav id="nav"> ... </nav>
    <div id="tagline"><img src="images/header.gif" alt=""/></div>
  </header>
  <section id="columnleft"> ... </section>
  <section id="columnmid">  ... </section>
  <aside id="columnright">  ... </aside>
  <footer id="footer"></footer>
</main>
```

Description

- This page includes a header with a logo that's floated to the left of a horizontal navigation menu, followed by a scalable image; two sections and an aside that are displayed in three columns; and a footer that's implemented as a background image.

- A *scalable image* scales to the size of the page. To create a scalable image, you remove its height and width attributes from the HTML, and you create a selector for the image that sets its max-width property to 100% and its height property to "auto".

Figure 7-8   A web page that uses Responsive Web Design

How to style the media query for a tablet in portrait orientation

When you finish implementing the desktop design for a web page, you can implement the media queries for the other screen widths. In figure 7-9, for example, you can see the result of the styles that I applied to the media query for a tablet in portrait orientation. Note that this page is displayed in Live view. Remember, though, that you can also display the page in a desktop browser that supports media queries and then reduce the width of the browser window to a size that's in the range specified by the media query. Then, you will see how the page transitions from the desktop design to the design shown here.

The table in this figure lists the selectors and properties that were added to this media query. As you can see, many of the properties simply change the widths of the structural elements within the page. For example, the width of the main element, the div that contains the scalable image (tagline), and the footer are reduced to 768 pixels, which is the minimum width for this media query. In addition, the width of the navigation menu is reduced so it will fit on the page without reducing the size of the logo. And the widths of the three columns are reduced so they fit on the page.

In addition to the widths, the top margin of the page is changed to zero so there's no space between the top of the page and the top of the browser window. Finally, the background image for the footer is changed to one that has the appropriate width for the page.

The web page in figure 7-8 for a tablet in portrait orientation

The selectors and properties used to implement the media query

Selector	Properties
main	width: 768px
	margin-top: 0px
#nav	width: 588px
#tagline	width: 768px
#columnleft	width: 235px
#columnmid	width: 238px
#columnright	width: 235px
#footer	width: 768px
	background-image: url('images/footer_tablet.gif')

Description

- The media query for a tablet in portrait orientation should reduce the width of the page to 768 pixels, which is the minimum width for this media query.

- The widths of any elements in the page should also be reduced so they fit within the width of the page, but the basic layout of the page can typically be maintained.

- Because the width of the background image that's used for the desktop version of this page is too wide for this media query, a smaller image must be used.

Figure 7-9   How to style the media query for a tablet in portrait orientation

How to style the media query for a smart phone in landscape orientation

Figure 7-10 shows the web page in figure 7-8 after the media query for a smart phone in landscape orientation is applied to it. The main difference here is that the content of the page is now displayed in a single column. The main selectors and properties used to implement this design are listed in the table in this figure.

First, the widths of the main element, the div that contains the scalable image (tagline), and the footer are reduced to 480 pixels, which is the minimum width for this query. In addition, the width of the div that contains the logo is set to 480 pixels so it occupies the entire width of the screen, and the image is centered in the middle of the screen. Similarly, the width of the navigation menu is reduced to 480 pixels, its height is set to 50 pixels, and it's centered on the screen.

In addition, the widths of all three columns on this page are increased to 460 pixels so the columns don't float next to each other. Although it's not shown here, the padding and margins for these columns are also changed so the total widths of the boxes are equal to the width of the page. For example, the padding-left property of the first column is set to 10 pixels initially, and no other padding or margins are set. For this media query, though, padding of 10 pixels is added to the right side of the column so the total of the padding on the right and left plus the width of the column is equal to 480 pixels.

Like the media query for a tablet in portrait orientation that you saw in the previous figure, this media query also uses a different background image for the footer. This image has a width of 480 pixels so it's the same width as the page.

The web page in figure 7-8 for a smart phone in landscape orientation

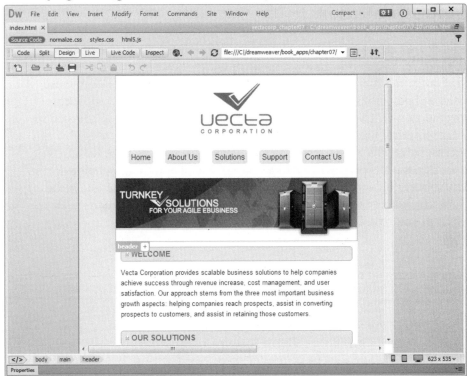

The main selectors and properties used to implement the media query

Selector	Properties
`main, #tagline`	`width: 480px`
`#logo`	`width: 480px` `text-align: center`

`#nav`	`width: 480px`
	`height: 50px`
	`text-align: center`

`#columnleft, #columnmid,` `#columnright`	`width: 460px`

`#footer`	`width: 480px`
	`background-image:`
	`    url('images/footer_mlandscape.gif')`

Description

- The media query for a smart phone in landscape orientation should reduce the width of the page to 480 pixels, which is the minimum width for this media query.

- The layout of the page is typically changed so it's displayed in a single column.

- In addition to the properties shown above, some of the margins and padding for some of the elements have been modified so they're appropriate for the screen size.

Figure 7-10   How to style the media query for a smart phone in landscape orientation

How to style the media query for a smart phone in portrait orientation

Figure 7-11 shows the web page in figure 7-8 after the media query for a smart phone in portrait orientation is applied. It also shows most of the selectors and properties that are used to implement this query. If you compare these selectors and properties to the ones shown in the previous figures, you'll see that they're similar. The main difference is that the widths have been adjusted so they're appropriate for the device width.

At this point, you have a responsive web page that transitions gracefully from the desktop all the way down to a smart phone in portrait orientation. Notice, however, that the navigation menu no longer fits on a single line in the smallest screen size. One way to fix that is to use a drop-down menu instead. You'll learn how to do that next.

The web page in figure 7-8 for a smart phone in portrait orientation

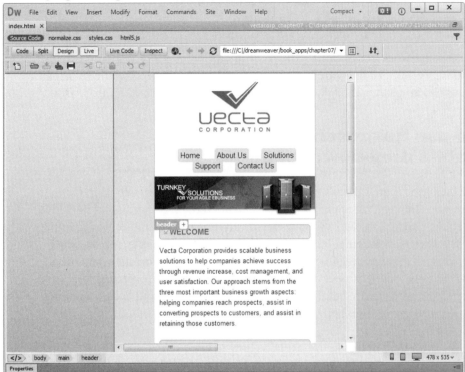

The main selectors and properties used to implement the media query

Selector	Properties
`main, #tagline`	`width: 320px`
`#logo`	`width: 320px` `text-align: center`

`#nav`	`width: 320px`
	`height: 50px`
	`text-align: center`

`#columnleft, #columnmid,` `#columnright`	`width: 300px`

`#footer`	`width: 320px`
	`background-image:`
	`    url('images/footer_mportrait.gif')`

Description

- The media query for a smart phone in portrait orientation should reduce the width of the page to 320 pixels, which is the minimum width for a smart phone.
- The layout of the page is typically changed so it's displayed in a single column.
- In addition to the properties shown above, some of the margins and columns for some of the elements have been modified.
- The navigation menu could also be improved by using a drop-down menu.

Figure 7-11   How to style the media query for a smart phone in portrait orientation

How to use third-party tools for responsive designs

Although a variety of third-party tools are available for developing responsive designs, most of them are beyond the scope of this book. Two that you can start using right away, though, are Responsive Menu and ProtoFluid.

How to use Responsive Menu to create a drop-down menu

One of the more difficult tasks of designing a responsive web page is converting a navigation menu from the standard vertical or horizontal menu into something that's usable on a mobile device. In the previous figure, for example, you saw that the horizontal menu that had displayed on a single line on larger screen sizes no longer fits on one line of a smart phone in portrait orientation. One solution to that problem would be to reduce the size of the menu items and the space between them, but that would make them difficult to access. A better solution is to convert the horizontal menu to a *drop-down menu* like the one shown in figure 7-12.

The procedure in this figure explains how to use a menu that was developed by Matt Kersley called Responsive Menu. Like most third-party Responsive Web Design tools, Responsive Menu works by using jQuery. To use it, you start by downloading its jQuery file to the root directory of your website. Next, you add two script elements to the head element for your page. The first one refers to the core jQuery library, which is required for using jQuery. In this case, the jQuery library is retrieved from a *Content Delivery Network* (*CDN*). Because of that, it doesn't have to be downloaded to your website. The second script element refers to the jQuery file for Responsive Menu that you need to download to your website.

To use Responsive Menu, you add a third script element with the jQuery code shown in this figure following the other script elements you just added. This code executes a function named mobileMenu on the element with an id of "menu" and adds the resulting drop-down menu to the nav element. For this to work, the ul element for the menu must have an id of "menu", and the menu must be defined within a nav element. Otherwise, you'll need to change the jQuery code so it's appropriate for the web page.

When this code is executed, the original navigation menu is converted to a single drop-down menu that includes all of the original menu items. In addition, an item is added at the top of the menu that instructs the user to select a page. Notice too that this code works with multi-tier menus. In this case, the Solutions menu item in the original menu included a submenu with three items. When this menu is converted, an additional item, Main, is added to the submenu. If the user selects this item, the page specified by the item in the main menu is displayed.

The navigation menu with Responsive Menu

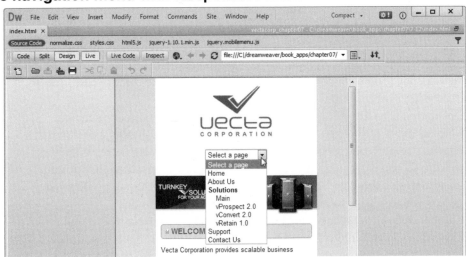

How to use the Responsive Menu plugin

1. Use your browser to navigate to http://github.com/mattkersley/Responsive-Menu. Then, right-click on the jquery.mobilemenu.js file and use the Save As command to save the file to the root directory of your website.

2. Display the HTML for the page that contains the menu, place the cursor just before the closing </head> tag, and choose Insert→Script to display the Select File dialog box. Then, enter the path to the latest version of jQuery in the File Name text box:

    http://code.jquery.com/jquery-1.10.1.min.js

3. Choose Insert→Script again and then use the Select File dialog box that's displayed to browse to the jquery.mobilemenu.js file in the root directory of your website. The script tag will be added to the code just below the jQuery script reference.

4. Add the jQuery code shown below after the two script elements you just added but before the closing </head> tag.

5. Add the unique id "menu" to the <ul> tag for the navigation menu.

jQuery code that triggers the responsive menu plugin functionality

```
<script>
    $(document).ready(function(){
        $('#menu').mobileMenu({prependTo:"nav"});
    });
</script>
```

Description

- You can use a jQuery plugin called Responsive Menu to convert a traditional navigation menu into a *drop-down menu*. By default, the menu is used for devices with screen sizes that are less than 480 pixels.

Figure 7-12   How to use Responsive Menu to create a drop-down menu

How to use ProtoFluid to test a responsive design

Because so many different devices with different screen sizes are available, it's important to test a web page that uses a responsive design on as many of those devices as possible. Although the best way to do that is to deploy the page and then display it on each device, that's not always possible. In that case, you'll need to consider other options.

One option is to use the device emulators and browser simulators that are available for many of the most popular mobile devices and browsers. To do that, you typically need to download the emulator or simulator from the manufacturer's website so you can run it on your desktop. In a few cases, though, you can run an emulator or simulator online. Before you can do that, though, you must first deploy the web page to a server so it can be accessed online.

Another option for testing a responsive web page is to use a web-based tool like ProtoFluid. ProtoFluid is a free, jQuery-based emulator that lets you view a web page in the screen sizes used by many different devices. In figure 7-13, for example, you can see how a web page will be displayed on an iPhone 5. Other options include Google Nexus, iPad, Microsoft Surface and Surface Pro, Facebook Page tab, several desktop sizes, and even Google Glass. ProtoFluid also lets you change the screen from portrait to landscape orientation, and it lets you extend the height of the frame so you can see more of the page. Although other, more complex testing tools are available, ProtoFluid is free and easy-to-use, and it provides for more of the screen sizes you need.

The ProtoFluid user interface

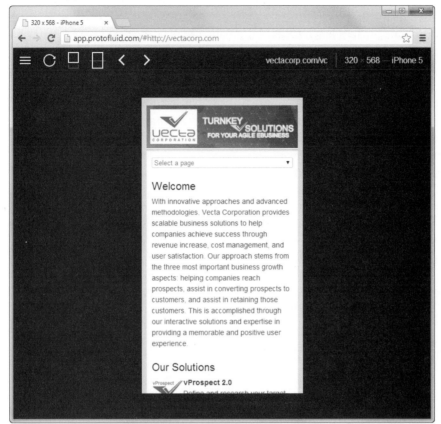

How to use ProtoFluid

- To start ProtoFluid, open a browser and navigate to http://app.protofluid.com. Then, click the URL link in the upper right to display the Location dialog box, enter the path to your website, and click Go to display the starting page in a frame.
- To cycle through the screen sizes, click the Next (**>**) and Previous (**<**) icons.
- You can also use the two icons to the left of the Previous and Next icons to extend or clip the height of the frame (▣) or to rotate the frame between portrait and landscape view (▦).

Description

- ProtoFluid is a free, easy-to-use application for quickly testing your responsive web designs in various screen sizes and for various devices.
- Before you can use ProtoFluid, you must deploy your website to a server. For more information, see chapter 13.

Figure 7-13   How to use ProtoFluid to test a responsive design

Perspective

The use of mobile devices has increased dramatically over the past few years. Because of that, it has become important to design websites that are easy to use from these devices. Although that often means more work, this can be a critical aspect of maintaining your presence in the business world.

Fortunately, the task of building a mobile website has become much easier with the advent of CSS3 media queries and Dreamweaver's support for them. No longer are mobile web pages limited to static pages containing simple paragraphs of text with small thumbnail images sprinkled throughout. Because of media queries, web developers can now build feature-rich, responsive websites that look and function the same on desktops, tablets, and smart phones.

In addition to media queries, though, you should know that responsive websites often use fluid layouts instead of the fixed layouts you've learned about so far. With fluid layouts, percents are used to specify the widths of the page and its main structural elements. Because of that, the widths increase or decrease based on the screen size. In the next chapter, you'll learn how to use Dreamweaver to develop fluid layouts that include media queries.

Terms

media query	viewport
Wireless Universal Resource File (WURFL)	scale
	breakpoint
Responsive Web Design (RWD)	scalable image
native mobile application	drop-down menu
wireframe	Content Delivery Network (CDN)

Summary

- The best way to provide web pages for mobile devices is to use CSS3 *media queries*. A media query can detect the width of the screen that's being used to display a page and then apply CSS to change the appearance of the page so it's appropriate for that size.

- Media queries are an integral part of *Responsive Web Design* (*RWD*), which refers to websites that adapt gracefully to the screen size.

- When you plan a responsive design, you should focus on making information easily accessible, making navigation menus easy to use, deciding what additional functionality to include for mobile devices, and creating a *wireframe* for each range of screen resolutions that shows the layout of the page.

- The *viewport* on a mobile device determines the content that's displayed on the screen. When you use media queries, the viewport should be set so the entire page is displayed on the screen.

- A media query is defined by a CSS3 @media selector that uses conditional expressions to determine when the styles it contains are applied.

- You can use the @Media pane of the CSS Designer to create and work with media queries.

- Dreamweaver provides several techniques for displaying a page at different screen sizes so you can see how the page will look when a media query is applied. You can also test a web page in any desktop browser that supports media queries by changing the size of the browser window.

- To create navigation menus that are easier to use on smaller mobile devices, you can use a jQuery plug-in called Responsive Menu to convert a standard menu to a *drop-down menu*.

- To quickly test a responsive design at a variety of screen sizes, you can use an online application like ProtoFluid.

Exercise 7-1   Add a media query to a web page

In this exercise, you'll add a media query to a web page so it will work for both desktop screens and mobile screens. That will give you a better idea of how media queries and responsive web design work. You will also use Responsive Menu to convert a navigation bar to a drop-down menu when the page is displayed on mobile devices.

Review the files for this exercise and add a meta element

1. Open the Exercises site, open the folder for this exercise, and open its index file.

2. Review the HTML and CSS for this page to see what you're going to be working with. Note that no media queries have been added to the CSS file. Then, switch to Live view to see that this page only works right for desktop screens.

3. With figure 7-4 as a guide, add a viewport meta element to the head element of the HTML for this page. Use the default settings, and switch to Code view to see the meta element that has been inserted into the code.

Add a media query and the styles within it

4. In Design view with figure 7-6 as a guide, add a media query with max-width set to 480 pixels.

5. With figure 7-6 as a guide, create main and footer selectors for the media query that you just created. Then, set the widths for both selectors to 320 pixels. (As you do this, be sure the media query is selected in the @Media pane. Otherwise, the settings will be added to the CSS file that's selected, but not within the media query.)

6. To view these changes in Dreamweaver, click on the phone icon in the status bar of the Document window. To view the changes in a browser, you can drag the browser's border to mimic the screen size of a phone. At this point, the display should be shaping up, but there's still a way to go.

7. Within the media query, create selectors for #logo and nav. Then, set their widths to 320 pixels, float to none, and align the text in the center of the page.

8. To hide the tagline image in the media query, create a selector for #tagline and set the display property to none.

9. To minimize the space between the logo and the navigation bar within the media query, create a selector for nav ul and set the top margin property to 0 pixels.

10. View the web page in Live view and in your browser in both full screen and mobile sizes. At this point, both views should work, but the menu items will be crowded in mobile view.

Use Responsive Menu to add a drop-down menu to the mobile view

11. To make it easier for you to use Responsive Menu to convert the navigation bar to a drop-down menu, the Responsive Menu file (jquery.mobilemenu.js) has already been added to the root directory for this exercise. Also, the script element for downloading the jQuery file from a CDN has been added to the head element.

12. Switch to Code view to display the HTML code and place the cursor in the code just before the </head> tag. Then, choose Insert→Script to display the Select File dialog box. Finally, browse to the jquery.mobilemenu.js file in the root directory for the exercises and double-click on it to add the script element to the HTML.

13. Switch back to Design view, and select the ul tag of the site's navigation bar. In the Property Inspector, set "menu" as its id property. This id will be used by the jQuery code that converts the navigation bar to a drop-down list when the width of the screen is less than 480 pixels.

14. With figure 7-12 as a guide, enter the jQuery code that converts the navigation bar to a responsive menu. Note that this code has to be exactly the same. (If needed, you can copy the code from the book app for this figure).

15. View the web page in Live view and in your browser in both full screen and mobile sizes. At this point, both views should work, but Live view for the mobile view won't be quite the same as it is in your browser.

Add media queries for other device sizes?

16. If you know how to add a media query for one device size, you should be able to add the media queries for other device sizes. So if you have the time and want the practice, try adding the media query for tablets with two columns.

How to work
with fluid layouts

In the last chapter, you learned how to use media queries to develop a responsive web design that adapts to desktop, tablet, and mobile screen sizes. As you saw in that chapter, the same media query is applied to a range of screen sizes. For example, the media query for a smart phone in landscape orientation will be applied to any screen size from 480 pixels to 767 pixels. Because of that, the media query limits the width of the page to 480 pixels.

To eliminate this problem, a responsive web design often uses a fluid layout instead of a fixed layout. When you use a fluid layout, the width of a page will expand to the percent of the screen width that you specify. In this chapter, you'll learn how you can use Dreamweaver's fluid grid layout feature to create a responsive web design that incorporates media queries with a fluid layout.

An introduction to fluid layouts

Up to this point, all of the websites you've seen in this book have used a *fixed layout* that results in pages and elements with fixed widths. Instead of using a fixed layout, though, you can create websites that use *fluid layouts*. With a fluid layout, the width of a page and its main structural elements are specified as a percent of the viewport width. That way, the page will expand or contract based on the size of the screen or, for a desktop, the size of the browser window.

Fluid layouts vs. fixed layouts

As you saw in the last chapter, creating a responsive design that uses a fixed layout can be time-consuming. First, you have to create a style sheet for the desktop design. Then, you have to add media queries for other screen sizes, and you have to add the styles to those queries that modify the desktop design.

Ordinarily, creating a responsive design that uses fluid layouts would require just as much work. As you'll see in this chapter, though, Dreamweaver provides strong visual support for developing fluid layouts that use media queries. That makes the process of creating a fluid layout easy and efficient when compared to creating a fixed layout.

So why would you choose fixed layouts over fluid layouts? As figure 8-1 shows, the main benefit of using fixed layouts is that you can get the measurements for each element directly from the wireframes. In this figure, for example, the illustration shows the exact measurements of a page and each of its major elements. Of course, you could also get other measurements from the wireframe such as margins and padding, but this should give you an idea of how this works. The bottom line is that if you want to create a page that looks exactly like the wireframe you created for it, you should use a fixed layout. Then, the layout of the page will change only when a breakpoint specified by a media query is reached.

In contrast, a page that uses a fluid layout adjusts to the size of the screen automatically. For example, the illustration in this figure indicates that the width of the page using a fluid layout is 90%. In other words, the page will fill all but 10% of the viewport. Then, the widths of the elements within the page always add up to 100%. For example, the width of the element at the top of the page that contains the logo is 25%, and the width of the element that contains the navigation menu is 75%. Note that these percents are relative to the size of the page, not the size of the viewport. So in this case, the width of the element that contains the logo is 22.5% of the viewport width (.25 x .90), and the width of the element that contains the navigation menu is 67.5% of the viewport width (.75 x .90).

A wireframe for a web page that compares fixed and fluid widths

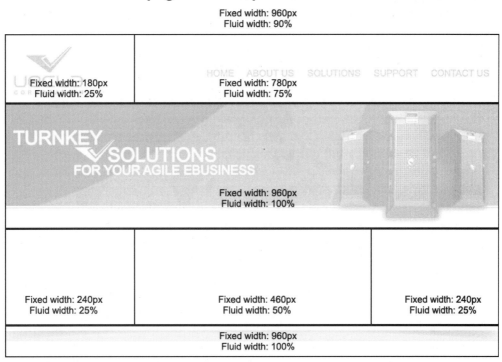

The benefits of using fixed layouts

- The measurements for each element can be taken directly from the wireframe for the page.
- The layout of a page can be adjusted for various screen sizes using media queries.
- They're typically more flexible in terms of setting margins, padding, and widths.

The benefits of using fluid layouts

- Page layouts are proportional to the size of the viewport, so they will fill the screen equally at all sizes.
- They are scalable, so when new screen sizes become available in the future, they will automatically adapt to those new sizes.
- CSS3 media queries aren't required in some cases, since relative measurements are used. In those cases, the pages are backward and cross-browser compatible.

Description

- A *fixed layout* uses absolute measurements to specify the widths of a page and its main structural elements. This guarantees that the final layout for a web page will look exactly the same as the wireframe for the page.
- A *fluid layout* uses percents to specify the widths of a page and its main structural elements. This meets the challenge of a web page adapting gracefully to all screen sizes, since the layouts are proportional rather than fixed.

Figure 8-1   Fluid layouts vs. fixed layouts

How to create a website that uses a fluid layout

Figure 8-2 shows how to create a website that uses a fluid layout. To do that, you select the Fluid Grid Layout option in the New Document dialog box. Then, options for mobile (smart phone), tablet, and desktop devices are displayed.

As you can see, the layout for each device is represented by a given number of columns. These are the grids of the fluid grid layout feature, and you'll learn more about how to use them in a minute. For now, you just need to know that you can use these columns to size and align the fluid elements on each page of the website. If you've created the wireframes for the page layouts, you can determine the number of columns you need, and you can adjust them here.

In addition to the number of columns, you can specify the total width of the page as a percent for each type of device. You can also specify the width of the margins between the columns for a mobile device. This width is specified as a percent of the column width. The values shown here are the defaults for a fluid layout, but you can change them as needed.

When you create a fluid layout, Dreamweaver automatically generates a style sheet that contains some style rules and media queries that are based on the values you entered in the New Document dialog box. Then, it displays the Save As dialog box so you can name this style sheet and save it to the root directory of the site. When the Document window is displayed, you should save the default page and then add the boilerplate.css and respond.min.js files when requested.

The boilerplate.css file is similar to the normalize.css file that you learned about in chapter 2, but it extends the function of that style sheet. The respond.min.js file is a JavaScript library that provides for responsive layouts in browsers that don't support CSS3 media queries. After these files are added, you can move them along with the main style sheet for the site to subfolders.

Before I go on, you should realize that once you create a website that uses a fluid layout, you don't add pages to it using the Blank Page option of the New Document dialog box like you would for a fixed layout. You also can't use the Fluid Grid Layout option again, because Dreamweaver will generate another style sheet if you do. Instead, you have to save an existing page with a new name. To do that, you can select the file in the Files panel and then choose File→Save As and enter a new name for the file in the dialog box that's displayed.

The New Document dialog box with Fluid Grid Layout selected

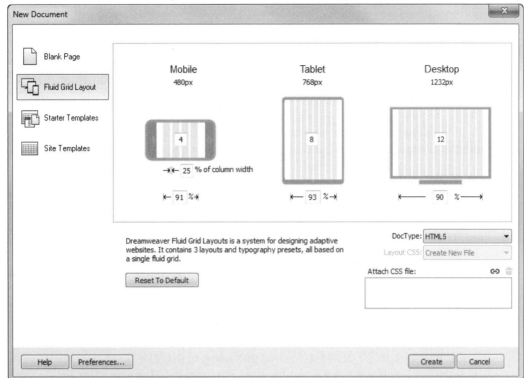

How to create a fluid layout

1. Choose File→New to display the New Document dialog box.
2. Select the Fluid Grid Layout option, make any necessary changes, and click Create to display the Save As dialog box.
3. Enter a name for the style sheet and then save it to the root directory of the site.
4. Save the page that's generated. If a dialog box is displayed indicating that the boilerplate.css and respond.min.js are required, click OK to add them.

Description

*   The boilerplate.css file extends the normalize.css file that you learned about in chapter 2. The respond.min.js file allows your website to be responsive in older browsers that don't support CSS3 media queries.
*   Dreamweaver uses columns as guides to help you size a layout appropriately for different types of devices. You can change the number of columns that are used from the New Document dialog box. You can also change the percent of the device width that's used, and you can change the space between the columns as a percent of the column width for a mobile device.

Figure 8-2   How to create a website that uses a fluid layout

How the style sheet for a fluid layout works

To help you understand how a fluid layout works, figure 8-3 presents the basic structure of the style sheet that's generated when you create a website with a fluid layout. If you review this structure, you'll see that it's different from the structure of a style sheet like the ones in the last chapter that use media queries to implement a responsive design. That's because a style sheet for a fluid layout is based on the concepts of *mobile first design*.

With mobile first design, you start by developing the mobile layout. By doing that, you're forced to focus on the most important components of the page. Then, once you complete the mobile layout, you can move on to the tablet layout and, finally, the desktop layout.

When you use mobile first design, the styles for the mobile layout are placed outside of any media queries in the style sheet. That means that these are the base styles for the page, but they can be overridden by the styles in the media queries. In this figure, for example, you can see that the style sheet includes two media queries. The styles in the first media query are applied if the screen is at least 481 pixels wide, and the styles in the second media query are applied if the screen is at least 769 pixels wide.

It's important to notice here that the conditions on the media queries specify a minimum screen width rather than a range of widths. Because of that, each media query inherits all of the styles that precede it in the style sheet. If a screen is at least 769 pixels wide, for example, it is also at least 481 pixels wide. So, after the styles outside the media queries are applied, the styles for the first media query are applied, followed by the styles for the second media query.

You should also notice in this example that the comment for the first media query indicates that it's for a tablet layout, and the comment for the second query indicates that it's for a desktop layout. However, the minimum widths used by these queries aren't the standard widths that we presented in the last chapter for tablets and desktops. For example, the media query shown here for a tablet is comparable to the media query for a smart phone in landscape orientation shown in the last chapter. Of course, you can change the minimum widths on these media queries any way you want. Until you've had a chance to experiment with the fluid grid layout feature, though, we recommend that you use the values that Dreamweaver generates.

The basic structure of the generated style sheet

```
/* Dreamweaver Fluid Grid Properties. */
   ...fluid styles go here

/* Mobile Layout: 480px and below. */
   ...mobile styles go here

/* Tablet Layout: 481px to 768px. Inherits styles from: Mobile Layout. */

@media only screen and (min-width: 481px) {
    ...tablet styles go here
}

/* Desktop Layout: 769px to a max of 1232px.  Inherits styles from: Mobile
Layout and Tablet Layout. */

@media only screen and (min-width: 769px) {
    ...desktop styles go here
}
```

Description

- The style sheet that's generated when you create a fluid layout contains some basic style rules and media queries for implementing a fluid design that's based on the concepts of *mobile first design*. With this design technique, you develop the mobile design first, followed by the designs for larger screen sizes.

- To implement a mobile first design, Dreamweaver places the styles for the mobile layout outside the media queries. These styles are applied to a screen of any size.

- The first media query is for a screen that has a minimum width of 481 pixels that's used for the tablet layout. If a screen meets this condition, the styles in this query will be applied after the styles for the mobile layout.

- The second media query is for a screen that has a minimum width of 769 pixels that's used for the desktop layout. If a screen meets this condition, the styles in this query will be applied after the styles for the mobile layout and the styles for the tablet layout.

Figure 8-3   How the style sheet for a fluid layout works

How to implement a mobile layout

Now that you understand how fluid grid layouts work and you know how to create a website that uses a fluid layout, you're ready to learn how to use the features Dreamweaver provides to implement a mobile layout.

How to use the visual aids for working with a fluid layout

Dreamweaver provides a number of visual aids that make it easy for you to work with fluid layouts. These visual aids are summarized in figure 8-4. To start, you can use the Show/Hide Fluid Grid Layout Guides toolbar button to show and hide these visual aids. Since these visual aids can help you size and align the fluid elements on a page, you'll leave them displayed most of the time.

The grid layout guides are the columns that are displayed in the Document window. The number of columns that are displayed depends on the numbers you entered in the New Document window when you created the website and the window size that's selected. To select the window size, you can use the three icons near the lower right of the Document window's status bar. Here, the Mobile Size icon is selected, which is the default when you start a fluid layout. Since I didn't change the default number of columns when I created the site, four columns are displayed.

When you create a website with a fluid layout, Dreamweaver creates a page with a single fluid element. When you select this element, or any other fluid element that you add to the page, handles appear at the left and right side of the element. You can drag these handles to size the element. Note that when you size an element, it will automatically snap to the guides. That makes it easy to create elements with the same width and to align elements on the page.

In addition to the handles, several icons appear when you select a fluid element. To start, a lock icon appears to the right of the element. You can click this icon to lock the element so it can't be modified. Later, if you need to modify the element, you can click this icon again to unlock it.

The icons that appear below, or sometimes above, a fluid element, let you hide or show the element, create a copy of the element below the selected element, or delete the element. In addition to these icons, other icons may appear as you work on a page. You'll learn about these icons later in this chapter.

The beginning of a fluid layout in Dreamweaver

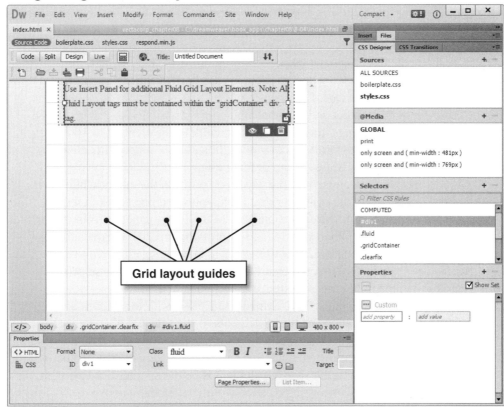

Description

- When you first create a website that uses a fluid layout, the starting page is displayed in mobile layout so you can design that layout first.
- You can use the Show/Hide Fluid Grid Layout Guides button (▦) in the Document toolbar to show and hide the visual aids for working with fluid layouts.
- The grid layout guides help you size fluid elements, since these elements always snap to the guides. To size a fluid element, you can use the handles that appear at the left and right edges of the element when it's selected.
- You can click the Lock icon (🔒) that appears to the right of a fluid element when it's selected to keep the element from being modified. Click this icon again to unlock the element.
- When you select a fluid element, three icons appear above or below it. The Show/Hide icon (⊘) lets you show or hide the element, the Duplicate icon (🗗) lets you create a copy of the element, and the Delete icon (🗑) lets you delete the element.
- You can use the icons near the right side of the Document window's status bar to display the window in mobile size (▯), tablet size (▯) or desktop size (🖳).

Figure 8-4   How to use the visual aids for working with a fluid layout

How to add and work with fluid elements

When you create a website with a fluid layout, Dreamweaver generates a page that includes two div elements. The first div is the main container for the page, and all other content must be added within this div. That includes the second div that's generated by default. You can see both of these divs in the Document window at the top of figure 8-5.

The default div element within the container div is assigned to a class named "fluid". Among other things, this class sets the width of the element to 100% so it stretches across all of the grid layout guides. In addition, it floats the element to the left so you can easily create two or more columns.

To add another fluid element to the page, you position the cursor where you want the element within the container div. Then, you select the type of element you want to insert from the Structure category of the Insert panel or from the Insert→Structure menu. When you do, an Insert dialog box like the one shown in this figure is displayed. Here, a section element is being inserted with an id of "welcome". Notice here that the Insert as Fluid Element option is selected. Because of that, the fluid class is assigned to the element as well.

After you add one or more fluid elements to a page, additional icons are displayed when you select one of those elements. If the selected element is above another fluid element, for example, an icon with a down arrow on it appears below the element. If you click this icon, the element and the one below it are swapped. Similarly, if the selected element is below another fluid element, an icon appears that lets you swap the element with the element above it.

If you select a fluid element that's below another fluid element, another icon appears in the group of icons for hiding or showing, duplicating, and deleting the element. This icon lets you float the element to the right of the element above it. This is useful for creating multi-column layouts and navigation menus for tablet and desktop layouts. You'll learn more about that later in this chapter.

A mobile web page after three fluid elements have been added

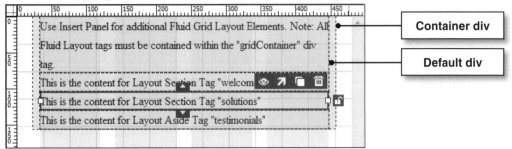

The Insert dialog box for inserting structural elements

Description

- The HTML that's generated for a page that uses a fluid layout consists of a container div element. By default, this element contains another div element with the id "div1" that contains placeholder text. Any other content you add to the page should also be added within the container div.

- The div that's added to the container div by default is assigned to the class named "fluid", which sets the width of the div to 100% of the width of the container div. Any other fluid elements you add should also be assigned to this class.

- To add a fluid element, position the cursor within the container div and then select the element from the Structure category of the Insert panel. When you do, an Insert dialog box like the one shown above is displayed. The Insert as Fluid Element option is selected by default, which is what you want.

- If you select a fluid element that's positioned above another fluid element, a Swap Down icon (▼) appears below the element. If the element is positioned below another fluid grid layout element, a Swap Up icon (▲) appears above the element. You can click these icons to move the element up and down.

- If you change the widths of two or more fluid elements so they will fit next to each other on the page, you can use the Move Up a Row icon (↗) to move an element so it floats to the right of the previous element. See figure 8-8 for more information.

Figure 8-5   How to add and work with fluid elements

How to add and format content

Figure 8-6 shows how to add content to a fluid layout and how to format that content. In general, you do that using the same techniques that you use to add and format content for a fixed layout. When you format the content for the mobile layout, though, you need to be sure that the styles are added outside the media queries. You can do that using one of two techniques.

The easiest way to format the content for a mobile layout is to just use the Selectors and Properties panes in the CSS Designer while the Mobile Size icon in the Document window's status bar is selected. You can tell if the correct layout is displayed by the number of columns that appear in the Document window. In this figure, for example, you can see that four columns are displayed. Because the icon that's selected can get out of sync with the layout that's displayed, you should always be sure that the layout is correct. If it's not, you can click the Mobile Size icon until the correct layout is displayed.

The second way to be sure that the styles you apply are added outside the media queries is to select the style sheet in the Sources pane and then select the GLOBAL option in the @Media pane. If you do that, though, you should realize that the page will be displayed in desktop layout. That's because Dreamweaver has no way of knowing what the screen size is outside of a media query. If you use this technique, then, you won't be able to see how the styles affect the mobile layout until you switch back to that layout. Because of that, this technique can be inefficient.

A mobile web page with basic content and formatting in a fluid layout

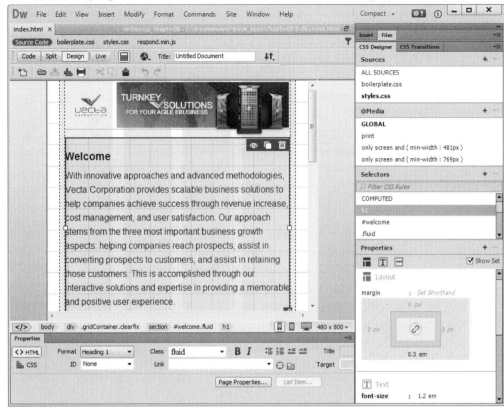

Description

- You can use the same techniques you use to add content to a fixed layout to add content to a fluid grid layout.

- If you insert an image into a fluid element, the width and height of the image aren't included in the HTML. Then, because the max-width property for images is set to 100% by default, the image will scale to the width of the element if it's at least as wide as that element.

- You can remove the div element that's added by default, or you can replace the placeholder text and modify the div as needed.

- To format a page for mobile layout, be sure that the Mobile Size icon in the Document window's status bar is selected. Then, use the Selectors and Properties panes of the CSS Designer just as you normally would. When you do, any styles you set are added outside the media queries.

Figure 8-6   How to add and format content

How to create a fluid navigation menu

In chapter 7, you learned how to use a jQuery plug-in called Responsive Menu to create a drop-down menu for a mobile layout. Another option when you use a fluid layout is to use a fluid navigation menu. Figure 8-7 shows how to create this type of menu.

To start, you add an unordered list as a fluid element so it will occupy the entire width of the container element. When you do that, you should specify an ID for the list that can be used to refer to the list in the CSS if needed. Next, you add a list item to the list that's also a fluid element. In this case, you should specify a class for the list item that can be used to refer to all the list items. Then, you replace the placeholder text for the list item with the text for the menu item, and you create a link to the file that you want to be displayed when the menu item is tapped.

After you create the first menu item, you can click the Duplicate icon for that item to create the next menu item. Then, you just need to modify the text and the path for the link. You can repeat this for each menu item you want to create. Finally, you can format the list, list items, and links any way you want.

A menu item after it's duplicated and modified

The complete navigation menu in a browser

How to create a fluid navigation menu

1. Position the cursor where you want to add the navigation menu.

2. Add an unordered list to the page as a fluid element. When you do, you should specify an ID in the Insert Unordered List dialog box.

3. Position the cursor within the unordered list, and add a list item as a fluid element. When you do, you should specify a class in the Insert List Item dialog box.

4. Replace the placeholder text for the list item with the text for the first menu item. Then, highlight the text and enter a path to the file to be displayed when the menu item is clicked in the Link text box of the Property Inspector.

5. Select the list item and then click the Duplicate icon to add a new menu item below the selected one. Then, change the text for the new item and the file that's displayed when the item is clicked.

6. Repeat step 5 for each additional menu item you want to add.

7. Set the list-style-type property of the unordered list to "none", and then format the menu item and the link any way you want.

Description

- You can use an unordered list to create a fluid navigation menu. This works much like a responsive menu, but it doesn't require jQuery.

- Because the list and list items are added as fluid elements, they will stretch across the width of a mobile screen.

Figure 8-7   How to create a fluid navigation menu

How to implement a tablet or desktop layout

Now that you know how to create a mobile layout, you're ready to learn how to modify that layout for a tablet or the desktop. To do that, you'll typically format the content in multiple columns. In addition, you may need to change some of the other formatting, and you'll want to modify the navigation menu so it's appropriate for larger screens.

How to create a multi-column layout

Dreamweaver's visual aids for working with fluid layouts make it easy to create multi-column layouts. To do that, you simply change the widths of two or more fluid elements so they will fit next to each other on the page. Then, you click the Move Up a Row icon that appears when an element is selected to float that element to the right of the element above it.

Figure 8-8 illustrates how this works. Here, you can see that one fluid element is already floated to the right of another fluid element, but the third fluid element is too wide to fit on the page next to the other elements. So, before it can be floated, its size has to be reduced. In this example, the right handle of the element is being dragged to resize the element. As it's resized, the width of the element is displayed as a percent of the total width of the container element. The number of columns that the element will occupy in the fluid grid layout is also displayed. In this case, the element will occupy four columns, which is the number of columns that remain to the right of the other elements.

Earlier in this chapter, I mentioned that each fluid element you create is assigned to the fluid class. I also mentioned that the float property of that class is set to "left". In addition, the clear property of that class is set to "both", which is why a fluid element doesn't float automatically when you reduce its size. If you want to float an element, then, you have to click the Move Up a Row icon. When you do that, the clear property of the element is set to "none".

A desktop layout as columns are created

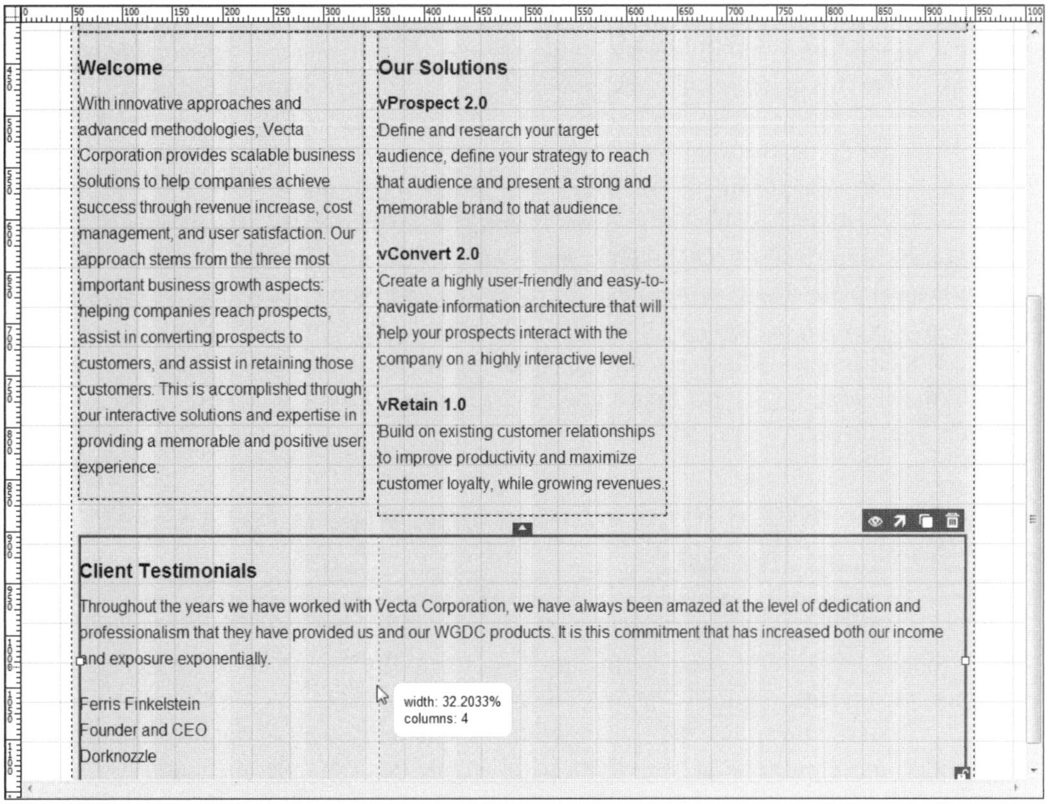

Welcome

With innovative approaches and advanced methodologies, Vecta Corporation provides scalable business solutions to help companies achieve success through revenue increase, cost management, and user satisfaction. Our approach stems from the three most important business growth aspects: helping companies reach prospects, assist in converting prospects to customers, and assist in retaining those customers. This is accomplished through our interactive solutions and expertise in providing a memorable and positive user experience.

Our Solutions

vProspect 2.0

Define and research your target audience, define your strategy to reach that audience and present a strong and memorable brand to that audience.

vConvert 2.0

Create a highly user-friendly and easy-to-navigate information architecture that will help your prospects interact with the company on a highly interactive level.

vRetain 1.0

Build on existing customer relationships to improve productivity and maximize customer loyalty, while growing revenues.

Client Testimonials

Throughout the years we have worked with Vecta Corporation, we have always been amazed at the level of dedication and professionalism that they have provided us and our WGDC products. It is this commitment that has increased both our income and exposure exponentially.

Ferris Finkelstein
Founder and CEO
Dorknozzle

width: 32.2033%
columns: 4

How to float fluid elements

1. Change the widths of the elements you want to float so they will fit next to each other. As you size a fluid element, Dreamweaver displays its width as a percent of the container width and indicates the number of columns it will occupy.

2. Select the element you want to float and then click the Move Up a Row icon (↗) to float that element to the right of the element above it. A margin is automatically added to the left of the floated element to create space between the two elements.

Description

- You can use Dreamweaver's visual aids for working with fluid layouts to create multi-column layouts by floating fluid elements.

- If you select a fluid element that has been floated to the right of another element, the Starts a New Row icon is displayed in place of the Move Up a Row icon. You can click this icon to move the element back to its position before it was floated.

Figure 8-8   How to create a multi-column layout

How to format tablet and desktop layouts

In addition to modifying the fluid elements of the tablet and desktop layouts so they're displayed in columns, you may need to change some of the other formatting for these elements or the elements they contain. For example, you may want to change some of the margins, padding, and font sizes. To do that, you need to change the styles for the appropriate media query.

To display the styles for a media query, you select the style sheet in the Sources pane of the CSS Designer and then select the media query in the @Media pane. Then, you can use the Selectors and Properties panes as you normally would to work with the styles for that query. Remember, though, that if you modify the media query for the tablet layout, those changes will be applied to the desktop layout too. So you don't need to repeat those changes for the desktop layout.

How to modify a fluid navigation menu for tablet and desktop layouts

Earlier in this chapter, you learned how to create a fluid navigation menu for a mobile layout. Once you do that, it's easy to modify the menu for tablet and desktop layouts. Figure 8-9 shows you how.

To start, you reduce the size of the first menu item so all of the menu items will fit in a single row at that width. In this figure, for example, the menu consists of four items, so each item can be two columns wide in a standard tablet layout. When you reduce the size of the first menu item, you'll notice that all of the other menu items are reduced as well. That's because the width property is set for the class you specified for the menu items when you created them.

Next, you select the second menu item and click its Move Up a Row icon. When you do, Dreamweaver floats as many menu items as it can to the right of the first menu item. Because a left margin is automatically added to each menu item, though, the last menu item may not fit. In that case, you can select the first menu item and click the icon to its left as shown here. This assigns a class to that item that sets its left margin to 0, which should make space for the last menu item to float into place.

A fluid navigation menu as it's created in tablet size

The complete navigation menu in a browser

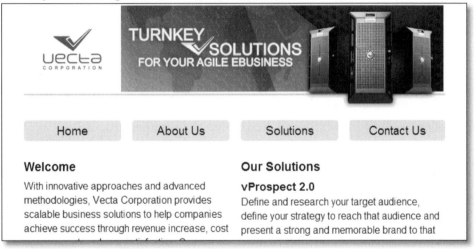

How to configure a navigation menu for tablet and desktop layouts

1. Display the web page that contains the menu in tablet layout.

2. Select the first menu item and then use the resize handle on its right side to reduce its width so all menu items can be displayed in a single row at that width. All of the other menu items will be resized automatically.

3. Select the second menu item and then click the Move Up a Row icon to float all of the menu items to the right of the first one. If the last menu item doesn't fit, select the first menu item again and then click the icon to its left to assign a class that removes the left margin from that item. Then, the last item should float into place.

4. Display the web page in desktop layout, and then repeat steps 2 and 3.

Description

- You can use the grid layout guides when resizing menu items to create a consistent width for all menu items. Then, you can float the menu items so they appear in a horizontal menu.

Figure 8-9   How to modify a fluid navigation menu for tablet and desktop layouts

Perspective

In this chapter, you learned how to use Dreamweaver's fluid grid layout feature to develop responsive websites with fluid layouts. You can use this feature to quickly develop web pages for mobile, tablet, and desktop layouts. But what happens when your pages become more complex?

In that case, you may not be able to create the page layouts you need using the fluid grid layout feature. Then, you can use the skills you learned in the previous chapter to develop your own media queries so your pages look just the way you want. If you do that, keep in mind that you can still use fluid layouts instead of fixed layouts. To do that, you just need to use percents for the widths of all main structural elements.

Terms

fixed layout	mobile first design
fluid layout	

Summary

- A page that uses a *fixed layout* will look exactly like the wireframe for the page since it uses absolute measurements for the width of the page and its main structural elements.

- A page that uses a *fluid layout* will adapt gracefully to all screens sizes since it uses percents for the width of the page and its main structural elements.

- When you create a fluid layout in Dreamweaver, you can specify the number of columns that will be used as guides in the Document window for the mobile, tablet, and desktop layouts. You can also specify the width of the screen that each page will occupy as a percent.

- The style sheet that Dreamweaver generates for a fluid layout is based on the concepts of *mobile first design*. That means that you develop the mobile layout first, followed by the tablet layout and then the desktop layout.

- The style sheet for a fluid layout includes a media query for tablet layout that inherits the styles for mobile layout. The style sheet also includes a media query for desktop layout that inherits the styles for mobile layout and the styles for tablet layout.

- Dreamweaver's visual aids for fluid layouts let you size, lock, duplicate, and delete fluid elements. They also let you swap the position of elements, create navigation menus, and create multi-column layouts.

Exercise 8-1   Modify a web page that uses the fluid grid layout

In this exercise, you'll work with a web page that uses the Fluid Grid Layout. This page was started by using the procedure in figure 8-2. At this point, the page has the headings and content for three columns, but it doesn't have navigation links at the top of the page and the columns haven't been formatted for mobile, tablet, and desktop screens.

Open and review the index page with the fluid grid layout

1. Open the Exercises site, open the folder for this exercise, and open the index.html file.

2. Review the HTML for this page to see what you're going to be working with. The first part was generated by Dreamweaver when the page was created. The second part consists of the section and aside elements that we added to the page, but the fluid class attributes were added by Dreamweaver.

3. Review the CSS for this page. Almost all of this code has been generated by Dreamweaver since this page is using the fluid grid layout. Note that this page already includes two @media selectors for pages over 480 and 768 pixels, but the media queries don't have any rules for the elements with the ids of div1, welcome, solutions, and testimonials.

4. Test the page in Live view and click the buttons at the bottom of the view to move from mobile to tablet to desktop size. Note that all three views work the same, but with wider pages. In this exercise, you're going to fix that.

Add a header image and navigation bar to the mobile design

5. In Design view for the mobile size, use the Insert panel to add an h1 heading at the top of the second section and set its text to Solutions. When the dialog box is displayed, uncheck the Insert as Fluid Element box and don't provide an id or class.

6. Still in Design view for the mobile size, click anywhere in the Dreamweaver generated text at the top of the page. Then, use the Insert panel to add the header.gif image that's in the images folder. This should insert an image that is going to scale with the page as the screen size changes. You can test that by clicking on the page size icons at the bottom of Design view. Now, delete the Dreamweaver generated text.

7. In Split view for the mobile size, move the insertion point below the header image. Then, use the Insert panel to add an unordered list. When the dialog box is displayed, be sure the Insert as Fluid Element box is checked, and provide an id named "menu" for the element.

8. Move the insertion point into the unordered list. Then, use the Insert panel to add a list item. When asked for an id or class name, choose class and name it "menu_list."

9. Replace the placeholder text for the list item with "Home". Then, select the text, and use the HTML Property Inspector to link this item to the index.html page.

10. With figure 8-7 as a guide, create three more list items by clicking on the Duplicate icon. Then, change the text for the items to "Solutions", "About Us", and "Contact Us".

11. At this point, you could use the Property Inspector to change the pages that the items link to, but you don't need to do that for this exercise.

12. Drag the handle on the right-side of the first list item box so the box covers only one column of the grid. This should resize all four list item boxes.

13. Select the second list item and click the Move Up a Row icon. This should put all of the list items on one line in mobile view. If it doesn't, you will need to select the first list item again and click the left-arrow. This will apply a class named zeroMargin_mobile. The style for this class was generated by Dreamweaver. As its name implies, it sets the left-margin property to zero.

Change the layout for tablets

14. Switch to tablet view, and note that the four list items are vertical. To convert them to a horizontal navigation bar, size the first list item so it covers two columns in the grid. Then, repeat step 13.

15. Size the two sections (Welcome and Solutions) so they will display in two side-by-side columns. To do that, drag the right borders so the sections are four grid columns wide. Then, select the second section and click the Move Up a Row icon. The Testimonials aside should still be the width of the page in tablet view.

Change the layout for desktops

16. Switch to desktop view, and note that the four list items are vertical again. To fix that, size the first list item so it covers two grid columns. Then, repeat step 13.

17. Size the two sections (Welcome and Solutions) and the aside (Testimonials) so they will display in three side-by-side columns. To do that, drag the right borders so the sections and aside are four grid columns wide. Then, use the Move Up a Row icon to move the second section and the aside to the right of the first section.

18. Test the page in a browser and adjust the size of the browser window to see how this responsive design works. Note that the three columns and the navigation bar don't align with the header image when the screen is in its widest view.

19. To fix this for the desktop display, select the media query that affects the desktop display and change the #gridContainer style rule so its maximum width is 960 pixels. Then, test the page again.

9

How to use templates and library items

As you develop a website, you'll find that many pages require some of the same elements like headers, navigation menus, and footers. The easiest way to create pages with common elements like this is to use templates. In addition, you can use library items to define individual components that can be used on more than one page. In this chapter, you'll learn how to use both templates and library items to simplify the development of a web site.

Basic skills for creating and using templates

A *template* is a master document that provides the common elements for two or more pages of a website. For instance, templates make it easy to include the headers, navigation menus, and footers that are used by those pages. In the topics that follow, you'll learn the basic skills for creating and using templates.

An introduction to templates

To understand how templates work, figure 9-1 shows the structure of a website whose pages are all based on a single template named main.dwt. Here, you can see that the pages are divided into two groups: those that are available internally (the intranet pages) and those that are available publicly (the Internet pages). Because each page is based on the same template, its basic design is the same. However, each page can contain different information.

This figure also presents four benefits of using templates. To start, they make it easy to maintain a consistent look throughout the pages of a website. In this figure, for example, each page includes the same header and navigation menu, and these elements can't be changed in the individual pages.

Templates also make the design and maintenance of a website more efficient. That's because, instead of repeating the elements that appear on each page, you can include them in the template and then base each page on that template. In addition, if you need to make a change to the design, you can do that by modifying the template rather than each page. Then, that change is applied to the *template-derived web pages*.

Templates also provide flexibility by including one or more editable regions. When you base a web page on a template, you can add content to the editable regions without affecting other areas of the page.

Finally, if you're working as part of a collaborative team, templates can improve the productivity of the members of that team. That's because templates make it possible for some members to focus on the design of the website, while others focus on the content.

Although the example in this figure shows pages that are all based on the same template, you should realize that's not always the case. For example, a different template could have been used for the internal pages of this site. Because each website is different, you'll have to decide what works best for the site you're developing.

A website whose pages are all based on a single template

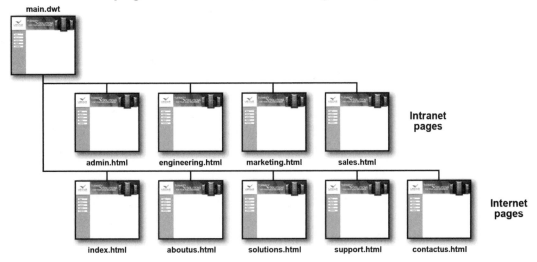

The benefits of using templates

The benefits of using templates

- **Templates provide an easy way to maintain consistency across a site.** Templates include common elements like headers and navigation menus that can't be changed in pages that are based on the template.

- **Templates provide an efficient mechanism for designing and maintaining a website.** Common elements don't have to be repeated on each page when you use templates. In addition, if you need to change the design of pages that are based on a template, you can do that by changing the template.

- **Templates include editable regions that determine the flexibility of the design.** The editable regions of a template allow changes to be made to a template-derived web page without affecting the overall design of the page.

- **Templates can enhance productivity among members of a collaborative team.** While some members of the team focus on designing and creating templates, others can focus on developing the content of pages that are based on those templates.

Description

- A Dreamweaver *template* is a master document that you can use to design the appearance and layout of two or more pages in a website.

- When you create a web page from a template, it inherits the elements of the template. This is known as a *template-derived web page*. Then, you can modify the page so it includes its own unique content. The areas that you can modify are defined by editable regions within the template.

- To make changes to the layout and appearance of the pages that are based on a template, you can simply change the template.

Figure 9-1   An introduction to templates

How to create a template

Dreamweaver provides two ways to create a template. If you've already developed a page with the basic design you want to use in the template, you can create a template from that page as described in the procedure in figure 9-2.

To start, you'll want to delete any content from the page that you don't want to include in the template. When you do that, keep in mind that you may want to delete the content from an element but keep the element so it's included in pages that are based on the template. For example, the page in this figure includes two empty elements between the navigation menu and the footer. You'll learn more about how to work with elements like these in the next figure.

Once the page contains just the content you want to include in the template, you can save the page as a template as described in this figure. Note that when you do that, a new folder named Templates is created and the template is saved in that folder. In addition, a dialog box is displayed that asks if you want to update links. Because the template is stored in a different folder than the original web page, you'll want to click Yes so the paths for any links are updated appropriately. After that, the template is displayed in the Document window so you can modify it as described in the topics that follow.

If you haven't developed any pages for your website yet, you can start by creating the template from scratch. To do that, you simply select the HTML Template option from the New Document dialog box. Then, you can add elements to the template just like you would any other document.

A web page that's being saved as a template

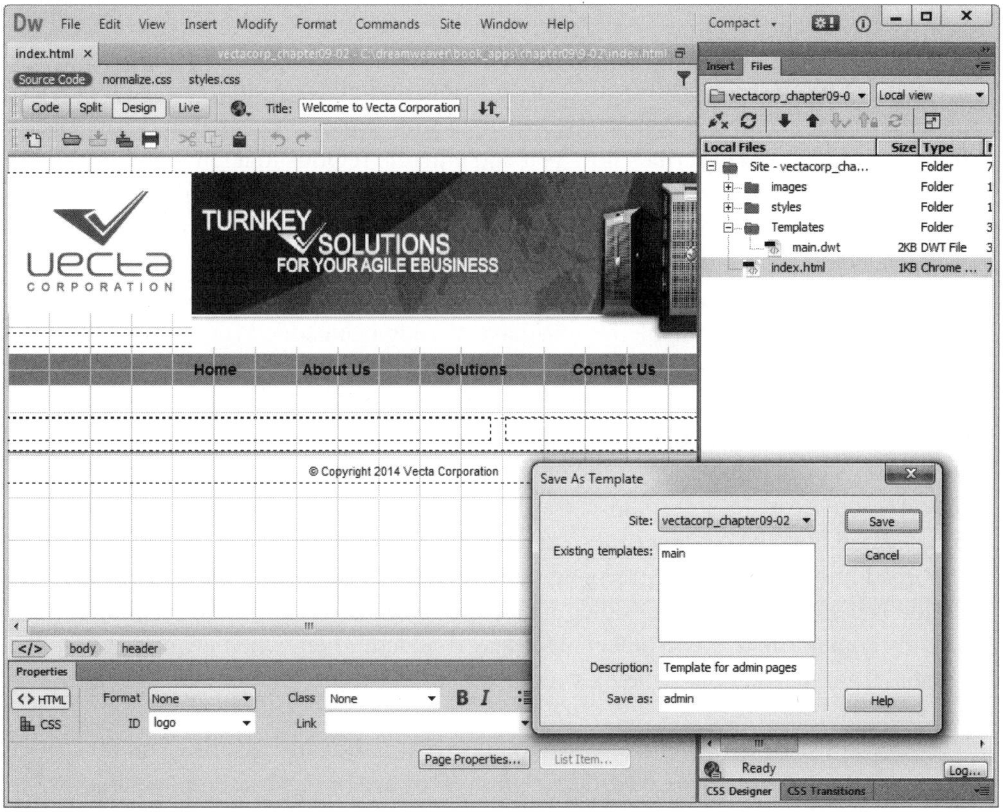

How to create a template from an existing web page

1. Display the page you want to base the template on and then delete any content from the page that you don't want to include in the template.

2. Select File→Save as Template to display the Save As Template dialog box. Enter a name and description for the template and click Save.

3. A dialog box that asks if you want to update links is displayed. Click Yes. A template with the extension .dwt (Dreamweaver template) is added to the website in a folder named Templates.

How to create a template from scratch

*   Select File→New to display the New Document dialog box. Then, display the Blank Page category, select HTML Template from the Page Type list, and click Create.

Description

*   It's easiest to create a template from a page with the layout you want to use. However, you can also create a template from scratch.

*   Because templates are stored in a separate folder, any links in the template must be updated so they point to the correct location of files like images and styles.

Figure 9-2   How to create a template

How to add editable regions to a template

In addition to the elements a template includes to define the basic design of a web page, it must include one or more editable regions. An *editable region* is an area within a template that can be modified from a page that's based on the template. Figure 9-3 describes how you add editable regions to a template.

To add an editable region, you start by placing the cursor within the element you want to be editable. If that element doesn't already exist, you can add it using standard techniques. Then, you display the New Editable Region dialog box, enter a name for the region, and click OK.

In this figure, two editable regions have already been added for the two columns. Here, the region names—Column 1 and Column 2—are displayed above the editable regions, the regions are displayed with a turquoise border around them to make them easy to identify, and placeholder text that consists of the region names is included in the regions. In most cases, you'll want to modify this text so it provides information for developers about how the region should be used and how the content of the region should look.

In addition to the two existing editable regions in this figure, another editable region is being added for the footer. Unlike the other two regions, this region already contains text, so no placeholder text is added. Then, when a web page is created from this template, the existing text is used by default, but this text can be changed if necessary.

As you work on a template, you should save it frequently just like you do your web pages. Note, however, that if you try to save or close a template that doesn't include any editable regions, an alert is displayed indicating that the template doesn't have any editable regions. For example, if you try to save a template right after you create it, an alert like this will be displayed. In most cases, you can just click OK to save the template. Just be sure to add one or more editable regions before anyone starts using the template.

A Dreamweaver template after editable regions have been added

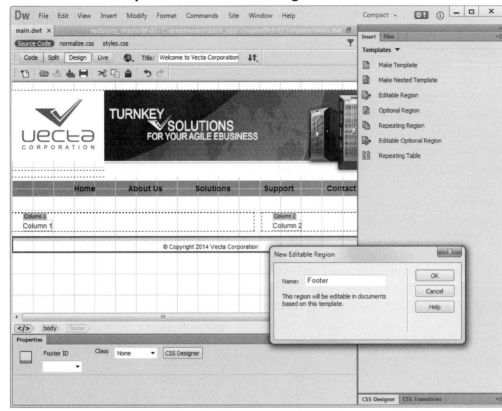

How to add an editable region to a template

1. Place your cursor within the element you want to be editable. If the element doesn't already exist, you must add it first.

2. Choose Insert→Template→Editable Region or choose Editable Region from the Templates category of the Insert panel to display the New Editable Region dialog box.

3. Enter a unique name for the region and click OK.

Description

*   An *editable region* provides an area where changes can be made to pages that are based on the template.

*   A template should include at least one editable region. If you try to save or close a template without adding any editable regions, an alert is displayed. Then, you can return to the template or you can save or close it and add editable regions later.

Figure 9-3   How to add editable regions to a template

How to base a web page on a template

After you add one or more editable regions to a template, you can create web pages that are based on that template. Figure 9-4 shows you how.

To start, you select the Site Templates category from the New Document dialog box. Then, a list of all the sites is displayed, and you can select the site that contains the template you want to use. Next, you can select the template you want to use. When you do, a preview of the template is displayed along with its description.

The Update option in this dialog box determines if the page is updated any time the template it's based on changes. It's selected by default, which is usually what you want. If you just want to use the template as the starting point for another page, though, you can remove the check mark from this option. Then, the page will be independent of the template, and you can make any changes to it that you want.

After you create a web page from a template, the page is displayed in the Document window with a yellow border around it to indicate that it's based on a template. In addition, the name of the template is displayed in the upper right of the window. Now, you can add content to the editable regions of the page using standard techniques. The editable regions will appear as shown in the previous figure, so they'll be easy to identify.

The New Document dialog box with a template selected

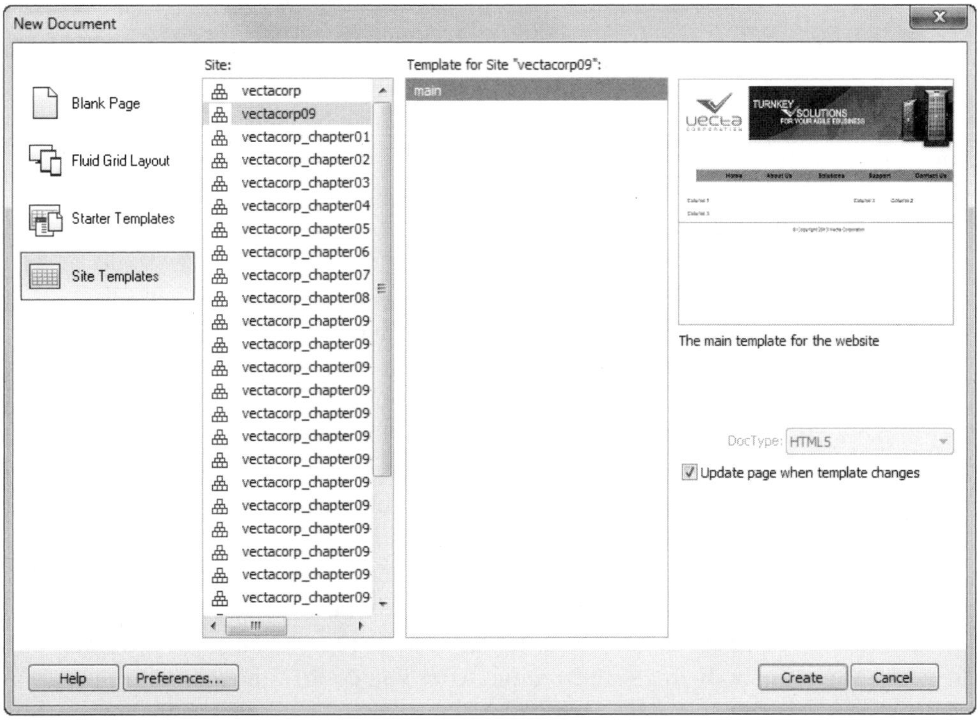

How to create a web page from an existing template

1. Select File→New to display the New Document dialog box.
2. Select the Site Templates category, select your site from the Site pane, and then select the template from the Template for Site pane.
3. Review the template preview and description to be sure you've selected the correct template, and then click Create.
4. Save the document as an HTML file, and then add the required content to the editable regions.

Description

*   The Site Templates category in the New Document dialog box contains a list of all the Dreamweaver sites, not just those that contain templates.
*   When you select a template from the New Document dialog box, a preview of the template and its description are displayed.
*   If you want the page to be updated when changes are made to the template, be sure that the Update option is selected.
*   After you create a web page from a template, it appears in the Document window with a yellow border around it. This indicates that the page is based on a template.
*   You can use the same techniques to add and work with content within the editable regions of a page that's based on a template that you would use to work with any other page.

Figure 9-4   How to base a web page on a template

How to apply a template to an existing web page

In some cases, you may need to apply a template to a page that already includes content. For example, you may start to develop a website and then realize that you should have used a template. When that happens, you have two choices. You can create a new page from the template and then copy and paste content from the original page to the new page, or you can apply the template to the original page.

Figure 9-5 shows how to apply a template to an existing web page. To do that, you choose Modify→Templates→Apply Template to Page and then select the template you want to use from the Select Template dialog box. Then, the Inconsistent Region Names dialog box is displayed. This dialog box lets you map regions of the page to editable regions of the template.

In most cases, the Inconsistent Region Names dialog box will list just two regions: Document body and Document head. Then, if either of these regions includes content that you want to assign to an editable region, you can select that region from the list and then select the editable region from the menu near the bottom of the dialog box. In this example, the content in the body of the document is being assigned to the region named Column 1. Note that you can't assign different areas of the body to different editable regions. Instead, you have to assign the entire body to a single region. After you do that, though, you can move content from one editable region to another.

If you don't want to include a region in the web page, you can select the Nowhere option for that region. Unless the document head contains an editable region, for example, you can select this option for this region. Then, the document head is excluded from the web page. Since the document head is almost always included in the template, that's usually what you want.

The Select Template dialog box

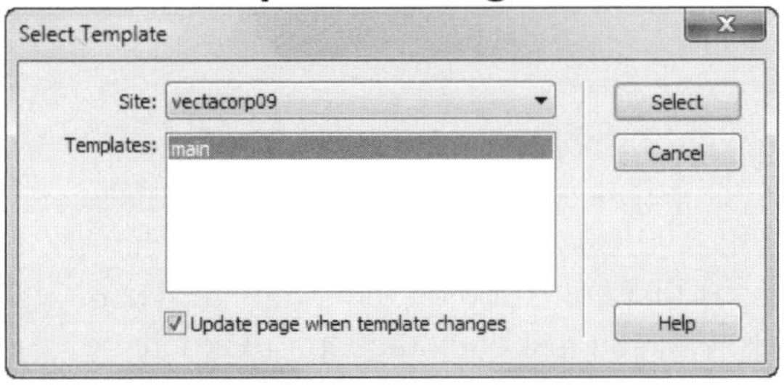

The Inconsistent Region Names dialog box

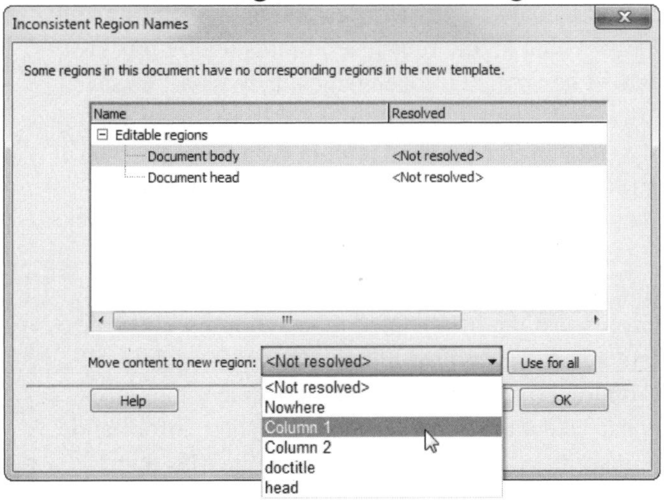

How to apply a template to an existing web page

1. Display the page that you want to apply a template to, and then choose Modify→Templates→Apply Template to Page to display the Select Template dialog box.

2. Select the template that you'd like to apply to the page and click Select. The Inconsistent Region Names dialog box is displayed.

3. To assign a region of the web page to an editable region in the template, select the region from the list and then select the editable region from the menu. You can also select the Nowhere option to remove the content of a region. Click OK to apply the template to the web page.

Description

*   If you create a page and then realize that you should have used a template, you can apply the template to the page instead of creating a new page from the template and then copying and pasting text from the original page.

*   The Inconsistent Region Names dialog box lets you map the content in specific regions of the page to editable regions of the template.

*   If you select the Nowhere option from the Inconsistent Region Names dialog box, any content in the selected region is deleted.

Figure 9-5   How to apply a template to an existing web page

How to update a site with changes made to a template

As you make changes to a template, you'll want to save it periodically so you don't lose your work. If you've created pages that are based on the template, the Update Template Files dialog box will be displayed each time you save the template. This dialog box lists all the pages that are based on the template. Then, if you're not ready to update those pages, you can just click the Don't Update button to return to the template and continue your work.

When you're ready to update the pages that are based on the template, you can click the Update button in the Update Template Files dialog box. Before you do that, though, you should be sure that all the files listed in this dialog box are closed. Although the changes will be applied to open pages, they won't be saved until those pages are explicitly saved. Then, if you don't save those pages for any reason, they'll become out of sync with the updated template. In that case, you'll have to either modify the template and then update the site again to apply the changes, or you'll have to update the web pages manually as described later in this chapter.

When the update is complete, the Update Pages dialog box is displayed. In this case, this dialog box indicates that the files named main, aboutus, and index were updated due to a template being updated. At this point, you can just click the Close button to close this dialog box. Or, if you want to display more information about the update, you can select the Show Log option. Then, information about the files that were examined, the files that were updated, the files that couldn't be updated, and the total time it took to perform the update is displayed at the bottom of the dialog box.

The Update Template Files dialog box

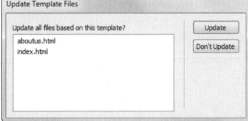

The Update Pages dialog box

How to modify and save a template

1. Close any pages that use the template, and then open the template and make any necessary changes.
2. Click the Save button or choose File→Save to display the Update Template Files dialog box.
3. Click the Update button to display the Update Pages dialog box.
4. If you'd like to see a log of the updates, click the Show Log check box.
5. Click the Close button to close the Update Pages dialog box.

Description

- You can make changes to a template just as you would any other web page.
- When you save a modified template, you can have Dreamweaver update any pages that are based on that template.
- The Update Template Files dialog box lists all of the files that are based on the template you're saving.
- The Update Pages dialog box lists the files that were updated, including the template file. To see additional information about the update, select the Show Log option.

Figure 9-6   How to update a site with changes made to a template

More skills for working with templates

So far, you've learned the skills you'll use most often when you work with templates. However, Dreamweaver provides some additional features you may want to use to develop more complex templates. You'll learn about those features now.

How to create and use optional regions

In addition to the editable regions that you've already learned about, you can add two types of optional regions to a template. A basic *optional region* is a region that can be displayed or hidden from a template-derived web page. However, the content of this region can't be changed. In contrast, the content of an *editable optional region* can be changed.

Figure 9-7 shows how to create and work with optional regions. When you add an optional region to a template, the Basic tab of the New Optional Region dialog box is displayed. Then, you enter a name for the region just like you do for any editable region. In addition, you set the Show by Default option to indicate if the region is displayed by default in template-derived web pages.

After you add an optional region, you can add content to it just as you normally would. When you're done, you should save the template and apply the changes to any template-derived pages. When you do, the Inconsistent Region Names dialog box you saw in figure 9-5 may be displayed. If it is, you can use it to map any editable regions within a web page to the new optional region. This is necessary, for example, if you replace an editable region with an optional region.

To show or hide an optional region from a template-derived web page, you use the Template Properties dialog box. This dialog box lists all the optional regions in the page. Then, you can select a region and check or uncheck the Show option to show or hide the region.

The New Optional Region dialog box

The Template Properties dialog box

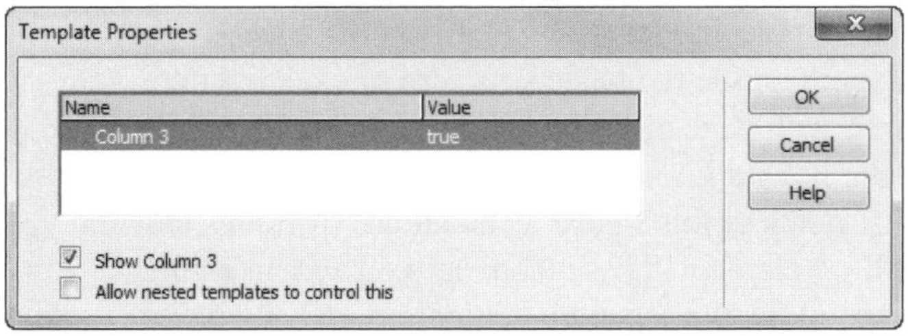

Types of optional regions

Region	Description
Optional region	A region that can be either shown or hidden from a template-derived page.
Editable optional region	An optional region whose content can be edited from a template-derived page.

How to add an optional region to a template

1. Open the template, place the cursor where you'd like the optional region to appear, and choose Insert→Template→Optional Region or Insert→Template→Editable Optional Region to display the New Optional Region dialog box.

2. Enter a name for the optional region and click OK to create it.

3. Add any content that you want to include in the region. Then, save the template and apply the changes to all template-derived pages. If the Inconsistent Region Names dialog box is displayed (see figure 9-5), you can map a previously created editable region to the optional region.

How to show or hide an optional region on a web page

1. Open a template-derived web page and select Modify→Template Properties to display the Template Properties dialog box.

2. To show an optional region, select it from the list and check the Show check box. To hide the region, uncheck the Show check box.

Description

- *Optional regions* add flexibility to template-derived web pages by allowing those regions to be shown or hidden. *Editable optional regions* can also be edited.

Figure 9-7   How to create and use optional regions

How to create and use repeating regions and repeating tables

Another type of region that you can add to a template is a repeating region. A *repeating region* consists of an element that contains one or more editable regions. Then, those regions can be repeated in a template-derived web page.

Figure 9-8 illustrates how repeating regions work. Here, the repeating region consists of an unordered list with a list item that is defined as an editable region. That list item contains an image that specifies a size but no source, along with h3 and <p> elements that contain placeholder text. Then, when a page is created from this template, the developer can see the basic structure of each list item.

In this figure, you can see a web page after the information for the first list item has been entered and a second list item has been added. To work with repeating elements like the list items in this figure, you can use the icons that are displayed above the repeating element. These icons let you add an element, delete the selected element, and move the selected element up and down.

In addition to repeating regions, you can add *repeating tables* to a template. You'll learn the basic skills for working with tables in chapter 11. For now, you just need to understand that a table consists of columns and rows, and a table can have repeating rows just like a repeating region can have repeating elements. Then, the content in the repeating rows can be modified from a web page that's created from the template.

This figure also presents the basic procedure for creating a repeating table. To do that, you use the Insert Repeating Table dialog box. Although this dialog box isn't shown here, you shouldn't have any trouble understanding how it works. For more information on setting up a table, though, please see chapter 11.

The New Repeating Region dialog box

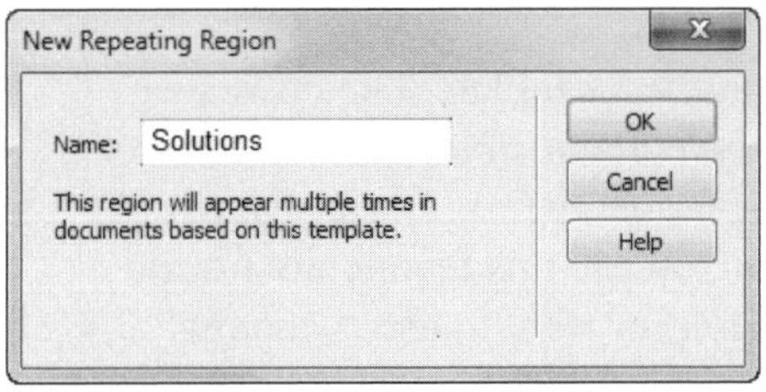

A web page with a repeating list

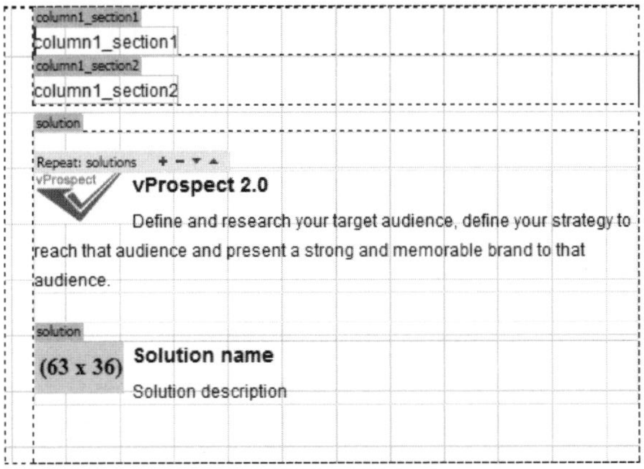

How to add a repeating region to a template

1. Select an element that contains one or more editable regions.
2. Choose Insert→Template→Repeating Region to display the New Repeating Region dialog box.
3. Enter a name for the region and click OK.

How to add a repeating table to a template

1. Place the cursor where you'd like the Repeating Table to appear in the template, and choose Insert→Template→Repeating Table to display the Insert Repeating Table dialog box.
2. Enter the information for the table, specify the rows that should be repeated, and enter a name for the region. Then, click OK.

Description

*   A *repeating region* contains one or more elements that repeat within another element. A *repeating table* contains one or more rows that repeat within the table.
*   You can add, delete, and move repeating elements in a web page that's based on the template using the **+**, **−**, **▼**, and **▲** icons that appear above the repeating elements.
*   Repeating regions and tables can be added within an optional region so you can show or hide the region.

Figure 9-8   How to create and use repeating regions and repeating tables

How to create and use editable tag attributes

In addition to letting you add editable regions to a template, Dreamweaver lets you add editable attributes to a tag. An *editable tag attribute* lets a web developer change an attribute of a tag in a non-editable region. Because most of the attributes that Dreamweaver generates when you use this feature are invalid in HTML5, you should use it sparingly. If you do ever want to use it, though, figure 9-9 shows you how.

To add an editable tag attribute to a template element, you use the first procedure in this figure. To start, you select the element and display the Editable Tag Attributes dialog box. Then, you enter the name of the attribute you want to be editable, along with a label that you will use to refer to the attribute from a template-derived web page. You must also select an attribute type, which can be Text, URL, Color, True/False, or Number, and a default value for the attribute. You should also be sure that the Make Attribute Editable option is selected so this works properly. In this example, I created an attribute that will allow the background color of the body element to be changed from its default color of white (#FFFFFF).

To change the value of an attribute from a template-derived web page, you just open the page and display the Template Properties dialog box as indicated in the second procedure in this figure. This dialog box lists any editable tag attributes that are available to the page. Then, you can select the attribute you want to change and specify a new value.

The Editable Tag Attributes dialog box

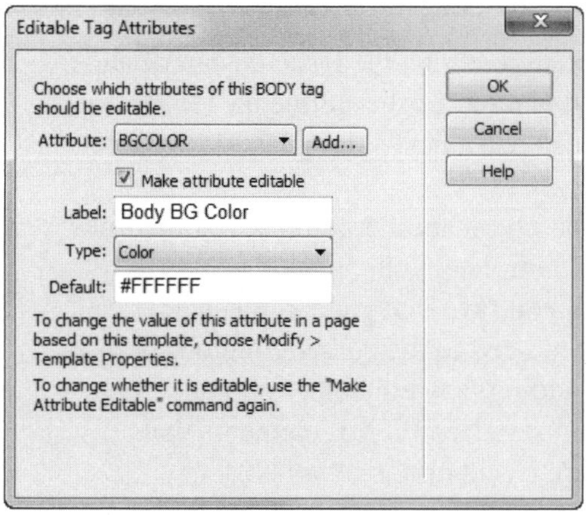

How to add an editable tag attribute to a template

1. Open the template and select the element whose attribute you want to make editable.
2. Choose Modify→Templates→Make Attribute Editable to display the Editable Tag Attributes dialog box.
3. Click the Add button to the right of the Attribute menu, and then enter the name of the attribute in the dialog box that's displayed.
4. Make sure that the Make Attribute Editable option is checked, and enter a unique name for the attribute in the Label text box.
5. Choose an option from the Type menu to indicate the type of attribute that's selected, and enter a default value for the attribute.
6. Click OK, then save the template and update the site.

How to change an attribute value from a web page

1. Open a web page that's based on the template with the editable tag attribute, and select Modify→Template Properties to display the Template Properties dialog box.
2. Select a property from the list of properties, set the value of that property, and click OK.

Description

- An *editable tag attribute* lets you change the value of a property for an element in a non-editable region of a template-derived web page.
- It's a good practice to name an editable tag attribute so it refers to both the element and the attribute that's being made editable.
- Dreamweaver generates invalid HTML5 for most of the attributes that you're likely to make editable. Because of that, you should limit your use of editable tag attributes.

Figure 9-9   How to create and use editable tag attributes

How to create and use nested templates

In most cases, you'll use a single template to define the basic design of all the pages in a website. However, you might want to further refine the design for a selected group of pages. To do that, you can use a nested template as described in figure 9-10.

A *nested template* is a template that's based on another template, sometimes called a *parent template*. To create a nested template, you create a web page that's based on the original template. Then, you save that page as a nested template. Finally, you make any changes you need to the editable regions defined by the original template. That can include adding new editable, optional, and repeating regions. It can also include adding standard HTML elements that won't be modifiable from web pages that are based on the template.

The nested template shown in this figure illustrates how this works. Here, Column 1 is an editable region that's defined in the original template. (Although you can't tell here, it's identified by an orange border.) The text at the top of this region indicates that you can add content to this region that can't be edited from web pages that are based on this template. In addition to this text, an editable region and an editable optional region have been added to the original region. Then, when a web page is based on this template, the content within these regions can be modified.

When you use nested templates, you should realize that you can only make changes to the editable regions of the parent template. Any other elements can only be changed from the parent template. If the parent template contains a header, a navigation menu, and three editable regions as shown in figure 9-3, for example, the header and navigation menu can only be changed from the parent template. If they are changed, though, the changes are applied to the nested template and then to any web pages that are based on the nested template.

A nested template after two editable regions have been added

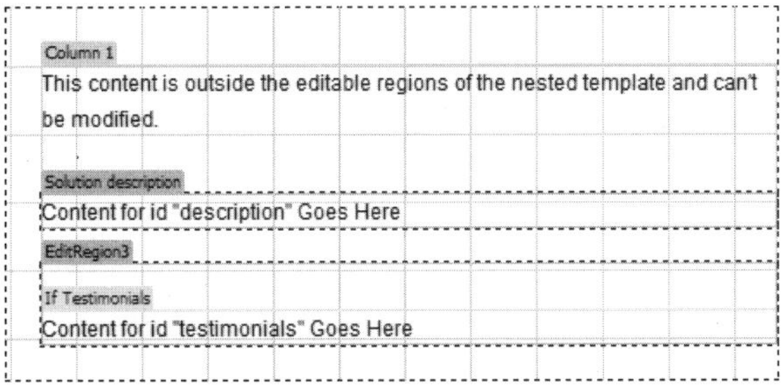

Column 1
This content is outside the editable regions of the nested template and can't be modified.

Solution description
Content for id "description" Goes Here

EditRegion3

If Testimonials
Content for id "testimonials" Goes Here

How to create a nested template

1. Create a template, add editable, optional, and repeating regions, and then save the template.

2. Create a new web page based on the template.

3. With the template-derived web page open, choose Insert→Template→Make Nested Template to display the Save As Template dialog box.

4. Enter a name and description for the nested template and click Save.

5. Make any changes needed to the editable regions of the nested template to further refine those regions.

6. Save the template.

How to create a web page from a nested template

- Follow the procedure in figure 9-4 for creating a web page from a template, but select the nested template from the New Document dialog box.

Description

- A *nested template* is a template that's based on another template. You can use nested templates to further refine the main template for a portion of a website.

- When you create a nested template, you can add new editable, optional, and repeating regions within the editable regions defined by the original template. Then, those regions can be modified in pages that are based on the nested template.

- You can also add standard HTML elements to the editable regions of the original template. Then, those elements can't be modified in pages that are based on the nested template.

Figure 9-10   How to create and use nested templates

How to use the Assets panel to work with templates

Another way to perform some of the functions for working with templates is to use the Assets panel. As chapter 12 explains, you can use this panel to manage a variety of assets for a site. Figure 9-11 describes some of the features of this panel for working with templates.

When you display the Templates category of the Assets panel, a list of all the templates defined in the site is displayed. You can use this list to display a preview of a selected template as shown here, to rename a template, and to display a template in the Document window. You can also use the Apply button at the left side of the toolbar to apply a template to the web page that's currently displayed in the Document window. And you can use the icons at the right side of the toolbar to refresh the list of templates, add a new template, open a template for editing in the Document window, and delete a template. If you delete a template, you should realize that the links to the template in any pages that are based on the template will be broken. Then, you can identify the pages with the broken links as described in chapter 4.

You can also work with templates using the options menu of the Assets panel. This figure lists three of the options that are available from this menu. You can use the Update Current Page option to apply any changes you've made to a template to a web page that's displayed in the Document window. This is useful if the web page was open when you made changes to the template and you didn't save the changes to the page. Then, you can use this option to apply the changes again.

The Update Site option displays an Update Pages dialog box similar to the one you saw in figure 9-6. In this case, though, the Look In menu gives you the option of either updating an entire site with the changes made to all the templates in that site or updating all the web pages in the current site that are based on a single template. A second menu is displayed depending on the option you choose that lets you specify a site or a template.

You can use the Copy to Site option to copy the selected template to another site. When you select this option, a submenu of the available sites is displayed so you can choose the site where you want to copy the template. Note that if the site doesn't already have a Templates folder, one will be created and the template will be placed in that folder.

The Templates category of the Assets panel

Some of the options that are available from the options menu

Option	Description
Update Current Page	Updates an open web page with the changes made to a template.
Update Site	Updates the template-based pages in a site manually after you make changes to a template. Use this option if the automated update fails for any reason.
Copy to Site	Copies the selected template to another site.

Description

- The Assets panel (Window→Assets) lets you work with a variety of *assets*, including images, scripts, templates, and library items.

- When the Templates category is selected at the left side of the panel, the templates defined in the site are listed at the bottom of the panel, and a preview of the selected template is displayed at the top of the panel.

- To rename a template, select it, click on its name, and then enter a new name. If any pages are based on the template, the Update Links dialog box is displayed asking if you want to update links to the template. Click Yes from this dialog box.

- To display a template in the Document window, double-click on it in the list.

- You can use the icons at te right side of the toolbar to refresh the list of assets, to add a new template, to display the selected template in the Document window so you can edit it, and to delete the selected template.

- You can use the Apply button at the left side of the toolbar to apply the selected template to a web page.

- You can also use the options menu in the Assets panel to work with templates. This menu includes some options that aren't available anywhere else.

Figure 9-11   How to use the Assets panel to work with templates

Other template features you should know about

In addition to the features for working with templates that you've already learned about in this chapter, Dreamweaver provides some other features you may want to know about. These features are summarized in figure 9-12. Although you probably won't use these features often, you should at least know that they're available if you every do need to use them.

For example, you can use the Detach from Template option in the Modify→Templates menu if you ever need to detach a web page from the template it's based on. Similarly, you can use the Open Attached Template option to open the template that a web page is based on. And you can use the Description option to change the description of a template.

If you review the features in this figure, you'll see that some of them refer to the markup code that Dreamweaver adds to the HTML file when it creates a template. This *template markup* is proprietary to Dreamweaver, and it's used to identify items like editable regions and attributes. Because you don't need to see this code to understand how templates work, we haven't shown it in this chapter. If you're interested, though, you can look at this generated code by displaying the HTML for a template in Code view.

Template features available in the Modify→Templates menu

Feature	Description
Detach from Template	Detaches a web page from its template.
Open Attached Template	Opens the template that a web page is based on.
Check Template Syntax	Checks the syntax of the markup code that's inserted when you create a template. Because Dreamweaver checks the syntax when you save a template, this isn't usually necessary unless you modify the code yourself and want to check it before saving the template.
Export without Markup	Lets you export a template-based web page to another site without including the template markup. This is useful if you want to use the page as a starting point for a template in another site.
Remove Template Markup	Removes any proprietary template markup from a web page. This is typically done to reduce the size of the web page just before the website goes live.
Description	Lets you change the description of a template.
New Entry After Selection	Adds a new repeating region after the currently selected repeating region. This is similar to using the **+** icon.
New Entry Before Selection	Adds a new repeating region before the currently selected repeating region.
Move Entry Up	Moves a repeating element up in a repeating region. This is similar to using the ▲ icon.
Move Entry Down	Move a repeating element down in a repeating region. This is similar to using the ▼ icon.

Template features available in the File menu

Feature	Description
Export Template Data as XML	Lets you export the editable regions of a template along with their content to an XML file so you can work with them outside of Dreamweaver. Available by choosing File→Export→Template Data as XML.
Import XML into Template	Lets you import properly formatted XML into a template as editable regions with content. Available by choosing File→Import→XML into Template.

Description

- The features described above are used infrequently, but you should at least be aware of them.
- You might want to export template data to XML so you can import into a spreadsheet program. Then, after you revise the data and export it back to XML, you can import it into a template.

Figure 9-12   Other template features you should know about

How to create and use library items

Unlike a template, which represents the overall design of a page, a *library item* is an individual component that can be used in one or more web pages or templates. They're typically used for content that's likely to change. That's because whenever you change a library item, any pages that use that item are updated automatically.

How to create a library item

Figure 9-13 shows how you create a library item. To do that, you have to add the content you want to include in the library item to a document. Then, when you create the library item, it's given a generic name and is stored in a folder named Library. You'll want to change this generic name so it reflects the content of the library item. You can do that from the Files panel or the Assets panel shown in the next figure.

Note that when you create a library item, Dreamweaver displays a warning indicating that the content may not look the same in other documents because the information in the style sheets isn't copied. Because of that, you'll want to be sure that you either use the same style sheet for other web pages that use the library item, or that you include the style rules used by the library item in the style sheets used by those web pages.

In this figure, you can see a library item that was created for a footer. (Dreamweaver identifies it as a library item by displaying it against a yellow background.) Because this footer includes a copyright year, it's a perfect candidate for a library item. Then, any time the year changes, the change can be made to the library item and it will be reflected in any web pages that use that item.

After you create a library item, you can add it to other pages or templates. To do that, you use the Assets panel as described in the next figure. This panel is opened by default when you create a library item.

A footer that's saved as a library item

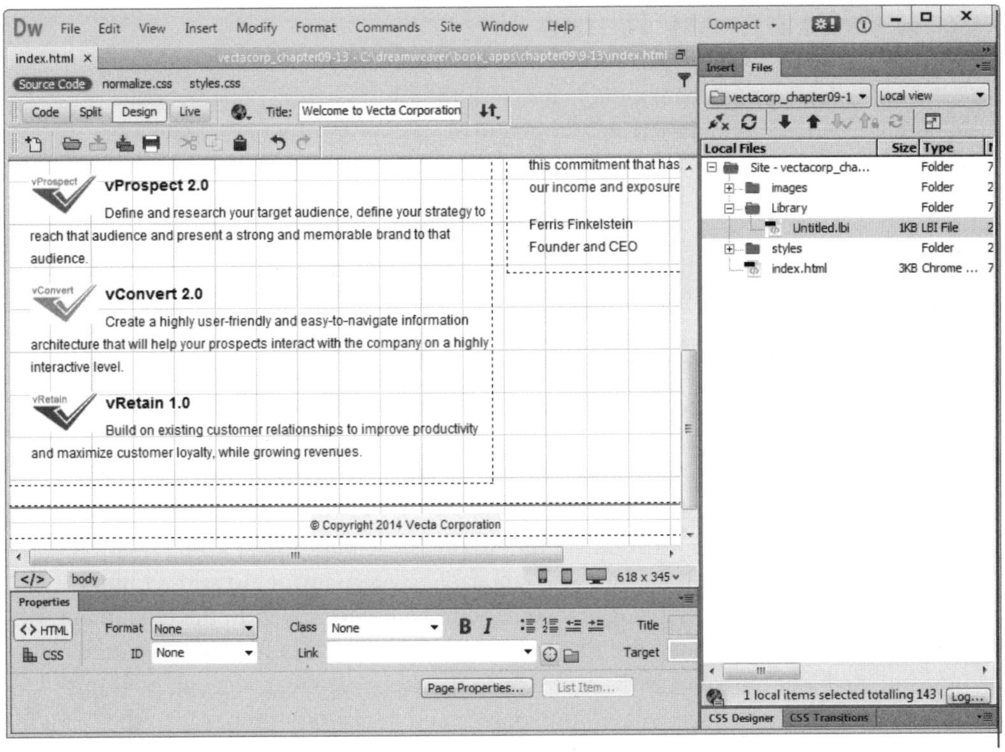

How to create a library item

- Open the document you want to add the library item to, and select the content you want to include in the library item.
- Choose Modify→Library→Add Object to Library. A warning is displayed indicating that the selection may not look the same in other documents because the information in the style sheets isn't copied with it. Click OK.
- A library item with the default name Untitled.lbi (library item) is added to the website in a folder named Library, and the Library category of the Assets panel is displayed.

Description

- A *library item* contains HTML code that can be used in one or more pages of a website.
- Library items are stored as separate files, and each page that uses a library item contains a link to that item. That way, if you make a change to a library item, the change is reflected in every page that uses that item.
- You can create a library item from any element in the body section of a document. Once you do that, the element will be displayed with a yellow background to identify it as a library item.
- You can also use library items with templates. See figure 9-15 for details.

Figure 9-13   How to create a library item

How to use the Assets panel
to work with library items

Figure 9-14 shows the Assets panel with the Library category selected. When this panel is first displayed, the name of the library item is selected as shown here so you can enter a name that reflects the content of the library item. In addition, a preview of the library item is displayed in the top pane.

You can use the Assets panel to perform a variety of functions. For example, you can use the icons at the right side of the toolbar to refresh the list of library items, add a new library item, edit the selected library item, and delete the selected library item. You use these icons similarly to the way you use them to work with templates. The main difference is that before you can add a new library item, you have to open a web page and select the content you want to include in the item.

You can also use the options that are available from the options menu to work with library items. Again, these options work like the options you use to work with templates. For more information, please see figure 9-11.

In addition to these functions, you can use the Assets panel to add a library item to a web page. To do that, the web page must be displayed in the Document window. Then, you can drag the library item you want to add from the list of items to the location you want to add it to in the web page. Or, you can position the cursor in the web page where you want to add the library item, select the item in the Assets panel, and click the Insert button.

The Library category of the Assets panel as a library item is renamed

Description

- To display a preview of a library item in the top pane of the Assets panel (Window→Assets), select it in the bottom pane.

- To rename a library item, select it, click its name, and then enter the new name. When the Update Files dialog box is displayed, click Update to update the links in all web pages that use the library item.

- To insert a library item into a web page, drag the item from the list in the Assets panel onto the page where you want the library item to appear. Or, position the cursor in the web page, select the library item from the list of items in the Assets panel, and click the Insert button.

- You can use the icons at the right side of the toolbar to refresh the list of assets, to add a new library item, to display the selected library item in the Document window so you can edit it, and to delete the selected library item.

- Before you add a new library item from the Assets panel, you must open a web page that contains the content you want it to include and then select that content.

- When you modify and then save a library item, the Update Library Items dialog box is displayed with a list of the web pages that are linked to the library item. Click Update from this dialog box and then click Close from the Update Pages dialog box that's displayed. This works just like it does for templates.

- You can also display, rename, and delete library items from the Files panel.

Note

- Although you might think that you could insert a library item by dragging it to a web page from the Files panel, that doesn't work. Instead, this adds a hyperlink to the page with the name of the library item and its URL.

Figure 9-14   How to use the Assets panel to work with library items

How to use library items with templates

Library items are particularly useful if you need to give developers a choice between two or more items. To do that, you can add the items to optional regions within a template. Then, when a web page is created from that template, the developer can decide what region to display and what regions to hide. Figure 9-15 illustrates how this works. Note that this is the same website that you saw back in figure 9-1 that contains both private and public web pages.

Here, the template contains two optional regions, and each optional region contains a different navigation menu that's implemented as a library item. Because the Show option was selected for both of these optional regions when they were created, both of the library items will be displayed by default when a web page is created from the template. Then, the developer can hide the item that won't be used. In this figure, for example, you can see that the second library item has been hidden in all the private web pages, and the first library item has been hidden in all the public web pages. This is just one more way to add flexibility to your websites.

A website with a template that uses library items to provide for two different navigation menus

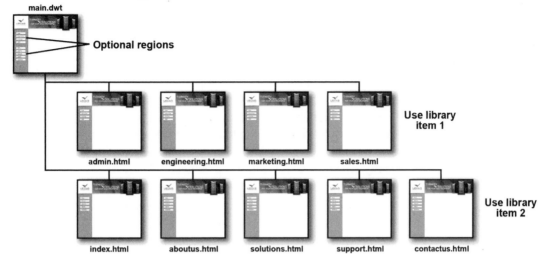

Description

- You can create library items in templates using the same technique you use to create them in web pages. Then, if the library item is placed in an editable region, it can be changed from pages that are based on the template. Otherwise, it can't be changed.

- If you place a library item in an optional region, it can be displayed or hidden from a web page that's based on the template. This is useful if a web page will use one of two or more library items. Then, one can be displayed and the others can be hidden.

- You can also use a library item with template-derived web pages. To do that, the template must contain an editable region where the library item can be inserted.

Figure 9-15   How to use library items with templates

Perspective

In this chapter, you learned that Dreamweaver templates are a powerful feature that lets you create a design for your website that includes elements that are common to all pages. When you create web pages from a template, you can be sure that the design for each page is consistent. In addition, if you ever need to make a change to the design, you can change the template and all the pages that use that template are updated automatically.

Library items are similar to templates, but they're individual components that you can add to the pages of a website. Like templates, they can help make a website more consistent. In addition, any web pages that use a library item are updated automatically when the library item is changed.

Terms

template	repeating table
template-derived web page	editable tag attribute
editable region	nested template
optional region	parent template
editable optional region	template markup
repeating region	library item

Summary

- *Templates* provide a way to create a master design that defines the appearance and layout for the pages of a website. Templates ensure consistency throughout a website.

- A *template-derived web page* is a page that's based on a template. These pages are linked to the template so if any changes are made to the template, those changes are applied to the template-derived pages.

- A template can include content that can't be changed from pages that are created from the template. A template must also contain at least one *editable region* that can be changed from template-derived pages.

- If a template contains an *optional region*, the developer of a template-derived page can show or hide that region. In addition, the developer of a template-derived page can make changes to an *editable optional region*.

- A *repeating region* is an element such as a list that contains one or more repeating elements such as list items. Repeating elements can be added, deleted, and repositioned from a template-derived page.

- A *repeating table* is an HTML table that contains one or more repeating rows.

- An *editable tag attribute* is an attribute within the tag of a non-editable region of a template that can be changed from a template-derived page.

- A *nested template* is a template that exists within the editable region of another template, called a *parent template*.

- Dreamweaver uses *template markup* to identify the various components of a template such as editable regions and editable tag attributes.

- *Library items* provide a way of creating components that can be reused in a site. They are typically used for items that are expected to change. When a change is made to a library item, all the web pages that use that item are updated.

Exercise 9-1   Create and use templates and library items

In this exercise, you'll create a template from an existing web page, add editable regions and a library item, and make changes to the template. The template will consist of the header, the navigation bar, and the footer that's shown in this web page:

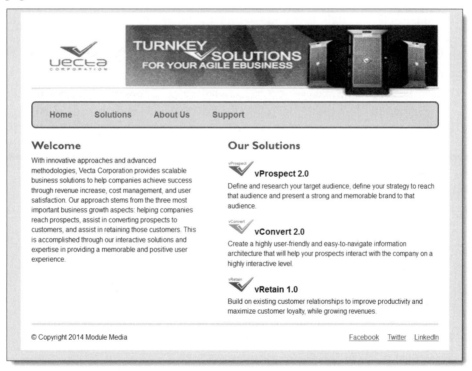

Open and review folders and files for this exercise

1. Open the Exercises website, open the folder for this exercise, and note that it contains three html files with _old attached to their names. These are the index, solutions, and aboutus pages that were started without a template, and you're going to rebuild them with a template.

2. Open the index_old.html file, and review its HTML and CSS. This is the page that you will use for creating the template.

Create a template from the index_old.html page

3. To create a template from the index_old page, start by deleting the aside and template elements because they shouldn't be part of the template. Everything else should be.

4. Choose File→Save as Template…, name the template "master", and describe it as "Master Site Template". When prompted to update the links on this page, click OK. This template will be saved as master.dwt in a Templates folder under the Exercises folder, and it will become the open document in the Document window.

5. In Code view, you can see that two editable regions were automatically added to the head element.

6. To create an editable region in the body element of the master.dwt file, put the cursor between the header and footer elements. Then, choose the Insert→Template→Editable Region command, and name this region Main Editable.

7. In Split or Design view, select the paragraph element that contains the copyright notice in the footer element. Then, choose Insert→Template→Editable Region, and name this region Copyright Editable.

8. In Design view, select just the text for the copyright notice, choose Modify→Library→Add Object to Library, which will open the Assets panel, name the file "copyright", and close the Assets panel. This should create a library file named copyright.lbi in a Library folder at the same level as the Template folder. This should also add the library item to the template.

9. Save and close the template.

Create three pages from this template

10. To create a page from the template you just created, choose File→New, select Site Templates in the dialog box that follows, select the template you just created under the Exercises site, and click the Create button. Then, save the new file as index.html in the ex09-01 folder.

11. Open the index_old.html file, copy its aside and section elements in Code view, and paste them into the main editable region in the index.html file in Code view. Then, switch to Live view for the index.html file to see that the copy has been integrated with the template and formatted by the style sheet specified in the template.

12. Repeat steps 10 and 11 for a page named solutions.html, and copy the content from the solutions_old.html file into its main editable region.

13. Repeat steps 10 and 11 for a new page named aboutus.html, and copy the content from the aboutus_old.html file into it. Then, to apply custom formatting to that page, drag the aboutus.css style sheet in the styles folder to the second editable region in the head element for the file. That should attach this style sheet.

14. Test all three pages in your browser to make sure that everything looks and works right.

Change the template and update the pages built from it

15. Close all of the html files that are open. This is necessary if you want to update these files when you update the template without having to save each open file that's built from the template.

16. Open the master.dwt file in the Exercises folder. Then, in Code view, add a fifth list item and link to the navigation bar. The text for the link should be "Forum" and the href attribute should be "forum.html" even though that file doesn't exist. Then, save the template and approve the updates to the pages that are built from this template.

17. Open and view the index, solutions, and aboutus files to make sure this worked.

18. Open the index.html file, select Modify→Template Properties, and uncheck the "Show Social Editable" box. Then, note that the social links aren't displayed on the page. That shows how an optional region can be used.

Change the library item

19. Open the copyright.lbi file in the Library folder of the Exercises site. Then, update the date in the file from "2014" to "2015", save this file, and click on Update to update the template and the three pages created from it.

20. Check the updated pages to make sure this worked. Then, do a final test in your browser to make sure everything is working right.

10

How to add audio, video, and animations to a website

In this chapter, you'll learn how to add audio and video to your website. As you will see, Dreamweaver provides for audio and video using the new HTML5 audio and video elements. You'll also learn how to use Flash animations and the successor to Flash animations, Edge Animate compositions. Finally, you'll learn how to use HTML5 Canvas to draw graphics programmatically using JavaScript.

An introduction to media on the web

Before I show you how to include media files in a web page, you need to be familiar with the various media types and codes that are used for video and audio. You also need to know what media types and encoders work with the browsers that are used today.

Common media types for video and audio

When most of us think about *media types*, a short list comes to mind: MPEG, AVI, MP3, and maybe even AAC. The reality, though, is that there are dozens of media types for both video and audio. Some of them are summarized in figure 10-1.

These media types are nothing more than containers of information that are used by *media players* to play the content that the types contain. For example, an MPEG file contains a video track, which is what the users see, and one or more audio tracks, which is what the users hear. To keep the video coordinated with the audio, a media type can also contain markers that help the audio sync up with the video. In addition, a media type can contain metadata, such as the title of the video, any still imagery related to the video (cover art), the length of the video, and digital rights management information.

For some media types, a browser will require a *plugin* that plays that type. These plugins are generally released by the player manufacturers. For instance, Apple provides a QuickTime plugin, Windows provides a Windows Media Player plugin, and Adobe provides a Flash Player plugin. If a browser supports a media type without requiring a plugin, you can say that the browser "natively" supports that media type.

Common media types for video

Type	Description
MPEG-4	Commonly found with either an .mp4 or .m4v extension. The MPEG-4 media type is loosely based on Apple's QuickTime (.mov) media type. Although movie trailers on Apple's website are still delivered in the older QuickTime .mov media type, iTunes uses the newer MPEG-4 media type for delivering video.
Flash Video	Commonly found with either the .flv or .f4v extension. Flash Video, developed by Adobe, is currently the most common media type for delivering video on the web. At this writing, YouTube delivers its video using this format.
Ogg	Usually found with the .ogv extension. Ogg is an open-source, open-standard media type currently supported natively by Firefox 3.5 and above, Chrome 4 and above, and Opera 10.5 and above. The video stream of an Ogg media type is technically referred to as Theora.
WebM	A relatively new file format that is usually found with the .webm extension. WebM is currently supported natively by Chrome, Firefox, and Opera, and Adobe has recently announced that future releases of Flash will also support WebM video.
ASF	The Advanced Systems Format is commonly found with the .asf extension. ASF is a Microsoft proprietary media type and is specifically meant for streaming media. The video stream of an ASF media type is typically Windows Media Video (WMV).
AVI	Audio Video Interleave is commonly found with the .avi extension and is another Microsoft proprietary media type. It is one of the oldest media types and was introduced in 1992 when computer-based video was largely a hope for the future.

Common media types for audio

Type	Description
MP3	MPEG-1 Audio Layer 3, which is commonly known as MP3, is one of the most widely-used media types for audio.
AAC	Advanced Audio Coding or AAC is the format that Apple uses to deliver audio for iTunes. AAC was originally designed to deliver better quality audio than MP3.
Ogg	Usually found with the .ogg extension. Ogg is an open-source, open-standard media type currently supported natively by Firefox 3.5+, Chrome 4+, and Opera 10.5+. The audio stream of an ogg media type is technically referred to as Vorbis.
WMA	Windows Media Audio or WMA are usually found with the .wma extension. The audio stream of an ASF media type is typically Windows Media Audio.

Description

- A *media type* is a container for several components, including an encoded video track, one or more encoded audio tracks, and metadata.
- To play a media type, a browser requires a *media player* for that type.
- For specific media players, browsers often require special *plugins*. These plugins are generally released by the player manufacturers, and include QuickTime, Windows Media Player, and Adobe Flash Player.
- To say that a browser "natively" supports a media type means that the browser doesn't require a plugin for it.

Figure 10-1   Common media types for video and audio

Video codecs

Within a media type, a video is encoded with a specific type of code. Although there are dozens of different codes used for video, figure 10-2 summarizes the three that are most noteworthy. H.264 is usually mentioned in the same breath as MPEG since it was developed by MPEG in 1993. Theora is the video stream portion of the Ogg media type. And VP9 was developed by Google, who acquired its predecessor, VP8, in 2010 from On2 Technologies.

When a media player plays a media type, it has to do the five tasks that are summarized in this figure. Of these tasks, it's the decoding of the video and audio tracks that is the most difficult.

To decode, media players use software components called *codecs*. This name is derived from COmpressor/DECompressor, because video and audio are compressed when they're encoded and decompressed when they're decoded. You can also think of codec as COder/DECoder. Once the codecs have been used to "crack the codes," the media players display a series of images (also known as frames) on the screen.

Video codecs

Codec	Description
H.264	Developed by the MPEG group in 1993. The goal of the Movie Picture Experts Group (MPEG) was to provide a single "all inclusive" codec that would support low bandwidth, low-CPU devices (think mobile phones); and high bandwidth, high-CPU devices (think your computer); and everything in between.
Theora	Theora is a royalty free codec which can produce video streams that can be embedded in virtually any format. Theora is typically mentioned in the same breath as Ogg.
VP9	VP9 is an open-source, royalty-free encoder. It is a successor to VP8, which was originally developed by On2 Technologies and purchased by Google in May 2010.

What a media player does when it plays a video

- Determines the media type that the user is attempting to play.
- Determines whether it has the capability of decoding its video and audio streams.
- Decodes the video and displays it on the screen.
- Decodes the audio and sends it to the speakers.
- Interprets any metadata and makes it available.

Description

- A *codec* (derived from COmpressor/DECompressor or COder/DECoder) is a software component that is used is to code and decode the algorithms that are used for a media type.
- A codec also compresses the code so it will load faster in a browser and decompresses the code before it is played.
- Although there are dozens of codecs for video, the three most common are H.264, Theora, and VP9.

Figure 10-2   Video codecs

Audio codecs

Like video, dozens of audio codecs are available. In fact, it's safe to say that there are many more audio codecs than there are video codecs. That's because there's a multi-billion dollar industry that revolves around the delivery of audio streams via MP3 players as well as tablets and smart phones. Figure 10-3 summarizes a few of these audio codecs.

An audio codec is used to decode the audio portion of an audio or video file, convert it to audible waveforms, and send it to the speakers of a system, which convert those waveforms into sound. The biggest difference between video and audio is that audio can store channels that let the sound be delivered to different speakers at the same time.

Most audio files contain two channels, which represent the left and right speakers, but it's common for video media types to have several channels of audio that represent left, right, and center speakers plus speakers in the rear. This is commonly referred to as "surround sound."

Unlike video, where the codecs have different names than their media types, audio codecs often have names that are the same as or similar to their media types. MP3 is one example, which can be played on a dedicated MP3 player or as part of a video track. Another example is AAC, which was adopted by Apple and is currently supported by all of Apple's products, including iTunes, iPod, iPad, and iPhone. Similarly, Vorbis is commonly used for the Ogg media types (both audio and video), and Windows Media Audio (WMA) is commonly used for Microsoft's WMA and ASF media types.

Audio codecs

Codec	Description
AAC	AAC is one of the most common media types and is also the encoding standard for the media type. It is currently used on all Apple products, as well as Nintendo's DSi and Wii, Sony's Playstation 3 and Portable, as well as several mobile devices including phones powered by Sony Ericsson, Nokia, Android, and WebOS.
FLAC	Free Lossless Audio Codec (FLAC) is a free, open-source codec that has seen its popularity increase over the years due in large part to its high compression ratio. Audio files that use FLAC can have their file sizes reduced by up to 60%.
MP3	MPEG-1 Audio Layer 3, commonly known as MP3, is one of the most widely-used media types for audio.
Vorbis	Typically packaged within the .ogg extension and commonly referred to as Ogg Vorbis. Vorbis is a free, open source format that is supported natively by most popular Linux installations as well as the newer editions of Chrome, Firefox, and Opera browsers.
WMA	Windows Media Audio (WMA) is usually found with the .wma extension. The audio stream of an ASF media type is typically Windows Media Audio.

Description

- Although there are more than a dozen codecs for audio, the five most common are those in the table above.

- When you watch a video or listen to audio in your browser, your media player is responsible for interpreting the media type. It is also responsible for decoding the audio so it can direct the sound to the speakers on your device.

- Unlike video codecs, audio codecs often have the same name as their media type or a similar name.

Figure 10-3   Audio codecs

Audio and video support in current browsers

One of the problems when adding audio or video to a website is that there isn't a single combination of codecs that will work on all browsers. This is shown by the first two tables in figure 10-4.

One solution to this problem is to encode your media in the Flash file format (SWF) and rely on the browser's Flash Player plugin to play your media. Although this has worked well for many years, it presents three problems. First, you're forcing your users to rely on a plugin to view your media. Although it's true that 97% of desktop users have the Flash plugin installed, this plugin consumes resources and that still leaves 3% who won't be able to play your media. Second, what about the ever-expanding use of mobile devices such as tablets and smart phones that don't support Flash? That segment, which currently represents 30 to 40% of Internet traffic, is also left out. Third, the Flash player is unstable in some browsers so it sometimes crashes, which is one of the biggest reasons why many smart phones and tablets don't support Flash.

This is where HTML5 and its new video and audio elements come in. To use them, though, you need to encode your media into multiple formats so they can be run on all browsers. You'll learn how to do that next.

Audio codec support in current browsers

Browser	Ogg Vorbis	MP3	AAC
Chrome	5.0+	10.0+	6.0+
IE	-	9.0+	9.0+ (with VP9 codec)
Firefox	3.6+	-	-
Safari	with QuickTime installed	3.0+	5.0+
Opera	10.5+	-	-

Video codec support in current browsers

Browser	Ogg Theora	H.264	WebM
Chrome	5.0+	10.0+	6.0+
IE	-	9.0+	9.0+ (with VP9 codec)
Firefox	3.5+	-	4.0+
Safari	-	3.0+	-
Opera	10.5+	-	10.6+

Description

- The most common audio codecs are Ogg Vorbis, MP3, and AAC. Chrome has the best audio codec support of the five browsers above.

- The most common video codecs are Ogg Theora, H.264, and WebM. Again, Chrome has the best support of the five browsers above.

- Mobile devices such as Apple's iPhone and Google's Android support H.264 video and AAC audio within the MPEG media type.

- One of the problems when adding audio or video to a website is that there isn't a single combination of codecs that will work on all browsers. To support all browsers, then, you need to encode your media into more than one media type.

Figure 10-4   Audio and video support in current browsers

How to encode media

Figure 10-5 shows how easy it is to use software products that can convert a media file from one type to another, like MPEG/AAC to Ogg Theora/Vorbis. A product like this can also convert a raw, uncompressed video or audio file that you've recently captured on a digital video camera into a compressed format that targets one of the codecs.

Although many free and commercial software packages are available for encoding media types, one free product that I like is Miro Converter (www.mirovideoconverter.com). It lets you convert a file from just about any media type into the types needed for web applications. Miro Converter also supports audio-only formats including MP3 and Ogg as well as formats for mobile devices.

To use Miro Converter, you just drag the media file that you'd like to convert into the file pane, select the media type/codec that you'd like to target from the Format drop-down menu, and click Convert. Depending on the size of your file, the conversion process will take anywhere from seconds to minutes to hours. When the conversion process is finished, your new media file will be in the same folder as the original file.

Other converters that warrant mention are: Apple's iTunes (for audio) and QuickTime Pro (for just about anything); Microsoft's Windows Media Encoder; Adobe's Media Encoder (great for Flash); Firefogg, which is a handy add-in to Firefox and specifically supports the Ogg file format; FFmpeg, which is great for batch encoding; and Handbrake, which is ideally suited for mobile device output and comes as a graphical user interface or command line install.

Miro Converter as it's about to convert a .mp4 file to WebM Video

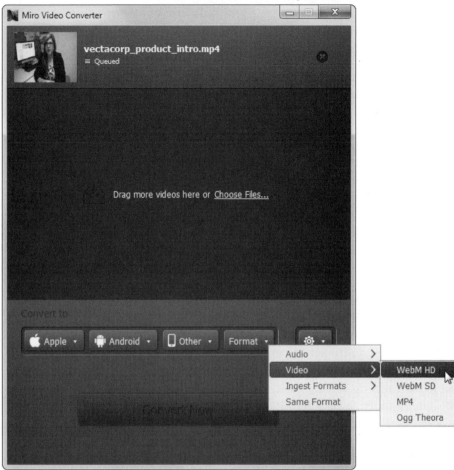

Description

- To encode audio and video files in the formats that you need, you can use one of the many encoders that are currently available, including Miro Converter, iTunes, QuickTime, Windows Media Encoder, Adobe Media Encoder, Firefogg, FFmpeg, and Handbrake.

- One encoder that I recommend is Miro Converter. It is a free program that lets you convert audio and video from one format to another as well as encode video for the popular media types including Ogg, WebM, and MPEG-4.

- Miro Converter also supports popular mobile devices including iPhone and Android.

Figure 10-5   How to encode media

How to add audio and video

With that as background, you're ready to learn how to add audio and video to your web pages. As you'll see, Dreamweaver makes doing that easy.

How to add HTML5 audio

Figure 10-6 shows how you add HTML5 audio to a web page. When you do that, an audio element is added to the HTML for the page and an audio icon appears on the page. Then, you can select that icon to set the properties for the audio element using the Property Inspector.

To start, you must specify the path to the audio file in the Source text box. In this example, the source file is named welcome.mp3, and it's stored in a folder named media. In addition to the MP3 file, the media folder also contains files in the Ogg and Flash formats. Then, to be sure that the audio will work in any browser, these files have been specified in the Alt Source 1 and Alt Source 2 text boxes.

Note that because either the MP3 or the Ogg file will play in any browser that supports HTML5, the Flash file is used only if the browser isn't HTML5-compliant. But even in that case, the Flash Player plugin must be installed. If it isn't installed and the user doesn't want to or can't install it, you'll want to provide text that's displayed in place of the audio file. You can specify this text in the Fallback Text text box.

The options in the lower left of the Property Inspector let you control the playback of the audio file. For example, you can check the Controls option if you want the browser's default controls to be displayed for the audio, and you can check the Autoplay option if you want the audio to begin playing automatically when the page loads. To quickly test these and other options, you can display the page in Live view.

The Property Inspector for HTML5 audio

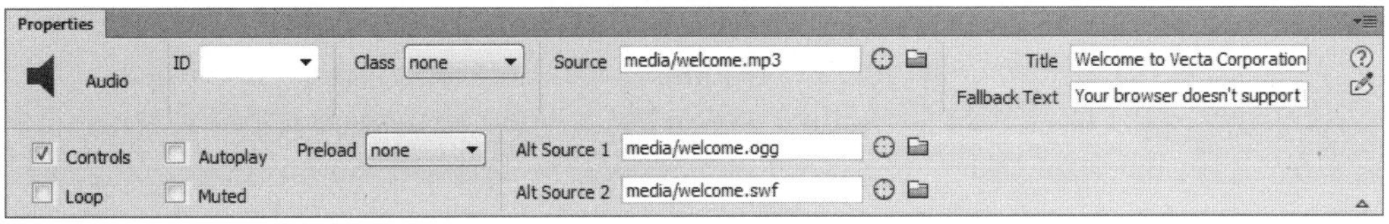

Controls for formatting HTML5 audio

Control	Description
Source text box	Specifies the path to the audio file to be played.
Title text box	Specifies a title for the audio. This text is displayed if you place the mouse pointer over the audio toolbar in a browser.
Fallback Text text box	Specifies the text that's displayed if the browser doesn't support the HTML5 audio element.
Controls check box	If checked, causes the default control toolbar to be displayed for the audio being played.
Loop check box	If checked, causes the audio to repeat playing when it reaches the end.
Autoplay check box	If checked, starts playing the audio as soon as the web page is loaded in the browser.
Muted check box	If checked, causes the audio to begin playing (if Autoplay is also set) with the volume muted.
Preload menu	Determines the data to be preloaded by the browser. The options are none (the default), metadata (only preload metadata like the track list), and auto (preload the entire media file).
Alt Source text boxes	Specify the paths to two alternate sources for the audio.

Description

- To insert HTML5 audio into a web page, position the cursor where you want to insert the audio and choose Insert→HTML5 Audio. You can also choose the HTML5 Audio option from the Media category of the Insert panel. An HTML5 Audio icon (◄) will appear within the web page.

- To format HTML5 audio, use the Property Inspector to set the properties of the audio. At the least, you need to enter the path to the audio file in the Source text box.

- If you want the audio to work in all browsers, you should also enter two alternate sources in the Alt Source 1 and Alt Source 2 text boxes.

- Audio files are typically stored in a folder named media.

Figure 10-6   How to add HTML5 audio

How to add HTML5 video

Figure 10-7 shows how you add HTML5 video to a web page. This works similarly to the technique for adding audio, but a video element is added to the HTML for the page and a video icon will appear on the page. Some additional properties are also available for a video.

Just as you do when you add audio, you should specify a source file and two alternate source files for a video. Because a video can have a variety of media types, though, you won't specify a Flash file for the second alternate source like you do for an audio file. In this figure, for example, you can see that the source is an MP4 file, the first alternate source is a WebM file, and the second alternate source is an Ogg video file. Then, if you want to include a Flash file that can be used if the browser doesn't support HTML5 or the other files aren't recognized, you can identify that file in the Flash Fallback text box.

When you set the source for a video, Dreamweaver automatically sets the width and height of the video based on the information in the video file. If you want to override this size to make the video smaller or larger, you can do that by entering new values in the W and H text boxes. Keep in mind, though, that if you enlarge a video, its quality may be reduced.

If a video doesn't start playing automatically when the page is loaded, you might want to display a static image until the user starts the video. To do that, you specify the path to the image in the Poster text box. In the example in this figure, the AutoPlay option is selected, so a static image isn't necessary.

The Property Inspector for HTML5 video

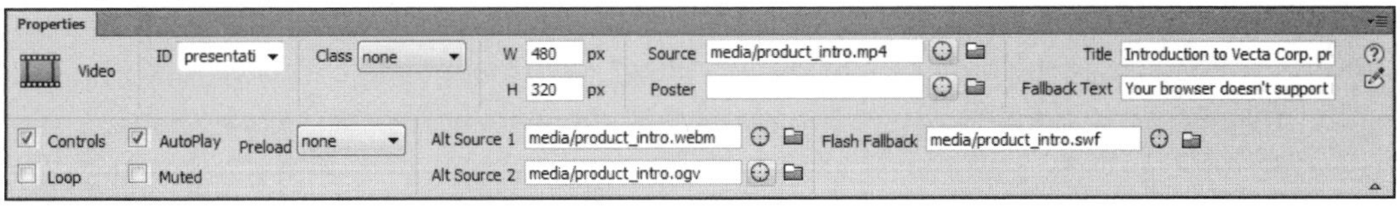

Controls for formatting HTML5 video

Control	Description
W and H text boxes	Specify the video's width and height in pixels.
Source text box	Specifies the path to the video file to be played.
Poster text box	Specifies the path to a static image to be displayed in place of the video until the video is played.
Title text box	Specifies a title for the video. This text is displayed if you place the mouse pointer over the video in a browser.
Fallback Text text box	Specifies the text that's displayed if the browser doesn't support the HTML5 video element.
Controls check box	If checked, causes the default control toolbar to be displayed below the video being played.
Loop check box	If checked, causes the video to repeat playing when it reaches the end.
Autoplay check box	If checked, starts playing the video as soon as the web page is loaded in the browser.
Muted check box	If checked, causes the video to begin playing (if Autoplay is also set) with the volume muted.
Preload menu	Determines the data to be preloaded by the browser. The options are none (the default), metadata (only preload metadata like dimensions and track list), or auto (preload the entire media file).
Alt Source text boxes	Specify the paths to two alternate sources for the video.
Flash Fallback text box	Specifies the path to the Flash file to be used if the source files aren't recognized or the browser doesn't support the HTML5 video element.

Description

- To insert HTML5 video into a web page, position the cursor where you want to insert the video and choose Insert→HTML5 Video. You can also choose the HTML5 Video option from the Media category of the Insert panel. An HTML5 Video icon (⊞) will appear within the web page.

- To format HTML5 video, use the Property Inspector to set the properties of the video as necessary. At the least, you need to enter the path of the video file in the Source text box. If you want the video to work in all browsers, you also need to enter two alternate sources and a Flash fallback file in the Alt Source 1, Alt Source 2, and Flash Fallback text boxes.

- Video files are typically stored in a folder named media.

Figure 10-7   How to add HTML5 video

How to add Flash video

Because of the problems using Flash that were mentioned earlier in this chapter, we don't generally recommend that you use Flash video except as a fallback. Instead, you should use the HTML5 video element as described in the last topic. If you ever need to use Flash video, though, figure 10-8 shows you how to add it to a web page.

When you add Flash video to a web page, the Insert FLV dialog box shown in this figure is displayed. The Video Type menu lets you choose from two different ways of delivering the video. If you choose the Progressive Download Video option, the video file is downloaded to the user's computer and it can start playing before the download is complete. When you use this option, the file can be stored with the other files for the website or in a separate location on the Web.

If you choose the Streaming Video option, the file must be stored on a streaming media server. Then, the file is streamed to the user's computer and can start playing after a small portion of the file is buffered. To include streaming Flash video in a website, you must have Adobe Media Server. For more information, see the Adobe website.

The Skin menu lets you choose from a variety of predefined Flash skins that determine the appearance of the control toolbar used by the Flash video. When you select one of these skins, a preview is displayed below this menu so you can be sure you've selected a skin with all the functions you need.

Next, you must define the width and height of the video. The easiest way to do that is to click the Detect Size button to have Dreamweaver get the size from the Flash file. Then, you can use the Width and Height text boxes to make the video larger or smaller if you need to. By default, the Constrain option is checked, so if you change one of the dimensions the other dimension will change so the aspect ratio of the video is maintained.

Like HTML5 audio and video, a Flash video will start playing automatically if the Auto Play option is checked. In addition, a Flash video includes the Auto Rewind option. If you select this option, the playback control in the video toolbar will return to the beginning of the video when the video ends. That way, the user can play the video again simply by clicking the Play button.

When you add a Flash video to a website, Dreamweaver automatically adds any files that are required for controlling and playing the video. In this case, that includes a file for the selected skin and a file to play the video progressively.

In addition to these files, when you save the web page that contains the video, a dialog box is displayed indicating that supporting files are required. The first file, swfobject_modified.js, is a JavaScript file that's used to detect if the required version of Adobe Flash Player is installed on the user's computer. If it isn't installed, the second file, expressInstall.swf, is used to upgrade or install it. Dreamweaver adds these files to the Scripts folder of your local website. It also adds content to your page that's displayed if a newer version of the player is required. You can edit this content by clicking the icon with an eye on it that appears next to the words "SWF: FLVPlayer" in the upper left of the flash video when you point to or select the video in Design view.

The Insert FLV dialog box for a progressive download

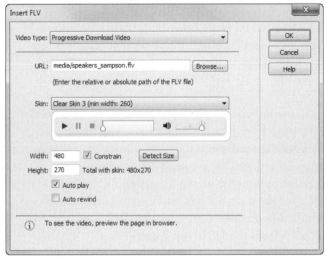

Controls in the Insert FLV dialog box for a progressive download

Control	Description
Video type menu	Determines whether the video will download progressively or stream from a streaming media server.
URL text box	Specifies the path to the Flash video file to be played. Can be a relative or an absolute path.
Skin menu	A list of skins that determine the appearance of the video toolbar. A preview of the selected skin is displayed below this menu.
Width and Height text boxes	Specify the width and height of the video player in pixels.
Detect Size button	Detects the width and height of the video file and sets the Width and Height controls to those values.
Constrain option	If checked, Dreamweaver maintains the aspect ratio of the video when you change the width or height.
Auto Play option	If checked, starts playing the video as soon as the web page is loaded in the browser.
Auto Rewind option	If checked, causes the playback control to return to the beginning when the video ends.

Description

- To insert Flash video into a web page, position the cursor where you want to insert the video and choose Insert→Media→Flash Video to display the Insert FLV dialog box. Or, choose the Flash Video option from the Media category of the Insert panel.
- To format Flash video, set the options in the Insert FLV dialog box. At the least, you need to specify the path to the Flash video, and you need to set the height and width of the video. When you click OK, a Flash Video icon (🎬) will appear within the web page.
- After you add a video file, you can set its properties using the Property Inspector.

Figure 10-8   How to add Flash video

How to add other types of media

Dreamweaver provides for adding media types other than HTML5 audio and video and Flash video. That includes QuickTime and Windows media, as well as others. As you learned earlier in this chapter, many of these media types require a plugin that plays the media type. Figure 10-9 shows how to add these types of media to a web page.

When you add a plugin-based media type to a page, it's defined by an embed object, and it's represented on the page by a generic plugin icon. You can select this icon to display the properties for the media in the Property Inspector. In this figure, for example, the properties for a QuickTime movie are displayed.

In the Src text box, you enter the path to the media file. Then, in the Plg URL text box, you enter the URL for the plugin that's required to play the media file. Then, if the plugin isn't installed in the user's browser, the web page will automatically attempt to download it from the URL you specify.

The other properties should be self-explanatory. Please note, though, that some of these options have been deprecated in HTML5, so you shouldn't use them. Also note that you have to enter the dimensions of the media player manually. They're not set automatically like they are for an HTML5 video, and you can't detect the size like you can for a Flash video.

In addition to the properties that you specify for a media file in the Property Inspector, you can specify parameters that are passed to the media player at runtime. When you use the QuickTime Player, for example, you can include parameters that cause the file to play automatically, that cause the file to loop when it reaches the end, and that set the initial volume. To do that, you click the Parameters button to display the Parameters dialog box. Then, you can use that dialog box to enter the name of each parameter and its value. For more information about the parameters that are available for each media player, you can search online.

The Property Inspector for a plugin

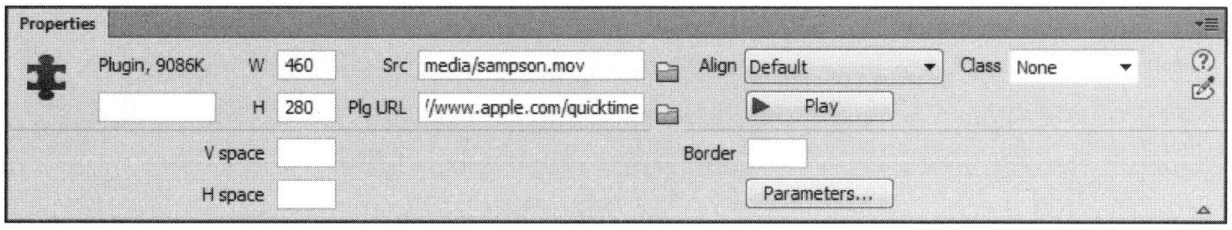

Controls for formatting a plugin

Control	Description
Name text box	Specifies a name for the media that can be used to refer to it from a script. (This is the unlabeled text box near the upper left corner of the Property Inspector.)
W and H text boxes	Specify the width and height of the media in pixels.
Src text box	Specifies the path to the media file.
Align menu	Determines the alignment of the media within its containing element. Deprecated in HTML5.
Plg URL text box	Specifies the path to the website where the plugin that's required to play the media file can be downloaded.
V and H space text boxes	Specify the amount of vertical and horizontal space around the media file in pixels. Deprecated in HTML5.
Play button	Plays the media within Dreamweaver.
Border text box	Specifies the width of the border that's displayed around the media file in pixels. Deprecated in HTML5.
Parameters button	Opens the Parameters dialog box, which lets you set parameters and values that are passed to the media player at runtime.

Description

- To insert other types of media such as QuickTime and Windows Media into a web page, select Insert→Media→Plugin or choose the Plugin option from the Media category of the Insert panel. Then, select the media file from the dialog box that's displayed. A generic plugin icon (▦) will appear within the web page.

- To format the media, use the Property Inspector. At the least, you'll want to set the height and width of the media. In most cases, you'll also want to set the plugin URL so users can download the plugin for the media player to their browsers if they don't already have it.

- Each media player accepts different parameters, which are passed to the player at runtime. When you add media types such as QuickTime and Windows Media to a web page, these parameters aren't available from the Property Inspector. Instead, you must use the Parameters dialog box to identify and set the values for these parameters.

Figure 10-9   How to add other types of media

A web page that offers both audio and video

Now that you've seen how to use Dreamweaver to add audio and video to your web pages, figure 10-10 presents a web page that uses both HTML5 audio and video. Here, both the audio and the video present an introduction to the products offered by the fictitious Vecta Corporation.

The main source for the audio is an MP3 file. Then, Ogg and Flash files are used as alternate sources. Similarly, the main source for the video is an MP4 file, and WebM and Ogg files are used as alternate sources. In addition, a Flash fallback file is specified. That way, you can be sure that the audio and video will work in any browser.

The default controls are also used for both the audio and video, and titles and fallback text are specified. Finally, a static image is displayed for the video when the page is first loaded since the video doesn't start automatically.

A web page that uses HTML5 audio and video

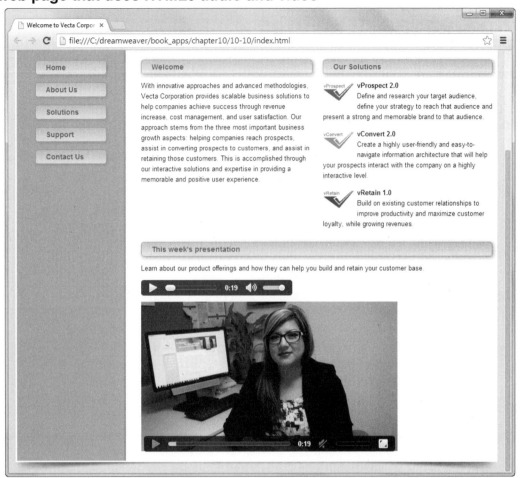

Description

- This web page includes both an audio and a video that present an introduction to the three products offered by Vecta Corporation.

- In addition to the main source file, two alternate sources are specified for the audio so it will work in any browser. Similarly, two alternate sources are specified for the video, along with a Flash fallback file, so the video will work in any browser.

- The controls property of both the audio and video is set so the default control toolbar is displayed.

- The poster property of the video is used to display a static image in place of the media type when the page is displayed. The poster file will be replaced with the actual video when the user clicks on the Play button.

Figure 10-10   A web page that offers both audio and video

How to add animations and Canvas drawings

Now that you've seen how to use Dreamweaver to work with audio and video, you're ready to learn how to use it to work with Flash animations, Adobe Edge Animate compositions, and HTML5 Canvas drawings.

How to add Flash animations

Earlier in this chapter, you learned how to add Flash video to a web page. But Flash can also be used to create animations, and you can use Dreamweaver to add those animations to a website. Figure 10-11 shows you how.

When you choose the Flash SWF option to add a Flash animation, a dialog box is displayed that lets you select the Flash file. Then, a second dialog box is displayed that lets you specify accessibility attributes for the animation. These attributes include a title, an access key, and a tab index. You can set these attributes just as you would for other elements.

After you add a Flash animation, the path to the Flash file is displayed in the File text box of the Property Inspector. In addition, the W and H text boxes are set to the width and height of the animation in pixels. Then, you can change the size of the animation if necessary. Since Flash animations are vector-based—meaning that they have both size and direction—enlarging an animation won't typically affect its quality.

You've already learned about some of the other controls for a Flash animation, so you shouldn't have any trouble understanding what they do. However, three of them require some additional explanation.

To start, the Quality option you choose determines the amount of anti-aliasing that's used. *Anti-aliasing* is a procedure for smoothing lines and removing distortions. If the quality is set to High, anti-aliasing is turned on, which can slow down playback considerably on slower computers. If the quality is set to Low, anti-aliasing is turned off. This option should be used only when quick playback is essential. The quality can also be set to Auto High or Auto Low. With Auto High, High quality will be used to start but the quality will switch to Low if playback is too slow. With Auto Low, Low quality will be used to start but the quality will switch to High if the user's computer is fast enough.

The Scale option you choose determines how the file fits within the area specified for the animation. By default, the entire file is displayed and its aspect ratio is maintained. Then, if the area has a different aspect ratio than the video, borders can appear on two sides of the animation. If you use the No Border option, the file will fill the area and the aspect ratio will be maintained, but no borders will be displayed. In that case, the content may be cropped. If you use the Exact Fit option, the file will fill the area but the aspect ratio won't be maintained. Because of that, the animation may be distorted.

The Wmode, or Window Mode, option determines how the animation is layered with other elements on the web page. The window option is used by default, which means that the animation runs in its own window. In that case, the browser determines how it's layered with other elements. If you use the opaque

The Property Inspector for a Flash animation

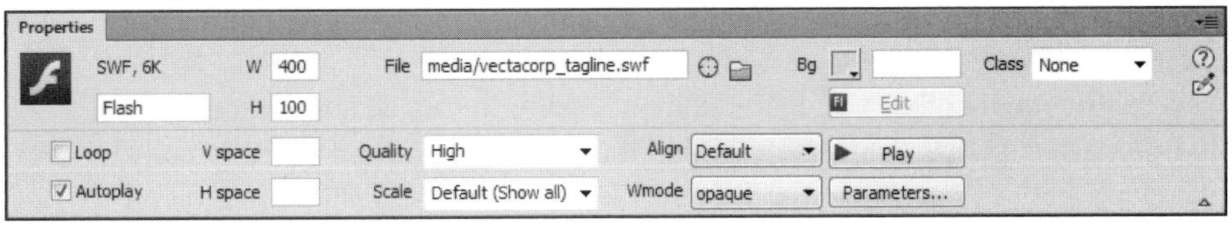

Controls for formatting a Flash animation

Control	Description
ID text box	Specifies the id for the Flash animation. A unique value is required. (This is the unlabeled text box near the upper left corner of the Property Inspector.)
W and H text boxes	Specify the width and height of the Flash animation in pixels.
File text box	Specifies the path to the Flash SWF file.
Bg color picker	Specifies the background color for the Flash animation.
Edit button	Launches Flash so you can edit the original Flash (FLA) file.
Loop option	If checked, causes the Flash animation to repeat playing when it reaches the end.
Autoplay option	If checked, starts playing the Flash animation as soon as the web page is loaded in the browser.
V and H space text boxes	Specify the amount of vertical and horizontal space around the animation.
Quality combo box	Determines the level of anti-aliasing that's used. The options are High, Low, Auto High, and Auto Low.
Scale combo box	Determines how the animation fits within the specified dimensions. The options are Default (Show all), No Border, and Exact Fit.
Align menu	Determines the alignment of the animation within its containing element.
Wmode menu	Determines the window mode for the animation. The options are window, opaque, and transparent.
Play/Stop button	Plays the Flash animation within Dreamweaver, or stops the animation when it's playing
Parameters button	Opens the Parameters dialog box, which lets you set parameters and values that are passed to the animation at runtime. The animation must be designed to receive these parameters.

Description

- To add a Flash animation to a web page, select Insert→Media→Flash SWF or choose the Flash SWF option from the Media category of the Insert panel. Then, select the SWF file from the first dialog box that's displayed, and enter accessibility options in the second dialog box that's displayed. When you're done, a Flash icon ( ) will appear within the web page.
- To format a Flash animation, use the Property Inspector.

Figure 10-11   How to add Flash animations

option, any elements behind the animation are hidden. In contrast, if you use the transparent option, any elements behind the animation show through the transparent background of the animation.

Like the media types you learned about earlier in this chapter that require a plugin, Flash supports the passing of parameters to animations. In fact, many of the values that you specify in the Property Inspector for a Flash animation are passed as parameters. If you want to set any other parameters, though, you can do that by clicking the Parameters button and then entering the parameter names and values in the dialog box that's displayed. For a complete list of the parameters that are supported by the Flash player, please visit the following web page: http://helpx.adobe.com/flash/kb/flash-object-embed-tag-attributes.html.

If you have Adobe Flash installed on your computer, you should realize that you can start it directly from the Property Inspector. To do that, just click the Edit button. When you do, a dialog box is displayed that lets you select the Flash (.fla) file you want to edit. (If this doesn't work, you'll want to use the File Types / Editors category of the Preferences dialog box to be sure that the .fla file extension is associated with Adobe Flash.) Then, if you make changes to that file, you can export it to a .swf file from Flash and save it over the original file.

How to add Edge Animate compositions

Adobe Edge Animate is a new multimedia authoring tool that is intended to be a successor to Flash. It can be used to create animations, called *compositions*, using HTML5 and JavaScript. The goal of Adobe Edge Animate is to create cross-browser and device-independent animations that run on a browser without the use of a plugin.

Figure 10-12 shows how to add an Edge Animate composition to a web page using Dreamweaver. The composition shown here consists of three tabs. When the web page is first loaded, the first tab is displayed. Then, the product title appears and shifts slightly from right to left, the description appears and shifts up slightly, and the line below the title is drawn from left to right. This process is repeated each time a different tab is displayed.

When you add an Edge Animate composition to a web page, it's added at its original size by default. If you need to, you can change its size from the Property Inspector. You can also change its id or specify a class like you can for any other element.

A web page with an Edge Animate composition

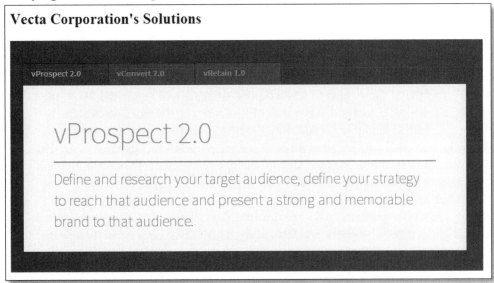

The Property Inspector for an Edge Animate composition

Description

- You can use Edge Animate to create *compositions* that are implemented using HTML5 and JavaScript and that don't require a plugin. The file extension for an Edge Animate composition is .oam.

- To insert an Edge Animate composition into a web page, select Insert→Media→Edge Animate Composition, or choose the Edge Animate Composition option from the Media category of the Insert panel. Then, select the .oam file from the Select Edge Animate Package dialog box that's displayed. When you click OK, an Animate icon (An) will appear within the web page.

- To change the size of a composition or to add an id or class attribute, use the Property Inspector.

- When you add an Edge Animate composition to a website, a number of supporting files are added along with the .oam file. These files are stored in folders named assets and edgeanimate_assets.

Figure 10-12   How to add Edge Animate compositions

How to add an HTML5 Canvas drawing

Canvas is a new HTML5 feature that provides a rich interface for programmatically drawing shapes and images and creating animations and other objects using JavaScript. Like other HTML5 features, Canvas is supported by most modern browsers.

Figure 10-13 shows how to add a Canvas drawing to a web page. Here, the drawing is a simple footer that consists of text and a horizontal line. Although you can create much more sophisticated drawings with Canvas, you need to know how to code JavaScript to do that. For the purposes of this book, then, I'll just describe how JavaScript works with the canvas element. This is the element that's created when you add a Canvas drawing to a web page.

After you insert a Canvas drawing, you should use the Property Inspector to set its size so it's appropriate for the drawing. You should also change the default id so it reflects the object that's being drawn. This id will be used to refer to the element in the JavaScript.

The JavaScript that draws the footer is coded in a script element within the header of the document as shown in the HTML in this figure. This element includes a function named drawFooter that contains the statements that create the footer. If you review this code, you should get a general idea of how this works. Notice, though, that to identify where the drawing will be placed, the first statement gets the element that has an id of "footer". This is the id that was assigned to the canvas element.

To draw the footer, you must execute the drawFooter function. To do that, you code the onload attribute on the body element, and you assign the name of the function to this attribute. Then, the function will be executed when the web page is loaded.

A web page with a footer drawn using HTML5 Canvas

Copyright 2014 - All Rights Reserved.

The Property Inspector for an HTML5 canvas

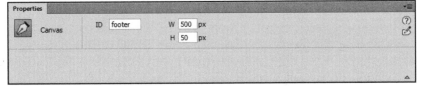

The HTML and JavaScript for the web page

```html
<!DOCTYPE html>
<html>
    <head>
        <meta charset="utf-8">
        <title>Welcome to Vecta Corporation</title>
        <script>
        function drawFooter() {
            var shape = document.getElementById("footer");
            var footer = shape.getContext("2d");
            footer.moveTo(0, 40);
            footer.lineTo(500, 40);
            footer.stroke();
            footer.font = "bold 14px sans-serif";
            footer.fillText("Copyright 2014 - All Rights Reserved.", 0, 25);
        }
        </script>
    </head>
    <body onload="drawFooter()">
        <canvas id="footer" width="500" height="50"></canvas>
    </body>
</html>
```

Description

- *Canvas* is a new HTML5 *API* (*Application Programming Interface*) that lets you use JavaScript to draw, fill, and animate elements within a browser. It can be used without third-party software or plugins.

- To support the Canvas API, HTML5 provides a canvas element that receives the output from the JavaScript. To insert a canvas element, you select Insert→Canvas or choose the Canvas option from the Common category of the Insert panel. Then, a Canvas icon ([🖋]) will appear within the web page.

- To change the size of a canvas element or to add an id attribute, use the Property Inspector. The id attribute is referred to in the script.

- In the future, Canvas is expected to be used in place of third-party, plugin based applications such as Flash.

- At the time of this writing, Dreamweaver supports only the canvas element. All of the JavaScript code must still be written by hand.

Figure 10-13   How to add HTML5 Canvas drawings

A web page with a Flash animation and an Edge Animate composition

To complete this chapter, I'll present a web page that includes a Flash animation and an Edge Animate composition. Since the Edge Animate composition is the same one that you saw earlier in this chapter, I'll focus on describing the Flash animation here. Keep in mind, though, that the best way to understand how both the animation and the composition work is to see them in action. You can do that by downloading the files for this book and then displaying this page in a browser.

The Flash animation on this web page consists of the three lines of text below the Welcome heading in the first column. When this page is first displayed, the area that the animation occupies is blank. Then, when the animation executes, the first line of text moves into view from the left, followed by the second line of text from the right, and finally the third line of text from the left. In addition, the first line of text initially appears in a larger font but is then reduced to the size shown here. Finally, after each line is displayed, a shadow of the text appears and then that shadow enlarges and fades out.

A web page that uses a Flash animation and an Edge Animate composition

Description

- The Flash animation is displayed below the Welcome heading when the page is loaded. This animation causes the three lines of text it contains to move into view from the left and right sides of the column. It also causes shadows of the text to enlarge and fade out.

- The Edge Animate composition is displayed below the Our Solutions heading and consists of three tabs for the three solutions. When the page is loaded, the text on the first tab moves into view and the line below the solution name is drawn. This is repeated each time a different tab is displayed.

Figure 10-14   A web page with a Flash animation and an Edge Animate composition

Perspective

Now that you know how to include media files in your web pages, here are two cautions about overusing them. First, remember that media files are often large, so web pages that include them are likely to load slowly. Second, remember that users who can't see or hear won't benefit from video or audio. So, before you decide to use media files, you should be sure that they support the goals of your website and enhance the user experience.

Terms

media type
media player
plugin
codec
anti-aliasing

Adobe Edge Animate
composition
Canvas
API (Application Programming
    Interface)

Summary

- A browser uses a *media player* to play an audio or video *media type* when media are embedded in a web page.

- Some browsers require *plugins* for the media players that play specific media types.

- Audio and video files come in a variety of media types. MPEG, Ogg, and WebM are common types for video, and AAC and MP3 are common types for audio.

- A *codec* is a software component that's used by browsers to decipher the algorithms in a media type.

- The HTML5 audio and video elements are supported by modern browsers and will play media without the need for special plugins.

- Because Flash requires a plugin, isn't supported by many mobile browsers, and can be unstable, it's typically used only as a backup to other audio and video formats.

- You can use Dreamweaver to add HTML5 audio and video, Flash video, and other media types such as Apple's QuickTime and Microsoft's Windows Media Video to a web page.

- Animations have traditionally been developed using Adobe Flash, but Adobe Edge Animate and HTML5 Canvas can now be used instead.

- *Adobe Edge Animate* is a new multimedia authoring tool that can be used to create *compositions* using HTML5 and JavaScript.

- *Canvas* is a new HTML5 feature that provides for drawing a variety of objects with JavaScript, including shapes, images, and animations.

Exercise 10-1   Add video, canvas, and flash to a web page

In this exercise, you'll add video, canvas, and flash to a web page so it looks like the one that follows:

Open and review the Solutions page

1. Open the Exercises website, open the folder for this exercise, and open the solutions.html file.

2. Review the starting HTML for this page to see that it includes header, main, and footer elements.

Add a video to the page

3. Place your cursor in the main element after the Solutions h1 element. Then, choose Insert→HTML5 Video. This will add a video icon to the page.

4. Select the icon, and use the Property Inspector to add the three different types of files for the intro video from the media folder: mp4, webm, and ogv. If necessary, use figure 10-7 as a guide. Then, set the width of the video to 660 pixels, check the Controls box, and make sure AutoPlay is unchecked.

5. Test the page in Live view and in your browser.

6. Select the video icon again, and use the Property Inspector to add the poster.png file from the media folder to the poster text box. Then, test again.

Add a canvas drawing to the footer

7. Before you add the canvas element, review the HTML for the page to see that a script element that contains the JavaScript code for drawing the footer has already been added to the head element.

8. Choose Insert→Canvas to add a canvas element inside the footer element, and use the Property Inspector to set its id to "footer". This id is used by the JavaScript function. Then, set the width of this element to 700 pixels and the height to 50 pixels.

9. To have the drawing displayed when the page is loaded into a browser, add this attribute to the body element:

   ```
   onload="drawFooter()"
   ```

   It runs the drawFooter function that's in the script element in the head section.

10. Test the page in Live view and your browser. Note that the footer line doesn't go across the entire page and the footer text is above the line instead of below it.

11. To fix that, adjust the JavaScript in the head element so the moveTo values are 0, 5 and the lineTo values are 700, 5. Those are the horizontal and vertical values for the start and end of the line. Now test those changes.

12. To indent and lower the text in the footer, adjust the JavaScript so the last two fillText values are 20, 30. Then, test that change.

Add a flash animation

13. In Code view, put the cursor in the main element right after the video element. Then, select Insert→Media→Flash SWF and choose the tagline.swf file from the media folder.

14. Test this addition in both Live view and in your browser.

15. Review the HTML to see the code that has been added for this animation, including a script element in the head section, another script element after the footer, and an object element in the body. Besides that, a Scripts folder that contains two files has been added to the root directory of the Exercises folder.

How to work with tables

If you look at the HTML for some of the websites that are in use today, you'll see that many of them still use tables to control the page layout. As you learned in chapter 6, though, the right way to do that is to use CSS. As a result, you should only use tables to display tabular data. In this chapter, you'll learn how to do that.

Basic skills for working with tables

In the topics that follow, you'll learn the basic skills for working with tables in Dreamweaver. But first, I want to introduce you to the structure of a table. That will help you understand the features for working with tables that are built into Dreamweaver.

An introduction to tables

Figure 11-1 presents a simple table and points out its various components. To start, a *table* consists of one or more *rows* and *columns*. As you'll see in the next figure, you build a table in Dreamweaver by defining its rows and columns.

Within each row, a table can contain two different kinds of *cells*. *Header cells* identify what's in the columns and rows of a table, and *data cells* contain the actual data of the table. For example, the two cells in the first row of the table in this figure are header cells that identify the contents of the columns. In contrast, the cells in the next five rows are data cells. Note that by default, the content of a header cell is boldfaced and centered in the cell, and the content of a data cell is left-aligned. If that's not what you want, you can use CSS to control this formatting.

This table also contains a *caption* that summarizes what's in the table. This can help visually-impaired users decipher the contents of the table. This caption is centered above the table by default.

This figure also presents some of the HTML for this table so you can see the elements it uses. To start, the table element includes one tr (table row) element for each row in the table. Then, each table row includes a td (table data) element for each data cell or a th (table header) element for each header cell. In addition, if the table contains a caption, it includes a caption element.

A simple table with basic formatting

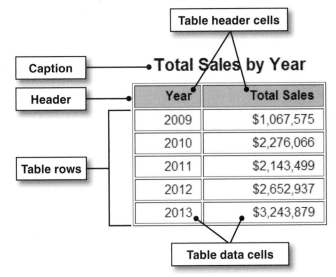

The HTML for the table

```
<table>
  <caption>
    Total Sales by Year
  </caption>
  <tr>
    <th>Year</th>
    <th>Total Sales</th>
  </tr>
  <tr>
    <td>2009</td>
    <td>$1,067,575</td>
  </tr>
    .
    .
    .
  <tr>
    <td>2013</td>
    <td>$3,243,879</td>
  </tr>
</table>
```

Description

- A *table* consists of *rows* and *columns* that intersect at *cells*.
- Cells that contain the data of the table are called *data cells*.
- The *header* for a table consists of a row with *header cells* that identify the data in the columns.
- The *caption* for a table provides information about the data in the table.
- Now that CSS can be used for page layout, you should only use tables for tabular data.

Figure 11-1   An introduction to tables

How to insert a table

Figure 11-2 shows the Insert Table dialog box that you use to insert a table in Dreamweaver. This dialog box lets you specify the number of rows and columns in the table, whether the table contains a header and where that header is located, and a caption for the table.

This dialog box also lets you specify other values, but the attributes that are generated if you do that are deprecated in HTML5 and will cause warnings when you validate the page. That includes the table width, the width of the border around the cells, the padding between the content of a cell and its border, the space between the cells, and a summary of the table's contents. Because of that, you should delete the values from these text boxes and use CSS to provide this formatting instead.

At this point, you should know that even if you don't set the width of a table when you create it, Dreamweaver will create a table with narrow columns. Then, you can enter the data for the table into the cells of those columns. As you do that, Dreamweaver will adjust the widths of the columns based on the data you enter.

Also, if you specify the width of a table in CSS, the column widths are equal by default. But again, Dreamweaver will adjust the widths as you enter data. If that's not what you want, you can specify the exact width for each column in CSS.

You can include a header at the top of a table, at the left side of a table, or at both the top and left side. If you include a header, you'll want to be sure to specify the table size accordingly. If you include a header at the top of a table, for example, you'll want to include an extra row for the header. And if you include a header at the left side of a table, you'll want to include an extra column.

The Insert Table dialog box

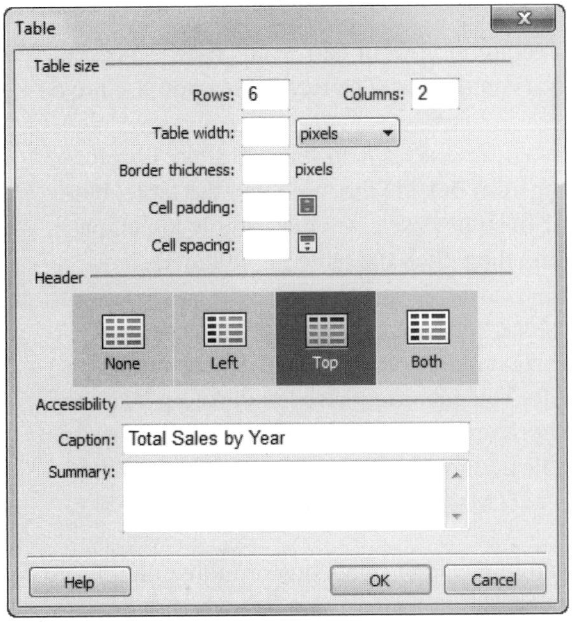

How to insert a table into your web page

1. Position the cursor in the document where you want to insert the table, and choose Insert→Table or click the Table object in the Common category of the Insert panel to display the Table dialog box.

2. Set the number of rows and columns for the table.

3. If you want to include a header, select one of the options to indicate where it should be positioned.

4. If you want to make the table more accessible to visually-impaired users, enter a caption.

5. Click OK to insert the table.

Description

*   You use the Insert Table dialog box to create the initial structure for a table. Then, you can add data to the individual table cells.

*   Although the Table dialog box lets you set the table width, border thickness, cell padding, cell spacing, and summary, these attributes are deprecated in HTML5. So you should delete any values from these text boxes and use CSS to format the table instead as shown in chapters 5 and 6.

*   You can also create a table by importing tabular data. You'll learn how to do that later in this chapter.

Figure 11-2   How to insert a table

How to select tables, columns, rows, and cells

Before you can work with a table, column, row, or cell, you have to select it. Figure 11-3 describes several ways you can do that. The techniques you use are a matter of preference.

This figure starts by presenting five different ways to select a table. I prefer to select a table by dragging the cursor from outside the table into the table, but it can be difficult to use this technique in some cases. Another simple technique is to click anywhere inside the table and then click the table tag in the Tag selector.

When you select a table, a thick black border appears around it as shown in this figure. This border includes resize handles on the right side, the bottom, and the bottom right corner of the table. You can drag these handles to resize the table horizontally, vertically, or both horizontally and vertically. Note, however, that using these handles to resize a table adds width and height attributes to the table element, which are deprecated in HTML5. Because of that, you shouldn't size a table this way.

In addition to selecting an entire table, you can select one or more columns, rows, or cells. Some of the techniques for doing that are also described in this figure. When you select one or more columns, rows, or cells, a thick black border appears around each cell in the selection so you can tell what's selected. Unfortunately, you won't be able to see these borders if you apply a solid black border to the cells using CSS. Because of that, you may want to wait to add a border like this until your table is complete.

Before I go on, you should notice the visual aid that's displayed above the table in this figure. This visual aid is reminiscent of classic hand drafting techniques for displaying widths from one point to another. In this case, the outer lines indicate the width of the table, and the inner lines indicate the widths of the columns. If the widths of the table and its columns are set in the HTML for the table, these widths are displayed to the left of the down arrows in the center of the lines. But, again, since we don't recommend specifying widths in the HTML, you should never see the actual widths in this visual aid.

If you want to, you can hide this visual aid by choosing View→Visual Aids→Table Widths. Keep in mind, though, that this visual aid does more than just identify the widths of the table and its columns. It also provides access to context menus that you can display by clicking on a down arrow (▼). These menus let you perform functions such as clearing the heights and widths for the table or inserting a column to the right or left of another column. Although we don't include the skills for using this visual aid in this book, you might want to review its menus to see what you can do.

A table after it's selected

Year	Total Sales
2011	$2,143,499
2012	$2,652,937
2013	$3,243,879

Five ways to select a table

- Drag the cursor from just outside the table into the table.
- Place your cursor within a cell and then click the <table> tag in the Tag selector.
- Roll your cursor over the edge of the table until a red border is displayed around the table, and then click to select the table.
- Right-click within any cell and then choose Table→Select Table from the context menu that appears.
- Click in any cell of the table and then choose Modify→Table→Select Table.

How to select columns and rows

- To select a single column, place the mouse pointer just above the top of the column until it turns into a down arrow and a red border is displayed around the column, and then click.
- To select two or more columns, select the first column and continue to hold down the mouse button as you drag across the other columns. Or, hold down the Ctrl key (Windows) or the Cmd key (Mac) as you select the columns.
- To select one or more rows, use the same techniques for selecting one or more columns, but position the mouse pointer just to the left of the row until it turns into a right arrow.

How to select cells

- To select a single cell, place your cursor in it and then press Ctrl+A (Windows) or Cmd+A (Mac).
- To select two or more cells, hold down the Ctrl key (Windows) or the Cmd key (Mac) and then click on the cells you want to select. Or, click in one cell and then drag across the other cells you want to select.

Description

- When a table is selected, a thick black border appears around the table.
- When one or more rows, columns, or cells are selected, a thick black border appears around each cell in the selection.

Figure 11-3   How to select tables, columns, rows, and cells

How to use the Property Inspector to work with tables

When you select a table in the Document window, the Property Inspector shown in figure 11-4 is displayed. Like the Table dialog box that you use to insert a table, the Property Inspector generates some attributes that have been deprecated in HTML5. When that's the case, I've indicated the CSS property you should use instead in this figure. For example, instead of entering a value in the CellPad text box, you should use the CSS padding properties.

If you want to add rows or columns to a table, you can do that by increasing the value in the Rows or Cols text box. If you increase the number of rows, new rows are added at the bottom of the table. If you increase the number of columns, new columns are added at the right side of the table. If you want to insert rows or columns in the middle of a table instead, you can use the techniques you'll learn later in this chapter.

You can also use the Rows and Cols text boxes to delete rows and columns. To do that, just decrease the values in these text boxes. Then, rows are deleted from the bottom of the table and columns are deleted from the right side of the table.

The icons near the bottom left of the Property Inspector let you work with the widths and heights of the table. For example, you can use the Clear Column Widths and Clear Row Heights icons to remove any widths or heights that been specified in the HTML for the table. You might want to do that if you're updating the table to use HTML5. Then, you can specify the widths and heights in the CSS instead.

The other two icons let you convert any widths specified in the HTML for the table to pixels or percents. That includes the widths of columns and the width of the table. Since you shouldn't specify widths in the HTML for a table, you probably won't use these icons.

Although you're not likely to use the other controls in the lower portion of the Property Inspector, you may want to know what they're for. But first, you should realize that before the use of CSS became popular, page layouts were defined using tables. To make it easier to define a layout, many web developers used a product called Adobe Fireworks to prototype the layout. Then, that prototype could be exported to a proprietary Fireworks HTML file that implemented the design using tables. If you identified that file in the Src text box of the Property Inspector, the HTML would be updated automatically if the design was changed in Fireworks.

The Property Inspector for a table

Properties							
Table	Rows 4	W	pixels ▼	CellPad	Align Default ▼	Class None ▼	⑦
▼	Cols 2			CellSpace	Border		☑

Common controls for formatting a table

Control	Description
ID combo box	Adds an id attribute to the selected element with the value you specify. You can also select an existing id selector from the list. (This control is near the left side of the Property Inspector and isn't labeled.)
Rows text box	Sets the number of rows in the table.
Cols text box	Sets the number of columns in the table.
W (Width) controls	Set the width of the table in either pixels or percent. Use the CSS width property instead.
CellPad text box	Sets the space between the cell contents and the outer edge of the cells. Use the CSS padding properties instead.
CellSpace text box	Sets the space between cells. Use the CSS border-spacing property instead.
Align menu	Sets the horizontal alignment of the table within the block element that contains it. The options are Left (the default), Center, or Right. Use the CSS float property instead.
Border text box	Sets the thickness of the border around the table. Use the CSS border property instead.
Class combo box	Adds a class attribute to the selected element with the value you select. Can also be used to remove the current class, rename a class, or attach an external style sheet.
Clear icons (🔲 and 🔲)	Remove any widths or heights that have been applied to the columns or rows of the table using HTML.
Convert icons (🔲 and 🔲)	Convert the table width and any column widths specified in the HTML to pixels or percents.

Description

- Before you can modify the properties of a table, you must select the table as described in figure 11-3.
- Some of the table attributes that are generated when you use the controls in the Property Inspector have been deprecated in HTML5. Because of that, you should use the CSS properties as indicated in the table above instead.

Figure 11-4   How to use the Property Inspector to work with tables

How to use the Property Inspector to work with table cells

Figure 11-5 describes some of the properties that are available from the Property Inspector when one or more cells are selected. Note that the controls in the top half of this panel are the same as those that you use to format text. You can use the HTML and CSS icons at the left side of the panel to switch between the HTML and CSS controls. The icon you choose doesn't affect the controls that are displayed in the bottom half of the panel.

Like the properties that are available for tables, many of the attributes that are generated by the Property Inspector for cells have been deprecated in HTML5. That includes the attributes that specify the horizontal alignment, the vertical alignment, the width, the height, the wrapping, and the background color. Instead of using the controls that generate these attributes, then, you should use the CSS properties indicated in the table in this figure.

The two icons near the lower left corner of the Property Inspector let you merge two or more cells and split a cell into two or more cells. You'll learn more about how this works later in this chapter.

The only other control you may want to use is the Header check box. If you select this check box, the selected cells are converted from data cells to header cells. That can be useful if you insert a table and then later realize that you didn't include a row or column for the header. Then, you can insert a new row or column as described in the next figure and convert the data cells that are generated to header cells. When you do that, remember that header cells are automatically centered and boldfaced. If that's not what you want, you can format these cells using CSS.

The Property Inspector for table cells

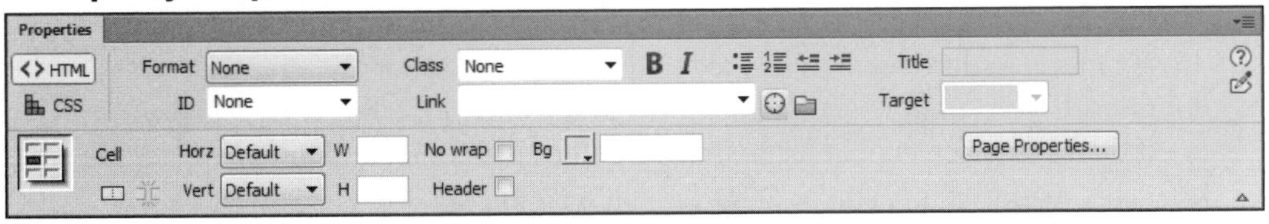

Common controls for formatting table cells

Control	Description
Merge icon (⊞)	Merges the selected cells. See figure 11-7 for more information.
Split icon (⚶)	Splits the selected cell into two or more columns or rows. See figure 11-7 for more information.
Horz menu	Sets the horizontal alignment of text within the selected cells. The options are Left (the default), Center, or Right. Use the CSS text-align property instead.
Vert menu	Sets the vertical alignment of text within the selected cells. The options are Top, Middle, Bottom or Baseline. Use the CSS vertical-align property instead.
W text box	Sets the width of the selected cells in pixels. Use the CSS width property instead.
H text box	Sets the height of the selected cells in pixels. Use the CSS height property instead.
No Wrap check box	If checked, prevents text within the selected cells from wrapping to the next line. If the text exceeds the width of a cell, the cell is expanded to make room for the text. Use the CSS white-space property instead.
Header check box	If checked, converts the selected cell into a table header cell (<th>).
Bg color picker and text box	Set the background color of the selected cells. Use the CSS background-color property instead.

Description

- Before you can modify the properties of one or more cells, you must select the cells as described in figure 11-3.
- The top half of the Property Inspector for a cell contains standard controls for formatting text using HTML or CSS.
- Some of the cell attributes that are generated when you use the controls in the Property Inspector have been deprecated in HTML5. Because of that, you should use the CSS properties as indicated above instead.

Figure 11-5   How to use the Property Inspector to work with table cells

How to insert and delete rows and columns

Figure 11-6 describes several techniques you can use to insert rows and columns. If you simply need to add a row at the end of a table, the easiest way to do that is to place the cursor in the last cell of the table and then press the Tab key. This works well if you're entering that data into a table one row at a time. Then, you can just press the Tab key at the end of each row to create the next row.

If you want to insert a single row above another row, you can right-click in that row and then choose Table→Insert Row from the context menu that's displayed. Similarly, you can insert a single column to the left of another column by right-clicking in that column and then choosing Table→Insert Column.

You can also use the context menu that's displayed when you right-click a row or column to insert more than one row or column. To do that, choose the Insert Rows or Columns option to display the Insert Rows or Columns dialog box shown here. This dialog box lets you specify whether you want to insert rows or columns, the number of rows or columns you want to insert, and where you want the rows or columns inserted. This is the most flexible technique for inserting rows and columns.

This figure also presents several techniques for deleting rows and columns. If you need to delete a single row or column or two or more consecutive rows or columns, you can select them and press the Delete key. Alternatively, you can right-click in a row or column or select two or more rows or columns and then right-click in the selection. Then, you can use the options in the Table submenu of the context menu that's displayed to delete the rows or columns.

As you learned earlier in this chapter, you can also use the Property Inspector for a table to add or delete rows or columns. To do that, you just change the value in the Rows or Cols text box. Then, rows are added to or deleted from the bottom of the table and columns are added to or deleted from the right side of the table.

The Insert Rows or Columns dialog box

```
Insert Rows or Columns                    [X]

    Insert:  ⦿ Rows                    [  OK  ]
             ◯ Columns
    Number of rows:  1  [▲▼]           [ Cancel ]

    Where:  ◯ Above the Selection
            ⦿ Below the Selection      [  Help  ]
```

How to insert rows and columns

- To insert a row at the end of a table, place the cursor within the last cell of the table and press the Tab key.
- To insert a row above another row, right-click in a cell within the row and choose Table→Insert Row.
- To insert a column to the left of another column, right-click in a cell within the column and choose Table→Insert Column.
- To insert two or more rows or columns, right-click in a cell and choose Table→Insert Rows or Columns to display the Insert Rows or Columns dialog box. Then, select an option to insert rows or columns, enter the number of rows or columns you want to insert, and indicate if you want to insert the rows above or below the current row or insert the columns to the left or right of the current column.
- To add one or more rows at the end of the table or one or more columns to the right side of the table, select the table and then use the Property Inspector as described in figure 11-4 to increase the number of rows or columns.

How to delete rows and columns

- To delete one or more consecutive rows or columns, select them and then press the Delete key.
- To delete a single row or column, right-click in a cell within the row or column and choose Table→Delete Row or Table→Delete Column.
- To delete two or more rows or columns, select the rows or columns. Then, right-click on the rows or columns and choose Table→Delete Row or Table→Delete Column.
- To delete one or more rows from the bottom of a table or one or more columns from the right side of a table, select the table and then use the Property Inspector as described in figure 11-4 to decrease the number of rows or columns.

Description

- You can also insert and delete rows and columns using the Modify→Table submenu.

Figure 11-6   How to insert and delete rows and columns

How to merge and split cells

For complicated tables, it often makes sense to *merge* some of the cells. This is illustrated in figure 11-7. Here, five cells are merged in the first row so "Sales" spans the last five columns of the table. Also, two cells are merged in the first column so there isn't an empty cell above the cell that contains "Year".

To merge cells like this, you can use one of the two techniques shown here. To start, you select the cells you want to merge. Then, you can right-click on the cells and choose Table→Merge Cells, or you can click the Merge icon in the Property Inspector.

When you merge cells in a row, a colspan attribute is added to the resulting cell. This attribute indicates the number of columns that the cell spans. Similarly, when you merge cells in a column, a rowspan attribute is added to the resulting cell that indicates the number of rows that the cell spans.

You can also *split* a cell into two or more cells. To do that, you use the Split Cell dialog box shown in this figure. This dialog box lets you indicate if you want to split the cell into rows or columns and the number of rows or columns you want to create. If a cell was previously merged, Dreamweaver will set the number of rows or columns based on the value of the colspan or rowspan attribute. Otherwise, it will set this value to 2. You can change this value any way you want, though.

A table after two cells in a column and five cells in a row have been merged

Year	Sales				
	Quarter 1	Quarter 2	Quarter 3	Quarter 4	Total Sales
2009	$242,533.00	$211,065.00	$302,332.00	$311,645.00	$1,067,575.00
2010	$420,303.00	$313,045.00	$480,452.00	$600,133.00	$2,276,066.00
2011	$506,345.00	$478,949.00	$512,432.00	$750,002.00	$2,143,499.00
2012	$640,322.00	$590,040.00	$612,342.00	$810,233.00	$2,652,937.00
2013	$750,323.00	$720,322.00	$823,002.00	$950,232.00	$3,243,879.00

The Split Cell dialog box

Split Cell

Split cell into: ○ Rows
● Columns

Number of columns: 2

OK   Cancel   Help

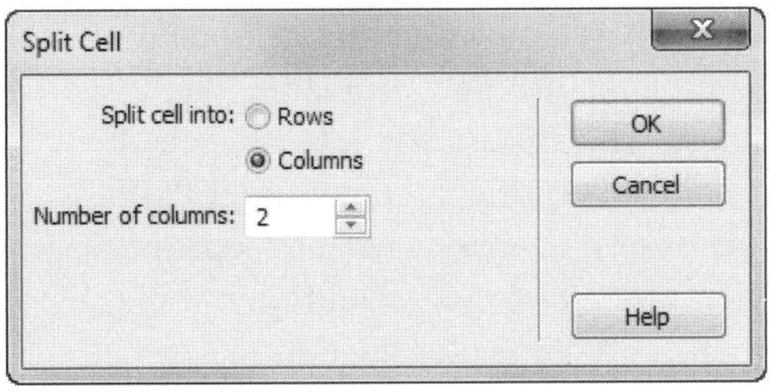

Two ways to merge cells

- Select two or more cells in a table, right-click on them, and then choose Table→Merge Cells.
- Select two or more cells and then click the Merge icon (▦) in the Property Inspector.

Two ways to split a cell into two or more columns or rows

- Right-click the cell you'd like to split and choose Table→Split Cell to display the Split Cell dialog box. Select an option to split the cell into rows or columns, and then indicate the number of rows or columns.
- Place the cursor in a cell and then click the Split icon (✣) in the Property Inspector to display the Split Cell dialog box.

Description

- You can *merge* one or more cells in a table into one cell, and you can *split* a single cell into two or more cells.
- You can also merge and split cells using the Modify→Table submenu.

Figure 11-7   How to merge and split cells

Other skills for working with tables

Now that you've learned the basic skills for working with tables, you're ready to learn two additional skills that may be useful from time to time. That includes importing data from an external file into a table and sorting the data in a table.

How to import tabular data

In some cases, the data that you want to include in a table will already exist in another form outside of Dreamweaver. For example, it might be stored in a spreadsheet. Then, if the data can be converted to a delimited text file, it can be imported into Dreamweaver as described in figure 11-8.

A *delimited text file* is a file whose data is separated by a delimiter, such as a tab or a comma. To import this type of file into Dreamweaver as a table, you use the Import Tabular Data dialog box shown here. This dialog box lets you select the file that contains the delimited text. It also lets you select the delimiter that's used to separate the values in this file. In this example, a tab is used to separate the values. If the delimiter used by the file isn't included in the Delimiter menu, you can select the Other option from this menu and then enter the delimiter in the text box that's provided.

The middle section of this dialog box lets you determine how the width of the imported table is set. In most cases, you'll use the Fit to Data option so the width of each column in the table accommodates the data it contains. That's the option that was used to create the table shown in this figure.

If you choose the Set To option instead, you can specify a value for the width of the table in either pixels or a percent. Then, the widths of the columns are set based on that width and the data they contain. Because Dreamweaver adds a width attribute to the table when you use this option, though, we don't recommend you use it. Instead, you should use the CSS width property.

The lower section of this dialog box lets you specify formatting options for the table. That includes cell padding, cell spacing, and a border. We recommend that you clear these three text boxes since the attributes that Dreamweaver generates for them aren't compliant with HTML5.

The menu in the lower section of this dialog box lets you apply basic formatting to the first row of a table. Although you can use the options in this menu to boldface, italicize, or both boldface and italicize the data in this row, it's typically better to convert the cells in this row to header cells as described in figure 11-5. Then, the data is boldfaced by default, and you can apply additional formatting using CSS.

A table with imported data after it's formatted

Year	Q1	Q2	Q3	Q4	Total Sales
2009	$242,533.00	$211,065.00	$302,332.00	$311,645.00	$1,067,575.00
2010	$712,857.00	$313,045.00	$650,031.00	$600,133.00	$2,276,066.00
2011	$506,345.00	$478,949.00	$408,203.00	$750,002.00	$2,143,499.00
2012	$640,322.00	$590,040.00	$612,342.00	$810,233.00	$2,652,937.00
2013	$750,323.00	$720,322.00	$823,002.00	$950,232.00	$3,243,879.00

The Import Tabular Data dialog box

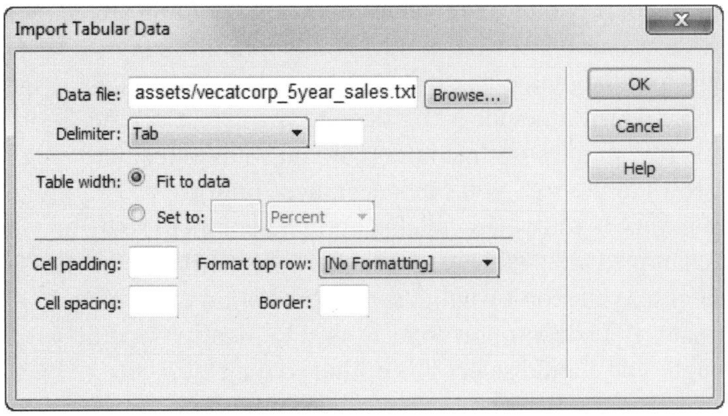

How to import tabular data

1. Choose File→Import→Tabular Data to display the Import Tabular Data dialog box.
2. Enter the path to the delimited text file you want to import, or click the Browse button to locate and select the file.
3. Choose the delimiter that's used by the file from the Delimiter menu, or choose the Other option from this menu and then enter the delimiter in the text box.
4. Choose the Fit to Data option to have Dreamweaver determine the width of the table based on its contents. (Because the Set To option causes a width attribute to be generated, which is deprecated in HTML5, you shouldn't use it.)
5. Be sure that the Cell Padding, Cell Spacing, and Border text boxes are empty, since the attributes they generate are deprecated in HTML5.
6. Select an option from the Format Top Row menu to boldface, italicize, or boldface and italicize the data in the first row. A better alternative is to convert this row to a header row.
7. Click OK to create a table with the imported data.

Description

- You can import tabular data from a *delimited text file* into a table. This is particularly useful for large tables that were created outside of Dreamweaver.

Figure 11-8 How to import tabular data

How to sort a table

Dreamweaver also lets you sort a table by one or two columns. This is illustrated in figure 11-9. Here, the table that was shown in the previous figure has been sorted by the Total Sales column in descending sequence.

To sort a table, you use the Sort Table dialog box shown here. This dialog box lets you select the column you want to sort by, the order in which you want to sort the column (alphabetically or numerically), and whether you want to sort it in ascending or descending sequence.

If it's possible for the column you're sorting to have duplicate values, you may want to sort by a second column. To do that, you use the second set of controls in this dialog box. Then, if two or more values in the first column are the same, the rows with those values are sorted by the second column.

The options at the bottom of the dialog box let you control how the sort works. For example, if a table doesn't include a header row, you can select the option that includes the first row in the sort. In contrast, if you want to include any header rows or footer rows in the sort, you can select those options.

The last option is useful only if you've applied background colors to some of the rows in the table. For example, some tables are formatted so alternating rows are different colors. In that case, you won't want to select this option or the row colors will no longer alternate. If a background color is used to identify specific rows by their content, though, you should select this option so the colors are maintained.

A table that's sorted in descending sequence by the last column

Year	Q1	Q2	Q3	Q4	Total Sales
2013	$750,323.00	$720,322.00	$823,002.00	$950,232.00	$3,243,879.00
2012	$640,322.00	$590,040.00	$612,342.00	$810,233.00	$2,652,937.00
2010	$712,857.00	$313,045.00	$650,031.00	$600,133.00	$2,276,066.00
2011	$506,345.00	$478,949.00	$408,203.00	$750,002.00	$2,143,499.00
2009	$242,533.00	$211,065.00	$302,332.00	$311,645.00	$1,067,575.00

The Sort Table dialog box

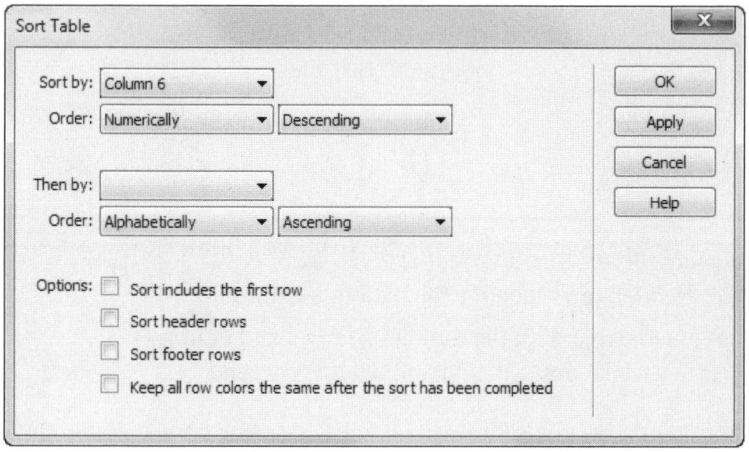

How to sort table data

1. Select the table that you want to sort and choose Commands→Sort Table to display the Sort Table dialog box.

2. Choose the number of the first column you want to sort by from the Sort By menu. Then, choose an option from the first Order menu to determine if the column will be sorted alphabetically or numerically, and choose an option from the second Order menu to determine if the column will be sorted in ascending or descending sequence.

3. To sort by a second column, select the column number from the Then By menu and then choose options from the two Order menus below that menu.

4. Check any of the options that are available to customize the sort.

5. To preview the sort, click the Apply button. Then, click the OK button to accept the sort, or click the Cancel button to return the table to its unsorted sequence.

Description

- You can sort a table by the data in one or two columns. If you sort by two columns and the data in two or more rows of the first column is the same, the data will be sorted by the second column.

Figure 11-9   How to sort a table

Perspective

As you've seen in this chapter, it's relatively easy to create tables. Remember, though, that you should only use tables when you're presenting tabular data. You should use CSS, not tables, for page layout.

Terms

table	header cell
row	caption
column	merge cells
cell	split a cell
data cell	delimited text file
header	

Summary

- A *table* consists of *rows* and *columns* that intersect at *cells*. *Data cells* contain the data of a table. *Header cells* identify the data in a column or row.

- You can insert a table into a web page with the number of rows and columns you specify. Once you create a table, you can add and delete rows and columns as necessary.

- Dreamweaver lets you *merge* two or more cells in a column or row into a single cell. It also lets you *split* a single cell into two or more cells.

- You can import tabular data from a *delimited text file* into a table. Then, you can work with that table from Dreamweaver just like any other table.

- You can sort the data in a table by one or two columns. Each column can be sorted alphabetically or numerically in ascending or descending sequence.

Exercise 11-1 Import and modify a table

In this exercise, you'll create a web page that imports a table, modifies it, and formats it, so it looks like the one below. This will give some quick practice with the use of tables.

Open the folder for this exercise and review its folders and files

1. Open the Exercises site, open the folder for this exercise, and open the sales.html file. Then, review the HTML and CSS for this page.

2. Note the assets folder and the salesdata.txt file that it contains. That's the file that contains the table that you will import into the sales.html page.

Add a table to a web page

3. In Code view, place the insertion point after the h1 element. Then, with figure 11-8 as a guide, import the tabular data from the salesdata.txt file. The delimiter is a Tab character, and you shouldn't set any of the other values.

4. Right-click in a cell in the left column of the table, and add a new column to its left. Then, add the names of the Vecta Corp products to the last three cells in the column as shown above.

5. Select the cells in the top row of the table and use the Property Inspector to convert them to th elements by clicking on the Header check box. Then, note the changes in Live view.

6. Select the cells in the left column of the table, use the Property Inspector to convert them to th cells, and note the changes in Live view.

7. Select a cell in the top row of the table, and add a new row above it. Then, merge all of the cells in this top row, and add this text to the merged row: "Total Sales by Product."

Format the table

8. To align the data in the cells of the table, use the CSS Designer to create a style rule for the table selector that sets the text-align property to right. Since most of the data is numeric, right alignment works for most of the cells.

9. To add a border around the table, set the border-width property for the table to 1 pixel and the border-style property to solid.

10. To add space above and below the text in each cell of the table, first set the border-collapse property for the table to collapse. Then, create a style rule for the th and td elements (th, td) that sets the left and right padding to 1em and the top and bottom padding to .5em.

11. To center the heading at the top of the table, select the merged cell and use the Property Inspector to set its id to tableHeader. Then, use the CSS Designer to add a style rule for this id (#tableHeader) that aligns the text in the center of the cell.

12. To left align the product names in the first column of the table, first create a style rule for the left class (.left) that sets the text-align property to left. Then, select the three cells that contain the product names and use the Property Inspector to set their class values to left.

13. When you're through experimenting, close and save all files.

12

How to work more efficiently in Dreamweaver

In this chapter, you'll learn how to use some of the often overlooked features that can improve how you work in Dreamweaver. Although you may not use these features on a regular basis, you should at least know they're available so you can use them whenever that makes sense.

How to use snippets

Snippets are blocks of predefined code that you can add to a web page. Dreamweaver comes with a number of built-in snippets that range from a simple footer with bulleted links to JavaScript functions and calculations. You can also create your own custom snippets. Then, these snippets are available from any website you create.

How to use the Snippets panel to work with Snippets

To work with snippets, you use the *Snippets panel* shown in figure 12-1. As you can see, the snippets are organized into folders. Here, the Footers folder has been expanded and the second footer snippet has been selected. A preview of this snippet is displayed in the pane at the top of the panel.

Once you locate the snippet you want to use, the technique you use to insert it depends on whether you want to insert it at a specific location on the web page or wrap it around a selection in the web page. To insert a snippet at a specific location, you can either drag it from the Snippets panel to that location, or you can position the cursor at that location and then select the snippet and click the Insert button. To wrap a snippet around a selection, you have to make the selection first and then select the snippet and click the Insert button. Then, part of the snippet is placed before the selection and part of it is placed after the selection.

After you insert a snippet, you can customize it so it looks and works the way you want it to. For instance, after you insert the footer snippet shown here, you'll want to modify the text so it's appropriate for your site. You'll also need to modify the href attributes for the links so they point to the correct files. And you may need to change the styles for the inserted elements. Keep in mind, though, that when you insert a snippet that contains formatting, the formatting is implemented using inline styles. Because of that, you may want to move these styles to an external style sheet before you change the formatting.

You can also use the Snippets panel to perform other functions related to snippets. To do that, you use the icons at the right side of the toolbar. The first icon lets you create a new folder for storing snippets. You may want to do that if you create a custom snippet that doesn't fit into any of the existing folder categories. You may also want to do that so you can store the snippets you use most often in a separate folder. If you create a new folder, you can add snippets to it by simply dragging them into the folder.

The second icon lets you create a custom snippet. You'll learn how to do that in the next figure. The third icon lets you edit an existing snippet using the same dialog box you use to create a snippet. And the fourth icon lets you delete an existing snippet.

The Snippets panel with a footer snippet selected

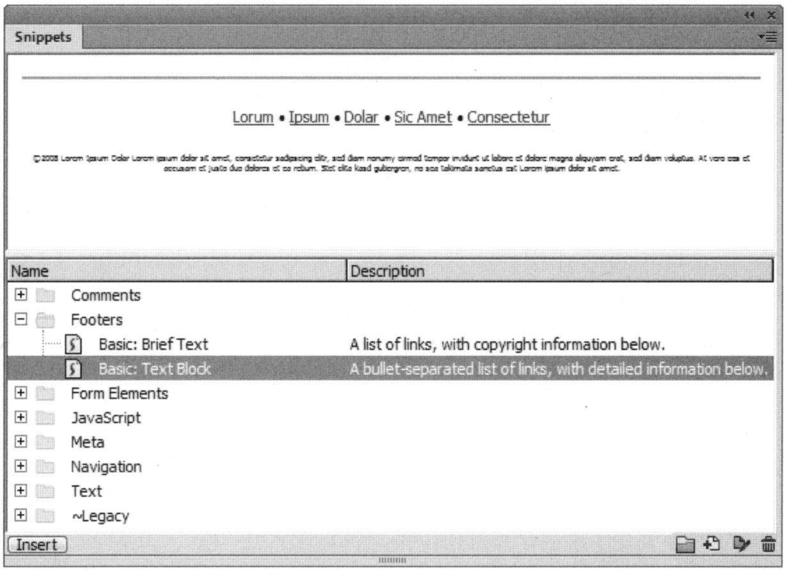

Description

- A *snippet* consists of predefined content that you can add to your web pages. To work with snippets, you use the *Snippets panel* (Window→Snippets).

- To display a preview of a snippet in the Snippets panel, locate and select the snippet in the list of snippets that's displayed.

- To insert a snippet into a web page, drag it from the Snippets panel to the location where you want it to appear on the web page. Or, position the cursor where you want the snippet to appear, and then select the snippet in the Snippets panel and click the Insert button at the left side of the toolbar.

- Some snippets wrap around a selection in a web page. In other words, part of the snippet is inserted before the selection, and part of it is inserted after the selection. Before you insert this type of snippet, you must make a selection in the web page.

- After you insert a snippet, you'll need to edit the inserted content so it's appropriate for your web page. You may also need to add CSS to format the content.

- Snippets that insert HTML use inline styles for formatting. Because of that, you'll want to move these styles to an external style sheet and then change the formatting so the elements appear the way you want them to.

- You can use the icons at the right side of the toolbar to create a new folder for storing snippets (⌹), to create a new snippet (⌹), to edit the selected snippet (⌹), and to delete the selected snippet (🗑). If you create a new folder, you can drag any snippets you want into that folder.

- Both the snippets that come with Dreamweaver and any custom snippets you define are available from any website.

Figure 12-1   How to use the Snippets panel to work with snippets

How to create custom snippets

Instead of using the snippets that come with Dreamweaver, you can create your own custom snippets. The easiest way to do that is to add the code you want to include in the snippet to your website. If the snippet has a visual interface, you can do that from Design view. Then, you select the code for the snippet in Code view, select the folder where you want to store the snippet in the Snippets panel, and click the New Snippet icon to display the Snippet dialog box shown in figure 12-2. When you do that, the code you selected is placed in the Insert Code text box. Of course, you can also enter code directly into this text box.

The code shown in this figure is for a horizontal navigation menu. Notice here that the styles for the menu are coded inline. That's because a snippet can be used in any web page in any website, so all of its code must be self-contained.

To complete the snippet, you need to enter a name and description for it and choose a Snippet Type option to determine if the snippet will wrap around a selection or be inserted as a block at a specific location. If you choose the Wrap Selection option, the Insert Code text box is replaced by Insert Before and Insert After text boxes. As their names imply, any code in the Insert Before text box will be inserted before the selection that's made when the snippet is used, and any code in the Insert After text box will be inserted after the selection. For example, you could create a simple snippet that displays selected text as a superscript by entering ^{in the Insert Before text box and} in the Insert After text box.

Finally, you need to choose a Preview Type option. If the snippet has a visual interface, you'll want to choose the Design option. Then, the snippet will appear in the Preview pane of the Snippets panel as shown in the previous figure. Otherwise, you can select the Code option so the code for the snippet is displayed in the Preview pane.

Like the snippets that come with Dreamweaver, the snippet shown here provides generic code that you could use in any website. Although you might think that you would create snippets that are specific to a particular website, that's not usually the case. Instead, you would store code like that in a library item. Then, you have the added advantage of being able to modify the library item to change every occurrence of it in the website. To learn more about how this works, please see chapter 9.

The Snippet dialog box with a custom snippet

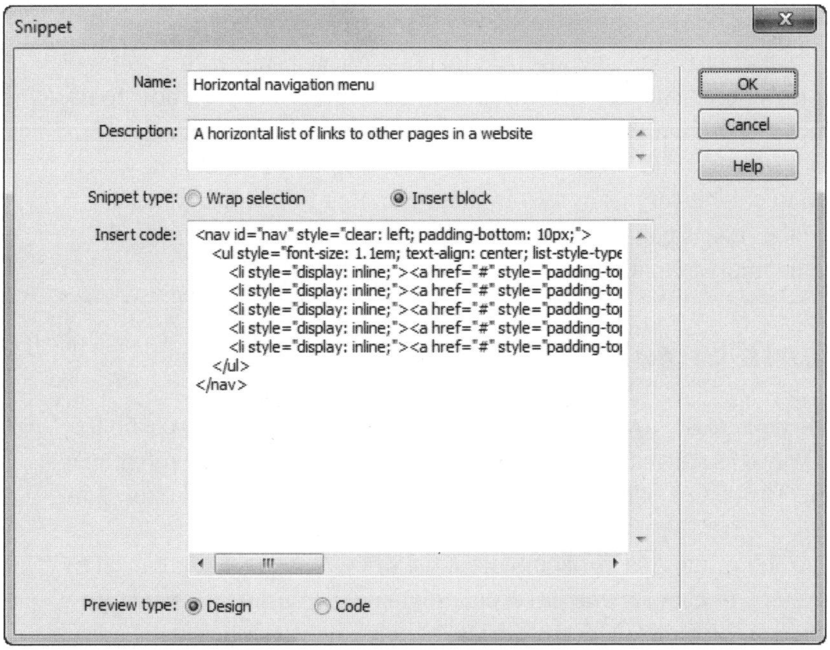

```
Snippet                                                    X

         Name:  Horizontal navigation menu                       OK

   Description:  A horizontal list of links to other pages in a website    Cancel

                                                                  Help

 Snippet type:  ○ Wrap selection          ◉ Insert block

   Insert code:  <nav id="nav" style="clear: left; padding-bottom: 10px;">
                   <ul style="font-size: 1.1em; text-align: center; list-style-type
                     <li style="display: inline;"><a href="#" style="padding-to
                     <li style="display: inline;"><a href="#" style="padding-to
                     <li style="display: inline;"><a href="#" style="padding-to
                     <li style="display: inline;"><a href="#" style="padding-to
                     <li style="display: inline;"><a href="#" style="padding-to
                   </ul>
                 </nav>

                  ◀    III              ▶

  Preview type:  ◉ Design        ○ Code
```

The snippet after it's inserted into a web page

| Item 1 | Item 2 | Item 3 | Item 4 | Item 5 |

How to create a snippet that inserts a block of code

1. Highlight the code you want the snippet to contain in Code view.

2. Select the folder where you want to store the snippet in the Snippets panel, and then click the New Snippet icon (⬚) to display the Snippet dialog box. The code you selected appears in the Insert Code text box.

3. Enter a name and description for the snippet, and make sure that the Insert Block option is selected.

4. Select the Design or Code option to determine whether the design or code for the snippet is displayed in the Preview pane of the Snippets panel.

5. Click OK to create the snippet and return to the Snippets panel.

How to create a snippet that wraps around text

1. Select the Wrap Selection option in the Snippet dialog box. The Insert Code text box is replaced with Insert Before and Insert After text boxes, and any code you selected before you displayed the Snippet dialog box is displayed in the Insert Before text box.

2. Enter the code you want inserted before and after the selection you make when you insert the snippet.

Figure 12-2   How to create custom snippets

How to use the Assets panel

The *Assets panel* provides a centralized location for working with a variety of objects. If you've read chapter 9, for example, you've already seen how to use the Assets panel to work with templates and library items. But you can also use the Assets panel to work with other objects that you include in a website, which can be referred to collectively as *assets*. In the topics that follow, I'll present an overview of the Assets panel. Then, I'll show you how you can identify the assets you use the most to make them easy to work with.

How the Assets panel works

When you add an asset to a website, it's stored in Dreamweaver's cache for that site. That way, Dreamweaver can track that asset to make sure its references are maintained. The Assets panel lets you work with the assets that are stored in the cache.

Figure 12-3 shows the Assets panel with a list of the images that are used by the current website. To choose what assets are displayed, you select a category from the left side of the panel. The categories include images, colors, URLs, SWF files, videos, scripts, templates, and library items. When you select a category, the assets in that category are displayed in the bottom pane, and you can select an asset to display a preview of it in the top pane.

The information that's displayed for each type of asset varies. In this figure, for example, you can see that the information for an image includes its physical dimensions, the size of the image file, the image file type, and the path to the file within the website. In contrast, the information for a color includes just the color value and an indication of whether it's a web-safe color.

The preview that's displayed also varies depending on the type of asset. If the asset has a visual interface, for example, that interface is displayed. Otherwise, the preview might consist of code like it does for a script or a link like it does for a URL.

Finally, the functionality that's available from the toolbar in the Assets panel varies depending on the type of asset. For example, you can add or delete templates and library items, but not other assets. In contrast, you can't add a template or library item to your list of favorites, but you can add any other asset to this list. Similarly, you insert some assets like images and movies, but you apply other assets like colors and templates.

You can also initiate the editing of some assets from the Assets panel by double-clicking on the asset or selecting it and clicking the Edit icon. Then, if an editor is available for that asset, the editor is opened and the asset is displayed. Note, however, that most assets require an external editor. To edit an image file, for example, you must have an image editor installed on your computer. In addition, the file type for the image must be associated with the image editor in Dreamweaver. To create this association, you can display the File Types / Editors category in the Preferences dialog box (Edit→Preferences) and then select the file extension and editor.

The Assets panel with the Images category selected

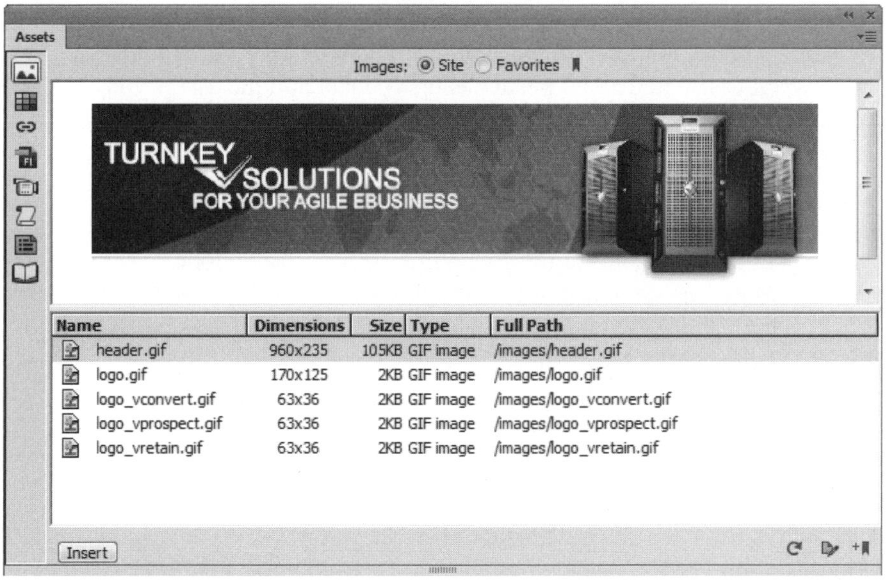

Description

- You can use the *Assets panel* (Window→Assets) to work with any of the *asset* categories listed down the left side of the panel. These categories include all the images, colors, URLs, SWF files, videos, scripts, templates, and library items in your website that have been cached by Dreamweaver.

- When you select an asset category, a list of the assets in that category is displayed in the bottom pane of the panel along with information about each asset. In addition, a preview of the selected asset is displayed in the top pane.

- The features that are available for each type of asset differ. In all cases, though, the Assets panel includes a button at the left side of the toolbar that lets you insert or apply the asset. It also includes an icon near the right side of the toolbar that lets you refresh the list of assets for the site.

- In some cases, the toolbar also includes icons for creating a new asset, editing an asset, deleting an asset, or adding an asset to your list of favorites.

- If an asset can be stored in your list of favorites, options appear at the top of the panel to let you choose to display all assets in the site or just your favorite as See figure 12-4 for more on working with favorites.

- You can use the Assets panel to rename some assets. To do tha then click its name and enter a new name.

- To edit an asset, double-click on it to display it i available.

Figure 12-3

How to create and work with favorites

If a website includes a large number of assets, it can be difficult to find one when you want to use it. To make that easier, you can add the assets you use most often to a list of favorites within any category except for templates or library items. Figure 12-4 shows you how to do that.

To add an asset to the list of favorites for a category, you simply select the asset and click the Add to Favorites icon. You can also select two or more assets to add them to the list of favorites at the same time. When you're done, you can select the Favorites option at the top of the Assets panel to display just the assets in your favorites list.

Unlike other assets in the Assets panel, you can organize your favorite assets into folders. To do that, you start by clicking the New Favorites Folder icon that becomes available when the favorites are displayed. Then, the new folder will appear in the bottom pane and you can enter a name for it. To add favorites to the folder, you simply drag them into the folder.

You can also remove one or more assets or folders from a favorites list as described in this figure. If you delete a folder, you should realize that any assets it contains are also rʳ   ʳed from the favorites list. Note, however, that any assets you remoᵛ   ᵛorites list aren't removed from your website. So they're still lʲ   ʲ the Site option at the top of the Assets panel.

How the Assets panel works

the appropriate editor if one is

select the asset and

sets.

The Assets panel with favorite image assets inside a folder

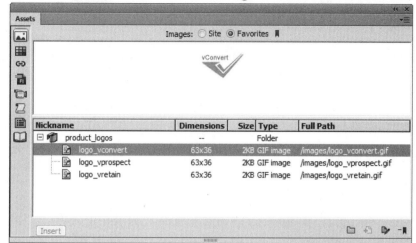

How to add assets to a favorites list

1. Select the asset category you want to work with, and then select one or more assets from the list that's displayed.

2. Click the Add to Favorites icon (+▮) at the right side of the toolbar. An alert indicating that the assets have been added to your favorites will appear. Click OK.

How to create a folder to organize your favorites

1. Click the Favorites option at the top of the Assets panel to see a list of the favorites.

2. Click the New Favorites Folder icon (▢) near the right side of the toolbar. The new folder will appear in the favorites list, and you can enter a name for the folder.

3. Drag any assets that you want to move to the folder into the folder.

How to remove assets or folders from your favorites list

- Click the Favorites option at the top of the Assets panel to display a list of your favorites.

- To remove one or more assets, select those assets using standard techniques and then click the Remove from Favorites icon (-▮) near the right side of the toolbar.

- To remove one or more folders and any favorites they contain, select the folders and then click the Remove from Favorites icon.

Description

- *Favorites* are assets that you use often and want to be able to access quickly. To display the favorites for an asset category, click the Favorites option at the top of the Assets panel.

- To make favorites even easier to work with, you can organize them into folders.

- When you remove an asset from your favorites list, the asset isn't deleted from your website. The reference to the asset is simply removed from the favorites list.

Figure 12-4   How to create and work with favorites

How to use the find and replace feature

Dreamweaver provides a powerful find and replace feature that you can use to find and replace text or source code. This feature lets you select the area you want to search, from a selection in a single document all the way up to an entire site. It also lets you specify advanced search options, and it lets you perform special actions on the tag you specify.

How the find and replace feature works

Figure 12-5 describes the basic techniques for using the find and replace feature. To perform a find and replace operation, you use the Find and Replace dialog box shown at the top of this figure. The Find In menu lets you choose where you want to search. In this example, the entire site will be searched. However, you can also search within selected text, a document, all open documents, selected documents, or a folder within the site.

The Search menu lets you choose the type of content you want to search for. To search for a text string, you can use the Source Code option as shown here. Note that when you use this option, Dreamweaver includes the HTML in the search. If that's not what you want, you can use the Text option instead. Then, Dreamweaver will ignore any HTML that interrupts the text. The other menu options let you search using advanced options and search for specific tags. You'll learn more about using these search options later.

After you identify the type of content you want to search for and where you want to search, you specify the value you want to search for in the Find text box. In addition, if you want to replace any occurrences of the search value, you need to enter a replacement value in the Replace text box.

To further refine a search, you can use the options at the bottom of this dialog box. For example, if you only want to search for values that have the same case as the value you specify, you can check the Match Case option. In this example, I've selected the Ignore Whitespace option. That way, Dreamweaver will include occurrences of the search value that have more than one space between "vRetain" and "1.0".

To perform a find operation, you use the Find Next or Find All button. If you click Find Next, the next occurrence of the search value is selected. If you click Find All, all occurrences of the search value are displayed in the Search Panel. You'll learn more about this panel in the next figure.

To perform a replace operation, you use the Replace and Replace All buttons. If you click Replace, the current occurrence of the search value is replaced with the replacement value and Dreamweaver selects the next occurrence. If you click Replace All, all of the occurrences of the search value are replaced with the replacement value, and a list of the replacements is displayed in the Search panel.

By the way, you should realize that if you perform a replace operation on documents that aren't currently open, the operation can't be undone. Because of that, Dreamweaver displays a warning message when that's about to happen.

The Find and Replace dialog box

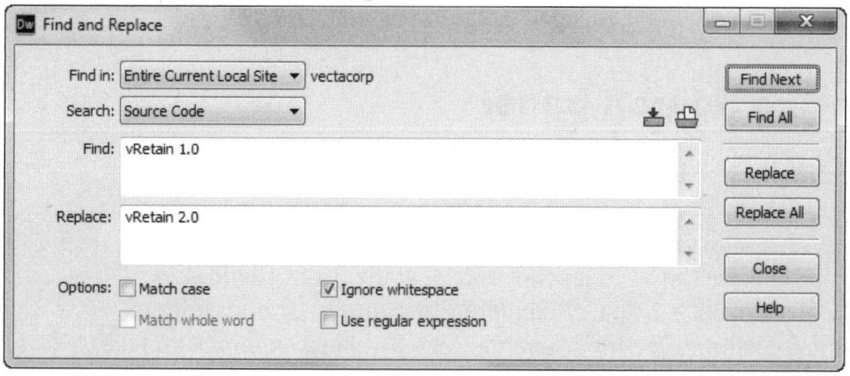

Description

- The Find and Replace dialog box makes it possible to find and, optionally, replace text or source code within selected text, a document, all open documents, selected documents, a folder within the site, or the entire site. To display this dialog box, choose Edit→Find and Replace.

- To determine where the search is performed, choose an option from the Find In menu. If you choose the Folder option, a folder icon will appear and you can click it to choose the folder. If you choose the Selected Files In Site option, you must select the folders or files you want to search in the Files panel.

- To determine the type of content that's searched for, choose an option from the Search menu. If you choose the Source Code option, Dreamweaver searches for the exact text string you specify. If you choose the Text option, Dreamweaver ignores any HTML that interrupts the text string. See figure 12-7 for details on the Text (Advanced) option.

- The Find and Replace text boxes specify the value to be searched for and replaced. If you choose the Specific Tag option from the Search menu, these options aren't available. See figure 12-8 for details.

- The four check boxes determine whether Dreamweaver searches only for values that match the case of the value entered in the Find text box; searches only for values that are whole words; ignores whitespace; and searches for values with the pattern you specify in the Find text box using regular expressions.

- After you perform a search, or *query*, you can click the Save Query icon (⬇) to save the query as a .dwr file anywhere on your computer. Then, you can click the Load Query icon (📂) to load the saved query so you can run it again.

- The Find Next button causes the next occurrence of the search value to be selected. Then, you can click the Replace button to replace that occurrence, or you can click the Find Next button again to find the next occurrence.

- The Find All button causes all occurrences of the search value to be located and displayed in the Search tab of the Results panel. See figure 12-6 for details.

- The Replace All button causes all occurrences of the search value to be replaced with the replacement value.

Figure 12-5   How the Find and Replace feature works

Then, before you perform the operation, you may want to review the occurrences of the search value that will be changed using the Search panel.

How to use the Search panel

In the last topic, you learned that if you click the Find All or Replace All button in the Find and Replace dialog box, Dreamweaver displays the Search panel. Figure 12-6 shows this panel and describes how you use it.

You'll typically use the Search panel to review the list of found occurrences before you replace them. This panel includes two columns of information. The first column identifies the file where the search value was found, and the second column displays the search value underlined in red along with some of the surrounding text. Then, if you need to, you can double-click on any item in the list to display that item in the Document window with the search value highlighted.

If you want to change a find operation, you can do that by clicking the Find and Replace icon at the top left of the Search panel. This redisplays the Find and Replace dialog box. Then, you can change the options any way you want and click the Find All button again to update the list in the Search panel.

When you're satisfied with the results of the find operation, you can replace the found occurrences. To do that, you can click the Find and Replace icon to display the Find and Replace dialog box. Then, you can enter the replacement text if you haven't already done so and click the Replace All button. This updates the Search panel with the results of the replace operation. To indicate that the occurrences have been replaced, a large green dot appears to the left of the file name as shown here.

The Search panel with the results of a find and replace operation

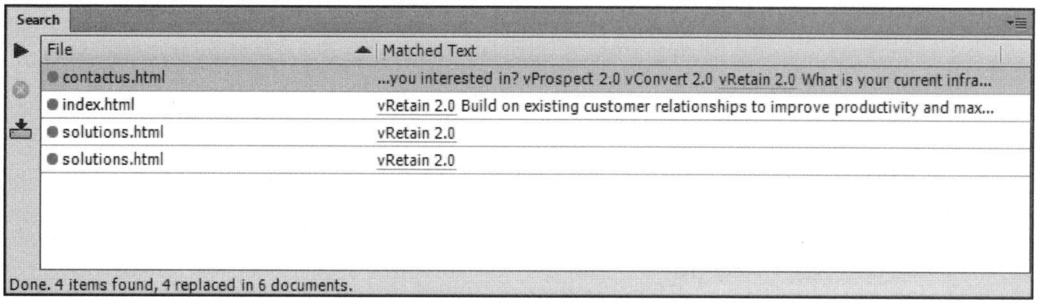

Description

- If you want to review all of the occurrences of the search value before replacing it, you can click the Find All button in the Find and Replace dialog box. Then, a list of the found occurrences is displayed in the Search panel.

- You can also click the Replace All button in the Find and Replace dialog box to replace all occurrences of the search value with the replacement value. Then, a list of the replaced occurrences is displayed in the Search panel.

- If an occurrence has been replaced, a large green dot appears to the left of the file name.

- The two columns in the Search panel indicate the name of the file where the search value was found and a portion of the text that surrounds that value. The actual search or replacement value is underlined in red.

- You can double-click on an item in the Search panel to display that item in the Document window with the search or replace value highlighted.

- You can use the Find and Replace icon (▶) at the left side of the Search panel to redisplay the Find and Replace dialog box. Then, you can use this dialog box to replace the search value or change the find operation.

Figure 12-6   How to use the Search panel

How to use the advanced options for finding text

In addition to the search options you saw in figure 12-5, Dreamweaver provides some advanced options that you can use to find text. To display these options, you select the Text (Advanced) option from the Search menu in the Find and Replace dialog box. Figure 12-7 shows how these advanced options work.

When you first select the Text (Advanced) option, the initial controls identified in this figure are displayed. The menu lets you select whether the search value occurs inside or outside a tag, and the combo box lets you enter or select the tag. You can also select [any tag] from the combo box, in which case the search value can occur within any tag. In this example, the search value must occur within an <a> tag.

To further refine the search, you can click the **+** button to the left of the initial controls. Then, additional controls are displayed below the initial controls as shown here. This time, the menu that's displayed includes the six options that are summarized in the second table in this figure.

The first two options, With Attribute and Without Attribute, let you specify whether the opening tag for the search value contains the attribute you specify. If you use the With Attribute option, you must also specify a relational operator and a value for the attribute. In most cases, you'll use the equals (=) operator so Dreamweaver will search for an attribute with the value you specify. In this example, an <a> tag that contains the search value must include a class attribute with the value "solutions". Dreamweaver can also search for values that are greater than (>), less than (<), or not equal to (!=) the specified value.

The next two options, Containing and Not Containing, let you specify whether the tag that contains the search value also contains the specified text or tag. If you select one of these options, another menu is displayed that lets you choose if you want to specify text or a tag. If you select the Text option, a text box is displayed where you can enter the text. If you select the Tag option, a combo box is displayed that lets you enter or choose a tag.

The last two options, Inside Tag and Not Inside Tag, are the same as the two options in the initial menu. They let you specify whether the search value occurs inside or outside a tag. The Inside Tag option is particularly useful if you want to search for a value that occurs within a tag that's nested within another tag.

The Find and Replace dialog box with the Text (Advanced) option selected

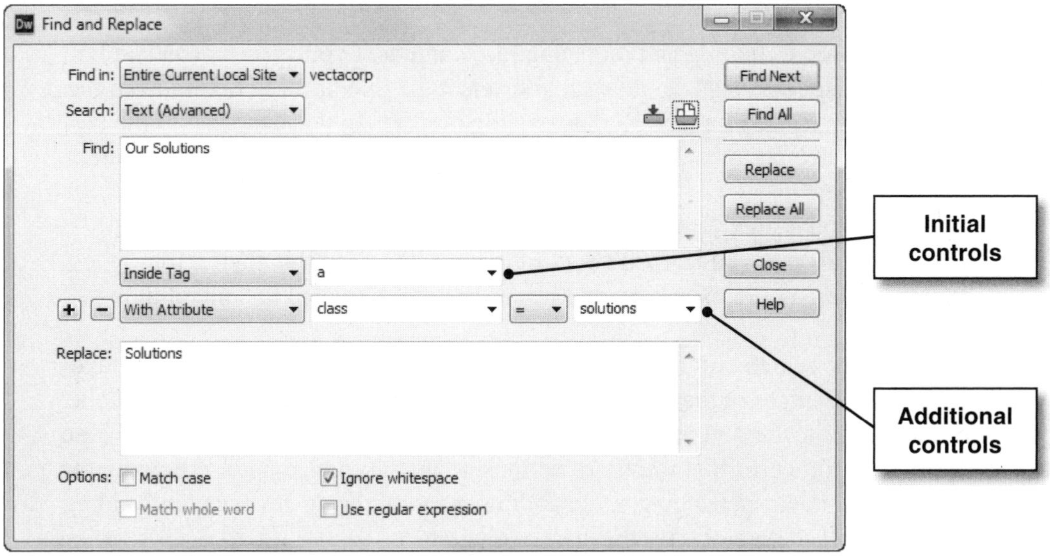

Initial advanced options

Option	Description
Inside Tag	The search text must occur within the specified tag.
Not Inside Tag	The search text must not occur within the specified tag.

Additional advanced options

Option	Description
With Attribute	The tag must have the specified attribute. The attribute can be equal to, not equal to, greater than, or less than the specified value.
Without Attribute	The tag must not have the specified attribute.
Containing	The tag must contain the specified text or tag.
Not Containing	The tag must not contain the specified text or tag.
Inside Tag	The tag must occur within the specified tag.
Not Inside Tag	The tag must not occur within the specified tag.

Description

- When you choose the Text (Advanced) option from the Search menu in the Find and Replace dialog box, additional controls become available. You can use these controls to further refine the search operation.

- By default, the initial controls identified above are displayed when you select the Text (Advanced) option. If you click the **+** button, the additional controls shown above are displayed so you can further limit the search operation. These controls change depending on which option you choose from the menu.

- Each time you click the **+** button, another set of controls is displayed. You can also click the **−** button to remove a set of controls.

Figure 12-7   How to use the advanced options for finding text

How to find and replace specific tags

In addition to finding and replacing the search text you specify, you can find and replace specific tags. To do that, you select the Specific Tag option from the Search menu in the Find and Replace dialog box. Then, you can specify the tag you want to search for as shown in figure 12-8. Here, Dreamweaver will search for an <a> tag.

When you search for a specific tag, you can also include the additional search options that you learned about in the last figure. In this figure, for example, the <a> tag must have an href attribute that's equal to "oursolutions. html".

Once the search criteria are set, you can specify the action you want to take on any occurrences of the tag that meet those criteria. To do that, you select one of the Action menu options that are summarized in the table in this figure. These options let you perform a variety of actions, including replacing or removing the tag and its contents, changing a tag, adding or removing an attribute, and adding text or HTML before or after the start or end tag.

When you choose one of the action options, additional controls are displayed that let you provide the required information. In this figure, for example, the Set Attribute option is selected. This option lets you add an attribute to a tag. To do that, you must specify the attribute and its value as shown here.

The Find and Replace dialog box with the Specific Tag option selected

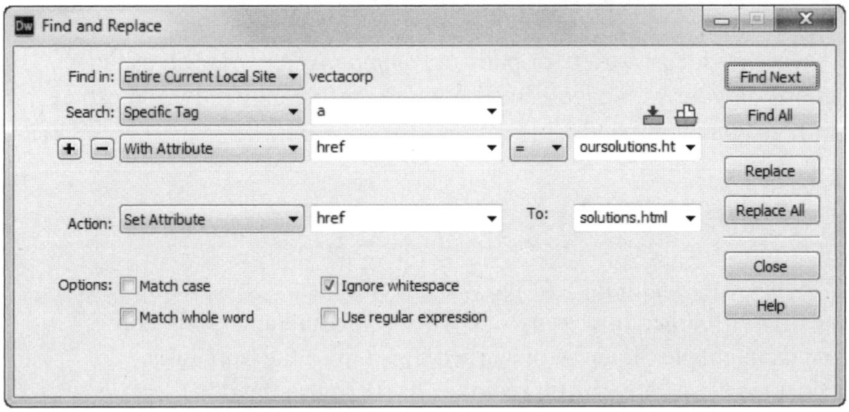

Action menu options

Option	Description
Replace Tag & Contents	Replaces the tag and contents with the specified text.
Replace Contents Only	Replaces the contents of the tag with the specified text.
Remove Tag & Contents	Removes the tag and its contents.
Strip Tag	Removes the tag but leaves its contents.
Change Tag	Changes the tag to the specified tag.
Set Attribute	Adds the specified attribute with the specified value to the tag.
Remove Attribute	Removes the specified attribute from the tag.
Add Before Start Tag	Adds the specified text or HTML before the start tag.
Add After End Tag	Adds the specified text or HTML after the end tag.
Add After Start Tag	Adds the specified text or HTML after the start tag.
Add Before End Tag	Adds the specified text or HTML before the end tag.

Description

- When you choose the Specific Tag option from the Search menu in the Find and Replace dialog box, you can enter or select the tag you want to search for in the combo box to the right of this menu.

- The additional advanced options described in figure 12-7 are also available when you choose the Specific Tag option. In addition, you can perform any of the actions described in the table above when the search conditions are satisfied.

Figure 12-8   How to find and replace specific tags

How to work with commands

Dreamweaver provides a variety of built-in *commands* that you can use to perform functions on your web pages. In addition to these commands, you can create your own custom commands.

A summary of the built-in commands

Figure 12-9 presents a summary of the built-in commands that Dreamweaver provides. You already learned how to use the Check Spelling and Optimize Image commands in chapter 4, and you learned how to use the Sort Table command in chapter 11. Although you're not as likely to use the other commands, they can come in handy from time to time.

In particular, if you find yourself working on a website that wasn't created with Dreamweaver, you might want to use the Apply Source Formatting or Apply Source Formatting to Selection command. These commands apply Dreamweaver's formatting preferences to an entire document or the code you select, and they can make it easier to work with a document in Code view. If you want to change any of Dreamweaver's formatting preferences before using these commands, you can do that from the Code Format category of the Preferences dialog box (Edit→Preferences).

The commands in the Commands menu

Command	Description
Check Spelling	Checks the spelling in the current document. See chapter 4 for details.
Apply Source Formatting	Applies Dreamweaver's current formatting preferences such as indentation and tabs to an existing HTML document.
Apply Source Formatting to Selection	Applies Dreamweaver's current formatting preferences to the selected code while in Code view.
Clean Up HTML	Displays a dialog box that lets you select the cleanup you want to perform. That includes removing empty tags, redundant nested tags, and special markup that Dreamweaver may add. You can also remove one or more tags that you specify.
Clean Up Word HTML	Displays a dialog box that lets you clean up HTML that is copied in from a Word document. That includes removing word-specific markup, cleaning up CSS and font tags, fixing invalidly nested tags, and applying source formatting.
Clean Up Web Fonts Script Tag	Checks which web fonts are being used on the current page and removes unnecessary values from the script tag. This ensures that only fonts that will actually be used on the web page are downloaded.
Externalize JavaScript	Moves inline JavaScript code or embedded script tags to an external JavaScript .js file. Dreamweaver also adds a new script tag to the HTML that links to the new external file.
Remove FLV Detection	Removes Flash Player detection code that's placed outside the object tag that identifies the FLV file. This is only necessary if you delete a Flash video that was added using Dreamweaver CS3 or earlier. In later versions, the Flash Player detection code is placed directly in the object tag.
Optimize Image	Displays a dialog box that lets you adjust the quality and size of an image. See chapter 4 for details.
Sort Table	Sorts a table by the columns you specify. See chapter 11 for details.

Description

- Dreamweaver comes with several *commands* that are available from the Commands menu. You've already learned about some of these commands, and you're not likely to use the others often. But you should at least be aware of what these commands do.

Figure 12-9   A summary of the built-in commands

How to use the History panel

To create custom commands, you use the History panel. Before you learn how to do that, though, you need to understand how the History panel works. This panel is described in figure 12-10.

The *History panel* lists the changes you've made to a document since that document was opened. In this figure, for example, you can see that four changes have been made to the current document. When working in this panel, each change is referred to as a step.

One of the basic functions of the History panel is to let you undo or redo changes. To undo changes, you can simply drag the slider at the left side of the panel up past the steps you want to undo. Alternately, you can click to the left of a step in the list. Then, the slider automatically moves to that step and any changes after that step are undone.

Similarly, you can redo a change by dragging the slider down to the last step you want to redo. Or, you can click to the left of a step to redo all changes through that step. Note that if you undo one or more changes and then make additional changes, you can no longer redo the original changes.

Of course, you can also use the Undo or Redo buttons in the Standard toolbar or the Undo or Redo option in the Edit menu to undo or redo a change. When you use these techniques, though, you can only undo or redo one change at a time. In addition, if you use the Undo or Redo button, you don't know what the changes are.

You can also use the History panel to repeat one or more steps. Before you do that, you must either position the cursor in the Document window where you want the steps to be repeated, or you must select the text or element you want the steps applied to. Then, you can select the steps you want to repeat in the History panel and click the Replay button.

You can also copy one or more steps from the current document and play them back in another document. To do that, you select the steps and then click the Copy Steps icon. Then, you can switch to the other document, position the cursor or select an element, and then click the Paste button in the Standard toolbar or choose Edit→Paste.

If you think you'll want to repeat a sequence of steps regularly, you can create a custom command that includes those steps. To do that, you select the steps and then click the Save As Command icon. You'll learn more about how that works next.

The History panel with four steps

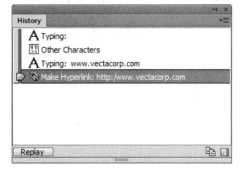

Description

- The *History panel* displays a list of the steps you performed within a document in the order you performed them. To display the History panel, choose Window→History.

- You can drag the slider at the left side of the History panel up to undo previous steps or down to redo previous steps. You can also undo or redo steps by clicking to the left of a step in the list.

- The Replay button at the left side of the toolbar lets you repeat the steps you select. Before you click this button, you must position the cursor in the Document window where you want the steps repeated or select the text or element you want the steps applied to.

- You can use the Copy Steps icon (⧉) to copy steps to the clipboard. Then, you can use the Edit→Paste command or the Paste button in the Standard toolbar in another document to play the steps back in that document.

- You can use the Save As Command icon (⊟) to save steps as a named command. See figure 12-11 for details.

- By default, the History panel displays a maximum of 50 steps. To change this number, choose Edit→Preferences to display the Preferences dialog box. Then, display the General category, and change the value in the Maximum Number of History Steps text box.

- When you close a document, its history is cleared. To clear the history without closing the document, right-click in the History panel and choose Clear History from the context menu that's displayed.

Figure 12-10   How to use the History panel

How to create and work with custom commands

In addition to the commands that come with Dreamweaver, you can create your own custom commands. You might want to do that if you find yourself repeating the same sequence of steps frequently. Figure 12-11 shows how to create your own custom commands.

When you select the steps you want to include in the command from the History panel and click the Save As Command icon, Dreamweaver displays the Save As Command dialog box shown at the top of this figure. This dialog box lets you enter a name for the command. Once you do that, the command will appear at the bottom of the Commands menu, and you can use it just as you would if you were replaying the steps from the History panel.

You can also rename or delete custom commands. To do that, you use the Edit Command List dialog box. To rename a command, you just click on it and then enter a new name. To delete a command, you click on it and then click the Delete button.

The Save As Command dialog box

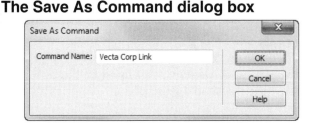

The Edit Command List dialog box with a custom command

How to create a command

1. Open the History panel and select one or more steps.
2. Click the Save As Command icon to display the Save As Command dialog box.
3. Enter a unique name for the Command and click OK.

How to apply a command

1. Position the cursor in the document window where you want the command applied, or select the text or element you want the command applied to.
2. Choose Commands→<command name>.

How to rename or delete commands

*   Choose Commands→Edit Command List to display the Edit Command List dialog box.
*   To rename a command, click on it and then enter the new name.
*   To delete a command, click on it and then click the Delete button.

Description

*   If you think you may need to reuse a set of steps in the History panel, you can save them as a command.
*   Unlike the steps in the History panel, a command is available after you close a document and exit from Dreamweaver. Commands you create are also available from any site.
*   Custom commands appear at the bottom of the Commands menu.

Figure 12-11   How to create and work with custom commands

Other skills
for improving your efficiency

In addition to the skills you've already learned, Dreamweaver provides three more skills for improving your efficiency that you should know about.

How to use Element Quick View

Element Quick View is a new feature of Dreamweaver CC 2014 that lets you display and work with the structure of an HTML document in a quick and easy way. To display Element Quick View, you click the </> icon at the left side of the Tag selector. Then, the elements of the document are displayed in a hierarchical tree as shown in figure 12-12.

To display the elements that another element contains, you can click on that element to expand it. To display the structure shown in this figure, for example, I started by clicking the body element to expand it. Then, I clicked on the main and aside elements to expand those elements.

If you click on an element that's already expanded, that element is collapsed. In addition, when you click on any element in Element Quick View, it's selected in the Document window.

Element Quick View is most useful for modifying the structure of an HTML document. To start, you can move an element from one location in the document to another by simply dragging it. In this figure, for example, I clicked the aside element and then dragged it before the main element. When I did that, the main element was shaded and a green line appeared above it to indicate where the aside element would be positioned. Then, when I dropped the aside element, it was moved before the main element in the HTML.

You can also drag an element and drop it on the shaded element (the reference element) rather than above it. When you do that, no green line is displayed, and the element is positioned as the first child element of the reference element. If I had dropped the aside element on the main element instead of above it, for example, the aside element would have been positioned before the first h2 element within the main element. Another way to do this would be to just drag the aside element above the h2 element. If the main element didn't contain any child elements, though, dropping the aside element on the main element would be the only way to make it a child element.

In addition to moving elements, you can also use Element Quick View to copy, paste, duplicate, and delete elements. To do that, you use the context menu that's displayed when you right-click on an element. Note that when you copy an element, any child elements it contains are also copied. Then, when you paste the element, it's placed below the selected element. A duplicated element also includes child elements and is placed below the original element.

Element Quick View as an element is being moved

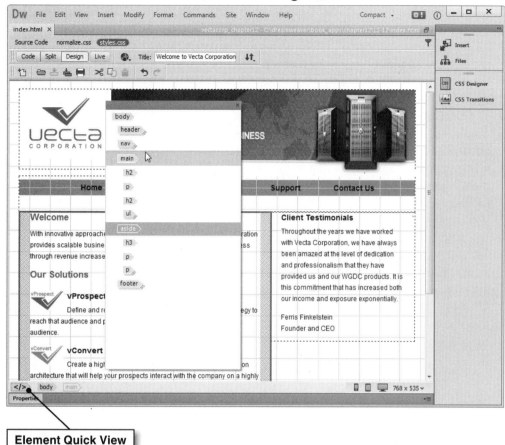

Element Quick View

Figure 12-12   How to use Element Quick View

Description

- You can use *Element Quick View* to display the elements of an HTML document in a hierarchical tree. To display Element Quick View, click the </> icon at the left side of the Tag selector or choose View→Element Quick View.

- To expand an element, just click on it. This also selects the element in the Document window. To collapse an expanded element, just click on it again.

- To move an element in the tree, just drag it. A green line appears indicating the new position of the element. When you drop the element, it's repositioned in the HTML before the shaded element (the reference element).

- If you drag and drop an element on the reference element instead of before that element, the element you're moving will be positioned as the first child element of the reference element.

- You can copy, paste, duplicate, or delete elements from Element Quick View using the context menu that's displayed when you right-click an element. If you copy or duplicate an element, any child elements it contains are copied or duplicated as well.

How to create and manage custom layouts

In chapter 1, you learned that you can customize your workspace layout by docking and undocking panels, collapsing and expanding panels, hiding and displaying panels, and repositioning panels. Once you get your workspace the way you want it, you may want to save it as a custom layout. Figure 12-13 describes how you do that.

To create a custom layout, you use one of the techniques in this figure to display the New Workspace dialog box and enter a name for the layout. When you click OK, the new layout will appear at the top of the Workspace Layout menu so you can quickly switch to this layout. Note that in addition to organizing the panels the way you want them, a custom layout can include just the toolbars you want. So you'll want to be sure those toolbars are displayed when you create the layout.

After you create a custom layout, you can rename or delete it from the Manage Workspaces dialog box as described in this figure. You can also change a custom layout and then save those changes. You might want to do that as you get more experience working with Dreamweaver and discover more efficient ways to organize a layout. Or, if you make changes to a layout and later decide that you don't want to save them, you can reset the layout to the previously saved layout.

The New Workspace dialog box

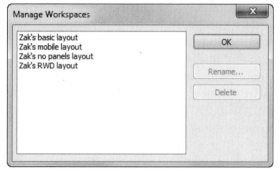

The Manage Workspaces dialog box with custom layouts

How to create a workspace layout

1. Organize your panels the way you'd like them displayed. You can also display or hide toolbars in the Document window for a layout using the View→Toolbars command.

2. Choose New Workspace from the Workspace Layout menu in Dreamweaver's menu bar, or choose Window→Workspace Layout→New Workspace to display the New Workspace dialog box.

3. Enter a name for the layout and click OK to create the layout. The new layout will be added to the Workspace Layout menu as well as to the Window→Workspace Layout submenu.

How to manage workspace layouts

- Choose Manage Workspaces from the Workspace Layout menu, or choose Window→Workspace Layout→Manage Workspaces to display the Manage Workspaces dialog box.

- To rename a layout, select the layout and click the Rename button to display the Rename Workspace dialog box. Enter a new name and click OK.

- To delete a layout, select the layout and click the Delete button. Then, respond to the dialog box that's displayed to confirm the deletion.

- To save changes to an existing layout, choose Save Current from the Workspace Layout menu or choose Window→Workspace Layout→Save Current.

- To reset a layout to its original settings after making changes, choose Reset <layout name> from the Workspace Layout menu, or choose Window→Workspace Layout→Reset <layout name>.

Figure 12-13   How to create and manage custom layouts

How to set keyboard shortcuts

Dreamweaver provides *keyboard shortcuts* for many of its operations. For example, you can use the standard Ctrl+X, Ctrl+C, and Ctrl+V keys (Windows) or Cmd+X, Cmd+C, and Cmd+V keys (Mac) to cut, copy, and paste a selection. Although you won't want to change standard keyboard shortcuts like these, you may want to change some of the keyboard shortcuts that are specific to Dreamweaver, and you may want to add keyboard shortcuts for commands that don't currently have them. To do that, you use the Keyboard Shortcuts dialog box as described in figure 12-14.

To start, you should know that you can't change the set of keyboard shortcuts that comes with Dreamweaver. Because of that, you have to create your own set of shortcuts. To do that, you start by duplicating an existing set of shortcuts. When the Keyboard Shortcuts dialog box is first displayed, for example, the Dreamweaver Standard set of shortcuts is displayed. Then, you can click the Duplicate Set icon to the right of the Current Set menu to duplicate this set and enter a custom name for it.

After you create a new set of keyboard shortcuts, you can choose the type of commands you want to change from the Commands menu. In this figure, the menu commands are selected. Then, the commands in the menus along with their keyboard shortcuts are displayed in the list below the Commands menu.

If you want to assign a shortcut to a command, you select that command and click the Add Item (+) icon above the Shortcuts list. Then, you enter the keyboard shortcut in the Press Key text box and click the Change button. Note that if you enter a shortcut that's already assigned to another command, Dreamweaver alerts you so you can enter a different shortcut.

You can also change the keyboard shortcut that's currently assigned to a command. To do that, select the command to display its shortcut in the Shortcuts list. Then, click the Remove Item (−) icon to remove the current shortcut. Finally, click the Add Item icon and then enter the new shortcut in the Press Key text box and click the Change button. Of course, you can also assign more than one shortcut to a command, but you're not likely to do that.

The Keyboard Shortcuts dialog box

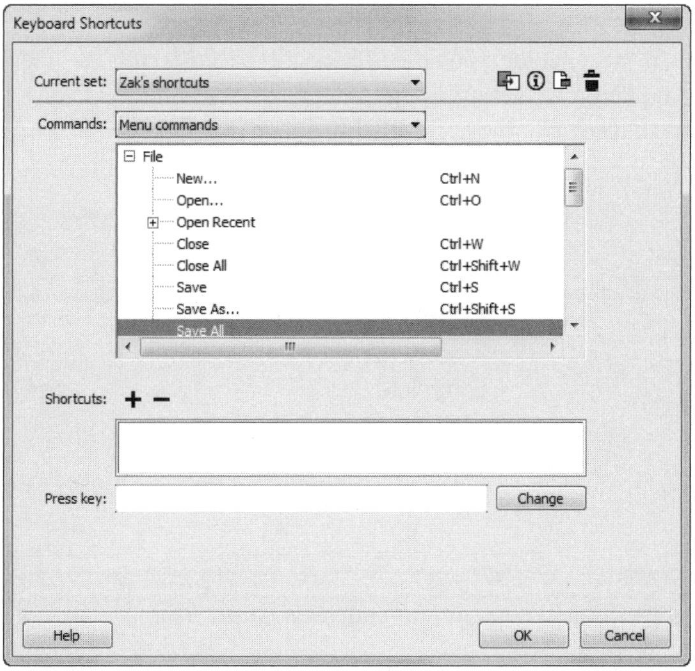

Description

- *Keyboard shortcuts* provide a way to access Dreamweaver commands using the keyboard. To create your own set of keyboard shortcuts, you use the Keyboard Shortcuts dialog box.

- To display the Keyboard Shortcuts dialog box, choose Edit→Keyboard Shortcuts (Windows) or Dreamweaver→Keyboard Shortcuts (Mac).

- To change the set of keyboard shortcuts that are currently in use or to work with a set of keyboard shortcuts, select the set from the Current Set menu.

- To create a new set of keyboard shortcuts, select the set you want to base it on, click the Duplicate Set icon (🖼) to the right of the Current Set menu, enter a name for the set in the Duplicate Set dialog box that's displayed, and then click OK.

- To work with the shortcuts for a command, select a command category from the Commands menu to display the commands in that category. Then, locate and select the command in the list.

- When you select a command, its shortcuts are displayed in the Shortcuts list. Then, you can select a shortcut and click the Remove Item button (–) to delete the shortcut.

- To add a shortcut, click the Add Item button (+). Then, enter a key combination in the Press Key box and click the Change button. If the shortcut is already assigned to a command, Dreamweaver displays an alert when you enter the key combination.

- Because you can't change the set of keyboard shortcuts that come with Dreamweaver, you have to create your own set of shortcuts. You'll typically do that to add shortcuts for commands that don't have them.

Figure 12-14   How to set keyboard shortcuts

Perspective

Now that you've completed this chapter, you should have all the skills you need for working efficiently in Dreamweaver. Although you may not use these skills all the time, you'll at least know that they're available when you do need them.

Terms

snippet	query
Snippets panel	History panel
Assets panel	command
asset	Element Quick View
favorite	keyboard shortcut

Summary

- You can use *snippets* to insert predefined content into your web pages. You can also create your own custom snippets.

- You can use the *Assets panel* to work with the *assets* used by a website. Assets include images, colors, URLs, SWF files, videos, scripts, templates, and library items.

- You can define *favorites* for most categories of assets to make those assets easier to access. You can also organize favorites into folders.

- Dreamweaver provides a powerful feature for finding and replacing text and source code. You can also use this feature to find a specific tag and then perform actions on that tag, such as replacing the content of the tag or adding or removing an attribute.

- You can use Dreamweaver's built-in *commands* to perform a variety of functions on your web pages. You can also create your own custom commands by saving a series of steps that you've performed from the *History panel*.

- You can use *Element Quick View* to display the structure of an HTML document in a hierarchical tree. Then, you can quickly move, copy and paste, duplicate, and delete elements.

- You can create custom workspace layouts with panels that are organized just the way you want them. Then, you can work with those layouts just like you do Dreamweaver's predefined layouts.

- You can change Dreamweaver's *keyboard shortcuts* and create new shortcuts so Dreamweaver works just the way you want it to.

Exercise 12-1   Experiment with the efficiency skills

In this exercise, you'll work with snippets, assets, find and replace, the history panel, commands, Element Quick View, and shortcut keys. This will give you a chance to experiment with some of the skills that you learned in this chapter.

Open the folder for this exercise and review its pages

1. Open the Exercises site, and open the folder for this exercise.

2. Open the index.html and solutions.html files and review the HTML code for these pages.

Add a Dreamweaver snippet to the index.html page

3. In Code view for the index.html file, place the insertion point between the head and body elements. Then, choose Window Snippets to open the Snippets panel, expand the Comments folder, select the Development Note snippet, and click the Insert button to add the snippet to the index.html page. Now, close the Snippets panel.

4. In Code view, select the "Development Note" text that was generated by Dreamweaver, and replace it with a note something like this:

   ```
   Developed by (your name). For questions, email: (your email
   address)
   ```

   This shows how you can insert and modify any snippet.

Use the Assets panel to insert images into the solutions.html file

5. Use Window→Assets to open the Assets panel. This shows all of the assets for all of the exercises because the exercises folder is treated as a single site.

6. Add the three gif images for the products to Favorites. To do that, select all three gif product images with "fav" in front of the name, and click on the Add to Favorites icon.

7. In Design view for the index.html file, note that there are no product images next to the product names. To add the first of these images to the index.html page, place the cursor in front of the "vProspect" text in the first h3 element. Next, in the Assets panel, select the Favorites radio button to display only the files in Favorites. Then, select the fav_vprospect.gif image, and click on the Insert button.

8. Repeat this procedure to insert the fav_vconvert.gif and fav_vretain.gif images into the next two h3 headings. Then, close the Assets panel.

Use the Find and Replace command

9. In Code view, note that the images you just inserted have empty alt attributes. To fix that, the next three steps have you use the Find and Replace command to put "Product Image" into the alt attributes for these img elements as well as those on the solutions.html page.

10. Choose Edit→Find and Replace, select Folder in the Find In menu in the dialog box that follows, and browse to and select the folder for this exercise (exercises/ex12-01). This means that the command will search the three HTML files in this folder.

11. Still in the Find and Replace dialog box, select the Specific Tag option from the Search menu, and select the img tag from the drop-down list. Next, to find only the product images (not all images), select the With Attribute option and set the width attribute equal to 63 (meaning pixels). Then, from the Action menu, select the Set Attribute option, select the alt tag, and enter text that reads "Product Image".

12. Still in the Find and Replace dialog box, start the function by clicking on the Find Next button. If the correct image tag is displayed, click on the Replace button. Then, repeat this for all of the img elements in both the index.html and solutions.html pages. But stop when you return to the first image that has already been updated.

Use Element Quick View

13. With figure 12-12 as a guide, use Element Quick View to review the HTML structure for the aboutus.html page. That's a quick way to make sure that the structure for a page is okay.

14. Use Element Quick View to drag the h2 heading and paragraph for Damon ahead of the h2 heading and paragraph for Agnes. Then, note the change in Live view.

Experiment with the History panel, Dreamweaver commands, and shortcut keys

15. In Design view for the solutions.html page, choose Window→History to open the History panel. Then, use this panel to undo the three Replace steps. To do that, you just slide the control up to the first of the three Replace steps. If this works correctly, all three Replace steps will be grayed out in the History panel, and the alt attributes in Code view for the three img elements on the solutions.html page will be reset to blank.

16. Switch to the index.html page, and review the History panel for it. Note that it shows more than three steps that can be undone, and the three Replace steps for this page haven't been undone yet. Now, undo those Replace steps.

17. In Code view for the index.html file, choose Commands→Apply Source Formatting. Note, how the HTML code is reformatted so it's easier to read.

18. With figure 12-14 as a guide, create a shortcut key of F11 for the Validate command (File→Validate→Validate Current Document (W3C)). Then, use that key to validate the three HTML pages for this exercise.

13

How to deploy a website and collaborate with a team

Once you've developed and tested a website on your local computer, you're just a few steps away from making that website available to anyone in the world who is connected to the Internet. To do that, you just need to transfer the files for your website to a web server that's connected to the Internet. This can be done easily using Dreamweaver's site management features.

Dreamweaver also provides features for working as part of a collaborative team. These features can help maintain the integrity of a website as well as help team members work more easily together.

How to get a web host and domain name

Before you can *deploy* (or *publish*) a website to the Internet, you need to have access to a web server that's connected to the Internet. If you already have access to an Internet web server, you can use that server. Otherwise, you can search the Internet for a web host as described in this topic. If you want to register a domain name for your site, a web host can usually do that for you too.

How to find a web host

Figure 13-1 shows how to find a *web host*, or *web hosting service*. To do that, you can search the web for "web host" or "web hosting service". Then, you can follow the links until you find a web host that has all the features you need. For small websites like the ones presented in this book, you only need a small amount of disk space. For larger websites, you may need more disk space, access to a database server, and a server-side programming language such as PHP, JSP, or ASP.NET.

In addition, most web hosts provide one or more *FTP (File Transfer Protocol)* accounts. This provides a way for you to transfer the files for your website to and from your web host. When you use Dreamweaver, though, you won't need this because Dreamweaver provides its own FTP facility.

Most web hosts charge a monthly fee. For a small website, the price may be as little as $5 per month. Also, some web hosts provide some services for free. If you search the Internet, you'll find a wide range of services and prices.

If you already pay an *Internet service provider* (*ISP*) to connect to the Internet, you can check to see if it provides free web hosting as part of its monthly fees. If so, you can check to see if it provides the web hosting features that you need for your website.

When you get a web host, you will receive an *IP address* in this format: 64.46.106.120. You can use this address to access your website. Later, when you get your domain name, you can access your site with either the IP address or the domain name. Internally, the Internet uses IP addresses to address websites, but people use domain names because they're easier to remember.

A web host

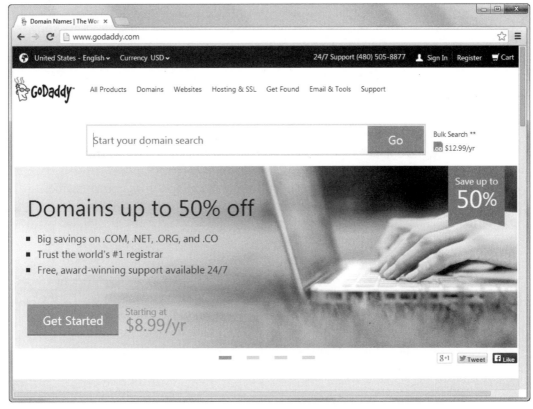

Description

- A *web host*, or *web hosting service*, provides space on a server computer that's connected to the Internet, usually for a monthly fee. You can use a web host to make your website accessible via the Internet.

- *File Transfer Protocol* (*FTP*) allows you to transfer the files for your website to and from your web host.

- To find a web host, search the web for "web host" or "web hosting service". Then, follow the links until you find a web host that has all the features you need.

- An *Internet service provider* (*ISP*) often includes free web hosting as part of its monthly fees. As a result, if you have an ISP, you can check to see if it provides the web hosting features that you need for your website.

Figure 13-1   How to find a web host

How to get a domain name

If you're using a web host, you can often use its *domain name* to access your website. For example, if your web hosting company has a domain name of

```
olive.forest.net
```

you may be able to access your website using a *subdomain* like this:

```
www.vectacorp.olive.forest.net
```

Or, you may be able to access your website using a subfolder like this:

```
www.olive.forest.net/vectacorp
```

Either way, the domain name of the web host is included in the URL that's used to access your website.

For most professional websites, you'll want to get your own domain name. That way, you can access your website without including the domain name of the web host in the URL. For example, you can access a website with the domain name vectacorp.com like this:

```
www.vectacorp.com
```

To get a domain name, you can use a website like GoDaddy, as shown in figure 13-2. But first, you need to decide what extension you want to use for the website. The .com extension was originally intended to be used for commercial websites, .net was intended to be used for networking websites, and .org was intended to be used for other organizations. However, many other extensions are now available, such as those for military (.mil), government (.gov), and business (.biz) websites.

When you use a site like the one shown here, you typically enter one or more domain names. Then, the *domain name registry* is searched to see which of the names is available, and you can choose to purchase any available name for a specific amount of time. Most web hosts also provide these services.

A search for a domain name

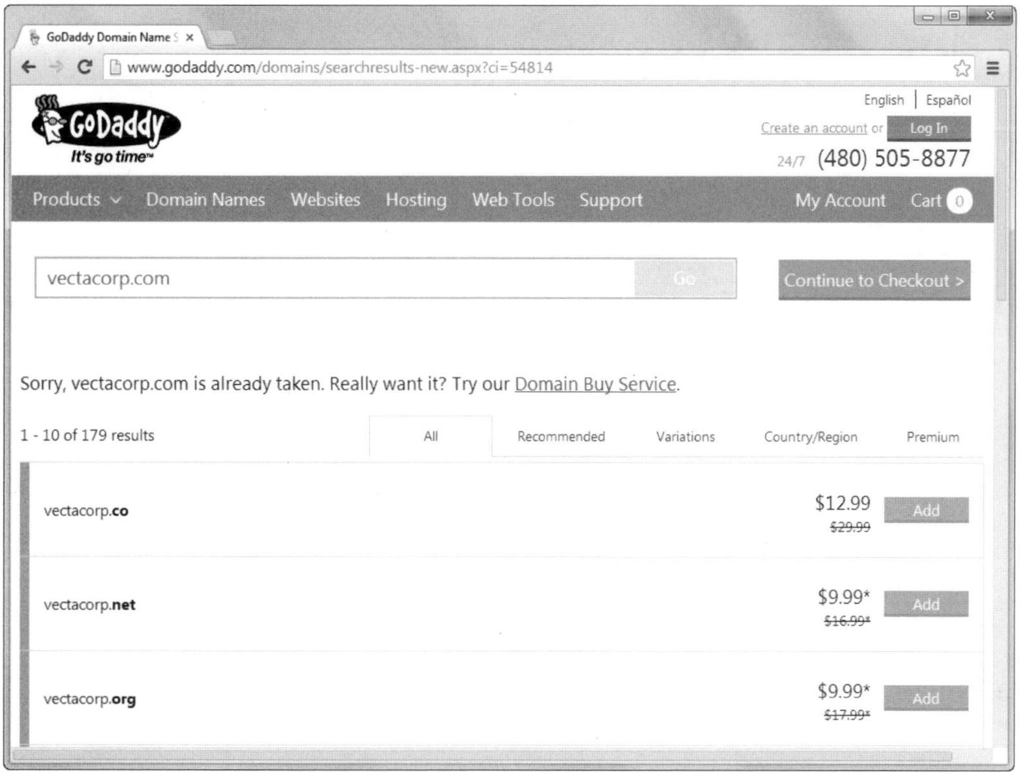

Description

- A *domain name* is a user-friendly name that's used to locate a resource that's connected to the Internet. For example, google.com is a domain name.

- A domain name can have one or more *subdomains*. For example, mail.google.com is a subdomain.

- The .com, .net, and .org extensions are popular endings for domain names. These extensions were originally intended to be used for commercial websites (.com), networking infrastructure websites (.net), and other types of organizations (.org).

- The *domain name registry* is a database of all registered domain names.

- If you are using a web hosting service, you can often use that service to register the domain name for you. To start, you can use your web hosting service to find a domain name that hasn't been registered yet. Then, you can have your web hosting service register that domain name for you.

Figure 13-2   How to get a domain name

How to transfer files to and from your web host

Once you have a web host and domain name, you can publish your website to the Internet by transferring the files for your website from your local computer to the correct folder on the web host's server. To do that, you can use the FTP client that's built into Dreamweaver.

How to define a remote server

Figure 13-3 shows you how to set the properties for a remote server. To do that, you start by displaying the Servers category of the Site Setup dialog box for the site. If any remote servers are already defined, they will be listed in this dialog box. To add a server, you click the Add New Server icon to display the Server Settings dialog box.

From the Server Settings dialog box, you enter the name you want to use for the server in the Server Name text box. Then, you select the connection method you want to use from the Connect Using menu. In most cases, you'll use FTP, but Dreamweaver also provides other connection methods.

Next, you enter the address of the server where you will upload the files for your website in the FTP Address text box. In addition, you must enter your user name and password for connecting to the server. At that point, you can click the Test button to test the connection. If the connection is successful, Dreamweaver will display a message to that affect. Otherwise, it will display an error message. Then, you'll need to review the message carefully and make the changes necessary to correct the problem.

Once you're able to connect to the server, you need to enter the root directory for the website along with its URL. In this figure, for example, you can see that the root directory is webroot/vc/. This is the directory where the files for your website will be stored. Then, the URL is just the complete web address, including the protocol and the root directory.

In most cases, you'll define a single remote server where you can upload the files for a website. You should realize, though, that you can define as many servers as you like. Before you upload a website to a live environment, for example, you might want to upload it to a testing server. Then, once you're sure it works correctly in that environment, you can upload it to its final location.

To indicate whether a server is a remote server or a testing server, you can check the appropriate option for the server in the Site Setup dialog box. If you define more than one server, you should realize that you can only select one of them as the current remote server and one as the current testing server. Then, to determine which server Dreamweaver will use, you can use the expanded Files panel as described in figure 13-5.

The Site Setup dialog box for defining a remote server

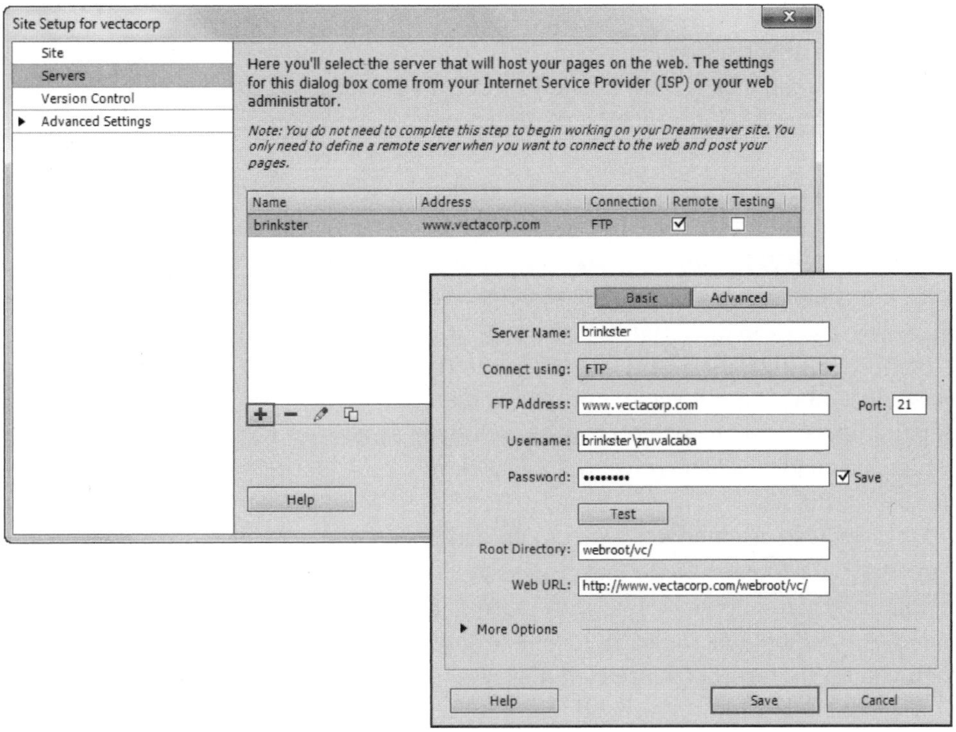

How to define a remote server

1. Double-click the menu of sites in the Files panel to display the Site Setup dialog box, and then choose the Servers category.

2. Click the Add New Server icon (**+**) to display the Server Settings dialog box.

3. Enter a name for the server, choose the connection method you'll use to copy files to and from the server, and enter any additional information that's required.

4. Click the Test button to be sure you can connect to the server. Then, click Save to close the Server Settings dialog box, and click Save again to save the remote server definition.

Description

- Before you can connect to your web host, you must set the properties for the remote server. Then, you can transfer files between the local and remote sites.

- For the Connect Using option, you typically use FTP. However, Dreamweaver also provides for Secure FTP (SFTP), FTP over SSL/TLS, Local/Network, WebDAV, and RDS.

- The information that's required to define a remote server varies depending on the connection type you choose. For FTP, you need to enter the FTP address, your username, and your password. In addition, you need to specify the root directory where the files for your website will be stored and the URL for your website.

Figure 13-3   How to define a remote server

How to upload and download files

After you define a remote server, you can *upload files* to that server. Then, you can *download files* from the remote server to the local site whenever that's necessary. Figure 13-4 describes several ways that you can upload and download files.

If you need to upload or download a single file, you can do that using the Put or Get options in the Site menu or the File Management menu in the Document toolbar. For this to work, the file you want to upload or download must be displayed in the Document window. Note that when you download a file, it will overwrite the file if it exists in your local site. If you've made changes to the local file, then, they will be lost. Similarly, if you upload a file, you could overwrite a more current version of the file on the remote server. That might happen if more than one person is working on the same site. To prevent these problems, you can use Dreamweaver's Check In/Check Out feature as described later in this chapter.

You can also use the Files panel to upload or download a single file or two or more files or folders. To do that, you select the files and folders and then click the Put or Get icon in the toolbar at the top of the Files panel. You can also use the Get and Put options in the Site menu or the context menu that's displayed when you right-click on the selected files and folders.

When you upload or download multiple files, you'll want to be particularly careful that you don't overwrite newer versions of the files. One way to do that is to expand the Files panel so you can see the files on the remote server. You'll learn how to do that in a minute.

When you upload or download files, you should realize that you don't have to explicitly upload or download other files that they refer to. For example, you don't have to explicitly upload or download the style sheets that a web page refers to. Instead, Dreamweaver will display a Dependent Files dialog box that asks if you want to include those files in the transfer. If the referenced files haven't been modified since they were last uploaded or downloaded, you can click No. If the files have been modified, though, or they haven't been uploaded or downloaded, you should click Yes.

Before it uploads or downloads files, Dreamweaver automatically connects to the remote server. Because of that, you won't need to connect manually unless you want to display the files on the remote server. You'll see how to do that next.

The File Management menu in the Document toolbar

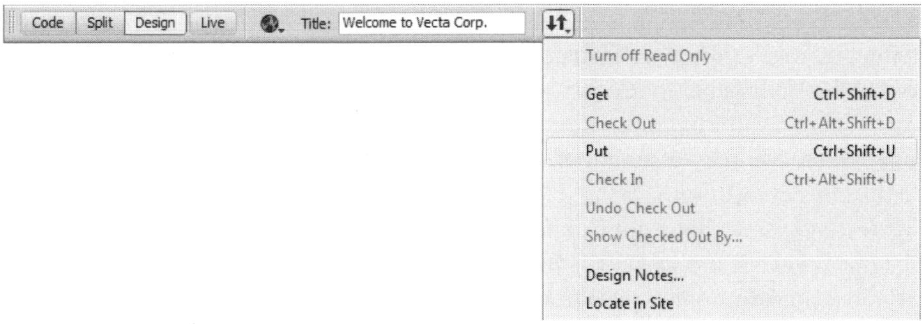

| Code | Split | Design | Live | 🌐 | Title: | Welcome to Vecta Corp. | ↕↑ |

Turn off Read Only	
Get	Ctrl+Shift+D
Check Out	Ctrl+Alt+Shift+D
Put	Ctrl+Shift+U
Check In	Ctrl+Alt+Shift+U
Undo Check Out	
Show Checked Out By...	
Design Notes...	
Locate in Site	

The icons in the Files panel toolbar for uploading and downloading files

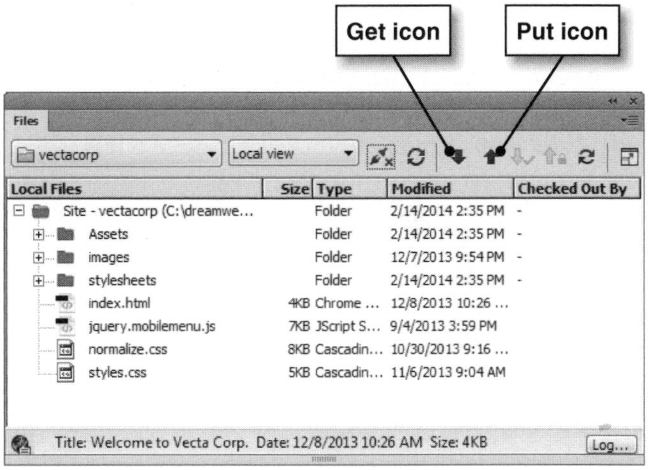

[Get icon]   [Put icon]

Files

| vectacorp ▼ | Local view ▼ | | | | | | |

Local Files	Size	Type	Modified	Checked Out By
Site - vectacorp (C:\dreamwe...		Folder	2/14/2014 2:35 PM	-
Assets		Folder	2/14/2014 2:35 PM	-
images		Folder	12/7/2013 9:54 PM	-
stylesheets		Folder	2/14/2014 2:35 PM	-
index.html	4KB	Chrome ...	12/8/2013 10:26 ...	
jquery.mobilemenu.js	7KB	JScript S...	9/4/2013 3:59 PM	
normalize.css	8KB	Cascadin...	10/30/2013 9:16 ...	
styles.css	5KB	Cascadin...	11/6/2013 9:04 AM	

Title: Welcome to Vecta Corp. Date: 12/8/2013 10:26 AM Size: 4KB   [Log...]

Two ways to upload or download the file in the Document window

- With the focus in the Document window, choose Put from the File Management menu to upload the file to the remote server, or choose Get to download the file from the remote server.
- With the focus in the Document window, choose Site→Put or Site→Get.

Three ways to upload or download files and folders from the Files panel

- Select the files and folders and then click the Put icon in the toolbar to upload them to the remote server, or click the Get icon to download them from the remote server.
- Select the files and folders and then choose Site→Get or Site→ Put.
- Select the files and folders and then right-click on them and choose Get or Put from the context menu that's displayed.

Description

- Dreamweaver automatically connects to the remote server when you upload or download files, so you don't have to do that manually.

Figure 13-4   How to upload and download files

How to use the expanded Files panel

In the previous figure, you learned how to use the File Management and Site menus and the Files panel to quickly upload files to or download files from a remote server. One shortcoming of these techniques is that you can't see the files on the remote server. Because of that, you can't be sure that you're uploading files to the correct location.

Figure 13-5 shows how you expand the Files panel so it shows the files in both the local and remote websites. To do that, you simply click the Expand icon in the toolbar, make sure that the Remote Server icon is selected, and then click the Connect icon. Then, the files on the remote server are displayed in the left pane of the panel, and the local files are displayed in the right pane.

With the expanded Files panel displayed, you can upload files and folders to the remote server by selecting them in the Local Files pane and then clicking the Put icon. Similarly, you can download files and folders from the remote server by selecting them in the Remote Server pane and then clicking the Get icon. You can also select the files and folders and then drag them from one pane to another to upload or download them.

Just like it does when you upload or download files using the techniques in figure 13-4, Dreamweaver displays a Dependent Files dialog box that asks if you want to include any files that are referenced by the files you're uploading or downloading. If that's not what you want, you can use the Site category of the Preferences dialog box to change when this dialog box is displayed as described in this figure. You can also use the Site category of the Preferences dialog box to switch the two panes of the expanded Files panel so the local files are displayed on the left and the remote files are displayed on the right.

You can also use the expanded Files panel to work directly with the files on the remote server. That includes creating, renaming, deleting, and moving folders and files. For example, suppose you upload a file and then later decide to change the name of the file in the local site. Then, you could rename the file in the remote site too. Or, suppose you upload a file to the root directory of the remote site and later decide to store the file in a new folder of the local site. Then, you could create the new folder in the remote site and move the file to that folder.

Although this figure shows how to work with a remote server, you can also use the expanded Files panel to work with a testing server that you've defined. To do that, you just click the Testing Server icon instead of the Remote Server icon. Then, you can upload files to and download files from the testing server, and you can work directly with the files on the server.

Note that the last server you work with from the expanded Files panel becomes the server that Dreamweaver uses by default when you upload and download files. That's true even if you work from the standard Files panel. This is just one more reason that it's better to work from the expanded Files panel.

The expanded Files panel showing remote and local files

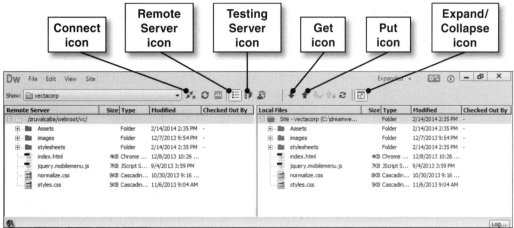

How to upload and download files

- Make sure that the Remote Server icon is selected. Then, click the Connect icon to establish a connection to the remote server. The files in the remote website will be displayed in the left pane of the panel.

- To upload files to the remote site, select the files in the Local Files view and then click the Put icon. Or, select the files and then drag them to the Remote Server view.

- To download files from the remote site, select them in the Remote Server view and then click the Get icon. Or, select the files and then drag them to the Local Files view.

How to set basic preferences

- To change whether the Dependent Files dialog box is displayed when you upload or download files with dependent files, choose Edit→Preferences and select the Site category from the Preferences dialog box that's displayed. Then, check or uncheck the two Prompt options in the Dependent Files group of options.

- To reverse the locations of the Remote Server and Local Files panes, change the Always Show options so the local files are always displayed on the left or the remote files are always displayed on the right.

Description

- The expanded Files panel lets you display files on both the remote server and your local computer as you upload and download files. To expand the Files panel, click the Expand/Collapse icon in the toolbar. To collapse this panel, click this icon again.

- You can create, rename, delete, and move folders and files in the Remote Server pane just as you would in the Local Files pane.

- When you upload and download files, Dreamweaver gives you the option of uploading and downloading any dependent files, such as style sheets.

Figure 13-5   How to use the expanded Files panel

How to synchronize a website

Instead of uploading and downloading the files and folders you select, you can synchronize all the files and folders for a site to be sure that the local and remote sites are the same. This is useful when two or more people are working on the same website or when a single person is working on a website from more than one computer. Then, after changes are made to the local site, the remote site can be synchronized with that site so it contains the most current files. Similarly, before the local site is modified by another person or from another computer, that site can be synchronized with the remote site so the local site contains the most current files.

Figure 13-6 describes the procedure for synchronizing a local and remote site. To start, you display the Synchronize with Remote Server dialog box. Then, to synchronize an entire site, you choose the Entire <site name> Site from the Synchronize menu as shown here. You can also synchronize just some of the files in the local or remote site by selecting those files in the Files panel and then choosing Selected Local Files or Selected Remote Files from the Synchronize menu.

The Direction menu in the Synchronize with Remote Server dialog box determines the direction of the synchronization. The options in this menu let you upload files from the local site to the remote site if they're newer than files in the remote site; download files from the remote site to the local site if they're newer than files in the local site; and both upload and download newer files. You can also delete files from the remote site that aren't in the local site by checking the Delete Remote Files Not On Local Drive option.

Next, you click the Preview button to display the Synchronize dialog box. This dialog box lists all the files that will be synchronized and the action that will be taken to synchronize them. In this figure, for example, you can see that the four images in this list will be uploaded to the remote site. If you want to see all of the files in the site instead of just those that will be synchronized, you can check the Show All Files option.

If you want to change the action that will be performed on any of the files in the list, you can do that using the icons in the lower left corner of the dialog box. These icons let you change the direction of the synchronization, delete files, ignore files so they're not synchronized, and mark files as synched. In this figure, the four text files in the Assets folder will be ignored.

You can also compare the local and remote versions of a file if you're not sure which version you want to keep. To do that, though, you must have a third-party file comparison program installed and you must associate that program with Dreamweaver using the File Compare category of the Preferences dialog box (Edit→Preferences (Windows) or Dreamweaver→Preferences (Mac)). Three programs that I've found useful in the past are Scooter Software's Beyond Compare, Grig Software's Compare It!, and WinDiff . These programs show the files side-by-side and identify the differences in each line of code.

When you're satisfied that the correct action will be taken for each file, you can click OK. Then, Dreamweaver will perform the synchronization.

The Synchronize with Remote Server dialog box

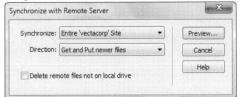

The Synchronize dialog box

How to synchronize a website

1. Click the Synchronize icon in the Files panel toolbar (🗘), or choose Site→Synchronize Sitewide to display the Synchronize with Remote Server dialog box.

2. Choose the Entire <site name> Site option from the Synchronize menu to synchronize the entire site.

3. Choose an option from the Direction menu. To upload files in the local site that are newer than files in the remote site, choose Put Newer Files To Remote. To download newer files from the remote site, choose Get Newer Files From Remote. To both upload and download newer files, choose Get And Put Newer Files.

4. Click Preview to display the Synchronize dialog box. Then, make any changes to how the files will be handled by using the buttons in the bottom left corner of the dialog box, and click OK.

Description

*   When you synchronize a website, you make sure that all the folders and files in your local and remote sites are the same.

*   The Synchronize dialog box lets you change the direction that files are copied (⬇ and ⬆), delete files (🗑), ignore files (⊘), mark files as synched (🗘), and compare files (🔲).

*   You can also synchronize just some of the local or remote files in a site by selecting them in the Files panel and then selecting the Selected Remote Files or Selected Local Files option from the Synchronize menu.

Figure 13-6   How to synchronize a website

How to use the Check In/Check Out feature

If you're working as part of a collaborative team, you may want to consider using Dreamweaver's Check In/Check Out feature. This feature requires that you check out a web page when you want to work on it. Then, no one else can work on it until you check it back in. This keeps members of a team from overwriting work done by other members.

How to configure the Check In/Check Out feature

Before you can use the Check In/Check Out feature, each team member must configure their local site in Dreamweaver. But first, if the files for the website have already been uploaded to the remote server, they should be checked to be sure they're up to date. If they're not, the most current files should be uploaded using one of the techniques presented in this chapter.

In contrast, if the files for the website haven't yet been uploaded to the remote server, the team member who has the current files can check them in after they enable the Check In/Check Out feature. You'll learn how to check in files in the next figure.

Figure 13-7 presents the procedure for configuring the Check In/Check Out feature. This procedure assumes that you've already created a local site. It also assumes that you've defined a remote server as described earlier in this chapter.

To start, you display the Site Setup dialog box and choose the Servers category as shown in figure 13-3. Then, you select the server you want to configure, click the Edit icon, and display the Advanced tab shown here. Finally, you check the Enable File Check-Out option and enter your name and email address. The Check Out files When Opening option is selected by default, which is usually what you want.

Before you begin working on a website that's configured to use the Check In/Check Out feature, you'll need to download the files from the remote website. That's true even if you already have the files on your local computer. The only exception is if you have the current files for the website and you haven't uploaded the files to the remote server. Then, you can check them in as described next. In either case, a small lock icon will be displayed next to each file in the Files panel to indicate that the file is locked and can't be changed without checking it out.

The Advanced tab of the Server Settings dialog box

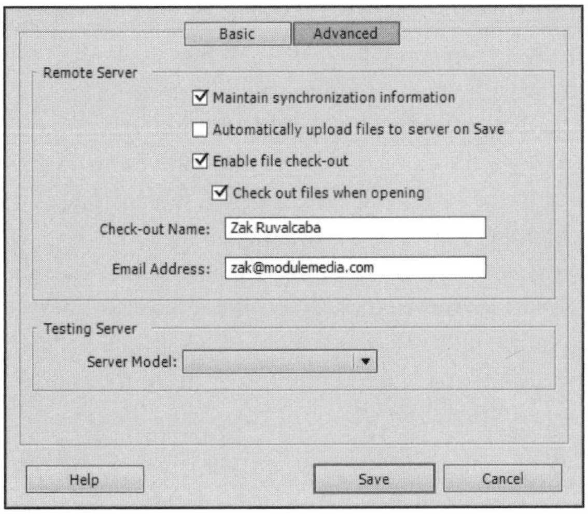

How to configure a website to use the Check In/Check Out feature

1. Double-click the menu of sites in the Files panel to display the Site Setup dialog box, and then choose the Servers category.

2. Select the server you want to configure, and then click the Edit icon (🖉) below the server list to display the basic settings for the server.

3. Click the Advanced button to display the advanced settings. Then, check the Enable File Check-out option, enter your name in the Check-out Name text box, and enter your email address in the Email Address text box.

4. Click Save to save your settings and close the Server Settings dialog box. Click Save again to close the Site Setup dialog box.

Description

- You can use Dreamweaver's Check In/Check Out feature to keep track of which files in a website are being used by another member of a collaborative team.

- If someone checks a file out, no one else can check the file out until the file is checked back in. That way, one team member won't overwrite the work of another team member.

- When you check a file out, it's downloaded from the remote server so you can be sure you're working on the most current version of the file. When you check a file in, it's uploaded to the remote server so other team members have access to the most current version.

- When you use the Check In/Check Out feature, you shouldn't use other techniques to upload and download files.

- If the remote site resides on a server that uses WebDAV, you can use the HTTP extensions it provides for versioning. You can also use an open source program called Subversion for version control. See Dreamweaver help for more information.

Figure 13-7   How to configure the Check In/Check Out feature

How to check in files

Before the members of a collaborative team can use the Check In/Check Out feature with a remote website, the files must be *checked in* to the remote website. If the files were already uploaded to the remote server before this feature was enabled, each member must download those files as described in the previous topic. If the files haven't been uploaded to the remote server, though, the current files must be checked in before other members have access to them.

Figure 13-8 describes three techniques for checking in files. The first two techniques let you check in some or all of the files in a site. You'll need to use one of these techniques to check in an entire site to make it available to other members of a team. You can also use it if you've checked out one or more files and you want to check them back in. In contrast, you can only check in a single file with the third technique.

When you check in files, Dreamweaver connects to the server and uploads the files to the remote website. In addition, it displays a Dependent Files dialog box that asks if you want to include dependent files in the transfer. If you're checking in files after having checked them out and you checked out the dependent files, you should click Yes to check them back in. Otherwise, you can click No. In either case, any files in the website that are checked in appear with a lock icon next to them in the Files panel. In this figure, for example, the jquery.mobilemenu.js and normalize.css files are checked in.

How to check out files

To work with one or more files in a website that uses the Check In/Check Out feature, you must first *check the files out*. To do that, you can use one of the three techniques described in figure 13-8. When you check out files, Dreamweaver connects to the server and downloads the files. It also displays the Dependent Files dialog box just like it does when you check in files. Then, if you need to have access to a dependent file such as a style sheet, you can check out the dependent files as well.

When you check out files, you have exclusive editing rights to those files. Although other members of your team will still be able to display those files, they won't be able to make changes to them. Because of that, you'll want to check files back in as soon as you're done working with them.

When you have a file checked out, a green check mark appears next to it in the Files panel. In contrast, if someone else has a file checked out, a red check mark appears next to it. In addition, the name of the member who has a file checked out appears in the Checked Out By column. In this figure, for example, you can see that two files are checked out to two different people. Note that these names are configured as email links. That way, you can click on a link to send an email to another member.

When you use the Check In/Check Out feature, you should realize that you shouldn't use any other techniques for uploading and downloading files. Otherwise, the files on the remote site can get out of synch.

Two checked out files and two checked in files in the Files panel

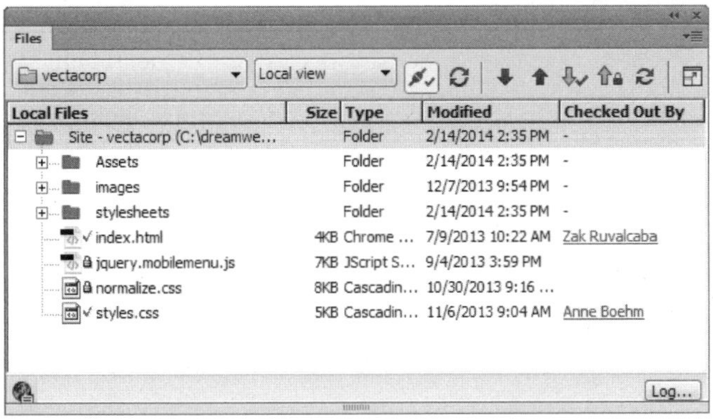

Three ways to check in files

- Select one or more files and folders in the Files panel and then click the Check In icon (⬆🔒) in the toolbar.
- Select one or more files and folders and then choose Site→Check In.
- Display the file in the Document window and then choose Check In from the File Management menu in the Document toolbar.

Three ways to check out files

- Select one or more files and folders in the Files panel and then click the Check Out icon (⬇✓) in the toolbar.
- Select one or more files and folders and then choose Site→Check Out.
- Display the file in the Document window and then choose Check Out from the File Management menu in the Document toolbar.

Description

- Before any member of a collaborative team can *check out files* from the remote server, all the files in the site must be *checked in*.
- When a file is checked in, a lock icon appears next to the file name in the Files panel. Then, you can't edit the file until you check it out.
- When a file is checked out, a checkmark icon appears next to the file name. If you check it out, the checkmark is green indicating that you can edit it. If someone else has the file checked out, the checkmark is red indicating that it can't be edited.
- The Checked Out By column in the Files panel displays the name of the person who has the file checked out. You can click this name to send the person an email.
- You can undo a check-out operation by choosing Site→Undo Check Out. This checks in the checked out file or files without uploading changes to the server.
- You can display the name of the person who has a file checked out without displaying the Files panel by choosing Site→Show Checked Out By.

Figure 13-8   How to check in and check out files

How to export, import, and duplicate a site

Occasionally, you may want to export a Dreamweaver site to create a backup for yourself. You may also want to export a site so it can be used on another computer. Then, you can import it onto that computer. You may also want to duplicate a site to create a site with the same settings. You perform all three of these operations from the Manage Sites dialog box as shown in figure 13-9.

How to export a site

To *export a site*, you select the site and then click the Export Site icon. Then, you can use the Export Site dialog box that's displayed to identify the location where you want to save the site file (.ste) and to name the file. By default, the site file is given the same name as the site.

If you've defined a remote server for your site, another dialog box is displayed before the Export Site dialog box. This dialog box lets you select what settings are included in the site file. If you're exporting the site for your own use, you can select the option that will include your login, password, and local paths. If you're exporting the site for another user, though, you'll want to select the option that excludes this information.

How to import a site

To *import a site* that was previously exported to a .ste file, you click the Import Site button and then locate and select the site file in the dialog box that's displayed. You might want to do that if you've experienced some type of computer failure and need to restore your site. Or, you may want to do that if you've purchased a new computer and you want to recreate the site on that computer. Finally, you may want to do that if another developer has given you a site file to work on or review.

How to duplicate a site

In chapter 3, you learned that you can use the Manage Sites dialog box to *duplicate a site*. To do that, you simply select the site and click the Duplicate Site icon. Then, another site is created with the name of the original site appended with "copy".

The main reason for duplicating a site is if you need to create a site that has many of the same settings as another site. For example, suppose you keep each website you work on in a different directory on your remote server. Then, to create a new site, you can just duplicate an existing site and only have to change the server directory. All of the other information for the server will remain the same. All other custom settings for your site such as workspace layouts will also be duplicated.

The Manage Sites dialog box with one site

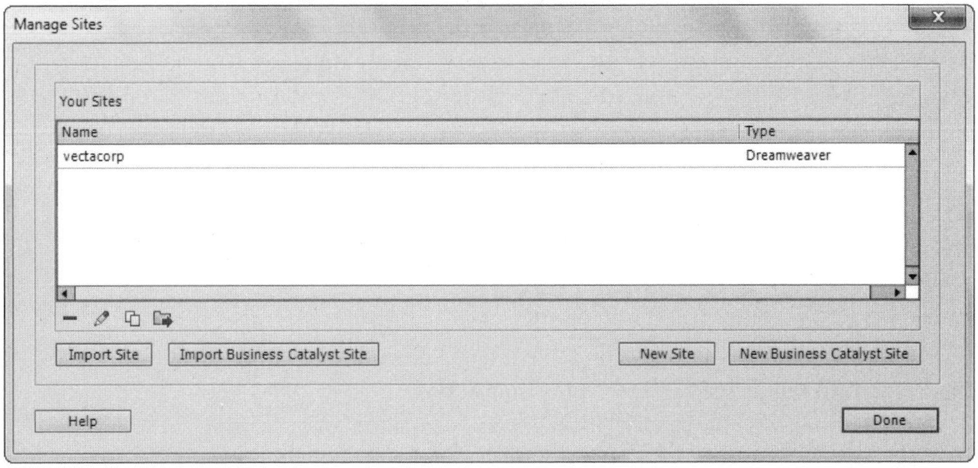

How to export a site

1. Select the site that you want to export from the Manage Sites dialog box, and then click the Export Site icon (▐➔) to display the Export Site dialog box.

2. Browse to the location where you want to store the site file, enter a name for the file, and click Save.

How to import a site

1. Click the Import Site button in the Manage Sites dialog box to display the Import Site dialog box.

2. Browse to and select the site file for the site you want to import and then click Open.

How to duplicate a site

- Select the site that you want to duplicate in the Manage Sites dialog box and then click the Duplicate Site icon (▐). A site with the name "<site name> copy" is created.

Description

- To display the Manage Sites dialog box, select Site→Manage Sites.

- If a remote server is defined for the site, the Exporting site '<site name>' dialog box is displayed when you click the Export Site icon. Then, you can select an option to determine what information is saved with the site.

- If you're exporting a site for your own use, select the Back Up My Settings option from the Export Site dialog box. Then, your login, password, and local paths are included.

- If you're exporting a site so you can share it with other users, select the Share Settings With Other Users option so your login, password, and local paths aren't included.

Figure 13-9   How to export, import, and duplicate a site

How to work with design notes

As you work on a website, you may want to create notes for yourself or for other members of a collaborative team that contain information about the files in the website. In Dreamweaver, these notes are referred to as *design notes*. In the topics that follow, you'll learn how to create and customize design notes and how to display custom design note values in the Files panel.

How to create a design note

Figure 13-10 shows how you create a basic design note. To do that, you use the Basic Info tab of the Design Notes dialog box.

At the top of this dialog box, you can see the name and location of the file that the note will be associated with. Then, you can choose an option from the Status menu that indicates the status of the file. These options include draft, revision1, revision2, revision3, alpha, beta, final, and needs attention.

You enter the actual note in the Notes text box. You can also include a date stamp in this text box by clicking the Insert Date icon. Finally, if you want the Design Notes dialog box to be displayed when you open a file that has a design note associated with it, you can select the Show When File is Opened option.

When you create a design note, it's stored in a file with the same name as the file it's associated with, appended with the file extension .mno. This file is stored in a folder named _notes in the root directory of your website. This directory is hidden, though, so you won't be able to see it from Dreamweaver. Instead, you'll need to use your computer's file explorer to see it. You may need to do that, for example, if you want to delete the note.

You may also need to delete design notes if you delete the files that they're associated with, since Dreamweaver doesn't do that automatically. In this case, though, you shouldn't delete the notes using your computer's file explorer. Instead, you should display the Site Setup dialog box for your site, expand the Advanced Settings category, choose Design Notes, and then click the Clean up Design Notes button.

You can also set other options from the Design Notes tab of the Site Setup dialog box. To start, you can disable the Design Notes feature by removing the check mark from the Maintain Design Notes option. You're not likely to do that, though. If you're working with a collaborative team, you can select the Enable Upload Design Notes for Sharing option. Then, design notes that are associated with files that are uploaded to or downloaded from a remote server are included with those files so other team members have access to them.

By default, you won't be able to tell by looking at a file in the Files panel if it has a design note associated with it. If you want to include an indicator in this panel, you have to display the Notes column. Then, a note icon like the one shown in this figure is displayed in this column if a design note is associated with the file. You'll learn how to display the Notes column later in this chapter.

The Design Notes dialog box after a date stamp and note are inserted

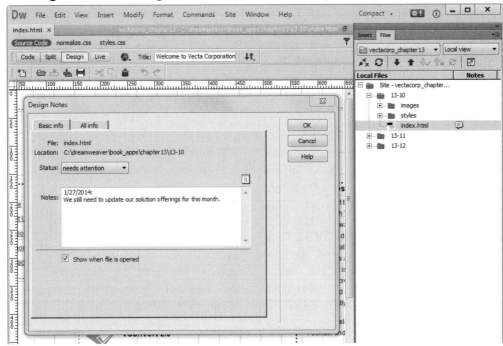

How to create a design note

- Select the file that you want to add a design note to in the Files panel and choose File→Design Notes to display the Design Notes dialog box.
- Select an option from the Status menu to indicate the status of the note.
- To insert a date stamp in the Notes text box, click the Insert Date icon (🗓). Then, enter the note.
- If you want the notes for a file to be displayed when the file is opened, check the Show When File is Opened option.

Description

- You can use the Design Notes feature to associate notes with the files in a site.
- You can also use the Design Notes dialog box to modify an existing design note. If this dialog box isn't displayed when the file it's associated with is opened, you can display it by choosing File→Design Notes.
- The notes for a file are stored within your website in a hidden folder named _notes. A note file has the same name as the file it's associated with appended with the extension .mno.
- The Design Notes feature is enabled by default, but note sharing is not enabled. To enable sharing, display the Site Setup dialog box, expand the Advanced Settings group, select the Design Notes category, and then select the Enable Upload Design Notes For Sharing option.

Figure 13-10   How to create a design note

How to customize a design note

When you create a design note as shown in the previous figure, the information you enter is saved in *name/value pairs*. For example, the value you select from the Status menu is saved with the name status. If you want to enter additional information for a design note to customize that note, you can do that by entering additional name/value pairs. To do that, you use the All Info tab of the Design Notes dialog box shown in figure 13-11.

Here, you can see that the first three name/value pairs in the Info list box are for the information that was entered in the Basic Info tab. The other name/value pairs provide custom information for the design note. For example, the item named hoursWorked has been assigned a value of 8.

To add a name/value pair, you simply click the Add Item icon and then enter a name and a value in the text boxes that are provided. Later, if you want to change the name or value for an item, you can do that by selecting that item in the Info list box to display its name and value in the text boxes. You can also delete an item by selecting it and then clicking the Delete Item icon. Note that you can change the names of the default items as well as the custom items you create. You can also delete the default items, although we don't recommend you do that.

The Design Notes dialog box with a custom design note

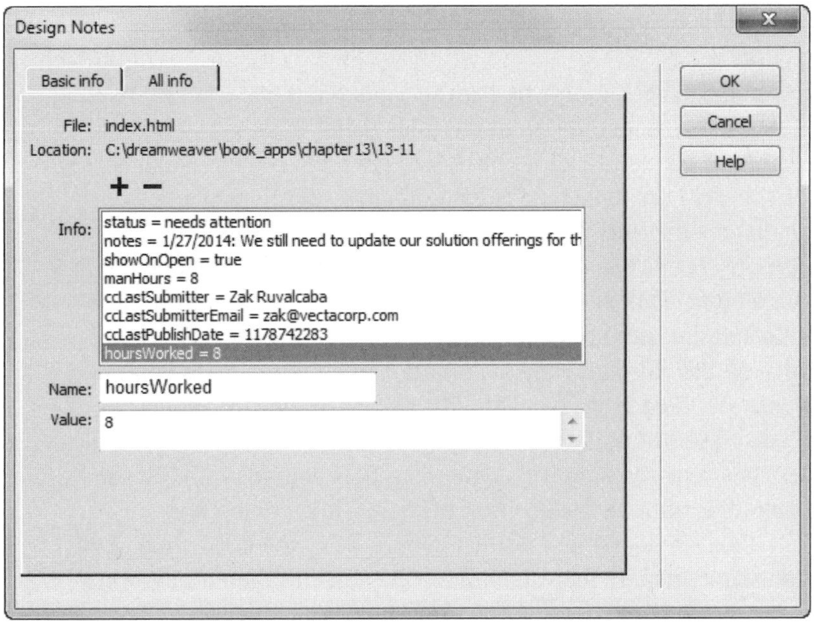

How to create a custom design note

1. Select the file that you want to add a design note to in the Files Panel and choose File→Design Notes to display the Design Notes dialog box.

2. Enter information into the Basic Info tab as described in figure 13-10, and then click the All Info tab.

3. Click the Add Item icon (+) to add a name/value pair. Then, enter a name in the Name text box and a value in the Value text box. Repeat for each name/value pair you want to create.

Description

- Design notes are stored as a series of *name/value pairs*. When you create a basic design note, three name/value pairs are generated with the names status, notes, and showOnOpen and the values you specify on the Basic Info tab.

- To create additional name/value pairs, you use the All Info tab of the Design Notes dialog box.

- You can change the name and value of any item by selecting that item in the Info list box and changing the values in the Name and Value text boxes.

- You can delete a name/value pair by selecting it in the Info list and clicking the Delete Item icon (−).

- You can display custom design notes in custom columns in the Files panel. See figure 13-12 for more information.

Figure 13-11   How to customize a design note

How to display design note values in the Files panel

After you customize a design note by adding a custom item, you can display the value of an item in a custom column in the Files panel. That way, you can quickly see the value of the item without having to open the Design Notes dialog box. Figure 13-12 shows how to add a custom column to the Files panel.

To start, you display the File View Columns category of the Site Setup dialog box for the site. Then, you click the Add Column icon to display the File View Column dialog box. This dialog box lets you enter the name you want to use for the column and the name of the custom design note item whose value you want to display in the column. Here, a column named Hours will display the value of the hoursWorked item. Note that the names of the custom design note items aren't displayed in the list portion of the Associate with Design Notes combo box, since they're associated with individual files and not with the site. So you have to enter the name in the text box portion of the combo box.

The File View Column dialog box also lets you specify the horizontal alignment that will be used to display the value. Since the value of the hoursWorked item is numeric, for example, it should be right-aligned. You should also be sure that the Show option is selected so the column will be displayed in the Files panel. Finally, if you want other members of a collaborative team to be able to see the column, you should check the Share with All Users of This Site option.

When you click Save, the new column is displayed at the bottom of the column list. If you want to change its position in the list, you can use the Move icons. In this figure, for example, I moved the Hours column up so it will appear after the Type column.

As I mentioned earlier, a note icon isn't automatically displayed when you add a design note to a file. That's because, by default, the Show option of the Notes column isn't selected. To display this column, you can just select the Notes column, click the Edit icon, and then select the Show option. Then, a note icon like the one you saw in figure 13-10 is displayed.

The Site Setup dialog box as a column is added to the Files panel

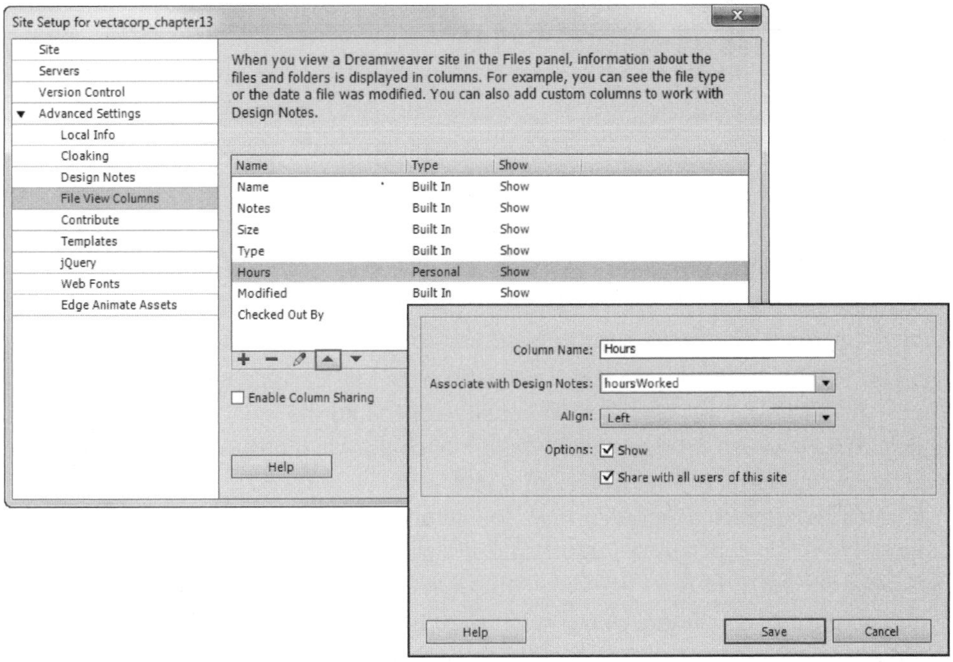

How to create a custom column for a design note

1. Double-click the menu of sites in the Files panel to display the Site Setup dialog box, expand the Advanced Settings group, and choose the File View Columns category.

2. Click the Add Column icon (**+**) to display the File View Column dialog box. Then, enter the name you want displayed for the column and the name of your custom design note item, select an alignment, make sure that the Show option is selected, and select the Share option if you want other users to see the column.

3. Click Save to save your settings and close the Add Column dialog box. Click Save again to close the Site Setup dialog box.

Description

- After you create custom design notes, you can display the values of those notes in custom columns in the Files panel. If you want other users to be able to see your custom columns, you can also select the Enable Column Sharing option.

- After you add a custom column, you can use the Move icons (▲ and ▼) to move the column up and down in the list to control where it appears in the Files panel.

- By default, the Notes column that indicates if a design note is associated with a file is hidden. To display this column, select it in the list of columns, click the Edit icon (✎), and then select the Show option. A note icon will be displayed in the Notes columns for each file that has a note.

Figure 13-12   How to display design note values in the Files panel

Three more skills for deploying a website

After you deploy your website to a remote web server, you need to test it. You also need to get your site indexed by the popular search engines so they will deliver people to your site.

How to test a website that has been uploaded to the web server

Figure 13-13 shows how to test a new web page that has just been uploaded to an existing website. In that case, you need to check all the links that go to it and from it. You also need to check that all its content is there and working correctly, including images, scripts, and styles.

For instance, a web page often links to one or more HTML files, CSS files, and image files. Then, if you forget to upload a supporting file, one of the links won't work correctly. In that case, you can solve the problem by uploading the supporting file. If you include all referenced files when you upload a web page from Dreamweaver as described earlier in this chapter, this shouldn't be a problem.

To test an entire website that has just been uploaded to a web server, you need to methodically review each of the pages on the site, including all of the links to and from each page. You should do that even if you've checked for broken links in Dreamweaver, because nothing takes the place of testing it online. The larger the site, of course, the more difficult the testing is, and the more methodical you need to be. To complicate the task, you need to do this for all of the browsers that your users are likely to use.

A website on the Internet

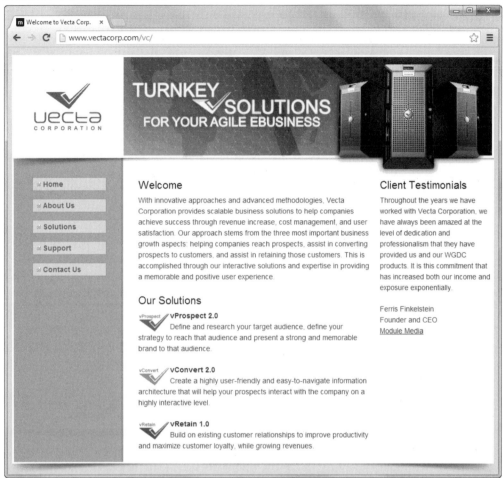

How to test a web page that you've just added to your site

- Start your web browser, go to your home page, and navigate to the new page using every route that your site has for getting there.
- Review the contents for the page, and make sure it's all there and it all works, including the images, JavaScript features, and jQuery features.
- Test all the links on the page to make sure they work correctly.
- Retest the page in all of the other browsers to make sure it works correctly in those browsers too.

How to test a new website

- Methodically review all of the pages and test all of the links, one page at a time.
- Do this for each of the browsers that your users might be using.

Figure 13-13   How to test a website that has been uploaded to the web server

How to get your website into search engines and directories

After you deploy and test your website, you will want to get your pages into the major search engines and directories so they can deliver visitors to your site. To do that, you go to the URLs in the table in figure 13-14, or you can search for "submit site to ..." These URLs take you to submission pages like the Google page shown in this figure.

At the submission page, you only need to submit the URL of your home page. Then, if your site is linked properly, the search engine's *robot* will "crawl" through the rest of your pages by following the links in your site. As it crawls, the robot will score your pages. Those scores will later determine how high your pages come up in the searches, and of course you want them to come up as high as possible.

The trouble is that the search engines use different algorithms for determining the scores of your pages. For instance, some search engines improve the score of a page if it has links to other sites. Some improve the score if the pages of other websites link to the page. To complicate the process, the search engines change their algorithms from time to time without any notice.

To find out more about the scoring algorithms that are used, you can go to the sites for the search engines or directories that you're submitting your site to. Most of these sites also give advice for optimizing your site for their engines. You can also search the web for information on search engine optimization.

Once you've submitted your website for indexing, you don't have to do it again, even if you've made significant enhancements to the site. That's because the robot for a search engine periodically crawls through all of the sites and indexes the pages again, sometimes with a new algorithm for scoring.

Last, you should be aware that most web hosts offer statistics packages that tell you where your visitors are coming from. You can also buy third-party packages that do that, or you can sign up for a free Google Analytics account (www.google.com/analytics). This data can help you figure out what's working…and what isn't working…so you can make changes that will improve your site.

Two additional free tools that you may find useful as you test and deploy a website are Google Webmaster Tools (www.google.com/webmasters) and Web Site Grader by HubSpot (http://websitegrader.com). You can use Google Webmaster Tools to perform a variety of functions, including checking links site wide, showing search rankings per page, uploading a sitemap.xml file to provide for better crawling and rankings, and making recommendations for improvement to the site. You can use Web Site Grader to determine how much traffic your site is getting and whether it has any search engine optimization problems.

But what if you don't want a search engine to index some of your pages? And what happens if you delete a page that is still in the index for a search engine? You can find out how to handle those conditions in the next figure.

The URLs for the major search engines and directory

Site name	Site type	Web URL
Google	Search engine	http://www.google.com/addurl
MSN/Bing	Search engine	http://www.bing.com/webmaster/SubmitSitePage.aspx
Yahoo	Search engine	http://search.yahoo.com/info/submit.html
DMOZ	Directory	http://www.dmoz.org/add.html

The Google web page for submitting your site

Description

- After you deploy and test your site, you'll want to get your pages into search engines and directories that can deliver visitors to your site. To submit your site to the three major search engines and the major directory, go to the websites in the table above.

- When you submit your site to a search engine or directory, you only need to provide the URL for your home page. Then, the *robot* (or *spider*) for that engine or directory "crawls" through the pages of your site and indexes them.

- After your site has been indexed the first time, the robot will periodically crawl through your site again to update the index based on any changes you've made.

- Each search engine or directory has its own algorithms for scoring pages, and those scores determine how high a page will be placed in the search results for specific keywords.

- At the site for each search engine or directory, you can get information that you can use to help your pages do better in the search results.

- Most web hosts offer statistics packages that track which sites and search engines are sending you visitors.

Figure 13-14   How to get your website into search engines and directories

How to control which pages are indexed and visited

Many websites contain pages and maybe even folders of pages that you don't want indexed. For instance, you usually don't want your shopping cart pages indexed. To stop pages from being indexed, you can use one of the two methods shown in figure 13-15.

First, you can set up a robots.txt file in the root folder of your website that specifies which folders or files to exclude from indexing. This is illustrated by the first set of examples in this figure. Here, the * for user-agent means that it applies to all search engines and directories. As these examples show, you can use a robots.txt file to eliminate one or more folders or files from indexing.

Second, you can code a robots meta tag with the content set to "noindex" and "nofollow". This means that the robot shouldn't index the page, and it also shouldn't follow any of the links on the page as it crawls through the pages of the site.

Now, back to the question of what happens if you delete a page on your website that has already been indexed. Unfortunately, it will still come up in the search results until your site is re-indexed. In the meantime, if somebody clicks on its link, the page won't be found and a 404 error page will be displayed. Since this indicates to the user that your site isn't being properly maintained, you certainly don't want that to happen.

One way to get around this problem is to delete the content from the page, but not the page itself. Then, you can add a refresh meta tag like the one in this figure that will redirect the user to another page. In this tag, the content attribute should be set to zero (0) so the redirection is done right away (no delay). Then, the url attribute should be set to the page that you want the old page to be redirected to.

Unfortunately, the refresh meta tag isn't supported by all browsers, so you need to provide alternatives for it. Since your web server determines how each HTTP request is handled, this is usually handled by server-side code that redirects the request to a current page.

Three robots.txt files

A file that tells all search engines not to index the pages in the cart folder
```
User-agent: *
Disallow: /cart/
```

A file that tells all search engines not to index the pages in two folders
```
User-agent: *
Disallow: /cart/
Disallow: /private/
```

A file that tells all search engines not to index one folder and one file
```
User-agent: *
Disallow: /cart/
Disallow: /backlist/private.html
```

A meta tag that tells a robot not to index a page or follow its links
```
<meta http-equiv="robots" content="noindex, nofollow">
```

A meta tag that redirects the user from a deleted page to a current page
```
<meta http-equiv="refresh" content="0" url="../index_vb.html">
```

How to control which pages are indexed

- If you don't want the robot to index the pages in a folder of the site, you can add a text file named robots.txt to the root folder of your website. You can also use this file to specify single pages that you don't want the robot to index.

- Another way to stop a robot from indexing a page is to add a robots meta tag to the page. In the content attribute, "noindex" tells the robot not to index the page and "nofollow" tells the robot not to follow the links on the page.

How to control which pages are visited from the search results

- When you delete a page from your website, it will remain in the index for a search engine until the robot for that engine crawls through your site again, and maybe even longer.

- To prevent users from going to a page that you've deleted before your site is re-indexed, you can delete the content of the page but not the page itself. Then, you can add a refresh meta tag to the page.

- In the refresh meta tag, the content attribute should be 0 so the redirection is done immediately (0 delay), and the url attribute should specify the page that the user should be redirected to.

- Not all browsers support the refresh meta tag, so you should provide a server-side alternative to this whenever possible.

Figure 13-15   How to control which pages are indexed and visited

Perspective

In this chapter, you learned the skills you need for deploying a website to a remote server. You also learned about the features Dreamweaver provides for working with a collaborative team. In particular, you learned how to use the Check In/Check Out feature to prevent more than one member of the team from changing the same file.

Now, if you've completed all of the chapters in section 2, you should be able to create and deploy professional websites of your own. But there's still more to learn. So, the next section will teach you how to create websites that provide for a variety of user interactions. It will also teach you how to use a jQuery library called jQuery Mobile to build mobile websites. Like the chapters in section 2, you can read the chapters in section 3 in whatever sequence you prefer.

Terms

deploy	download a file
publish	name/value pair
web host	check in a file
web hosting service	check out a file
FTP (File Transfer Protocol)	export a site
ISP (Internet Service Provider)	import a site
IP address	duplicate a site
domain name	design note
subdomain	robot
domain name registry	spider
upload a file	

Summary

- To *deploy* (or *publish*) a website, you can use a *web host*, or *web hosting service*, that will make your website accessible from the Internet.

- You can use *File Transfer Protocol* (*FTP*) to transfer the files for your website to and from your web host.

- An *IP address* uniquely identifies a website, and so does a *domain name*.

- To find a *domain name* for your website, you search the *domain name registry*, which is a database of all registered domain names.

- Once you have a domain name, you can have one or more *subdomains* that address portions of the domain.

- You can use Dreamweaver to define a remote server for a site and then *upload files* to and *download files* from that server.

- You can use Dreamweaver to synchronize a website to be sure that all the folders and files in the local and remote websites are the same.

- The Check In/Check Out feature is useful when working with a collaborative team. Then, while a member of the team has a file *checked out*, no other members can make changes to the file until it's *checked in*.

- You can use the Manage Sites dialog box to export a site for your own use or so you can share it with other users. You can also use it to import a previously exported site and to create a duplicate copy of a site.

- You can use *design notes* to add notes to the files in a site. You can also add custom information to a note, and you can display that information in a custom column in the Files panel.

- To test a web page that has been uploaded to a remote web host, start your web browser, navigate to the URL for the web page, and click on all links to make sure they work correctly.

- To get your website into a search engine, go to the URL for its submission page. Then, its *robot* (or *spider*) will crawl through your pages and score them for later searches that are based on keywords.

- To stop pages from being indexed by a search engine, you can use a robots.txt file or robots meta tags. To redirect the request for an inactive page on your website to another page, you can use a refresh meta tag.

Exercise 13-1   Deploy a website

If you have access to a remote server that you can deploy your website on, this exercise steps you through the process.

1. If you've been working on a website other than the ones for the book exercises, open it so you can deploy it in this exercise. Otherwise, you can open the Exercises website, open the folder for this exercise, and then deploy that website on the remote server.

2. Get the information for defining the remote server from your instructor, ISP, or web manager. Then, with figure 13-3 as a guide, define the remote server and test that connection to make sure it works.

3. In the Files panel, select the folders and files that you want to upload to the server, and the click the Put icon, as shown in figure 13-4.

4. Expand the File panel by clicking on the Expand/Collapse icon, as shown in figure 13-5. Then, to reverse the locations of the Remote Server and Local Files pane, choose Edit Preferences, select the Site category in the dialog box that's displayed, and change the Always Show options.

5. Start your web browser and go to the home page of the site that you've just uploaded. Then, test the pages of the site as summarized in figure 13-13.

6. If you find any errors or omissions, use Dreamweaver to fix the files that have errors. Then, use Dreamweaver to upload the fixed or missing folders and files.

Section 3

How to create interactive and mobile web pages

This section consists of four chapters that present Dreamweaver skills that are often used in professional websites. To start, chapter 14 shows you how to work with forms. That includes using classic HTML controls and validation techniques as well as the new HTML5 controls and validation features.

Next, chapter 15 shows you how to use Dreamweaver behaviors and CSS3 transitions. As you will see, behaviors are predefined JavaScript components that let you add a variety of functions to your web pages without writing any JavaScript code. In contrast, CSS3 transitions let you perform simple animation without using JavaScript.

Chapter 16 shows you how to use jQuery UI, a JavaScript library that extends the base jQuery library. With jQuery UI, you can add interactive features such as accordions, tabs, and effects to your web pages. In addition, this chapter shows you how to use jQuery plugins, which are JavaScript applications that use the jQuery library.

Finally, chapter 17 introduces you to another jQuery library called jQuery Mobile. With jQuery Mobile, you can create web pages for mobile devices. jQuery Mobile provides an alternative to using the Responsive Web Design techniques you learned about in chapters 7 and 8.

14

How to work with forms

To create dynamic web pages, you use forms that let the user enter data. Then, the user can click on a button to submit the data to a web server for processing.

In this chapter, you'll learn how to work with forms and the controls they contain. You'll also learn how to use the new HTML5 features for data validation and how to use the new HTML5 controls.

How to use forms and controls

A *form* contains one or more *controls* such as text boxes and buttons. In the topics that follow, you'll learn how to use Dreamweaver to create a form and add the classic controls that are currently supported by all browsers.

How to create a form

Figure 14-1 shows a simple form that contains three controls: a label, a text box, and a button. To add a form and its controls to a web page, you can use the items in the Insert→Form submenu. To insert a form, for example, you choose Insert→Form→Form. To insert a text box with a label that identifies it, you can choose Insert→Form→Text. And to insert a button that submits the form to the web server, you can choose Insert→Form→Submit Button. The form and control objects are also available from the Form category of the Insert panel.

When you add a form to a web page, it's identified by a red dashed outline in the Document window. Then, you can click on this outline to select the form element and display its properties in the Property Inspector. The most common properties for a form are summarized in this figure.

The two most important properties for a form are the Action and Method properties. The Action property specifies the file on the web server that should be used to process the data when the form is submitted. The Method property specifies the HTTP method that should be used for sending the form to the web server.

In the example in this figure, the form will be submitted to the server using the HTTP "post" method. This happens when the user clicks the Subscribe button. Then, the data in the form will be processed by the code that's stored in the file named contactus.asp.

When you use the post method, the form data is packaged as part of an HTTP request and isn't visible in the browser. Because of that, the submission is more secure than it is when you use the "get" method, but the resulting page can't be bookmarked.

When you use the get method, the form data is sent as part of the URL for the HTTP request. That means that the data is visible and the page can be bookmarked. This is illustrated by the URL in this figure. Here, the URL is followed by a question mark and name/value pairs. In this case, one value is submitted: the email address that has been entered.

After you create a form, you can add controls to it. As you'll learn in the topics that follow, many of the HTML controls are implemented as input elements. Then, the type of control is determined by the value of the Type property. For example, the value of the Type property for a button that submits a form is "submit". You'll learn more about the values that are used for different controls as you progress through this chapter.

A simple form in a web browser

Please enter your email address to subscribe to our newsletter.

Email: zak@modulemedia.com

Subscribe

The Property Inspector for a form

Properties

Form ID contactform Class None ▼ Action http://www.vectacorp.com/vc/scripts/contac 📁 Title

Method POST ▼

☐ No Validate Enctype Default ▼ Target Default ▼ Accept Charset ▼
☐ Auto Complete

Common properties of a form

Property	Description
ID	A name that can be referred to by client-side or server-side code.
Action	The URL of the file that will process the data in the form.
Method	The HTTP method for submitting the form data. It can be set to Default, GET, or POST. Default uses the browser's default, which is usually GET.
Target	Determines where the page that's specified in the action property is opened. If you specify _blank, the page is opened in a new window or tab.
Enctype	Determines how the data is encoded when it's sent to the server for processing. Options include Default, which removes this property, application/x-www-form-urlencoded (the default), and multipart/form-data.
No Validate	When checked, the browser won't use its native validation to validate controls on the web page.
Auto Complete	Enables or disables the browser's native auto-completion functionality.

The URL that's used when the form is submitted with the get method

`http://www.vectacorp.com/vc/scripts/contactus.asp?email=zak@modulemedia.com`

Description

- A *form* contains one or more *controls* like text boxes, radio buttons, lists, or check boxes that can receive data.
- To insert a form or control, choose the appropriate option from the Insert→Form submenu or the Form category of the Insert panel.
- When you insert a form, it appears with a red dotted line around it. You can click on this line to select the form.
- When a form is submitted to the server for processing, the data in the controls is sent along with the HTTP request.
- For the get method, the URL is followed by a question mark and name/value pairs that are separated by ampersands. For the post method, the data is hidden.

Figure 14-1   How to create a form

How to use text fields

Figure 14-2 shows how to create three types of *text fields*, also referred to as *text boxes*. To do that, you use the Text, Password, and Hidden controls. All three of these controls are illustrated in the example in this figure.

The first text box is a standard text field that accepts input from a user. You can see the Property Inspector for this text field here, along with a description of some of the most common properties.

When you add a text field, Dreamweaver includes Name and ID properties. However, you can't change the ID property from the Property Inspector. Instead, when you change the Name property, the ID property is automatically changed to the same value. Either of these properties can be used to refer to the control from client-side or server-side code. Because of that, they should be unique.

This text field also shows how to use the Max Length property. Here, this attribute is set to 50. As a result, the user can enter a maximum of fifty characters into this field. This is useful if you're working with a database that limits the number of characters that can be stored in a field.

If you want to put a starting value into a text field, you use the Value property. Then, the user has the option of changing that value. An alternative is to use the new HTML5 Place Holder property. Like the Value property, the Place Holder property displays a value within the text field. The difference is that the placeholder value disappears when the focus is moved to the control, but the user has to delete the value that's specified for the Value property.

Another property you may use for a standard text field is the Read Only property. If you select this property, the user can't enter data into the field. However, the field can receive the focus, and the data in the field is submitted with the form. In contrast, if you select the Disabled property, the field is grayed out, the field can't receive the focus, and the data in the field isn't submitted with the form.

A new HTML5 property that you may find useful is the Auto Focus property. If you select this property, the browser puts the focus in the field when the page is loaded.

The second text box in this figure is a *password field*, which works much like a standard text field. However, the value in the field is displayed as bullets or asterisks. This improves the security of an application by preventing others from reading a password when a user enters it.

When you add a standard text field or password field, you should realize that Dreamweaver also adds a label that contains default text. You can change this text to identify the field as shown in this figure.

The third text box in this figure is a *hidden field*. Although it works much like the other fields, it isn't displayed by the browser. Nevertheless, you can use client-side or server-side code to work with the value that's stored in this field. Because the user can't enter text into a hidden field, you usually code a Value property for it. In fact, this is one of the few properties that's available from the Property Inspector for a hidden field.

Text fields in a web browser

Username: [   ]

Password: [   ]

Hidden:

The Property Inspector for a Text control

```
Properties

 I    Text    Name Username    Class None  ▼    Size [    ]  Value [        ]    Title [        ]    ?
                                           Max Length [50]                 Place Holder [        ]    ☑

        □ Disabled    □ Required    □ Auto Complete   Form [    ▼]   Pattern [    ]   Tab Index [    ]   List [    ▼]
        □ Auto Focus  □ Read Only                                                                        ▲
```

Common properties for text fields

Property	Description
Name	A unique name that can be referred to by client-side or server-side code. If you change this property, the ID for the control is changed to the same value.
Size	The width of the field in characters based on the average character width of the font. However, it's better to use CSS to set the size of a field.
Max Length	The maximum number of characters that the user can enter in the field.
Value	The initial value for the field, but the user can change this value. If a reset button is clicked, the field will revert to this value.
Place Holder	A default value or hint for the field. Unlike the Value property, this value is removed when the field receives the focus.
Disabled	When checked, the field is disabled. The field can't receive the focus and the content can't be selected.
Auto Focus	When checked, the browser sets the focus on the field when the page is loaded.
Read Only	When checked, the user can't change the control's value. The control can't receive the focus but the content can be selected.

Description

- You can use the Text control, Password control, and Hidden control to create three different types of *text fields*.

- A standard text field and a *password field* both accept data from the user, but the entry for a password field is obscured by bullets or asterisks.

- A *hidden field* isn't displayed by the browser, but you can see the data in the field if you view the source code for the web page.

- A text field is implemented by an input element with its Type property set to "text", "password", or "hidden". Dreamweaver precedes the input element for a standard or password field with a label element that's used to identify the field. You can change the default text by selecting it in the Document window. See figure 14-8 for more information on labels.

Figure 14-2   How to use text fields

How to use buttons

Figure 14-3 shows four different types of *buttons*. The first button is a generic button that you create using the Button control. When the user clicks this type of button, client-side code is usually run. For instance, JavaScript can be used to validate the data on the form. Then, if the data is valid, the script can submit the form to the server.

The second button is a *reset button* that you create using the Reset Button control. When it is clicked, the values in all of the controls on the form are reset to their default values.

The third button is a *submit button* that you create using the Submit Button control. When it is clicked, the form and its data are submitted to the server for processing. Unlike a generic button, a submit button sends the data to the server automatically without using client-side code.

The Property Inspector for a submit button is shown in this figure. Here, the Value property determines the text that's displayed on the button. This is also the value that's submitted to the server when the button is clicked. Although it's not listed here, you'll typically set the Name property as well. When you do that, the ID property is set to the same value just like it is for a text field. That's true of most of the other controls you'll learn about in this chapter too.

The fourth button shown in this figure is an *image button* that you create using the Image Button control. This button works like a submit button. The difference is that an image button displays an image rather than text. When you insert an Image Button control, Dreamweaver displays a dialog box that lets you select the image you want to display. Then, the Src property of the control is set so it points to this image. You can also specify text that's displayed if the image can't be displayed using the Alt property. And you can change the size of the image using the Width and Height properties.

Buttons in a web browser

[Button] [Reset] [Submit] (REGISTER ▷)

The Property Inspector for a submit button

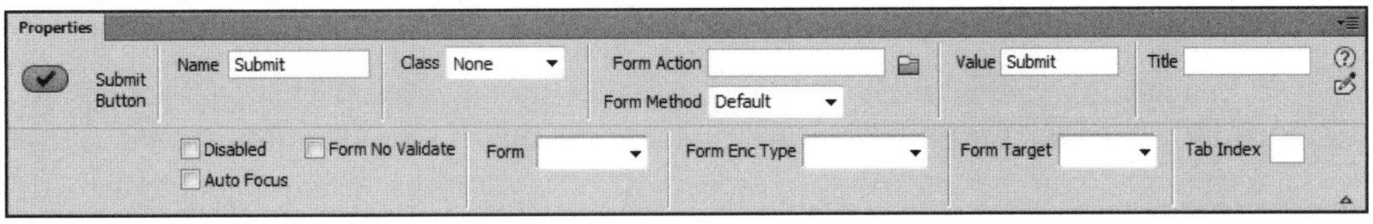

Properties							
✓ Submit Button	Name Submit	Class None ▼	Form Action		Value Submit	Title	⑦
			Form Method Default ▼				
	☐ Disabled ☐ Form No Validate ☐ Auto Focus		Form ▼	Form Enc Type ▼	Form Target ▼	Tab Index	

Common properties for buttons

Property	Description
Value	The text that's displayed on the button and submitted to the server when the button is clicked.
Src	For an image button, the relative or absolute URL of the image to display.
Alt	For an image button, alternate text to display in place of the image if the image can't be displayed.
Height	For an image button, the height of the button in pixels.
Width	For an image button, the width of the button in pixels.

Description

- You can use the Button control, Submit Button control, Reset Button control, and Image Button control to create four different types of *buttons*.
- When you click on a *submit button,* the form data is sent to the server as part of an HTTP request.
- An *image button* functions like a submit button, but you can use your own custom-designed image.
- When you click on a *reset button*, the data in all of the controls is reset to the default values.
- A generic button is used in cases where you don't want to submit or reset the form. Instead, it's typically used to run a client-side script.
- A button is implemented by an input element with its Type property set to "button", "submit", "image", or "reset".

Figure 14-3   How to use buttons

How to use radio buttons and check boxes

Figure 14-4 shows how to use *radio buttons* and *check boxes*. Although check boxes work independently of each other, radio buttons are typically set up so the user can select only one radio button from a group of buttons. In the example in this figure, for instance, you can select only one of the two radio buttons. However, you can select or deselect any combination of the three check boxes.

You create a radio button by adding a Radio Button control. Then, a label is added to the right of the radio button, and you can change the default text so it describes the radio button. You can repeat this process for each radio button you want to add to the page.

To group two or more radio buttons, you set the Name property for all of the radio buttons in the group to the same value. That way, the user will only be able to select one of the radio buttons at a time. Note, however, that each of the buttons must have a different Value property. That way, your client-side or server-side code can get the value of the selected control.

To create a check box, you add a Checkbox control. Then, if you want to refer to two or more check boxes as a group from your client-side or server-side code, you can set the Name property of those check boxes to the same value. Unlike the radio buttons in a group, though, the user will be able to select any of the check boxes in the group.

If you want a radio button or check box to be selected by default, you can select the Checked property. In this figure, for example, the first radio button has been selected by default.

Radio buttons and check boxes in a web browser

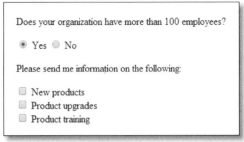

The Property Inspector for a radio button

Common properties for radio buttons and check boxes

Property	Description
Value	The value to submit to the server when the control is checked and the form is submitted.
Checked	When checked, the control is preselected in the browser. If a reset button is clicked, the control reverts to the checked state.

Description

- You can use the Radio Button control to create a *radio button*, and you can use the Checkbox control to create a *check box*.

- Only one radio button in a group can be selected at one time. The radio buttons in a group must have the same name, but different values.

- Check boxes are unrelated, so more than one check box can be checked at the same time. Each check box must have a different value.

- A radio button is implemented by an input element with its Type property set to "radio". A check box is implemented by an input element with its Type property set to "checkbox".

- Dreamweaver includes a label element after the input element for a radio button or check box that contains the text that identifies the control. The user can click the text for the label to select the associated control. See figure 14-8 for more information.

Figure 14-4   How to use radio buttons and check boxes

How to use radio button and check box groups

If you need to add several radio buttons to a group of radio buttons, you may want to use the Radio Button Group control instead of adding individual radio buttons. When you add this control to a web page, Dreamweaver displays the Radio Group dialog box shown in figure 14-5. You can use this dialog box to enter the value that's used for the Name property of each radio button. Then, you can enter the value for each radio button in the group and the label that's used to describe it. When you click OK, Dreamweaver generates code for each radio button in the list.

You can use a similar technique to create a group of check boxes. Just add a Checkbox Group control to the web page and then complete the Checkbox Group dialog box that's displayed. Note that when you use this technique, the same value is assigned to the Name property of each check box. If you want to use this property to access the check boxes from client-side or server-side code, you'll need to change this property for each control so it's unique.

A radio button group and a check box group in a web browser

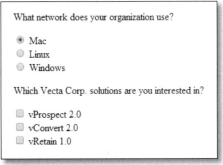

The Radio Group dialog box

Description

- You can use the Radio Button Group and Checkbox Group controls to simplify the addition of a series of radio buttons or check boxes. When you add one of these controls, the Radio Group or Checkbox Group dialog box is displayed.

- When the Radio Group and Checkbox Group dialog boxes are first displayed, two default items are included in the list. To change the text that's displayed for an item, click on the value in the Label column and then enter the text. To change the value for an item, click on the value in the Value column and then enter the value.

- To add additional items, click the Add Item icon (+) and then enter the text and value for the item.

- By default, the radio buttons and check boxes in a group are laid out using line breaks. If you want to use a table instead, you can select the Table option.

- Each radio button or check box in a group is implemented by an input element with its type property set to "radio" or "checkbox". Dreamweaver places the input element within a label element that contains the text for the radio button or check box. The user can click the text for a label to select the associated control.

- Unlike individual check box controls, the check box controls in a group are all given the same name by default.

Figure 14-5   How to use radio button and check box groups

How to use drop-down lists and list boxes

Figure 14-6 shows how to create two types of lists: a *drop-down list* and a *list box*. With a drop-down list, the user can select one option from a list of options. To display the list of options, the user must click the arrow at the right side of the control. In this figure, for example, you can see a drop-down list that includes ranges of employees.

Unlike a drop-down list, two or more options are always displayed in a list box. The list box in this figure, for example, displays the three solutions offered by Vecta Corporation. You can also define a list box so two or more options can be selected at the same time.

To create a drop-down list or list box, you add a Select control. You can see the Property Inspector for this control in this figure. The value of the Size property determines whether a drop-down list or a list box is displayed. If the value of this property isn't set or if it's set to 1, a drop-down list is displayed. If it's set to a value greater than 1, a list box is displayed with the number of options specified by this property.

To enter the options you want to appear in the list, you click the List Values button to display the List Values dialog box shown here. Then, you enter a label for each option, which is the value that's displayed in the list. You also enter the value that's assigned to the Value property of each option.

When a drop-down list is first displayed, the first option in the list is selected by default. If that's not what you want, you can choose the option you want to be selected by default from the list for the Selected property. You can also use this property to select a default option for a list box.

By default, the user can select only one option from a list box. In some cases, though, it makes sense to let the user select two or more options. To do that, you check the Multiple property. Then, the user can select multiple options by holding down the Ctrl key in Windows or the Command key in Mac OS and clicking on the options. When you check the Multiple property, you can also choose two or more options from the list for the Selected property and they will be selected by default.

A drop-down list and a list box in a web browser

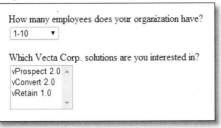

How many employees does your organization have?

1-10   ▼

Which Vecta Corp. solutions are you interested in?

vProspect 2.0
vConvert 2.0
vRetain 1.0

The Property Inspector for a drop-down list or list box

Properties

Select   Name employees   Class None ▼   Size   Title

☐ Disabled   ☐ Required   Form   Selected 1-10 / 11-100 / 101-1000   List Values...   Tab Index
☐ Auto Focus   ☐ Multiple

Common properties for drop-down lists and list boxes

Property	Description
Size	The number of items to be displayed in the control. If not set or set to 1, a drop-down list is displayed. If greater than 1, a list box is displayed.
Selected	The item that's selected by default when the page is loaded. The first item in a drop-down list is selected by default.
Multiple	When checked, allows multiple selections in a list box.

The List Values dialog box

List Values

➕ ➖   ▲ ▼   OK

Item Label	Value
1-10	1-10
11-100	11-100
101-1000	101-1000
1000+	1000+

Cancel

Help

Description

- You can use the Select control to create drop-down lists and list boxes.
- A *drop-down list* lets the user select an option from the list that's displayed when the user clicks the arrow at the right side of the control.
- The user can select one or more options from a *list box*. The number of options that are displayed at one time is determined by the value of the Size property.
- To add items to a list, use the List Values dialog box that's displayed when you click the List Values button in the Property Inspector.
- A drop-down list or list box is implemented by a select element with an option element for each item in the list. Dreamweaver precedes the select element with a label element that contains the text that identifies the list.

Figure 14-6   How to use drop-down lists and list boxes

How to use text areas

Figure 14-7 shows a *text area field*, or just *text area*. Although a text area is similar to a text field, a text area can display multiple lines of text. As the user enters text into a text area, the text is automatically wrapped to the next line when necessary. Or, the user can start a new line by pressing the Enter or Return key. If the user enters more lines than can be displayed at one time, the browser adds a scroll bar to the text area as shown in the example in this figure.

To create a text area, you add a Text Area control. Then, you can use the Property Inspector to set the properties for the control. For example, you may want to use the Place Holder property to display text that disappears when the text area receives the focus.

You can also set the Rows property to specify the approximate number of visible rows the text area will contain, and you can set the Cols property to specify the approximate number of columns. Although these properties were required with older versions of HTML, they are no longer required with HTML5. As a result, it's better to size the area by using CSS.

A text area with a placeholder in a web browser

The text area after text has been entered into it

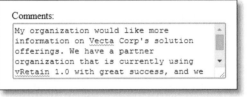

The Property Inspector for a text area

Properties									
I Text Area	Name Comments	Class None ▾	Rows 5	Max Length	Value		Title		⑦
			Cols 40	Wrap Default ▾			Place Holder If you have any		
	☐ Disabled ☐ Auto Focus	☐ Required ☐ Read Only	Form ▾	Tab Index					

Common properties for text areas

Property	Description
Rows	The approximate number of rows (height) in the text area. It's better to use the CSS height property.
Cols	The approximate number of columns (width) in the text area. It's better to use the CSS width property.
Max Length	The maximum number of characters that the user can enter.
Wrap	Specifies how the text should wrap when submitted to the server. Possible options include Default, which removes this property, Soft (no wrapping), and Hard (wrap using new line characters). The Cols property must be specified to use Hard.
Value	The initial value for the text area. If a reset button is clicked, the text area will revert to this value.
Place Holder	A default value or hint for the text area. This value is removed when the text area receives the focus.

Description

- You can use a Text Area control to create a *text area field* (or just *text area*) that can be used to get multi-line text entries. A scroll bar is added if the user enters more text than can be displayed at one time.

- A text area is implemented by an input element with its Type property set to "textarea". Dreamweaver precedes the input element with a label element that contains the text that identifies the text area.

Figure 14-7   How to use text areas

How to use labels

Figure 14-8 shows how Dreamweaver uses *labels* to display text that identifies the contents of a related control. When I added the three check boxes shown in this figure, for example, Dreamweaver added a label to the right of each box with default text. Then, I modified this text so it describes the check boxes.

When Dreamweaver adds a label like this, it sets the For property of the label to the ID property of the related control. If you later change the ID property of the related control, you may also need to change the For property of the label. To do that, you can place the cursor anywhere in the text for the label, click the label element in the Tag selector, and then change the For property in the Property Inspector. Note, though, that if the ID property of a control is changed automatically when the Name property is changed, the For property of the related label is also changed. So you'll only need to change the For property for controls such as radio buttons that have the same name but different IDs.

Later in this chapter, you'll learn that the use of labels provides an easy way to align the controls of a form with CSS. As shown in this figure, though, labels can also be used to improve the accessibility of radio buttons and check boxes. When you use labels like this, the user can click on the label text to turn a radio button or check box on or off. This makes the buttons and check boxes more accessible to users who lack the motor control to click on the smaller button or box.

The use of labels with radio buttons and check boxes also makes it easier for assistive devices such as screen readers to read the text associated with a control and tell it to the user. If labels weren't used in this way, the assistive devices would have to scan the text around a control and guess which snippet of text is associated with the control.

Although Dreamweaver adds labels along with other controls whenever needed, you can also add them explicitly using the Label control. When you do that, you should know that Dreamweaver doesn't include any default text for the label. Because of that, the label can be difficult to locate on the web page. To make the label easier to work with, then, Dreamweaver automatically displays the Document window in Split view and places the cursor between the opening and closing tags for the generated label element. Then, you can enter any default text for the label between these tags, and you can enter any required attributes such as an id attribute.

A check box in a browser as the user clicks on its label to select it

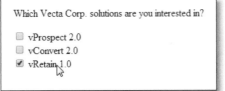

Which Vecta Corp. solutions are you interested in?

☐ vProspect 2.0
☐ vConvert 2.0
☑ vRetain 1.0

The Property Inspector for a label

Common property for labels

Property	Description
For	The ID of the related control.

Description

- A *label* is commonly used to identify a related control. Dreamweaver automatically adds a label with default text to most controls. Then, you can modify the text as necessary in the Document window.
- If you delete the text for a label in the Document window, the label is deleted. If that's not what you want, you can select the text in the label and then enter the new text instead.
- Dreamweaver sets the For property of a label to the ID of the related control when you insert the control. If you change the ID of the related control, you can change the For property of the label using the Property Inspector.
- Labels are used with radio buttons and check boxes to improve the accessibility of those controls. Then, the user can click on the text for a label to select the control.
- The label that's generated for each radio button or check box in a group doesn't include the For property. Because the input element for the control is coded within the label element, though, the user can still click on the text for the label to select the control.
- The use of labels also helps assistive devices such as screen readers that can read the text in the label to the user.
- Labels make it easier to align the controls on a form. For more information, see figure 14-12.
- You can also add a label to a form manually using the Label control whenever that's necessary.

Figure 14-8   How to use labels

How to use fieldsets to visually group controls

In many cases, you'll want to group related controls on a form to make it easy for users to see that they're related. To group controls, you use a *fieldset* as shown in figure 14-9. Then, the group is displayed with a thin gray border around it by default. If you want to change the appearance of the border, you can use CSS.

To create a fieldset, you add a Fieldset control. When you do, the Fieldset dialog box is displayed. This dialog box lets you enter a *legend* that's displayed at the top of the fieldset. In this figure, for example, you can see that legends have been added to both fieldsets. If you don't want to include a legend, you can just leave the Legend text box blank.

If you know that you want to include controls in a group, you'll want to add the fieldset before adding the controls. Then, you can add the controls directly to the group. If you add controls and then later decide to group them with a fieldset, you can do that too. Just select the controls before you add the fieldset and the controls will be enclosed within the fieldset. You can also add the fieldset and then drag existing controls from outside the fieldset to within the fieldset.

Two groups of controls with legends in a web browser

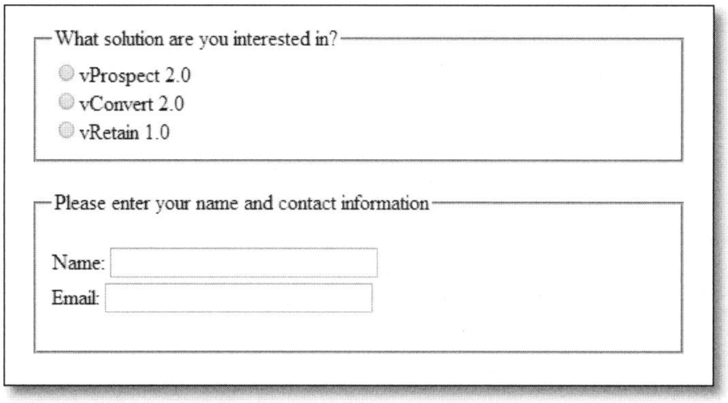

```
┌─ What solution are you interested in? ─────────────────────────┐
│  ○ vProspect 2.0                                               │
│  ○ vConvert 2.0                                                │
│  ○ vRetain 1.0                                                 │
└────────────────────────────────────────────────────────────────┘

┌─ Please enter your name and contact information ───────────────┐
│                                                                │
│  Name: [                          ]                            │
│  Email: [                          ]                           │
│                                                                │
└────────────────────────────────────────────────────────────────┘
```

The Fieldset dialog box

```
Fieldset                                          [X]

  Legend:  What solution are you int      [  OK  ]
                                           [ Cancel ]
```

Description

- You can use the Fieldset control to create a *fieldset* that visually groups controls on a web page. By default, the group is displayed with a thin gray border around it, but you can change the appearance of the border using CSS.

- When you insert a fieldset, the Fieldset dialog box is displayed. This dialog box lets you enter the *legend* you want to be displayed for the group. If you leave the Legend text box blank, no legend is displayed.

- If you select one or more controls before inserting a fieldset, those controls will be enclosed within the fieldset.

- After you add a fieldset, you can drag existing controls into the fieldset to add them to the group. You can also add new controls directly to the group.

- A fieldset is implemented by the fieldset element. A legend is implemented by a legend element that's coded within the fieldset element.

Figure 14-9   How to use fieldsets to visually group controls

How to use file-upload fields

Figure 14-10 shows how to use *file-upload fields*. These fields let users upload one or more files to the web server. You'll typically use a file-upload field with a server-side programming language such as PHP or ASP.NET, which performs the actual transfer. To create a file-upload field, you use the File control.

The example at the top of this figure shows a file-upload field in the Chrome browser. Note that this field may appear differently in other browsers. In Firefox, for example, the value that's displayed on the button is "Browse..." and the message to the right of the button is "No files selected."

When the user clicks the button for the file-upload field, the Open dialog box is displayed. This dialog box lets the user select the file or files to be uploaded. By default, only a single file can be selected. If you want the user to be able to select more than one file, you can check the Multiple property in the Property Inspector.

When using the file-upload field, the Method property of the form should be set to "POST". In addition, the Enctype property of the form should be set to multipart/form-data. This is typically the only time this property will be modified for a form.

A file-upload field in the Chrome browser

The Property Inspector for a file-upload field

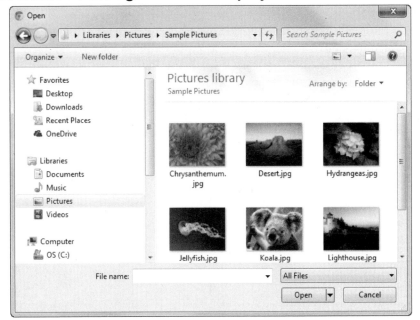

Common property for file-upload fields

Property	Description
Multiple	When checked, lets the user upload more than one file.

The Windows dialog box that's displayed when Choose Files is clicked

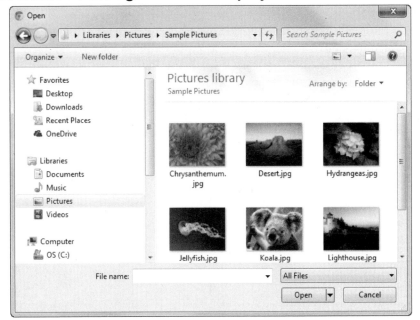

Description

- You use the File control to create a *file-upload field* that lets users select the files they want to upload to the web server.
- A file-upload field is implemented by an input element with its Type property set to "file". Dreamweaver precedes the input element with a label element.
- The Method property for the form that contains the file-upload field must be set to POST, and the Enctype property must be set to multipart/form-data.

Figure 14-10   How to use file-upload fields

A web page with a form
that uses the classic HTML controls

Figure 14-11 presents a web page with a form that uses some of the classic HTML controls you've just learned about. That includes a submit button that sends the data in the controls to the server when it's clicked. The Action property of the form is set so this data is processed by a server-side script named contact.asp on the Vecta Corporation server. This script simply extracts the information entered on the page and lists it on another page. If you've downloaded the files for this book as described in appendix A, you can try this yourself by displaying the web page in a browser, completing the form, and then clicking the Submit Now button.

This form includes four standard text boxes that let the user enter contact information. It also includes a check box group that lets the user select one or more products and a radio button group that lets the user select an operating system. Next, it includes a drop-down list that lets the user select the number of employees in the company and a list box that lets the user indicate how they heard about Vecta Corporation. Finally, it includes a text area that lets the user enter comments or questions.

Although you can't tell by looking at this web page, none of the controls in the form are validated. Because of that, the user could submit this form without entering any data. In most cases, that's not what you want. In the topics that follow, then, you'll learn some of the techniques for data validation. But first, you'll learn some additional skills for working with controls that make them easier to use.

A web page with a form that uses some of the classic HTML controls

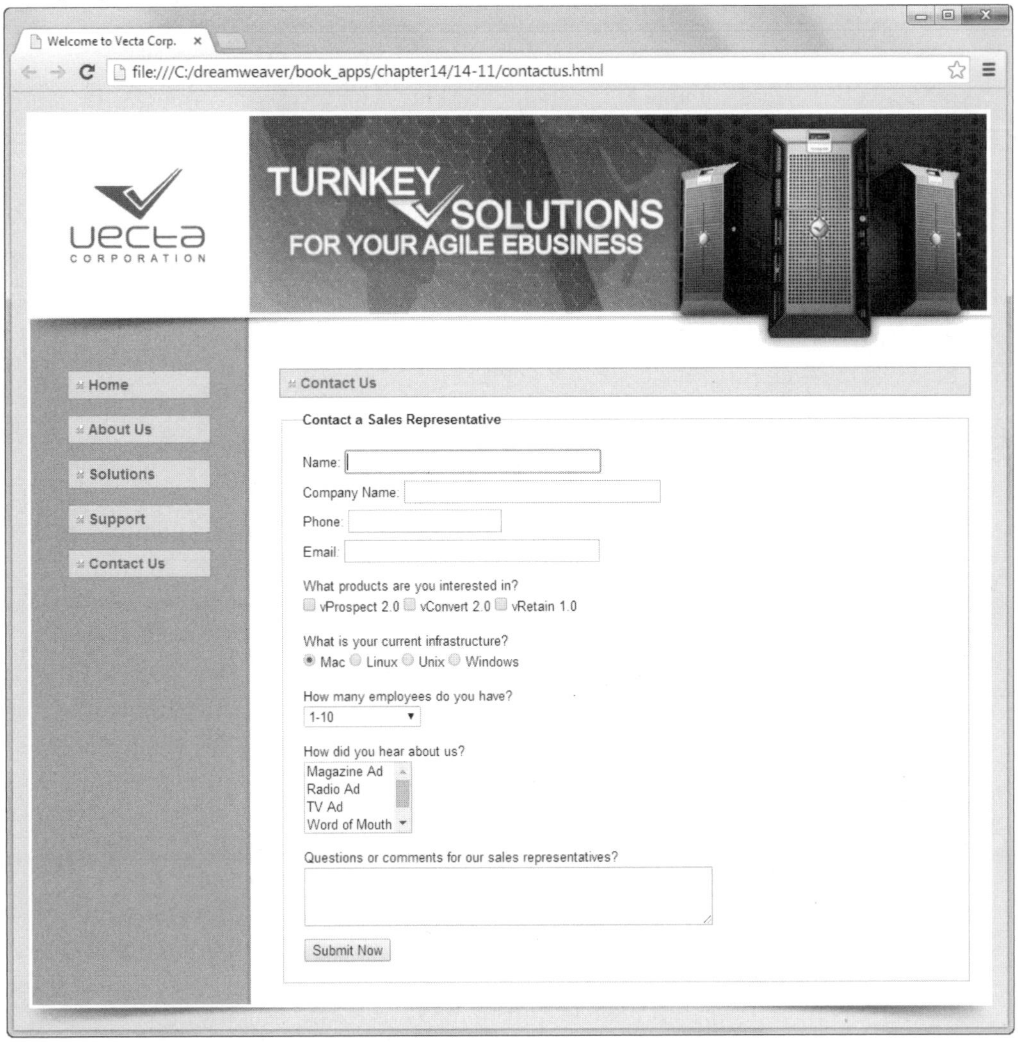

Description

- This web page includes a form that uses several of the classic HTML controls. All of the controls are placed within a fieldset that includes a legend.

- CSS is used to control the appearance of some of the controls. That includes the font weight of the legend, the width and spacing of the text fields, and the width and height of the text area.

- The Auto Focus property is used for the first control in the form so the tab order doesn't need to be changed. Otherwise, the navigation links would come before the form controls in the tab order.

- The form includes a submit button that the user can click to send the form data to the server.

Figure 14-11   A web page with a form that uses classic HTML controls

Other skills for working with forms

Now that you know how to create forms using classic HTML controls, you're ready to learn some other skills for working with forms and controls. In particular, you should know how to use CSS to align and format controls. You should also know how to set the tab order of the controls on a form and how to assign access keys to the controls. Finally, you should know how to use HTML5 properties, CSS3 selectors, and regular expressions to validate the data on a form.

How to align controls

The best way to align controls is to use the technique shown in figure 14-12. Here, the input element for each text box is preceded by a label element with a for attribute that associates the label with the text box. As you know, Dreamweaver generates this code automatically when you add a Text control.

The style rule for the labels starts by floating the labels to the left. Next, the style rule sets the width property so all the labels are the same width, and it sets the text-align property so the labels are aligned at the right. This makes the form more readable.

After the style rule for labels, a style rule is coded for the input controls. Here, the margin-left property increases the space between the labels and text boxes to 1 em. Then, the margin-bottom property sets the space after the text boxes to .5 ems.

The last style rule aligns the buttons on the form by adjusting the left margin of the Register button to 7 ems. To do that, it uses the Register button's ID as the selector. This aligns that button with the text boxes above it. Then, the Reset button is 1 em to the right of the Register button because the left margin for all input controls is set to 1 em.

You should notice in this code that the input element for each text box is followed by a br element. This causes the element that follows to be displayed on the next line, and this is the easiest way to align controls. If you know that you want to align controls like this, then, you should insert a br element after each control you're aligning instead of pressing the Enter or Return key, which places both the label and the control in a paragraph.

Label, text box, and button controls aligned on a form

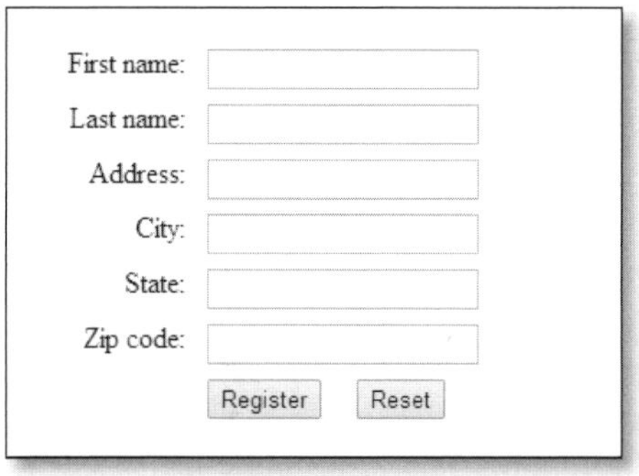

First name: [   ]
Last name: [   ]
Address: [   ]
City: [   ]
State: [   ]
Zip code: [   ]

[Register] [Reset]

The HTML for the form controls

```
<label for="firstname">First name:</label>
<input type="text" name="firstname" id="firstname"><br>
<label for="lastname">Last name:</label>
<input type="text" name="lastname" id="lastname"><br>
<label for="address">Address:</label>
<input type="text" name="address" id="address"><br>
<label for="city">City:</label>
<input type="text" name="city" id="city"><br>
<label for="state">State:</label>
<input type="text" name="state" id="state"><br>
<label for="zip">Zip code:</label>
<input type="text" name="zip" id="zip"><br>
<input type="submit" name="register" id="register" value="Register">
<input type="reset" name="reset" id="reset">
```

The CSS for the controls

Selector	Property
label	float: left width: 5em text-align: right
input	margin-left: 1em margin-bottom: .5em
#register	margin-left: 7em

Description

- If a form includes a series of controls and labels that identify them, you can align the labels by floating them to the left of the controls and setting a width that provides enough space for all the labels. Then, you can set a left margin for the controls to add space between the labels and the controls.

- A series of labels is typically more readable if the labels are aligned at the right, particularly if there is a sizable variance in length.

Figure 14-12   How to align controls

How to format controls

In the last topic, you learned how to use a few of the CSS properties to align the controls on a form. But you can also use CSS properties to format controls. Figure 14-13 shows how this works. The form shown here has the same HTML that's in the previous figure, but with some additional formatting.

First, the font-size property is used to change the font size for all text within the page. Additionally, the font-family property is used to change the font for all text within the web page. This not only affects the label elements but also the text that the user enters into the controls and the font on the buttons.

Second, the color for the labels has been set to navy. This is done by using a selector for all labels.

Third, the :focus pseudo-class is used to change the appearance of the text box that has the focus. In this case, a 2-pixel solid navy border is added to the text box. You can see that in the first text box in the browser.

Last, the widths of all of the text boxes and both of the buttons have been increased. That way, the text boxes should be wide enough to display all the data the user enters, and the buttons are aligned with the text boxes.

The form in figure 14-12 with some additional formatting

First name: [   ]
Last name: [   ]
Address: [   ]
City: [   ]
State: [   ]
Zip code: [   ]

[Register]   [Reset]

The CSS for the form

Selector	Properties
body	font: 90% font-family: Arial, Helvetica, sans-serif margin: 20px
label	color: #000080 float: left width: 8em font-weight: bold text-align: right
input	width: 15em margin-left: 1em margin-bottom: .5em
input:focus	border: 2px solid #000080
#register, #reset	width: 7em
#register	margin-left: 10.5em

Description

- You can use many of the properties you learned about in chapters 5 and 6 to format controls.

- You can use the :focus pseudo-class to change the appearance of a control when it has the focus. This class is not supported in older versions of Internet Explorer.

Figure 14-13   How to format controls

How to set the tab order and assign access keys

Figure 14-14 shows how to set the tab order of the controls on a form and how to assign access keys to controls. By default, when the user presses the Tab key on a web page, the focus moves from one control to another in the sequence that the controls appear in the HTML, not including labels. This sequence is referred to as the *tab order* of the controls, and it includes any links on the form.

To change this default tab order, you can set the Tab Index property for any control using the Property Inspector. To remove a control from the tab order, for example, you assign a negative number to its Tab Index property. To include a control in the order, you start the Tab Index property at zero or any positive number and then increment the index by any amount as you add more controls. You can also set the same Tab Index value for more than one control. Then, within those controls, the tab order will be the sequence that the controls appear in the HTML.

Controls that aren't assigned a Tab Index value will also receive the focus in the sequence that the controls appear in the HTML. These controls will receive the focus after all the controls that are assigned Tab Index values. As a result, you usually assign Tab Index values to all of the controls on a form if you assign values to any of the controls.

With HTML5, though, you can use the Auto Focus property to put the focus in the control that you want the user to start with. This is often all you need to do to get the tab order the way you want it.

When you work with the tab order, you should be aware of browser variations. That is, when you press the Tab key right after a page is loaded, the focus may move to a browser control like the address bar instead of the first control on the page. In fact, you may have to press the Tab key several times before the focus is moved to the first control. Here again, you can use the Auto Focus property to get around this problem.

When you provide an *access key* for a control, the user can press that key in combination with one or more other keys to move the focus to the control. If the page is displayed in Chrome, for example, the user can move the focus to a control by pressing the Alt key and the access key.

Unfortunately, you can't define an access key for a control using the Property Inspector. Instead, you must add the accesskey attribute directly to the HTML for the control as shown in this figure. The value of this attribute is the keyboard key you want to use to move the focus to the control. In the example in this figure, you can see that the accesskey attribute is coded for the three text boxes on the form. The access key for the First name text box is "F", the access key for the Last name text box is "L", and the access key for the Email text box is "E". Here, the letters that are used for the access keys are underlined in the labels that are associated with the controls. This is a common way to identify the access key for a control.

The properties for setting the tab order and an access key

Property	Description
`tabindex`	To set the tab order for a control, use a value of 0 or more. To take a control out of the tab order, use a negative value like -1.
`accesskey`	A keyboard key that can be pressed in combination with a control key to move the focus to the control.

Three labels with access keys

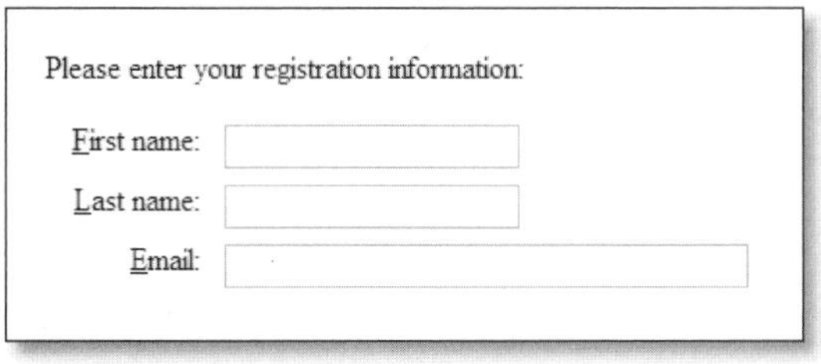

Please enter your registration information:

First name: _____

Last name: _____

Email: _____

The HTML for the controls

```
<label for="first"><u>F</u>irst name:</label>
<input type="text" name="first" id="first" accesskey="F"
       tabindex="0"><br>
<label for="last"><u>L</u>ast name:</label>
<input type="text" name="last" id="last" accesskey="L" tabindex="1"><br>
<label for="email"><u>E</u>mail:</label>
<input type="text" name="email" id="email" accesskey="E" tabindex="2">
```

Accessibility guideline

- Setting a proper tab order and providing access keys improves the accessibility for users who can't use a mouse.

Description

- The *tab order* for a form is the sequence in which the controls receive the focus when the Tab key is pressed. By default, the tab order is the order of the controls in the HTML, not including labels, and most browsers also include links.

- *Access keys* are shortcut keys that the user can press to move the focus to specific controls on a form. If you assign an access key to a label, the focus is moved to the control that's associated with the label since labels can't receive the focus.

- You can set the tab order of a control by entering a value in the Tab Index text box in the Property Inspector.

- To assign an access key to a control, you add the accesskey attribute to the control in Code view. You should also underline the access key in the label for the control so the user knows what it is.

- To use an access key, you press a control key plus the access key. For IE, Chrome, and Safari, use the Alt key. For Firefox, use Alt+Shift. And for Opera, use Alt+Esc to get a list of available access keys.

Figure 14-14   How to set the tab order and assign access keys

How to use the HTML5 properties and CSS3 selectors for data validation

HTML5 provides new features that let you validate some of the data the user enters into a form without using client-side or server-side code. In this topic, you'll learn about the three new properties that HTML5 provides for *data validation*. These properties are summarized in figure 14-15.

The Auto Complete property instructs a browser to use its *auto-completion feature* to display a list of entry options when the user starts the entry for a control. These options will be based on the entries the user has previously made for controls with similar names. If you're using a modern browser, you may have noticed that your browser does this by default. However, that depends on the browser and browser version you're using. To ensure that this feature is used for all browsers, then, you can check the Auto Complete property in the Property Inspector for a form or individual controls.

In some cases, you'll want to turn the auto-completion feature off. For instance, you may want to turn this feature off for controls that accept credit card numbers. To do that, you start by checking the Auto Complete property in the Property Inspector to turn this feature on. Then, you uncheck this property to turn the feature off. If you don't do that, the Auto Complete property won't be set and the browser's default will be used.

The Required property causes the browser to check whether a field is empty before it submits the form for processing. If the field is empty, it displays a message like the one in this figure. Some browsers also highlight all of the fields that require entries but are empty when the submit button is clicked. However, the message, how it's displayed, and how the empty fields are highlighted vary from one browser to another.

If you would like to stop all controls within a form from being validated, you can do that too. Just check the No Validate property for the form in the Property Inspector.

To format required, valid, and invalid fields, you can use the new CSS3 pseudo-classes that are listed in this figure. For instance, you can use the :required pseudo-class to format all required fields. If your browser doesn't support these pseudo-classes, you can still format the required fields by using the attribute selector shown in this figure.

The HTML5 properties for data validation

Property	Description
Auto Complete	Determines whether auto-completion is used. This can be set for a form or a control.
Required	Determines whether a value is required for a field. If the form is submitted and the field is empty, the browser displays its default error message.
No Validate	Determines whether the browser uses its native validation to validate the controls on a form.

The error message and highlighting used by Chrome

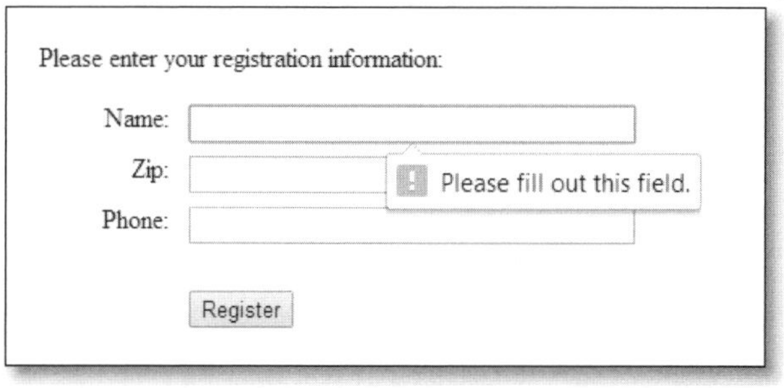

Please enter your registration information:

Name:

Zip: Please fill out this field.

Phone:

Register

The CSS3 pseudo-classes for required, valid, and invalid fields

```
:required
:valid
:invalid
```

A CSS attribute selector for all controls with the required attribute

```
input[required]
```

Description

- The *auto-completion feature* causes a browser to display entry options when the user starts an entry. These options will be based on previous entries for controls with similar names.

- If the Required property is set for a field, the browser checks whether the field is empty when the form is submitted. If it is, the browser displays its default error message for the field. But what this message says and how it's displayed are browser-dependent.

- You can style controls in their required, valid, and invalid states by using the new CSS3 pseudo-class selectors.

- To select all the input elements with the required attribute, you can also use the attribute selector shown above.

Figure 14-15   The HTML5 properties and CSS3 selectors for data validation

How to use regular expressions for data validation

A *regular expression* is a standard language that provides a way to match a user entry against a *pattern* of characters. As a result, regular expressions can be used for validating user entries that have a standard pattern, such as credit card numbers, zip codes, dates, phone numbers, URLs, and more. Regular expressions are supported by many programming languages including JavaScript, PHP, and ASP.NET, and now regular expressions are supported by HTML5.

As figure 14-16 shows, HTML5 provides a Pattern property that specifies the regular expression that will be used to validate the entry for a control. You can use the Property Inspector to enter the value for this property. In the example, regular expressions are used for the zip code and phone text boxes. As a result, the user must enter a zip code that has either 5 digits or 5 digits, a hyphen, and 4 more digits. And the phone number must be 3 digits, a hyphen, 3 more digits, another hyphen, and 4 more digits. If the entries don't match those patterns when the user clicks the submit button, an error message is displayed by the browser and the form isn't submitted. Here again, the message that is displayed and how that message is formatted, depends on the browser.

If you set the Title property for a control that is validated by a regular expression, the value of that property is displayed when the mouse hovers over the control. In some browsers, this value is also displayed at the end of the browser's standard error message for an entry that doesn't match the regular expression. In the example, the browser's standard message is: "Please match the requested format:", which is followed by the value of the title attribute. But here again, the message that's displayed and how it's displayed are browser-dependent.

The trick of course is adding the regular expressions that you need, and that can be difficult. For more information or to find the expressions that you need, you can search the web. Or, you can refer to our JavaScript or PHP book, which give detailed instructions on how to create regular expressions.

Properties for using regular expressions

Property	Description
Pattern	The regular expression that is used to validate the entry.
Title	Text that is displayed in the tooltip when the mouse hovers over a control. This text is also displayed after the browser's error message.

Patterns for common entries

Used for	Pattern
Password (6+ alphanumeric)	`[a-zA-Z0-9]{6,}`
Zip code (99999 or 99999-9999)	`\d{5}([\-]\d{4})?`
Phone number (999-999-9999)	`\d{3}[\-]\d{3}[\-]\d{4}`
Date (MM/DD/YYYY)	`[01]?\d\/[0-3]\d\/\d{4}`
URL (starting with http:// or https://)	`https?://.+`
Credit card (9999-9999-9999-9999)	`^\d{4}-\d{4}-\d{4}-\d{4}$`

A form in Chrome with an error message for an invalid pattern

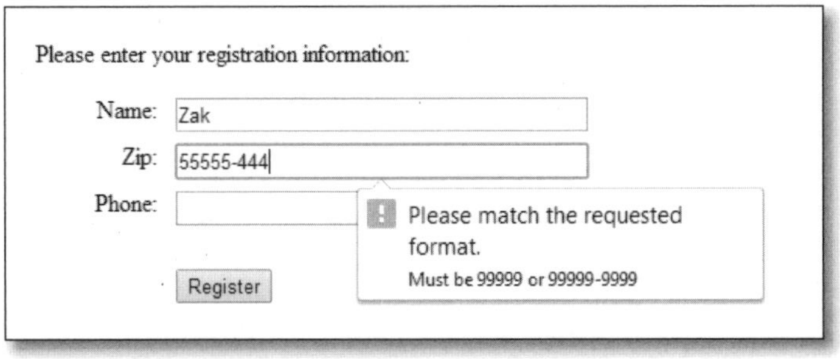

Please enter your registration information:

Name: Zak
Zip: 55555-444
Phone:

Please match the requested format.
Must be 99999 or 99999-9999

Register

Description

- To use *regular expressions* to validate entries in text fields, you enter the expression for the Pattern property in the Property Inspector for the control. Then, the user's entry must have the *pattern* that's defined by the regular expression.
- You can use the Title property to provide a hint to your users about the format of an entry.
- To learn how to code regular expressions, you can search the web or use our JavaScript or PHP book.

Figure 14-16   How to use regular expressions for data validation

How to use the HTML5 controls

Besides the validation features that you've just learned, HTML5 provides several new controls. Some of these do some validation, some provide better ways to enter data, and all of them are good semantically. In the topics that follow, you'll learn about the controls that are supported by Dreamweaver's visual interface. Just like the classic HTML controls, these controls are available from the Insert→Form submenu and the Form category of the Insert panel.

How to use the Email, Url, and Tel controls

Figure 14-17 presents the new Email, Url, and Tel controls. These controls are good to use for semantic reasons because the Type property of each control clearly indicates what type of data the control is for: an email address, a URL, or a telephone number.

Beyond that, a browser that supports the Email and Url controls will validate the data in the controls when the form is submitted. For instance, the browser in this figure is displaying its error message for an invalid email address. This works the same for a Url control. This prevents you from having to define a regular expression in the Pattern property for emails and URLs like you would if you were using a generic text box.

At this writing, though, validation isn't done for Tel controls. That's because the format of telephone numbers can vary so much from one country to another. However, this may change as browsers evolve.

If a browser doesn't support these controls, they are treated as text boxes. Since this doesn't cause any problems, you can start using these controls right away. That way, you still get the semantic benefits.

The Email, Url, and Tel controls

Control	Description
Email	A control for receiving an email address. This implies that the entry will be validated as an email address by the browser when the form is submitted.
Url	A control for receiving a URL. This implies that the entry will be validated as an Internet URL by the browser when the form is submitted.
Tel	A control for receiving a telephone number, but currently this doesn't imply validation because the formats vary from one country to another.

A form in Chrome with an error message for an invalid email entry

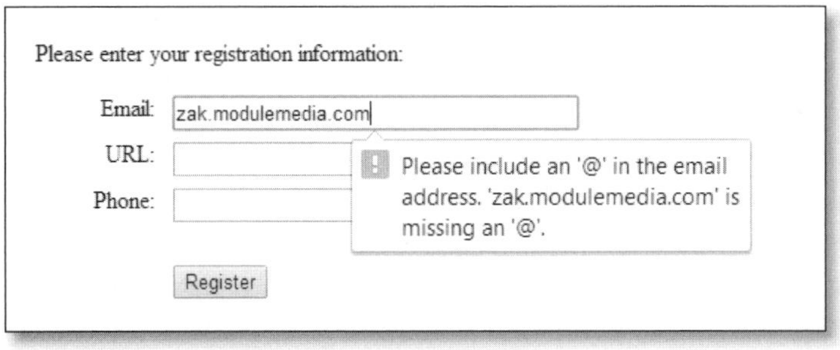

Description

- The HTML5 Email, Url, and Tel controls are designed for email address, URL, and telephone number entries. The first two imply that validation will be done by the browser when the form is submitted, but phone numbers aren't validated.

- The Email, Url, and Tel controls are implemented by an input element with its Type property set to "email", "url", or "tel". Dreamweaver precedes the input element with a label element.

- It's good to use these controls for semantic reasons because they indicate what type of data each control is for.

- The wording of the error messages and the way they're displayed depends upon the browser.

- If you want to refine the validation that's done for any of these controls, you can include regular expressions as described in figure 14-16.

Figure 14-17   How to use the Email, Url, and Tel controls

How to use the Number and Range controls

Figure 14-18 shows how to use the Number and Range controls. In browsers that support these controls, the Number control is presented as a text box with up and down arrows that can increase or decrease the value in the box. And the Range control is presented as a slider that the user can use to increase or decrease the initial value.

When you add these controls, you usually include the Min, Max, and Step properties, which you can set from the Property Inspector. Those properties set the minimum and maximum values that the control will accept, as well as the amount to increase or decrease the value when a number arrow is clicked or the slider is moved.

The examples in this figure show how this works. Here, the Number control has 100 as its minimum value, 1000 as its maximum value, and 100 as the step value when an arrow is clicked. In contrast, the Range control has 1 as its minimum value, 5 as its maximum value, and 1 as the step value.

If you set the Value property for a Number control, it will appear in the text box as the starting value. Otherwise, no value is displayed. If you set the Value property for a Range control, the slider will be set to that value. Otherwise, it will be set to the middle of the slider.

Here again, if a browser doesn't support these controls, they are treated as text boxes. Since this doesn't cause any problems, you can start using these controls right away. That way, you still get the semantic benefits.

A form with a Number and a Range control in Chrome

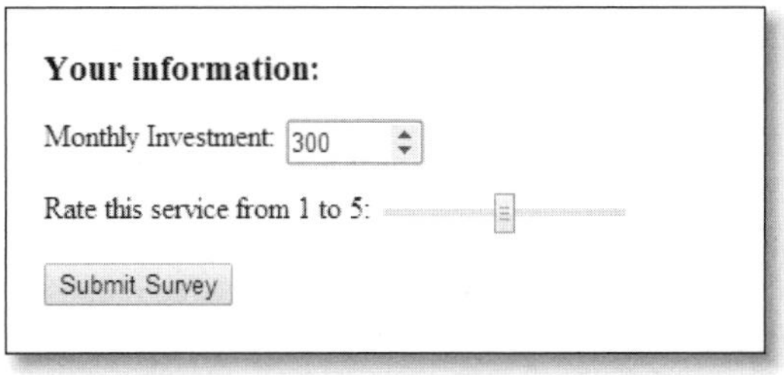

Your information:

Monthly Investment: [300 ⇕]

Rate this service from 1 to 5: ━━━━━[⊟]━━━━━

[Submit Survey]

The Property Inspector for a Number control

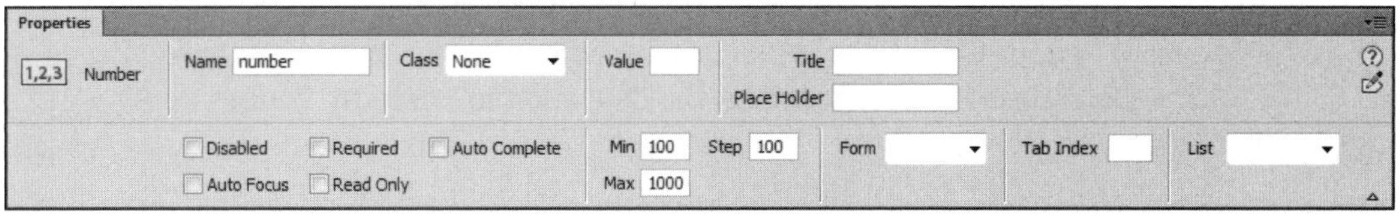

Properties

| [1,2,3] Number | Name [number] | Class [None ▼] | Value [ ] | Title [ ] | | ⑦ |
| | | | | Place Holder [ ] | | ✍ |

☐ Disabled   ☐ Required   ☐ Auto Complete   Min [100]   Step [100]   Form [▼]   Tab Index [ ]   List [▼]
☐ Auto Focus   ☐ Read Only   Max [1000]

Properties for the Number and Range controls

Property	Description
Min	The minimum value that may be entered.
Max	The maximum value that may be entered.
Step	The value that the entry is increased or decreased by when the user clicks on the up or down arrow for a Number control or moves the slider for a Range control.

Description

- The Number and Range controls are designed for numeric entries. These controls are implemented by an input element with its Type property set to "number" or "range". Dreamweaver precedes the input element with a label element.

- It's good to use these controls for semantic reasons because they indicate what type of data each control is for.

- In Chrome, Opera, and Safari, a text box with up and down arrows is rendered for the Number control and a slider is rendered for the Range control.

- If these controls aren't supported by a browser, a text box is displayed.

Figure 14-18   How to use the Number and Range controls

How to use the date and time controls

Figure 14-19 shows how to use the date and time controls for user entries. The example in this figure shows what each of these controls looks like in Opera.

When the user clicks on the down arrow for any one of the date controls, the calendar is displayed as shown by the last control in this figure. Then, the user can select the date, month, or week. When the user clicks on the up or down arrow for a time, the time is increased or decreased.

If you study the examples, controls, and properties for each control, you can see how they differ. For example, the only difference between the Date Time and Date Time Local controls is that Date Time is formatted in Coordinated Universal Time, or UTC. This is the time by which the world sets its clocks. In contrast, Date Time Local is based on the date and time used by your system's clock.

At this writing, Firefox, Internet Explorer, and Safari treat these controls as text boxes. Chrome supports these controls but not the popup calendar, and Opera has the best support for these controls. Nevertheless, it's good to use these controls for semantic reasons. And there's no harm done if they're rendered as text boxes.

The date and time controls in Opera

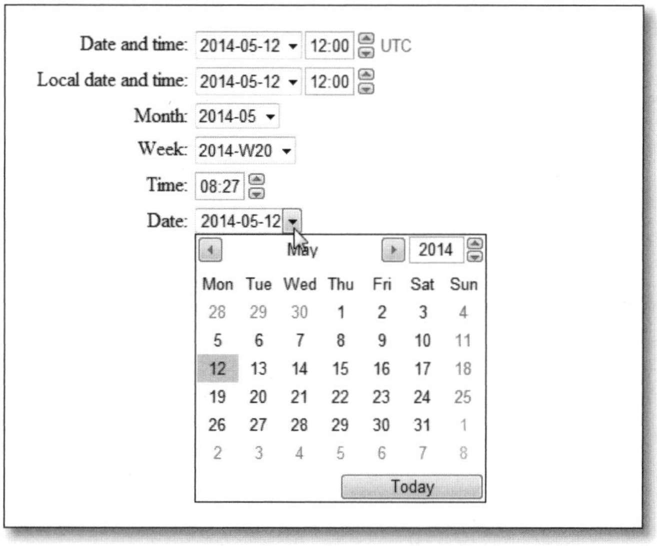

The Property Inspector for a Date control

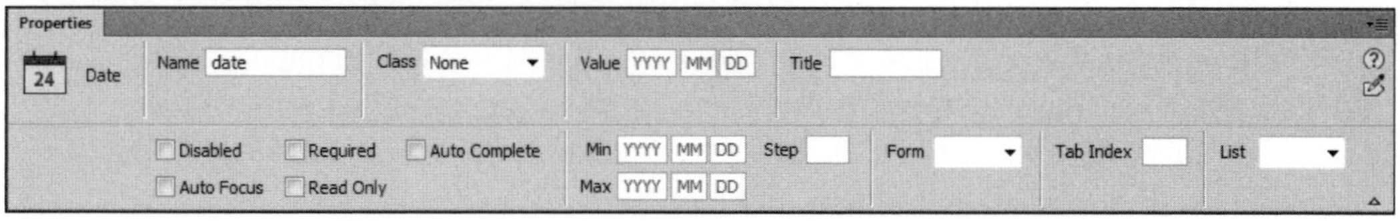

Properties for the date and time controls

Property	Description
Max	The maximum year, month, day, hours, minutes, and seconds that may be entered within a date or time field. How this property appears within the Property Inspector varies by control.
Min	The minimum year, month, day, hours, minutes, and seconds that may be entered within a date or time field. How this property appears within the Property Inspector varies by control.
Step	The value that the entry is increased or decreased by when the user interacts with arrows and buttons within the various date and time controls.

Description

- The HTML5 Date, Date Time, Date Time Local, Month, Week, and Time controls are designed for date and time entries. These controls are implemented by an input element with its Type property set to "date", "datetime", "datetime-local", "month", "week", or "time". Dreamweaver precedes the input element with a label element.

- Here again, it's good to use these controls for semantic reasons.

- At this writing, Safari, Firefox, and Internet Explorer ignore the date and time controls and render text fields instead. In contrast, Chrome has some support for these controls, and Opera fully supports them by showing calendar widgets.

Figure 14-19   How to use the date and time controls

How to use the Search control
for a search function

Figure 14-20 shows how you can add a search function to a website. To do that, you use the new Search control along with two Hidden controls and a submit button to create a form that submits the search data to a search engine.

At the top of this figure, you can see the two controls that are needed for a search function: a Search control for the search entry and a submit button with the value "Search" that submits the search entry to the search engine. This is the standard way to set up the controls for a search function, and this mimics the way Google uses these controls. If you want to vary from this at all, you can use a Go button instead of a Search button, but users expect all search functions to look this way. You should also make the text box large enough for a typical entry.

If you look at the HTML code for the search form, you will see that the form is submitted to www.google.com/search, which is the Google search engine. That's why the results of the search are displayed on the standard Google results page.

In the code for this search form, the first input element is for the Search control. Although a text box would also work, the new Search control is rendered differently in the browser. For instance, as the Safari browser at the top of this figure shows, the search box is highlighted and has an "x" at the right of the box. This is meant to mimic the look of other Apple products such as the iPad, iPhone, iPod, the Apple website, and more.

To limit the search to www.murach.com, this HTML uses two hidden fields that pass the required data to the Google search engine. To use this HTML for a Google search of your site, you just need to change the value attribute in the two hidden fields to the URL for your website.

The trouble with the standard Google search engine is that sponsored links may be displayed on the results page. That's why it's better to use a search engine that can be customized so it returns results that are appropriate for users of your site. To find a search engine like this, you can search the web for "add search function to website." Some of these search engines are free, and some like Google Site Search charge a nominal fee like $100 a year for a small site.

A search function that uses a Search control in the Safari browser

The results of a search when the Google search engine is used

![JavaScript - Google Search browser window showing Google search results for "JavaScript site:http://www.murach.com", with results including "Murach's JavaScript and DOM Scripting" (www.murach.com/books/mdom) and "Murach's JavaScript and jQuery" (www.murach.com/books/qury/)]

The HTML for using the Google search engine

```
<form method="get" action="http://www.google.com/search">
    <input type="search" name="q" size="30" maxlength="255">
    <input type="hidden" name="domains" value="http://www.murach.com">
    <input type="hidden" name="sitesearch" value="http://www.murach.com">
    <input type="submit" name="search" value="Search">
</form>
```

Description

- To implement a search function, you use an HTML form to submit the search text and other required data to the search engine.

- It's good to use the Search control to accept the entry for semantic reasons. This control is implemented by an input element with its Type property set to "search". Dreamweaver precedes the input element with a label element.

- The Search control should be followed by a submit button that says Search or Go. The form must also include one hidden field to specify the domain for the search and another one to specify that only that domain should be searched.

- If you use a search engine like Google, you have no control over the search results. If you want to customize the results, you can use a search engine like Google Site Search.

- At this writing, Safari and Chrome are the only browsers that stylize the Search control when the user enters data into it. Other browsers treat this control as a text box.

Figure 14-20   How to use the Search control for a search function

How to use the Color control

Figure 14-21 demonstrates the use of the new Color control. The example in this figure shows how this control works in Opera, since it's the only browser that fully supports it at this time. Here, the control is displayed as a small color box with a down arrow. When the user clicks this arrow, the color palette shown at the top of this figure is displayed, and the user can select a color from this palette.

The user can also click the Other button below the color palette to display the color palette that's used by the operating system. For example, the color palette for Windows is shown here. The user can select a basic color from this palette or create a custom color.

The Color control works similarly in Chrome, but it's displayed as a rectangular box with no down arrow. Then, the user can click this box to display the color palette for the operating system. Other browsers treat the Color control as a text box. But here again, it's good to use this control for semantic reasons, and there's no harm done if the control is treated as a text box.

The Color control in Opera

The Windows color palette

Description

- Use the Color control to let users select a color from a color palette. The Color control is implemented by an input element with its Type property set to "color". Dreamweaver precedes the input element with a label element.

- When the form is submitted, the hexadecimal value for the selected color is used as the data for the control.

- At this writing, only Opera fully supports this control. With that browser, the user can select a color from the palette that's displayed when the down arrow is clicked. Or, the user can click the Other button to display the color palette for the operating system and then select a basic color or create a custom color.

- In Chrome, a box with the current color is displayed for the Color control, and the user can click on this box to display the color palette provided by the operating system.

- Other browsers treat the Color control as a text box. But here again, using this control is good for semantic reasons.

Figure 14-21   How to use the Color control

A web page with a form that uses HTML5 controls and data validation

Figure 14-22 presents a web page with a form that uses two of the new HTML5 controls: a Tel control for the phone number and an Email control for the email address. The Required property is also set for all of the controls except the check box group, radio button group, and text area, so the user must enter values into these controls. And a regular expression is used for the phone number so it must be entered in this format: 999-999-9999.

When the user clicks the Submit Now button, the data validation is performed before the data is sent to the server. Then, if one or more fields don't pass validation, the result depends on the browser you're using. In this figure, for example, Firefox is used. This browser highlights all of the fields that didn't pass validation and then displays an error message for the first field. Other browsers, such as Chrome and Opera, highlight just the first field that didn't pass validation.

In addition to using HTML5 controls and data validation, CSS has been used to align the controls on the form. If you compare this form with the one you saw in figure 14-11, you'll see that this makes the form easier to read and work with.

A web page in Firefox with a form that uses HTML5 controls and data validation

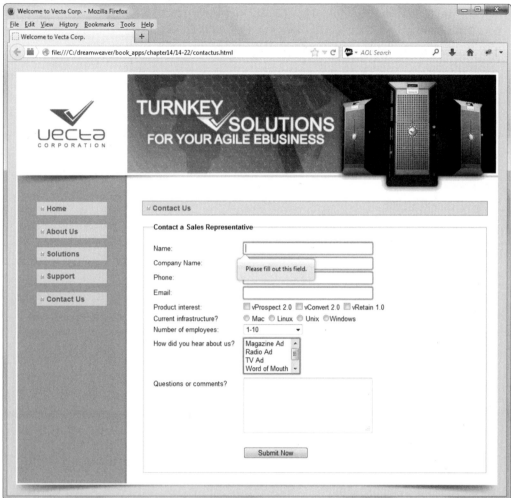

Description

- The form in this web page uses many of the classic HTML controls that were presented in this chapter, as well as some of the new HTML5 controls.

- All four of the text boxes as well as the drop-down list and list box are validated using the Required property. The phone number is also validated using a regular expression.

- Some browsers, like Chrome and Opera, highlight just the first field in error. Other browsers, like Firefox and Internet Explorer, highlight all fields in error as shown above.

- The Auto Focus property is used for the first control in the form so the tab order doesn't need to be changed. Otherwise, the navigation links would come before the form controls in the tab order.

Figure 14-22   A web page with a form that uses HTML5 controls and data validation

Perspective

Now that you've completed this chapter, you should have all the skills you need for creating forms, including forms that use HTML5 controls. You should also be able to use the HTML5 features for data validation. You should know, however, that you can do a better job of data validation by using JavaScript. On the other hand, data validation should always be done on the server too, so the client-side data validation doesn't have to be foolproof.

At present, the main problem with the HTML5 features for data validation is that they aren't supported consistently by all browsers. Until that changes, it's okay to use the new controls because they are treated as text boxes if they aren't supported. But for client-side data validation, JavaScript is still the best solution.

Terms

form	list box
control	text area
text field	label
text box	fieldset
password field	legend
hidden field	file-upload field
button	tab order
submit button	access key
reset button	data validation
image button	auto-completion feature
radio button	regular expression
check box	pattern
drop-down list	

Summary

- A *form* contains one or more *controls* like text boxes, radio buttons, or check boxes that can receive data. When a form is submitted to the server for processing, the data in the controls is sent along with the HTTP request.

- When the get method is used to submit a form, the data is sent as part of the URL for the next web page. When the post method is used, the data is hidden.

- A standard *text field* is used to get data from a user. A *password field* also gets data from the user, but its data is obscured by bullets or asterisks. A *hidden field* contains data that is sent to the server, but the field isn't displayed on the form.

- A *submit button* submits the form data to the server when the button is clicked. A *reset button* resets all the data in the form when it is clicked. Buttons can also be used to start client-side scripts when they are clicked.

- *Radio buttons* let the user choose one option from a group of options. In contrast, *check boxes* are unrelated, so more than one check box can be selected at the same time.

- The options in a *drop-down list* aren't displayed until the user clicks the down arrow at the right side of the control. In contrast, a *list box* displays two or more options at the same time.

- A *label* is commonly used to identify a related control. To do that, the For property of the label is set to the value of the ID property of the control.

- You can use a *file-upload field* to upload a file from the user's system. Then, server-side code is used to store the file on the web server.

- You can use CSS to align controls by floating the labels to the left of the controls. You can also use CSS to format the controls.

- The *tab order* of a form is the order in which the controls receive the focus when the Tab key is pressed. By default, this is the sequence in which the controls appear in the HTML. To change that, you can use the Tab Index property.

- *Access keys* are shortcut keys that the user can press to move the focus to specific controls on a form. To assign an access key to a control, you add an accesskey attribute in code. To let the user know that an access key is available, you can underline the access key in the label for the control.

- HTML5 introduces some properties for *data validation*, and CSS3 introduces some pseudo-classes for formatting required, valid, and invalid controls. The HTML5 properties for data validation include the Required property and the Pattern property that provides for *regular expressions*.

- HTML5 also introduces some input controls including the Email, Url, Tel, Number, Range, Date, Time, Search, and Color controls. These are good semantically because they indicate what types of data the controls are for.

Exercise 14-1 Build a form

In this exercise, you'll build a form like the one that follows. That will demonstrate some of the intricacies of working with forms and controls.

Open the page and add a form to it

1. Open the Exercises website, open the folder for this exercise, and open the contactus.html file. Then, review the HTML for the page to see that it includes header, section, and h1 elements.

2. In Live view, use the Insert panel to add a form element right after the h1 element. This form element should have "contactform" as its name and id attributes, "get" as the method attribute, and "submit.html" as the action attribute. The submit.html page is just an HTML page that uses JavaScript to get and display the data that's submitted. Since the get method is used, the JavaScript can get the data from the URL when the form is submitted.

Add the four text boxes and the submit button

When you insert controls into a form, the HTML that's inserted varies depending on whether you're working in Code view, Design view, or Live view. In general, you want to work in either Design view or Live view because the right code gets inserted for you. But to make sure that the right code gets inserted in the right place, it's often best to work in the Design or Live portion of Split view and then check the code that gets inserted in the Code portion. As you go through this exercise, you'll develop your own preferences for which views work best.

3. In Split view, delete the text that has been inserted into the form element, and put the cursor right after the opening tag of the form element. Then, in Design or Live view, use the Insert panel or the Insert menu to insert a Text control. This should insert both a label and an input element.

4. In Design view, select the text box and use the Property Inspector to change its name to "name". Then, (1) change the label text to "Name:"; (2) move the cursor to the right of text box (either by clicking to the right of it or pressing the End key); and use Insert→Character→Line Break or its shortcut key to enter a line break. Now, check the HTML code to make sure this worked correctly, because this can be tricky.

5. In Design view, put the cursor after the line break, and add another Text control, a Tel control, and an Email control. The names for these controls should be company, phone, and email, and the labels should be the ones shown above. Then, check the HTML code to make sure this worked correctly, and add a line break after each box.

6. Insert a submit button after the last line break. Then, note that its name is submit and the text on the button is Submit so you don't have to change these values. At this point, the formatting needs work, but you'll fix that later.

Add the check boxes and radio buttons

7. Insert a label right before the Submit button, and change its text to "Products of Interest;" as shown above. Then, in Design view, move the cursor to the right of the label, insert a check box, use the Property Inspector to set its name to vProspect, and change the text in the label to "vProspect 2.0".

8. Move the cursor to the right of the first check box, and insert two more check boxes. Their names should be vConvert and vRetain, and their labels should be like the ones shown above. Then, insert a line break after the third check box.

9. Insert a label and change its text to "Operating system:". Then, in Design view, insert a Radio Group with three buttons, as shown in figure 14-5. The name for the buttons should be "system", and both the labels and values for the three buttons should be "Windows", "Mac", and "Linux". Now, add a line break.

10. At this point, the radio buttons are on three different lines. To put them all on the same line like the check boxes, switch to Code view and delete the br elements between the lines.

Add the drop-down list, list box, and fieldset element

11. In Design view with figure 14-6 as a guide, add a drop-down list after the third radio button. Start by inserting a Select control. Then, use the Property Inspector to name the control "employees" and to set the list labels to "1-10", "11-100", and "Over 100" and the list values to 1-10, 11-100, and 100+. Now, add a line break.

12. Still in Design view with figure 14-6 as a guide, add a list box. To do that, insert a Select control and use the Property Inspector to set the name to hearAbout, the size to 3 (that's what makes it a list box), the list labels to

Word of Mouth, FaceBook, Twitter, LinkedIn, and Other and their values to word, facebook, twitter, linkedin, and other. To let the user select more than one option, check the Multiple box.

13. In Code view, select all of the controls in the form element, but not the starting or ending tag of the form element. Next, insert a fieldset element and set its legend to "Contact a Sales Representative". That should enclose all of the controls within the fieldset.

14. At this point, you can review the page in Live view or in your browser, and you can look at the HTML code to make sure it all looks right.

Format the form

This part of the exercise will guide you through the process of formatting the labels and fields of a form. This will also give you some insight into the difficulties of doing that. After each step, note the changes in Live view.

15. Use the CSS Designer to add a style rule for the fieldset element that sets the padding on all four sides to 20px.

16. Add a style rule for label elements that floats them to the left and sets their widths to 12em. Notice that this messes up the formatting for the check boxes and radio buttons, but you'll fix that later.

17. Add a style rule for the four text boxes by using their ids: #name, #company, #phone, and #email. Then, set their widths to 20em.

18. Add a style rule for the input and select elements that sets the bottom margin to .75em and the left margin to 1em.

19. Add a style rule for the submit button (#submit) that sets its width to 9em, its left margin to 13em, and its bottom margin to 0. Then, test these changes. At this point, the text boxes and button should look like those in the page at the start of this exercise...except for the check boxes and radio buttons.

20. To fix the check boxes and radio buttons, create a style rule for a class named defaults (.defaults) that sets the width back to auto and the float back to none. Then, add a "defaults" class to the six labels that are used for the check boxes and radio buttons. To do that, use Code view to enter the class attribute (class="defaults") into the starting tags of the six label elements.

Test the form and add some HTML5 attributes

21. Use the Property Inspector to add the autofocus attribute to the first text box on the form. Then, test the form in your browser by clicking on the Submit button before you enter any data into the form. This should submit the form, which shows that no validation has been done in the browser.

22. Use the Property Inspector to add required attributes to the four text boxes on the form, and test the form again by clicking the Submit button before you enter any data. Then, enter valid data for the first three fields but an invalid email address, and test again. Last, test again with all valid data. The page that follows should show you the submitted data. You should also be able to see the submitted data in the URL for the page since the get method was used.

15

How to use Dreamweaver behaviors and CSS transitions

In this chapter, you'll learn how to use a feature of Dreamweaver called behaviors. As you'll see, behaviors let you perform functions such as changing the property of an element, displaying a pop-up dialog box, and swapping images. This is done using JavaScript, which is generated for you when you create a behavior using Dreamweaver's visual interface. That makes it easy to *use* JavaScript even if you don't *know* JavaScript.

This chapter also shows you how to use a new feature of CSS3 called transitions. You can use transitions to perform simple animations using just the CSS3 transition properties. Like behaviors, Dreamweaver provides a visual interface that makes creating transitions easy.

An introduction to JavaScript and behaviors

When you create a behavior, Dreamweaver generates the JavaScript that's needed to perform the operation that's provided by the behavior. In the topics that follow, you'll learn the general procedure for creating a behavior. You'll also learn how to change when a behavior is triggered. But first, I'll show you how JavaScript works so you can compare it to the way that behaviors work.

How JavaScript works

As you learned in the chapter 1, *JavaScript* is a scripting language that provides for client-side processing. In the browser in figure 15-1, for example, JavaScript is used to display a pop-up dialog box with the current date when a button is clicked.

For this to work, a JavaScript *function* named displayDateTime is coded in a script element within the head element of the web page. Although it's not important for you to understand how this function works, you should get a general idea by reviewing its code. Then, if you want to learn more about how JavaScript works, you can read *Murach's JavaScript and jQuery*.

Because the function in this example is executed when the user clicks the button, the code for the button must include a *function call*. Here, you can see that the function call is coded as an attribute that identifies the *event* that causes the function to be executed. In this case, the Click event of the button is used. Then, the value of this attribute is the name of the function.

JavaScript that displays the current date when a button is clicked

```
<script>
    function displayDateTime() {
      var today = new Date();
      window.alert(today.toDateString());
    }
</script>
    .
    .
    .
<input type="button" value="What is today's date?"
       onClick="displayDateTime()">
```

The current date displayed in a pop-up dialog box

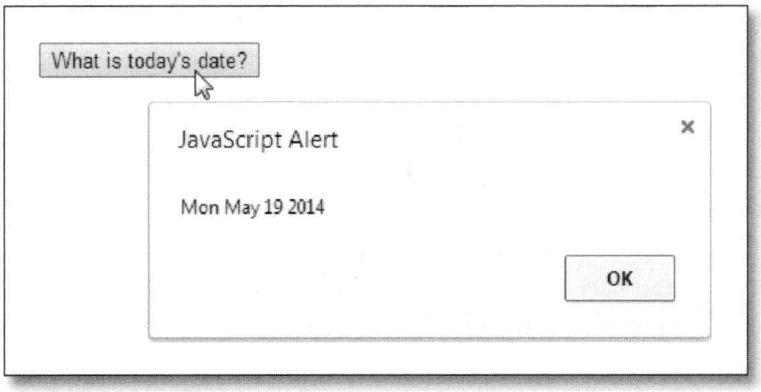

Description

- *JavaScript* is a scripting language that is run by the *JavaScript engine* of a browser. As a result, the work is done on the client, not the server.

- JavaScript can modify the contents of a web page when an event occurs on an *object* such as a button.

- An *event* is a signal that's sent by the browser indicating that something has happened, such as the user clicking a button. Then, a JavaScript *function* called an *event handler* can be executed in response to that event.

Figure 15-1   How JavaScript works

How to use behaviors

Figure 15-2 shows you how to use a Dreamweaver *behavior*. In Dreamweaver, a behavior is a predefined JavaScript function that performs a specific action. To use a behavior, you attach it to an *object* such as a button, image, or link. Then, the behavior is executed when the most common event of that object occurs. If you attach a behavior to a button, for example, it's executed when the button is clicked. If that's not what you want, you can change the event as described in the next figure.

To attach a behavior to an object, you start by selecting the object in the Document window. Then, when you display the Behaviors panel (Window→Behaviors), the selected object is identified at the top of the panel. For example, the panel shown here indicates that an input tag is selected.

Next, you click the Add Behavior icon to display a list of the behaviors that are available for the selected object. Then, when you choose a behavior, a dialog box is displayed that lets you enter any information needed to create the behavior. You'll see the dialog boxes for many of the behaviors in this chapter.

When you complete the dialog box for a behavior, the behavior is listed in the Behaviors panel for the event that triggers it. In addition, the code that implements the behavior is added to the web page. In this figure, for example, you can see the code that's used to implement the Popup Message behavior. This behavior displays a pop-up dialog box like the one you saw in figure 15-1 when a button is clicked. If you compare the code in these two figures, you'll see the similarities. Remember, though, that you don't have to know JavaScript to use behaviors.

The Add Behavior list in the Behaviors panel

How to attach a behavior to an object

1. Select the object you want to attach the behavior to. Then, in the Behaviors panel (Window→Behaviors), click the Add Behavior icon (**+**) to display the Add Behavior list.

2. Choose the behavior you want to use to display the dialog box for that behavior.

3. Complete the dialog box and then click OK to attach the Behavior to the object.

Code generated by the Popup Message behavior

```
<script type="text/javascript">
    function MM_popupMsg(msg) { //v1.0
        alert(msg);
    }
</script>
...
<input name="button" type="button" id="button" value="Display Message"
    onClick="MM_popupMsg(''+((new Date()).toDateString())+'')">
```

Description

- A *behavior* consists of a predefined JavaScript function that performs an action in response to an event on an object. The HTML for the object includes an attribute that identifies the event and the function to be called when the event occurs.

- You can use the Behaviors panel to attach one or more behaviors to an object. If you attach more than one behavior to an object, you can use the up and down arrows to determine the order in which the behaviors are executed.

- To modify a behavior, double-click on it in the Behaviors panel. To remove a behavior, select it and then click the Remove Event icon (**–**).

Figure 15-2   How to use behaviors

How to change the event that triggers a behavior

When you attach a behavior to an object as described in the previous figure, the behavior is executed when the most common event of the object occurs. In most cases, that's what you want. If you want to change the event that triggers a behavior, though, you can do that as shown in figure 15-3.

Here, you can see the Popup Message behavior that was attached to a button in the previous figure. As you can see, this behavior is currently set to be triggered by the Click event of the button. To change the event that triggers this behavior, you can drop down the event list for the behavior and then select the event attribute you want to use.

Notice here that the Behaviors panel shows only those events that have behaviors associated with them. That's because, unlike the panel in figure 15-2, the Show Set Events icon is selected. That can make it easier to review and change the events for a behavior. To switch back so all of the events are shown, you select the Show All Events icon.

This figure also lists the most common events that are supported by Dreamweaver and indicates when they're triggered. These events relate directly to the event attributes that are available from the Behaviors panel. If you review these events, you shouldn't have any trouble understanding when to use them. You'll see examples that use a few of these events as you progress through this chapter.

The Behaviors panel with the event list for a behavior

Common Dreamweaver-supported events

Event	Description
Click/DblClick	Triggered when an object is clicked or double-clicked.
Error	Triggered when an error is detected.
Focus/Blur	Triggered when an object receives or loses focus.
KeyDown	Triggered when a key on the keyboard is being pressed.
KeyPress	Triggered when a key on the keyboard has been pressed.
KeyUp	Triggered when a key on the keyboard is released after being presesed.
Load/Unload	Triggered when a document or object is loaded or unloaded.
MouseDown	Triggered when a mouse button is pressed over an object.
MouseMove	Triggered when the mouse pointer is moving while it is over an object.
MouseOut	Triggered when the mouse pointer is moved out of an object.
MouseOver	Triggered when the mouse pointer is moved onto an object.
MouseUp	Triggered when a mouse button is released over an object.

Description

- When you attach a behavior to an object, it's attached to the most common event for that object by default.
- To change the event that a behavior is attached to, you drop down the event list for the behavior and select the event you want to use.
- The events that are available in the event list depend on the object that the behavior is attached to.
- To show just the events that currently have behaviors attached to them as shown above, you click the Show Set Events icon ( ). To show all events, you click the Show All Events icon ( ).

Figure 15-3   How to change the event that triggers a behavior

A summary of the Dreamweaver behaviors

Figure 15-4 summarizes the behaviors that are provided by Dreamweaver. You'll learn about many of these behaviors in the topics that follow. Because you'll rarely use the Call JavaScript and Drag AP Element behaviors, though, they're not covered here. In addition, because the Effects set of behaviors are part of Dreamweaver's integration with jQuery and jQuery UI, they're covered in the next chapter.

Two other behaviors that aren't presented explicitly in this chapter are Swap Image Restore and Preload Images. These behaviors are added automatically when you add a Swap Image behavior. Because of that, I'll describe them when I describe that behavior. Keep in mind, though, that you can use the Load Images behavior with behaviors other than Swap Image, such as the Show-Hide Elements behavior.

You can also use behaviors in addition to the ones that are listed in this figure. To do that, just click the Get More Behaviors item at the bottom of the Add Behaviors list. When you do, the Adobe Add-ons website is displayed. This website contains behaviors, commands, and objects that have been created by third-party developers and packaged as add-ons. Then, you can search for the functionality you need and, if you find it, you can install the add-on that provides it. Note that although most add-ons are free, others cost a nominal fee.

The Dreamweaver behaviors

Behavior	Description
Call JavaScript	Used to write inline JavaScript code for an object without having to switch to Code view.
Change Property	Used to programmatically change a CSS property for an object.
Check Plugin	Used to check if a plugin exists on the user's browser.
Drag AP Element	Used to create a draggable object. The object must be an absolutely positioned div element.
Effects	Used to add effects to objects.
Go To URL	Used to redirect the user to a new URL.
Jump Menu	Used to add redirection functionality to the items in a drop-down list.
Jump Menu Go	Used to force the redirection of a selected item in a drop-down list that has the Jump Menu behavior already attached to it.
Open Browser Window	Used to open a new browser window with the dimensions and features you specify.
Popup Message	Used to display a simple message in a pop-up dialog box.
Preload Images	Used to preload any images that may be used by other behaviors. This behavior will make other behaviors that rely on images, such as the Swap Image behavior, run more quickly.
Set Text	Used to insert text into text fields, a frame, a container, or the browser's status bar.
Show-Hide Elements	Used to show or hide an element.
Swap Image	Used to replace one image with another image. When you use this behavior, the Preload Images and Swap Image Restore behaviors are automatically added for you.
Swap Image Restore	Used to redisplay an image that was previously swapped out. You rarely need to add this behavior since the Swap Image behavior adds it for you automatically.
Validate Form	Used to perform basic validation on a form.

Description

- Dreamweaver provides for a variety of behaviors that perform functions ranging from displaying a simple pop-up dialog box to changing the properties of an object.

- The behaviors include a set of effects that are part of Dreamweaver's jQuery support. You'll learn about effects and other jQuery features in chapter 16.

Figure 15-4   A summary of the Dreamweaver behaviors

How to use
the most common behaviors

At this point, you should understand how behaviors work and you should understand the general procedure for using them. Now, you're ready to learn more about the most common behaviors.

How to use the Popup Message behavior

Figure 15-5 shows how to use the Popup Message behavior to create a pop-up dialog box like the one you saw in figure 15-1. This type of dialog box displays an OK button that lets the user acknowledge the message that's displayed. Because of that, a pop-up dialog box should be used only to display information to the user.

To use the Popup Message behavior, you enter the message you want to display in the Popup Message dialog box. This message can include text as well as one or more JavaScript expressions. To include an expression, you must enclose it in braces. For example, you could include the current date formatted as a date string using this expression:

```
{(new Date()).toDateString()}
```

Of course, you need to know more about JavaScript to use expressions like this. To get that knowledge, we recommend *Murach's JavaScript and jQuery*.

The Popup Message dialog box

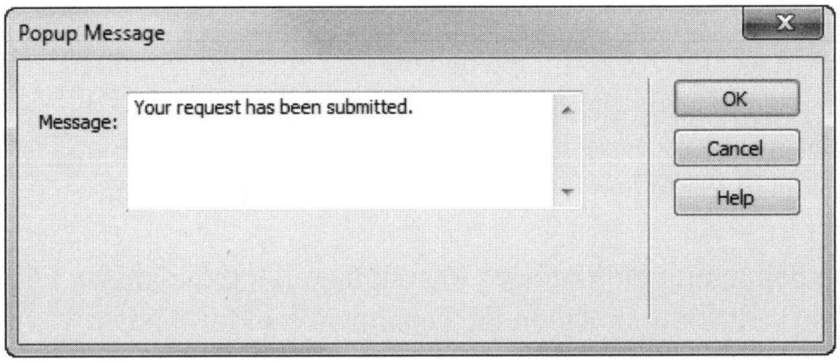

The dialog box that's displayed when the button is clicked

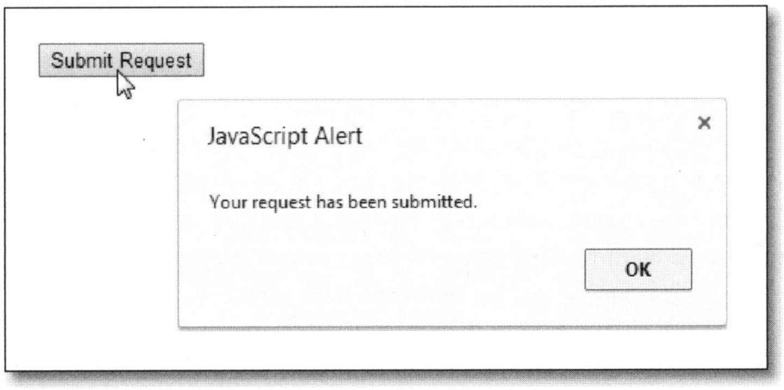

Description

- The Popup Message behavior displays a message in a pop-up dialog box. Because the dialog box includes just an OK button, it should be used only to provide information to the user.

- You use the Popup Message dialog box to specify the message you want to display. In addition to text, you can include any JavaScript expression in the message. To do that, you must enclose the expression in braces ({}). If you want to include a brace in the message, you must precede it with a backslash (\).

- The exact appearance of the dialog box is determined by the browser.

Figure 15-5   How to use the Popup Message behavior

How to use the Swap Image behavior

Figure 15-6 shows how to use the Swap Image behavior to perform an *image rollover*. An image rollover occurs when the mouse hovers over an image and the image is replaced by another image of the same size. In this figure, for example, the Swap Image behavior is used to change the image that's displayed for each item in a navigation menu.

To use the Swap Image behavior, you first need to assign an ID to the image you want to swap. Then, you select that image in the Document window and display the Swap Image dialog box. When you do, that image is selected in the list of images by default, and you can specify the image you want to display in its place when the mouse hovers over it. In this figure, for example, you can see that an image named nav_home2.gif will replace the image with an ID of "home". This replacement image has red text instead of the white text of the original image.

One common mistake when using the Swap Image behavior with more than one image as shown here is to set all of the swapped images at the same time. For example, you might think that you could select each image in the Images list and then specify the image you want to display in its place before you click OK. If you do that, though, all of the images will be swapped when the mouse hovers over the image that the behavior is attached to. Since that's not what you want, you should be sure to attach the Swap Image behavior to each image separately.

By default, when you attach the Swap Image behavior to an image, the Preload Images behavior is attached to the Load event of the page. This behavior lets you load images when the page is loaded, even if the images aren't displayed initially. With image rollovers, for example, the replacement images aren't displayed until the mouse hovers over the original image. If the Preload Images behavior is used, though, these images don't have to be loaded the first time they're displayed, which makes the process of switching between the images more efficient. If you don't want to preload an image for an image rollover, you can remove the checkmark from the Preload Images option.

In addition to preloading the replacement image, the Swap Image Restore behavior is attached to the MouseOut event of the original image by default. This behavior causes the original image to be redisplayed when the user moves the mouse off the image. If that's not what you want, you can remove the checkmark from the Restore Images onMouseOut option.

You can also create an image rollover at the same time that you insert the original image. To do that, you choose Insert→Image→Rollover Image to display the Insert Rollover Image dialog box. This dialog box lets you assign an ID to the img element that's inserted and specify the original image and the rollover image. It also lets you indicate whether the rollover image is preloaded. When you complete this dialog box, the Swap Image and Swap Image Restore behaviors are generated for you, as well as the Preload Images behavior if you selected that option.

The Swap Image dialog box

An image-based navigation menu with rollover menu items

Description

- The Swap Image behavior replaces one image with another image of the same size when the mouse hovers over the image. This can be referred to as an *image rollover*.

- The Swap Image dialog box lists all of the images on the web page with id attributes, and the image that the behavior is being attached to is selected by default. Then, you can set its replacement image.

- When you use the Swap Image behavior, the Preload Images and Swap Image Restore behaviors are added by default. The Preload Images behavior loads the replacement images when the page is loaded, which makes the switching of images more efficient. The Swap Image Restore behavior causes the original image to be redisplayed when the user moves the mouse off the replacement image.

- You can also generate Swap Image, Swap Image Restore, and Preload Images behaviors when you insert the original image by choosing Insert→Image→Rollover Image and then completing the dialog box that's displayed.

Figure 15-6   How to use the Swap Image behavior

How to use the Show-Hide Elements behavior

Figure 15-7 shows you how to use the Show-Hide Elements behavior to change the visibility of one or more elements. One use of this behavior is to create a photo gallery like the one in this figure. Here, the page consists of four thumbnail images, followed by larger versions of those images with IDs set to image01, image02, image03, and image04. Then, when the user clicks one of the thumbnail images, the larger image is displayed and all of the other larger images are hidden.

Although you can't see it here, it's important for you to understand how the CSS for these images is set. First, the visibility property is set to "hidden" so none of the images appear when the page is first displayed. Another option would be to hide all but the first image so that image is displayed initially.

Next, the position property is set to "absolute" and the top and bottom properties are set so the images will all appear in the same location when they're displayed. That's necessary because the images are placed one after the other in the HTML for the page, and hidden images aren't removed from the flow of the page.

To use the Show-Hide Elements behavior with this photo gallery, you attach it to each of the thumbnail images. To do that, you use the Show-Hide Elements dialog box to indicate which elements are hidden and which are displayed when the thumbnail is clicked. In this case, the four larger image elements are the only elements that are listed, since they're the only ones with id attributes. Then, you can select each element and click the Show, Hide, or Default button to set its visibility. The settings for the first thumbnail are shown here, which show the first image and hide the others.

If you use the Show-Hide Elements behavior with images that change as the user interacts with the page, you should also consider using the Preload Images behavior. As explained in the previous topic, this can make the switching of images more efficient.

Of course, you can use the Show-Hide Elements behavior for more than just creating a photo gallery like the one shown here. For example, you could use it to display additional information about an element such as an image when the mouse hovers over that element. Or, you could use it to display a submenu when the mouse hovers over a menu item.

The Show-Hide Elements dialog box

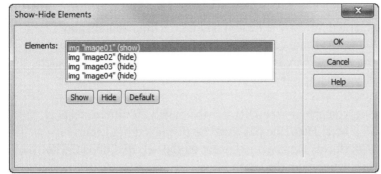

A photo gallery created using the Show-Hide Elements behavior

Description

- The Show-Hide Elements behavior lets you change the visibility of one or more elements on a web page.
- The Show-Hide Elements dialog box lists all elements with an id attribute. Then, you can select an element and click the Show, Hide, or Default button to show the element, hide the element, or set the visibility of the element to its default.
- If you use the Show-Hide Elements behavior with images as shown above, you should consider using the Preload Images behavior to make the process of switching between images more efficient. This behavior lets you specify the images you want to preload.

Figure 15-7   How to use the Show-Hide Elements behavior

How to use the Go To URL behavior

In chapter 4, you learned how to create text and image links that display another page when clicked. In some cases, though, you'll want to create links for other objects. For example, you may want to create a link for a form object such as a button. To do that, you can use the Go To URL behavior shown in figure 15-8.

To use this behavior, you specify the URL for the page you want to display in the Go To URL dialog box. Then, the page will be displayed in the current window when the user performs the specified event on the selected object. This is referred to as the Main window in the Open In list.

If you're developing a frames-based website, a list of frames will be included in the Open In list. Then, you can display the web page in the current window or the frame you select. Because frames-based websites are rarely used anymore, they're not covered in this book.

The Go To URL dialog box

Description

- The Go To URL behavior opens another web page in the current window. It can be used to create hyperlinks for elements that don't otherwise support hyperlinks.
- The Go To URL dialog box lets you specify the URL of the web page you want the user to be redirected to.
- If you're developing a frames-based website, you can also select the frame where you want the web page displayed from the Open In list. Otherwise, the main window is the only option.

Figure 15-8   How to use the Go To URL behavior

How to use the Open Browser Window behavior

The Open Browser Window behavior is similar to the Go To URL behavior, but it opens a web page in a new browser window instead of the current window. When this behavior is executed in response to an event like the Load event of a page, it's referred to as a pop-up ad. Because the use of these ads has been abused, most web browsers now include pop-up blockers. As a result, a window that's opened by the Open Browser Window behavior will likely be blocked, unless you open the window in response to a user action such as clicking a button.

Figure 15-9 shows you how to use the Open Browser Window behavior. To do that, you specify the URL for the web page you want to display in the Open Browser Window dialog box, along with the size and attributes for the window. If you don't specify the size and attributes, the new window will have the same size and attributes as the browser window that displays it. In contrast, if you set the size of the new window or one or more of its attributes, only the specified size and attributes will be used.

For example, if the first window includes a navigation toolbar and a menu bar and you don't set any attributes for the new window, the new window will have the toolbar and menu bar too. In the dialog box in this figure, though, the size and one attribute of the new window are set. As a result, it won't include the toolbar and menu bar because these attributes aren't selected.

The Open Browser Window dialog box

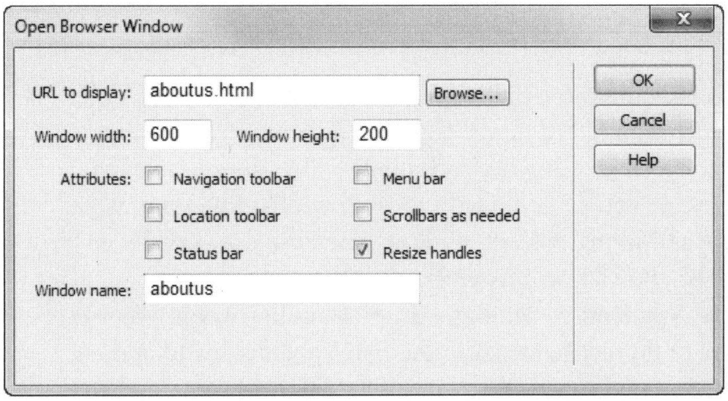

The browser window that's displayed when a button is clicked

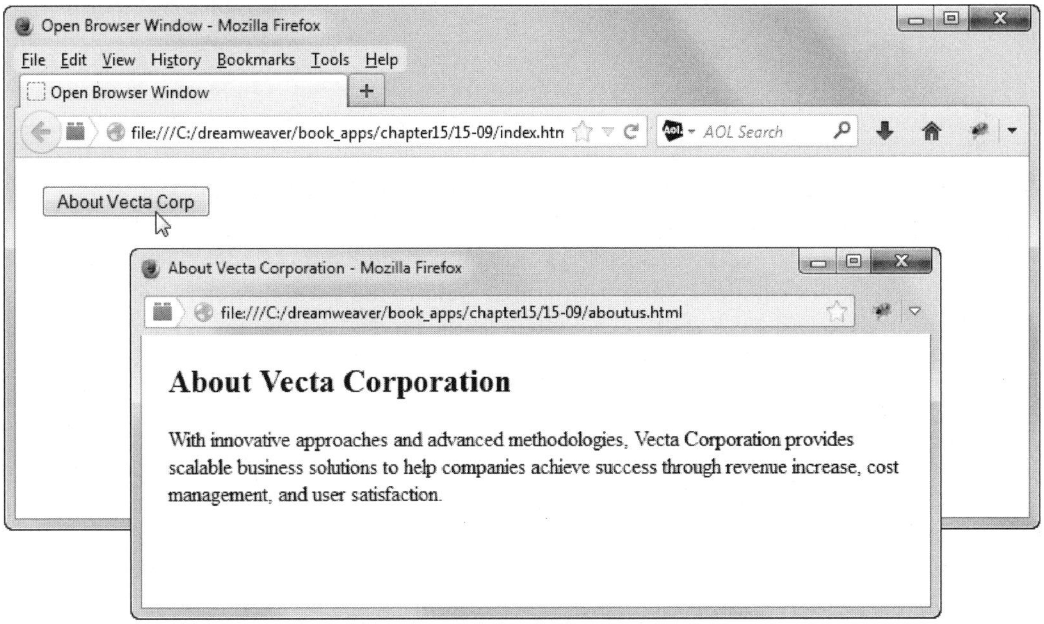

Description

- The Open Browser Window behavior lets you display a web page in another browser window.
- You specify the URL for the web page you want to display, along with the size and attributes for the browser window, in the Open Browser Window dialog box.
- By default, the browser window has the same size and attributes as the browser window that displays it. If you set the size of the browser window or any of its attributes, however, none of the other attributes of the original window are used.
- If you want to be able to link to the window or refer to it in JavaScript, you can give it a name.

Figure 15-9   How to use the Open Browser Window behavior

How to use the Jump Menu and Jump Menu Go behaviors

If you've read chapter 14, you know that a drop-down list is a form object that lets you select an item from a list of items. Then, you can use client-side or server-side code to perform processing depending on which item is selected. With the Jump Menu behavior, you can convert a drop-down list to a *jump menu* that displays another web page in the current window when the user selects an item in the list. Figure 15-10 shows how this works.

To create a jump menu, you start by adding a drop-down list. Then, you use the Jump Menu dialog box to define the items in the list. Specifically, to add an item, you click the Add Item icon (**+**) and then enter the text you want displayed for the item in the Text text box and the URL for the web page you want to be displayed when the item is selected in the When Selected, Go To URL text box. Then, that item is added to the Menu Items list box. In this figure, for example, four items have been added to this list.

When you use the Jump Menu behavior, you should realize that one item in the list—usually the first item—is selected by default. Unfortunately, that means that you can't select that item to redirect to the web page that's associated with it without first selecting another item. You can use one of two techniques to work around this problem, though.

First, you can add an item at the beginning of the list that doesn't cause redirection. For example, you might add an item to the list shown here with the text set to "-- SELECT ONE --" and the URL set to "#". Then, this item will be selected when the list is displayed, and the user will be able to select any of the other items.

Second, you can add a Go button for use with the jump menu as shown in this figure. Then, you can attach the Jump Menu Go behavior to this button to associate it with the jump menu. When you do that, redirection doesn't occur when the user selects an item from the jump menu. Instead, the user must click the Go button to display the web page that's associated with the selected item.

The Jump Menu dialog box

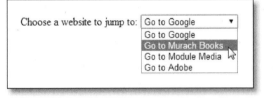

The jump menu in a web browser

The jump menu with a Go button

Description

- The Jump Menu behavior lets you create a drop-down list called a *jump menu* that displays other web pages when items in the list are selected. To add a drop-down list to a web page, you can choose Insert→Form→Select.

- The Jump Menu dialog box lets you enter the text you want to be displayed for each item in the jump menu, along with the URL of the page you want to be displayed when the item is selected.

- If you're developing a frames-based website, you can also select the frame where you want the web page displayed from the Open URLs In menu. Otherwise, the main window is the only option.

- The Jump Menu Go behavior lets you add a Go button to a jump menu. When you use this behavior, no redirection occurs until the user clicks the Go button.

- The Jump Menu Go dialog box lets you select the ID of the jump menu that the Go button is associated with.

- The Jump Menu Go behavior is particularly helpful if you want to be able to redirect to the web page specified by the item that's currently selected in the jump menu without first redirecting to the page specified by another item.

Figure 15-10   How to use the Jump Menu and Jump Menu Go behaviors

How to use the Change Property behavior

Figure 15-11 shows you how to use the Change Property behavior. This behavior lets you change one of several properties of an element when an event occurs on an object. In this figure, for example, the behavior changes the background color of a div element when a button is clicked.

When you choose the Change Property Behavior, the Change Property dialog box is displayed. You use this dialog box to choose the type of element whose property you want to change, along with the ID of the specific element. Note that the types of elements you can use this behavior with are limited.

Next, you select the property of the element you want to change. You can do that by choosing the Select option and then selecting a property from the menu. Or, if you want to change a property that doesn't appear in the list, you can choose the Enter option and then enter the property name into the text box. Finally, you enter the new value for the property. Then, when this behavior is executed, the current value of the property will be changed to the new value.

The Change Property dialog box

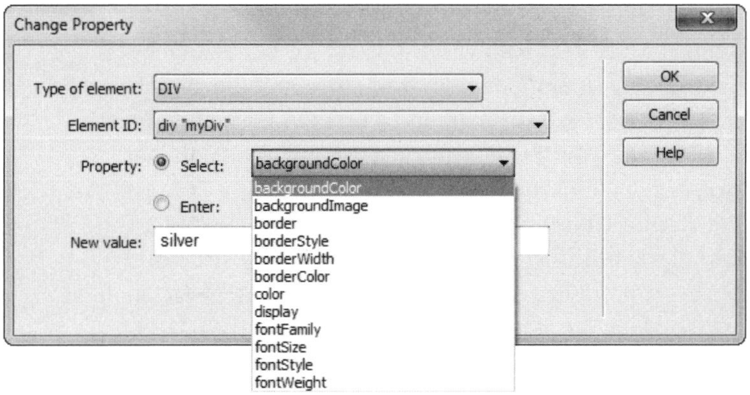

The div before and after the Change Property behavior is applied

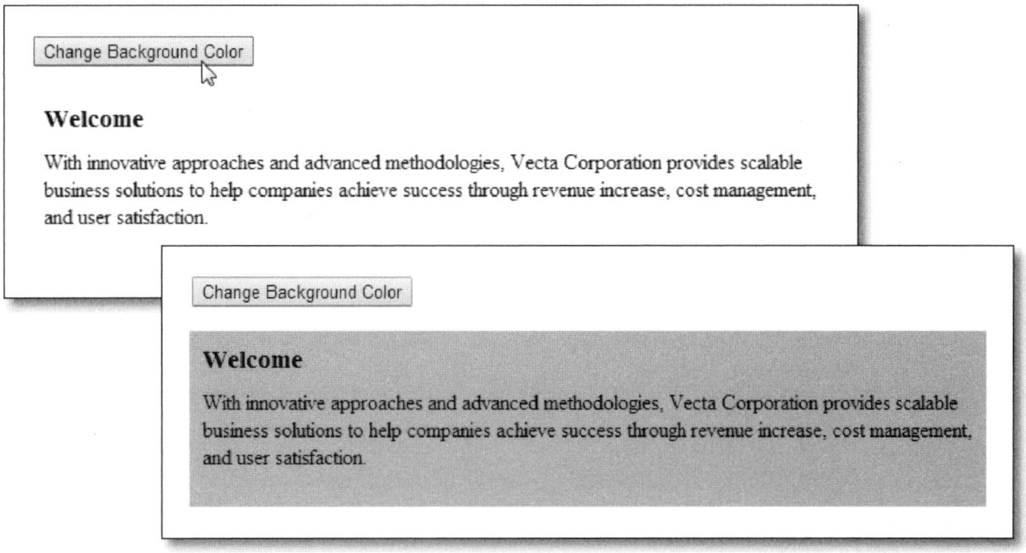

Description

- The Change Property behavior lets you change common CSS properties for several HTML elements. You use the Change Property dialog box to identify the element and property you want to change and how you want to change it.

- You choose the type of element whose property you want to change from the Type of Element menu, and you choose the specific element from the Element ID menu. Every element of the type you select that has an id attribute is included in the Element ID menu.

- You can use the Select menu that's available when you choose the Select option to select the property you want to change. Or, you can choose the Enter option and then enter the name of the property into the text box.

- You enter the value you want to change the selected property to in the New Value text box.

Figure 15-11   How to use the Change Property behavior

How to use the Set Text behaviors

Figure 15-12 presents the Set Text behaviors. These four behaviors let you replace the content in a container element, a frame if you're developing a frames-based website, the browser's status bar, and a text field. The Set Text of Container behavior is the one you'll use most often, and it's the one that's illustrated in this figure.

You can use the Set Text of Container behavior to set the content of any block element. That includes a heading, a paragraph, an HTML5 structural element, a div element, a form, or even a body element. The content can include any valid HTML, as well as JavaScript expressions.

In this figure, the Set Text of Container behavior is attached to three different buttons. Then, different text is displayed in a div element when each button is clicked. Here, the Set Text of Container dialog box shows the settings for the first button. That includes the container where the content will be displayed as well as the actual content. To choose a container, an ID must be assigned to it.

Another behavior you may use is the Set Text of Text Field behavior, which replaces the content of a text field on a form. One situation where this can be useful is if you want to remove the starting value of a field when the user moves the focus to that field. If you're creating a search field, for example, you might set the initial value of the text field to "Enter your search here." Then, you could use the Set Text of Text Field behavior to remove this value when the control receives the focus, and you could use it again to add the value back when the control loses the focus. This works like the Place Holder property you learned about in chapter 14 that was introduced with HTML5. When you use the Set Text of Text Field behavior, though, you don't have to worry about whether the code is backwards compatible.

You'll rarely, if ever, use the Set Text of Frame and Set Text of Status Bar behaviors. That's because frames aren't typically used anymore, and Internet Explorer is the only browser that lets you set the text that's displayed in the status bar.

The Set Text behaviors

Behavior	Description
Container	Sets the content of a container element such as a div, HTML5 structural element, paragraph, heading, or form.
Frame	Sets the text in a frame. For more information, see Dreamweaver help.
Status Bar	Sets the text in a status bar. Doesn't work in all browsers and may require special settings in other browsers.
Text Field	Sets the text in a text field.

The Set Text of Container dialog box

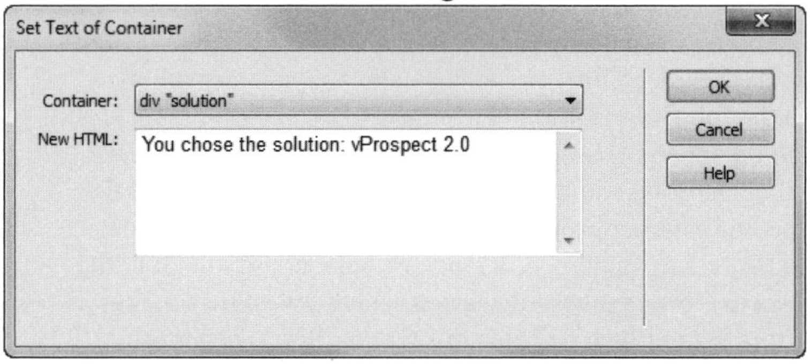

The text that's displayed in the div when the first button is clicked

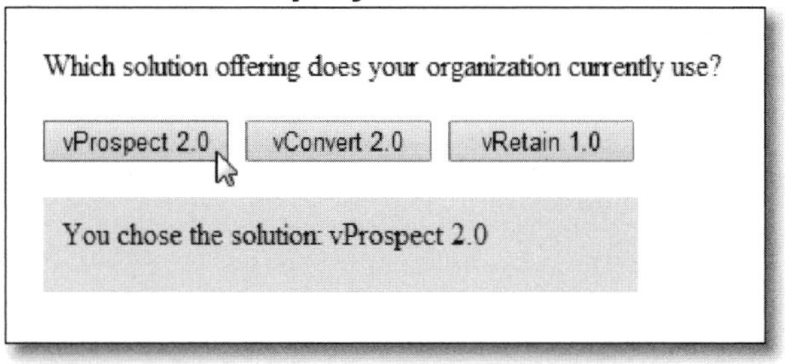

Description

- The Set Text behaviors let you replace the content of a container, a frame, the browser's status bar, or a text field. These behaviors are available from the Set Text submenu of the Add Behavior list.

- To use the Set Text of Container behavior, you select the container where you want to display the content and the content you want to display in the Set Text of Container dialog box. The content can be any valid HTML source code.

- To use the Set Text of Status Bar behavior, you specify the message you want to display in the Set Text of Status Bar dialog box.

- To use the Set Text of Text Field behavior, you select the field where you want to display the content and enter the content you want to display in the Set Text of Text Field dialog box.

- You can include any valid JavaScript expression in the replacement content. For information on how to do that, see figure 15-5.

Figure 15-12   How to use the Set Text Behaviors

How to use the Validate Form behavior

In chapter 14, you learned how to validate some of the fields on a form using HTML5 properties, regular expressions, and the Email and URL controls. Another way to perform simple validation on text fields is to use the Validate Form behavior. This behavior is shown in figure 15-13.

In most cases, you'll want to validate all the text fields on the form that require validation when the form is submitted to the server. To do that, you can attach the Validate Form behavior to the form or to the submit button for the form. In either case, the behavior will be executed when the Submit event of the form occurs.

To use the Validate Form behavior, you select each field you want to validate from the Fields list in the Validate Form dialog box. This list includes all of the input elements on the form, along with the elements' IDs and a summary of their current validation options. Then, you can select an element and check the Required option if an entry is required for that field. You can also select the Email address, Number, or Number From…To option if you want to validate the entry for an email address, a number, or a range of numbers. By default, the Anything option is selected, which allows the user to enter any value.

The web page in this figure illustrates how this works. Here, entries are required for all three fields. In addition, a number must be entered for the phone number, and an @ sign must be included in the email address. If any of the fields aren't valid when the form is submitted, a pop-up dialog box with an error message for each error is displayed as shown here.

The Validate Form dialog box

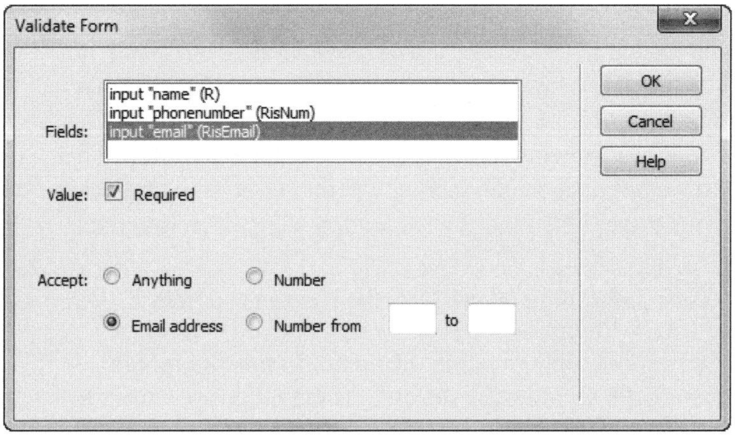

An error message is shown detailing the errors of a submitted form

Description

- The Validate Form behavior lets you perform simple validation tasks on the text fields in a form. If one or more fields don't pass validation, the errors are listed in a pop-up dialog box.
- The Validate Form dialog box lists all of the fields on the form with id attributes. Then, you can select a field and check the Required option if the user must enter a value in the field. You can also select an Accept option to validate the entry for an email, a number, or a number within a range.
- You can validate individual fields when the Blur or Change event occurs. You can validate all the fields on a form when the Submit event of the form occurs.

Figure 15-13   How to use the Validate Form behavior

How to use the Check Plugin behavior

If you develop a web page that requires a plugin, you may want to check if that plugin is installed on the user's browser. To do that, you can use the Check Plugin behavior shown in figure 15-14.

In most cases, you'll want this behavior to run when the page is loaded. That way, you can display a different page depending on whether or not the plugin is installed. For this behavior to run when the page is loaded, you attach it to the body element.

To use the Check Plugin behavior, you start by specifying the plugin you want to check for in the Check Plugin dialog box. To do that, you can select the Select option and then choose a plugin from the menu. In this figure, for example, you can see that the Flash plugin is selected. If the plugin you want to check for isn't included in the Select menu, you can select the Enter option and then enter the name of the plugin in the text box that's provided.

If the plugin you're checking for is found, the current web page is typically displayed. If you want to display a different page, though, you can enter the URL for that page in the If Found text box. Similarly, if the plugin isn't found, you can enter the URL for the page you want to display in the Otherwise text box. For example, the URL in this figure is for the page that lets the user download the Flash player. Another option is to display a page that doesn't use Flash.

If you're using an older version of Internet Explorer, the Check Plugin behavior won't be able to check if a plugin is installed. In that case, the user will be redirected to the URL in the Otherwise text box by default. If that's not what you want, you can check the Always Go To First URL If Detection Is Not Possible option. Then, it will be assumed that the plugin is installed, and the content will be displayed if it is installed. You'll typically select this option if the plugin content is integral to the web page.

The Check Plugin dialog box

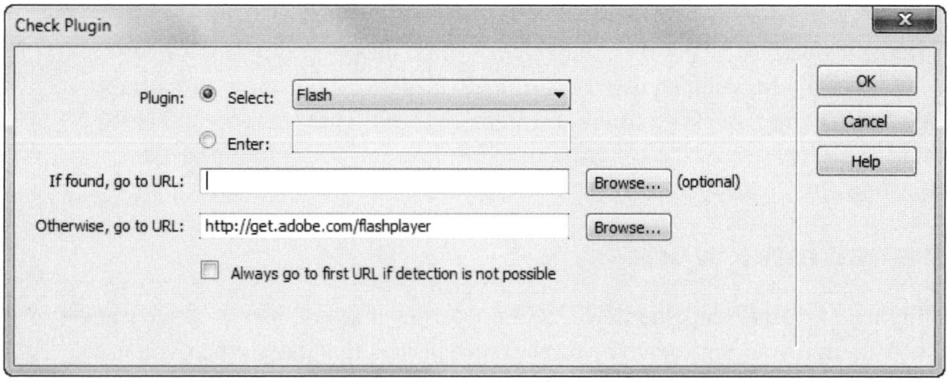

Description

- The Check Plugin behavior lets you check if the browser supports the plugin you specify. This behavior is typically attached to the Load event of the body element so it's executed when the web page is loaded.

- The Check Plugin dialog box lets you specify the plugin you want to check for. You can use the Select menu that's available when you choose the Select option to choose the Flash, Shockwave, LiveAudio, QuickTime, or Windows Media Player plugin. Or, you can choose the Enter option and then enter the name for a plugin.

- If you want another page to be displayed if the plugin is found, you can specify the URL for that page in the If Found text box. If no URL is entered, users will stay on the same page.

- If you want another page to be displayed if the plugin isn't found, you can specify the URL for that page in the Otherwise text box. In most cases, you'll specify the URL of a web page that provides for downloading the plugin. If no URL is entered, users will stay on the same page.

- If it isn't possible to check for the plugin, it will be assumed that the plugin isn't found and the user will be redirected to the web page specified in the Otherwise text box so the plugin can be downloaded. If that's not what you want, you can check the Always Go To First URL If Detection Is Not Possible option.

Figure 15-14   How to use the Check Plugin behavior

An introduction to CSS3 transitions

In the last two topics of this chapter, you'll be introduced to *CSS3 transitions*. As you'll see, you can use transitions to change one or more properties of an element when the state of that element changes. That lets you add basic animation effects to a web page without using JavaScript or plugin-based applications for creating animations.

How transitions work

Figure 15-15 presents the new CSS3 properties that you use to create transitions. Although you don't have to set these properties manually when you use Dreamweaver, it's important that you understand how they work. Then, in the next figure, you'll see how to use Dreamweaver to generate these properties.

The transition in this figure causes the height of the div element shown here to increase when the mouse hovers over it. That way, more of the content of the div is displayed. In the two web pages in this figure, for example, you can see that only the heading at the beginning of the div is displayed before the transition. After the transition, though, the paragraph that follows the heading is also displayed.

The CSS shown in this figure accomplishes this transition. To start, the style rule for the div element sets the initial height of the element to 38 pixels, which will accommodate just the heading. Then, the overflow property of the div is set to "hidden" so that any content that extends beyond the 38 pixels won't be displayed.

Next, the transition-property property is set to the property that the transition will affect, in this case, height. The transition-duration property is set to the time it will take for the duration to complete, in this case, 1 second. And the transition-timing-function property is set to the speed curve for the transition, in this case, ease-in-out. This causes the beginning and end of the transition to occur more slowly than the middle of the transition. Because this particular transition only lasts for a second, though, this difference in speed isn't noticeable.

A style rule is also included for the hover pseudo-class of the div element. This style rule specifies what happens when the mouse hovers over the div causing the transition to occur. As indicated by the transition-property property of the style rule for the div element, this style rule changes the height of the div. In this case, the div is increased to 150 pixels so the paragraph that follows the heading is visible.

In this case, the transition starts as soon as the mouse moves over the div element. If that's not what you want, you can include the transition-delay property to indicate the delay before the transition starts.

Although the transition properties shown in the example in this figure are coded separately, you should know that they can also be coded on the shorthand transition property. In fact, when you use Dreamweaver to create a transition, it uses the transition property rather than the individual properties by default. If you want to change this, you can uncheck the Transition option in the CSS Styles category of the Preferences dialog box (Edit→Preferences).

The CSS3 transition properties

Property	Description
transition-property	The CSS property that the transition will affect.
transition-duration	The seconds or milliseconds the transition will take to complete.
transition-timing-function	The speed curve for the transition. Possible values include ease, linear, ease-in, ease-out, ease-in-out, and cubic-bezier.
transition-delay	The delay in seconds or milliseconds before the transition starts.
transition	The shorthand property for setting the four properties above.

The HTML for a div element

```
<div>
    <h2>About Vecta Corporation</h2>
    <p>With innovative approaches and advanced methodologies, Vecta
    Corporation provides scalable business solutions to help ... </p>
</div>
```

CSS that applies a transition to the div element

```
div {
    width: 300px; height: 38px; background: #DFE3E6;
    padding-top: 5px; padding-bottom: 5px; padding-left: 10px;
    overflow: hidden;
    transition-property: height;
    transition-duration: 1s;
    transition-timing-function: ease-in-out;
}
div:hover {
    height: 150px;
}
```

The div before and after the transition

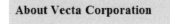

About Vecta Corporation

About Vecta Corporation

With innovative approaches and advanced methodologies, Vecta Corporation provides scalable business solutions to help companies achieve success through revenue increase, cost management, and user satisfaction.

Description

- A CSS3 *transition* causes one or more properties of an element to change when the state of that element changes.

- CSS3 transitions let you add basic animation effects to elements without using JavaScript or plugin-based applications such as Flash or Adobe Edge Animate.

- CSS3 transitions are supported in all modern browsers except Internet Explorer before version 10.

Figure 15-15   How transitions work

How to create a transition in Dreamweaver

Figure 15-16 shows you how to use Dreamweaver to create a CSS transition like the one you saw in the previous figure. To do that, you start by displaying the CSS Transitions panel, which is grouped with the CSS Designer panel by default. Then, you click the Create New Transition icon to display the New Transition dialog box.

From this dialog box, you start by identifying the element the transition will affect. To do that, you can select the CSS selector for an existing style rule from the Target Rule combo box, or you can enter a new selector in this combo box. In this example, the transition will affect the div element you saw in the previous figure. However, you can also specify other types of selectors such as an ID selector.

Next, you indicate when you want the transition to occur by selecting a state from the Transition On menu. The available states include active, checked, disabled, enabled, focus, hover, indeterminate, and target. In this example, the hover state is selected so the transition will occur when the mouse hovers over the div element.

The remaining group of settings defines the transition that will occur. To start, if the transition will change a single property, you can specify the duration, delay, and timing function for the transition. Then, you can click the **+** icon below the Property list to display a list of properties, select the property you want to change, and then enter the value that the property will be changed to in the End Value text box. Here, the transition is defined just as it was in the example in the previous figure.

If the transition will change more than one property, you can use the menu at the top of this group of settings to determine if the same duration, delay, and timing function are used for each property. If you choose to use the same transition, you can just set the duration, delay, and timing function once and then select each property you want to change and set its end value. If you choose to use a different transition, the options will change so you can specify a different duration, delay, and timing function for each property.

When you create a transition, Dreamweaver generates any required CSS code for you. The menu at the bottom of the New Transition dialog box lets you choose where this CSS is created. The options that are available from this menu depend on whether any external style sheets are attached to the document and whether any styles are embedded in the document. In the example shown here, a single external style sheet is attached to the document and no embedded styles are defined. Because of that, the CSS will automatically be added to the external style sheet.

After you create a transition, it appears in the CSS Transitions panel as shown here. This simply indicates the element that the transition affects, the state that causes the transition to occur, and the number of transitions that are applied. Then, you can delete a transition by selecting the state, clicking the Remove icon, and then completing the Remove Transition dialog box that's displayed. And you can edit a transition by double-clicking on the state or selecting the state and then clicking the Edit icon.

The CSS Transitions panel with the transition for a div element

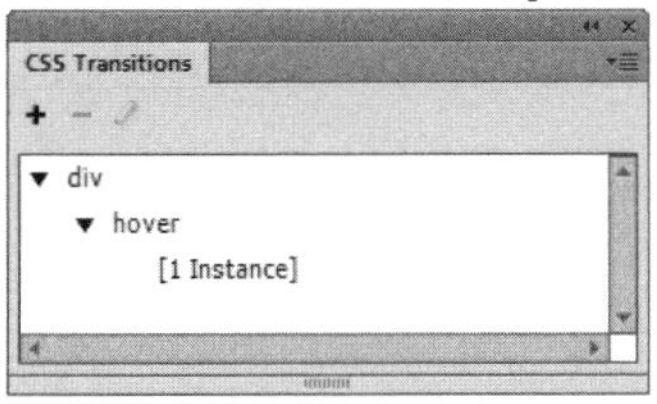

The New Transition dialog box

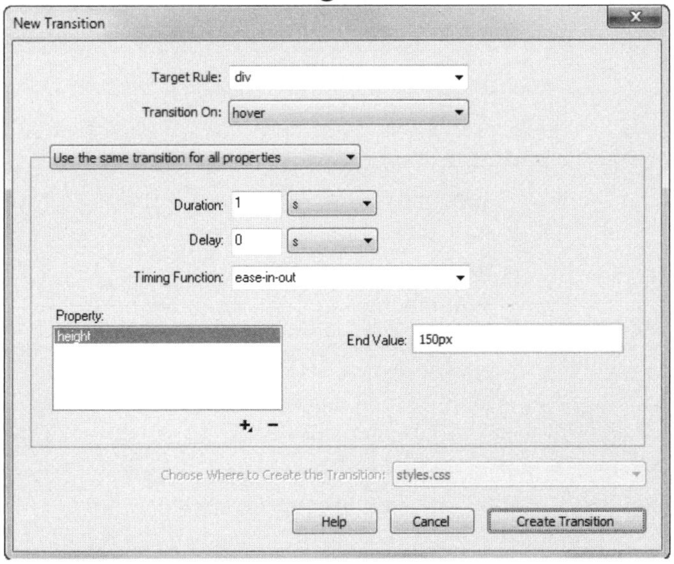

How to create a CSS3 transition in Dreamweaver

1. In the CSS Transitions panel (Window→CSS Transitions), click the Create New Transition icon (**+**) to display the New Transition dialog box.

2. Select or enter the selector for the element you want to create a transition for in the Target Rule combo box.

3. Select a state from the Transition On menu to indicate when the transition will occur.

4. If the transition will affect more than one property, choose whether to use the same transition for all properties or to create a different transition for each property.

5. Specify the duration, the delay, and the timing function for the transition.

6. Click the **+** icon, select the property you want to change from the list that's displayed, and then enter the new value for the property in the End Value text box.

Description

- When you create a transition, Dreamweaver generates the required CSS code automatically. That includes the transition property and the style rule for the element that will be changed by the transition. It also includes a -webkit-transition property to support older versions of Chrome and Safari and an -o-transition property to support older versions of Opera.

Figure 15-16   How to create a transition in Dreamweaver

Perspective

As you have seen in this chapter, you can use Dreamweaver behaviors to generate JavaScript that performs a variety of functions. Remember, though, that you need little or no knowledge of JavaScript to use behaviors. That lets you quickly add a broad range of interactivity to your web pages.

You were also introduced to transitions, which are a new feature of CSS3. Transitions let you change one or more properties of an element when the state of that element changes. This provides a simple way to add animation to a web page without using JavaScript or a plugin-based application for creating animations.

Terms

JavaScript	function call
JavaScript engine	behavior
object	add-on
event	jump menu
function	image rollover
event handler	transition

Summary

- *JavaScript* is a scripting language that is run on the client by the *JavaScript engine* of a browser.

- When an *event* occurs on an *object*, a JavaScript *function* can be called in response to that event. For example, a function can respond to the user clicking on a button.

- In Dreamweaver, a *behavior* consists of a predefined JavaScript function that's called in response to an event on an object. To use a behavior, you attach it to an object. Then, it's called in response to the most common event for that object. If that's not what you want, you can use the Behaviors panel to select another event.

- When you attach a behavior to an object, you must provide information that's specific to that behavior.

- In addition to the behaviors that are provided by Dreamweaver, you can download and install behaviors created by third-party developers from the Adobe Add-ons website.

- You can use CSS3 *transitions* to add basic animation effects to a web page. Transitions work by changing one or more properties of an element when the state of the element changes.

- When you create a transition in Dreamweaver, the CSS for the transition is generated for you.

Exercise 15-1   Use a behavior and a CSS transition

In this exercise, you'll use the Show-Hide Elements behavior to create an image gallery like the one below. You'll also add a transition that changes the size and color of the heading at the top of the page when the user moves the mouse over it.

Open the page and review its HTML and CSS

1. Open the Exercises website, open the folder for this exercise, and open the index.html file.

2. Review the HTML for the page to see that it consists of an h1 element, four img elements with the class set to "thumbnail", and four img elements with unique id attributes.

3. Review the CSS in the style sheet to see that the visibility property for the four img elements with ids is set to "hidden", but the visibility property for the image with "image01" as its id is later set to "visible". Since that overrides the earlier setting of "hidden", only this image is displayed when the page is loaded.

4. Still in the CSS, note that the position property for the body is set to relative, and the position property for the four img elements with ids is set to absolute positioning within the body element. Then, all four images are positioned 180 pixels from the top of the body container and 20 pixels from its left side. Remember, though, that only one image will show at a time.

5. Test the page in Live view and in your browser to see that no behaviors or CSS transitions have yet been applied to this page.

Create the image gallery by using the Show-Hide Elements behavior

6. Use Window→Behaviors to display the Behaviors panel.

7. Select the first thumbnail image in Design view, click the Add Behavior icon in the Behaviors panel, and select the Show-Hide Elements behavior to display the dialog box shown in figure 15-7. Then, use the Show/Hide buttons to set the elements so the first image is shown when the user clicks on the thumbnail, and the last three images are hidden.

8. Repeat this for the second thumbnail image, but show the second image and hide the other images. Then, repeat this for the third and fourth thumbnails using the same logic for showing and hiding. Then, test these behaviors in your browser to make sure they work correctly.

9. Review the HTML for the page to see that a script element has been added to the head section of the document. It provides the JavaScript code for the function that performs this behavior. Note too that onClick attributes have been added to the four img elements. These attributes call the JavaScript function.

10. Use the procedure in figure 15-3 to change the events for the four thumbnail images from the Click event to the MouseOver event. Then, test these changes.

11. Use the Behaviors panel to preload the four images with ids when the load event for the body element occurs. You won't notice anything when you test this change, but this can make a difference in performance when a page has dozens of images on it.

12. Review the HTML code to see the JavaScript function that has been added to the script element for the PreLoad Images behavior as well as the onLoad attribute that has been added to the body element.

Add a CSS transition to the page

13. With figure 15-16 as a guide, create a CSS transition that changes the h1 heading on the page when the mouse hovers over it. This transition should change the font-size property to 250% and the color property to a shade of blue. To start, try a duration of 3 seconds and the ease-in timing function.

14. Test this change in Live view and in your browser, and note changes to the location of the rest of the items on the page. This should give you a quick idea of how easy it is to work with CSS transitions.

15. Review the CSS in the style sheet and notice that a style rule has been added for the h1:hover selector that changes the font size and color. In addition, the transition property has been added to the style rule for the h1 element. Here, the transition property is the shorthand property for the first four properties in the table in figure 15-15. In addition, -webkit-transition and -o-transition properties have been added so the transition will work in older versions of Chrome, Safari, and Opera. That's all this transition requires because this is a CSS3 feature.

16

How to use jQuery
and jQuery UI

In this chapter, you'll get off to a fast start with jQuery UI by learning how to use its widgets and effects within the context of Dreamweaver. As you will see, widgets can add useful features to your web pages with minimal development time. That's why they're used by many websites. Effects are also easy to add in Dreamweaver and can be used to animate elements when their visibility changes.

You'll also be introduced to jQuery plugins in this chapter. Like widgets, plugins can add useful features to your web pages. Unlike widgets, though, Dreamweaver doesn't provide a visual interface for defining plugins. Because of that, you typically have to write jQuery code to implement plugins.

An introduction to jQuery and jQuery UI

In this introduction, you'll learn what jQuery and jQuery UI are. You'll also learn how Dreamweaver helps you work with jQuery and jQuery UI by including the required files when you add a widget or effect.

What jQuery and jQuery UI are

As figure 16-1 summarizes, *jQuery* is a free, open-source, JavaScript library that provides dozens of methods for common web features that make JavaScript programming easier. Beyond that, jQuery functionality is coded and tested for cross-browser compatibility, so it'll work in all browsers.

Those are two of the reasons why jQuery is used by more than half of the 10,000 most-visited websites today. And that's why jQuery is commonly used by professional web developers. In fact, you can think of jQuery as one of the four technologies that every web developer should know how to use: HTML, CSS, JavaScript, and jQuery. But don't forget that jQuery is actually JavaScript.

One interesting note about jQuery is that it's entirely code based. Because of that, there's no visual support for jQuery in Dreamweaver. That means that you have to enter jQuery code directly into Code view. To learn more about how to write jQuery code, you can refer to *Murach's JavaScript and jQuery*.

Although jQuery is code based, visual *plugins* have been developed over the years that make it easier to work with jQuery. One such plugin is *jQuery UI (User Interface)*. jQuery UI is a free, open-source, JavaScript library that extends the use of the core jQuery library by providing higher-level features that you can use with a minimum of code. To provide those features, the jQuery UI library uses the jQuery library. In fact, you can think of jQuery UI as the official plugin library for jQuery.

jQuery provides three core types of features. *Widgets* are objects that you can add to a web page like accordions, tabs, and date pickers. In this chapter, you'll learn how to use many of the widgets that are currently provided by jQuery UI and that are also included in Dreamweaver. Then, you'll learn how to use *effects*, which are visual animations that you can attach to objects. Although interactions are also a part of jQuery UI, Dreamweaver has no visual support for them so they won't be presented in this book. To learn more about any of these features, you can visit the jQuery UI website shown in this figure.

The jQuery UI website

The URL for jQuery UI

`http://jqueryui.com`

Description

- *jQuery* is a free, open-source, JavaScript library that provides methods that make JavaScript programming easier. Today, jQuery is used by more than 50% of the 10,000 most-visited websites, and its popularity is growing rapidly.

- *jQuery UI* is a free, open-source, JavaScript library that extends the jQuery library by providing higher-level features like widgets, effects, and interactions. jQuery UI uses jQuery and can be thought of as the official *plugin* library for jQuery.

- Dreamweaver doesn't provide visual support for jQuery, but it does provide visual support for jQuery UI widgets and effects. Because of that, you don't need to know much about jQuery UI to use these features from Dreamweaver.

Figure 16-1   What jQuery and jQuery UI are

How Dreamweaver implements jQuery and jQuery UI

Dreamweaver makes it easy to work with widgets and effects by automatically adding the required files to the site when you add a widget or effect. It also adds any link and script elements to the web page that are required to use those files. This is illustrated in figure 16-2.

The first code example in this figure shows the three link and two script elements that Dreamweaver adds for a Tabs widget. The first two link elements are for style sheets that include the core styles and the generic theme styles used by the jQuery UI widgets. Although jQuery UI provides many themes other than the core theme, Dreamweaver currently supports only the generic theme.

The third link element is for a style sheet that's specific to the Tabs widget. Finally, the script elements are for the jQuery core library and the Tabs widget. Notice that all five of these elements refer to files that are stored in the site, since Dreamweaver downloads these files to the site when you add the widget.

In addition to the link and script elements shown in the first example, most widgets require another script element like the one shown in the second example. This element uses jQuery code to initialize the widget. Here, the code calls the tabs method of an element with an ID of "Tabs1". This element, and any others that are needed to create the widget, are generated for you along with the jQuery code that initializes the widget. Then, as you'll see later in this chapter, you can use the Property Inspector to change how the widget works. When you do, the jQuery and HTML code are updated for you automatically. This is much easier than having to write this code yourself.

The third example in this figure shows the two script elements that are added when you add a jQuery UI effect to a web page. Like the script elements for a widget, these elements refer to files that are downloaded to the site when the effect is added. The first one is for the jQuery core library and the second one is for all of the jQuery UI effects.

When you add an effect, it's implemented as a behavior like the ones you learned about in the last chapter. If you look back at figure 15-2, you'll see the code that's used for a simple behavior. It includes a script element that contains a JavaScript function for the behavior, as well as an event attribute that calls the function when the triggering event occurs. Dreamweaver also adds code like this when you add an effect to a web page.

The jQuery and jQuery UI files for a web page that uses the Tabs widget

```
<!-- The jQuery UI core styles -->
<link href="jQueryAssets/jquery.ui.core.min.css" rel="stylesheet"
    type="text/css">

<!-- The jQuery UI generic theme styles -->
<link href="jQueryAssets/jquery.ui.theme.min.css" rel="stylesheet"
    type="text/css">

<!-- The jQuery UI styles for the Tabs widget -->
<link href="jQueryAssets/jquery.ui.tabs.min.css" rel="stylesheet"
    type="text/css">

<!-- The jQuery core library -->
<script src="jQueryAssets/jquery-1.8.3.min.js" type="text/javascript">
</script>

<!-- The jQuery UI code for the Tabs widget -->
<script src="jQueryAssets/jquery-ui-1.9.2.tabs.custom.min.js"
        type="text/javascript"></script>
```

The jQuery code that initializes the jQuery UI functionality

```
<script type="text/javascript">
$(function() {
    $( "#Tabs1" ).tabs()
});
</script>
```

The jQuery and jQuery UI files for a web page that uses an effect

```
<script src="jQueryAssets/jquery-1.8.3.min.js" type="text/javascript">
</script>
<script src="jQueryAssets/jquery-ui-effects.custom.min.js"
        type="text/javascript"></script>
```

Description

- When you add a jQuery UI widget or effect to a web page, Dreamweaver adds the jQuery core library to the site and then adds a script element for that library to the page.

- When you add a jQuery UI widget to a web page, Dreamweaver also adds the jQuery UI core and generic theme style sheets to the site and then adds link elements for those style sheets to the page. It also adds one or more style sheets and a JavaScript file that are specific to the widget to the site and then adds link and script elements for those files to the page. And it adds jQuery code that initializes the widget.

- When you add a jQuery UI effect to a web page, Dreamweaver adds a JavaScript file for all the effects and a script element for that file to the page. It also adds a script element with a JavaScript function for the behavior that implements the effect.

- Some of the jQuery UI widgets use interactions. In that case, a separate style sheet may be included for the interaction.

Figure 16-2   How Dreamweaver implements jQuery and jQuery UI

How to use the jQuery UI widgets

The best way to get off to a fast start with jQuery UI is to begin using its widgets. That will show you how you can quickly add features like accordions and tabs to your web pages with little or no code. In the topics that follow, you'll learn how to use six of the widgets that are currently supported by jQuery UI and made available through Dreamweaver.

How to use any widget

The next five figures show how to define specific widgets using Dreamweaver's Property Inspector. That may be all you need to know to use these widgets in your own web pages. However, it can be helpful to see how the widgets work before you use them. To do that, you can review the jQuery UI documentation for the widgets, which is excellent. You can also use this documentation to review all the options, methods, and events for a widget. Then, if you want to use a feature that isn't available from the Property Inspector, you can implement it directly in Code view.

To illustrate how the documentation for the widgets works, figure 16-3 shows the documentation for the Accordion widget. You can display a page like this by clicking on the widget name in the left sidebar of the jQuery UI home page. When you do, a widget that uses its default functionality is displayed and you can interact with that widget to see how it works. To see how other features of the widget work, you can click on the other examples in the right sidebar. You can also click on the View Source link to see the source code that makes the example work. After that, you can review the options, methods, and events for the widget by clicking on the API Documentation link.

Once you understand how a widget works, you can use Dreamweaver to add it to a web page. To do that, you can choose the widget from the Insert→jQuery UI submenu or from the jQuery UI category of the Insert panel. Note that not all of the widgets that are provided by jQuery UI are available from Dreamweaver. If you ever want to use any of these widgets, then, you'll need to add the code for implementing them yourself. After you gain some experience using widgets in Dreamweaver, you should be able to do that by referring to the jQuery UI documentation for the widget you want to use.

You may also notice that Dreamweaver includes three widgets that aren't listed on the jQuery UI website: Buttonset, Checkbox Buttons, and Radio Buttons. These widgets are actually different forms of the Button widget, but Dreamweaver makes them easier to create by listing them as separate widgets. If you want to find out more about these forms of the Button widget, you can refer to the documentation for that widget.

The documentation for the Accordion widget on the jQuery UI website

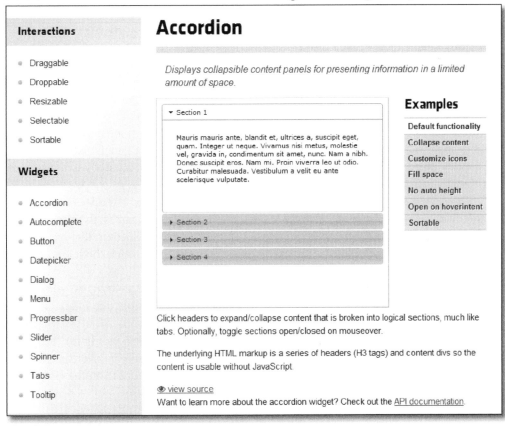

How to use the jQuery UI documentation

- From the home page of the jQuery UI website, click on a widget name in the left sidebar to display an overview.
- In the right sidebar, click on an example name to see a working example of the widget.
- Click the API Documentation link to display information about the widget's options, methods, and events.

How to add a jQuery widget

- Choose the widget from the Insert→jQuery UI submenu or from the jQuery UI category of the Insert panel.

Description

- Although Dreamweaver provides a visual interface for working with widgets, it can be helpful to see how a widget works before you use it and to learn about its various options, methods, and events. To do that, you can use the jQuery UI documentation.

Figure 16-3   How to use any widget

How to use the Accordion widget

Figure 16-4 shows how to use an Accordion widget, which consists of two or more headings and the content for those headings. By default, an accordion starts with the panel for the first heading displayed, and only one panel can be open at a time. Then, when the user clicks on one of the other headings, the contents for that heading are displayed and the contents for the first heading are hidden.

When you first add an accordion to a web page, it consists of three panels with default headings and content. If you want to add or remove a panel, you can use the Add Panel or Remove Panel icon to the right of the Panels list in the Property Inspector. Then, you can change the heading for each panel by entering it directly into Design view.

You can also enter the content for a panel into Design view, but only one panel is displayed at a time. To display the content for another panel, though, you can select the panel from the Panels list in the Property Inspector. Or, you can point to the heading for the panel in Design view and then click the icon with the eye on it that appears at the right side of the heading.

To set the panel that will be expanded by default when the page loads, you enter the index of the panel in the Active text box. In this example, the index is set to 0, which refers to the first panel. This is the default.

By default, a panel is expanded when the user clicks on the heading for that panel. Another option is to expand the panel when the mouse hovers over the heading. To make that change, you can select the mouseover item from the Event menu.

Another property you may want to change is the Collapsible property. If this property is checked, it means that all of the panels can be closed at the same time. To close the open panel, the user can click on its heading or move the mouse over its heading depending on the event that's selected.

The last property you may want to change is the Animate property. Its menu lets you select the animation that you want to use when the panels are expanded and collapsed. Then, the box to its right lets you specify the time in milliseconds for the animation. If, for example, you set this property to "swing" and the duration to 1000, the panels will take one second (1000 milliseconds) to expand and collapse and the swing animation will be used. For usability, though, you're always okay with the default setting.

An Accordion widget

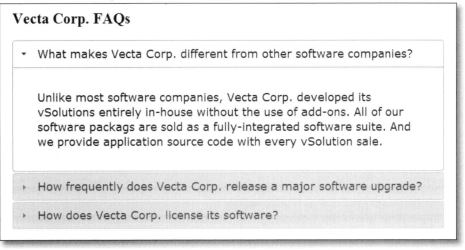

The Property Inspector for an Accordion widget

Properties of an Accordion widget

Property	Description
ID	The unique ID of the widget.
Panels	The panels in the accordion listed by heading. To add a panel, use the Add Panel icon (+). To delete a panel, use the Remove Panel icon (–). To change the sequence of the panels, use the repositioning arrows (▲ and ▼).
Active	The zero-based index of the panel that's expanded by default.
Event	The event that causes the contents for a heading to be displayed.
Height Style	Determines the height of each panel. To set all panels to the height of the tallest panel based on its content, use "auto". To set all panels to the height available within the parent element, use "fill". And to set each panel to the height required for its content, use "content".
Disabled	When checked, disables the widget.
Collapsible	When checked, the expanded panel can be collapsed so no content is displayed.
Animate	The type of animation that's used to expand and collapse a panel and the duration of the animation in milliseconds.
Icons	The icons that will appear to the left of an active and inactive heading.

Description

- The jQuery UI Accordion widget provides for two or more panels that contain a header and content. When the content of one panel is displayed, the panel whose content is currently displayed is hidden. The content of all panels can also be hidden.

Figure 16-4   How to use the Accordion widget

How to use the Tabs widget

Figure 16-5 shows how to use the Tabs widget. This widget has the same general function as the Accordion widget, but it displays the contents of a panel when the related tab is clicked.

Like the Accordion widget, three panels are added by default for a Tabs widget. Then, you can use the Panels list and controls in the Property Inspector to add and delete panels, and you can enter the headings and contents for the panels in Design view.

Also like the Accordion widget, the first panel of the Tabs widget is displayed by default when the page loads. To change that, you can enter the index of the panel in the Active text box. In this figure, for example, the index is set to 1 so the second panel will be displayed.

A unique property of the Tabs widget is Orientation. By default, horizontal orientation is used, which means that the tabs are displayed at the top of the widget as shown here. If you choose vertical orientation instead, the tabs will be displayed down the left side of the widget.

A Tabs widget

Vecta Corp. Management Team

| Agnes | Damon | Herbert | Mike | Wilbur |

Director of Development
Damon creates learning materials for Vecta Corp. and consults with customers to integrate vSolutions into their production pipeline and business processes.

The Property Inspector for a Tabs widget

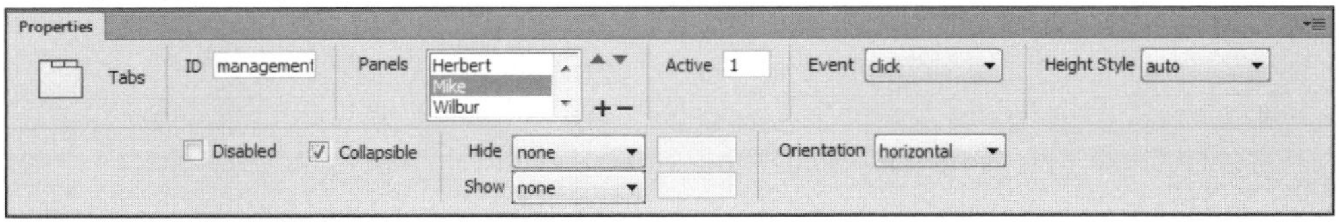

Properties

Tabs   ID management   Panels Herbert / Mike / Wilbur   Active 1   Event click   Height Style auto

Disabled   ☑ Collapsible   Hide none   Orientation horizontal

Show none

Properties of a Tabs widget

Property	Description
ID	The unique ID of the widget.
Panels	The panels in the widget listed by heading. To add a new panel, click the (+) icon. To remove a panel, click the (–) icon. To change the sequence of the panels, use the repositioning arrows (▲ and ▼).
Active	The zero-based index of the panel that's displayed by default.
Event	The event that causes the contents for a heading to be displayed.
Height Style	Determines the height of each panel. To set all panels to the height of the tallest panel based on its content, use "auto". To set all panels to the height available within the parent element, use "fill". And to set each panel to the height required for its content, use "content".
Disabled	When checked, disables the widget.
Collapsible	When checked, the current panel can be collapsed so no content is displayed.
Hide/Show	The effect that's used to hide and show the panel and the duration of the effect.
Orientation	The orientation of the tabs. If set to "horizontal", the tabs are displayed at the top. If set to "vertical", the tabs are displayed down the left side.

Description

- The jQuery UI Tabs widget provides for displaying the content in one of two or more panels using a tabbed interface. The content of the current panel can also be hidden so only the tabs are displayed.

Figure 16-5   How to use the Tabs widget

How to use the Datepicker widget

Figure 16-6 shows how to use a Datepicker widget that is associated with a text box. Then, when the focus moves to the text box, a calendar is displayed. After the user selects a date, the calendar is hidden and the selected date appears in the text box.

One of the basic properties of the Datepicker widget is Date Format. This property determines the format of the date that's displayed in the text box. The default format is "mm/dd/yy" as shown here, but you can select from several other common formats.

Four other properties have also been set for the widget shown here. First, the Change Month and Change Year properties have been selected. This causes the month and year at the top of the calendar to be displayed as drop-down lists rather than as standard text. That way, the user can change the month and year by selecting values from the lists.

Second, the Show Button Panel property has been selected. This causes a panel with two buttons on it to be displayed at the bottom of the calendar. The user can click the Today button to select the current date in the calendar. Note that this doesn't close the calendar, though. To do that, the user can click the Done button.

Finally, the Number of Months property has been set to 2. By default, this property is set to 1 so that only one calendar month is displayed at a time.

Two other properties you may want to set are Min Date and Max Date. These properties determine the minimum and maximum dates the user can select. The value you enter for these properties must be a positive or negative integer that represents the number of days before or after the current date. If you enter 30 for the Max Date property, for example, the user can select a date up to 30 days after the current date.

In addition to displaying the calendar when the focus moves to the text box, it can be displayed when the user clicks on a button. To do that, you select the Button Image property. Then, you select the image you want displayed on the button, and the button appears to the right of the text box.

A Datepicker widget

The Property Inspector for a Datepicker widget

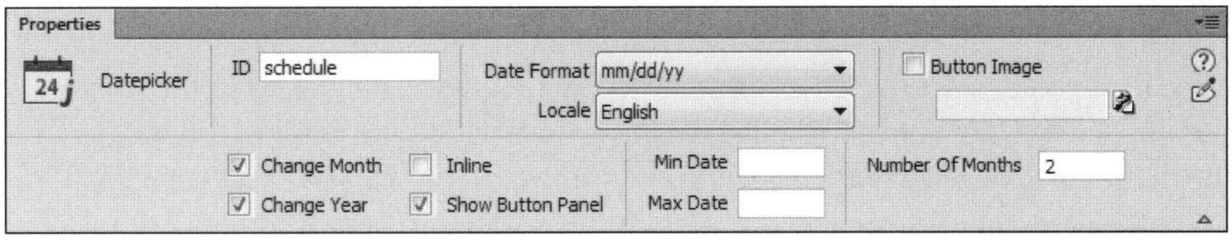

Properties of a Datepicker widget

Property	Description
ID	The unique ID of the widget.
Date Format	The format for the date that's displayed in the text box.
Locale	The language used for the date display.
Button Image	When checked, you can specify an image that can be clicked to show the calendar.
Change Month	When checked, displays a drop-down list for the month.
Change Year	When checked, displays a drop-down list for the year.
Inline	When checked, no text field is displayed and the calendar appears by default.
Show Button Panel	When checked, a toolbar appears at the bottom of the calendar. The Today button can be clicked to select the current date, and the Done button can be clicked to close the calendar.
Mix/Max Date	The number of days from the current date that the user can select.
Number of Months	The number of months to display at any one time.

Description

- The Datepicker widget provides a calendar from which the user can select a date. By default, the calendar is displayed when the user moves the focus into the text box, and the current date is highlighted.

Figure 16-6   How to use the Datepicker widget

How to use the Button and Dialog widgets

Figure 16-7 shows how the Button and Dialog widgets work. A Button widget is similar to a standard HTML button. In fact, Dreamweaver implements this widget as a button element. When the button is initialized by jQuery code, though, the HTML for the button is converted into a button that uses the jQuery UI theme. Because of that, you might want to use it when you include other widgets on a web page so all the widgets use the same theme. Other than that, the button works its normal way. In this example, when the user clicks the button, the dialog box is displayed.

Although the Property Inspector for a Button widget isn't shown in this figure, you shouldn't have any trouble using it. In most cases, you'll just set the ID property to a unique ID. However, you can also set properties that determine whether text, icons, or both text and icons are displayed on the button and the text and icons that are displayed.

The Dialog widget displays a dialog box like the one shown in this figure. After you add this widget to a web page, you can enter the content for the dialog box in Design view. You can also set several properties for it using the Property Inspector.

To start, you can set the Title property to the text that's displayed in the title bar of the dialog box. You can use the Position property to set the initial position of the dialog box relative to the edges of the browser window. And you can use the Width and Height properties to set the initial width and height of the dialog box.

By default, a dialog box is 300 pixels wide and tall enough to fit all of its content. However, the user can resize a dialog box by dragging its edges. If that's not what you want, you can remove the check mark from the Resizable property. Another option, though, is to limit the size of the dialog box. To do that, you can use the Min Width, Min Height, Max Width, and Max Height properties. By default, the Min Width and Min Height properties are set to 300 pixels, but the Max Width and Max Height properties aren't set.

The user can also move a dialog box by default by dragging it by its title bar. If that's not what you want, you can remove the check mark from the Draggable property.

When you first add a Dialog widget to a web page, the Auto Open property is selected. That causes the dialog box to be displayed when the page loads. In most cases, that's not what you want. Instead, you'll want it to be displayed in response to an event such as the clicking of a button. To do that, you can set the Trigger Button property to the ID of the button whose event will trigger the display, and you can set the Trigger Event property to the event.

A Dialog widget that's displayed by a Button widget

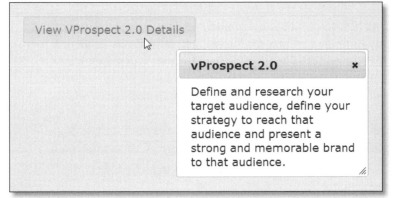

The Property Inspector for a Dialog widget

Properties

Dialog   ID `vprospect-dialog`   Title `vProspect 2.0`   Position `center ▼`   Width `300`   Min Width `150`   Max Width `____`

Height `auto`   Min Height `150`   Max Height `____`

☑ Draggable   ☑ Close On Escape   ☑ Resizable   Hide `none ▼`   `____`   Trigger Button `Button1 ▼`

☐ Auto Open   ☑ Modal   Show `none ▼`   `____`   Trigger Event `click ▼`

Properties of a Dialog widget

Property	Description
ID	The unique ID of the widget.
Title	The title that's displayed in the title bar of the dialog box.
Position	The position of the dialog box relative to the edges of the browser window. Possible values include center (the default), top, left, right, and bottom.
Width/Height	The initial width and height of the dialog box in pixels.
Min Width/Height	The minimum width and height of the dialog box in pixels.
Max Width/Height	The maximum width and height of the dialog box in pixels.
Draggable	When checked, the user can drag the dialog box to a new location.
Auto Open	When checked, the dialog box appears automatically when the page loads.
Close On Escape	When checked, the user can press the Esc key to close the dialog box.
Modal	When checked, the dialog box is modal. The user can't interact with other items on the page until the dialog box is closed.
Resizable	When checked, the user can resize the dialog box.
Hide/Show	The effect that's used to open and close the dialog box and the duration of the effect.
Trigger Button	The ID of the button that will trigger the opening of the dialog box.
Trigger Event	The event for the selected button that will trigger the opening of the dialog box.

Description

- The Dialog widget displays a modal or non-modal dialog box within a web page. You typically use a Button widget to trigger the display of a Dialog widget.

Figure 16-7   How to use the Button and Dialog widgets

How to use the Autocomplete widget

Figure 16-8 shows how to use an Autocomplete widget. As the user types one or more characters into the text box for this widget, a list drops down that shows the items that contain those characters. Then, the user can select one of those items by clicking on it or by pressing the down-arrow key to go to an item and the Enter or Return key to select that item. That item then replaces what's typed in the text box.

Note that the items that are displayed in the list don't have to start with the letters you type. If I entered the letter "c" in this widget, for example, both vProspect 2.0 and vConvert 2.0 would be listed even though they don't start with that letter.

To use the Autocomplete object, you must specify the list of items you want to include for the Source property. The easiest way to do that is to code an array of strings as shown in this figure. Another option, though, is to store the list in a *JavaScript Object Notation* (*JSON*) file. JSON is a popular format for storing and exchanging large amounts of data. If you use JSON with the Autocomplete widget, you should be aware that additional code may be required for it to work correctly across all browsers.

Some of the other properties for the Autocomplete widget let you determine how many characters must be entered before the list is displayed, what HTML element the list is appended to, and whether the focus moves to the text box when the page loads. You may want to experiment with these properties to see how they work.

An Autocomplete widget

The Property Inspector for an Autocomplete widget

Properties of an Autocomplete widget

Property	Description
ID	The unique ID of the widget.
Source	An array or a JSON file that contains the items for the list in the Autocomplete widget.
Min Length	The minimum number of characters that should be entered before the auto complete list is displayed.
Delay	The delay in milliseconds before the list is displayed.
Append To	The HTML element that the list will be appended to. The list can be positioned relative to that element using CSS positioning properties.
Auto Focus	When checked, the focus is moved to the text box when the page loads.
Position	The position of the items relative to the list and the list relative to the text box.

The array that contains the list of values

```
["vProspect 2.0","vConvert 2.0","vRetain 1.0"]
```

Description

- The Autocomplete widget displays the items in a list that match an entry in a text box and then lets the user select an item. This works similarly to Google's AutoSuggest functionality.

- The items for an autocomplete list can be coded as an array in the format shown above, or they can be stored in a *JSON (JavaScript Object Notation)* file. Additional code may be required for JSON to work across all browsers.

Figure 16-8   How to use the Autocomplete widget

A web page that uses jQuery UI widgets

Figure 16-9 presents the user interface for a web page that uses four of the widgets you just learned about. To start, the Read More button is implemented as a Button widget. When this button is clicked, a Dialog widget is used to display a dialog box that contains additional information about Vecta Corporation.

Information about the three solutions the company offers is displayed in a Tabs widget. By default, the first panel is displayed, but the user can click on the tab for either of the other two panels to display the information about that solution. Similarly, the first panel in the Accordion widget is displayed by default, but the user can click on the heading for another panel to display the information in that panel. This widget displays testimonials from clients who use Vecta Corp. solutions.

A web page that uses jQuery UI widgets

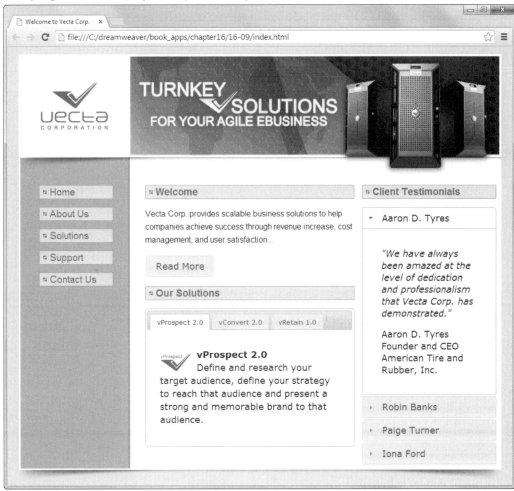

Description

- A Dialog widget that displays additional information about the company is displayed when the user clicks the Button widget labeled Read More.
- The Tabs widget displays information about the three solutions offered by the company.
- The Accordion widget displays client testimonials from people who have used the company's solutions.

Figure 16-9   A web page that uses jQuery UI widgets

An introduction to the jQuery UI effects

In the two topics that follow, you'll learn the basic skills for using the jQuery UI effects that Dreamweaver provides. As you'll see, these effects are implemented as behaviors. Because of that, you shouldn't have any trouble using them if you've read chapter 15.

How to use any effect

jQuery UI provides for four types of core effects. Color transitions provide for animating background color, border colors, text color, and outline color. Class transitions provide for changing the class that's assigned to one or more elements over a specified period of time so the change is gradual. Easings determine the way that an animation is performed. For instance, an animation can start slowly and pick up speed as it goes. Or, an animation can start or end with a little bounce. Finally, visibility transitions provide for applying an individual effect to an element while showing, hiding, or toggling the element.

The only effects that are supported visually in Dreamweaver are the *visibility transitions*. You access these effects from the Behaviors panel as shown in figure 16-10. Before you use these effects, though, you'll want to see how they work. To do that, you can go to the URL shown in this figure. There, you'll see that Dreamweaver doesn't include all of the effects provided by jQuery UI.

Because effects are implemented as behaviors, you attach an effect to an object just like you do a behavior. Then, the effect takes place when an event occurs on that object. When the user clicks a button, for example, the Slide effect could be used to slide an element into view.

To add an effect to an element, you choose the effect you want to use from the Effects submenu of the Add Behavior menu. Then, you complete the dialog box that's displayed for that effect to set its options. In the next figure, for example, you'll see the dialog box for the Blind effect.

The Effects submenu in the Behaviors panel

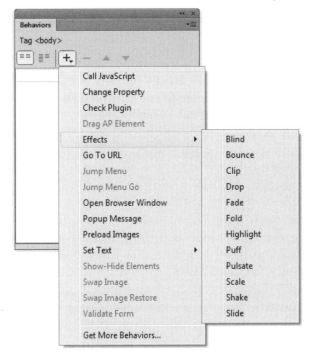

The URL for demonstrations of all of the jQuery UI effects

`http://jqueryui.com/effect`

How to add an effect to an object

1. Select the object you want to add the effect to and then click the Add Behavior icon (**+**) in the Behaviors panel to display the Add Behavior menu.

2. Choose Effects to display the Effects submenu and then choose the effect you want to use.

3. Complete the dialog box that's displayed to define the effect and then click OK.

Description

- The jQuery UI *effects* extend jQuery functionality by providing color transitions, class transitions, easings, and visibility transitions. The only effects supported by Dreamweaver are the *visibility transitions*, which animate an element as it's displayed or hidden.

- In Dreamweaver, an effect is a behavior that you attach to an object from the Behaviors panel. For more information on using the Behaviors panel, please see chapter 15.

- For more information on the jQuery UI effects, you can refer to the jQuery UI website. It provides documentation and demonstrations for the effects just like it does for widgets.

Figure 16-10   How to use any effect

How to set the options for an effect

When you choose an effect from the Behaviors panel, a dialog box like the one shown in figure 16-11 is displayed. Here, the dialog box is for the Blind effect. This effect works something like the blinds on a window.

To set the options for this effect, you start by selecting the element that the effect will be applied to from the Target Element menu. In this example, the effect will be applied to a div element with an ID of "welcome". Then, you enter the duration of the effect in milliseconds. Here, the effect will last 1,000 milliseconds, or one second. Next, you select an option from the Visibility menu to determine if the effect will hide the element, show the element, or toggle the element. If you select the toggle option, the element will be hidden if it's displayed and displayed if it's hidden.

Finally you select an option from the Direction menu to determine the direction from which the element will be displayed or hidden. If you select "up" as shown here, the effect will work like standard vertical blinds. You can also select other options, though, such as "down", "left", and "right".

The example in this figure illustrates how this effect works. Here, the effect is attached to the Click event of a button. Before this button is clicked, the entire div element, which consists of a heading and a paragraph, is displayed as shown in the first window. But when the button is clicked, the effect is applied and the "blinds are pulled up" as shown in the second window.

Now that you've seen how the Blind effect works, you should be able to use most of the other effects without any trouble. Just keep in mind that some of the effects include options other than the ones shown here. The easiest way to learn more about these options is to click the Help button in the dialog box for the effect. This will take you to the documentation for the effect on the jQuery UI website.

The dialog box for the Blind effect

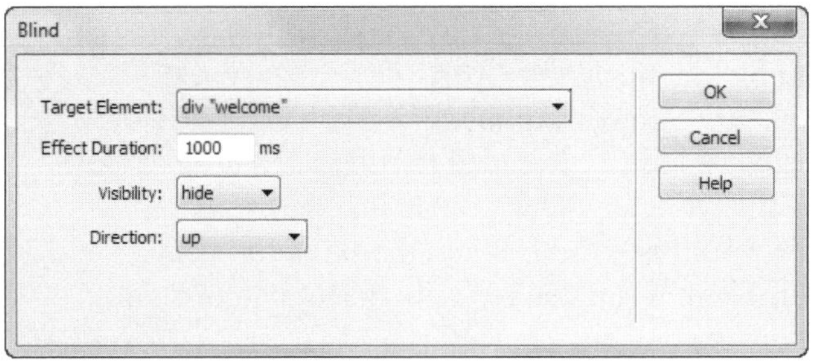

The Blind effect as it's applied to the div element

Description

- For each effect, you must specify the element it will affect, the duration of the effect, and whether the effect hides or shows the element. An element can also be toggled so it's hidden if it's currently shown and shown if it's currently hidden.

- Most effects also include other options. To learn more about these options, you can click the Help button in the dialog box for an effect to display the jQuery UI documentation for that effect.

Figure 16-11   How to set the options for an effect

An introduction to jQuery plugins

In addition to the jQuery UI plugin, many third-party developers have created plugins that perform a variety of tasks. Although you can use these plugins in Dreamweaver, no visual support is provided for them. Because of that, you have to download any files and write any jQuery code that they require.

In the two topics that follow, you'll be introduced to the skills for using jQuery plugins in Dreamweaver. Then, when you're ready to learn more about writing jQuery code, we recommend you get a copy of *Murach's JavaScript and jQuery*.

How to use any plugin

Figure 16-12 presents a general procedure for using a plugin. Before you can use this procedure, though, you have to find a plugin that performs the task you need. The easiest way to do that is to search the Web. You may also be able to find the plugin you need on the Adobe Add-ons website. To display this website, choose Window→Browse Add-ons.

Once you find the plugin you want to use, you can download it to your computer. This download is often in the form of a zip file, which you can then unzip to extract the individual files it contains. The download will always include at least one JavaScript file for the plugin. In addition, it may include CSS or image files that are used by the plugin, as well as an HTML file that demonstrates how the plugin works. After you extract these files, you can store them in your site.

Next, you code link elements for any CSS files that are required to use the plugin, along with script elements for any required JavaScript files. That includes a script element for the core jQuery library, since the plugins use this library. Note that if this library isn't already included in your site, you can download it from the jQuery website. Also note that the script element for this library must come before the script element for the plugin.

Once you've coded the link and script elements, you're ready to use the plugin. To do that, you start by adding the necessary HTML and CSS for the page so it's appropriate for the plugin. In most cases, you can do that using Dreamweaver's visual interface. To find out what's required, you can refer to the documentation for the plugin. Finally, you code the jQuery for the plugin. You'll see an example of that in the next figure.

But first, I want to point out that you don't have to download the jQuery library to your site to use it. Instead, you can include a script element that refers to the version of this library that you want to use on the jQuery *Content Delivery Network* (*CDN*). This is illustrated in the first code example in this figure.

In some cases, you can also refer to a plugin on the developer's CDN instead of downloading the plugin. For instance, the second code example in this figure shows a script element that refers to a plugin named bxSlider on the developer's CDN. You'll see an example of this plugin in the next figure.

General steps for using a plugin within your web pages

1. Download the files for the plugin from the developer's website, and save them in one of the folders of your site.

2. In the head element of the page, code the link elements for any CSS files that are included in the download for the plugin.

3. In the head element, code a script element for the jQuery library. If your website doesn't already include this library, you can download it from the jQuery website at http://jquery.com/download/.

4. In the head element, code script elements for the JavaScript files that are included in the download for the plugin. The script elements for the plugin must be after the one for the core jQuery library because all jQuery plugins use the core library.

5. Add the necessary elements and styles to the page as needed by the plugin.

6. If necessary, add the jQuery code that uses the methods and options of the plugin to a script element in the head element.

A script element that refers to a jQuery library on the jQuery CDN

```
<script src="http://code.jquery.com/jquery-1.11.0.min.js"></script>
```

A script element that refers to a plugin on the developer's CDN

```
<script src="http://bxslider.com/sites/default/files/
            jquery.bxSlider.min.js"></script>
```

Two cautions

*   Make sure that you include a script element for jQuery, and make sure that the script element for the plugin comes after it. Not doing one or the other is a common error.

*   Some plugins won't work with the latest version of jQuery. So if you have any problems with a plugin, check its documentation to see which version of jQuery it requires.

Description

*   jQuery *plugins* are JavaScript applications that extend the functionality of jQuery. These plugins require the use of the jQuery library just like jQuery UI does.

*   Plugins are available for hundreds of web functions like slide shows, carousels, tabs, menus, text layout, data validation, and mobile application development. To locate a plugin, you can search the Web or visit the Adobe Add-ons website.

*   Instead of downloading the current version of jQuery to your site and referring to that file from a script element, you can add a script element that retrieves the jQuery library from the *Content Delivery Network* (*CDN*) on the jQuery website.

*   The files for some plugins can also be referred to from a CDN on the developer's website. In that case, you don't need to download them to your site.

*   Most plugins require the use of jQuery code to call methods and set options. A few, however, only require that you code the HTML in a specific way.

Figure 16-12   How to use any plugin

The code for a sample plugin

To illustrate how a typical plugin works, figure 16-13 presents the bxSlider plugin. This plugin is used to create a carousel like the one shown here. In this example, the plugin displays two images at a time, and the user can move to the next or previous images by clicking on the buttons to the right or left of the images. However, you can change many aspects of how this plugin works by setting its options.

If you download the JavaScript file for this plugin, you can refer to it using a script element like the one shown in this figure. As part of the download, you'll also get a set of images that you can use with this plugin. Another way to access the JavaScript file is to get it from the bxSlider.com site, as you saw in the previous figure. If you don't need to use the images that come in the download for the plugin, you can use whichever technique you want.

The easiest way to set up the HTML for this plugin is to add the images you want to use to your web page. Then, you can highlight the images and convert them to an unordered list using the Property Inspector. You will also need to assign an ID to the list so you can refer to it from your jQuery code. In the example shown here, the list includes five images and it has an ID of "slider".

To run the carousel using its default options, you code this jQuery statement within the ready function of a jQuery application:

```
$("#slider").bxSlider();
```

To set some of its options, you code a set of braces that contains name/value pairs as shown in the example in this figure. Here, the number of slides that are displayed at one time is set to 2, and the number of slides that are moved when the next or previous button is clicked is also set to 2.

By default, the bxSlider plugin will display next and prev links in the bottom left corner of the carousel. But you can change the text links to buttons by setting the nextImage and previousImage options so they point to the images you want to use. Beyond that, this plugin provides many other options that affect the way the carousel works. To get a better understanding of that, you can review the examples on this plugin's web site. Then, you can review the documentation for the options to see what's available.

To change the placement of the next and previous links or images, you also need to add some CSS that uses the bx.next and bx.prev classes. You won't find these classes in the HTML, though, because they're added to the DOM by the plugin. You can also use these classes to change the default links to images, which is the way the application in this example works. To see the CSS that's used, you can review the CSS file for the downloaded application.

Now that you've seen how this plugin works, you should realize that you can use some plugins without writing any jQuery code. For example, the Cycle2 plugin for creating slide shows only requires that you code a class attribute with the value "cycle-slideshow" on the div element that contains the images for the slide show. Then, it just works!

A web page that uses the bxSlider plugin for a carousel

The script element for the bxSlider plugin

```
<script src="jQueryAssets/jquery.bxSlider.min.js"></script>
```

The HTML for the bxSlider plugin

```
<ul id="slider">
    <li><img src="images/building_01_thumb.jpg"></li>
    <li><img src="images/building_02_thumb.jpg"></li>
    <li><img src="images/building_03_thumb.jpg"></li>
    <li><img src="images/building_04_thumb.jpg"></li>
    <li><img src="images/building_05_thumb.jpg"></li>
</ul>
```

The jQuery for using the plugin

```
$(document).ready(function(){
    $("#slider").bxSlider(
        { displaySlideQty:2,
          moveSlideQty:2 }
    );
});
```

Description

- The bxSlider plugin makes it easy to develop a carousel like the one above.

- The HTML for the images can be an unordered list that contains one list item for each slide as shown above. Or, it can be a top-level div element that contains one div element for each slide.

- The bxSlider plugin provides many options. Two of the most useful are displaySlideQty and moveSlideQty. The first one determines how many slides are displayed at one time; the second one determines how many slides are moved at one time.

- By default, "next" and "prev" links that move to the next or previous slide appear below the slides. To change the location of the links and to change the links to buttons, you can use CSS to apply styles to the bx.next and bx.prev classes that are added to the DOM by the plugin. You can see how this works in the downloaded application.

- It's a good practice to set the width and height attributes for img elements to the exact sizes of the images. Then, the browser can reserve the right amount of space for the images and continue rendering the page while the images are being loaded.

Figure 16-13   The code for a sample plugin

Perspective

Now that you've completed this chapter, you should be able to build a web page that uses the jQuery UI widgets you learned about. You should be able to use jQuery UI effects to add animation to elements when their visibility changes. And you should have a general idea about how to use jQuery plugins for tasks like displaying carousels or slide shows.

Of course, you can do a lot more with jQuery than what Dreamweaver provides for. So when you're ready to learn how to use jQuery and jQuery UI without relying on Dreamweaver, don't forget *Murach's JavaScript and jQuery*.

Terms

jQuery	modal dialog box
plugin	JavaScript Object Notation (JSON)
jQuery UI (User Interface)	visibility transition
widget	Content Delivery Network (CDN)
effect	

Summary

- *jQuery* is a JavaScript library that provides methods that make JavaScript programming easier. These methods have been tested for cross-browser compatibility.

- *jQuery UI* and *plugins* are JavaScript libraries that use the jQuery library to build higher-level features.

- The most widely-used jQuery UI components are the *widgets* that include the Accordion, Tabs, Button, Dialog, Autocomplete, and Datepicker widgets.

- When you add a widget in Dreamweaver, all the required CSS and JavaScript files are downloaded to your site, and link and script elements that refer to those files are added to the web page.

- Dreamweaver also adds starting HTML and jQuery code for a widget when you add it to a page. Then, you can use the Property Inspector to customize the widget and the code will be modified for you.

- Although jQuery UI provides for four types of *effects*, the only type supported by Dreamweaver are the *visibility transitions*. This type of effect is applied when the visibility of an element changes.

- Effects are implemented as behaviors in Dreamweaver, which means that you attach an effect to an object using the Behaviors panel. Then, you can use the dialog box that's displayed to customize the effect.

- If you need a common function for a web page, chances are that a plugin is already available for it. Because Dreamweaver doesn't provide a visual interface for plugins, you have to add any jQuery code that's required by hand.

- To find the plugin you need, you can search the Web or use a code repository like the Adobe Add-ons website.

- To use a plugin, you can download it from the developer's website and then add link and script elements for any CSS and JavaScript files that the plugin requires. You also need to include a script element for the jQuery library before the script element for the plugin.

Exercise 16-1   Add a widget to a page

In this exercise, you'll add an Accordion widget to a web page. This is one of the widgets that you'll use the most, and it will give you a solid insight into how the other widgets are used.

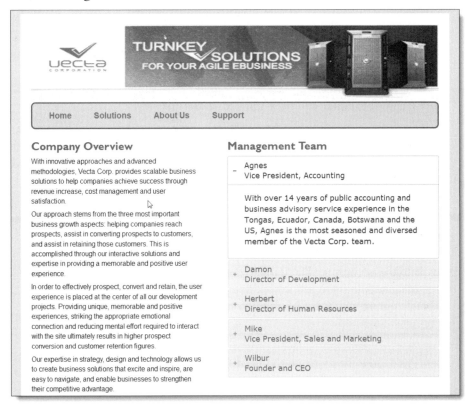

Open the page and review its HTML

1. Open the Exercises website, open the folder for this exercise, and open the aboutus.html file.

2. Review the HTML code to see that it contains an aside element that is followed by a section element that starts with an h2 element that contains "Management Team". Beneath that h2 heading, you can see an h3 heading and a paragraph for each of the five people listed on the management team.

Convert the Management Team content to an accordion

3. In Design view, put the insertion point after the h2 element for Management Team and before the h3 element that follows it. Then, use the Insert menu or Insert panel to insert an accordion into the page.

4. In Code view, review the code that has been inserted for the accordion to see that it consists of three h3 elements for the headers on the accordion and three div elements for the content beneath those headers. Also, check the head element to see that the link and script elements for the accordion have been added there, and check the end of the file to see another script element.

5. In Design view, select the heading content for the first manager below the accordion, cut it, select the heading for the first accordion panel, and paste the content into it. Then, select the paragraph content for the first manager, cut it, select the content for the first accordion panel, and paste the content into it. Now, test what you have so far in Live view, and note the size of the content panel.

6. Select the accordion either by clicking on its tag in Design view or by clicking in it and selecting div#Accordion1 in the Tag selector. Then, in the Property Inspector, change the Height Style to content. Also, in the Panels menu, select Section 2 so that panel will be displayed in Design view.

7. In Design view, select the heading content for the second manager below the accordion, drag it into the heading for the second accordion panel, and delete the text that had been there. Then, select the paragraph content for the second manager, drag it into the second accordion panel, and delete the text that had been there. Now, test what you have so far in Live view, and note the size of the content panel.

8. Select the accordion again in Design view. Then, in the Property Inspector, click the Add Panel icon (+) for the Panels menu twice to add two more panels to the accordion. Then, move the headings and content for the last three managers into the accordion, delete any code that's left over from the original content, and use Live view to make sure that everything is working right.

9. Now, test this page in your web browser and note that one panel is always open. Also, note the icons on the headings for the accordion.

Change some of the settings for the accordion

10. In Design view, select the accordion, and use the Property Inspector to check the Collapsible box. Then, test to see that you can now close all of the panels.

11. Use the Header and Active Header menus in the Property Inspector to change the icons for those headers to the plus sign and the minus sign. Then, test that change.

12. Use the Animate menu in the Property Inspector to change the effect to easeInOutBounce (the last one in the list). Next, set the duration to 2000 milliseconds. Then, test that change to see that effects can be counterproductive in terms of usability.

17

How to use jQuery Mobile

In chapters 7 and 8, you learned how to use media queries and fluid layouts to create web pages with a responsive design that adapts to mobile devices with different screen sizes. In some cases though, it makes more sense to create a dedicated website for mobile devices. Then, you can use a jQuery library called jQuery Mobile to build websites that are optimized for use on these devices.

An introduction to jQuery Mobile

When you have a website for large-screen devices that consists of dozens or hundreds of pages, converting it to a responsive web design that works on screens of all sizes is difficult, time-consuming, and expensive. In that case, it often makes sense to build a separate website for mobile users, and to use jQuery Mobile to build that website.

How to redirect a user to a mobile website

One of the first questions that comes up when you build a separate mobile website is how to direct your users from the full-screen version to the mobile version. One way to do that is to provide links on the full version that link to the mobile version. But a better way is to automatically detect a mobile device when it accesses the full version of your site and redirect it to your mobile version.

To detect mobile devices and redirect them to the mobile versions of the sites, the full versions of the sites can use either client-side or server-side code. For instance, JavaScript or jQuery can be used to do that in the browser, and a scripting language like PHP can be used to do that on the web server.

Because there are so many different types of mobile devices and mobile browsers, it would be difficult to code and maintain a JavaScript application that redirects mobile browsers to the mobile version of a website. So when you need to do that, a good way to get started is to look for a plugin that does what you want.

One website that provides scripts for detecting browsers is the Detect Mobile Browsers site at the URL shown in figure 17-1. It provides scripts for clients and servers that detect mobile browsers and redirect them to the mobile versions of the sites. It provides these scripts in many different languages, including ASP. NET, JSP, PHP, and Python for servers as well as JavaScript and jQuery for browsers.

The procedure in this figure shows how to use the JavaScript version of this application. In brief, you download the JavaScript file, which has a txt extension. Then, you use your editor to modify the URL at the end of the file so it points to the home page in your mobile website, rename the file so it has a js instead of a txt extension, and deploy the file to your web server. From that point on, you code a script element that includes this file in any web page that you want redirected to the mobile site when a mobile browser is detected.

The Home pages for a full website and the mobile version of the site

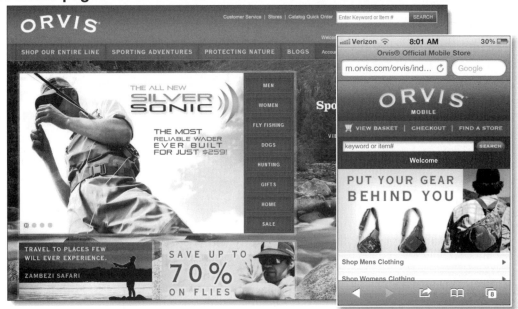

How to redirect a user to the mobile version of the site

- Use JavaScript or a server-side scripting language such as PHP to detect mobile devices and redirect them to the mobile version of the site.

The URL for a site that provides plugins for browser-detection

http://www.detectmobilebrowser.com

The script element for any page that uses the JavaScript plugin

```
<script src="detectmobilebrowser.js"></script>
```

How to use the JavaScript plugin for mobile browser detection

1. Go to the URL above. Then, click on the JavaScript button under the Download Scripts heading to download a file named detectmobilebrowser.js.txt.

2. Open the file in your text editor, and move the cursor to the end of the JavaScript code, which will include a URL. Then, change this URL to the path of the mobile site that you want the user redirected to.

3. Save your work, close the file, and rename the file so the .txt extension is removed. Then, deploy the file to your web server.

4. In any web page that you want to redirect to the mobile website, code a script element like the one above that refers to the file that you've just deployed.

Description

- The Detect Mobile Browsers website offers many server-side and client-side scripts that will redirect a mobile device from the full version of a site to the mobile version.

Figure 17-1   How to redirect a user to a mobile website

What jQuery Mobile is

As figure 17-2 summarizes, *jQuery Mobile* is a free, open-source, cross-platform, JavaScript library that you can use for developing mobile websites. This library lets you create pages that look and feel like the pages of a native mobile application. In addition, these pages are touch-optimized so they're easier to use on mobile devices.

Although jQuery Mobile is fairly new, the current version provides all of the features that you need for developing an excellent mobile website. Also, since jQuery Mobile's popularity is increasing rapidly, newer versions are in the works. At this writing, the current stable version is 1.4.2.

When you use jQuery Mobile, the CSS associated with jQuery Mobile automatically formats your web pages to look like a traditional, native iPhone application. Unlike native applications, though, you don't have to know the complex frameworks, tools, and coding languages required to create them. Instead, when you use Dreamweaver, you just need to know the jQuery Mobile attributes.

The jQuery Mobile website

The URL for jQuery Mobile

`http://jquerymobile.com`

Description

- *jQuery Mobile* is a free, open-source, JavaScript library that makes it much easier to develop websites for mobile devices. Like jQuery UI, jQuery Mobile is used in combination with the core jQuery library.

- jQuery Mobile lets you store multiple pages in a single HTML file; create dialog boxes, buttons, and navigation bars; format your pages without coding your own CSS; lay out pages within columns, collapsible content blocks, and accordions; and much more.

- jQuery Mobile is supported by most mobile operating systems including iOS, Android, BlackBerry, and Windows Phone.

- The jQuery Mobile website features all of the documentation and sample code that you need for working with jQuery Mobile.

Figure 17-2   What jQuery Mobile is

How Dreamweaver implements jQuery Mobile

When you add a jQuery Mobile component to a web page for the first time, Dreamweaver displays the jQuery Mobile Files dialog box shown in figure 17-3. This dialog box lets you determine whether the files that are required for jQuery Mobile are included in your website or retrieved from a Content Delivery Network. A *Content Delivery Network* (*CDN*) is a web server that hosts open-source software, and the jQuery website provides a CDN for getting the jQuery libraries.

To determine which technique is used, you select a Link Type option from the jQuery Mobile Files dialog box. Note that if you select the Remote (CDN) option, the jQuery CDN is used by default. Although you can change this CDN by entering different URLs, there's usually no reason to do that.

If you select the Local option, another text box labeled jQuery Library Source becomes available. Then, you can use the Browse button to the right of this text box to identify the directory that contains the required files. When you click OK and then save your page, these files will be stored in a folder named jquery-mobile in your site.

The CSS Type options in this dialog box let you choose whether you want to use the jQuery Mobile generic theme or a custom theme. If you choose the Combined option as shown here, the CSS for the generic theme is combined with the core jQuery Mobile CSS file. If you select the Split option, another text box labeled Theme becomes available where you can enter the URL for your custom theme. Then, the CSS for the custom theme is stored in a file that's separate from the jQuery Mobile CSS file.

Although we won't present it here, you should know that you can create a custom theme using the ThemeRoller application that's available on the jQuery Mobile website. This application lets you set custom properties for the jQuery Mobile elements as a whole, set the properties for swatches a, b, and c, and create new swatches. You'll learn more about swatches later in this chapter.

The first code example in this figure shows the link and script elements that are generated for you if you select the Remote (CDN) and Combined options. That includes a link element for the jQuery Mobile styles, a script element for the jQuery core library, and a script element for the jQuery Mobile library. Here, you can see that each element refers to a file on the CDN at http://code.jquery.com.

The second code example shows the link and script elements that are generated for you if you select the Local and Combined options. Here, each element refers to a file in the jquery-mobile folder of the website.

The last code example shows a meta element that you should add to the head element of any HTML document that uses jQuery Mobile. This element sets the width of the viewport to the width of the device to ensure that the entire width of the web page is displayed on the screen. For more information on the viewport, please see figure 7-4 in chapter 7.

The jQuery Mobile Files dialog box

```
jQuery Mobile Files                                                    [  x  ]

        Link Type:  ⦿ Remote (CDN)                          [    OK    ]
                    ○ Local                              [ Reset to defaults ]
                                                          [   Cancel   ]
        CSS Type:   ○ Split (Structure and Theme)          [    Help    ]
                    ⦿ Combined

jQuery Mobile Javascript:  http://code.jquery.com/mobile/1.3.0/jquery.mobile-1.3.0.min.js
     jQuery Mobile CSS:    http://code.jquery.com/mobile/1.3.0/jquery.mobile-1.3.0.min.css
            jQuery:        http://code.jquery.com/jquery-1.8.3.min.js


                           jQuery Mobile Updates
```

Code generated for the jQuery Mobile remote CDN library

```html
<!-- The jQuery Mobile styles -->
<link href="http://code.jquery.com/mobile/1.3.0/jquery.mobile-1.3.0.min.css"
rel="stylesheet">
<!-- The jQuery core library -->
<script src="http://code.jquery.com/jquery-1.8.3.min.js"></script>
<!-- The jQuery Mobile library -->
<script src="http://code.jquery.com/mobile/1.3.0/jquery.mobile-1.3.0.min.js">
</script>
```

Code generated for the jQuery Mobile local library

```html
<!-- The jQuery Mobile styles -->
<link href="jquery-mobile/jquery.mobile-1.3.0.min.css" rel="stylesheet">
<!-- The jQuery core library -->
<script src="jquery-mobile/jquery-1.8.3.min.js"></script>
<!-- The jQuery Mobile library -->
<script src="jquery-mobile/jquery.mobile-1.3.0.min.js"></script>
```

A meta element for a page that uses jQuery Mobile

```html
<meta name="viewport" content="width=device-width, initial-scale=1">
```

Description

- The first time you add a jQuery Mobile component to a web page, the jQuery Mobile Files dialog box is displayed.

- The Link Type option determines whether the jQuery Mobile files reside on a remote CDN or will be copied to your site. These files include a jQuery Mobile CSS file, the core jQuery library, and the jQuery Mobile library.

- The CSS Type option determines if the jQuery Mobile CSS structure and theme files are separated into two different files or combined into one file.

- The meta element shown above prevents the browser from scaling the page. To insert this element, choose Insert→Head→Viewport.

Figure 17-3   How Dreamweaver implements jQuery Mobile

How to create one web page with jQuery Mobile

To give you an idea of how jQuery Mobile works, figure 17-4 shows how to create one web page with it. When you insert a page into an HTML document, the Page dialog box in this figure is displayed. This dialog box lets you enter an ID for the page and select whether a header and a footer are included in the page.

If you include both a header and a footer, Dreamweaver generates the code shown in this figure. Here, you can see that the page is coded as a div element that contains three more div elements. The first one is for the header, the second one is for the main content of the page, and the third one is for the footer. Each of these div elements includes a data-role attribute that identifies the component it defines. In addition, the header is defined as an h1 element, and the footer is defined as an h4 element.

In the page that's displayed, you can see how jQuery Mobile automatically formats these components. Here, the text for both the header and footer is centered in white type against a black background, while the text for the content is black against a gray background. This is the default styling that's done by jQuery Mobile, and it's similar to the styling for a native iPhone application. Within the header, footer, and content components, you can code the HTML for whatever content you need. You'll see this illustrated in the examples that follow. However, this simple example should give you some idea of how easy it is to create a single web page.

The page dialog box and the jQuery Mobile page it creates

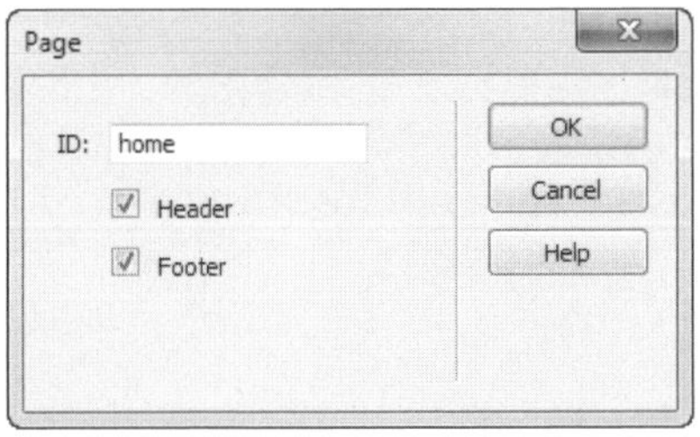

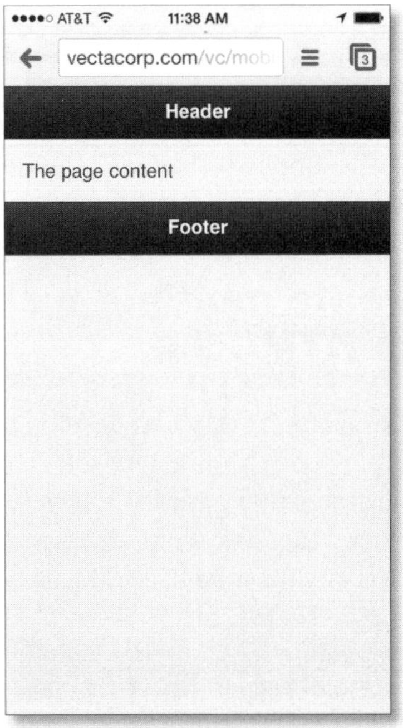

The HTML for the mobile web page

```
<div data-role="page" id="home">
    <div data-role="header">
        <h1>Header</h1>
    </div>
    <div data-role="content">The page content</div>
    <div data-role="footer">
        <h4>Footer</h4>
    </div>
</div>
```

Description

- To insert a jQuery Mobile page into an HTML document, choose Insert→jQuery Mobile→Page to display the Page dialog box. Then, enter an ID for the page and indicate whether you want to include a header or footer.

- Dreamweaver defines a mobile web page and each of its components (header, content, and footer) with a div element. The data-role attribute is used to identify the different components, and the style sheet for jQuery Mobile formats the web page based on the values in this attribute.

- In the header, the content is coded within an h1 element. In the footer, the content is coded within an h4 element. You can change this content, but not the element.

- In the div with "content" as its data-role attribute, you can code whatever elements you need.

- You can also add a mobile web page or any other jQuery Mobile object using the jQuery Mobile category of the Insert panel.

Figure 17-4   How to create one web page with jQuery Mobile

How to use jQuery Mobile to create a mobile website

In the four topics that follow, you'll learn the basic techniques for creating the pages of a mobile website. That will include the use of dialog boxes, buttons, and navigation bars.

How to create multiple web pages in a single HTML file

In contrast to the way you develop the web pages for a website that targets the desktop, jQuery Mobile lets you create multiple pages in a single HTML file. This is illustrated by figure 17-5. Here, you can see two pages of a site. When the user clicks on a link within the first page, the second page is opened just as it would be on any other website. What's surprising is that both pages are created within a single HTML file.

The procedure in this figure summarizes the process for creating multiple pages in a single HTML file. To do that, you insert the pages one after the other, making sure that you enter a unique ID for each page. As you insert each page, you need to be sure that the cursor is positioned after the closing div tag for the previous page. One way to do that is to click on the boundary of the page in Design view to select the page and then press the Right-arrow key to move past the end of the page. Another way is to position the cursor in Code view.

To link between the pages in the HTML file, you use placeholders as shown in figure 4-14 of chapter 4. For instance, the first <a> element in the first page in this example goes to "#vprospect" when the user taps on the link. This refers to the div element with "vprospect" as its id attribute, which means that tapping the link takes the user to the second page in the file.

Although this example shows only two pages, you can code many pages within a single HTML file. Remember, though, that all of the pages along with their images, JavaScript, and CSS files are loaded with the single HTML file. As a result, the load time will become excessive if you store too many pages in a single file. When that happens, you can divide your pages into more than one HTML file.

Two web pages that use jQuery Mobile

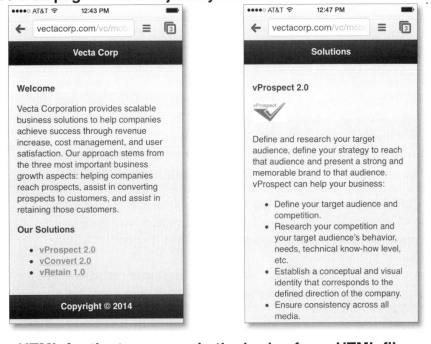

The HTML for the two pages in the body of one HTML file

```
<div data-role="page" id="home">
    <div data-role="header">...</div>
    <div data-role="content">
        ...
        <li><a href="#vprospect">vProspect 2.0</a></li>
        ...
    </div>
    <div data-role="footer">...</div>
</div>
<div data-role="page" id="vprospect">
    ...
</div>
```

How to create a multi-page layout

1. Create a single web page as described in figure 17-4. Be sure to assign an ID that uniquely identifies the page. This ID will act as a placeholder.

2. Position the cursor after the div for the first page and then add another page. Here again, be sure to assign an ID that uniquely identifies the page.

3. Repeat step 2 for any additional pages you want to include.

4. To link to one page from another, add a hyperlink that points to the placeholder for that page.

Description

*   When you use jQuery Mobile, you don't have to create a separate HTML file for each page. Instead, you can add as many pages as you need within a single file.

*   To link between pages in an HTML file, you use placeholders.

Figure 17-5   How to create multiple web pages in a single HTML file

How to use dialog boxes and transitions

When you display a mobile web page, you can display it as a standard web page or as a *dialog box*. Figure 17-6 illustrates the difference between these two types of pages. As you can see, the jQuery Mobile CSS file formats a dialog box differently than a normal web page. By default, a dialog box will have a dark background with white foreground text, and the header and footer won't span the width of the page. A dialog box will also have an "X" in the header that the user must tap to close the dialog box and return to the previous page.

To display a page as a dialog box, you code a data-rel attribute with a value of "dialog" in the <a> element that goes to that page. This is illustrated in the first code example in this figure. Note that you must enter this attribute directly into Code view, since Dreamweaver doesn't provide a visual interface for generating it. When you enter an attribute like this, though, you'll see that Dreamweaver provides code hints that can help you select the correct attribute and set its value.

When you code an <a> element that goes to another page or dialog box, you can also use the data-transition attribute to specify one of the nine *transitions* that are summarized in this figure. Each of these transitions is meant to mimic an effect that a mobile device like an iPhone uses. Like the data-rel attribute, the data-transition attribute must be entered directly into Code view.

A mobile page shown as a web page and as a dialog box

The web page

The dialog box

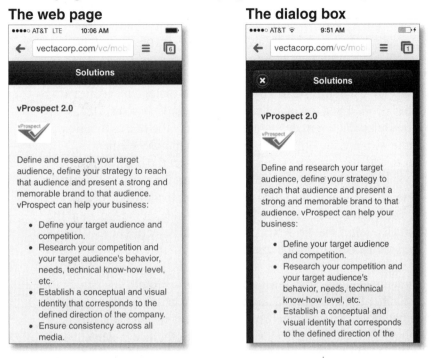

The transitions that can be used

pop	flow	slidefade
flip	fade	slideup
turn	slide	slidedown

HTML that opens the page as a dialog box with the "pop" transition

```
<a href="#vprospect" data-rel="dialog" data-transition="pop">
vProspect 2.0</a>
```

HTML that opens the page with the "fade" transition

```
<a href="#vprospect" data-transition="fade">vProspect 2.0</a>
```

Description

- You create a *dialog box* the same way you create any page. However, the <a> element that links to the page includes the data-rel attribute with "dialog" as its value. To close the dialog box, the user taps the X in the header of the box.

- To specify the way a page or a dialog box is opened, you can use the data-transition attribute with one of the values shown above. If a device doesn't support the *transition* that you specify, the attribute is ignored.

- You must enter the data-rel and data-transition attributes directly in Code view.

Figure 17-6   How to use dialog boxes and transitions

How to create buttons

When you develop a jQuery Mobile website, you can use buttons to navigate from one page to another. Figure 17-7 shows some of the types of buttons you can create.

To add buttons to a mobile web page in Dreamweaver, you can use the Button dialog box shown in this figure. By default, this dialog box creates a single button that's coded as a link and that doesn't include an icon. This is illustrated by the Delete button in this figure. To identify the link as a button, a data-role attribute with a value of "button" is added to the <a> element.

If you want to add an icon to a button, you can select the one you want to use from the Icon menu. Then, you can select a position for the icon from the Icon Position menu. By default, the icon is displayed at the left side of the button as shown here, but it can also be displayed at the right side, at the top, or at the bottom. You can also select the No Text option from this menu. Then, only the icon is displayed on the button. That's true even if text is specified for the <a> element.

If you want to create more than one button at the same time, you can do that by selecting a number from the Buttons menu. When you do, the Position menu becomes available. If you select Inline from this menu, a div element is generated with the number of <a> elements you specified. Both the div element and the <a> elements include a data-inline attribute with a value of "true". Then, the buttons will appear side by side as illustrated by the Cancel and OK buttons.

You can also create a group of buttons by selecting Group from the Position menu. Then, the <a> elements for the buttons are coded within a div element whose data-role attribute is set to "controlgroup". When you create a group of buttons, you can also select one of the Layout options. For the Yes, No, and Maybe buttons shown here, the Horizontal option was selected. Because of that, a data-type attribute with a value of "horizontal" was included on the div element.

Notice that two of the buttons in this group include icons. Unfortunately, even if you create more than one button from the Button dialog box, you can select only one icon and that icon is included on each button. Because of that, you probably won't select an icon when you add two or more buttons at the same time. Instead, you can set the data-icon attribute for each button in code. Or, you can use the jQuery Mobile Swatches panel to select an icon. You'll see this panel in figure 17-10.

The code for the last <a> element shown in this figure is for a Back button, which causes the previous page to be displayed. To create a button like this, you add a button with the Back icon. Then, you add a data-rel attribute to the button in Code view and set its value to "back".

The last two buttons on the web page in this example show how buttons appear in the footer for a page. Here, the icons and text are white against a black background.

In addition to using <a> elements to create buttons, you can use button and input elements like the ones you use with forms. To do that, you can select the Button or Input option from the Button Type menu. If you select the Input

The Button dialog box and a mobile web page with buttons

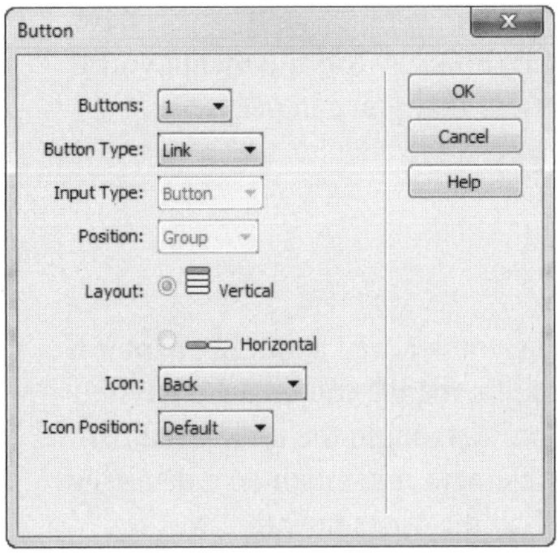

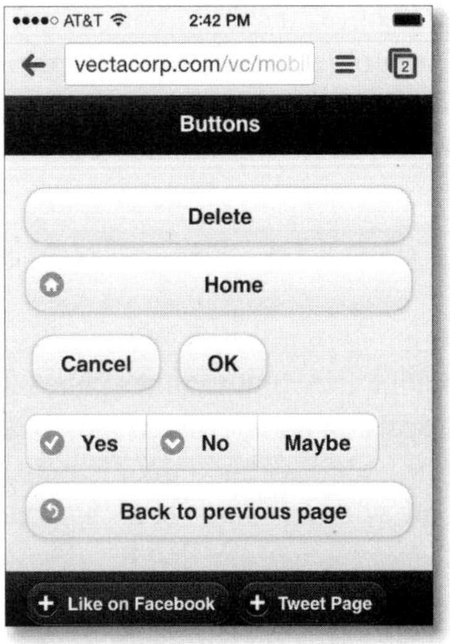

The HTML for the buttons

```
<!-- For a single button with no icon, use the defaults -->
<a href="#" data-role="button">Delete</a>
<!-- To add an icon to a button, select it from the Icon menu -->
<a href="#" data-role="button" data-icon="home">Home</a>
<!-- For inline buttons, set Position to Inline -->
<div data-inline="true">
    <a href="#" data-role="button" data-inline="true">Cancel</a>
    <a href="#" data-role="button" data-inline="true">OK</a>
</div>
<!-- To group buttons, set Position to Group and select a Layout option -->
<div data-role="controlgroup" data-type="horizontal">
    <a href="#" data-role="button" data-icon="check">Yes</a>
    <a href="#" data-role="button" data-icon="arrow-d">No</a>
    <a href="#" data-role="button">Maybe</a>
</div>
<!-- To code a Back button, set the data-rel attribute to back -->
<a href="#" data-role="button" data-icon="back" data-rel="back">
Back to previous page</a>
```

Description

- To add a button to a mobile web page, choose Insert→jQuery Mobile→Button to display the Button dialog box. Then, choose the number of buttons you want to add and the button type, and set any other options.

- If you add two or more buttons at the same time, you can group them vertically or horizontally, or you can display them inline as separate buttons.

- You can choose only one icon even if you add more than one button. Because of that, you may want to set the data-icon attribute in code. An alternative is to use the jQuery Mobile Swatches panel as shown in figure 17-10.

- To create a back button, you must set the data-rel attribute to "back".

Figure 17-7   How to create buttons

option, you can also select an option from the Input Type menu to create a generic button, a submit button, a reset button, or an image button. If you review the list of objects that are available from the Insert→jQuery Mobile menu, you'll see that jQuery mobile provides many other controls that you can use with forms. For more information on these controls, please see chapter 14.

How to create a navigation bar

A *navigation bar* is like the navigation menus you learned about in chapter 6 that let the user link to other pages. Like a navigation menu, you create a navigation bar using an unordered list. With jQuery Mobile, though, the unordered list must be coded within a div element, and the div element must include a data-role attribute with its value set to "navbar". Figure 17-8 illustrates how this works.

Here, you can see that the div element for the navigation bar is coded within the header for the page. You can create this element and the unordered list it contains using standard techniques. For example, the easiest way to create the unordered list is to add the <a> elements and then use the Property Inspector to convert them to a list.

After you create the list, you can use Code view to set the data-role attribute of the div element. Then, if you want to include an icon on each item, you can add a data-icon attribute to the <a> elements. In addition, you'll typically want to assign the "ui-btn-active" class to the active item. That makes the color of the item lighter than the color of the other items in the navigation bar.

Note that, even though the <a> elements in this example don't include a data-role attribute, these elements are treated as buttons. That's because these elements are coded within a div element whose data-role attribute is set to "navbar". In addition to causing the <a> elements to be formatted as buttons, this attribute causes the icons to be displayed above the text on the buttons by default. If you want to change this default formatting, you can use the jQuery Mobile Swatches panel as described later in this chapter.

A mobile web page with a navigation bar

The HTML for the navigation bar

```
<div data-role="header">
    <h1>Vecta Corp</h1>
    <div data-role="navbar">
        <ul>
            <li><a href="#home" class="ui-btn-active"
                    data-icon="home">Home</a></li>
            <li><a href="#solutions"
                    data-icon="grid">Solutions</a></li>
            <li><a href="#contactus"
                    data-icon="info">Contact Us</a></li>
        </ul>
    </div>
</div>
```

Description

- A *navigation bar* consists of an unordered list, where each item includes a link to another page. The unordered list must be coded within a div element in the page's header, and the data-role attribute of the div must be set to "navbar".
- To include an icon above the text for each link, set the data-icon attribute to the icon of your choosing.
- To display the active item in a color that's lighter than the other items in the navigation bar, set its class attribute to "ui-btn-active".

Figure 17-8   How to create a navigation bar

How to format content with jQuery Mobile

As you've already seen, jQuery Mobile automatically formats the components of a web page based on its own style sheet. Now, you'll learn more about that, as well as how to adjust the default styling that jQuery Mobile uses.

The default styles that jQuery Mobile uses

Figure 17-9 shows the default styles that jQuery Mobile uses for common HTML elements. For all of its styles, jQuery Mobile relies on the browser's rendering engine so its own styling is minimal. This keeps load times fast and minimizes the overhead that excessive CSS would impose on a page.

In general, jQuery Mobile's styling is so effective that you shouldn't need to modify its styling by providing your own CSS style sheet. For instance, the spacing between the items in the unordered list and the formatting of the table are both acceptable the way they are. Also, the black type on the gray background is consistent with the formatting for native mobile applications.

The default styles for common HTML elements

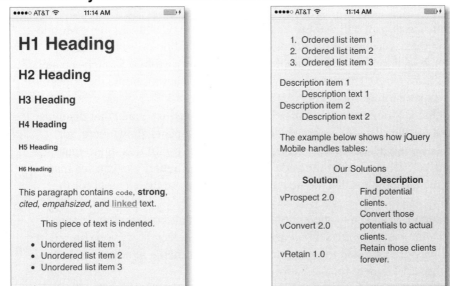

Description

- By default, jQuery Mobile automatically applies styles to the HTML elements for a page. These styles are not only attractive, but also mimic a browser's native styles.

- By default, jQuery Mobile applies a small amount of padding to the left, right, top, and bottom of each mobile page.

- By default, links are slightly larger than normal text. This makes it easier for the user to tap the links.

- By default, links are underlined with blue as the font color.

Figure 17-9   The default styles that jQuery Mobile uses

How to use swatches to apply themes

In some cases, you will want to change the default styles that jQuery Mobile uses. To do that, you can use the *themes* that jQuery Mobile provides. These themes—a, b, c, d, and e—are available from the jQuery Mobile Swatches panel shown in figure 17-10. Here again, these themes are meant to mimic the appearance of a native mobile application.

The jQuery Mobile Swatches panel is a context-sensitive panel that displays the options for the currently selected element. The first panel shown here, for example, is for the header in the second example at the top of this figure that uses theme "e". If you look at the code example in this figure, you can see that a data-theme attribute for this theme has been added to the div element for the header.

The second panel shows the options that are available for a button. In this case, the Home button in the second navigation bar is selected. As you can see, theme "d" has been applied to this button and the data-theme attribute has been added to the <a> element for the button.

In addition to specifying the theme for a button, the jQuery Mobile Swatches panel lets you choose the icon that's displayed on the button and the position of the icon. This makes it easier to format buttons, as well as other elements, using a visual interface.

By the way, you should notice the Refresh icon in the lower right corner of this panel. Although this panel should be updated automatically when you select a different element, it may not always do that right away. In that case, you can click this icon to refresh the panel.

Two headers and navigation bars that illustrate the use of themes

Header "a", bar "b"

Header "e", bar "d"

The jQuery Mobile Swatches panel for a header and a button

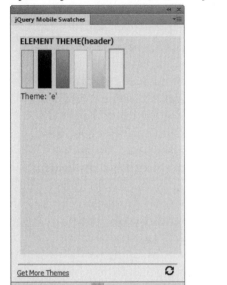

The HTML for the second header and navigation bar

```
<div data-role="header" data-theme="e">
    <h1>Vecta Corp</h1>
    <div data-role="navbar">
        <ul>
            <li><a href="#home" class="ui-btn-active" data-icon="home"
                data-theme="d">Home</a></li>
            <li><a href="#solutions" data-icon="grid"
                data-theme="d">Solutions</a></li>
            <li><a href="#contactus" data-icon="info"
                data-theme="d">Contact Us</a></li>
        </ul>
    </div>
</div>
```

Description

- You can use the jQuery Mobile Swatches panel (Window→jQuery Mobile Swatches) to apply *themes* to elements, add icons to buttons, set the position of icons within buttons, and more.

- By using the five themes that are included with jQuery Mobile, you can make appropriate adjustments to the default styles for the HTML elements.

Figure 17-10   How to use jQuery Mobile Swatches to apply themes

How to use jQuery Mobile for page layout

In the next four topics of this chapter, you'll learn how to use jQuery Mobile to create special page layouts.

How to lay out your content in two columns

Figure 17-11 shows how you can lay out the content for a page in two columns. This can be useful for a photo gallery or product list because it can reduce the amount of scrolling that's needed to see all of the items.

To create a two-column layout, you use the Layout Grid dialog box with the settings shown here. In this case, each column will consist of a single row. Then, Dreamweaver generates code that consists of a div element for the grid and a div element for each column. As you can see in the code example in this figure, the class "ui-grid-a" is assigned to the div for the grid, and the classes "ui-block-a" and "ui-block-b" are assigned to the two columns. Then, you can add any content you want for the columns.

In this example, the content for each testimonial consists of a single paragraph. Also, all of the testimonials for the first column are coded in the first block, and all of the testimonials for the second column are coded in the second block. However, you could also format this content as a series of "a" and "b" blocks where each block contained a single testimonial. To do that, you would increase the number of rows in the Layout Grid dialog box. If you set the number of rows to 2, for example, Dreamweaver would generate two sets of blocks. Then, you could place the content for the first column of the first row in the first "a" block. You could place the content for the second column of the first row in the first "b" block. You could place the content for the first column of the second row in the second "a" block. And you could place the content for the second column of the second row in the second "b" block.

Before I go on, you should notice that, unlike some of the web pages you've seen in this chapter, the footer for this page is displayed at the bottom of the page even though the content doesn't fill the page. To do that, a data-position attribute with a value of "fixed" has been added to the div element for the footer. This is a common layout technique that's used with mobile web pages.

The Layout Grid dialog box and a web page with two columns

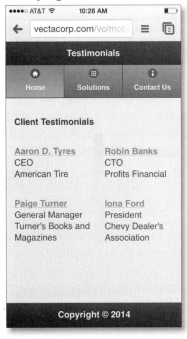

The HTML for the two columns

```
<div class="ui-grid-a">
    <div class="ui-block-a">
        <!-- The content for column one goes here -->
    </div>
    <div class="ui-block-b">
        <!-- The content for column two goes here -->
    </div>
</div>
```

Description

- To create a two-column layout, you display the Layout Grid dialog box (Insert→jQuery Mobile→Layout Grid) and then select 1 from the Rows menu and 2 from the Columns menu.

- The ui-block-a and ui-block-b classes are formatted by jQuery Mobile so they float left. As a result, the div elements are displayed in two columns.

- Although you can lay out content in more than two columns, you're not likely to do that. However, you might include more than one row in each column.

Note

- You can display the footer at the bottom of the page as shown above by coding the data-position attribute with a value of "fixed" on the div element for the footer.

Figure 17-11   How to lay out your content in two columns

How to create an accordion

Figure 17-12 shows how you can display content in an *accordion*. Like the Accordion widget that's provided by jQuery UI, a jQuery Mobile accordion includes two or more blocks that contain a heading and the content for that heading. By default, all of the blocks are collapsed so only the headings are visible. Then, the user can click on a heading to display its content. Note that if the content for one heading is already displayed when the user clicks on another heading, the content for the first heading is hidden. In other words, only one block can be expanded at a time.

To create an accordion in Dreamweaver, you choose Insert→jQuery Mobile→Collapsible Block. Then, an accordion with three blocks is generated. The code for this accordion starts with a div element with its data-role attribute set to "collapsible-set". Then, each block within the accordion is defined by a div element with its data-role attribute set to "collapsible". These div elements include an h3 element for the heading and a <p> element for the content.

In addition to the data-role attribute, the div element for each block except the first one includes a data-collapsed attribute with the value "true". This indicates that the block will be collapsed. This attribute isn't required for the first block because it's collapsed by default. If you want one of the blocks to be displayed by default, though, you can set this attribute to "false".

A mobile web page with an accordion

With all blocks collapsed   ### With the third block expanded

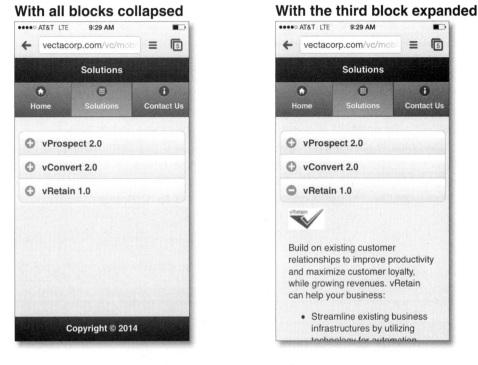

The HTML for the accordion

```html
<div data-role="collapsible-set">
    <div data-role="collapsible">
        <h3>vProspect 2.0</h3>
        <p>Define and research your target audience, define your ...</p>
    </div>
    <div data-role="collapsible" data-collapsed="true">
        <h3>vConvert 2.0</h3>
        <p>Create a highly user-friendly and easy-to-navigate ...</p>
    </div>
    <div data-role="collapsible" data-collapsed="true">
        <h3>vRetain 1.0</h3>
        <p>Build on existing customer relationships to improve ...</p>
    </div>
</div>
```

Description

- To add an *accordion*, choose Insert→jQuery Mobile→Collapsible Block to create an accordion that consists of three blocks. Then, add the heading and content for each block in the areas provided.

- Only one block in an accordion can be expanded at once. If you want a block to be expanded when the page loads, set its data-collapsed attribute to "false".

Figure 17-12   How to create an accordion

How to create collapsible content blocks

Figure 17-13 shows how you can display content in *collapsible content blocks*. Collapsible content blocks work like an accordion, except that more than one block can be expanded at the same time. That's because collapsible content blocks work independently of each other rather than as a group like the blocks in an accordion.

To create collapsible content blocks, you start by creating an accordion. Then, you delete the outer div element that groups the blocks as shown here. When you do, each block appears separately on the page. If you compare the headings shown in this figure with the headings shown in the accordion in the previous figure, for example, you'll see that there's space between the collapsible content blocks but there's no space between the blocks of an accordion.

A mobile web page with collapsible content blocks

With all blocks collapsed

With the third block expanded

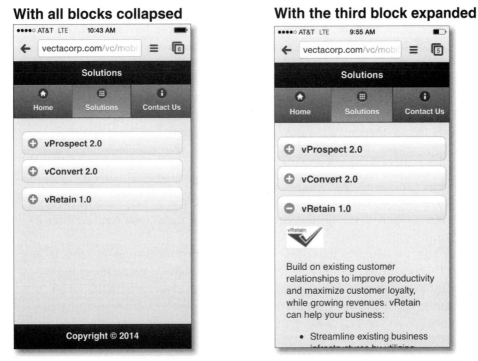

The HTML for the collapsible content blocks

```
<div data-role="collapsible">
    <h3>vProspect 2.0</h3>
    <p>Define and research your target audience, define your ... </p>
</div>
<div data-role="collapsible" data-collapsed="true">
    <h3>vConvert 2.0</h3>
    <p>Create a highly user-friendly and easy-to-navigate ... </p>
</div>
<div data-role="collapsible" data-collapsed="true">
    <h3>vRetain 1.0</h3>
    <p>Build on existing customer relationships to improve ... </p>
</div>
```

Description

- To add *collapsible content blocks*, choose Insert→jQuery Mobile→Collapsible Block to create an accordion with three blocks like the one shown in figure 17-12. Then, switch to Code view and remove the div element with the data-role attribute that's set to "collapsible-set".

- In contrast to an accordion, more than one content block can be expanded at the same time.

Figure 17-13   How to create collapsible content blocks

How to create a contents list

Figure 17-14 shows how to create a *contents list* that can be used to link to other pages. In this example, the user can click anywhere on a list item to go to a page that gives more information about the solution.

To create a contents list, you use the List View dialog box. The List Type menu in this dialog box lets you choose whether an unordered or ordered list is used. In most cases, you'll use an unordered list. If you choose to use an ordered list, though, the numbers may require special formatting to line them up the way you want. Regardless of the type of list you use, a data-role attribute with a value of "listview" is added to the ul or ol element.

To determine how many items are included in the list initially, you select a value from the Items menu. The default value is 3, but you can create a list with up to ten items. Then, if you need to include additional items, you can add them in Code view.

By default, each item in the list includes just the text for the <a> element it contains. If you want to include additional content, though, you can select the Text Description option as shown here. Then, each <a> element includes an h3 element and a <p> element by default.

Another option you may want to use is Inset. This option causes the list to appear inset from the edges of the screen. You'll see an example of this in the next figure.

If the items in a list represent categories, you may want to use the Text Bubble option. This option causes a text bubble to be displayed at the right side of each list item. Then, you can set the number for each bubble so it represents the number of items in the category.

The Aside option lets you float some of the content of the list items to the right of the other content. For example, this would be an easy way to display an image at the left side of the list items and text at the right side.

The last option, Split Button, determines whether a line is included between the content of the list items and the icon at the right side of the list items. You typically choose this option if you want one page to be displayed when the user clicks on the content of the list item and another page to be displayed when the user clicks the icon. To accommodate that, a second <a> element is included within each list item. If you select the Split Button option, you'll typically choose a different icon from the Split Button Icon menu as well. Then, a data-split-icon attribute is added to the ul or ol element.

The List View dialog box and a mobile web page with a contents list

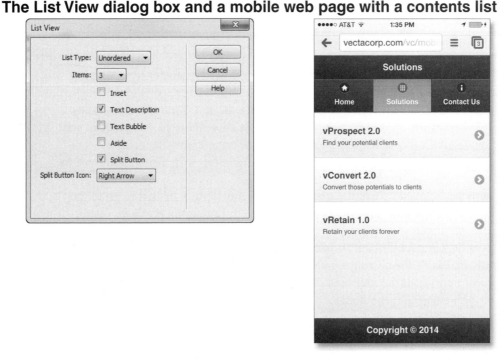

The HTML for a contents list

```html
<ul data-role="listview">
    <li><a href="#vprospect"><h3>vProspect 2.0</h3>
        <p>Find your potential clients</p></a>
    </li>
    <li><a href="#vconvert"><h3>vConvert 2.0</h3>
        <p>Convert those potentials to clients</p></a>
    </li>
    <li><a href="#vretain"><h3>vRetain 1.0</h3>
        <p>Retain your clients forever</p></a>
    </li>
</ul>
```

Description

- A *contents list* is a list that links to other pages when the user clicks an item. It typically includes a heading, text, and an action icon.
- To create a contents list, choose Insert→jQuery Mobile→List View to display the List View dialog box. Then, select the type of list you want to use and the number of items you want to include in the list, and set any other options.
- If you want the list to appear inset, choose the Inset option. If you want to include content other than just the text for each link, choose the Text Description option. And if you want to link to a different page when the user clicks the icon, choose the Split Button option. You can also choose a different icon from the Split Button Icon menu if you choose the Split Button option.

Figure 17-14   How to create a contents list

A mobile website
that uses jQuery Mobile

To show how the features you've just learned work together in a complete website, figure 17-15 presents four pages of the Vecta Corp website that uses jQuery Mobile. That includes the Home, Solutions, and Contact Us pages, as well as one of the individual solution pages. On all of these pages, you can see the navigation bar that lets the user go from one page to another.

On the Home page, you can see some introductory text. This is followed by an accordion that provides client testimonials.

On the Solutions page, the user can tap on any item in the list to go to the page for that solution. This list is like the one you saw in the previous figure, except that it is inset.

On the Contact Us page, you can see an address, a phone number, and an email address. If the user taps on the phone number, the user's device will try to call that number. If the user taps on the email address, the user's device will try to start an email to that address.

The page layouts for a mobile website that uses jQuery Mobile

The Home page   ### The Solutions page

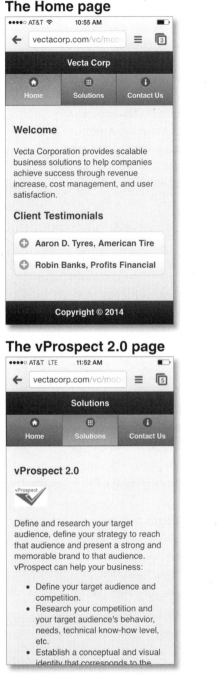

The vProspect 2.0 page   ### The Contact Us page

Description

- When the user taps a solution on the Solutions page, a page for that solution is opened.
- When the user taps the phone number on the Contact Us page, the device's phone feature will try to call the number. If the user taps the email address on this page, the user's device will try to start an email to the address.

Figure 17-15   A mobile website that uses jQuery Mobile

Perspective

The use of mobile devices has increased dramatically over the past few years. Because of that, it has become increasingly important to design websites that are easy to use from these devices. Although that sometimes means developing a separate website as shown in this chapter, this can be a critical aspect of maintaining your presence on the Internet.

Fortunately, the task of building a touch-optimized mobile website has become much easier with the advent of jQuery Mobile. No longer are mobile web pages limited to static pages that contain headings, paragraphs, links, and thumbnail images. With jQuery Mobile, web developers can now build feature-rich websites that look and feel like native mobile applications.

Terms

jQuery Mobile	theme
CDN (Content Delivery Network)	accordion
dialog box	collapsible content blocks
transition	contents list
navigation bar	

Summary

- *jQuery Mobile* is a JavaScript library that's designed for developing mobile websites. jQuery Mobile uses the core jQuery library along with its own CSS file.

- The first time you add a jQuery Mobile component to a web page, you can choose whether to retrieve the jQuery and jQuery Mobile files from a *CDN* or include them in your site.

- jQuery Mobile lets you code the HTML for many mobile pages in a single HTML file. jQuery Mobile also supports the use of dialog boxes, transitions, buttons, navigation bars, accordions, collapsible content blocks, and more.

- By default, jQuery Mobile provides formatting that relies on a browser's native rendering engine. jQuery Mobile also provides five *themes* that you can use to adjust the default formatting without using CSS style sheets of your own.

Exercise 17-1   Experiment with a mobile website

In this exercise, you'll first test a mobile version of the Vecta Corp website like the one that's presented in figure 17-15. Then, you'll make some modifications to it. You'll also add a new Solutions page that looks like this:

Open the mobile website and review its HTML

1. Open the Exercises site, and open the folder for this exercise. Note that this folder contains an images folder that contains three images and an index.html file.

2. Open the index.html file, switch to Live view, and click the Mobile size icon at the bottom of this view to show the first page in mobile size. Then, navigate through the pages by clicking on its various buttons and links. Note that the vProspect page opens as a dialog box, but the other two product pages open as regular pages.

3. Review the HTML for the index.html file to see that this single file contains the code for the five pages and one dialog box. For your convenience, each of these pages is preceded by an HTML comment that identifies the page.

Modify the way the pages work and test these changes

4. Modify the Solutions page so the vConvert and vRetain pages open as dialog boxes. Also, set the transitions for these links to slide and flip. (The transition for the vProspect link has already been set to pop.) Then, test this mobile site in Chrome, Firefox, or Safari to see how the transitions work.

5.   With figure 17-7 as a guide, add a button at the bottom of the Contact Us page that goes back to the page that called it. The icon for the button should be the Back icon, and the text should be "Return to Previous Page." Then, test this change with both the Home and the Solutions pages.

Add a new page to the site that replaces the Solutions page

6.   In Code view, put the insertion point after the div tag near the end of the index.html file. Then, use the jQuery Mobile category of the Insert panel to add a new page to the file. This page should have a header and a footer, and its id attribute should be "solutions2".

7.   Change the id for the earlier Solutions page from "solutions" to "old_solutions". Then, change the id for the new page from "solutions2" to "solutions". That way, all of the links to the old Solutions page will now go to the new one.

8.   In Design view, copy the navigation bar from the header in the old_solutions page and paste it into the header of the new page.

9.   In Design view, select the "contents" text for the new page, and choose Insert→jQuery Mobile→Collapsible Block to replace the contents with an accordion. Then, change the three accordion headings as shown in the example above. Now, test this change in Live view.

10.   In Design view, scroll to the vProspect page, copy its image and text, scroll back to the first collapsible block on the new Solutions page, select the "contents" text for this block, and paste the image and text. Then, test this change in Live view.

11.   Repeat step 10 for the next two blocks in the accordion. Then, test this in Live view and also in your browser.

12.   With figure 17-7 as a guide, add three link buttons to the footer of the page so they look like the ones in the example above, but don't bother setting the href attributes for them.

13.   When you're through experimenting, close the file.

Appendix A

How to set up your computer for this book

To build the websites presented in this book, you need to have the Creative Cloud and Dreamweaver CC installed on your system. In addition, to test these websites, you need to have one or more browsers installed. This appendix shows you how to install this software on both Windows and Mac OS X systems. It also shows you how to download and install the source code for this book.

As you read these descriptions, please remember that most websites are continually upgraded. As a result, some of the procedures in this appendix may have changed since this book was published. Nevertheless, these procedures should still be good guides to installing the software.

How to install the Creative Cloud and Dreamweaver CC

Before you can install Dreamweaver CC, you must have a Creative Cloud membership. In addition, you must have the Creative Cloud installed on your system. To make this process easier, the Creative Cloud is installed automatically when you purchase a membership to any Creative Cloud product, including Dreamweaver CC.

On a Windows system

Figure A-1 shows how to download and install the Creative Cloud and Dreamweaver CC on a Windows system.

On a Mac OS X system

Figure A-1 also shows how to download and install the Creative Cloud and Dreamweaver CC on a Mac OS X system.

The website address for downloading the Creative Cloud

`https://creative.adobe.com/plans?tt=v10`

How to install the Creative Cloud and Dreamweaver CC on a Windows system

1. Go to the website address above.

2. Click the Join button for the Single App membership on the Individuals tab or, if you're affiliated with an institution, the Complete membership on the Students and Teachers tab.

3. Select Dreamweaver from the page that's displayed, and then click the Join button.

4. Follow the instructions to create an Adobe ID.

5. Review the membership details and provide your payment information. If you're purchasing a membership as a student or teacher, you'll also need to enter information about your academic status.

6. Confirm your purchase, and the Creative Cloud setup file will begin to download to your computer. If you're asked if you want to run or save the Creative Cloud setup file, click Save.

7. When the download finishes, use Windows Explorer to find the exe file, and double-click on it to start it. Log in with your Adobe ID when prompted, and the Creative Cloud and Dreamweaver CC will be installed.

How to install the Creative Cloud and Dreamweaver CC on a Mac OS X system

1. Complete steps 1 through 6 above to purchase a membership and download the Creative Cloud setup file.

2. When the Download finishes, double-click on the dmg file in the Downloads folder to display the Creative Cloud Installer window.

3. Double-click the Creative Cloud Installer folder to start the installation. Login in with your Adobe ID when prompted, and the Creative Cloud desktop application and Dreamweaver CC will be installed.

Description

- The Creative Cloud and Dreamweaver CC run on Windows and Mac OS X systems.

- You can also get a free 30-day trial of Dreamweaver CC at this website: https://creative.adobe.com/products/download/creative-cloud?version=2.0

Figure A-1   How to install the Creative Cloud and Dreamweaver CC

How to install Chrome

When you develop web pages and websites, you need to test them on all of the browsers that the users of the application are likely to use. For a commercial application, that usually includes Chrome, Internet Explorer, Firefox, Safari, and Opera. Then, if an application doesn't work on one of those browsers, you need to fix it.

As you do most of the exercises for this book, though, you can test your web pages on just two browsers. Windows users should use Internet Explorer plus Chrome, and Mac OS X users should use Safari and Chrome. Then, because Chrome and Safari support most of the HTML5 features, you'll be able to see how those features work. In the rare case that a feature isn't supported, you can install other browsers such as Opera. For example, Opera is currently the only browser that fully supports the date and time controls.

In figure A-2, you can see the procedure for downloading and installing Chrome. As you respond to the dialog boxes for the installer, we recommend that you make Chrome your default browser. Then, if you want to install Firefox, Safari, and Opera, you can use similar procedures.

The website address for downloading Chrome

`https://www.google.com/intl/en-US/chrome/browser/`

How to install Chrome

1. Go to the website address above.
2. Click on the Download Chrome button.
3. Review the Google Chrome Terms of Service that are displayed. Then, indicate if you want Chrome to be your default browser and if you want to automatically send usage statistics and crash reports to Google.
4. Click the Accept and Install button.
5. If a dialog box is displayed with a security warning, click the Run button.
6. If you're asked if you want to allow the program to make changes to your computer, click the Yes button.
7. The installer is downloaded and Chrome is installed and started.
8. When the Welcome to Chrome dialog box is displayed asking you to set the default browser, click the Next button and then select a browser.
9. When the Set up Chrome tab is displayed, you can log in using your email address and password so your bookmarks, history, and settings are updated on all the devices where you use Chrome. Or, you can click the "Skip for now" link to skip this step.
10. A tab is displayed with the Google home page.

Other popular browsers

*   Firefox
*   Safari
*   Opera

Description

*   Chrome and Microsoft's Internet Explorer are the most popular browsers today. That's why we suggest that you test all of the exercises that you do for this book on both of those browsers.
*   Because Firefox, Safari, and Opera are also popular browsers, you'll want to install them so you can see what level of support they provide for HTML5.
*   If you have a Windows system, Internet Explorer will already be on it, but you will have to install Chrome.
*   If you have a Mac, Safari will already be on it, and you won't be able to install Internet Explorer because it doesn't run on Macs.
*   To install Firefox, Safari, and Opera, you can use procedures that are similar to the one for Chrome. However, you may need to save the exe file for the installation to your computer and then run it to install the browser.

Figure A-2   How to install Chrome

How to install and use the source code for this book

The next two figures show how to install and use the source code for this book. One figure is for Windows users, the other for Mac OS X users.

On a Windows system

Figure A-3 shows how to install the source code for this book on a Windows system. This includes the source code for the applications and significant examples in this book, as well as the starting files and solutions for the exercises.

When you finish this procedure, the applications, exercises, and solutions will be in the three folders that are listed in this figure, but the exercises will also be in the second folder that's shown. Then, when you do the exercises, you use the subfolders and files in this folder:

        `c:\dreamweaver\exercises`

but you have backup copies of these subfolders and files in this folder:

        `c:\murach\dreamweaver\exercises`

That way, you can restore the files for an exercise by copying the files from the second folder to the first.

As you do the exercises, you may want to copy code from a book application or example into a file that you're working with. That's easy to do because the folders for the applications and examples are preceded by the figure numbers that present them. For instance, this folder

        `c:\murach\dreamweaver\book_apps\ch06\6-10`

contains the files for the web page in figure 6-10 in chapter 6. And this folder

        `c:\murach\dreamweaver\book_apps\ch16\16-04`

contains the files for the example that's in figure 16-4 in chapter 16.

If you want to experiment with the code in the book applications or examples, you may want to copy the folder first so the original files won't be changed. For instance, you can copy the book_apps folder from this folder

        `c:\murach\dreamweaver\`

to this folder

        `c:\dreamweaver\`

Then, you will have backup copies.

The Murach web site

`www.murach.com`

The default installation folder for the source code on a Windows system

`c:\murach\dreamweaver`

The Windows folders for the applications, exercises, and solutions

`c:\murach\dreamweaver\book_apps`
`c:\murach\dreamweaver\exercises`
`c:\murach\dreamweaver\solutions`

The Windows folder for doing the exercises

`c:\dreamweaver\exercises`

How to download and install the source code on a Windows system

1. Go to www.murach.com and find the page for *Murach's Dreamweaver CC 2014*.

2. Scroll down the page until you see the "FREE Downloads" tab and then click on it. Then, click the "All book files" link for the self-extracting zip file. This will download a setup file named drmw_allfiles.exe onto your hard drive.

3. Use Windows Explorer to find the exe file on your hard drive. Then, double-click this file. This installs the source code for the book applications, exercises, and solutions into the folders shown above. After it does this install, the exe file copies the exercises folder to c:\dreamweaver so you have two copies of the exercises.

How to restore an exercise file

- Copy it from its subfolder in
     `c:\murach\dreamweaver\exercises`
  to the corresponding subfolder in
     `c:\dreamweaver\exercises`

Description

- The exe file that you download stores the exercises in two different folders. That way, you can do the exercises using the files that are stored in one folder, but you have a backup copy in case you want to restore the starting files for an exercise.

- As you do the exercises, you may want to copy code from a file that's presented in the book into the file you're working on. That's easy to do because all of the websites and all of the significant examples in the book are available in the book_apps folder.

- In the book_apps folder, the prefixes on the folders refer to the number of the figure that presents the website or example.

Figure A-3   How to install the source code for this book on a Windows system

On a Mac OS X system

Figure A-3 shows how to install the source code for this book on a Mac OS X system. This includes the source code for the applications and significant examples in this book, as well as the starting files and solutions for the exercises.

When you finish this procedure, the applications, exercises, and solutions will be in the three folders that are listed in this figure, but the exercises will also be in the second folder that's shown. Then, when you do the exercises, you use the subfolders and files in this folder:

`documents\dreamweaver\exercises`

but you have backup copies of these subfolders and files in this folder:

`documents\murach\dreamweaver\exercises`

That way, you can restore the files for an exercise by copying the files from the second folder to the first.

As you do the exercises, you may want to copy code from a book application or example into a file that you're working with. That's easy to do because the folders for the applications and examples are preceded by the figure numbers that present them. For instance, this folder

`documents\murach\dreamweaver\book_apps\ch06\6-10`

contains the files for the web page in figure 6-10 in chapter 6. And this folder

`documents\murach\dreamweaver\book_apps\ch16\16-04`

contains the files for the example that's in figure 16-4 in chapter 16.

If you want to experiment with the code in the book applications or examples, you may want to copy the folder first so the original files won't be changed. For instance, you can copy the book_apps folder from this folder

`documents\murach\dreamweaver\`

to this folder

`documents\dreamweaver\`

Then, you will have backup copies.

The Murach web site

www.murach.com

The Mac OS X folders for the applications, exercises, and solutions

documents\murach\dreamweaver\book_apps
documents\murach\dreamweaver\exercises
documents\murach\dreamweaver\solutions

The Mac OS X folder for doing the exercises

documents\dreamweaver\exercises

How to download and install the source code on a Mac OS X system

1. Go to www.murach.com and find the page for *Murach's Dreamweaver CC 2014*.
2. Scroll down the page until you see the "FREE Downloads" tab and then click on it. Then, click the "All book files" link for the regular zip file. This will download a setup file named drmw_allfiles.zip onto your hard drive.
3. Move this file into the Documents folder of your home folder. Then, use Finder to go to your Documents folder.
4. Double-click the drmw_allfiles.zip file to extract the folders for the book applications, exercises, and solutions. This will create a folder named dreamweaver in your documents folder that will contain the book_apps, exercises, and solutions folders.
5. To create two copies of the exercises folder, copy this folder from
   documents\murach\dreamweaver
   to
   documents\dreamweaver

How to restore an exercise file

- Copy it from its subfolder in
  documents\murach\dreamweaver\exercises
  to the corresponding subfolder in
  documents\dreamweaver\exercises

Description

- This procedure stores the exercises in two different folders. That way, you can do the exercises using the files that are stored in one folder, but you have a backup copy in case you want to restore the starting files for an exercise.
- As you do the exercises, you may want to copy code from a file that's presented in the book into the file you're working on. That's easy to do because all of the websites and all of the significant examples in the book are available in the book_apps folder.
- In the book_apps folder, the prefixes on the folders refer to the number of the figure that presents the website or example.

Figure A-4   How to install the source code for this book on a Mac OS X system

Index

E

Easings, 542, 543
Edge Animate, 338, 339
Editable optional region (template), 292, 293
Editable region (template), 284, 285
Editable tag attribute (template), 296, 297
Effect, 524, 525
Effects, *see jQuery UI effects*
Effects behaviors, 495
Element
  article, 57
  aside, 57
  audio, 326
  body, 46, 47, 50, 51
  br, 82
  canvas, 340, 341
  caption, 348, 349
  div, 54, 55, 56, 57
  fieldset, 455
  figure, 57
  footer, 57
  head, 46, 47, 50, 51
  header, 57
  input, 441, 443, 445, 447, 451, 457, 566
  label, 440, 441, 445, 447, 449, 451, 457
  legend, 455
  link, 58, 59, 98, 99, 526, 527, 546, 547, 558, 559
  main, 56, 57
  meta, 50, 51, 234, 235, 558, 559
  nav, 57
  option, 449
  script, 526, 527, 546, 547, 558, 559
  section, 56, 57
  select, 449
  span, 54, 55
  style, 58, 59
  table, 348, 349
  td, 348, 349
  th, 348, 349
  title, 50, 51
  tr, 348, 349
  video, 328
Element Live Display, 24, 25, 96, 97
Element Quick View, 392, 393
Elements
  formatting with Property Inspector, 84, 85
  formatting with the Insert panel, 86, 87
Email control, 470, 471
Email link, 142, 143
Embedded style sheet, 58, 59
Empty tag, 52, 53
Enctype property (form), 439
  with file-upload field, 456, 457

Event, 488, 489, 490, 491
  changing for a behavior, 492, 493
Event handler, 489
Event property
  Accordion widget, 530, 531
  Tabs widget, 533
Events (Dreamweaver), 492, 493
Expanded Files panel, 410, 411
Expanded layout, 32, 33
Export a site, 418, 419
External links, 146, 147
External style sheet, 58, 59, 98-105
  attaching, 102, 103
  creating, 98, 99

F

Favorites (Assets panel), 376, 377
FFmpeg, 324, 325
Fieldset, 454, 455
Fieldset control, 454, 455
fieldset element, 455
figure element, 57
File control, 457
File Transfer Protocol (FTP), 402, 403
Files, saving, 78, 79
Files panel, 21, 26, 27
File-upload field, 456, 457
Find and replace, 378, 379, 380
  advanced options for text, 382, 383
  for tags, 384, 385
  Search panel, 380, 381
Firefogg, 324, 325
Firefox, 10, 11
Fixed layout, 182, 258, 259
Fixed positioning, 216, 217, 218, 219
FLAC (Free Lossless Audio Codec), 321
Flash animation, 336, 337, 338
Flash video, 317, 330, 331
float property, 210, 211
Floating, 210-215
  2-column layout, 212, 213
  3-column layout, 214, 215
  fluid elements, 272, 273
Floating panel, 35
Fluid elements
  floating, 272, 273
  working with, 264, 265, 266, 267
Fluid layouts, 257-275
  creating, 260, 261
  style sheet, 262, 263
Fluid navigation menu
  mobile, 270, 271
  tablet or desktop, 274, 275

XYZ

100% Guarantee

When you order directly from us, you must be satisfied. Our books must work better than any other programming books you've ever used...both for training and reference...or you can send them back within 60 days for a prompt refund. No questions asked!

Mike Murach, Publisher

Ben Murach, President

Related Book

Have you mastered HTML and CSS?

The more you know about HTML and CSS, including HTML5 and CSS3, the more productive you'll be with Dreamweaver. That's why *Murach's HTML5 and CSS3* is the perfect companion to our Dreamweaver book.

Books for web developers

Murach's Dreamweaver CC 2014	$54.50
Murach's HTML5 and CSS3	54.50
Murach's JavaScript and jQuery	54.50
Murach's JavaScript and DOM Scripting	54.50
Murach's PHP and MySQL	54.50

Books for Java programmers

Murach's Android Programming	$57.50
Murach's Java Programming	57.50
Murach's Java Servlets and JSP (3rd Ed.)	57.50

Books for .NET developers

Murach's ASP.NET 4.5 Web Programming w/ C# 2012	$57.50
Murach's C# 2012	54.50
Murach's ASP.NET 4.5 Web Programming w/ VB 2012	$57.50
Murach's Visual Basic 2012	54.50

Books for database programmers

Murach's SQL Server 2012 for Developers	$54.50
Murach's MySQL	54.50
Murach's Oracle SQL and PL/SQL (2nd Ed.)	54.50

Prices and availability are subject to change. Please visit our web site or call for current information.

We want to hear from you

Do you have any comments, questions, kudos to pass on to us? It would be great to hear from you! Please share your feedback in whatever way works best.

www.murach.com

twitter.com/MurachBooks

1-800-221-5528
(Weekdays, 8 am to 4 pm Pacific Time)

facebook.com/murachbooks

murachbooks@murach.com

linkedin.com/company/
mike-murach-&-associates

What software you need for this book

- Adobe Creative Cloud and Dreamweaver CC 2014.
- To test the web pages that you develop on a Windows system, we recommend that you use Internet Explorer and Chrome. On a Mac OS X system, we recommend that you use Safari and Chrome. All three browsers are free.
- To help you install these products, appendix A provides the website addresses and procedures that you'll need.

The downloadable applications and files for this book

- All of the applications that are presented in this book.
- All of the significant examples that are presented in this book.
- The starting files for the exercises in this book.
- The solutions for the exercises.

How to download the applications and files

- Go to www.murach.com, and go to the page for *Murach's Dreamweaver CC 2014*.
- Locate and click the "FREE downloads" tab.
- If you're using a Windows system, click the "All book files" link for the self-extracting zip file. That will download an exe file named drmw_allfiles.exe. Then, find this file in Windows Explorer and double-click on it. That will install the files for this book in this directory: c:\murach\dreamweaver.
- If you're using a Mac, click the "All book files" link for the regular zip file. That will download a zip file named drmw_allfiles.zip onto your hard drive. Then, move this file into the Documents folder of your home directory, use Finder to go to your Documents folder, and double-click on the zip file. That will create a folder named murach\dreamweaver in your Documents folder that contains all the files for this book.
- For more information, please see appendix A.

www.murach.com